Teacher Wraparound Edition

Glencoe McGraw-Hill

California
Mathematics

Concepts, Skills, and Problem Solving

6

D1364001

Volume 2

Authors

Day • Frey • Howard • Hutchens
Luchin • McClain • Molix-Bailey
Ott • Pelfrey • Price
Vielhaber • Willard

 Glencoe

New York, New York   Columbus, Ohio   Chicago, Illinois   Woodland Hills, California

About the Cover

In 1880, the first San Diego County Fair was organized to bring area farmers together to share ideas and hold competitions. Since then the fair has been held almost every year and its permanent home in Del Mar was opened in 1936. The fair is now one of the largest in the United States with an average daily attendance over 54,000 people. You'll learn how to compute averages and find other statistical measurements in Chapter 9.

About the Graphics

Created with *Mathematica*. A rectangular array of circles is progressively enlarged and rotated randomly. For more information, and for programs to construct such graphics, see: www.wolfram.com/r/textbook.

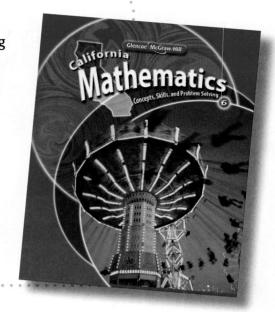

Image Credits: T2 Roy Ooms/Masterfile; **T11** F. Lukasseck/Masterfile

 **Glencoe**

The *McGraw·Hill* Companies

Send all inquiries to:
Glencoe/McGraw-Hill
8787 Orion Place
Columbus, OH 43240-4027

ISBN: 978-0-07-877848-3 *(Student Edition)*
MHID: 0-07-877848-4 *(Student Edition)*
ISBN: 978-0-07-877849-0 *(Teacher Wraparound Edition, Vol. 1)*
MHID: 0-07-877849-2 *(Teacher Wraparound Edition, Vol. 1)*
ISBN: 978-0-07-879262-5 *(Teacher Wraparound Edition, Vol. 2)*
MHID: 0-07-879262-2 *(Teacher Wraparound Edition, Vol. 2)*

Printed in the United States of America.

1 2 3 4 5 6 7 8 9 10 055/073 16 15 14 13 12 11 10 09 08 07

Contents in Brief

Authors

Rhonda J. Molix-Bailey
Mathematics Consultant
Mathematics by Design
DeSoto, Texas

Roger Day, Ph.D.
Mathematics Department
   Chair
Pontiac Township High
   School
Pontiac, Illinois

Patricia Frey, Ed.D.
Math Coordinator at
   Westminster Community
   Charter School
Buffalo, New York

Arthur C. Howard
Mathematics Teacher
Houston Christian
   High School
Houston, Texas

**Deborah A. Hutchens,
   Ed.D.**
Principal
Chesapeake, Virginia

Beatrice Luchin
Mathematics Consultant
League City, Texas

Contributing Author

Viken Hovsepian
Professor of Mathematics
Rio Hondo College
Whittier, California

Kay McClain, Ed.D.
Assistant Professor
Vanderbilt University
Nashville, Tennessee

Jack M. Ott, Ph.D.
Distinguished Professor
  of Secondary Education
  Emeritus
University of South Carolina
Columbia, South Carolina

Ronald Pelfrey, Ed.D.
Mathematics Specialist
Appalachian Rural
  Systemic Initiative and
  Mathematics Consultant
Lexington, Kentucky

Jack Price, Ed.D.
Professor Emeritus
California State
  Polytechnic University
Pomona, California

Kathleen Vielhaber
Mathematics Consultant
St. Louis, Missouri

Teri Willard, Ed.D.
Assistant Professor
Department of Mathematics
Central Washington
  University
Ellensburg, Washington

Contributing Author

FOLDABLES Dinah Zike
Educational Consultant
Dinah-Might Activities, Inc.
San Antonio, Texas

California Mathematics Advisory Board

Glencoe wishes to thank the following professionals for their invaluable feedback during the development of the program. They reviewed the table of contents, the prototype of the Teacher Wraparound Edition, and the California Standards Review chapter.

Cheryl L. Avalos
Mathematics Consultant
Retired Teacher
Hacienda Heights, California

William M. Bokesch
Rancho Bernardo High
School
San Diego, California

Patty Brown
Teacher
John Muir Elementary
Fresno, California

David J. Chamberlain
Secondary Mathematics
Resource Teacher
Capistrano Unified School
District
San Juan Capistrano, California

Eppie Chung
K-6 Teacher
Modesto City Schools
Modesto, California

Lisa Marie Cirrincione
Middle School Teacher
Lincoln Middle School
Oceanside, California

Carol Cronk
Mathematics Program
Specialist
San Bernardino City Unified
School District
San Bernardino, California

Ilene Foster
Teacher Specialist–
Mathematics
Pomona Unified School
District
Pomona, California

Grant A. Fraser, Ph. D.
Professor of Mathematics
California State University,
Los Angeles
Los Angeles, California

vi

Suzanne Bocskai Freire
Teacher
Kingswood Elementary
Citrus Heights, California

Beth Holguin
Teacher
Graystone Elementary
San Jose, California

Donna M. Kopenski, Ed. D.
Mathematics Coordinator K-5
City Heights Educational
    Collaborative
San Diego, California

Kelly Mack
6th Grade Teacher
Captain Jason Dahl
    Elementary
San Jose, California

Juvenal Martinez
Dual Immersion/ESL
    Instructor
Aeolian Elementary
Whittier, California

John McGuire
Associate Principal
Pacific Union School
Arcata, California

Dr. Donald R. Price
Teacher, Adjunct Professor
    Motivational Speaker
Rowland Unified School
    District
Rowland Heights, California

Kasey St. James
Mathematics Teacher
Sunny Hills High School
Fullerton, California

Arthur K. Wayman, Ph. D.
Professor of Mathematics
    Emeritus
California State University,
    Long Beach
Long Beach, California

Beverly Wells
First Grade Teacher
Mineral King Elementary
    School
Visalia, California

Frances Basich Whitney
Project Director, Mathematics
    K-12
Santa Cruz County Office of
    Education
Capitola, California

Consultants

Glencoe/McGraw-Hill wishes to thank the following professionals for their feedback. They were instrumental in providing valuable input toward the development of this program in these specific areas.

Mathematical Content

Viken Hovsepian
Professor of Mathematics
Rio Hondo College
Whittier, California

Grant A. Fraser, Ph. D.
Professor of Mathematics
California State University, Los Angeles
Los Angeles, California

Arthur K. Wayman, Ph. D.
Professor of Mathematics Emeritus
California State University, Long Beach
Long Beach, California

Differentiated Instruction

Nancy Frey, Ph. D.
Associate Professor of Literacy
San Diego State University
San Diego, California

English Language Learners

Mary Avalos, Ph. D.
Assistant Chair, Teaching and Learning
Assistant Research Professor
University of Miami, School of Education
Coral Gables, Florida

Jana Echevarria, Ph. D.
Professor, College of Education
California State University, Long Beach
Long Beach, California

Josefina V. Tinajero, Ph. D.
Dean, College of Education
The University of Texas at El Paso
El Paso, Texas

Gifted and Talented

Ed Zaccaro
Author
Mathematics and science books for gifted children
Bellevue, Iowa

Graphing Calculator

Ruth M. Casey
Mathematics Teacher
Department Chair
Anderson County High School
Lawrenceburg, Kentucky

Jerry Cummins
Former President
National Council of Supervisors of Mathematics
Western Springs, Illinois

Learning Disabilities

Kate Garnett, Ph. D.
Chairperson, Coordinator
   Learning Disabilities
School of Education
Department of Special Education
Hunter College, CUNY
New York, New York

Mathematical Fluency

Jason Mutford
Mathematics Instructor
Coxsackie-Athens Central School District
Coxsackie, New York

Pre-AP

Dixie Ross
AP Calculus Teacher
Pflugerville High School
Pflugerville, Texas

Reading and Vocabulary

Douglas Fisher, Ph. D.
Director of Professional Development and Professor
City Heights Educational Collaborative
San Diego State University
San Diego, California

Lynn T. Havens
Director of Project CRISS
Kalispell School District
Kalispell, Montana

California Reviewers

 Each California Reviewer reviewed at least two chapters of the Student Edition, giving feedback and suggestions for improving the effectiveness of the mathematics instruction.

Mariana Alwell
Teacher & Mathematics Coach
Garden Gate Elementary
Cupertino, California

Cheryl Anderson
District Mathematics Resource Teacher
Cupertino School District
Cupertino, California

Aimey Balderman
Mathematics Teacher
Tommie Kunst Junior High School
Santa Maria, California

Kristine A. Banfe
Mathematics Teacher
Hyde Middle School
Cupertino, California

Dianne Chrisman
Mathematics Teacher
Coronado High School
Coronado, California

Patricia Elmore
6th Grade Mathematics Teacher
Heritage Intermediate School
Fontana, California

Jill Fetters
Mathematics Teacher
Tevis Jr. High
Bakersfield, California

Rosalee Hrubic
Staff Development Specialist, Secondary
  Mathematics
Riverside Unified School District
Riverside, California

Derrick Chun Kei Hui
Certified BCLAD Mathematics Teacher
Natomas Middle School
Sacramento, California

Robin Ingram
Mathematics Instructor/Department Chair
Alta Sierra Intermediate School
Clovis, California

Debra C. Lonso
Mathematics Teacher
Dover Middle School
Fairfield, California

Roxanne Mancha
Mathematics Department Chair
Crystal Middle School
Suisun City, California

Mary Beth Moon
Mathematics Teacher/Consulting Teacher
Earl Warren Jr. High School
Bakersfield, California

Grāinne O'Malley
Middle School Mathematics Coordinator
Crossroad Middle School
Santa Monica, California

Candice Richards
Mathematics Teacher
Newport Mesa Unified School District
Costa Mesa, California

Steven Robitaille
Mathematics Instructor
Trabuco Hills High School
Mission Viejo, California

Rudy C. Sass
Mathematics Chair
Orangeview Junior High School
Anaheim, California

David Schick
Mathematics Teacher
Wangenheim Middle School
San Diego, California

James Douglas Sherman
Pre-Algebra/Algebra Instructor, 7th/8th
  grade
Miller Middle School
San Jose, California

Charles P. Toots
Mathematics Department Chairperson
Le Conte Middle School
Los Angeles, California

Judith Vincent
Teacher
Cavitt Junior High School
Granite Bay, California

Carrie M. Wong
6th/7th Mathematics Teacher
Taylor Middle School
Millbrae, California

TEACHER HANDBOOK

California Teacher Handbook

Table of Contents

Welcome to California Mathematics

Concepts • Skills • Problem Solving

The only true vertically aligned K–12
Mathematics Curriculum

What is Vertical Alignment?

Vertical alignment is a process that provides learners with an articulated, coherent sequence of content. It ensures that content standards and units of study are introduced, reinforced, and assessed and that instruction is targeted on student needs and California Standards.

Why is Vertical Alignment Important?

Strong vertical alignment accommodates a wide variety of developmental levels. It allows teachers increased precision in their teaching because they are not teaching content that is covered elsewhere or that students have previously mastered.

5 Keys to Success

1 Back-Mapping

According to The College Board, about 80% of students who successfully complete Algebra I and Geometry by 10th grade attend and succeed in college. That 80% is nearly constant regardless of race. (*Changing the Odds: Factors Increasing Access to College,* 1990) *California Mathematics: Concepts, Skills, and Problem Solving* was conceived and developed with the final result in mind– student success in Algebra I and beyond. The authors, using the California Mathematics Standards as their guide, developed this brand-new series by "back-mapping" from the desired result of student success in Algebra I, Geometry, and beyond.

California Mathematics: Concepts, Skills, and Problem Solving

California Math Triumphs is designed for students who need intensive intervention to meet grade-level standards.

| Kindergarten | Grade 1 | Grade 2 | Grade 3 | Grade 4 | Grade 5 |

The K–8 mathematics program prepares students for success in Algebra I by using consistent vocabulary and concept presentation throughout the program.

② Balanced, In-Depth Content

California Mathematics: Concepts, Skills, and Problem Solving was developed to specifically target the skills and topics that give students the most difficulty.

Grades K–2	Grades 3–5
1. Problem Solving	1. Problem Solving
2. Money	2. Fractions
3. Time	3. Measurement
4. Measurement	4. Decimals
5. Fractions	5. Time
6. Computation	6. Algebra

Grades 6–8	Grades 9–12
1. Fractions	1. Problem Solving
2. Problem Solving	2. Fractions
3. Measurement	3. Algebra
4. Algebra	4. Geometry
5. Computation	5. Computation
	6. Probability

– K–12 Math Market Analysis Survey, Open Book Publishing, 2005

③ Ongoing Assessment

California Mathematics: Concepts, Skills, and Problem Solving includes diagnostic, formative, and summative assessment; data-driven instruction; intervention options; and performance tracking, as well as remediation, acceleration, and enrichment tools throughout the program.

④ Intervention and Differentiated Instruction

In order for students to overcome difficulties with mathematics learning, attention is paid to their backgrounds, the nature of their previous instruction, and underlying learning differences. *California Mathematics: Concepts, Skills, and Problem Solving* includes a two-pronged approach to intervention.

Strategic Teachers can use the myriad of intervention tips and ancillary materials to address the needs of students who need strategic intervention.

Intensive For students who are two or more years below grade level, *California Math Triumphs* provides step-by-step instruction, vocabulary support, and data-driven decision making to help students succeed.

For students not ready for Algebra I in Grade 8, *California Algebra Readiness* provides highly focused instructional materials to help students rebuild foundational skills and concepts and prepare for algebra success.

⑤ Professional Development

California Mathematics: Concepts, Skills, and Problem Solving includes many opportunities for teacher professional development. Additional learning opportunities in various formats—video, online, and on-site instruction—are fully aligned and articulated from grade K through Algebra II.

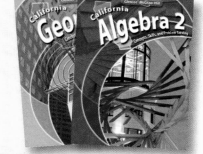

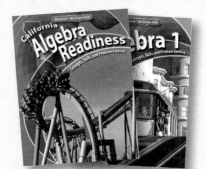

Grade 6	Grade 7	Algebra Readiness/Algebra I	Geometry	Algebra II

California Algebra Readiness is for students who are not ready for Algebra I in 8th grade.

Program Development

Checklist

Articulation Macmillan/McGraw-Hill and Glencoe/McGraw-Hill's suite of fully articulated programs include:

- *Mathematics: Concepts, Skills, and Problem Solving,* PreKindergarten
- *California Mathematics: Concepts, Skills, and Problem Solving,* Grades K–7
- *California Math Triumphs: Intervention for Intensive Students,* Grades 4–7
- *California Algebra Readiness: Concepts, Skills, and Problem Solving*
- *California Algebra 1: Concepts, Skills, and Problem Solving*
- *California Geometry: Concepts, Skills, and Problem Solving*
- *California Algebra 2: Concepts, Skills, and Problem Solving*

These brand new programs form a comprehensive, standards-based K–12 program that follows the specific requirements of the Mathematics Framework for California Public Schools to ensure success in your classroom.

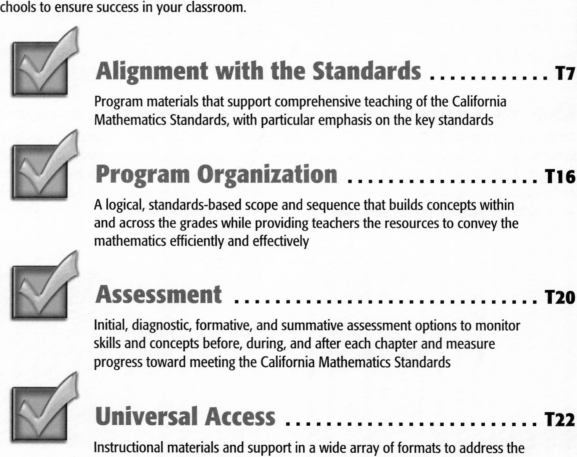

Alignment with the Standards

California Content Standards, Grade 6 Correlated to *California Mathematics: Concepts, Skills, and Problem Solving,* Grade 6

⚷ denotes Key standards
* denotes standards assessed on the California High School Exit Examination (CAHSEE)

Standard	Text of Standard	Primary Citations	Supporting Citations
Number Sense			
⚷ **1.0**	**Students compare and order positive and negative fractions, decimals, and mixed numbers. Students solve problems involving fractions, ratios, proportions, and percentages.**	192-210, 215-220, 230-246, 250-270, 282-312, 316-322, 342-365, 369-383, 540-545, CA4-CA6	80-87, 323, 329-332, 366-367, 460-497, 518-523, 670
⚷ **1.1**	Compare and order positive and negative fractions, decimals, and mixed numbers and place them on a number line.	84-87, 215-220, CA4, CA6	80-83, 196-210, 230-235, 282-286, 294-305, 670
⚷ **1.2**	Interpret and use ratios in different contexts (e.g., batting averages, miles per hour) to show the relative sizes of two quantities, using appropriate notations (a/b, a to b, $a:b$).	282-293, CA4, CA6	206-210, 215-220, 294-311, 316-322, 369-374, 460-497
⚷ **1.3**	Use proportions to solve problems (e.g., determine the value of N if $\frac{4}{7} = \frac{N}{21}$, find the length of a side of a polygon similar to a known polygon). Use cross-multiplication as a method for solving such problems, understanding it as the multiplication of both sides of an equation by a multiplicative inverse.	306-311, 316-322, 350-354, 540-545, CA4, CA5, CA6	312, 323
⚷ **1.4**	Calculate given percentages of quantities and solve problems involving discounts at sales, interest earned, and tips.	342-365, 375-383, CA5, CA6	202-205, 349, 366-367, 518-523
⚷ **2.0**	**Students calculate and solve problems involving addition, subtraction, multiplication, and division.**	24-69, 80-118, 180-220, 230-270, 282-332, 342-383, CA7-CA9	128-168, 396-449, 460-497, 510-562, 572-625, 636-659
2.1	Solve problems involving addition, subtraction, multiplication, and division of positive fractions and explain why a particular operation was used for a given situation.	236-246, 252-257, 265-270, CA7, CA8	230-235, 248-251, 314-322, 584-588, 646-647
2.2	Explain the meaning of multiplication and division of positive fractions and perform the calculations $\left(\text{e.g.,} \frac{5}{8} \div \frac{15}{16} = \frac{5}{8} \times \frac{16}{15} = \frac{2}{3}\right)$.	252-257, 264-270, CA9	250-251
⚷ **2.3**	Solve addition, subtraction, multiplication, and division problems, including those arising in concrete situations, that use positive and negative integers and combinations of these operations.	93-99, 101-111, 114-118, CA7, CA8, CA9	24-29, 38-41, 44-47, 53-56, 112-113, 314-315
⚷ **2.4**	Determine the least common multiple and the greatest common divisor of whole numbers; use them to solve problems with fractions (e.g., to find a common denominator to add two fractions or to find the reduced form for a fraction).	186-189, 192-195, 211-214, CA7, CA9	180-185, 192-195, 202-205, 215-220, 236-241, 242-246, 252-257, 282-286

Standard	Text of Standard	Primary Citations	Supporting Citations
Algebra and Functions			
1.0	**Students write verbal expressions and sentences as algebraic expressions, solve simple linear equations, and graph and interpret their results.**	38-41, 44-56, 128-146, 258-263, CA10-CA12	57-62, 63-67, 69, 80-82, 112-118, 151-161, 163-168, 196-200, 230-235, 252-257, 306-311, 316-322, 344-348, 350-354, 361-365, 375-382, 409, 434-437, 524-531, 540-545, 572-576, 578-582, 613-624, 636-639, 649-653
1.1	Write and solve one-step linear equations in one variable.	49-52, 134-146, 258-263, CA10, CA12	63-67, 151-161, 230-235, 252-263, 306-311, 316-322, 350-354, 361-365, 375-378, 434-437, 524-531, 540-545
1.2	Write and evaluate an algebraic expression for a given situation, using up to three variables.	44-47, 128-133, CA11, CA12, CA34	57-61, 62, 69, 103-106, 112-113, 114-118, 156-161, 163-167, 252-257, 379-382, 572-576, 578-582, 613-618, 636-639, 649-653
1.3	Apply algebraic order of operations and the commutative, associative, and distributive properties to evaluate expressions; and justify each step in the process.	38-41, 53-56, CA11, CA12	44-47, 80-82, 578-582
1.4	Solve problems manually by using the correct order of operations or by using a scientific calculator.	38-41, CA11, CA35	44-47, 69, 80-82, 151-155, 168, 409, 619-623
2.0	**Students analyze and use tables, graphs, and rules to solve problems involving rates and proportions.**	142-146, 287-292, 294-305, CA13-CA15	63-68, 156-161, 163-168, 282-286, 293, 422, 518-523
2.1	Convert one unit of measurement to another (e.g., from feet to miles, from centimeters to inches).	294-305, CA13, CA15	160, 168
2.2	Demonstrate an understanding that *rate* is a measure of one quantity per unit value of another quantity.	287-292, CA13, CA14, CA15	293
2.3	Solve problems involving rates, average speed, distance, and time.	142-146, 287-292, CA13, CA15, CA34, CA35	63-67, 163-167, 282-286
3.0	**Students investigate geometric patterns and describe them algebraically.**	156-161, 546-551, 572-593, 596-599, CA16-CA18	47, 128-133, 162, 600-601, 613-618, 640-645, 649-653, 656-659
3.1	Use variables in expressions describing geometric quantities (e.g., $P = 2w + 2\ell$, $A = \frac{1}{2}bh$, $C = \pi d$ – the formulas for the perimeter of a rectangle, the area of a triangle, and the circumference of a circle, respectively).	156-161, 577-588, 596-599, CA16, CA17, CA18, CA37, CA39	162, 572-576, 589-593, 640-645, 649-653, 656-659

Standard	Text of Standard	Primary Citations	Supporting Citations
3.2	Express in symbolic form simple relationships arising from geometry.	156-161, 546-551, 572-593, 596-599, CA16, CA17, CA18, CA36, CA37, CA38, CA39	47, 128-133, 162, 600-601, 613-618, 640-645, 649-653, 656-659
Measurement and Geometry			
1.0	**Students deepen their understanding of the measurement of plane and solid shapes and use this understanding to solve problems.**	524-529, 532-538, 540-562, 572-593, 596-601, 603-623, CA19-CA21, 649-659	639, 645
1.1	Understand the concept of a constant such as π; know the formulas for the circumference and area of a circle.	583-593, CA19, CA20, CA21	656-659
1.2	Know common estimates of π (3.14; $\frac{22}{7}$) and use these values to estimate and calculate the circumference and the area of circles; compare with actual measurements.	584-593, CA19, CA21	619-623, 656-659
1.3	Know and use the formulas for the volume of triangular prisms and cylinders (area of base x height); compare these formulas and explain the similarity between them and the formula for the volume of a rectangular solid.	613-623, CA20, CA21	639, 645
2.0	**Students identify and describe the properties of two-dimensional figures.**	510-517, 524-529, 532-538, 540-551, CA22-CA24	156-161, 568, 569
2.1	Identify angles as vertical, adjacent, complementary, or supplementary and provide descriptions of these terms.	510-517, CA22, CA24, CA38	529, 568
2.2	Use the properties of complementary and supplementary angles and the sum of the angles of a triangle to solve problems involving an unknown angle.	514-517, 524-529, CA22, CA23, CA24	569
2.3	Draw quadrilaterals and triangles from given information about them (e.g., a quadrilateral having equal sides but no right angles, a right isosceles triangle).	524-529, 533-538, CA23, CA24	156-161, 530-531
Statistics, Data Analysis, and Probability			
1.0	**Students compute and analyze statistical measurements for data sets.**	396-408, 402-408, 410-414, CA25-CA27	415-422, 424-425, 426-449
1.1	Compute the range, mean, median, and mode of data sets.	396-408, CA25, CA27, CA36	402-414
1.2	Understand how additional data added to data sets may affect these computations.	396-408, CA26, CA27	410-414
1.3	Understand how the inclusion or exclusion of outliers affects these computations.	410-414, CA26, CA27	396-408
1.4	Know why a specific measure of central tendency (mean, median, mode) provides the most useful information in a given context.	402-408	409-414
2.0	**Students use data samples of a population and describe the characteristics and limitations of the samples.**	409, 438-449, CA28-CA30	312, 396-408, 410-422, 424-425, 432-433, 438-443
2.1	Compare different samples of a population with the data from the entire population and identify a situation in which it makes sense to use a sample.	438-443	312

Standard	Text of Standard	Primary Citations	Supporting Citations
⚷ 2.2	Identify different ways of selecting a sample (e.g., convenience sampling, responses to a survey, random sampling) and which method makes a sample more representative for a population.	438-443 CA28, CA29, CA30	434-437
⚷ 2.3	Analyze data displays and explain why the way in which the question was asked might have influenced the results obtained and why the way in which the results were displayed might have influenced the conclusions reached.	444-449	415-422, 424-425, 432-433, 438-443
⚷ 2.4	Identify data that represent sampling errors and explain why the sample (and the display) might be biased.	444-449	438-443
⚷ 2.5	Identify claims based on statistical data and, in simple cases, evaluate the validity of the claims.	409, 426-431, 434-443, CA28, CA30	438-443
3.0	**Students determine theoretical and experimental probabilities and use these to make predictions about events.**	460-478, 486-497, CA31-CA33	128-133, 190-191, 480-485, 523, 623, 665
⚷ 3.1	Represent all possible outcomes for compound events in an organized way (e.g., tables, grids, tree diagrams) and express the theoretical probability of each outcome.	465-478, CA31, CA33, CA37, CA39	128-133, 190-191
3.2	Use data to estimate the probability of future events (e.g., batting averages or number of accidents per mile driven).	486-491, CA35	484-485
⚷ 3.3*	Represent probabilities as ratios, proportions, decimals between 0 and 1, and percentages between 0 and 100 and verify that the probabilities computed are reasonable; know that if P is the probability of an event, $1-P$ is the probability of an event not occurring.	460-464, CA31, CA33, CA35	465-478, 484-497
3.4	Understand that the probability of either of two disjoint events occurring is the sum of the two individual probabilities and that the probability of one event following another, in independent trials, is the product of the two probabilities.	492-497, CA32	523, 623, 665
⚷ 3.5	Understand the difference between independent and dependent events.	492-497, CA32, CA33	523, 623, 665
Mathematical Reasoning			
1.0	**Students make decisions about how to approach problems.**	*Used throughout the text.* For example, 25-29, 148-149, 594-595, CA34-CA35.	
1.1	Analyze problems by identifying relationships, distinguishing relevant from irrelevant information, identifying missing information, sequencing and prioritizing information, and observing patterns.	25-29, 42-43, 107-111, 148-149, 180, 190-191, 248-249, 532, CA34, CA35	57-67, 84-87
1.2	Formulate and justify mathematical conjectures based on a general description of the mathematical question or problem posed.	93-94, 101-102, 530-531, CA34, CA35	69, 134-135, 168, 409, 415-422, 426-431, 434-437, 491, 552, 577, 624, 654-655
1.3	Determine when and how to break a problem into simpler parts.	594-595, CA34, CA35	25-29, 53-56, 95-99, 150, 607, 649-653, 656-659

Standard	Text of Standard	Primary Citations	Supporting Citations
2.0	**Students use strategies, skills, and concepts in finding solutions.**	*Used throughout the text.* For example, 134-135, 151-155, 190-191, CA36-CA37.	
2.1	Use estimation to verify the reasonableness of calculated results.	148-149, 355-360, CA37	25-29, 236-246, 312
2.2	Apply strategies and results from simpler problems to more complex problems.	546-551, 594-595, CA37	62, 180
2.3	Estimate unknown quantities graphically and solve for them by using logical reasoning and arithmetic and algebraic techniques.	424-431	49-52, 136-146, 151-155, 230-235, 350-354, 426-431, 434-437
2.4	Use a variety of methods, such as words, numbers, symbols, charts, graphs, tables, diagrams, and models, to explain mathematical reasoning.	62-67, 69, 134-135, 162-168, 314-315, 424-425, 484-485, 518-523, 607-612, 624, 646-647, CA36, CA37	30-41, 44-47, 49-52, 80-82, 88-94, 95-106, 114-118, 128-146, 151-155, 163-167, 180, 185, 196-200, 202-205, 230-241, 252-263, 265-270, 282-286, 293, 316-322, 324-332, 342-349, 369-374, 355-360, 396-409, 415-422, 426-437, 532, 553-562, 600-601, 607, 624, 636-645, 654-655, 649-653, 656-659
2.5	Express the solution clearly and logically by using the appropriate mathematical notation and terms and clear language; support solutions with evidence in both verbal and symbolic work.	38-41, 128-133, CA37	53-56, 136-146, 151-161, 258-263, 350-354, 383, 409, 510-513, 540-545
2.6	Indicate the relative advantages of exact and approximate solutions to problems and give answers to a specified degree of accuracy.	584-588, CA37	300-305, 344-348, 350-354, 361-365, 369-378, 546-551, 572-576, 578-582, 589-593, 636-639, 656-659
2.7	Make precise calculations and check the validity of the results from the context of the problem.	148-149, CA36, CA37	24-29, 42-43, 136-146, 151-155, 265-270
3.0	**Students move beyond a particular problem by generalizing to other situations.**	*Used throughout the text.* For example, 426-431, 438-443, 594-599, CA38-CA39.	
3.1	Evaluate the reasonableness of the solution in the context of the original situation.	366-367, CA39	24-29, 42-43, 236-241, 265-270, 324-328, 355-365, 518-531, 553-557, 572-576, 619-623, 640-645
3.2	Note the method of deriving the solution and demonstrate a conceptual understanding of the derivation by solving similar problems.	24-29, CA38, CA39	42-43, 62, 93-94, 101-102, 112-113, 134-135, 148-149, 190-191, 248-249, 314-315, 342-343, 366-367, 424-425, 484-485, 530-531, 594-595, 646-647
3.3	Develop generalizations of the results obtained and the strategies used and apply them in new problem situations.	93-94, 101-102, 250-251, 577, 583, 600-601, CA38, CA39	62, 162, 168, 323

Alignment with the Standards

California Mathematics: Concepts, Skills, and Problem Solving, Grade 6, Correlated to California Content Standards, Grade 6

Boldfaced standards indicate primary citations.

Lesson	Page(s)	Standard(s)
Reading Word Problems: Making Sense	24	**6MR3.1,** 🔑 **6NS2.3**
1-1 A Plan for Problem Solving	25–29	**6MR1.1, Reinforcement of** 🔑 **5NS2.1,** 🔑 6NS2.3, 6MR1.3, 6MR2.1, 6MR2.7, 6MR3.1, 6MR3.2
1-2 Powers and Exponents	30–33	**Reinforcement of 5NS1.3,** 6MR2.4
1-3 Squares and Square Roots	34–37	**Preparation for 7NS2.4,** 6MR2.4
1-4 Order of Operations	38–41	**6AF1.3, 6AF1.4,** 🔑 6NS2.3, 6MR2.4, 6MR2.5
1-5 **PSI:** Guess and Check	42–43	**6MR1.1, Reinforcement of** 🔑 **5NS2.1,** 6MR2.7, 6MR3.1, 6MR3.2
1-6 **Algebra:** Variables and Equations	44–47	**6AF1.2, 6AF1.4,** 🔑 6NS2.3, 6AF1.3, 6AF3.2, 6MR2.4
1-7 **Algebra:** Equations	49–52	🔑 **6AF1.1,** 6MR2.3, 6MR2.4
1-8 **Algebra:** Properties	53–56	**6AF1.3,** 🔑 6NS2.3, 6MR1.3, 6MR2.4, 6MR2.5
1-9 **Algebra:** Arithmetic Sequences	57–61	**6AF1.2,** 6MR1.1
Extend 1-9 Algebra Lab: Exploring Sequences	62	**6AF1.2, 6MR2.4,** 6MR1.1, 6MR2.2, 6MR3.2. 6MR3.3
1-10 **Algebra:** Equations and Functions	63–67	**6AF1.2, 6MR2.4,** 🔑 6AF1.1, 6AF2.3, 6MR1.1
Extend 1-10 Graphing Calculator Lab: Functions and Tables	68	**6AF1.2, 6MR2.4,** 6AF1.4, 6MR1.2
2-1 Integers and Absolute Value	80–83	**Preparation for** 🔑 **6NS1.1,** 6AF1.3, 6AF1.4, 6MR2.4
2-2 Comparing and Ordering Integers	84–87	**Preparation for** 🔑 **6NS1.1,** 6MR1.1, 6MR2.4
2-3 The Coordinate Plane	88–92	**Reinforcement of 5AF1.4, 6MR2.4,** 6MR2.4
Explore 2-4 Algebra Lab: Adding Integers	93–94	**6MR3.3,** 🔑 6NS2.3, 6MR1.2, 6MR2.4, 6MR3.2
2-4 Adding Integers	95–99	🔑 **6NS2.3,** 6MR1.3, 6MR2.4
Explore 2-5 Algebra Lab: Subtracting Integers	101–102	**6MR3.3,** 🔑 6NS2.3, 6MR1.2, 6MR2.4, 6MR3.2
2-5 Subtracting Integers	103–106	🔑 **6NS2.3,** 6AF1.2, 6MR2.4
2-6 Multiplying Integers	107–111	🔑 **6NS2.3,** 6AF1.2, 6MR2.4
2-7 **PSI:** Look for a Pattern	112–113	**6MR1.1,** 🔑 6NS2.3, 6MR3.2
2-8 Dividing Integers	114–118	🔑 **6NS2.3,** 6AF1.2, 6MR2.4
3-1 Writing Expressions and Equations	128–133	**6AF1.2,** 6AF3.2, 6SDAP3.1*, 6MR2.4, 6MR2.5
Explore 3-2 Algebra Lab: Solving Equations Using Models	134–135	🔑 **6AF1.1, 6MR2.4,** 6MR1.2, 6MR3.2
3-2 Solving Addition and Subtraction Equations	136–141	🔑 **6AF1.1, 6MR2.4,** 6MR2.2, 6MR2.5, 6MR2.7
3-3 Solving Multiplication Equations	142–146	🔑 **6AF1.1, 6AF2.3,** 6MR2.2, 6MR2.4, 6MR2.5, 6MR2.7
3-4 **PSI:** Work Backward	148–149	**6MR2.7,** 🔑 6NS2.3, 6MR1.1, 6MR2.1, 6MR3.2
Reading Word Problems: Simplify the Problem	150	**6MR1.3, Preparation for** 🔑 **7AF4.1**

Lesson	Page(s)	Standard(s)
3-5 Solving Two-Step Equations	151–155	**Preparation for** 🔑 **7AF4.1,** 🔑 **6AF1.1,** 6AF1.4, 6MR2.2, 6MR2.4, 6MR2.5, 6MR2.7
3-6 Measurement: Perimeter and Area	156–161	**6AF3.1, 6AF3.2,** 🔑 6AF1.1, 6AF1.2, 6AF2.1, 6MG2.3, 6MR2.5
Explore 3-7 Measurement Lab: Representing Relationships	162	**6AF3.2, 6MR2.4,** 6AF3.1, 6MR3.3
3-7 Functions and Graphs	163–167	**6AF2.3, 6MR2.4,** 6AF1.2
Extend 3-7 Graphing Calculator Lab: Graphing Relationships	168	**6AF2.1, 6MR2.4,** 6AF1.4, 6MR1.2, 6MR3.3
Explore 4-1 Math Lab: Exploring Factors	180	**Preparation for** 🔑 **6NS2.4, 6MR1.1,** 6MR2.2, 6MR2.4
4-1 Prime Factorization	181–184	**Preparation for** 🔑 **6NS2.4**
Reading Word Problems: Everyday Meaning	185	**6MR2.4,** Preparation for 🔑 6NS2.4
4-2 Greatest Common Factor	186–189	🔑 **6NS2.4**
4-3 PSI: Make an Organized List	190–191	**6MR1.1, Preparation for 6SDAP3.1*,** 6MR2.4, 6MR3.2
4-4 Simplifying Fractions	192–195	🔑 **6NS2.4**
4-5 Fractions and Decimals	196–200	**Preparation for** 🔑 **6NS1.1,** 6MR2.4
4-6 Fractions and Percents	202–204	**Preparation for** 🔑 **6NS1.1,** 🔑 6NS1.4, 🔑 6NS2.4, 6MR2.4
4-7 Percents and Decimals	206–210	**Preparation for** 🔑 **6NS1.1,** 🔑 6NS1.2
4-8 Least Common Multiple	211–214	🔑 **6NS2.4**
4-9 Comparing and Ordering Rational Numbers	215–220	🔑 **6NS1.1,** 🔑 **6NS2.4,** 🔑 6NS1.2
5-1 Estimating with Fractions	230–235	**6NS2.1,** 🔑 6NS1.1, Key 6AF1.1, 6MR2.3, 6MR2.4
5-2 Adding and Subtracting Fractions	236–241	**6NS2.1,** 🔑 **6NS2.4,** 6MR2.1, 6MR2.4, 6MR3.1
5-3 Adding and Subtracting Mixed Numbers	242–246	**6NS2.1,** 🔑 **6NS2.4,** 6MR2.1
5-4 PSI: Eliminate Possibilities	248–249	**6MR1.1, 6NS2.1,** 6MR3.2
Explore 5-5 Math Lab: Multiplying Fractions	250–251	**6MR3.3, 6NS2.2,** 6NS2.1
5-5 Multiplying Fractions and Mixed Numbers	252–257	**6NS2.1, 6NS2.2,** 🔑 6NS2.4, 🔑 6AF1.1, 6AF1.2, 6MR2.4
5-6 Algebra: Solving Equations	258–263	🔑 **6AF1.1,** 6MR2.4, 6MR2.5
Reading Word Problems: Meaning of Division	264	**6NS2.2**
5-7 Dividing Fractions and Mixed Numbers	265–270	**6NS2.1, 6NS2.2,** 6MR2.4, 6MR2.7, 6MR3.1
6-1 Ratios	282–286	🔑 **6NS1.2,** 🔑 6NS1.1, 🔑 6NS2.4, 6AF2.3, 6MR2.4
6-2 Rates	287–292	🔑 **6NS1.2,** 🔑 **6AF2.2, 6AF2.3**
Extend 6-2 Algebra Lab: Rate of Change	293	🔑 **6NS1.2,** 🔑 **6AF2.2,** 🔑 6NS1.1, 6AF2.3, 6MR2.4
6-3 Measurement: Changing Customary Units	294–299	**6AF2.1,** 🔑 6NS1.1, 🔑 6NS1.2
6-4 Measurement: Changing Metric Units	300–305	**6AF2.1,** 🔑 6NS1.1, 🔑 6NS1.2, 6MR2.6
6-5 Algebra: Solving Proportions	306–311	🔑 **6NS1.3,** 🔑 6NS1.1, 🔑 6NS1.2, 🔑 6AF1.1
Extend 6-5 Statistics Lab: Wildlife Sampling	312	**6SDAP2.1, 6MR2.1**
6-6 PSI: Draw a Diagram	314–315	**6MR2.5, 6NS2.1,** 🔑 6NS2.3, 6MR2.4, 6MR3.2
6-7 Scale Drawings	316–322	🔑 **6NS1.3,** 🔑 6NS1.1, 🔑 6NS1.2, 6NS2.1, 6AF1.1, 6MR2.4
Extend 6-7 Spreadsheet Lab: Scale Drawings	323	🔑 **6NS1.3, 6MR3.3**

Lesson	Page(s)	Standard(s)
9-7　Theoretical and Experimental Probability	486–490	**6SDAP3.2,** ◆— 6NS1.2, ◆— 6SDAP3.3*
Extend 9-7 Probability Lab: Simulations	491	**6SDAP3.2, 6MR1.2,** ◆— 6NS1.2, Key 6SDAP3.3*
9-8　Compound Events	492–497	**6SDAP3.4,** ◆— **6SDAP3.5*,** ◆— 6NS1.2, ◆— 6SDAP3.3*
10-1　Angle Relationships	510–513	**6MG2.1,** 6MR2.5
10-2　Complementary and Supplementary Angles	514–517	**6MG2.1,** ◆— **6MG2.2**
10-3　**Statistics:** Display Data in a Circle Graph	518–523	**Reinforcement of 5SDAP1.2,** ◆— 6NS1.4, 6MR2.4, 6MR3.1
10-4　Triangles	524–529	◆— **6MG2.2,** ◆— **6MG2.3,** ◆— 6AF1.1, 6MR3.1
10-5　**PSI:** Use Logical Reasoning	530–531	**6MR1.2,** ◆— **6MG2.3,** ◆— 6AF1.1, 6MR3.2, 6MR3.1
Explore 10-6 Geometry Lab: Investigating Quadrilaterals	532	**6MR1.1,** ◆— **6MG2.3,** 6MR2.4
10-6　Quadrilaterals	533–538	◆— **6MG2.3**
10-7　Similar Figures	540–545	◆— **6NS1.3,** ◆— 6AF1.1, 6MR2.5
10-8　Polygons and Tessellations	546–551	**6MR2.2, 6AF3.2,** 6MR2.2, 6MR2.6
Extend 10-8 Geometry Lab: Tessellations	552	**Preparation for 7MG3.4, 6MR2.2,** 6MR1.2
10-9　Translations	553–557	**Preparation for 7MG3.2,** 6MR2.4, 6MR3.1
10-10　Reflections	558–562	**Preparation for 7MG3.2,** 6MR2.4
11-1　Area of Parallelograms	572–576	**6AF3.1, 6AF3.2,** 6AF1.2, 6MR2.6, 6MR3.1
Explore 11-2 Measurement Lab: Triangles and Trapezoids	577	**6AF3.2, 6MR3.3,** 6AF1.2, 6AF3.1, 6MR1.2
11-2　Area of Triangles and Trapezoids	578–582	**6AF3.1, 6AF3.2,** 6AF1.2, 6MR2.6
Explore 11-3 Measurement Lab: Circumference of Circles	583	◆— **6MG1.1, 6MR3.3,** 6AF3.1, 6AF3.2
11-3　Circles and Circumference	584	◆— **6MG1.1, 6MG1.2,** 6AF3.1, 6AF3.2, 6MR2.6
11-4　Area of Circles	589	◆— **6MG1.1, 6MG1.2,** 6AF3.1, 6AF3.2, 6MR2.6
11-5　**PSI:** Solve a Simpler Problem	594–595	**6MR1.3, 6MR2.2, 6NS2.1,** 6MR3.2
11-6　Area of Complex Figures	596–599	**6AF3.1, 6AF3.2,** 6MR2.2
Extend 11-6 Measurement Lab: Nets and Surface Area	600–601	**Preparation for 7MG3.5, 6MR3.3,** 6AF3.2, 6MR2.4
11-7　Three-Dimensional Figures	603–606	◆— **Preparation for 7MG3.6**
Explore 11-8 Geometry Lab: Three-Dimensional Figures	607	◆— **Preparation for 7MG3.6, 6MR2.4,** 6MR1.3
11-8　Drawing Three-Dimensional Figures	608–612	**Reinforcement of 5MG2.3, 6MR2.4**
11-9　Volume of Prisms	613–618	**6MG1.3,** 6AF1.2, 6AF3.2
11-10　Volume of Cylinders	619–623	**6MG1.3,** 6AF1.4, 6MG1.2, 6MR1.2, 6MR2.4, 6MR3.1
Extend 11-10 Graphing Calculator Lab: Graphing Geometric Relationships	624–625	**6AF3.2, 6MR1.2, 6MR2.4**
12-1　Estimating Square Roots	636–639	**Preparation for 7NS2.4,** 6AF1.2, 6MR2.4, 6MR2.6
12-2　The Pythagorean Theorem	640–645	**Preparation for** ◆— **7MG3.3,** 6AF3.1, 6AF3.2, 6MR2.4, 6MR3.1
12-3　**PSI:** Make a Model	646–647	**6MR2.4, 6NS2.1,** 6MR3.2
12-4　Surface Area of Rectangular Prisms	649–653	**Preparation for 7MG2.1, 6AF3.2,** 6AF1.2, 6AF3.1, 6MR1.3, 6MR2.4
Extend 12-4 Measurement Lab: Changes in Volume and Surface Area	654–655	**Preparation for 7MG2.4, 6MR2.4,** 6MR1.2
12-5　Surface Area of Cylinders	656–659	**Preparation for 7MG2.1,** 6AF3.1, 6AF3.2, ◆— 6MG1.1, 6MG1.2, 6MR1.3, 6MR2.4, 6MR2.6

Program Organization

Alignment McGraw-Hill's *California Mathematics: Concepts, Skills, and Problem Solving*, **Grade 6** differs from other mathematics programs because it:

- is fully aligned to the California Mathematics Standards for Grade 6.
- is paced to ensure in-depth coverage of all assessed standards by the test date.
- provides for comprehensive review of the California Standards before the test date.

Standards

Students and parents know exactly which **California Standards** are addressed by the lesson. The portion of the standard in bold is the specific part being addressed in the lesson.

Vocabulary

Both **New Vocabulary** and **Review Vocabulary** help students identify terms being presented.

Key Concepts

Key Concepts use multiple representations to demonstrate the skills being presented.

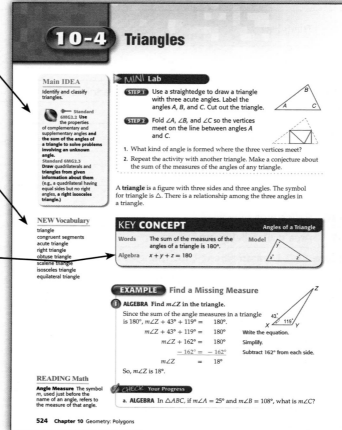

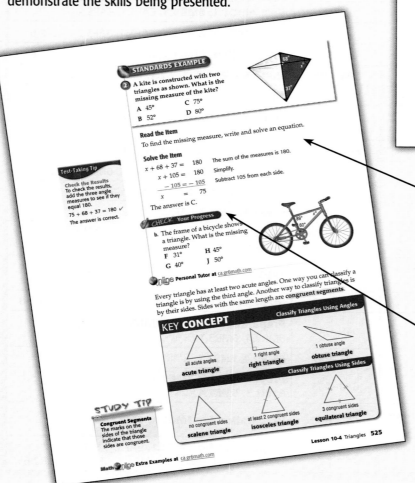

Examples

Fully worked-out **Examples** enable students and parents to see how to solve problems step by step. **California Standards Examples** help students practice the Standards using multiple-choice questions.

Check Your Progress

Check Your Progress exercises act as *diagnostic assessment* by showing you whether students understand the concepts presented.

Check Your Understanding

Check Your Understanding exercises can be used as *formative assessment* to monitor student progress and guide your instruction toward helping students achieve the standards.

Multi-Step Word Problems

Multi-step word problems are not simple computation problems using the numbers given. Students must analyze exactly what the problem is asking and how to use the information given. These problems are starred in the Teacher Wraparound Edition.

Homework Help

Homework Help guides students and parents to an example that is similar to the problems they are trying to solve.

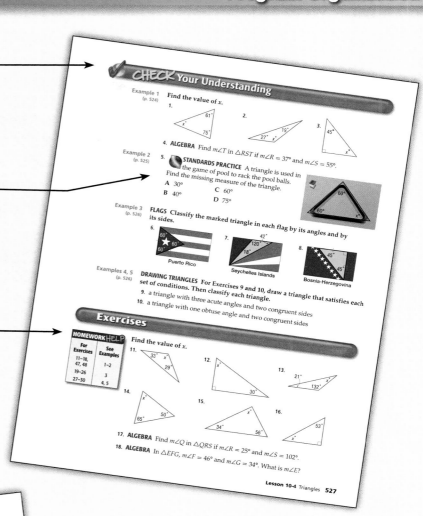

H.O.T. Problems

H.O.T. Problems require students to use **Higher Order Thinking** skills to solve problems.

Standards Practice

Every lesson includes **California Standards Practice** questions that are similar to those found on state assessments. The assessed California Standards are noted in the Teacher Wraparound Edition.

Spiral Review

Spiral Review provides constant reinforcement of skills from previous lessons. The last few exercises let you assess whether students have the **prerequisite skills** for the next lesson.

Program Organization

Balance McGraw-Hill's *California Mathematics: Concepts, Skills, and Problem Solving,* **Grade 6** is designed to provide students a balanced approach to mathematics learning by offering them the opportunity to:

- investigate concepts and build their conceptual understanding,
- review, learn, and practice basic computational and procedural skills, and
- apply mathematics to problem solving in real-world situations.

Standards Review

This special chapter gives students additional review of the California Standards and additional practice in how to become better test takers.

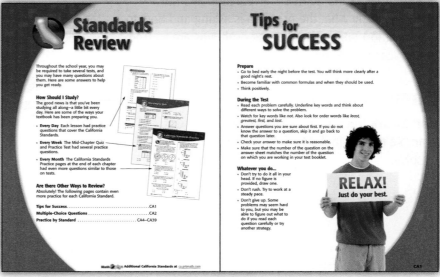

Problem-Solving Investigations

Problem-Solving Investigations help students learn different problem-solving strategies for attacking word problems.

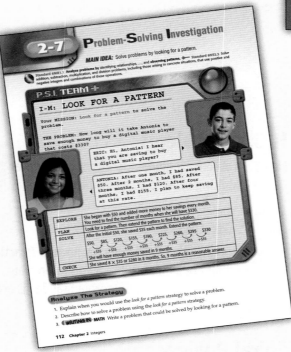

Reading Math

Helps students understand and interpret mathematical language.

Hands-On Labs

Some labs act as an introduction to a mathematical topic, while others extend the topic just presented. **Algebra, Geometry, Measurement, Statistics,** and **Probability** labs use models to bridge the gap between concrete understanding and mathematical symbolism.

Concepts in Motion

Concepts in Motion are online illustrations of key concepts through animations, Interactive Labs, and BrainPOPs®.

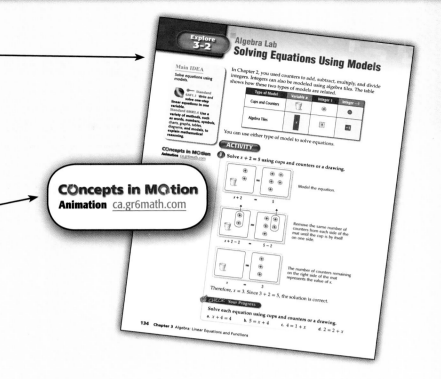

COncepts in MOtion
Animation ca.gr6math.com

Three Built-In Workbooks in the Student Edition

1 Prerequisite Skills

Use the **Prerequisite Skills** with students who need a review of previously taught concepts.

2 Extra Practice

For additional exercises that are modeled after the exercises in each lesson, refer to the **Extra Practice** section.

3 Mixed Problem Solving

Additional word problems for each chapter are provided in **Mixed Problem Solving**.

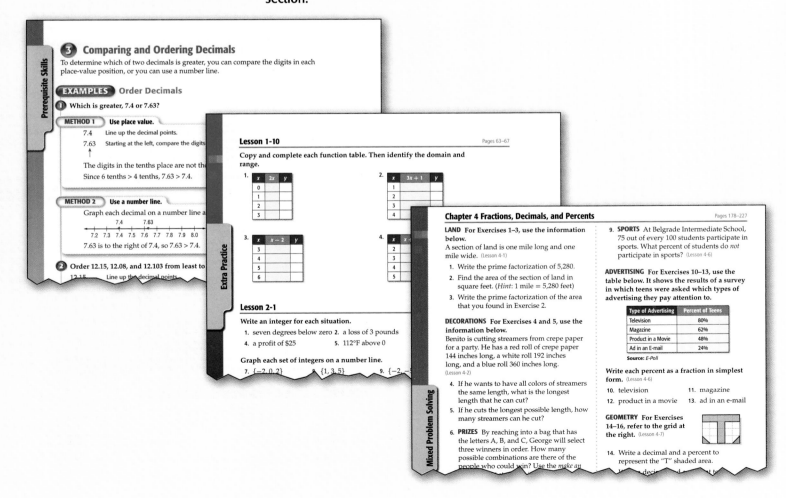

 # Assessment

Data-Driven Decision Making

McGraw-Hill's *California Mathematics: Concepts, Skills, and Problem Solving,* **Grade 6** offers frequent and meaningful assessment of student progress within the curriculum structure and teacher support materials.

California Assessment and Intervention System

1 Diagnostic

3 Summative

2 Formative

1 Diagnostic

Initial Assessment Assess students' prior knowledge **at the beginning of the year** with the *Diagnostic and Placement Tests.* This booklet will help you determine whether your students need additional materials and resources to meet the grade-level or intensive intervention standards.

Entry Level Assessment Assess students' prior knowledge **at the beginning of a chapter or lesson** with one of the following options.

Student Edition
- Get Ready for the Chapter
- Get Ready for the Next Lesson

Teacher Wraparound Edition
- Chapter Assessment Planner

Other Resources
- Chapter Resource Masters
- ExamView Assessment Suite
- Chapter Readiness at ca.gr6math.com

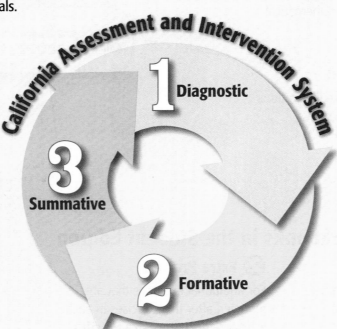

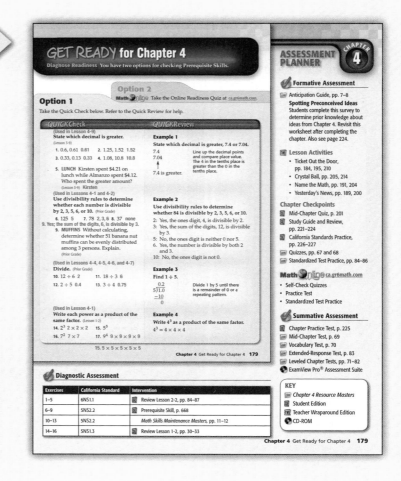

Formative

Progress Monitoring Determine if students are progressing adequately as you teach each lesson, and use the assessments to differentiate lesson instruction and practice.

Student Edition
- Check Your Progress
- Check Your Understanding
- Mid-Chapter Quiz
- Study Guide and Review

Teacher Wraparound Edition
- Chapter Assessment Planner
- Step 4 (Assess) of the Teaching Plan
- Data-Driven Decision Making

Other Resources
- Chapter Resource Masters
- ExamView Assessment Suite
- Self-Check Quizzes at ca.gr6math.com

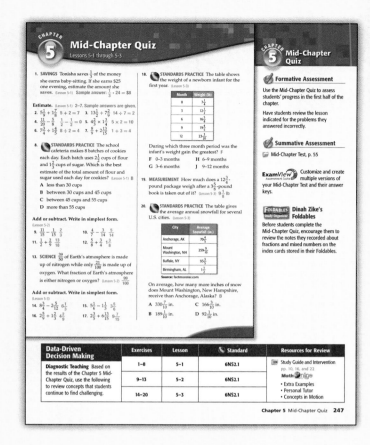

Summative

Summative Evaluation Assess student success in learning the concepts in each chapter.

Student Edition
- Chapter Practice Test
- California Standards Practice

Teacher Wraparound Edition
- Chapter Assessment Planner
- Data-Driven Decision Making

Other Resources
- Chapter Resource Masters
  - 6 forms of Chapter Tests
  - 4 Quizzes
  - Vocabulary Test
  - Extended-Response Test
  - Standardized Test Practice
- ExamView Assessment Suite
- Chapter Tests at ca.gr6math.com

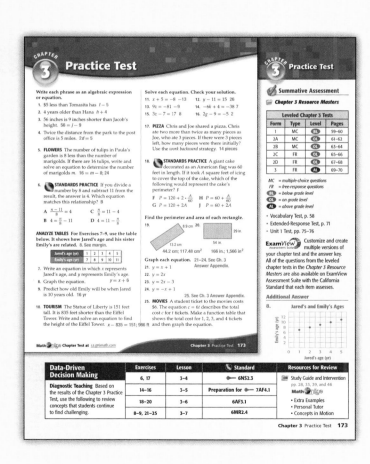

Universal Access

Options McGraw-Hill's *California Mathematics: Concepts, Skills, and Problem Solving,* Grade 6 provides extensive support for universal access.

Leveled Resources

All of the blackline masters and transparencies that accompany the program, as well as all of the Teacher Wraparound Edition pages, are available on the TeacherWorks Plus™ CD-ROM. Resources and assignments are leveled for students who are **below grade level** **BL**, **on grade level** **OL**, and **above grade level** **AL**, and for students who are **English learners** **ELL**.

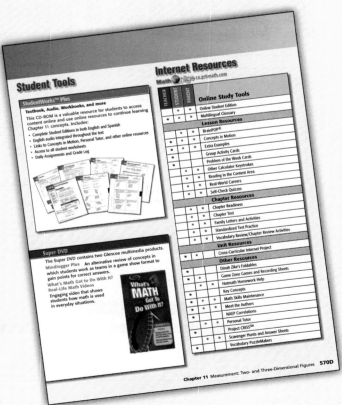

Technology

In addition to the Student Edition and Teacher Wraparound Edition, *California Mathematics: Concepts, Skills, and Problem Solving,* Grade 6 includes extensive resources online, on CD-ROM, and on DVD.

Online Resources for teachers, students, and parents can be found at ca.gr6math.com. These resources include a variety of activities to teach, reinforce, review, and assess mathematical concepts.

CD-ROM/DVD In addition to all of the Student Edition pages, all of the student workbooks that accompany the program are available on the StudentWorks Plus™ CD-ROM. This resource offers full audio of the text to support students with hearing challenges or language difficulty.

Additional tools for class presentations and assessment are available on a variety of CD-ROMs and DVDs.

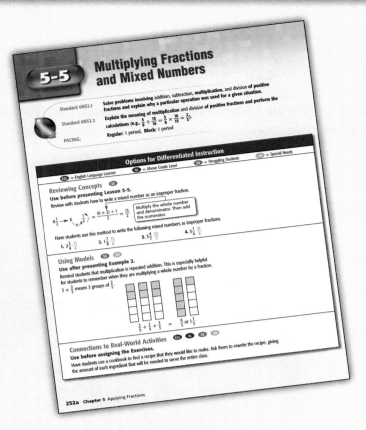

Differentiated Instruction

Diagnostic Teaching Every chapter and lesson includes suggestions for identifying and meeting your students' needs. Strategies include differentiation in pacing and student grouping, alternate approaches, ways to enhance instruction with manipulatives, questions to promote higher order thinking, and language hints.

Personalize instruction for:

- Struggling students
- English language learners
- Students with special needs
- Students who are above grade level in their comprehension of mathematics

Intervention

Strategic Resources and assignments that are coded for students who are below level may be used to provide strategic intervention in your classroom. **Teaching Tips** and other margin resources in the Teacher Wraparound Edition can also be used to target your instruction.

The data-driven decision-making tools in the Teacher Wraparound Edition help teachers identify intensive students, implement targeted intervention, and accelerate students' learning.

In addition, you may want to suggest that students use the *Quick Review Math Handbook* to review mathematical concepts.

Intensive *California Math Triumphs* can accelerate achievement for students who are two or more years below grade level. The content addresses foundational skills from grades K–7. Each volume presents content in small chunks with math "the visual way" to promote differentiated instruction.

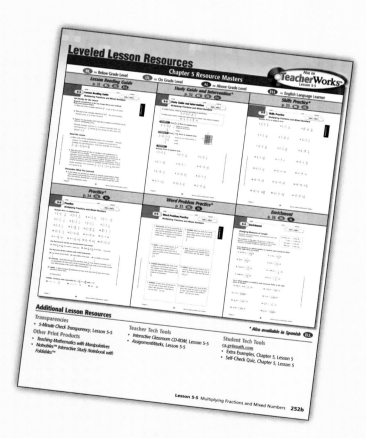

Advanced Learners

Acceleration and Enrichment Resources and assignments that are coded for students who are above level may be used with advanced learners. In particular, the **Enrichment Masters** may provide students with valuable opportunities for extending your lessons. **Pre-AP Activities** provide additional opportunities for extension.

 **Universal Access**

Intensive Intervention McGraw-Hill's *California Mathematics: Concepts, Skills, and Problem Solving*, Grade 6 and *California Math Triumphs* provides extensive support for universal access.

How Can I Accelerate Learning for Intensive Students?

Students who have significant gaps in their understanding of mathematics may need intensive intervention in order to meet grade-level mathematics standards.

California Math Triumphs provides step-by-step instruction, vocabulary support, and data-driven decision making to help students succeed.

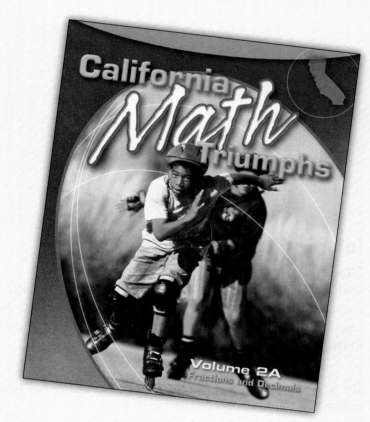

Provide Personalized Instruction

Consumable volumes and minimal preparation requirements allow for flexibility and personalized instruction in any setting.

- After school
- Summer school
- Before school
- Intersession
- Tutoring
- Pull-out/Resource room

For more information, contact your sales representative at 1-800-334-7344 or visit glencoe.com.

Intensive Intervention

1. **Diagnose**—Students can complete the Online Readiness Quiz or the Quick Quiz at the start of each chapter. Teachers can also administer online or print-based diagnostic assessments for each volume, chapter, and lesson.

2. **Prescribe**—Students follow a personalized remediation plan to accelerate their understanding of specific mathematics skills.

   - **Print:** Interactive, full-color study guides provide explicit skills instruction
   - **Hands-On:** *Active Problem Solving for Differentiated Instruction* offer engaging, cooperative learning experiences
   - **Technology:** Online assessments evaluate students' success

3. **Assess**—Measure student success and inform future instruction through frequent, meaningful assessment, both online and in print.

How Does *California Math Triumphs* Support *California Mathematics?*

The table below shows how the prerequisite skills for *California Mathematics, Concepts, Skills, and Problem Solving,* **Grade 6,** correlate to *California Math Triumphs*. Specific suggestions are provided in each chapter.

California Mathematics Grade 6	Prerequisite Skills	Standards	Use *California Math Triumphs*
Chapter 1: Introduction to Algebra and Functions	Compare and order, operations with integers	6NS2.3, 3AF1.0	Volume 2, Chapter 4 Volume 4, Chapter 1
Chapter 2: Integers	Compare real numbers, evaluate algebraic expressions	6NS1.1, 6AF1.1	Volume 2, Chapter 4 Volume 4, Chapter 3
Chapter 3: Algebra: Linear Equations and Functions	Graph ordered pairs, add, subtract, divide integers	5SDAP1.4, 6NS2.3	Volume 5, Chapter 2 Volume 1, Chapter 6
Chapter 4: Fractions, Decimals, and Percents	Compare decimals, use exponents as repeated multiplication	6NS1.1, 4NS4.1	Volume 2, Chapter 4 Volume 1, Chapter 1
Chapter 5: Applying Percents	Multiply and divide decimals, write equivalent fractions	6NS2.3, 6NS1.1	Volume 2, Chapters 2 and 4
Chapter 6: Ratios and Proportions	Multiply and divide multi-digit numbers, convert decimals to fractions	4NS3.2, 4NS1.6	Volume 1, Chapters 4-5 Volume 2, Chapter 4
Chapter 7: Applying Percents	Solve one-step equations, convert percents to decimals	6AF1.2, 5NS1.2	Volume 4, Chapter 3 Volume 3, Chapter 3
Chapter 8: Statistics: Analyzing Data	Compare decimals, evaluate numerical expressions	6NS1.1, 6AF1.2	Volume 2, Chapter 4 Volume 4, Chapter 3
Chapter 9: Probability	Multiply whole numbers, multiply and simplify fractions	4NS3.2, 5NS2.5	Volume 1, Chapter 4 Volume 2, Chapter 3
Chapter 10: Geometry: Polygons	Multiply and divide decimals, solve equations	5NS2.1, 5AF1.2	Volume 2, Chapter 4 Volume 4, Chapter 3
Chapter 11: Measurement: Two- and Three-Dimensional Figures	Multiply rational numbers, evaluate exponents	5NS2.5, 6NS2.3, 4NS4.1	Volume 2, Chapters 3-4 Volume 1, Chapter 4
Chapter 12: Looking Ahead to Grade 7: Geometry and Measurement	Evaluate exponents and algebraic expressions	4NS4.1, 6AF1.2	Volume 1, Chapter 4 Volume 4, Chapter 3

Accelerate Learning

- Step-by-step instruction, scaffolded practice, and frequent assessments reinforce skills for long-term retention.
- Motivate reluctant learners through meaningful real-world applications.
- Comprehensive Teacher Edition helps identify common errors and misconceptions, differentiate instruction, and accommodate English Learners.

Use Data-Driven Decision Making

- Diagnostic, formative, and summative assessments help teachers match instruction to students' intervention needs.
- Assessments monitor progress and content mastery.

Instructional Planning and Support

Strong Pedagogy McGraw-Hill's *California Mathematics: Concepts, Skills, and Problem Solving,* **Grade 6** has a strong instructional model that includes:

- differentiated instructional options,
- reteaching, reinforcement, and extension options,
- Teacher Tips to help address various learners,
- Pre-AP/Advanced items, and
- assessment linked with instruction.

Planning for Success

The **Chapter Overview** helps you plan your instruction by showing the objectives to be covered, the California Standards to be mastered, and the suggested pacing.

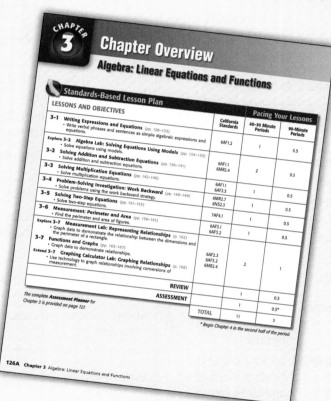

Vertical Alignment

Topics are presented to build upon prior skills and concepts and to serve as a foundation for future topics.

What the Research Says

Citations from **research** help to validate McGraw-Hill's *California Mathematics* program.

Reading and Writing in Mathematics

Resources such as **Reading in the Content Area, Noteables™ Interactive Study Notebook,** and **Recommended Outside Reading** help mathematics students become better readers. **Project CRISS^SM** strategies improve reading and comprehension.

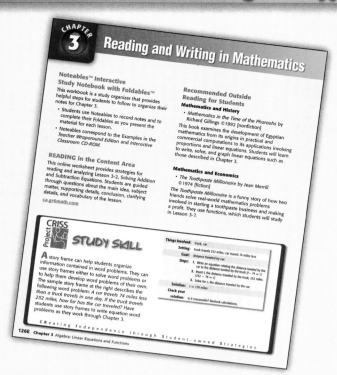

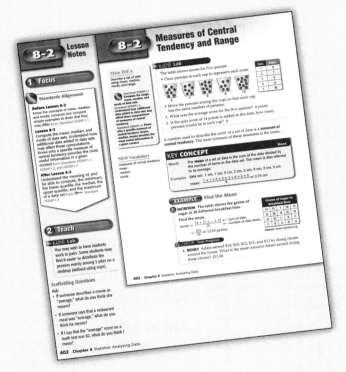

Four-Step Teaching Plan

Organizes your instruction as you **Focus** and **Teach** and help your students **Practice** and **Assess** what they've learned.

Standards Alignment

California Standards Alignment shows the Standards that lead into and follow the current lesson's content for a coherent K–12 scope and sequence.

Scaffolding Questions

Each lesson contains **Scaffolding Questions** for you to use to help students investigate and understand the main ideas of the lesson.

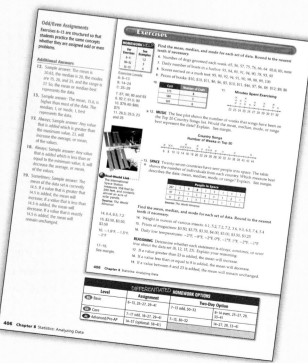

Additional Examples

Each **Additional Example** mirrors the Example in the Student Edition. The Additional Examples are also available as a PowerPoint® presentation on the **California Interactive Classroom** CD-ROM. Students also have access to these examples in their **California Noteables: Interactive Study Notebook**.

Differentiated Homework Options

Because most classrooms include students at a wide range of ability levels, **Differentiated Homework Options** allow you to customize your assignments.

 Instructional Planning and Support

Professional Development McGraw-Hill Professional Development provides a comprehensive professional development plan for mathematics that is fully aligned and articulated with *California Mathematics: Concepts, Skills, and Problem Solving.*

Textbook Implementation Modules

These are video-enhanced CD programs in which users see an experienced teacher showing a new teacher how to use McGraw-Hill Teacher Editions, Student Editions, and program ancillaries to enhance classroom instruction.

Video Workshops

- **Self-Study** Users watch video clips of classroom lessons and guest educators who discuss issues and best practices. Then they complete short, self-paced lessons and activities in which they analyze the demonstrated teaching strategies and consider how to apply them in their classrooms.

- **Mentor-Led** Groups watch video clips of classroom lessons and guest educators. Then school coaches or facilitators use the videos as springboards for discussion and group professional development activities.

Accredited Online Courses

(Available for purchase)

Each 3- to 5-hour online module emphasizes the strategies and techniques used to teach mathematics. Users watch video clips of classroom lessons, complete interactive exercises, and develop electronic portfolios that can be printed and submitted to verify course completion. University credit is available for an additional charge.

Customized On-Site Training Materials

These workshop materials allow coaches to create a customized sequence of mathematics professional development sessions that directly address the specific needs of a school or district.

Mini-Clip Video Library

The video library includes several hundred short video clips that are referenced at point of use in the *California Mathematics: Concepts, Skills, and Problem Solving* Teacher Editions. These clips illustrate math content or instructional strategies and may include demonstrations or commentaries by curriculum specialists.

Mc Graw Hill Professional Development

Targeted professional development has been articulated throughout the *California Mathematics: Concepts, Skills, and Problem Solving* series. The **McGraw-Hill Professional Development Video Library** provides short videos that support the Key Standards. For more information, visit ca.gr6math.com.

Professional Development Web Sites

- **MHPD Online** (mhpdonline.com) is a Web site for K-12 educators where they can view video clips of instructional strategies, link to Web sites for relevant educational information, download grade-level student activities and worksheets, review monthly book suggestions, and read about the latest news and issues in education.

- **Teaching Today** (glencoe.com/sec/teachingtoday/index.phtml) is a Web site for secondary teachers of all disciplines that makes use of the extensive resources and expertise available from all of Glencoe/McGraw-Hill's secondary subject areas.

Program Components

	Grade K	Grade 1	Grade 2	Grade 3	Grade 4	Grade 5	Grade 6	Grade 7
Chapter Resource Masters	●	●	●	●	●	●	●	●
Mastering the California Standards		●	●	●	●	●	●	●
Daily Reteach Transparencies	●	●	●	●	●	●		
5-Minute Check Transparencies		●	●	●	●	●	●	●
California Noteables							●	●
Hands-On Activity Tools	●	●	●	●	●	●		
Teaching Math with Manipulatives							●	●
Science and Math Lab Manual							●	●
ELL Guide	●	●	●	●	●	●		
Strategic Intervention Guide		●	●	●	●	●		
Problem of the Day/Week	●	●	●	●	●	●	●	●
Learning Station Cards	●	●	●	●	●	●		
Math Routines on the Go	●	●	●					
Quick Review Math Handbook							●	●
Visual Vocabulary Cards	●	●	●	●	●	●		
Transition Blackline Masters				●				
Math Skills Maintenance							●	●
Problem Solving Leveled Readers	●	●	●	●	●	●		
Graphic Novels							●	●
Dinah Zike's Teaching with Foldables	●	●	●	●	●	●	●	●
Diagnostic and Placement Tests	●	●	●	●	●	●	●	●
StudentWorks Plus CD-ROM	●	●	●	●	●	●	●	●
TeacherWorks Plus DVD	●	●	●	●	●	●	●	●
ExamView CD-ROM		●	●	●	●	●	●	●
Interactive Classroom PowerPoint™			●	●	●	●	●	●
Math Adventures with Dot and Ray CD-ROM	●	●	●	●	●	●	●	
Classroom Games CD-ROM	●	●	●	●	●	●		
AssignmentWorks CD-ROM								●
Math Songs CD-ROM	●	●	●	●	●	●		
Individual Manipulative Kit	●	●	●	●	●	●	●	●
Classroom Manipulative Kit	●	●	●	●	●	●	●	●
Overhead Manipulative Kit	●	●	●	●	●	●	●	●
Teacher Tool Kit	●	●	●	●	●	●		
Magnetic Manipulative Kit	●	●	●	●	●	●		
Student Edition Flip Book	●							
Activity Flip Chart	●							
Robot Puppet	●	●	●					
Workmats	●		●	●	●	●		
Professional Development	●	●	●	●	●	●	●	●

Program Manipulatives

Manipulative	Suggested Alternative	Grade K	Grade 1	Grade 2	Grade 3	Grade 4	Grade 5	Grade 6	Grade 7
Attribute Buttons	real buttons, pasta	●							
Color Tiles	blocks, buttons	●							
Graphing Mats	posterboard	●							
Attribute Blocks	pasta, buttons	●	●	●					
Student Clock	paper plate, brads	●	●	●	●	●	●		
Demonstration Clock	paper plate, brads	●	●	●	●	●	●		
Connecting Cubes	paper clips	●	●	●	●	●	●		
Number Cubes	spinner, cards	●	●	●	●	●	●	●	●
Spinners	construction paper, paperclip, pencil		●	●	●	●	●	●	●
Two-Colored Counters	buttons, coins, beans	●	●	●	●	●	●	●	
Pattern Blocks	construction paper	●	●	●	●	●	●	●	●
Geometric Solids	cans, boxes, balls		●	●	●	●	●		
Bucket Balance	ruler, paper cups, string	●	●	●	●	●			
Base-Ten Blocks	grid paper		●	●	●	●		●	●
Money	real money, construction paper		●	●	●	●	●		
Ruler	straightedge, book		●	●	●	●	●	●	●
Fraction Circles	construction paper		●	●	●	●	●		
Fraction Models					●	●	●		
Geoboards			●	●	●	●		●	●
Compass					●	●	●	●	●
Protractor					●	●	●	●	●
Plastic Cups	paper cups				●	●	●	●	●
Algebra Tiles	block, buttons, coins							●	●
Centimeter Cubes	block							●	●
Equation Mats	construction paper							●	●
Stopwatch	clock, watch							●	●
Measuring Cups	paper cups							●	●
Geomirrors								●	●
Tangrams	construction paper							●	●

Contents

Start Smart
Be a Better Problem Solver

Unit 1
Algebra and Functions

Integers

For formative and summative
assessment options, see page 79.

For formative and summative assessment options, see page 127.

Prerequisite Skills
- Get Ready for Chapter 3   127
- Get Ready for the Next Lesson   133, 141, 146, 155, 161

Reading and Writing Mathematics
- Reading in the Content Area   136
- Reading Word Problems   150
- Writing in Math   132, 141, 146, 148, 155, 161, 167

🌊 **California Standards Practice**
- Multiple Choice   126, 131, 133, 141, 147, 155, 161, 167
- Worked Out Example   130

H.O.T. Problems
Higher Order Thinking
- Challenge   132, 141, 146, 155, 161, 167
- Find the Error   132, 146
- Open Ended   132, 160, 167
- Select the Operation   149
- Select a Technique   155
- Which One Doesn't Belong?   141

Unit 2
Number Sense: Fractions

CHAPTER 4
Fractions, Decimals, and Percents

For formative and summative assessment options, see page 179.

Prerequisite Skills

- Get Ready for Chapter 4   179
- Get Ready for the Next Lesson   184, 189, 195, 200, 205, 210, 214, 220

Reading and Writing Mathematics

- Reading Word Problems   185
- Vocabulary Link   197, 211
- Writing in Math   184, 189, 190, 195, 200, 205, 210, 214, 220

California Standards Practice

- Multiple Choice   184, 189, 195, 200, 205, 210, 214, 220
- Worked Out Example   217

H.O.T. Problems
Higher Order Thinking

- Challenge   184, 189, 195, 200, 205, 210, 214, 220
- Find the Error   195, 210
- Number Sense   184, 191
- Open Ended   184, 194, 200, 210, 214
- Reasoning   213
- Select the Operation   191
- Select a Technique   214
- Which One Doesn't Belong?   205, 220

CHAPTER 5 Applying Fractions

For formative and summative assessment options, see page 229.

Prerequisite Skills
- Get Ready for Chapter 5   229
- Get Ready for the Next Lesson   235, 241, 246, 257, 262

Reading and Writing Mathematics
- Reading in the Content Area   236
- Reading Word Problems   264
- Vocabulary Link   258
- Writing in Math   235, 240, 246, 247, 257, 262, 270

California Standards Practice
- Multiple Choice   235, 241, 246, 257, 260, 262, 270
- Worked Out Example   260

H.O.T. Problems
Higher Order Thinking
- Challenge   234, 240, 246, 257, 262, 269
- Find the Error   240, 269
- Number Sense   234, 246
- Open Ended   234, 240, 257
- Reasoning   262
- Select the Operation   248
- Select a Technique   235
- Select a Tool   269
- Which One Doesn't Belong?   262

Unit 3

Algebra and Number Sense: Proportions and Percents

CHAPTER 6

Ratios and Proportions

For formative and summative assessment options, see page 281.

Prerequisite Skills

Reading and Writing Mathematics

California Standards Practice

H.O.T. Problems
Higher Order Thinking

CHAPTER 7 Applying Percents

For formative and summative
assessment options,
see page 341.

Prerequisite Skills
- Get Ready for Chapter 7   341
- Get Ready for the Next Lesson   348, 354,
  360, 365, 374, 378

Reading and Writing Mathematics
- Reading Math   380
- Reading Word Problems   349
- Writing in Math   348, 354, 360, 361, 365,
  374, 378, 382

California Standards Practice
- Multiple Choice   348, 354, 360, 365, 372,
  374, 378, 382
- Worked Out Example   371

H.O.T. Problems
Higher Order Thinking
- Challenge   348, 354, 359, 365, 374, 378,
  382
- Find the Error   359, 374
- Number Sense   359, 373
- Open Ended   348, 354, 359, 365, 373,
  378, 382
- Select the Operation   360
- Select a Technique   348
- Select a Tool   368
- Which One Doesn't Belong?   378 220

Unit 4

Statistics, Data Analysis, and Probability

CHAPTER 8

Statistics: Analyzing Data

For formative and summative
assessment options, see page 395.

Prerequisite Skills

Reading and Writing Mathematics

California Standards Practice

H.O.T. Problems
Higher Order Thinking

Prerequisite Skills
- Get Ready for Chapter 9   459
- Get Ready for the Next Lesson   464, 470, 474, 478, 483, 490

Reading and Writing Mathematics
- Reading in the Content Area   471
- Reading Math   460, 462, 492
- Vocabulary Link   480
- Writing in Math   464, 469, 474, 478, 483, 484, 490, 497

California Standards Practice
- Multiple Choice   464, 467, 470, 474, 478, 483, 490, 497
- Worked Out Example   466

H.O.T. Problems
Higher Order Thinking
- Challenge   464, 469, 474, 478, 483, 490, 497
- Find the Error   469, 483
- Open Ended   464
- Select the Operation   485
- Select a Tool   469, 477, 490
- Which One Doesn't Belong?   464, 474

Unit 5

Geometry and Measurement

Geometry: Polygons

For formative and summative
assessment options, see page 509.

Prerequisite Skills

- Get Ready for Chapter 10   509
- Get Ready for the Next Lesson   513, 517, 523, 529, 538, 545, 551, 557

Reading and Writing Mathematics

- Reading in the Content Area   510
- Reading Math   510, 511, 515, 524, 541, 546, 547, 553
- Writing in Math   513, 517, 523, 529, 537, 545, 551, 556, 562

California Standards Practice

- Multiple Choice   513, 517, 523, 529, 537, 545, 551, 557, 562
- Worked Out Example   527

H.O.T. Problems
Higher Order Thinking

- Challenge   513, 517, 523, 529, 545, 550, 556, 562
- Find the Error   538
- Open Ended   529, 550, 562
- Reasoning   517, 537, 550, 556
- Which One Doesn't Belong?   556

Looking Ahead to Grade 7: Geometry and Measurement

For formative and summative assessment options, see page 637.

Student Handbook

Built-In Workbooks

Reference

California Grizzly Bear

California Content Standards, Grade 6, Correlated to *California Mathematics*, Grade 6 ©2008

●━━ = Key Standard defined by Mathematics Framework for California Public Schools
* = Standard assessed on the California High School Exit Exam (CAHSEE)

Standard	Text of Standard	Primary Citations	Supporting Citations
Number Sense			
●━ 1.0	**Students compare and order positive and negative fractions, decimals, and mixed numbers. Students solve problems involving fractions, ratios, proportions, and percentages.**		
●━ 1.1	Compare and order positive and negative fractions, decimals, and mixed numbers and place them on a number line.	215-220	80-87, 196-210, 230-235, 282-311, 316-322, 329-332, 670
●━ 1.2	Interpret and use ratios in different contexts (e.g., batting averages, miles per hour) to show the relative sizes of two quantities, using appropriate notations (*a/b, a* to *b, a:b*).	282-293	206-210, 215-220, 294-311, 316-322, 369-374, 460-497
●━ 1.3	Use proportions to solve problems (e.g., determine the value of N if $\frac{4}{7} = \frac{N}{21}$, find the length of a side of a polygon similar to a known polygon). Use cross-multiplication as a method for solving such problems, understanding it as the multiplication of both sides of an equation by a multiplicative inverse.	306-311, 316-322, 350-354, 540-545	312, 323
●━ 1.4	Calculate given percentages of quantities and solve problems involving discounts at sales, interest earned, and tips.	342-365, 375-383	202-205, 349, 366-367, 518-523
●━ 2.0	**Students calculate and solve problems involving addition, subtraction, multiplication, and division.**		
2.1	Solve problems involving addition, subtraction, multiplication, and division of positive fractions and explain why a particular operation was used for a given situation.	236-246, 252-257, 265-270	230-235, 248-251, 314-322, 584-588, 646-647
2.2	Explain the meaning of multiplication and division of positive fractions and perform the calculations $\left(e.g., \frac{5}{8} \div \frac{15}{16} = \frac{5}{8} \times \frac{16}{15} = \frac{2}{3}\right)$.	252-257, 264-270	250-251
●━ 2.3	Solve addition, subtraction, multiplication, and division problems, including those arising in concrete situations, that use positive and negative integers and combinations of these operations.	93-99, 101-106, 112-113, 114-118	24-29, 38-41, 44-47, 53-56, 107-111, 314-315
●━ 2.4	Determine the least common multiple and the greatest common divisor of whole numbers; use them to solve problems with fractions (e.g., to find a common denominator to add two fractions or to find the reduced form for a fraction).	186-189, 192-195, 211-214	180-185, 192-195, 202-205, 215-220, 236-241, 242-246, 252-257, 282-286
Algebra and Functions			
1.0	**Students write verbal expressions and sentences as algebraic expressions and equations; they evaluate algebraic expressions, solve simple linear equations, and graph and interpret their results.**		
●━ 1.1	Write and solve one-step linear equations in one variable.	49-52, 134-146, 258-263	63-67, 151-161, 230-235, 252-263, 306-311, 316-322, 350-354, 361-365, 375-378, 434-437, 524-531, 540-545

Standard	Text of Standard	Primary Citations	Supporting Citations
1.2	Write and evaluate an algebraic expression for a given situation, using up to three variables.	44-47, 128-133	57-61, 62, 69, 103-106, 112-113, 114-118, 156-161, 163-167, 252-257, 379-382, 572-576, 578-582, 613-618, 636-639, 649-653
1.3	Apply algebraic order of operations and the commutative, associative, and distributive properties to evaluate expressions; and justify each step in the process.	38-41, 53-56	44-47, 80-82, 578-582
1.4	Solve problems manually by using the correct order of operations or by using a scientific calculator.	38-41	44-47, 69, 80-82, 151-155, 168, 196-200, 344-348, 409, 619-624, 636-639
2.0	**Students analyze and use tables, graphs, and rules to solve problems involving rates and proportions.**		
2.1	Convert one unit of measurement to another (e.g., from feet to miles, from centimeters to inches).	294-305	156-161, 168
2.2	Demonstrate an understanding that *rate* is a measure of one quantity per unit value of another quantity.	287-292	293
2.3	Solve problems involving rates, average speed, distance, and time.	142-146, 287-292	63-67, 163-167, 282-286
3.0	**Students investigate geometric patterns and describe them algebraically.**		
3.1	Use variables in expressions describing geometric quantities (e.g., $P = 2w + 2\ell$, $A = \frac{1}{2}bh$, $C = \pi d$ – the formulas for the perimeter of a rectangle, the area of a triangle, and the circumference of a circle, respectively).	156-161, 577-588, 596-599	162, 572-576, 589-593, 640-645, 649-653, 656-659
3.2	Express in symbolic form simple relationships arising from geometry.	156-161, 546-551, 572-593, 596-599	47, 128-133, 162, 600-601, 613-618, 640-645, 649-653, 656-659
Measurement and Geometry			
1.0	**Students deepen their understanding of the measurement of plane and solid shapes and use this understanding to solve problems.**		
1.1	Understand the concept of a constant such as π; know the formulas for the circumference and area of a circle.	583-593	656-659
1.2	Know common estimates of π (3.14; $\frac{22}{7}$) and use these values to estimate and calculate the circumference and the area of circles; compare with actual measurements.	584-593	619-623, 656-659
1.3	Know and use the formulas for the volume of triangular prisms and cylinders (area of base x height); compare these formulas and explain the similarity between them and the formula for the volume of a rectangular solid.	613-623	639, 645
2.0	**Students identify and describe the properties of two-dimensional figures.**		
2.1	Identify angles as vertical, adjacent, complementary, or supplementary and provide descriptions of these terms.	510-517	529, 568
2.2	Use the properties of complementary and supplementary angles and the sum of the angles of a triangle to solve problems involving an unknown angle.	514-517, 524-529	569

Standard	Text of Standard	Primary Citations	Supporting Citations
⊶ 2.3	Draw quadrilaterals and triangles from given information about them (e.g., a quadrilateral having equal sides but no right angles, a right isosceles triangle).	524-529, 533-538	156-161, 530-531
Statistics, Data Analysis, and Probability			
1.0	**Students compute and analyze statistical measurements for data sets.**		
1.1*	Compute the range, mean, median, and mode of data sets.	396-408	402-414
1.2	Understand how additional data added to data sets may affect these computations.	396-408	410-414
1.3	Understand how the inclusion or exclusion of outliers affects these computations.	410-414	396-408
1.4	Know why a specific measure of central tendency (mean, median, mode) provides the most useful information in a given context.	402-408	409-414
2.0	**Students use data samples of a population and describe the characteristics and limitations of the samples.**		
2.1	Compare different samples of a population with the data from the entire population and identify a situation in which it makes sense to use a sample.	438-443	312
⊶ 2.2	Identify different ways of selecting a sample (e.g., convenience sampling, responses to a survey, random sampling) and which method makes a sample more representative for a population.	438-443	434-437
⊶ 2.3	Analyze data displays and explain why the way in which the question was asked might have influenced the results obtained and why the way in which the results were displayed might have influenced the conclusions reached.	415-422, 424-425, 432-433, 438-449	438-443
⊶ 2.4	Identify data that represent sampling errors and explain why the sample (and the display) might be biased.	444-449	438-443
⊶ 2.5*	Identify claims based on statistical data and, in simple cases, evaluate the validity of the claims.	409, 426-431, 434-443	438-443
3.0	**Students determine theoretical and experimental probabilities and use these to make predictions about events.**		
⊶ 3.1*	Represent all possible outcomes for compound events in an organized way (e.g., tables, grids, tree diagrams) and express the theoretical probability of each outcome.	465-478	128-133, 190-191
3.2	Use data to estimate the probability of future events (e.g., batting averages or number of accidents per mile driven).	486-491	484-485
⊶ 3.3*	Represent probabilities as ratios, proportions, decimals between 0 and 1, and percentages between 0 and 100 and verify that the probabilities computed are reasonable; know that if P is the probability of an event, $1-P$ is the probability of an event not occurring.	460-464	465-478, 484-497
3.4	Understand that the probability of either of two disjoint events occurring is the sum of the two individual probabilities and that the probability of one event following another, in independent trials, is the product of the two probabilities.	492-497	523, 623, 665
⊶ 3.5*	Understand the difference between independent and dependent events.	492-497	523, 623, 665

Standard	Text of Standard	Primary Citations	Supporting Citations
Mathematical Reasoning			
1.0	**Students make decisions about how to approach problems.**		
1.1	Analyze problems by identifying relationships, distinguishing relevant from irrelevant information, identifying missing information, sequencing and prioritizing information, and observing patterns.	25-29, 42-43, 107-111, 148-149, 180, 190-191, 248-249, 532	57-67, 84-87
1.2	Formulate and justify mathematical conjectures based on a general description of the mathematical question or problem posed.	93-94, 101-102, 530-531	69, 134-135, 168, 409, 415-422, 426-431, 434-437, 491, 552, 577, 624, 654-655
1.3	Determine when and how to break a problem into simpler parts.	594-595	25-29, 53-56, 95-99, 150, 607, 649-653, 656-659
2.0	**Students use strategies, skills, and concepts in finding solutions.**		
2.1	Use estimation to verify the reasonableness of calculated results.	148-149, 355-360	25-29, 236-246, 312
2.2	Apply strategies and results from simpler problems to more complex problems.	546-551, 594-595	62, 180
2.3	Estimate unknown quantities graphically and solve for them by using logical reasoning and arithmetic and algebraic techniques.	424-431	49-52, 136-146, 151-155, 230-235, 350-354, 426-431, 434-437
2.4	Use a variety of methods, such as words, numbers, symbols, charts, graphs, tables, diagrams, and models, to explain mathematical reasoning.	62-67, 69, 134-135, 162-168, 314-315, 424-425, 484-485, 518-523, 607-612, 624, 646-647	30-41, 44-47, 49-52, 80-82, 88-94, 95-106, 114-118, 128-146, 151-155, 163-167, 180, 185, 196-200, 202-205, 230-241, 252-263, 265-270, 282-286, 293, 316-322, 324-332, 342-349, 369-374, 355-360, 396-409, 415-422, 426-437, 532, 553-562, 600-601, 607, 624, 636-645, 654-655, 649-653, 656-659
2.5	Express the solution clearly and logically by using the appropriate mathematical notation and terms and clear language; support solutions with evidence in both verbal and symbolic work.	38-41, 128-133	53-56, 136-146, 151-161, 258-263, 350-354, 383, 409, 510-513, 540-545
2.6	Indicate the relative advantages of exact and approximate solutions to problems and give answers to a specified degree of accuracy.	584-588	300-305, 344-348, 350-354, 361-365, 369-378, 546-551, 572-576, 578-582, 589-593, 636-639, 656-659
2.7	Make precise calculations and check the validity of the results from the context of the problem.	148-149	24-29, 42-43, 136-146, 151-155, 265-270
3.0	**Students move beyond a particular problem by generalizing to other situations.**		
3.1	Evaluate the reasonableness of the solution in the context of the original situation.	366-367	24-29, 42-43, 236-241, 265-270, 324-328, 355-365, 518-531, 553-557, 572-576, 619-623, 640-645

Standard	Text of Standard	Primary Citations	Supporting Citations
3.2	Note the method of deriving the solution and demonstrate a conceptual understanding of the derivation by solving similar problems.	24-29	42-43, 62, 93-94, 101-102, 112-113, 134-135, 148-149, 190-191, 248-249, 314-315, 342-343, 366-367, 424-425, 484-485, 530-531, 594-595, 646-647
3.3	Develop generalizations of the results obtained and the strategies used and apply them in new problem situations.	93-94, 101-102, 250-251, 577, 583, 600-601	62, 162, 168, 323

Hearst Castle, San Simeon

Introduction

In this unit, students will use line plots and measures of central tendency to analyze data and make predictions. They also will learn to interpret statistical data through the use of stem-and-leaf plots, bar graphs, and histograms. Students will combine these skills as they analyze how data can be manipulated and displayed in a misleading fashion.

Students then will use tables, tree diagrams, and the Fundamental Counting Principle to find the number of possible outcomes of simple events. They will explore permutations and combinations of sets of objects. Finally, they will investigate theoretical and experimental probability and independent events.

Assessment Options

Unit 4 Test Pages 81–82 of the *Chapter 9 Resource Masters* may be used as a test or a review for Unit 4. This assessment contains both multiple-choice and short-response items.

Create additional customized Unit Tests and review worksheets for differentiated instruction.

Unit 4
Statistics, Data Analysis, and Probability

Focus

Calculate and use statistical measures to describe data, analyze data and sampling processes for possible bias, and calculate probabilities.

CHAPTER 8
Statistics: Analyzing Data

BIG Idea Compute and analyze statistical measurements for data sets.

BIG Idea Use measures of central tendency and range to describe a set of data.

BIG Idea Use data samples of a population and describe the characteristics and limitations of the samples.

CHAPTER 9
Probability

BIG Idea Determine theoretical and experimental probabilities and use these to make predictions about events.

392

What's MATH Got To Do With It?

Real-Life Math Videos engage students, showing them how math is used in everyday situations. Use Video 4 with this unit to discuss how stem-and-leaf plots, median, and mean are used in animal care and retail sales. (also available on one Super DVD combined with MindJogger Videoquizzes)

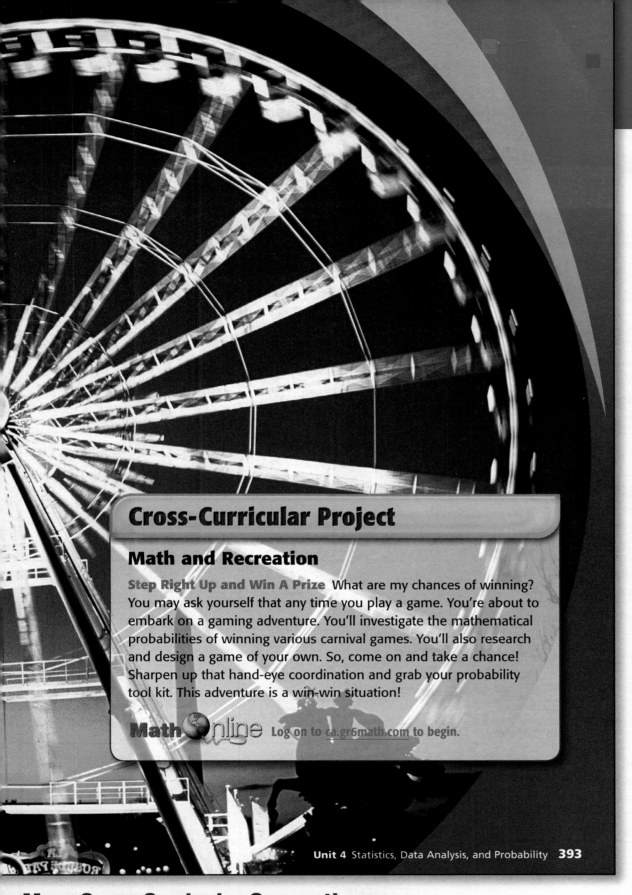

Math and Recreation

Step Right Up and Win A Prize This Cross-Curricular Project is an online project in which students do research on the Internet, gather data, and make presentations using word processing, graphing, page-making, or presentation software. In each chapter, students advance to the next step in their project. At the end of Chapter 9, the project culminates with a presentation of their findings.

Math Online
ca.gr6math.com Log on for teaching suggestions and sample answers for this project.

Team Teaching You can use this Cross-Curricular Project with your students' physical education teacher to make the connection from mathematics to the recreational activities your students are studying.

Cross-Curricular Project

Math and Recreation

Step Right Up and Win A Prize What are my chances of winning? You may ask yourself that any time you play a game. You're about to embark on a gaming adventure. You'll investigate the mathematical probabilities of winning various carnival games. You'll also research and design a game of your own. So, come on and take a chance! Sharpen up that hand-eye coordination and grab your probability tool kit. This adventure is a win-win situation!

Math Online Log on to ca.gr6math.com to begin.

Unit 4 Statistics, Data Analysis, and Probability **393**

More Cross-Curricular Connections

You may wish to share these suggestions with your students' other teachers.

Math and Social Studies
Research the history of carnivals around the world. Prepare a report including the significance of games, masks, and fatty foods in carnivals around the world. You may wish to focus on a particular place such as Venice, Italy; Rio de Janeiro, Brazil; or New Orleans in your report.

Math and Art
Design a poster for a carnival that is sure to attract customers. Include drawings of several carnival games and prizes, as well as foods, beverages, and entertainment. Use catchy names, attractive colors, and bold-sized graphics.

Chapter Overview

Statistics: Analyzing Data

Standards-Based Lesson Plan	Pacing Your Lessons		
LESSONS AND OBJECTIVES	California Standard	45–50 Minute Periods	90-Minute Periods
8-1 Line Plots (pp. 396–401) • Display and analyze data using a line plot.	6SDAP1.1 6SDAP1.2	1	0.5
8-2 Measures of Central Tendency and Range (pp. 402–408) • Describe a set of data using mean, median, mode, and range. **Extend 8-2 Graphing Calculator Lab: Mean and Median** (p. 409) • Use technology to calculate the mean and median of a set of data.	6SDAP1.1 6SDAP1.2 6SDAP1.4 6SDAP2.5 6MR2.5	1	0.5
8-3 Stem-and-Leaf Plots (pp. 410–414) • Display and analyze data in a stem-and-leaf plot.	6SDAP1.3 6SDAP1.1	1	0.5
8-4 Bar Graphs and Histograms (pp. 415–421) • Display and analyze data using bar graphs and histograms. **Extend 8-4 Spreadsheet Lab: Circle Graphs** (p. 422) • Use technology to create circle graphs.	6SDAP2.3 6MR1.2	2	1
8-5 Problem-Solving Investigation: Use a Graph (pp. 424–425) • Solve problems by using a graph.	6MR2.3 6SDAP2.3	1	0.5
8-6 Using Graphs to Predict (pp. 426–431) • Analyze line graphs and scatter plots to make predictions and inferences. **Extend 8-6 Spreadsheet Lab: Multiple-Line and-Bar Graphs** (pp. 432–433) • Use a spreadsheet to make a multiple-line graph and a multiple-bar graph.	6MR2.3 6SDAP2.5 6SDAP2.3 6MR2.4	2	1
8-7 Using Data to Predict (pp. 434–437) • Predict the actions of a larger group by using data.	6SDAP2.2 6SDAP2.5	1	0.5
8-8 Using Sampling to Predict (pp. 438–443) • Predict the actions of a larger group by using a sample.	6SDAP2.1 6SDAP2.2 6SDAP2.5	2	1
8-9 Misleading Statistics (pp. 444–449) • Recognize when statistics and graphs are misleading.	6SDAP2.3 6SDAP2.4	1	0.5
REVIEW		1	0.5
ASSESSMENT		1	0.5*
TOTAL		14	7

*The complete **Assessment Planner** for Chapter 8 is provided on page 395.*

* Begin Chapter 9 in the second half of the period.

Professional Development

California Standards Vertical Alignment

Before Chapter 8

Related Topics from Grade 5

- Organize and display single-variable data in appropriate graphs and representations and explain which types of graphs are appropriate for various data sets Standard 5SDAP1.2

- Know the concepts of mean, median, and mode; compute and compare simple examples to show that they may differ Standard 5SDAP1.1

- Identify ordered pairs of data from a graph and interpret the meaning of the data in terms of the situation depicted by the graph Standard 5SDAP1.4

Chapter 8

Topics from Grade 6

- Understand how additional data added to data sets may affect these computations of measures of central tendency

- Know why a specific measure of central tendency provides the most useful information in a given context

- Understand how the inclusion or exclusion of outliers affects measures of central tendency

- Analyze data displays

- Identify different ways of selecting a sample and which method makes a sample more representative for a population

- Identify claims based on statistical data

- Identify data that represent sampling errors and explain why the sample might be biased

See individual lessons for the specific Standards covered.

After Chapter 8

Preparation for Grade 7

- Understand the meaning of, and be able to compute, the minimum, the lower quartile, the median, the upper quartile, and the maximum of a data set Standard 7SDAP1.3

Back-Mapping

California Mathematics: Concepts, Skills, Problem Solving was conceived and developed with the final result in mind, student success in Algebra I and beyond. The authors, using the California Mathematics Standards as their guide, developed this brand-new series by "back-mapping" from the desired result of student success in Algebra I and beyond. McGraw-Hill's K-7 intervention program, *California Math Triumphs: Intensive Intervention* as well as *California Algebra 1, California Geometry, California Algebra 2,* and *California Algebra Readiness* were developed utilizing the same philosophy.

What the Research Says . . .

Guidelines by the American Statistical Association and Mathematical Association of America have three areas of emphasis: statistical thinking, data and concepts, and active learning.

- In Lessons 8-2, Extend 8-2, and 8-6, students use hands-on activities to explore statistical concepts.

- Each lesson in Chapter 8 uses real-world data to encourage students' statistical thinking.

McGraw Hill Professional Development

Targeted professional development has been articulated throughout the *California Mathematics: Concepts, Skills, and Problem Solving* series. The **McGraw-Hill Professional Development Video Library** provides short videos that support the Key Standards. For more information, visit ca.gr6math.com.

| Model Lessons | Instructional Strategies |

CHAPTER 8

Technology Solutions

Teacher Resources

TeacherWorks™ All-in-One Planner and Resource Center

All of the print materials from the Classroom Resource Masters are available on your TeacherWorks™ CD-ROM.

BL = Below Grade Level **OL** = On Grade Level **AL** = Above Grade Level **ELL** = English Language Learner

Chapter Resource Masters					8-1	8-2	8-3	8-4	8-5	8-6	8-7	8-8	8-9
BL	OL		ELL	Lesson Reading Guide	9	16	23	29		39	45	52	58
BL	OL		ELL	Study Guide and Intervention*	10	17	24	30	35	40	46	53	59
BL	OL			Skills Practice*	11	18	25	31	36	41	47	54	60
	OL	AL		Practice*	12	19	26	32	37	42	48	55	61
	OL	AL		Word Problem Practice*	13	20	27	33	38	43	49	56	62
	OL	AL		Enrichment	14	21	28	34		44	50	57	63
	OL	AL		Calculator and Spreadsheet Activities	15	22					51		64
	OL	AL		Chapter Assessments*	65–86								
BL	OL	AL		5-Minute Check Transparencies	✓	✓	✓	✓	✓	✓	✓	✓	✓
BL	OL			Teaching Mathematics with Manipulatives		✓					✓		✓

Also available in Spanish
Real-World Investigations for Differentiated Instruction, pp. 7–9, 11–13, 15–18

AssignmentWorks

Differentiated Assignments, Answers, and Solutions

- Print a customized assignment worksheet using the Student Edition exercises along with an answer key or worked-out solutions.
- Use default lesson assignments as outlined in the Differentiated Homework Options in the Teacher Wraparound Edition.
- Includes modified questions from the Student Edition for students with special needs.

Interactive Classroom

This CD-ROM is a customizable Microsoft® PowerPoint® presentation that includes:

- In-Class Examples
- Your Turn Exercises*
- 5-Minute Check Transparencies*
- Links to Online Study Tools
- Concepts in Motion

compatible with response pad technology

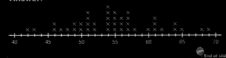

ExamView®Assessment Suite

- Create, edit, and customize tests and worksheets using QuickTest Wizard
- Create multiple versions of tests and modify them for a desired level of difficulty
- Translate from English to Spanish and vice versa
- Build tests aligned with your state standards
- Track students' progress using the Teacher Management System

Student Tools

StudentWorks™ Plus

Textbook, Audio, Workbooks, and more

This CD-ROM is a valuable resource for students to access content online and use online resources to continue learning Chapter 8 concepts. Includes:

- Complete Student Editions in both English and Spanish
- English audio integrated throughout the text
- Links to Concepts in Motion, Personal Tutor, and other online resources
- Access to all student worksheets
- Daily Assignments and Grade Log

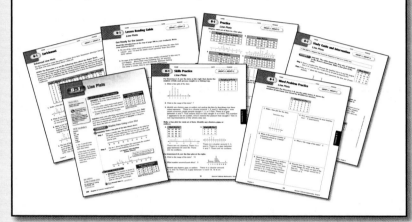

Super DVD

The Super DVD contains two Glencoe multimedia products.

MindJogger Plus An alternative review of concepts in which students work as teams in a game show format to gain points for correct answers.

What's Math Got to Do With It?
Real-Life Math Videos
Engaging video that shows students how math is used in everyday situations.

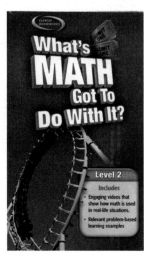

Internet Resources

Math Online ca.gr6math.com

TEACHER	STUDENT	PARENT	Online Study Tools
	•	•	Online Student Edition
•	•	•	Multilingual Glossary
			Lesson Resources
	•	•	BrainPOP®
•	•	•	Concepts in Motion
•	•	•	Extra Examples
•			Group Activity Cards
•			Problem of the Week Cards
	•	•	Other Calculator Keystrokes
	•	•	Reading in the Content Area
	•	•	Real-World Careers
	•	•	Self-Check Quizzes
			Chapter Resources
	•	•	Chapter Readiness
	•	•	Chapter Test
	•	•	Family Letters and Activities
	•	•	Standardized Test Practice
	•	•	Vocabulary Review/Chapter Review Activities
			Unit Resources
•	•		Cross-Curricular Internet Project
			Other Resources
•			Dinah Zike's Foldables
•	•		Game Zone Games and Recording Sheets
	•	•	Hotmath Homework Help
•			Key Concepts
•	•	•	Math Skills Maintenance
•	•	•	Meet the Authors
•			NAEP Correlations
	•	•	Personal Tutor
•			Project CRISS[SM]
	•	•	Scavenger Hunts and Answer Sheets
•			Vocabulary PuzzleMakers

Reading and Writing in Mathematics

Noteables™ Interactive Study Notebook with Foldables™

This workbook is a study organizer that provides helpful steps for students to follow to organize their notes for Chapter 8.

- Students use Noteables to record notes and to complete their Foldables as you present the material for each lesson.
- Noteables correspond to the Examples in the *Teacher Wraparound Edition* and *Interactive Classroom CD-ROM*.

READING in the Content Area

This online worksheet provides strategies for reading and analyzing Lesson 8-1, Line Plots. Students are guided through questions about the main idea, subject matter, supporting details, conclusion, clarifying details, and vocabulary of the lesson.

ca.gr6math.com

Recommended Outside Reading for Students

Mathematics and Manipulation

- *How to Lie with Statistics* by Darrell Huff ©1954, 1993 [nonfiction]

This classic book, illustrated by Irving Geis, warns readers of methods used to persuade an audience with statistics. Many techniques of manipulating statistics are explained, including the use of scale, presentation, and sample bias.

Mathematics and Everyday Life

- *Math Curse* by Jon Scieszka and Lane Smith ©1995 [fiction]

This book tells the funny story of a student who begins to see everything she encounters throughout the day as a math problem. Many questions arise which are related to different topics in mathematics, including the topic of *average.*

Project CRISS℠ STUDY SKILL

Vocabulary maps elaborate the meanings of vocabulary words by using multiple details. They are a useful way for students to organize their ideas while taking notes for a chapter. As students work through Chapter 8, have them complete vocabulary maps similar to the one shown at the right for vocabulary words related to statistics topics they encounter. You may wish to have them work in cooperative groups to make large versions of the maps that can be displayed on a bulletin board.

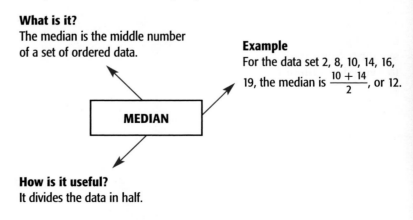

What is it?
The median is the middle number of a set of ordered data.

Example
For the data set 2, 8, 10, 14, 16, 19, the median is $\frac{10 + 14}{2}$, or 12.

MEDIAN

How is it useful?
It divides the data in half.

CReating **I**ndependence through **S**tudent-owned **S**trategies

Differentiated Instruction

Quick Review Math Handbook*

is Glencoe's mathematical handbook for students and parents.

Hot Words includes a glossary of terms.

Hot Topics consists of two parts:

- explanations of key mathematical concepts
- exercises to check students' understanding.

Lesson	Hot Topics Section	Lesson	Hot Topics Section
8-1	4•2	8-4	4•2, 9•4
8-2	4•4	8-6	4•2, 4•3
8-3	4•2	8-9	4•1, 4•3

Also available in Spanish

Teacher to Teacher

Bob Thompson
Thomas Jefferson
Middle School
Port Washington, WI

USE WITH LESSON 8-2

"I discuss how accurately the mean describes a set of data by asking the students to estimate the average age for the people in the classroom. Most students will answer an average student's age. But when my age is included in the data, the mean is higher."

Bob Thompson

Intervention Options

Intensive Intervention

Math Triumphs can provide intensive intervention for students who are at risk of not meeting the California standards addressed in Chapter 8.

Diagnose student readiness with the Quick Check and Quick Review on page 395. Then use *Math Triumphs* to accelerate their achievement.

Algebra: Integers

Prerequisite Skill	*Math Triumphs*
Compare decimals 6NS1.1	Volume 2, Chapter 4
Evaluate a numerical expression 6AF1.2	Volume 4, Chapter 3

See chart on page T24 for other *Math Triumphs* lessons that will support the prerequisite skills needed for success in *Glencoe California Mathematics, Grade 6.*

Strategic Intervention

For strategic intervention options, refer to the Diagnostic Assessment table on page 395.

FOLDABLES Study Organizer
Dinah Zike's Foldables

Focus This Foldable is designed to help students organize their notes about data analysis.

Teach Have students make the Foldable and label the tab for each lesson. Tell students that they should define terms, record key concepts, and write examples under the tab for each lesson. On the front of each tab, students should draw a graph, diagram, or picture that presents the main idea(s) of the lesson.

When to Use It As students work through each lesson, remind them to record notes under the corresponding tabs of their Foldables.

A version of a completed Foldable is shown on p. 450.

Differentiated Instruction

[CRM] Student-Built Glossary, p. 1

Students complete the chart by providing the definition of each term and an example as they progress through Chapter 8.

This study tool can be used to review for the chapter test.

CHAPTER 8 Statistics: Analyzing Data

BIG Idea

- **Standard 6SDAP2.0** Use data samples of a population and describe the characteristics and limitations of the samples.

Key Vocabulary

histogram (p. 416)

measures of central tendency (p. 402)

range (p. 397)

scatter plot (p. 427)

Real-World Link

Amusement Parks You can use a bar graph to display and then compare the speeds of various roller coasters.

FOLDABLES Study Organizer

Statistics: Analyzing Data Make this Foldable to help you organize your notes. Begin with nine sheets of notebook paper.

1 **Fold** 9 sheets of paper in half along the width.

2 **Cut** a 1" tab along the left edge through one thickness.

3 **Glue** the 1" tab down. Write the lesson number and title on the front tab.

4 **Repeat** Steps 2 and 3 for the remaining sheets. Staple them together on the glued tabs to form a booklet.

8-1 Line Plots

Materials Needed for Chapter 8

- pennies (Lesson 8-2)
- plastic cups (Lesson 8-2)
- grid paper (Lessons 8-4, 8-6, and 8-9)
- computers with a spreadsheet program (Extend 8-4 and Extend 8-6)

- measuring cup (Lesson 8-6)
- drinking glasses (Lesson 8-6)

- metric rulers (Lesson 8-6)
- marbles (Lesson 8-6)

GET READY for Chapter 8

Diagnose Readiness You have two options for checking Prerequisite Skills.

Option 1

Take the Quick Check below. Refer to the Quick Review for help.

Option 2

 Take the Online Readiness Quiz at ca.gr6math.com.

QUICK Check

(Used in Lessons 8-2 and 8-3)
Order from least to greatest. (Lesson 4-9)

1. 96.2, 96.02, 95.89 **95.89, 96.02, 96.2**

2. 5.61, 5.062, 5.16 **5.062, 5.16, 5.61**

3. 22.02, 22, 22.012 **22, 22.012, 22.02**

4. **JEANS** A store sells bootcut jeans for $49.97, classic for $49.79, and flared for $47.99. Write these prices in order from least to greatest. (Lesson 4-9)
$47.99, $49.79, $49.97

(Used in Lessons 8-2 and 8-3)
Order from greatest to least. (Lesson 4-9)

5. 74.65, 74.67, 74.7 **74.7, 74.67, 74.65**

6. 1.26, 1.026, 10.26 **10.26, 1.26, 1.026**

7. 3.304, 3.04, 3.340 **3.340, 3.304, 3.04**

(Used in Lesson 8-2)
Evaluate each expression. (Lesson 1-4)

8. $\dfrac{23 + 44 + 37 + 45}{4}$ **37.25**

9. $\dfrac{1.7 + 2.6 + 2.4 + 3.1 + 1.8}{5}$ **2.32**

10. **PIZZA** Four friends ordered a large pizza for $14.95, a salad for $3.75, and two bottles of soda for $2.25 each. If they split the cost evenly, how much does each person owe? (Lesson 1-4) **$5.80**

QUICK Review

Example 1

Order 47.7, 47.07, and 40.07 from least to greatest.

47.7
47.07   Line up the decimal points
40.07   and compare place value.
↑

The numbers in order from least to greatest are 40.07, 47.07, and 47.7.

Example 2

Order 2.08, 20.8, 0.28 from greatest to least.

2.08
20.8   Line up the decimal points
0.28   and compare place value.
↑

The numbers in order from greatest to least are 20.8, 2.08, and 0.28.

Example 3

Evaluate $\dfrac{3.4 + 4.5 + 3.8}{3}$.

$\dfrac{3.4 + 4.5 + 3.8}{3} = \dfrac{11.7}{3}$ Add 3.4, 4.5, and 3.8.

$= 3.9$ Divide 11.7 by 3.

Chapter 8 Get Ready for Chapter 8   **395**

ASSESSMENT PLANNER

CHAPTER 8

Formative Assessment

[CRM] Anticipation Guide, pp. 7–8
Spotting Preconceived Ideas
Students complete this survey to determine prior knowledge about ideas from Chapter 8. Revisit this worksheet after completing the chapter. Also see p. 454.

[TWE] Lesson Activities

• Ticket Out the Door, pp. 421, 431, 443
• Crystal Ball, pp. 401, 425, 437
• Name the Math, p. 408
• Yesterday's News, pp. 414, 449

Chapter Checkpoints

[SE] Mid-Chapter Quiz, p. 423
[SE] Study Guide and Review, pp. 450–454
[SE] California Standards Practice, pp. 456–457
[CRM] Quizzes, pp. 67 and 68
[CRM] Standardized Test Practice, pp. 84–86

Math Online ca.gr6math.com

• Self-Check Quizzes
• Practice Test
• Standardized Test Practice

Summative Assessment

[SE] Chapter Practice Test, p. 455
[CRM] Mid-Chapter Test, p. 69
[CRM] Vocabulary Test, p. 70
[CRM] Extended-Response Test, p. 83
[CRM] Leveled Chapter Tests, pp. 71–82
⊙ ExamView Pro® Assessment Suite

KEY

[CRM] *Chapter 8 Resource Masters*
[SE] Student Edition
[TWE] Teacher Wraparound Edition
⊙ CD-ROM

Diagnostic Assessment

Exercises	California Standards	Strategic Intervention
1–4	5NS2.5	*Math Skills Maintenance Masters*, pp. 32–33
5–7	5NS2.5	[SE] Prerequisite Skill, p. 670
8–10	6AF1.3, 6AF1.4	[SE] Review Lesson 1-4, pp. 38–41

8-1 Line Plots

Standard 6SDAP1.1   **Compute the range,** mean, median, and mode of data sets.

Standard 6SDAP1.2   **Understand how additional data added to data sets may affect these computations** of measures of central tendency.

PACING: **Regular:** 1 period, **Block:** 0.5 period

Options for Differentiated Instruction

ELL = English Language Learner   **AL** = Above Grade Level   **SS** = Struggling Students   **SN** = Special Needs

Kinesthetic Learners **ELL** **SS** **SN**

Use before presenting Example 1.

To create a line plot using classroom data, draw a number line on the board with a scale from 0 to at least 5. Give each student a sticky note and ask them to write the number of siblings they have on it. Then have each student come to the board and add their response to the line plot.

Ask:

- What is the most frequent response?
- What is the range of the data?
- What generalizations can you say about the number of siblings students have?
- If you were to survey a different class, do you think the line plot would look the same? Why or why not?

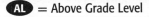
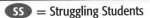
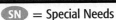

Creating Resource Sheets **ELL** **AL** **SS** **SN**

Use after presenting Examples.

Have students begin a resource sheet of questions to help them summarize data that are displayed in a line plot. Let them know that they will be adding to this sheet as they compare more sets of data and look at a variety of ways to display data. Sample questions are shown below.

- Which data value occurs most often on the line plot?
- What does the outlier on the line plot indicate?
- Around which point on the line plot are most of the data clustered?
- What is the range of the data?

Have students brainstorm other questions and add them to the list.

Building Vocabulary **ELL** **SS**

Use before assigning the Exercises.

Using the vocabulary of the lesson, have students work as a team to make a word web. Have four or five students write simultaneously on a large sheet of paper or on the board. Have them provide main concepts, supporting elements, and bridges showing relationships between ideas in a concept.

Leveled Lesson Resources

Chapter 8 Resource Masters

BL = Below Grade Level   **OL** = On Grade Level   **AL** = Above Grade Level   **ELL** = English Language Learner

Lesson Reading Guide
p. 9 **BL** **OL** **ELL**

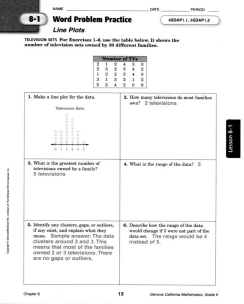

Study Guide and Intervention*
p. 10 **BL** **OL** **ELL**

Skills Practice*
p. 11 **BL** **OL**

Practice*
p. 12 **OL** **AL**

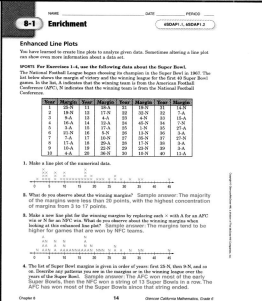

Word Problem Practice*
p. 13 **OL** **AL**

Enrichment
p. 14 **OL** **AL**

Additional Lesson Resources

Transparencies
- *5-Minute Check Transparency,* Lesson 8-1

Other Print Products
- *Noteables™ Interactive Study Notebook with Foldables™*

Teacher Tech Tools
- *Interactive Classroom CD-ROM,* Lesson 8-1
- *AssignmentWorks CD-ROM,* Lesson 8-1

Student Tech Tools
ca.gr6math.com
- Extra Examples, Chapter 8, Lesson 1
- Self-Check Quiz, Chapter 8, Lesson 1

8-1 **Lesson Notes**

 8-1 **Line Plots**

1 Focus

Standards Alignment

Before Lesson 8-1
Organize and display single-variable data in appropriate graphs and representations and explain which types of graphs are appropriate for various data sets from Standard 5SDAP1.2

Lesson 8-1
Compute the range. Understand how additional data added to data sets may affect these computations from Standards 6SDAP1.1 and 6SDAP1.2

After Lesson 8-1
Know various forms of display for data sets, including a stem-and-leaf plot or box-and-whisker plot; use the forms to display a single set of data or to compare two sets of data from Standard 7SDAP1.1

2 Teach

Scaffolding Questions

Tell the class you planted some wildflowers in two flower boxes.

Ask:

• If the tallest plant is 18 inches tall, and the shortest plant is 3 inches tall, what is the range in heights? 15 inches

• If I described the plants in the first box as "evenly spread out," what would that mean? The plants are spaced more or less evenly apart.

• If I described the plants in the second box as "clustered toward one end," what would that mean? Many of the plants are grouped, or bunched, together at one end.

Main IDEA
Display and analyze data using a line plot.

 Standard 6SDAP1.1 Compute the range, mean, median, and mode of data sets.
Standard 6SDAP1.2 Understand how additional data added to data sets may affect these computations of measures of central tendency.

NEW Vocabulary

statistics
data
line plot
cluster
outlier
range
analyze

1. Yes; 73 and 62 seem much greater than the other data values.

2. More than one building has 52 stories, 44 stories, 42 stories, and 39 stories. Without listing the data in order, this is not easy to determine.

READING in the Content Area

For strategies in reading this lesson, visit ca.gr6math.com.

GET READY for the Lesson

BUILDINGS The table shows the number of stories in 20 of the tallest buildings in Los Angeles.

1. Do any of the values seem much greater or much less than the other data values?

2. Do some of the buildings have the same height? Is this easy to see? Explain.

Los Angeles' Tallest Buildings Number of Stories				
73	48	55	52	44
62	52	40	54	39
52	45	52	42	53
39	42	44	52	42

Source: emporis.com

Statistics deals with collecting, organizing, and interpreting data. **Data** are pieces of information, which are often numerical. One way to show how data are spread out is to use a line plot. A **line plot** is a diagram that shows the data on a number line.

EXAMPLE Display Data Using a Line Plot

1 BUILDINGS Make a line plot of the data shown above.

Step 1   Draw a number line. The shortest building in the table has 39 stories, and the tallest has 73. You can use a scale of 35 to 75 and an interval of 5. Other scales and intervals could also be used.

Step 2   Put an × above the number that represents the number of stories in each building. Include a title.

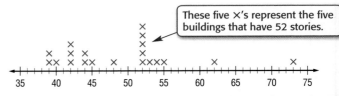

Los Angeles' Tallest Buildings Number of Stories

These five ×'s represent the five buildings that have 52 stories.

CHECK Your Progress

a. BUILDINGS The number of stories in the 15 tallest buildings in the world are listed at the right. Display the data in a line plot. **See margin.**

World's Tallest Buildings Number of Stories				
101	88	88	110	88
88	80	69	102	78
72	54	73	85	80

Source: The World Almanac

Online Personal Tutor at ca.gr6math.com

Additional Answer

a.

World's Tallest Buildings Number of Stories

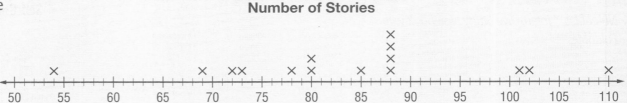

You can make some observations about the *distribution* of data, or how data are grouped together or spread out. Consider the line plot below.

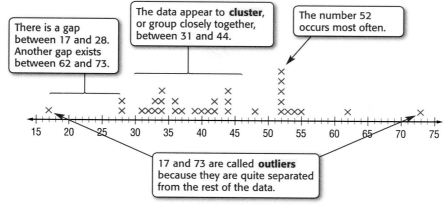

There is a gap between 17 and 28. Another gap exists between 62 and 73.

The data appear to **cluster**, or group closely together, between 31 and 44.

The number 52 occurs most often.

17 and 73 are called **outliers** because they are quite separated from the rest of the data.

In a line plot, you can easily find the **range**, or spread, of the data, which is the difference between the greatest and least numbers. When you **analyze** data, you use these observations to describe and compare data.

Vocabulary Link . . . .
Range
Everyday Meaning in music, all the notes between the high and low notes, as in a singer with a wide range.

Math Use the difference between the greatest number and least number in a set of data.

EXAMPLES Use a Plot to Analyze Data

2 **SHOES** The line plot below shows the prices for different basketball shoes. Identify any clusters, gaps, and outliers and find the range.

Prices ($) of Basketball Shoes

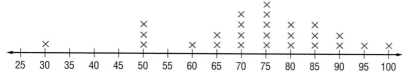

Many of the data cluster between $70 and $85.

There is a gap between $30 and $50.

Since $30 is apart from the rest of the data, it is an outlier.

The greatest price is $100, and the least price is $30. So, the range of the prices is $100 − $30 or $70.

STUDY TIP

Clusters
You can describe a cluster by stating a range of values or by giving a single value around which the data appear to be grouped.

3 Describe how the range would change if the data value $130 was added to the data set in Example 2.

The greatest price would change to $130, and the least price would remain the same at $30. So, the range of the prices would change from $70 to $130 − $30 or $100.

b–c. See Ch. 8
Answer Appendix.

CHECK Your Progress Refer to Example 1.

b. Identify any clusters, gaps, and outliers and find the range.

c. Describe how the range would change if the data value 50 was added to the data set.

Math Online Extra Examples at ca.gr6math.com

Answer for Additional Example 1

Age of Presidents at Inauguration

Focus on Mathematical Content

Statistics is the study of how to collect, display, and interpret data.

A good way to see how data are distributed is to make a **line plot**.

An **outlier** is less than or greater than the rest of the data and is relatively separated from them. *(The formal definition of outlier will be presented in the next grade level, where students use mathematical calculations to identify outliers.)*

The difference between the greatest and least values of a set of data is the **range**.

Formative Assessment

Use the Check Your Progress exercises after each Example to determine students' understanding of concepts.

ADDITIONAL EXAMPLE

1 **PRESIDENTS** The table below shows the ages of the U.S. presidents at the time of their inaugurations. Make a line plot of the data. See bottom margin.

Age at Inauguration				
57	51	54	56	61
61	49	49	55	52
57	64	50	51	69
57	50	47	54	64
58	48	55	51	46
57	65	55	60	54
61	52	54	62	68
54	56	42	43	
46	51	55	56	

Source: factmonster.com

Additional Examples are also in:
- Noteables™ Interactive Study Notebook with Foldables™
- Interactive Classroom PowerPoint® Presentations

★ indicates multi-step problem

CHECK Your Understanding

Example 1
(p. 396)

1–2. See Ch. 8 Answer Appendix.

Display each set of data in a line plot.

1.

Costs of Video Games ($)			
20	29	40	50
45	20	50	50
20	25	50	40

2.

Sizes of Tennis Shoes					
8	10	9	8	7	6
9	10	9	6	5	7
7	8	11	6	8	7

MUSIC For Exercises 3 and 4, analyze the line plot below.

Number of Music CDs Owned

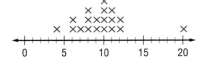

3. clusters: 6–12; gap: 12–20; outlier: 20; range: 20 — 4 or 16

Example 2
(p. 397)

3. Identify any clusters, gaps, and outliers and find the range of the data.

Example 3
(p. 397)

4. Describe how the range would change if the data value 3 was added to the data set. Sample answer: The range would change from 16 to 17.

8. Sample answer: The range would remain unchanged at 5.

SURVEYS For Exercises 5–8, analyze the line plot at the right and use the information below.

Jamie asked her classmates how many glasses of water they drink on a typical day. The results are shown.

Glasses of Water Consumed

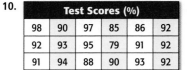

Example 2
(p. 397)

5. What was the most frequent response?

6. What was the least frequent response?

7. What is the range? 5 glasses

5. 1 or 2 glasses per day

6. 3 or 4 glasses per day

Example 3
(p. 397)

8. Describe how the range would change if an additional data value of 4 was added to the data set.

Exercises

Display each set of data in a line plot. 9–12. See Ch. 8 Answer Appendix.

9.

Heights of Desert Cacti (ft)				
30	10	1	15	10
10	10	10	2	10
20	3	2	15	5

10.

Test Scores (%)					
98	90	97	85	86	92
92	93	95	79	91	92
91	94	88	90	93	92

11.

Basketball Scores (pts)				
101	105	99	130	120
100	108	126	135	98
120	122	115	129	97

12.

Ages of Students (y)					
12	13	13	13	12	14
13	12	13	13	12	12
13	14	12	13	12	12

398 Chapter 8 Statistics: Analyzing Data

Example 2

Inches of Precipitation

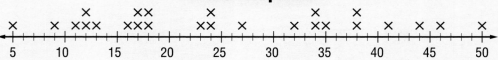

WEATHER For Exercises 13–16, analyze the line plot that shows the record high temperatures recorded by weather stations in each of the fifty states.

Record High Temperatures (°F)

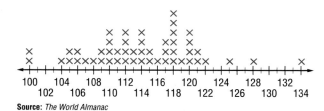

Source: *The World Almanac*

Real-World Link · · · ·
Death Valley National Park is the site of the highest temperature ever recorded in the United States, 134°F.
Source: *Death Valley Chamber of Commerce*

13. What is the range of the data? **34°F**

14. What temperature occurred most often? **118°F**

15. Identify any clusters, gaps, or outliers. **See margin.**

16. Describe how the range of the data would change if 134°F were not part of the data set. **The range would be 28°F rather than 34°F.**

MOVIES For Exercises 17–20, analyze the line plot below that shows the number of digital video discs various students have in their DVD collection.

Digital Video Disc (DVD) Collection

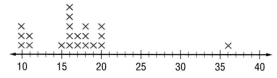

17. Find the range of the data. **36 − 10 or 26**

18. What number of DVDs occurred most often? **16 DVDs**

19. How many students have more than 15 DVDs in their collection? **15**

0. Sample answer: the range would change from 26 to 8.

20. Describe how the range would change if the data value 38 was added to the data set.

Determine whether each statement is *sometimes, always,* or *never* true. Explain your reasoning.

1. Sometimes; the range will only change if the new data value lies above or below the greatest and least points, respectively, if the original data set.

21. If a new piece of data is added to a data set, the range will change.

22. If there is a cluster, it will appear in the center of the line plot. **Sometimes; clusters may appear anywhere on the line plot.**

BOOKS For Exercises 23–25, analyze the line plot at the right.

23. How many students read 4 or more books? **10**

★ 24. How many more students read 1–2 books than 5–6 books? **3**

★ 25. About what percent of the students read less than 5 books? **about 72%**

Number of Books Read

					×				
					×				
	×	×		×	×		×		×
	×	×	×	×	×	×	×		×
—	—	—	—	—	—	—	—	—	—
0	1	2	3	4	5	6	7	8	

Lesson 8-1 Line Plots **399**

Tips for New Teachers

Justify Your Selection

As students construct line plots in the Exercises, have them also verbally justify why selecting a line plot is appropriate to display the data.

Sample answer: In Exercise 9, a line plot is appropriate since the data values are not too numerous and are not too spread out. There are some repeating data values. A line plot can be easily created to show individual data values.

Additional Answer

15. Sample answer: cluster 104°F–122°F, gaps 100°F–104°F, 122°F–125°F, 125°F–128°F, and 128°F–134°F, outliers 100°F and 134°F

Level	Assignment	Two-Day Option	
BL Basic	9–20, 31, 32, 34–44	9–19 odd, 35, 36	8–20 even, 31, 32, 34, 37–44
OL Core	9–19 odd, 21–32, 34–44	9–20, 35, 36	21–32, 34, 37–44
AL Advanced/Pre-AP	21–40 (optional: 41–44)		

DIFFERENTIATED HOMEWORK OPTIONS

27. Sample answer: range 34 yr; cluster 10–12 yr; outlier 40 yr

28. Sample answer: Most of the animals represented on the line plot have a life span of 10–20 years.

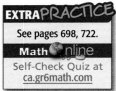

See pages 698, 722.

Self-Check Quiz at
ca.gr6math.com

H.O.T. Problems

33. See margin.

ANIMALS For Exercises 26–28, refer to the table.

Average Life Spans					
Animal	Span (yr)	Animal	Span (yr)	Animal	Span (yr)
black bear	18	giraffe	10	lion	15
camel	12	gorilla	20	pig	10
cat	12	grizzly bear	25	polar bear	20
chipmunk	6	horse	20	rhesus monkey	15
dog	12	kangaroo	7	squirrel	10
elephant	40	leopard	12	white rhinoceros	20

Source: *The World Almanac for Kids*

26. Display the data in a line plot. **See Ch. 8 Answer Appendix.**

27. Find the range and determine any clusters or outliers.

28. Use the line plot to summarize the data in a sentence or two.

★ **29.** The *maximum* life spans, in order, of the animals in the table above are 36, 50, 28, 10, 20, 77, 36, 54, 50, 50, 24, 23, 30, 27, 45, 37, 24, and 50, respectively. Display this data in a line plot. Compare this line plot to the line plot you made in Exercise 26. Include a discussion about clusters, outliers, range, and gaps in data. **See Ch. 8 Answer Appendix.**

30. COLLECT THE DATA Conduct a survey of your classmates to determine how
★ many hours of television they watch on a typical school night. Then display and analyze the data in a line plot. Use your analysis of the data to write a convincing argument about television viewing on a school night. **See students' work.**

31. REASONING Explain how the inclusion or exclusion of outliers affects the computation of the range of a data set. **See margin.**

32. FIND THE ERROR Ryan and Darnell are analyzing the data shown in the line plot at the right. Who is correct? Explain.
Darnell; 16 appears most often, but the greatest value is 20.

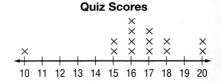

greatest data value: 20
least data value: 10

greatest data value: 16
least data value: 10

Ryan   Darnell

33. CHALLENGE Compare and contrast line plots and frequency tables. Include a discussion about what they show and when it is better to use each one.

34. **WRITING IN MATH** The last 14 bowling scores of two people are shown. Describe which person is more consistent and explain how you know.

Bowling Scores

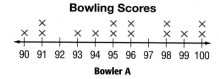

90 91 92 93 94 95 96 97 98 99 100

Bowler A

Bowling Scores

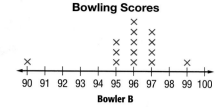

90 91 92 93 94 95 96 97 98 99 100

Bowler B

STANDARDS PRACTICE 6SDAP1.1, 6SDAP1.2

35. The graph shows the weight of the emperor penguins at a zoo. **C**

Emperor Penguins Weight (kg)

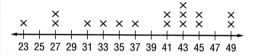

23 25 27 29 31 33 35 37 39 41 43 45 47 49

Which statement is *not* valid?

A More than half of these penguins weigh at least 41 kilograms.

B There are 16 emperor penguins at the zoo.

C Of these penguins, 30% weigh between 30 and 38 kilograms.

D The range of the emperor penguins' weight is 49 − 23 or 26 kilograms.

36. The table shows the math scores for 24 students in Mr. Baker's class. **G**

Math Test Scores							
90	86	96	89	85	91	82	89
100	65	73	85	85	93	77	93
71	70	75	80	82	99	84	75

How would the range of the test scores change if a score of 83 was added?

F The range would remain unchanged at 45.

G The range would remain unchanged at 35.

H The range would change from 45 to 83.

J The range would change from 35 to 17.

Spiral Review

Find the interest earned to the nearest cent for each principal, interest rate, and time. (Lesson 7-8)

37. $300, 10%, 2 years **$60**

38. $900, 5.5%, 4.5 years **$222.75**

39. **BASEBALL CARDS** What is the total cost of a package of baseball cards if the regular price is $4.19 and the sales tax is 6.5%? (Lesson 7-7) **$4.46**

40. Solve $m + 18 = 33$ mentally. (Lesson 1-7) **15**

▶ **GET READY for the Next Lesson**

PREREQUISITE SKILL Add or divide. Round to the nearest tenth if necessary.

41. $16 + 14 + 17$ **47**
42. $4.6 + 2.5 + 9$ **16.1**
43. $\frac{202}{16}$ **12.6**
44. $\frac{255}{7}$ **36.4**

 **Assess**

Crystal Ball Tell students that tomorrow's lesson is about finding the mean, median, and mode of a set of data. Have students write how they think what they learned today will connect with tomorrow's material.

FOLDABLES **Foldables™**
Study Organizer **Follow-Up**

Remind students to take notes about line plots under the tab for this lesson in their Foldables. Encourage them to draw and label a line plot on the front of the tab.

Additional Answer

34. Sample answer: Bowler B is more consistant because excluding the outlier of 90, the range of scores is 4 points, compared with a range of 10 for Bowler A. Bowler A has scores evenly spread out from 90 to 100.

Measures of Central Tendency and Range

Standard 6SDAP1.1	Compute the range, mean, median, and mode of data sets.
Standard 6SDAP1.2	Understand how additional data added to data sets may affect these computations of measures of central tendency.
Standard 6SDAP1.4	Know why a specific measure of central tendency (mean, median, mode) provides the most useful information in a given context.
PACING:	**Regular:** 1 period, **Block:** 0.5 period

Options for Differentiated Instruction

ELL = English Language Learner　　**AL** = Above Grade Level　　**SS** = Struggling Students　　**SN** = Special Needs

Visualizing the Concept ELL SS SN

Use while presenting the Examples.

Students may benefit from the use of a line plot when data are presented. For the examples, ask groups of students to create a line plot on the board or overhead transparency. A sample line plot is shown at the right.

Then refer to the plot as mean, median, and mode are discussed.

Creating a Checklist SS

Use before assigning the Exercises.

A common mistake that students make when finding the median is not ordering the data prior to finding the middle number.

Have students create a short checklist for finding the median of a set of data:
- Order the data from least to greatest.
- Count to make sure all pieces of data are included in the ordered set.
- Find the middle number.
- If there is an even number of data points, find the mean of the two middle numbers.

Challenge Beyond the Lesson Content AL

Use after completing Lesson 8-2.

Have students create four different data sets, each of which contains five data points and has a mean of 4. The requirement for each data set is listed below.

Data Set	Requirement
1	The mean is greater than the mode.
2	The mean equals the median.
3	The mean is greater than the median.
4	The mean, median, and mode are all equal.

Sample answers:
Set 1: 2, 2, 3, 4, 9;
Set 2: 2, 3, 4, 5, 6;
Set 3: 2, 2, 3, 4, 9;
Set 4: 3, 4, 4, 4, 5

Leveled Lesson Resources

Also on TeacherWorks™ — Lesson 8-2

Chapter 8 Resource Masters

BL = Below Grade Level **OL** = On Grade Level **AL** = Above Grade Level **ELL** = English Language Learner

---

Lesson Reading Guide
p. 16 **BL** **OL** **ELL**

NAME _____ DATE _____ PERIOD _____

8-2 Lesson Reading Guide 6SDAP1.1, 6SDAP1.2, 6SDAP1.4
Measures of Central Tendency and Range

Get Ready for the Lesson
Complete the Mini Lab at the top of page 402 in your textbook. Write your answers below.

1. What was the average score for the five quizzes? 8 points

2. If the quiz score of 14 points is added to the data, how many pennies would be in each cup? 9

Read the Lesson

3. Look at the data set 2, 5, 5, 6, 8, 11, 12. What is the mean? the median? the mode? 7; 6; 5

4. Match the measure of central tendency with the description of when it would be most useful.

   median ___b___   a. The data set has many identical numbers.

   mean ___c___   b. There are no big gaps in the middle of the data.

   mode ___a___   c. The data set has no outliers.

5. If you wanted to find the average height of all of the students in a classroom, which would be the most accurate to use—mean, median, or mode? Why? Sample answer: The mean would be the most accurate. It is very unlikely that the mode or median would reflect the true average.

Remember What You Learned

6. In baseball, a player has a batting average. What does this average measure tell you? What kind of data would you need to calculate a batting average? Sample answer: A batting average indicates how successful a player was at hitting given a number of opportunities (called "at bats"). To calculate a batting average you would need at least a number of hits and a number of at bats.

Chapter 8   16   Glencoe California Mathematics, Grade 6

Study Guide and Intervention*
p. 17 **BL** **OL** **ELL**

NAME _____ DATE _____ PERIOD _____

8-2 Study Guide and Intervention 6SDAP1.1, 6SDAP1.2, 6SDAP1.4
Measures of Central Tendency and Range

The **mean** is the sum of the data divided by the number of data items. The **median** is the middle number of the ordered data, or the mean of the two middle numbers. The **mode** is the number (or numbers) that occur most often. The mean, median, and mode are each **measures of central tendency**.

Example The table shows the number of hours students spent practicing for a music recital. Find the mean, median, and mode of the data.

Numbers of Hours Spent Practicing

3	12	10	8	7
18	11	12	10	3
8	6	0	1	5
8	2	15	9	12

mean = $\frac{3 + 12 + 10 + \ldots + 12}{20} = \frac{160}{20}$ or 8.

To find the median, the data must be ordered.

0, 1, 2, 3, 3, 5, 6, 7, 8, 8, 8, 9, 10, 10, 11, 12, 12, 12, 15, 18

$\frac{8+8}{2} = 8$

To find the mode, look for the number that occurs most often. Since 8 and 12 each occur 3 times, the modes are 8 and 12.

Exercises

Find the mean, median, and mode for each set of data. Round to the nearest tenth if necessary.

1. 27, 56, 34, 19, 41, 56, 27, 25, 34, 56
   mean, 37.5; median, 34; mode, 56

2. 7, 3, 12, 4, 6, 3, 4, 8, 7, 3, 20
   mean, 7; median, 6; mode, 3

3. 1, 23, 4, 6, 7, 20, 7, 5, 3, 4, 6, 7, 11, 6
   mean, 7.9 median, 6; mode, 7 and 6

4. 3, 3, 3, 3, 3, 3, 3
   mean, 3; median, 3; mode, 3

5. 2, 4, 1, 3, 5, 6, 1, 1, 3, 4, 3, 1
   mean, 2.8; median, 3; mode, 1

6. 4, 0, 12, 10, 0, 5, 7, 16, 12, 10, 12, 12
   mean, 8.3; median, 10; mode, 12

Chapter 8   17   Glencoe California Mathematics, Grade 6

Skills Practice*
p. 18 **BL** **OL**

NAME _____ DATE _____ PERIOD _____

8-2 Skills Practice 6SDAP1.1, 6SDAP1.2, 6SDAP1.4
Measures of Central Tendency and Range

Find the mean, median, and mode for each set of data. Round to the nearest tenth if necessary.

1. 5, 9, 6, 6, 11, 8, 4   7; 6; 6

2. 1, 3, 5, 2, 4, 8, 4, 7, 2   4; 4; 2 and 4

3. 1, 9, 4, 7, 5, 3, 16, 11   7; 6; none

4. 3, 4, 4, 4, 4, 3, 6   4; 4; 4

5. 3, 7, 2, 5, 5, 6, 5, 10, 11, 5   5.9; 5; 5

6. 19, 17, 24, 11, 19, 25, 15, 15, 19, 16, 16   17.8; 17; 19

7. 5, 8, 9, 9, 12, 6, 4
   Mean 7.6
   Median 8
   Mode 9

8. 3, 4, 9, 7, 6, 6, 2
   Mean 5.3
   Median 6
   Mode 6

9. [line plot] 7 8 9 10 11 12 13 14 15 16   11; 11; 12

10. [line plot] 25 26 27 28 29 30 31 32   29; 30; 26 and 32

11. [line plot] 14 15 16 17 18 19 20   17; 17; none

12. [line plot] 17 18 19 20 21 22 23   18.2; 17; 17

Chapter 8   18   Glencoe California Mathematics, Grade 6

Practice*
p. 19 **OL** **AL**

NAME _____ DATE _____ PERIOD _____

8-2 Practice 6SDAP1.1, 6SDAP1.2, 6SDAP1.4
Measures of Central Tendency and Range

Find the mean, median, and mode for each set of data. Round to the nearest tenth if necessary.

1. Number of parking spaces used: 45, 39, 41, 45, 44, 64, 51
   mean: 47 spaces; median: 45 spaces; mode: 45 spaces

2. Prices of plants: $10, $8, $20, $25, $14, $39, $10, $10, $8, $16
   mean: $16; median: $12; mode: $10

3. Points scored during football season: 14, 20, 3, 9, 18, 35, 21, 24, 31, 12, 7
   mean: 17.6 points; median: 18 points; mode: none

4. Golf scores: −3, −2, +1, +1, −1, −1, +2, −5
   mean: −1; median: −1 points; modes: −1 and +1

5. Percent increase: 3.3, 4.1, 3.9, 5.0, 3.5, 2.9, 3.9
   mean: 3.8; median: 3.9; mode: 3.9

6. **Dollars Spent Shopping**
   [line plot] 35 36 37 38 39 40 41 42 43 44
   mean: $40; median: $39; mode: $38

7. **CHILDREN** The table shows the number of children living at home in a neighborhood of 24 homes. Which measure best describes the data: mean, median, or mode? Explain. Sample answer: mean, 2.2; median, 2; or mode, 2. The data would best be described by any one of the three measures: mean, 2.2; median, 2; or mode, 2.

Children at Home

2	1	3	0	4	4	1	2
0	6	2	2	5	0	2	3
3	1	1	4	2	0	1	4

8. **WORK** The table shows the hours Sam worked each week during the summer. How many hours did he work during the twelfth week to average 20 hours per week? 22 hours

Hours Worked

| 18 | 24 | 20 | 19 | 15 | 21 |
| 20 | 19 | 18 | 22 | 22 | ? |

Chapter 8   19   Glencoe California Mathematics, Grade 6

Word Problem Practice*
p. 20 **OL** **AL**

NAME _____ DATE _____ PERIOD _____

8-2 Word Problem Practice 6SDAP1.1, 6SDAP1.2, 6SDAP1.4
Measures of Central Tendency and Range

SCHOOL For Exercises 1–6, use the table below. It shows the number of times per day that students go to their lockers.

Student Locker Visits

2	2	0	1	2	2	3	4
0	5	2	5	2	5	2	4
2	4	6	4	5	6	5	6
2	2	0	1	4	6	10	2

1. Make a frequency table of the data. Sample answer:

Number of Visits	Tally	Frequency
0–2		16
3–5		11
6–8		4
9–11		1

2. What is the range of the data? 10

3. Find the mean, median, and mode of the data. Round to the nearest tenth if necessary. mean: 3.3; median: 2.5; mode: 2

4. Would the mean, median, or mode best represent the data? Explain. Mode; the data has many identical numbers.

5. Explain why the mean does not best represent the data. Sample answer: The mean should not be used when the data has outliers, and 10 is an outlier.

6. If the value 10 were dropped from the data, find the median and the mode of the remaining data. median: 2; mode: 2

Chapter 8   20   Glencoe California Mathematics, Grade 6

Enrichment
p. 21 **OL** **AL**

NAME _____ DATE _____ PERIOD _____

8-2 Enrichment 7SDAP1.3

Quartiles

The median is a number that describes the "center" of a set of data. Here are two sets with the same median, 50, indicated by ◯.

25   30   35   40   45   ⦵50   55   60   ⟋65⟍   70   75

0   10   30   40   ⦵50   ⦵50   60   70   ⟋80⟍   90   100

But, sometimes a single number may not be enough. The numbers shown in the triangles can also be used to describe the data. They are called *quartiles*. The lower quartile is the median of the lower half of the data. It is indicated by ⟋⟍. The upper quartile is the median of the upper half. It is indicated by ⟋⟍.

Circle the median in each set of data. Draw triangles around the quartiles.

1. 29   52   44   37   27   46   43   60   31   54   36

2. 1.7   0.4   1.4   2.3   0.3   2.7   2.0   0.9   2.7   2.6   1.2

3. 1,150   1,600   1,450   1,750   1,500   1,300   1,200

4. 5   2   9   7   9   3   7   8   7   2   5   6   9   5   1

Use the following set of test scores to solve the problems.

71   57   29   37   53   41   25   37   53   27
62   55   75   48   66   53   66   48   75   66

5. Which scores are "in the lower quartile"? 25, 27, 29, and 37

6. How high would you have to score to be "in the upper quartile"? 66 or higher

Chapter 8   21   Glencoe California Mathematics, Grade 6

Additional Lesson Resources

Also available in Spanish **ELL**

Transparencies
- *5-Minute Check Transparency*, Lesson 8-2

Other Print Products
- *Teaching Mathematics with Manipulatives*
- *Noteables™ Interactive Study Notebook with Foldables™*
- *Science and Mathematics Lab Manual*, pp. 77–80

Teacher Tech Tools
- *Interactive Classroom CD-ROM*, Lesson 8-2
- *AssignmentWorks CD-ROM*, Lesson 8-2

Student Tech Tools
ca.gr6math.com
- Extra Examples, Chapter 8, Lesson 2
- Self-Check Quiz, Chapter 8, Lesson 2

8-2 # Measures of Central Tendency and Range

402 Chapter 8 Statistics: Analyzing Data

1 Focus

Standards Alignment

Before Lesson 8-2
Know the concepts of mean, median, and mode; compute and compare simple examples to show that they may differ from Standard 5SDAP1.1

Lesson 8-2
Compute the mean, median, and mode of data sets. Understand how additional data added to data sets may affect these computations. Know why a specific measure of central tendency provides the most useful information in a given context from Standards 6SDAP1.1, 6SDAP1.2, and 6SDAP1.4

After Lesson 8-2
Understand the meaning of, and be able to compute, the minimum, the lower quartile, the median, the upper quartile, and the maximum of a data set from ⟵ Standard 7SDAP1.3

2 Teach

▶MINI Lab

You may wish to have students work in pairs. Some students may find it easier to distribute the pennies evenly among 5 piles on a desktop (without using cups).

Scaffolding Questions

Ask:
- If someone describes a movie as "average," what do you think she means?

- If someone says that a restaurant meal was "average," what do you think he means?

- If I say that the "average" score on a math test was 82, what do you think I mean?

402 Chapter 8 Statistics: Analyzing Data

Main IDEA
Describe a set of data using mean, median, mode, and range.

Standard 6SDAP1.1 Compute the range, mean, median, and mode of data sets.
Standard 6SDAP1.2 Understand how additional data added to data sets may affect these computations of measures of central tendency.
Standard 6SDAP1.4 Know why a specific measure of central tendency (mean, median, mode) provides the most useful information in a given context.

NEW Vocabulary

measures of central tendency
mean
median
mode

▶MINI Lab

The table shows scores for five quizzes.
- Place pennies in each cup to represent each score.

8   7   9   6   10

Quiz	Score
1	8
2	7
3	9
4	6
5	10

- Move the pennies among the cups so that each cup has the same number of pennies.

1. What was the average score for the five quizzes? **8 points**

2. If the quiz score of 14 points is added to the data, how many pennies would be in each cup? **9**

A number used to describe the *center* of a set of data is a **measure of central tendency**. The most common of these measures is the mean.

KEY CONCEPT   Mean

Words	The **mean** of a set of data is the sum of the data divided by the number of items in the data set. The mean is also referred to as *average*.
Examples	data set: 1 cm, 1 cm, 5 cm, 2 cm, 2 cm, 4 cm, 2 cm, 5 cm
	mean: $\dfrac{1+1+5+2+2+4+2+5}{8}$ or 2.75 cm

EXAMPLE   Find the Mean

① **NUTRITION** The table shows the grams of sugar in 20 different breakfast bars.

Find the mean.

mean $= \dfrac{14 + 11 + \ldots + 12}{20}$ ⟵ sum of data
⟵ number of data items

$= \dfrac{253}{20}$ or 12.65 grams

Grams of Sugar in Breakfast Bars				
14	11	7	14	15
22	18	18	21	10
10	10	11	9	11
11	9	12	8	12

Source: www.cspinnet.org

CHECK Your Progress

a. **MONEY** Adam earned $14, $10, $12, $15, and $13 by doing chores around the house. What is the mean amount Adam earned doing these chores? **$12.80**

Two other common measures of central tendency are median and mode.

Vocabulary Link · · · ·
Median
Everyday Use the middle paved or planted section of highway, as in median strip.

Math Use the middle number of the ordered data.

KEY CONCEPT   Median

Words	In a data set that has been ordered from least to greatest, the **median** is the middle number if there is an odd number of data items. If there is an even number of data items, the median is the mean of the two numbers closest to the middle.
Example	data set: 7 yd, 11 yd, <u>15 yd, 17 yd</u>, 20 yd, 20 yd
	median: $\dfrac{15 + 17}{2}$ or 16 yd The median divides the data in half.

Mode

Words	The **mode** of a set of data is the number that occurs most often. If there are two or more numbers that occur most often, all of them are modes.
Example	data set: 50 mi, (45 mi, 45 mi,) 52 mi, 49 mi, (56 mi, 56 mi)
	modes: 45 mi and 56 mi

EXAMPLE   Find the Mean, Median, and Mode

2 **MOVIE RENTALS** The number of DVDs rented during one week at Star Struck Movie Rental is shown in the table. What are the mean, median, and mode of the data?

Star Struck Movie Rental Daily DVD Rentals						
S	M	T	W	TH	F	S
55	34	35	34	57	78	106

mean: $\dfrac{55 + 34 + 35 + 34 + 57 + 78 + 106}{7} = \dfrac{399}{7}$ or 57

median: 34, 34, 35, (55), 57, 78, 106   First, write the data in order.
                          ↓
                       median

mode: 34   It is the only value that occurs more than once.

The mean is 57 DVDs, the median is 55 DVDs, and the mode is 34 DVDs.

CHECK Your Progress

b. **BICYCLES** The sizes of the bicycles owned by the students in Ms. Garcia's class are listed in the table. What are the mean, median, and mode of the data? **24.25 in., 24 in., 24 in.**

Students' Bicycle Sizes (in.)			
20	24	20	26
24	24	24	26
24	29	26	24

c. **FOOTBALL** The points scored in each game by Darby Middle School's football team for 9 games are 21, 35, 14, 17, 28, 14, 7, 21, and 14. Find the mean, median, and mode. **19, 17, 14**

Focus on Mathematical Content

The **mean** of a data set is the sum of the data divided by the number of data.

The **median** of a data set is the middle value, or the mean of the two middle values.

The **mode** of a data set is the value that occurs most often.

✓ Formative Assessment

Use the Check Your Progress exercises after each example to determine students' understanding of concepts.

ADDITIONAL EXAMPLES

1 **ANIMALS** The table below shows the number of species of animals found at 30 major zoos across the United States. Find the mean.
436.37 species

Number of Species in Major U.S. Zoos				
300	400	283	400	175
614	700	700	715	280
800	290	350	133	400
195	347	488	435	640
232	350	300	300	400
705	400	800	300	659

2 **OLYMPICS** The table below shows the number of gold medals won by each country participating in the 2002 Winter Olympic games. Find the mean, median, and mode of the data. mean = 3.16, median = 2, mode = 0

2002 Winter Olympics: Gold Medals Won				
12	6	4	3	0
10	6	4	2	3
11	2	3	4	2
1	1	0	2	2
1	0	0	0	0

3 STANDARDS EXAMPLE The average weight in pounds of several breeds of dogs is listed below.

15, 45, 26, 55, 15, 30

If the average weight of the Golden Retriever, 70, is added to this list, which of the following statements would be true? C

A The mode would increase.
B The median would decrease.
C The median would increase.
D The mean would decrease.

Additional Examples are also in:

- Noteables™ Interactive Study Notebook with Foldables™
- Interactive Classroom PowerPoint® Presentations

Focus on Mathematical Content

Range is a measure of variation; it describes the spread of the data. The mean, median, and mode are all **measures of central tendency.** They describe the center of the data. When choosing between mean, median, mode, or range, remind students to only choose the range when they want to describe how far the data values are spread out.

Test-Taking Tip

Comparing Measures
Another way to solve Example 3 is to find the measures *before* 98 is added to the data set. Then find the measures *after* 98 is added to the data set. Then compare.

STANDARDS EXAMPLE 6SDAP1.2

3 The maximum length in feet of several whales is listed below.

46, 53, 33, 53, 79

If the maximum length of the Blue Whale, 98 feet, is added to this list, which of the following statements would be true?

A The mode would decrease.   **C** The mean would increase.
B The median would decrease.   **D** The mean would decrease.

Read the Item

You are asked to identify which statement would be true if the data value 98 was added to the data set.

Solve the Item

Use number sense to eliminate possibilities.
The mode, 53, will remain unchanged since the new data value occurs only once. So, eliminate answer choice A.

Since the new data value is greater than each value in the data set, the median will not decrease. So, eliminate answer choice B.

The remaining two answer choices refer to the mean. Since 98 is greater than each value in the data set, the mean will increase, not decrease. So, the answer is C.

CHECK Your Progress

d. If the maximum length of the Orca Whale, 30 feet, is added to the list in Example 3, which of the following statements would be true? J

F The mode would decrease.   **H** The mean would increase.
G The median would decrease.   **J** The mean would decrease.

 **Personal Tutor at** ca.gr6math.com

In addition to the mean, median, and mode, you can also use the range to describe a set of data. Below are some guidelines for using these measures.

CONCEPT Summary   Mean, Median, Mode, and Range

Measure	Most Useful When...
Mean	• data set has no outliers
Median	• data set has outliers • there are no big gaps in the middle of the data
Mode	• data set has many identical numbers
Range	• describing the spread of the data

STUDY TiP

Median
When there is an odd number of data, the median is the middle number of the ordered set. When there is an even number of data, the median is the mean of the two middle numbers.

EXAMPLE Choose Mean, Median, Mode, or Range

4 **TESTS** The line plot shows the test scores of the students in Mrs. Hiroshi's math class. Would the mean, median, mode, or range best represent the test scores?

Test Scores

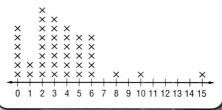

76 78 80 82 84 86 88 90 92 94 96

mean: $\dfrac{76 + 76 + 76 + \dots + 92}{18}$ or 83

median: $\dfrac{\text{9th term} + \text{10th term}}{2} = \dfrac{81 + 82}{2}$ or 81.5

mode: 89

range: $92 - 76$ or 16

The mode of 89 misrepresents the scores. Either the mean of 83 or the median of 81.5 best represents the scores.

✓ CHECK **Your Progress**

e. **GAMES** The table shows the cost of various board games. Would the mean, median, mode, or range best represent the costs? Explain.

Board Game Costs ($)

12	15	40	22
14	40	15	17
20	18	40	19
16	21	19	16

★ indicates multi-step problem

CHECK Your Understanding

Examples 1, 2
(pp. 402–403)

Find the mean, median, and mode for each set of data. Round to the nearest tenth if necessary.

. 52.3; 57; 59

1. Miles traveled on the weekend: 29, 14, 80, 59, 78, 30, 59, 69, 55, 50

. 9.5; 9.5; none

2.

Team	Number of Wins
Eagles	10
Hawks	8
Zipps	9
Falcons	11

. 44.6; 44; 44

3. **Quiz Scores**

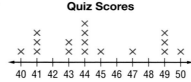

40 41 42 43 44 45 46 47 48 49 50

Example 3
(p. 404)
6SDAP1.2

4. **STANDARDS PRACTICE** During the week, the daily low temperatures were 52°F, 45°F, 51°F, 45°F, and 48°F. If Saturday's low temperature of 51°F is added, which statement about the data set would be true? **C**

A The mean would decrease.

B The median would decrease.

C The mode would increase.

D The mode would decrease.

Example 4 ★ 5.
(p. 405)

5. **SCHOOL** The line plot shows the number of times per day that students drink from the water fountain at school. Which measure best describes the data: mean, median, mode, or range? Explain. **See margin.**

Daily Drinks From the Water Fountain

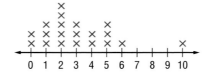

0 1 2 3 4 5 6 7 8 9 10

Additional Answer

5. Sample answer: Either the mean, median, or mode could be used to represent the data. The mean is slightly greater than most of the data items, and therefore is a less accurate description of the data.

ADDITIONAL EXAMPLE

4 **FIRST FAMILIES** The line plot below shows the number of children of United States presidents. Would the mean, median, or mode best represent the number of children? The mean, median, and mode are close, with values of 3.6, 3, and 2, respectively. Any of the three could be used to represent the data.

Children of US Presidents

0 1 2 3 4 5 6 7 8 9 10 11 12 13 14 15

3 Practice

✓ **Formative Assessment**

Use Exercises 1–5 to check for understanding.

Then use the chart on the next page to customize your assignments for students.

Intervention You may wish to use the Study Guide and Intervention Master on page 17 of the *Chapter 8 Resource Masters* for additional reinforcement.

Exercises

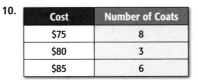

HOMEWORK HELP	
For Exercises	See Examples
6–11	1,2
30–32	3
12–13	4

Exercise Levels
A: 6–13
B: 14–24
C: 25–29

7. 87; 90; 80 and 93
8. 92.7; 91.5; 90
10. $79.40; $80; $75
11. 26.5; 25.5; 23 and 25

Find the mean, median, and mode for each set of data. Round to the nearest tenth if necessary.

6. Number of dogs groomed each week: 65, 56, 57, 75, 76, 66, 64 **65.6; 65; none**

7. Daily number of boats in a harbor: 93, 84, 80, 91, 94, 90, 78, 93, 80

8. Scores earned on a math test: 95, 90, 92, 94, 91, 90, 98, 88, 89, 100

9. Prices of books: $10, $18, $11, $6, $6, $5, $10, $11, $46, $7, $6, $8 **$12; $9; $6**

10.

Cost	Number of Coats
$75	8
$80	3
$85	6

11. **Minutes Spent Exercising**

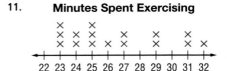

★ 12. **MUSIC** The line plot shows the number of weeks that songs have been on the Top 20 Country Songs list. Would the mean, median, mode, or range best represent the data? Explain. **See margin.**

Country Songs
Number of Weeks in Top 20

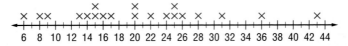

Real-World Link

The International Space Station measures 356 feet by 290 feet, and contains almost an acre of solar panels.
Source: *The World Almanac*

14. 6.4, 6.5, 7.2
15. $3.50, $3.50, $3.50
16. −1.9°F, −1.5°F, −2°F

17–19.
See margin.

··13. **SPACE** Twenty-seven countries have sent people into space. The table
★ shows the number of individuals from each country. Which measure best describes the data: mean, median, mode, or range? Explain. **See margin.**

People in Space								
267	1	9	8	1	1	1	1	1
97	1	1	1	3	1	1	2	1
11	2	1	1	5	1	1	1	1

Source: *The World Almanac*

Find the mean, median, and mode for each set of data. Round to the nearest tenth if necessary.

14. Weight in ounces of various insects: 6.1, 5.2, 7.2, 7.2, 3.6, 9.0, 6.5, 7.4, 5.4

15. Prices of magazines: $3.50, $3.75, $3.50, $4.00, $3.00, $3.50, $3.25

16. Daily low temperatures: −2°F, −8°F, −2°F, 0°F, −1°F, 1°F, −2°F, −1°F

REASONING Determine whether each statement is *always*, *sometimes*, or *never* true about the data set {8, 12, 15, 23}. Explain your reasoning.

17. If a value greater than 23 is added, the mean will increase.

18. If a value less than or equal to 8 is added, the mean will decrease.

19. If a value between 8 and 23 is added, the mean will remain unchanged.

406 Chapter 8 Statistics: Analyzing Data

DIFFERENTIATED HOMEWORK OPTIONS

Level	Assignment	Two-Day Option	
BL Basic	6–13, 25–27, 29–41	7–13 odd, 30–32	8–14 even, 25–27, 29, 33–41
OL Core	7–17 odd, 18–27, 29–41	7–13, 30–32	14–27, 29, 33–41
AL Advanced/Pre-AP	14–37 (optional: 38–41)		

DINOSAURS For Exercises 20–22, use the lengths of the dinosaurs shown below.

Tyrannosaurus Rex
Length: 480 inches

Corythosaurus
Length: 396 inches

Parasaurolophus
Length: 480 inches

20. What is the mean length of the dinosaurs? **452 inches**

21. One of the largest dinosaurs ever is the Brachiosaurus. Its length was 960 inches. If this data value is added to the lengths of the dinosaurs above, how will it affect the mean? Explain your reasoning.

22. Which measure best describes the data if the length of the Brachiosaurus is included: mean, median, mode, or range? If the length of the Brachiosaurus is *not* included? Explain any similarities or differences.

23. **SPORTS** The table shows the points scored by a lacrosse team so far this season. The team will play 14 games this season. How many points need to be scored during the last game so that the average number of points scored this season is 12? Explain. **10 points; See margin for explanation.**

Hawks Lacrosse Team Points Scored						
11	15	12	10	10	10	13
14	13	13	10	15	12	

24.  **FIND THE DATA** Refer to the California Data File on pages 16–19. Choose some data and then describe it using the mean, median, mode, and range. **See students' work.**

25. **OPEN ENDED** Give an example of a set of data in which the mean is not the best representation of the data set. Explain why not.

26. **Which One Doesn't Belong?** Identify the term that does not have the same characteristic as the other three. Explain your reasoning.

mean	median	range	mode

27. **REASONING** Determine whether the median is *sometimes*, *always*, or *never* part of the data set. Explain your reasoning. **See margin.**

28. **CHALLENGE** Without calculating, would the mean, median, or mode be most affected by eliminating 1,000 from the data shown? Which would be the least affected? Explain your reasoning. **See margin.**

50, 100, 75, 60, 75, 1,000, 90, 100

29. **WRITING IN MATH** According to the U.S. Census Bureau, the typical number of family members per household is 2.59. State whether this measure is a mean or mode. Explain how you know. **Mean; a mode must be a member of the data set, and it is impossible to have 2.59 family members.**

Lesson 8-2 Measures of Central Tendency and Range **407**

Pre-AP Activity Use after Exercise 25

Have students create line plots of three sets of data, one of which is best described by the mean, one of which is best described by the median, and one of which is best described by the mode.

 **Foldables™ Follow-Up**

Remind students to record notes about measures of central tendency under the tab in their Foldables for this lesson. Encourage them to draw a line plot on the front of the tab, showing where the mean, median, and mode are.

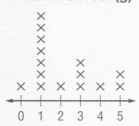 **Justify Your Selection** As students construct a line plot in Exercise 33, have them also verbally justify why selecting a line plot is appropriate to display the data. Sample answer: A line plot is appropriate since the data values are not too numerous and are close together in value. There are some repeating data values. A line plot can easily be created to show individual data values.

Additional Answer

33. Fiber in Cereal (g)

```
      ×
      ×
      ×
      ×
      ×        ×
      ×    ×   ×       ×
  ×   ×  × ×   ×   ×
  +---+---+---+---+---+---+
  0   1   2   3   4   5
```

STANDARDS PRACTICE 6SDAP1.1, 6SDAP1.1, 6SDAP1.2

30. The table below shows the number of soup labels collected in one week by each homeroom in grade 7.

Classroom	Number of Soup Labels
Mr. Martin	138
Ms. Davis	125
Mr. Cardona	89
Mrs. Turner	110
Mr. Wilhelm	130
Mrs. LaBash	?

Which number could be added to the set of data in order for the mode and median of the set to be equal? **C**

A 89

B 110

C 125

D 130

31. An antique dealer purchased 5 antiques for a total of $850.00. He later bought another antique for $758.00. What is the mean cost of all the antiques? **H**

F $151.60

G $170.00

H $268.00

J $321.60

32. Gina found the mean and median of the following list of numbers.

5, 7, 7

If the number 11 was added to this list, which of the following statements would be true? **A**

A The mean would increase.

B The mean would decrease.

C The median would increase.

D The median would decrease.

Spiral Review

33. **NUTRITION** The table shows the grams of fiber in one serving of 15 different cereals. Make a line plot of the data. (Lesson 8-1) **See margin.**

Fiber in Cereal (g)

5	5	4	3	3
3	1	1	1	2
1	1	1	1	0

Find the interest earned to the nearest cent for each principal, interest rate, and time. (Lesson 7-8)

34. $1,250, 3.5%, 2 years **$87.50**

35. $569, 5.5%, 4 months **$10.43**

36. **FOOD** The United States produced almost 11 billion pounds of apples in a recent year. Use the information in the graph to find how many pounds of apples were used to make juice and cider. (Lesson 7-1) **about 2.53 billion**

37. Name the property shown by the statement $4 \times 6 = 6 \times 4$. (Lesson 1-8) **Commutative (×)**

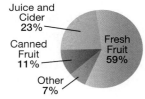

Uses of Apples in the United States

Juice and Cider 23%

Canned Fruit 11%

Fresh Fruit 59%

Other 7%

Source: usapple.org

GET READY for the Next Lesson

PREREQUISITE SKILL Name the place value of the underlined digit. (p. 669)

38. <u>5</u>81 **hundreds**

39. 6,29<u>5</u> **ones**

40. <u>4</u>,369 **thousands**

41. 2.8<u>4</u> **tenths**

Graphing Calculator Lab
Mean and Median

Main IDEA

Use technology to calculate the mean and median of a set of data.

 Standard **6SDAP2.5** Identify claims based on statistical data, **and in simple cases, evaluate the validity of the claims.** Standard **6MR2.5** Express the solution clearly and logically by using the appropriate mathematical notation and terms **and clear language; support solutions with evidence in both verbal and symbolic work.**

You can more efficiently calculate the mean and median of a large set of data using a graphing calculator.

ACTIVITY

COMPUTERS Kendrick surveys thirty seventh graders and asks them how many times they had to wait longer than 5 minutes during the previous week to use a computer in the school library. The results are shown below.

Number of Times a Student Had to Wait to Use the Library Computer									
5	2	9	1	1	2	1	2	5	2
3	4	2	1	4	0	4	2	2	5
4	2	2	3	2	1	3	9	5	2

Find the mean and median of the data.

STEP 1 Clear list L1 by pressing [STAT] [ENTER] [▲] [CLEAR] [ENTER].

STEP 2 Enter the number of times students had to wait in L1. Press 5 [ENTER] 2 [ENTER] . . . 2 [ENTER].

STEP 3 Display a list of statistics for the data by pressing [STAT] [▶] [ENTER] [2nd] 1 [ENTER].

The first value, x, is the mean.

Use the down arrow key to locate **Med**. The mean number of times a student waited was 3 and the median number of times was 2.

ANALYZE THE RESULTS

1. **WRITING IN MATH** Kendrick claims that, on average, students had to wait more than 5 minutes about 3 times last week. Based on your own analysis of the data, write a convincing argument to dispute his claim. (*Hint*: Create and use a line plot of the data to support your argument.) **See Ch. 8 Answer Appendix.**

2. **COLLECT THE DATA** Collect some numerical data from your classmates. Then use a graphing calculator to calculate the mean and median of the data. After analyzing the data, write a convincing argument to support a claim you can make about your data. **See students' work.**

STUDY TIP

Median The median, 2 times, means that half of the students waited more than 2 times to use a computer and half waited fewer than 2 times.

Math Online **Other Calculator Keystrokes at** ca.gr6math.com

Extend 8-2 Mean and Median **409**

1 Focus

Materials

• graphing calculator

Teaching Tip

If there aren't enough graphing calculators for every student, have students work in pairs or groups of three, sharing the calculators.

2 Teach

Activity You may want to suggest that students work in pairs, with one student reading the data from the table while the other student enters the data in the calculator. If students work in pairs, make sure they switch roles and repeat the Activity, with the data reader becoming the data enterer and vice versa.

3 Assess

Formative Assessment

Use Exercise 2 to determine whether students understand how to use a graphing calculator to find the mean and median of a data set.

From Concrete to Abstract Use Exercise 1 to bridge the gap between using a calculator to find measures of central tendency and understanding what those measures mean.

8-3 Stem-and-Leaf Plots

Standard 6SDAP1.3   Understand how the inclusion or exclusion of outliers affects measures of central tendency.

Standard 6SDAP1.1   Compute the range, mean, median, and mode of data sets.

PACING: **Regular:** 1 period,   **Block:** 0.5 period

Options for Differentiated Instruction

ELL = English Language Learner   **AL** = Above Grade Level   **SS** = Struggling Students   **SN** = Special Needs

Working in Pairs   ELL   SS   SN
Use with Example 1.

For Example 1, pair students together to create the stem-and-leaf plots. They should discuss how to set up each plot. Many students find it beneficial to have one partner read out the data points while the other partner writes them down in the plot.

Using Real-World Data   ELL   AL   SS
Use after presenting the Examples.

Have students research to find data about their favorite sports team. Have them display the information in a stem-and-leaf plot.

Give students ideas about the kind of data that they could use. Some suggestions are shown below.
- The number of homeruns hit by each player on a baseball team this season.
- The yards rushing per game for players on a football team.

Organizing Student Work   SN
Use before assigning the Exercises.

If students have organizational or fine motor skills difficulties, it may be helpful for them to use grid paper to keep the stems and leaves straight.

The stem-and-leaf plot for Exercise 1 is shown at right.
- Have students record each piece of data as they create the stem-and-leaf plot.
- Have them double count the points to make sure they haven't left any out.

Height of Trees						
Stem		**Leaf**				
0	8	8				
1	0	2	5	5	6	8
2	0	5				

1 | 0 = 10 feet

Leveled Lesson Resources

Chapter 8 Resource Masters

BL = Below Grade Level   **OL** = On Grade Level   **AL** = Above Grade Level   **ELL** = English Language Learner

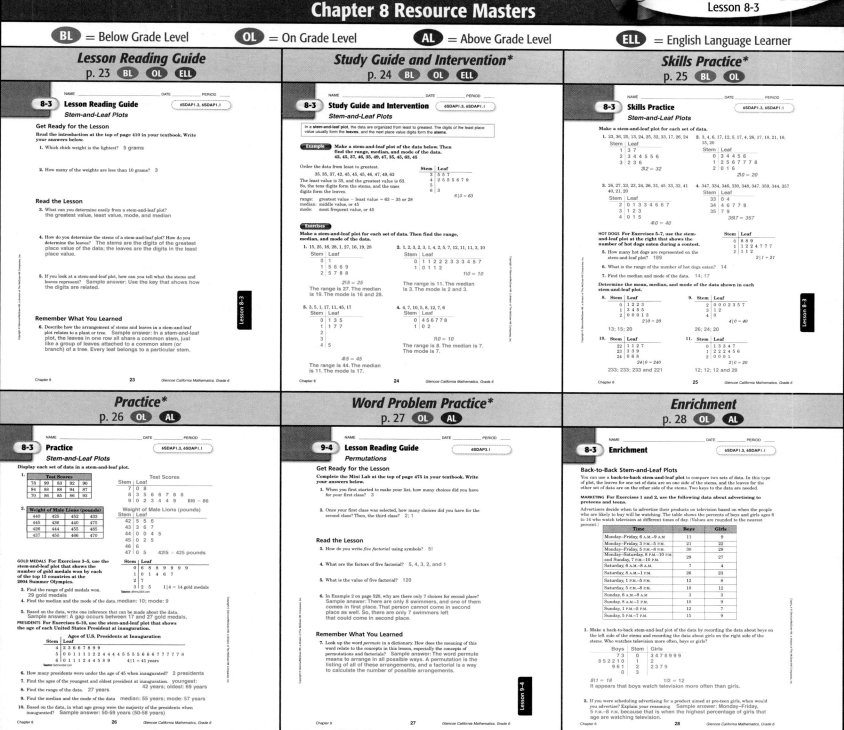

Additional Lesson Resources

Transparencies
- 5-Minute Check Transparency, Lesson 8-3

Other Print Products
- Noteables™ Interactive Study Notebook with Foldables™

Teacher Tech Tools
- Interactive Classroom CD-ROM, Lesson 8-3
- AssignmentWorks CD-ROM, Lesson 8-3

* Also available in Spanish **ELL**

Student Tech Tools
ca.gr6math.com
- Extra Examples, Chapter 8, Lesson 3
- Self-Check Quiz, Chapter 8, Lesson 3

1 Focus

Standards Alignment

Before Lesson 8-3
Organize and display single-variable data in appropriate graphs and representations and explain which types of graphs are appropriate for various data sets *from Standard 5SDAP1.2*

Lesson 8-3
Understand how the inclusion or exclusion of outliers affects measures of central tendency. Compute the range, mean, median, and mode of data sets *from Standards 6SDAP1.3 and 6SDAP1.1*

After Lesson 8-3
Know various forms of display for data sets, including a stem-and-leaf plot or box-and-whisker plot; use the forms to display a single set of data or to compare two sets of data *from Standard 7SDAP1.1*

2 Teach

Scaffolding Questions

As you ask the following questions, write each number on the board.

Ask:
- How many tens are in 17? 1
- How many tens are in 23? 2
- How many tens are in 6? 0
- How many tens are in 389? 38
- How many tens are in 102? 10

Formative Assessment

Use the Check Your Progress exercises after each Example to determine students' understanding of concepts.

8-3 **Stem-and-Leaf Plots**

Main IDEA
Display and analyze data in a stem-and-leaf plot.

Standard 6SDAP1.3 Understand how the inclusion or exclusion of outliers affects measures of central tendency.
Standard 6SDAP1.1 Compute the range, mean, median, and mode of data sets.

NEW Vocabulary
stem-and-leaf plot
leaf
stem

a. See Ch. 8 Answer Appendix.

GET READY for the Lesson

BIRDS The table shows the average chick weight in grams of sixteen different species of birds.

1. 5 grams
1. Which chick weight is the lightest?
2. How many of the weights are less than 10 grams? 3

Chick Weight (g)			
19	6	7	10
11	13	18	25
21	12	5	12
20	21	11	12

Source: upatsix.com

In a **stem-and-leaf plot**, the data are organized from least to greatest. The digits of the least place value usually form the **leaves**, and the next place value digits form the **stems**.

EXAMPLE   Display Data in a Stem-and-Leaf Plot

1 **BIRDS** Display the data in the table above in a stem-and-leaf plot.

Step 1 Choose the stems using digits in the tens place, 0, 1, and 2. The least value, 5, has 0 in the tens place. The greatest value, 25, has 2 in the tens place.

Step 2 List the stems from least to greatest in the *Stem* column. Write the leaves, the ones digits to the right of the corresponding stems.

Stem	Leaf
0	6 7 5
1	9 0 1 3 8 2 2 1 2
2	5 1 0 1

Step 3 Order the leaves and write a *key* that explains how to read the stems and leaves. Include a title.

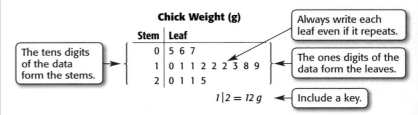

Chick Weight (g)

Stem	Leaf
0	5 6 7
1	0 1 1 2 2 2 3 8 9
2	0 1 1 5

The tens digits of the data form the stems.

Always write each leaf even if it repeats.

The ones digits of the data form the leaves.

$1|2 = 12\,g$ Include a key.

CHECK Your Progress

a. **HOMEWORK** The number of minutes the students in Mr. Blackwell's class spent doing their homework one night is shown. Display the data in a stem-and-leaf plot.

Homework Time (min)				
42	5	75	30	45
47	0	24	45	51
56	23	39	30	49
58	55	75	45	35

 Personal Tutor at ca.gr6math.com

410 **Chapter 8** Statistics: Analyzing Data

Justify Your Selection

Tips for New Teachers

As students construct a stem-and-leaf plot in Example 1, have them also verbally justify why selecting a stem-and-leaf plot is appropriate to display the chick weight data. Sample answer: A stem-and-leaf plot is an appropriate choice to display the data since the data can be grouped into intervals (stems) and the individual data values within those intervals can be plotted as the leaves.

Stem-and-leaf plots are useful in analyzing data because you can see all the data values, including the greatest, least, mode, and median value.

EXAMPLE — Describe Data

2 **CHESS** The stem-and-leaf plot shows the number of chess matches won by members of the Avery Middle School Chess Team. Find the range, median, and mode of the data.

range: greatest wins − least wins
         = 61 − 8 or 53

median: middle value, or 35 wins

mode: most frequent value, 40

Chess Matches Won

Stem	Leaf
0	8 8 9
1	9
2	0 0 2 4 4 8 9
3	1 1 2 4 5 5 6 6 7 7 8
4	0 0 0 3 8 9
5	2 4
6	1

3|2 = 32 wins

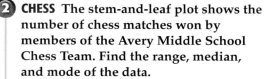

CHECK Your Progress

b. BIRDS Find the range, median, and mode of the data in Example 1.

_. 20 g; 12 g; 12 g_

EXAMPLE — Effect of Outliers

3 **NUTRITION** The average amount of pasta consumed in different countries each year is shown in the stem-and-leaf plot. Which measure of central tendency is most affected by the inclusion of the outlier?

The mode, 15, is not affected by the inclusion of the outlier, 59.

Amount of Pasta Consumed (lb)

Stem	Leaf
0	3 4 5 8 8 9 9
1	0 1 4 5 5 5 5 5 9
2	0 0 8
3	
4	
5	9

2|8 = 28 lb

Calculate the mean and median each without the outlier, 59. Then calculate them including the outlier and compare.

	without the outlier	including the outlier
mean:	$\dfrac{3 + 4 + \ldots + 28}{19} \approx 12.79$	$\dfrac{3 + 4 + \ldots + 28 + 58}{20} = 15.1$
median:	14	14.5

The mean increased by 15.1 − 12.79, or 2.31, while the median increased by 14.5 − 14, or 0.5. Since 2.31 > 0.5, the mean is most affected.

Real-World Career . . . .
How Does a Nutritionist Use Math?
Nutritionists use statistical graphs to summarize and compare the nutritional values of various foods.

Math Online
For more information, go to ca.gr6math.com.

CHECK Your Progress

c. CHESS Refer to Example 2. If an additional student had 84 wins, which measure of central tendency would be most affected? *mean*

 Math Online Extra Examples at ca.gr6math.com   **Lesson 8-3** Stem-and-Leaf Plots   **411**

Tips for New Teachers

Range

Although the range is not a measure of central tendency, it is interesting to calculate the range in Example 3 with and without the outlier, 59, and compare the results. The range including the outlier is 59-3, or 56. The range without the outlier is 28-3, or 25. Notice the impact of the outlier on the size of the range.

ADDITIONAL EXAMPLES

1 **BASEBALL** The table below shows the number of home runs that Babe Ruth hit during his career from 1914 to 1935. Make a stem-and-leaf plot of the data.

Home Runs

0	54	25	46	4
59	47	41	3	35
60	34	2	41	54
6	11	22	46	29
46	49			

Source: baberuth.com
See answer in bottom margin.

2 **FITNESS** The stem-and-leaf plot below shows the number of miles that Megan biked each day during July. Find the range, median, and mode of the data. *25; 12; 10*

Miles Megan Biked

Stem	Leaf
0	5 5 5 6
1	0 0 0 0 1 2 2 5 8 8 9
2	1 2 5 8
3	0

2|5 = 25 miles

3 **ANIMALS** The average life span of several animal species is shown in the stem-and-leaf plot. Which measure of central tendency is most affected by the inclusion of the outlier?

Life Spans

Stem	Leaf
0	3 4 6 8
1	0 0 2 2 2 5 5 6 8
2	0 0 0 0 2
3	
4	0

1|0 = 10 years

median

Additional Examples are also in:

- Noteables™ Interactive Study Notebook with Foldables™
- Interactive Classroom PowerPoint® Presentations

✔ CHECK Your Understanding

Focus on Mathematical Content

Focus on Mathematical Content

In a **stem-and-leaf plot**, data is organized so that it can be analyzed visually and mathematically.

The **stems** are the digits in the greatest common place value; the **leaves** are the digits in the remaining place value.

Inferences about data are conclusions supported by analysis of the data.

Example 1
(p. 410)

1–2. See Ch. 8 Answer Appendix.

Display each set of data in a stem-and-leaf plot.

1.

Height of Trees (ft)				
15	25	8	12	20
10	16	15	8	18

2.

Cost of Shoes ($)				
42	47	19	16	21
23	25	25	29	31
33	34	35	39	48

Examples 2, 3
(p. 411)

CAMP The stem-and-leaf plot at the right shows the ages of students in a pottery class.

3. What is the range of the ages of the students? **5**

4. Find the median and mode of the data. **11; 11**

5. If an additional student was 6 years old, which measure of central tendency would be most affected? **mean**

Ages of Students

Stem	Leaf
0	9 9 9
1	0 1 1 1 1 2 2 3 3 4

1|0 = 10 yr

---

3 Practice

✔ Formative Assessment

Use Exercises 1–5 to check for understanding.

Then use the chart at the bottom of this page to customize your assignments for students.

Intervention You may wish to use the Study Guide and Intervention Master on page 24 of the *Chapter 8 Resource Masters* for additional reinforcement.

Odd/Even Assignments

Exercises 6–19 are structured so that students practice the same concepts whether they are assigned odd or even problems.

Exercises

HOMEWORK HELP

For Exercises	See Examples
6–9	1
10, 11, 13, 14, 16–18	2
12, 15, 19	3

Exercise Levels
A: 6–19
B: 20–22
C: 23–26

6–9. See Ch. 8 Answer Appendix.

Display each set of data in a stem-and-leaf plot.

6.

Quiz Scores (%)			
70	96	72	91
80	80	79	93
76	95	73	93
90	93	77	91

7.

Low Temperatures (°F)				
15	13	28	32	38
30	31	13	36	35
38	32	38	24	20

8.

Floats at Annual Parade			
151	158	139	103
111	134	133	154
157	142	149	159

9.

School Play Attendance			
225	227	230	229
246	243	269	269
267	278	278	278

CYCLING The number of Tour de France titles won by eleven countries as of 2005 is shown.

10. Find the range of titles won. **35**

11. Find the median and mode of the data. **4; 1**

12. Which measure of central tendency is most affected by the outlier? **mean**

Tour de France Titles Won by Eleven Countries

Stem	Leaf
0	1 1 1 2 2 4 8 9
1	0 8
2	
3	6

0|4 = 4 titles

ELECTRONICS For Exercises 13–15, use the stem-and-leaf plot that shows the costs of various DVD players at an electronics store.

13. What is the range of the prices? **$45**

14. $108 and $115

14. Find the median and mode of the data.

15. If an additional DVD player cost $153, which measure of central tendency would be most affected? **mean**

Costs of DVD Players

Stem	Leaf
8	2 5 5
9	9 9
10	0 0 2 5 6 8
11	0 0 5 5 5 9 9
12	5 7 7

11|5 = $115

412 Chapter 8 Statistics: Analyzing Data

DIFFERENTIATED HOMEWORK OPTIONS

Level	Assignment	Two-Day Option	
BL Basic	6–19, 23, 25–35	7–19 odd, 27, 28	6–18 even, 23, 25, 26, 29–35
OL Core	7–19 odd, 20–23, 25–35	6–19, 27, 28	20–23, 25, 26, 29–35
AL Advanced/Pre-AP	20–33 (optional 34, 35)		

HISTORY For Exercises 16–19, refer to the stem-and-leaf plot below.

Ages of Signers of Declaration of Independence

Stem	Leaf
2	6 6 9
3	0 1 3 3 3 4 4 5 5 5 5 7 7 8 8 9 9
4	0 1 1 1 2 2 2 4 5 5 5 5 6 6 6 6 7 8 9
5	0 0 0 0 2 2 3 3 5 7
6	0 0 2 3 5 6
7	0

$3\,|\,1 = 31$ years

16. How many people signed the Declaration of Independence? **56 people**

17. What was the age of the youngest signer? **26**

18. What is the range of the ages of the signers? **44 years**

19. Based on the data, can you conclude that the majority of the signers were 30–49 years old? Explain your reasoning. **See margin.**

20. **GYMNASTICS** The scores for 10 girls in a gymnastics event are 9.3, 10.0, ★ 9.9, 8.9, 8.7, 9.0, 8.7, 8.5, 8.8, 9.3. Analyze a stem-and-leaf plot of the data to draw two conclusions about the scores. **See margin.**

21. **REPTILES** The average lengths of certain species ★ of crocodiles are given in the table. Analyze a stem-and-leaf plot of this data to write a convincing argument about a reasonable length for a crocodile. **See margin.**

Crocodile Average Lengths (ft)

8.1	16.3	16.3	9.8
16.3	16.3	11.4	6.3
13.6	9.8	19.5	16.0

Source: Crocodilian Species List

22. **FIND THE DATA** Refer to the California Data File on pages 16–19. Choose some data that can be presented in a stem-and-leaf plot. Then analyze the stem-and-leaf plot to draw two conclusions about the data. **See students' work.**

23. **FIND THE ERROR** Selena and Diana are analyzing the data in the stem-and-leaf plot at the right. Diana says half of the pieces of ribbon are between 20 and 30 inches in length. Selena says there are no pieces of ribbon more than 50 inches in length. Who is correct? Explain.

Cut Ribbon Length

Stem	Leaf
2	6 6 9
3	
4	6
5	3 6

$2\,|\,6 = 26$ in.

24. **CHALLENGE** Create a stem-and-leaf plot in which the median of the data is 25. **See margin.**

25. **WRITING IN MATH** Present the data shown at the right in a frequency table, a line plot, and a stem-and-leaf plot. Describe the similarities and differences among the representations. Which representation do you prefer to use? Explain your reasoning.
See Ch. 8 Answer Appendix.

Price of Jeans ($)

40	45	38	30
35	32	33	24
26	36	56	36
26	38	49	34
28	40	40	35

Lesson 8-3 Stem-and-Leaf Plots **413**

eal-World Link . . . .
ne saltwater
ocodile is the largest
ving reptile. Some
easuring 27–30 feet
 length have been
corded in the wild.
urce: pbs.org

XTRA PRACTICE
See pages 699, 722.

Math Online
Self-Check Quiz at
ca.gr6math.com

H.O.T. Problems . . . .

3. Diana; three out
f the six or 50% of
ne pieces of
bbon are 20–30
ches in length.

Additional Answers

19. Sample answer: Yes, Thirty-six of the 56 signers were 30–49 years. Since 36 out of 56 is greater than half, you can say that the majority of the signers were 30–49 years old.

20. **Gymnastics Scores**

Stem	Leaf
8	0 5 7 7 8
9	0 3 3 9
10	0

$8\,|\,0 = 8.0$

Sample answer: There is only one person who scored a perfect 10. An average score is about 9.0.

21. **Average Length (ft) of Crocodiles**

Stem	Leaf
6	3
7	
8	1
9	8 8
10	
11	4
12	
13	6
14	
15	
16	0 3 3 3 3
17	
18	
19	5

$13\,|\,6 = 13.6$ ft

Sample answer: A reasonable length for an average crocodile is about 16 feet.

24. Sample answer:

Stem	Leaf
1	1 2 3 4
2	5 5 6 7
3	
4	7 8

$2\,|\,5 = \$25$

Lesson 8-3 Stem-and-Leaf Plots **413**

Yesterday's News Remind students that yesterday's lesson was about using mean, median, and mode to describe data sets. Ask them to write how yesterday's concepts helped them with today's material.

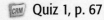

Formative Assessment

Check for student understanding of concepts in Lessons 8-1 through 8-3.

CRM Quiz 1, p. 67

Foldables™ Follow-Up

Remind students to record notes about stem-and-leaf-plots under the tab for this lesson in their Foldables. Encourage them to draw and label a stem-and-leaf plot on the front of the tab.

Additional Answers

29. 48.7; 50; 55

30. 4.3; 3.6; 3.6 and 2.4

34. Sample answer: 5; 0–20

35. Sample answer: 20; 20–120

---

26. COLLECT THE DATA Collect a set of data that represents the heights in inches of the people in your math class. Then write a question that can be solved by analyzing a stem-and-leaf plot of the data. Be sure to explain how the stem-and-leaf plot would be used to solve your problem. **See students' work**

STANDARDS PRACTICE 6SDAP1.3

27. Denzell's science quiz scores are 11, 12, 13, 21, and 35. Which stem-and-leaf plot best represents this data? **C**

A
Stem	Leaf
1	1
2	1
3	5

$3|5 = 35$

B
Stem	Leaf
1	3
2	1
3	5

$3|5 = 35$

C
Stem	Leaf
1	1 2 3
2	1
3	5

$3|5 = 35$

D
Stem	Leaf
1	1
2	1 1
3	5

$3|5 = 35$

28. The stem-and-leaf plot shows the points scored by the Harding Middle School basketball team. **H**

Points Scored
Stem	Leaf
4	7 8 8 8
5	0 0 2 3 7 9
6	1 6
7	
8	4

$7|0 = 70$

Which one of the following statements is true concerning how the measures of central tendency are affected by the inclusion of the outlier?

F The mode is most affected.

G The median is not affected.

H The mean is most affected.

J None of the measures of central tendency are affected.

Spiral Review

Find the mean, median, and mode for each set of data. Round to the nearest tenth if necessary. (Lesson 8-2) **29–30. See margin.**

29. 80, 23, 55, 58, 45, 32, 40, 55, 50

30. 3.6, 2.4, 3.0, 7.9, 7.8, 2.4, 3.6, 3.9

31. Make a line plot of the test scores shown. (Lesson 8-1) **See margin.**

32. SCHOOL The ratio of boys to girls in the sixth grade is 7 to 8. How many girls are in the sixth grade if there are 56 boys? (Lesson 6-1) **64**

33. Write $\frac{9}{24}$ in simplest form. (Lesson 4-4) $\frac{3}{8}$

Test Scores				
83	94	78	78	85
86	88	83	82	92
90	77	83	81	89
90	88	87	88	85
84	81	83	85	91

GET READY for the Next Lesson

PREREQUISITE SKILL Choose an appropriate interval and scale for each set of data. (Lesson 8-1) **34–35. See margin.**

34. 9, 0, 18, 19, 2, 9, 8, 13, 4

35. 30, 20, 60, 80, 90, 120, 40

31.

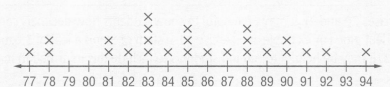

Bar Graphs and Histograms

Standard
6SDAP2.3

Analyze data displays and explain why the way in which the question was asked might have influenced the results obtained and why the way in which the results were displayed might have influenced the conclusions reached.

PACING: **Regular:** 2 periods, **Block:** 1 period

Options for Differentiated Instruction

ELL = English Language Learner   **AL** = Above Grade Level   **SS** = Struggling Students   **SN** = Special Needs

Comparing and Contrasting   ELL   SN

Use after presenting Examples 1 and 2.

Display the graphs in Examples 1 and 2 side-by-side so that students can more easily compare and contrast them.

Example 1

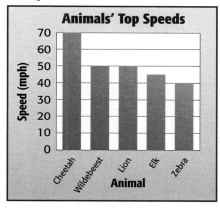

Example 2

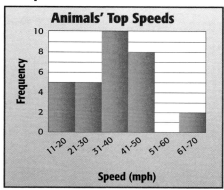

Have students describe the differences between the graphs. Sample answer: The graph in Example 1 has space between the bars and the bars represent the speeds of the animals listed on the horizontal axis. The graph in Example 2 has no space between the bars; the bars represent the number of animals that have the top speeds shown on the horizontal axis.

Research   AL

Use after presenting Lesson 8-4.

Have students find examples of bar graphs and histograms in newspapers and magazines.

Have them create a poster displaying all the graphs. In addition, have students identify the following:
- the name of the graph
- the label for the horizontal and vertical axis
- the scale and interval for the horizontal and vertical axis

Then have students write a two sentences about each one. Then have students write an explanation of the main objective in solving two-step equations. How does this relate to solving equations in Lessons 3-2 and 3-3?

Leveled Lesson Resources

BL = Below Grade Level   **OL** = On Grade Level   **AL** = Above Grade Level   **ELL** = English Language Learner

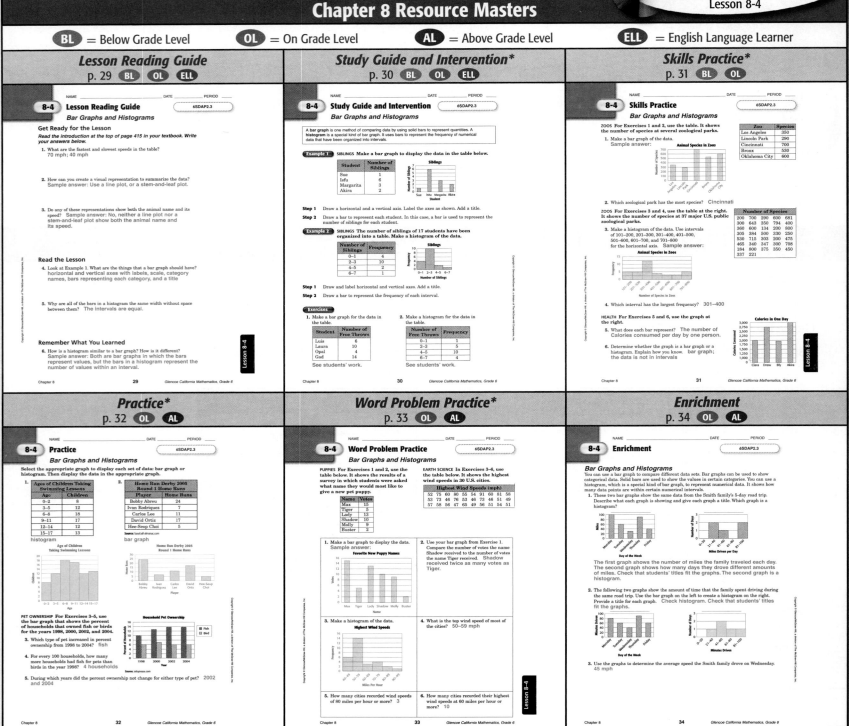

Additional Lesson Resources

Transparencies
- *5-Minute Check Transparency,* Lesson 8-4

Other Print Products
- *Noteables™ Interactive Study Notebook with Foldables™*

Teacher Tech Tools
- *Interactive Classroom CD-ROM,* Lesson 8-4
- *AssignmentWorks CD-ROM,* Lesson 8-4

* Also available in Spanish **ELL**

Student Tech Tools
ca.gr6math.com
- Extra Examples, Chapter 8, Lesson 4
- Self-Check Quiz, Chapter 8, Lesson 4

Main IDEA

Display and analyze data using bar graphs and histograms.

 Standard 6SDAP2.3 Analyze data displays and explain why the way in which the question was asked might have influenced the results obtained and why the way in which the results were displayed might have influenced the conclusions reached.

NEW Vocabulary

bar graph
histogram

3. Sample answer: No, neither a line plot nor a stem-and-leaf plot show both the animal name and its speed.

STUDY TiP

Bar Graphs
The bars should be of equal width with equal spacing between them.

▶ GET READY for the Lesson

ANIMALS The cheetah is the fastest known land animal. The table shows its fastest speed and the top speeds of four other land animals.

Animal	Speed (mph)
cheetah	70
wildebeest	50
lion	50
elk	45
zebra	40

Source: *The World Almanac*

1. What are the fastest and slowest speeds in the table? **70 mph; 40 mph**

2. How can you create a visual representation to summarize the data?

3. Do any of these representations show both the animal name and its speed? **2. Sample answer: Use a line plot or a stem-and-leaf plot.**

A **bar graph** is a method of comparing data by using solid bars to represent quantities.

EXAMPLE Display Data Using a Bar Graph

1. **Display the data in the table above in a bar graph.**

Step 1 Draw a horizontal axis and a vertical axis. Label the axes as shown. In this case, the scale on the vertical axis is chosen so that it includes all the speeds. Add a title.

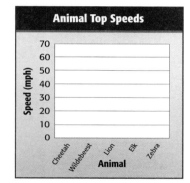

Step 2 Draw a bar to represent each category. In this case, a bar is used to represent the speed of each animal.

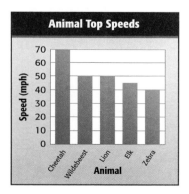

Lesson 8-4 Bar Graphs and Histograms **415**

 Justify Your Selection

As students construct a bar graph in Example 1, have them also verbally justify why selecting a bar graph is appropriate to display the data presented in the lesson opener. Sample answer: A bar graph is an appropriate choice to display the data because the data values show the speed of various individual animals and the data does not show intervals.

1 Focus

 Standards Alignment

Before Lesson 8-4
Organize and display single-variable data in appropriate graphs and representations and explain which types of graphs are appropriate for various data sets from Standard 5SDAP1.2

Lesson 8-4
Analyze data displays

from ━━ Standard 6SDAP2.3

After Lesson 8-4
Know various forms of display for data sets and use the forms to display a single set of data or to compare two sets of data from Standard 7SDAP1.1

2 Teach

Scaffolding Questions

Write the following caterpillar lengths on the board: 3 cm, 3.8 cm, 4.3 cm, 5.7 cm, 5.7 cm, 6.1 cm, 6.2 cm, and 6.9 cm.

Ask:

• How many caterpillars have lengths from 3 to 3.9 cm? 2

• How many caterpillars have lengths from 4 to 4.9 cm? 1

• How many caterpillars have lengths from 5 to 5.9 cm? 2

• How many caterpillars have lengths from 6 to 6.9 cm? 3

• If you used a histogram to display this data, which bar would be the largest? the bar for 6 to 6.9 cm

Formative Assessment

Use the Check Your Progress exercises after each Example to determine students' understanding of concepts.

Focus on Mathematical Content

A **bar graph** is a good way to compare different quantities.

A **histogram** shows the frequency of numerical data within equal intervals.

Inferences can be made about data by analyzing bar graphs and histograms.

a. See Ch. 8 Answer Appendix.

a. **FLOWERS** The table shows the diameters of the world's largest flowers. Display the data in a bar graph.

Flower	Maximum Size (in.)
Rafflesia	36
Sunflower	19
Giant Water Lily	18
Brazilian Dutchman	14
Magnolia	10

Source: *Book of World Records*

ADDITIONAL EXAMPLE

1️⃣ **TOURISM** Make a bar graph to display the data in the table below.

Country	Vacation Days per Year
Italy	42
France	37
Germany	35
Brazil	34
United Kingdom	28
Canada	26
Korea	25
Japan	25
United States	13

Source: *The World Almanac*

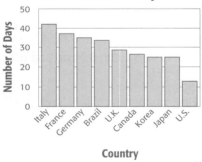

Additional Examples are also in:

• Noteables™ Interactive Study Notebook with Foldables™

• Interactive Classroom PowerPoint® Presentations

READING Math

Frequency
Frequency refers to the number of data items in a particular interval. In Example 2, the frequency of 10 in the third row means that there are 10 animals whose maximum speed is 31–40 mph.

STUDY TIP

Histograms
Because the intervals are equal, all of the bars have the same width, with no space between them. The space at 51–60 indicates that there are no data values on that interval.

A special kind of bar graph, called a **histogram**, uses bars to represent the frequency of numerical data that have been organized in intervals.

EXAMPLE Display Data Using a Histogram

2️⃣ **ANIMALS** The top speeds of thirty different land animals have been organized into a frequency table. Display the data in a histogram.

Maximum Speed (mph)	Number of Animals
11–20	5
21–30	5
31–40	10
41–50	8
51–60	0
61–70	2

Source: *The World Almanac*

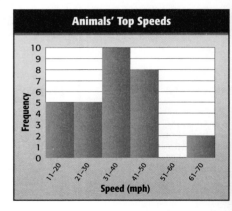

Step 1 Draw and label horizontal and vertical axes. Add a title.

Step 2 Draw a bar to represent the frequency of each interval.

The two highest bars represent a majority of the data. From the graph, you can easily see that most of the animals have a top speed of 31–50 miles per hour.

416 Chapter 8 Statistics: Analyzing Data

Tips for New Teachers

Using Graphs

Make sure students understand that bar graphs are used to show categorical data, such as animals' tops speeds, while histograms are used to show numerical data, such as the number of animals with top speeds within certain intervals.

Tips for New Teachers

Intervals

Point out that the data values in Example 2 are whole numbers that fall within the given intervals. If a value like 20.5 had been given, different intervals would be needed to include that value.

b. **EARTHQUAKES** The magnitudes of the largest U.S. earthquakes are organized into the frequency table shown. Display the data in a histogram.
See Ch. 8 Answer Appendix.

Magnitude	Frequency
7.0–7.4	4
7.5–7.9	14
8.0–8.4	5
8.5–8.9	2
9.0–9.4	1

Source: National Earthquake Information Center

 Personal Tutor at ca.gr6math.com

EXAMPLES Analyze Data to Make Inferences

WEATHER The bar graph shows the monthly number of tornadoes that occurred in the U.S. in 2004.

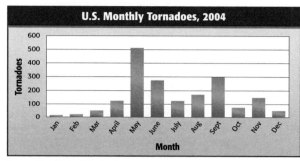

Source: NOAA National Weather Service

3 Which season had the least number of tornadoes? Justify your answer.

Look for the months with the least number of tornadoes. The graph shows that close to 0 tornadoes occurred in January and February. So, the least number of tornadoes occurred in winter.

4 Compare the number of tornadoes that occurred in May and June.

About 500 tornadoes occurred in May. About 275 tornadoes occurred in June. So, there were almost twice as many tornadoes in May than in June.

✓ CHECK Your Progress

MALLS The histogram shows the number of stores in the largest malls in the U.S.

c. How many malls are represented in the histogram? Explain your reasoning.

d. Compare the number of malls with 275–349 stores to the malls with 425–499 stores.

Source: Directory of Major Malls

c. 10 + 14 + 4 + 1 + 1 = 30; Sample answer: Find the sum of the heights of the bars in the histogram.

d. There are 4 times as many malls that have 275–349 stores than 425–499 stores.

Math Online **Extra Examples at** ca.gr6math.com

Lesson 8-4 Bar Graphs and Histograms **417**

2 **BASKETBALL** The number of wins for 29 teams of a basketball league for a season have been organized into a frequency table. Make a histogram of the data.

Number of Wins	Frequency
11–20	3
21–30	4
31–40	4
41–50	10
51–60	8

AUTOMOBILES The bar graph shows average prices for different kinds of cars.

3 Which kind of car was most expensive? Justify your answer. Luxury cars were most expensive. The bar graph shows that they cost almost $35,000, more than $5,000 more than the next most expensive car.

4 Compare the prices of mid-size cars and luxury cars. Mid-size cars cost about $17,000; luxury cars cost about $34,000. So, mid-size cars are about half as expensive as luxury cars.

✔ **Formative Assessment**

Use Exercises 1–4 to check for understanding.

Then use the chart at the bottom of this page to customize your assignments for students.

Intervention You may wish to use the Study Guide and Intervention Master on page 30 of the *Chapter 8 Resource Masters* for additional reinforcement.

Odd/Even Assignments

Exercises 5–15 are structured so that students practice the same concepts whether they are assigned odd or even problems.

Additional Answers

2.

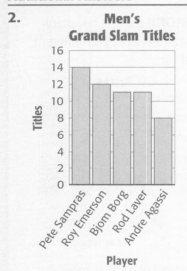

Men's Grand Slam Titles

4. Sample answer: The average number of pages in a health textbook is about 400. The average number of pages in a science textbook is about 800. Since 400 is half of 800, it is a reasonable statement.

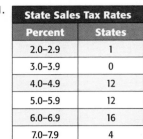 **CHECK Your Understanding**

Examples 1, 2
(pp. 415–417)

Select the appropriate graph to display each set of data: bar graph or histogram. Then display the data in the appropriate graph.

1. histogram; See Ch. 8 Answer Appendix for graph.

1.

State Sales Tax Rates	
Percent	**States**
2.0–2.9	1
3.0–3.9	0
4.0–4.9	12
5.0–5.9	12
6.0–6.9	16
7.0–7.9	4

Source: www.taxadmin.org

2. bar graph; See margin for graph.

2.

Men's Grand Slam Titles	
Player	**Titles**
Pete Sampras	14
Roy Emerson	12
Bjorn Borg	11
Rod Laver	11
Andre Agassi	8

Source: *Book of World Records*

Examples 3, 4
(p. 417)

TEXTBOOKS For Exercises 3 and 4, use the bar graph that shows the average number of pages in various textbooks.

3. On average, which textbook has the least number of pages? **health**

4. Is it reasonable to say that on average, a health textbook has half as many pages as a science textbook? Explain. **See margin.**

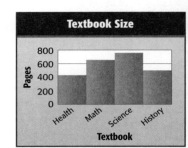

Exercises

HOMEWORK HELP

For Exercises	See Examples
5–8	1, 2
9–15	3

Exercise Levels
A: 5–15
B: 16–27
C: 28–30

Select the appropriate graph to display each set of data: bar graph or histogram. Then display the data in the appropriate graph.

5.

Most Threatened Reptiles	
Country	**Number of Species**
Australia	38
China	31
Indonesia	28
U.S.	27
India	25

Source: *Top 10 of Everything, 2005*

bar graph; See Ch. 8 Answer Appendix for graph.

6.

Home Run Leaders, 1985–2004	
Home Runs	**Frequency**
31–36	1
37–42	4
43–48	7
49–54	5
55–60	3

Source: *The World Almanac*

histogram; See Ch. 8 Answer Appendix for graph.

7.

Major U.S. Rivers	
Length (mi)	**Frequency**
600–999	15
1,000–1,399	5
1,400–1,799	3
1,800–2,199	3
2,200–2,599	2

Source: *The World Almanac*

histogram; See Ch. 8 Answer Appendix for graph.

8.

City Skyscrapers	
City	**Skyscrapers**
New York	176
Hong Kong	163
Chicago	81
Shanghai	49
Tokyo	44

Source: *Book of World Records*

bar graph; See Ch. 8 Answer Appendix for graph.

418 Chapter 8 Statistics: Analyzing Data

DIFFERENTIATED **HOMEWORK OPTIONS**

Level	Assignment	Two-Day Option	
BL Basic	5–15, 29–36	5–15 odd, 31, 32	6–14 even, 29, 30, 33–36
OL Core	5–15 odd, 16–27, 29–36	5–15, 31, 32	16–27, 29, 30, 33, 36
AL Advanced/Pre-AP	16–35 (optional: 36)		

GEOGRAPHY For Exercises 9–12, use the graph that shows the number of bordering states for each of the fifty states.

9. What is the most frequent number of states that borders another state? **4**

10. How many states are bordered by 6 states? **9**

11. How many states do not have any bordering states? Justify your answer.

12. **RESEARCH** Use the Internet or another source to find which states do not have any bordering states. Why do these states not have bordering states?
Hawaii and Alaska; Hawaii is surrounded by water and Alaska is bordered by Canada

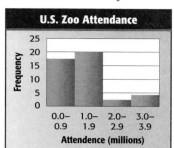

The State's Neighbors

ZOOS For Exercises 13–15, use the histogram that shows the attendance at the major U.S. zoos in a recent year.

13. About how many zoos does the graph represent? **43**

14. What is the range of attendance for most of the zoos?

15. Compare the number of zoos with 0.0–0.9 million visitors to the number of zoos with 3.0–3.9 million visitors.

U.S. Zoo Attendance

Source: The World Almanac

Match each characteristic to the appropriate graph(s).

16. data display based upon place value **c**   a. line plot

17. shows the frequency of data on a number line **a**   b. histogram

18. compares data using solid bars **d**   c. stem-and-leaf plot

19. data is organized using intervals **b**   d. bar graph

CELL PHONES For Exercises 20 and 21, use the bar graph shown below.

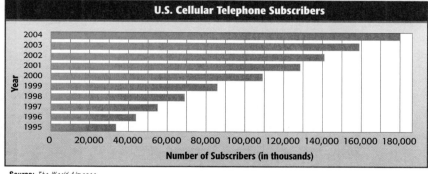

U.S. Cellular Telephone Subscribers

Source: The World Almanac

20. Describe how the number of cell phone subscribers has grown over the 10-year period. **See margin.**

21. Use the graph to predict the number of cell phone subscribers in 2010.
Sample answer: 210,000 thousand, or 210,000,000

Lesson 8-4 Bar Graphs and Histograms **419**

11. 2; The bar for 0 is 2 high.

14. 0.0–1.9 million people

15. Sample answer: The number of zoos with 0.0–0.9 million visitors is about 4 times the number of zoos with 3.0–3.9 million visitors.

 Exercise Alert!

Use the Internet Exercise 12 requires students to find information from the Internet.

Additional Answer

20. Sample answer: Cellular phone subscription in the U.S. increased dramatically over this time period. Every year, the amount of increase was larger than for the previous year's increase.

22. Refrigerator; the difference in annual costs between an old model and a new model is $106 — $56 or $50, which is greater than the differences for the other appliances.

ELECTRICITY For Exercises 22 and 23, use the multiple bar graph that compares the annual costs of using old model appliances and using equivalent new model appliances.

22. For which appliance is the difference in electricity costs between the old and new model the greatest? Explain.

23. Describe an advantage of using a multiple-bar graph rather than two separate graphs to compare data.

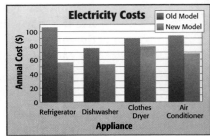

Source: *Association of Home Appliance Manufacturers*

Sample answer: It is easier to compare two sets of data.

EXERCISE For Exercises 24–27, refer to the graph below.

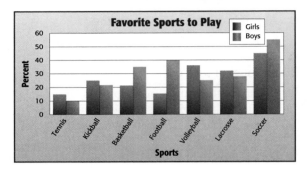

EXTRA PRACTICE

See pages 699, 722.

Math Online

Self-Check Quiz at ca.gr6math.com

24. Which sport did the girls surveyed prefer the most? **soccer**

25. Which sport is the least favorite for the boys? **tennis**

26. Based on this survey, boys prefer football 4 times more than what sport? **tennis**

27. Write a convincing argument telling why you think that approximately the same number of boys and girls like to play kickball. **See margin.**

H.O.T. Problems

28–30. See margin.

28. CHALLENGE The histograms show players' salaries for two major league baseball teams. Compare the salary distributions of the two teams.

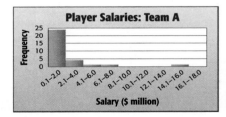

29. DATA SENSE Describe how to determine the number of values in a data set that is represented by a histogram.

30. WRITING IN MATH Can any data set be displayed using a histogram? If yes, explain why. If no, give a counterexample and explain why not.

31. The results of a survey are displayed in the graph. **C**

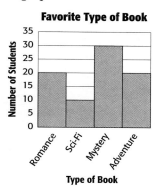

Favorite Type of Book

Which statement is valid about the survey?

A Twice as many students enjoy reading mysteries than romance.

B Most students enjoy reading adventure books.

C Twice as many students enjoy reading romance books than science fiction.

D Half as many students enjoy reading mysteries than romance.

32. The graph shows the average car sales per month at a car dealership. **H**

Average Monthly Sales

What is the best prediction for the number of station wagons the dealer sells in a year?

F 10

G 60

H 120

J 500

Spiral Review

SPORTS For Exercises 33 and 34, refer to the data that lists the number of games won by each team in a baseball league.

Number of Wins					
25	36	46	15	30	53
40	32	17	45	41	31
56	50	52	47	26	40
43	56	51	50	55	50
44	47	53	23	19	

33. Make a stem-and-leaf plot of the data. (Lesson 8-3) **See margin.**

34. What is the mean, median, and mode of the data? (Lesson 8-2) **about 40.4; 44; 50**

35. **SELECT A TECHNIQUE** The video game that Neil wants to buy costs $50. He has saved $\frac{1}{5}$ of the amount he needs. Which of the following techniques might Neil use to find how much more money he will need to buy the game? Justify your selection(s). Then use the technique(s) to solve the problem. (Lesson 5-5) **See margin.**

> mental math   number sense   estimation

GET READY for the Next Lesson

36. **WEATHER** At 5:00 P.M., the outside temperature was 81°F. At 6:00 P.M., it was 80°F. At 7:00 P.M., it was 79°F. Use the *look for a pattern* strategy to predict the outside temperature at 8:00 P.M. (Lesson 2-6) **78°F**

Lesson 8-4 Bar Graphs and Histograms   **421**

Tips for New Teachers

Describing Data

After students complete Exercise 34, have them write a verbal description of the data using the terms *mean, median,* and *mode.* Then have them find the range of the data and choose which measure best describes the center of the data. Have them provide a justification for the choice. Sample answer: The mean, or average, of the data is about 40.4. The median, or middle number, of the data is 44. The mode, or most frequently occurring number is 50. The range is 56–15, or 41. Either the mean or the median best represents the data since the mode is too high and the range is only used when describing the spread of the data.

---

4 Assess

Ticket Out the Door Write the following hamburger prices on the chalkboard: $2.79, $2.56, $1.99, $3.20, $2.95, $1.40, $2.75, $4.19, and $3.64. Have students write the intervals they would use to create a histogram of the prices.

FOLDABLES Study Organizer **Foldables™ Follow-Up**

Remind students to record notes about bar graphs and histograms under the tab for this lesson in their Foldable. Encourage them to draw and label a bar graph or histogram on the front of the tab.

Tips for New Teachers **Justify Your Selection**

As students construct a stem-and-leaf plot in Exercise 33, have them also verbally justify why selecting a stem-and-leaf plot is appropriate to display the number of games won by each team in a baseball league.

Sample answer: A stem-and-leaf plot is an appropriate choice to display the data since the data can be grouped in intervals (stems) and the individual data values within those intervals can be plotted as the leaves.

Additional Answers

33.

Number of Wins

Stem	Leaf
1	5 7 9
2	3 5 6
3	0 1 2 6
4	0 0 1 3 4 5 6 7 7
5	0 0 0 1 2 3 3 5 6 6

5|3 = 53 wins

35. Mental math; the numbers are easy to compute mentally. Sample answer: $\frac{1}{5}$ of $50 is $10 and $50 − $10 = $40. So, he will need an additional $40.

1 Focus

Materials

- computers with a spreadsheet program

Teaching Tip

If there aren't enough computers for every student in your class, have students work in pairs, sharing the computers.

2 Teach

Activity Make sure students understand that the circle graph shows the responses of all the students surveyed, or 100%. So each sector of the graph shows a part of the responses, or a percent less than 100%. Point out that students can estimate the percents shown by a circle graph by comparing the graph to a clock. For example, a sector showing $\frac{1}{4}$ or 25% would be equal to the sector of clock between the minute and hours hands at 3 o'clock.

3 Assess

Formative Assessment

Use Exercise 2 to determine whether students understand how to use a spreadsheet program to create a circle graph.

From Concrete to Abstract Use Exercise 1 to bridge the gap between using a spreadsheet program to create a circle graph and understanding how to interpret the graph.

Extend 8-4 | **Spreadsheet Lab**
Circle Graphs

Main IDEA

Use technology to create circle graphs.

 Standard 6SDAP2.3 Analyze data displays and explain why the way in which the question was asked might have influenced the results obtained and why the way in which the results were displayed might have influenced the conclusions reached.
Standard 6MR1.2 Formulate and justify mathematical conjectures based on a general description of the mathematical question or problem posed.

Another type of display used to compare categories of data is a *circle graph*. Circle graphs are useful when comparing parts of a whole.

ACTIVITY

MAGAZINES The table shows the results of a survey in which students were asked to indicate their favorite type of magazine. Use a spreadsheet to make a circle graph of these data.

Magazine Preferences	
Type	**Frequency**
Comics	2
Fashion	7
Entertainment	5
News	3
Sports	6
Other	1

STEP 1 Enter the data in a spreadsheet as shown.

Magazine Preferences.xls

	A	B	C	D	E	F
1	Comics	2				
2	Fashion	7				
3	Entertainment	5				
4	News	3				
5	Sports	6				
6	Other	1				
7						
8						
9						
10						
11						
12						

Magazine Preferences
- Comics
- Fashion
- Entertainment
- News
- Sports
- Other

Sheet 1 / Sheet 2 / Sheet 3

STEP 2 Select the information in cells A1 to B6. Click on the Chart Wizard icon. Choose the Pie chart type. Click Next twice. Enter the title Magazine Preferences. Then click Next and Finish.

STUDY TIP

Bar Graphs
To create a bar graph using a spreadsheet, follow the same steps used to create a circle graph, except choose Bar for the chart type.

ANALYZE THE RESULTS   1. See margin.

1. **MAKE A CONJECTURE** Use the graph to determine which types of magazines were preferred by about $\frac{1}{3}$ and 25% of the students surveyed. Explain your reasoning. Then check your answers.

2. **COLLECT THE DATA** Collect some data that can be displayed in either a circle or bar graph. Record the data in a spreadsheet. Then use the spreadsheet to make both types of displays. Which display is more appropriate? Justify your selection. See students' work.

Additional Answer

1. One-third of the students preferred fashion magazines since about $\frac{1}{3}$ of the circle is shaded to represent those who chose fashion magazines; Twenty-five percent of the students preferred sports magazines since about $\frac{1}{4}$ of the circle is shaded to represent those who chose sports magazines.

Mid-Chapter Quiz

Lessons 8-1 through 8-4

1. **STANDARDS PRACTICE** The table shows quiz scores of a math class. What is the range of test scores? (Lesson 8-1) **D**

Math Scores						
89	92	67	75	95	89	82
92	88	89	80	91	79	90

A 89 C 67
B 82 D 28

For Exercises 2–4, use the data below. (Lesson 8-1)

Age Upon Receiving Driver's License									
16	17	16	16	18	21	16	16	18	18
17	25	16	17	17	17	17	16	20	16

2. Make a line plot of the data. **2–3. See margin.**

3. Identify any clusters, gaps, or outliers.

4. Describe how the range of data would change if 25 was not part of the data set. **The range would be 5 rather than 9.**

5. **STANDARDS PRACTICE** The table shows the average April rainfall for 12 cities. If the value 4.2 is added to this list, which of the following would be true? (Lesson 8-2) **G**

Average Rain (in.)					
0.5	0.6	1.0	1.0	2.5	3.7
2.6	3.3	2.0	1.4	0.7	0.4

F The mode would increase.
G The mean would increase.
H The mean would decrease.
J The median would decrease.

6. **TREES** The heights, in meters, of several trees are 7.6, 6.8, 6.5, 7.0, 7.9, and 6.8. Find the mean, median, and mode. Round to the nearest tenth if necessary. (Lesson 8-2) **See margin.**

7. **SPEED** Display the data shown in a stem-and-leaf plot and write one conclusion based on the data. (Lesson 8-3) **See margin.**

Car Highway Speeds				
65	72	76	68	65
59	70	69	71	74
68	65	71	74	69

MAMMALS For Exercises 8–10, refer to the stem-and-leaf plot that shows the maximum weight in kilograms of several rabbits.

Maximum Weight of Rabbits (kg)

Stem	Leaf
0	8 9
1	0 2 4 6 8
2	7
3	
4	
5	4

$0|8 = 0.8\ kg$

8. Find the range of weights. **4.6 kg**

9. Find the median and mode of the data. **1.4 kg; no mode**

10. Which measure of central tendency is most affected by the inclusion of the outlier? Explain. **See margin.**

ATTENDANCE For Exercises 11 and 12, refer to the graph. (Lesson 8-4)

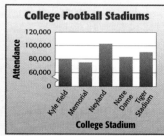

College Football Stadiums

Source: msnbc.com

11. About how many people does the graph represent? **about 430,000**

12. Which two stadiums house about the same number of people? **Notre Dame and Kyle Field**

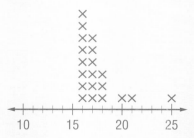
Data-Driven Decision Making	Exercises	Lesson	Standard	Resources for Review
Diagnostic Teaching Based on the results of the Chapter 8 Mid-Chapter Quiz, use the following to review concepts that students continue to find challenging.	1–4	8–1	6SDAP1.1	**CRM** Study Guide and Intervention pp. 10, 17, 24, and 30 **Math Online** • Extra Examples • Personal Tutor • Concepts in Motion
	5, 6	8–2	6SDAP1.4	
	7–10	8–3	6SDAP1.1	
	11, 12	8–4	🔑 6SDAP2.3	

8-5

Problem-Solving Investigation
USE A GRAPH

Standard 6MR2.3 **Estimate unknown quantities graphically** and solve for them by using logical reasoning and arithmetic and algebraic techniques.

Standard 6SDAP2.3 **Analyze data displays** and explain why the way in which the question was asked might have influenced the results obtained and why the way in which the results were displayed might have influenced the conclusions reached.

PACING: **Regular:** 1 period, **Block:** 0.5 period

Options for Differentiated Instruction

ELL = English Language Learner   **AL** = Above Grade Level   **SS** = Struggling Students   **SN** = Special Needs

Understanding the Concept   **ELL** **SS** **SN**

Use after presenting Lesson 8-5.

Make sure students understand that predicting from a graph involves estimation. They must understand that the trend in the data and the line drawn through the data are guides to their predictions. They can use the graph to justify their ideas, but real-life circumstances may alter the actual outcomes.

Choosing a Strategy   **ELL** **SS** **SN**

Use before assigning the Exercises.

Prior to assigning Exercises 5–8, read each exercise aloud and discuss with the class which strategy might be best to solve each problem. Possible discussion questions are listed below.
- What is the question asking for?
- Does it look like problems you have done in the past? If so which ones?
- What strategy do you think you will try to use?

Make sure that all students have chosen a strategy for each of the problems so that they can complete the assignment independently.

Working in Pairs   **ELL** **AL** **SS** **SN**

Use after students complete the Examples.

Display different graphs on the board or overhead, like those shown below.

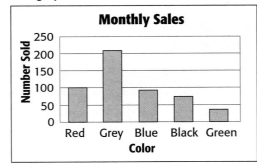

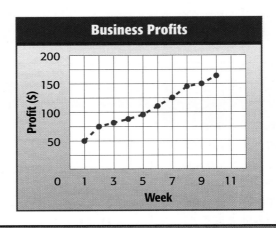

Have pairs of students write questions that can be answered using the graphs. Pairs should exchange questions and use the graphs to solve.

Leveled Lesson Resources

Chapter 8 Resource Masters

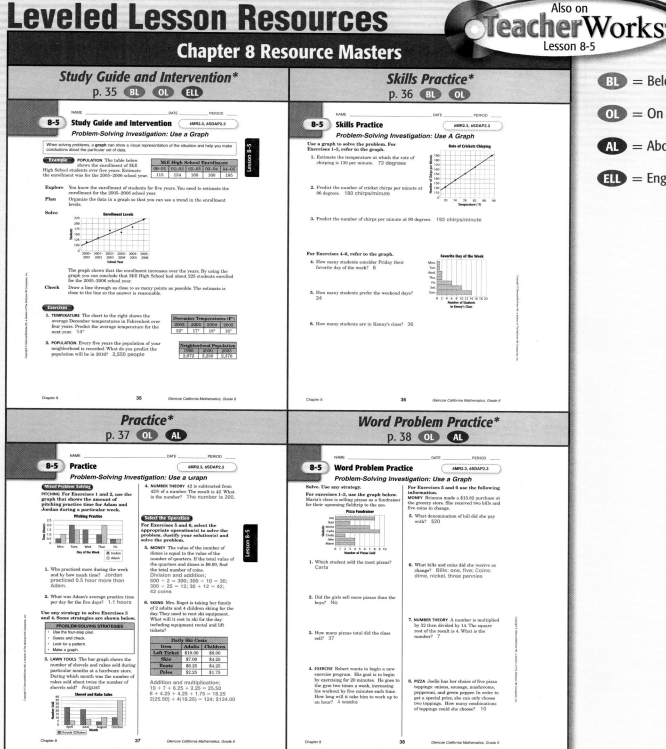

BL = Below Grade Level

OL = On Grade Level

AL = Above Grade Level

ELL = English Language Learner

* Also available in Spanish **ELL**

Additional Lesson Resources

Transparencies
- *5-Minute Check Transparency*, Lesson 8-5

Other Print Products
- *Noteables™ Interactive Study Notebook with Foldables™*

Teacher Tech Tools
- *Interactive Classroom CD-ROM*, Lesson 8-5
- *AssignmentWorks CD-ROM*, Lesson 8-5

Student Tech Tools
ca.gr6math.com
- Extra Examples, Chapter 8, Lesson 5
- Self-Check Quiz, Chapter 8, Lesson 5

8-5 Lesson Notes

1 Focus

Use a Graph Students have learned to solve problems and make inferences about data by analyzing graphs. This problem-solving strategy will be reinforced in later lessons when students learn how to make predictions from line graphs and scatter plots, and how to choose the best graphical representation for a set of data.

2 Teach

Scaffolding Questions

Ask:

• What would a graph of your *distance from home* look like as you were going to school? It would slope upward, or increase.

• What would a graph of your *distance from home* look like as you were going home? It would slope downward, or decrease.

• What would a graph of your *distance from home* look like as you were doing work around the house and garden? It would be more or less flat, with small increases and decreases.

ADDITIONAL EXAMPLE

Use a graph to solve.

CASSETTE SALES Based on the information in the table, how many music cassettes would you expect to be sold in 2004?

Cassette Sales (millions)	
Year	Cassettes Sold
1996	225
1997	173
1998	159
1999	124
2000	76

The graph shows a rapid downward trend. If it continued, no cassettes would be sold in 2004.

8-5 Problem-Solving Investigation

MAIN IDEA: Solve problems by using a graph.

 Standard 6MR2.3 Estimate unknown quantities graphically and solve for them by using logical reasoning and arithmetic and algebraic techniques. **Standard 6SDAP2.3 Analyze data displays** and explain why the way … might have influenced the results obtained and why the way … influenced the conclusions reached.

P.S.I. TEAM +

e-Mail: USE A GRAPH

YOUR MISSION: Use a graph to solve the problem.

THE PROBLEM: The table shows the study times and test scores of 13 students in Mrs. Collins' English class.

> Yolanda: Based on this data, what would be the test score of a student who studied for 80 minutes?

Study Time and Test Scores											
Study Time (min)	120	30	60	95	70	55	90	45	75	60	10
Test Score (%)	98	77	91	93	77	78	95	74	87	83	65

EXPLORE	You know the number of minutes studied. You need to predict the test score.
PLAN	Organize the data in a graph so you can easily see any trends.
SOLVE	The graph shows that as the study times progress, the test scores increase. You can predict that the test score of a student who studied for 80 minutes is about 88%.
CHECK	Draw a line that is close to as many of the points as possible, as shown. The estimate is close to the line so the prediction is reasonable.

Study Time and Test Scores

(graph showing scatter plot with Test Score (%) on y-axis from 65 to 95, Study Time (min) on x-axis from 0 to 100, with a trend line)

Analyze The Strategy

1. Explain why analyzing a graph is a useful way to quickly make conclusions about a set of data. **See Ch. 8 Answer Appendix.**

2. **WRITING IN MATH** Write a problem in which using a graph would be a useful way to check a solution. **See students' work.**

Additional Examples are also in:

• Noteables™ Interactive Study Notebook with Foldables™

• Interactive Classroom PowerPoint® Presentations

Answer to Additional Example

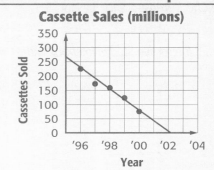

Cassette Sales (millions)

(line graph with Cassettes Sold on y-axis from 0 to 350, Year on x-axis from '96 to '04, showing downward trend)

★ indicates multi-step problem

For Exercises 3 and 4, solve by using a graph.

3. SCIENCE Refer to the graph. Suppose the trends continue. Predict the average high temperature for the month of July.
Sample answer: 95°F

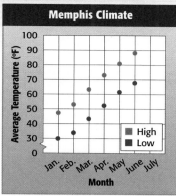

Source: weather.com

4. SCHOOL The graph shows the number of energy bars sold in the cafeteria. On which day did the cafeteria sell about half as many bars as it did on Friday? **Wednesday**

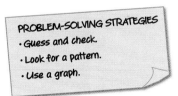

Use any strategy to solve Exercises 5–8. Some strategies are shown below.

> **PROBLEM-SOLVING STRATEGIES**
> • Guess and check.
> • Look for a pattern.
> • Use a graph.

5. ALGEBRA What are the next two numbers in the pattern 8, 18, 38, 78, …? **158, 318**

6. READING Maya read 10 pages of a 150-page book on Monday and plans to read twice as many pages each day than she did the previous day. On what day will she finish the book? **Thursday**
★

7. EXERCISE The graph shows the number of minutes Jacob exercised during one week. According to the graph, which two days did he exercise about the same amount of time? **Tuesday and Thursday**

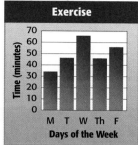

8. ALGEBRA Find two numbers with a sum of 56 and with a product of 783. **27, 29**
★

Select the Operation

For Exercises 9 and 10, select the appropriate operation(s) to solve the problem. Justify your selection(s) and solve the problem.

9. SAFETY An elevator sign reads *Do not exceed 2,500 pounds.* How many people, each weighing about 150 pounds, can be in the elevator at the same time?
division; 2,500 ÷ 150 is about 16 people

10. BOWLING Tariq and three of his friends are going bowling, and they have a total of $70 to spend. Suppose they buy a large pizza, four beverages, and each rent bowling shoes. How many games can they bowl if they all bowl the same number of games?
See margin.
★

Bowling Costs	
Item	**Price**
large pizza	$15.75
beverage	$1.50
shoe rental	$3.50
game	$4.00

Lesson 8-5 Problem-Solving Investigation: Use a Graph **425**

3 Practice

Using the Exercises

Exercises 1 and 2 can be used to check students' understanding of the use a graph strategy.

Exercises 3 and 4 give students an opportunity to practice the use a graph strategy.

Exercises 5–8 are structured so that students have the opportunity to practice many different problem-solving strategies. You may wish to have students review some of the strategies they have studied.

• Use the four-step plan p. 25
• Guess and check p. 42
• Look for a pattern p. 112
• Use a graph p. 424

Exercises 9 and 10 require students to select the appropriate operation(s) to solve the problem. Have students analyze each problem and its wording, asking themselves what kind of information is needed, and which operation(s) must be performed to get the information?

4 Assess

Crystal Ball Tell students that tomorrow's lesson is about using line graphs and scatter plots to make predictions. Ask students to write how they think what they learned today will connect with tomorrow's material.

Additional Answer

10. Using addition and multiplication, the amount spent is 15.75 + 4(1.50) + 4(3.50) or $35.75; Using subtraction, you find that they have $70 — $35.75 or $34.25 remaining to spend to play. If each person bowls 1 game, the cost will be $4 × 4 or $16. If each person bowls 2 games, the cost will be $4 × 4 × 2 or $32. So, they can bowl 2 games.

Pre-AP Activity Use after Exercise 2

Have students research on the Internet the population of Texas (or of your town or city) over the last 50 years. Have them graph the data, using five- or ten-year intervals. Finally, have them predict the population five or ten years in the future.

8-6 Using Graphs to Predict

Standard 6MR2.3 **Estimate unknown quantities graphically** and solve for them by using logical reasoning and arithmetic and algebraic techniques.

Standard 6SDAP2.5 **Identify claims based on statistical data,** and in simple cases, evaluate the validity of the claims.

PACING: **Regular:** 2 periods, **Block:** 1 period

Options for Differentiated Instruction

ELL = English Language Learner   **AL** = Above Grade Level   **SS** = Struggling Students   **SN** = Special Needs

Simplifying the Task SS SN

Use with the Mini Lab.

Give students copies of a coordinate grid like the one shown at the right to help them draw the graph in the Mini Lab. On the grid, provide lines for the title and axes labels.

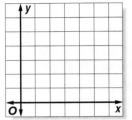

Creating Resources Sheets ELL SS SN

Use before assigning the Exercises.

Have students add to their resource sheet a list of questions to help them summarize data displayed in line graphs and scatter plots. Sample questions are shown below.

- The correlation of the scatter plot is __?__ , indicating that __?__ .
- The fluctuation in the line graph tells me that __?__ .
- I can tell there is no correlation in the data because __?__ .
- There is a strong positive correlation in the data, so I can predict that __?__ .

Have students brainstorm other questions and add them to the list.

Collecting Data ELL AL SS SN

Use after students complete Lesson 8-6.

Discuss with students the relationship between a person's foot length and their height.

Ask:

- Would it make sense to predict that a person with a long foot is probably tall?
- Could we collect data to support that hypothesis? If so, how?

Then collect data in the class of students' foot lengths and heights, both in centimeters. Have students create a scatter plot to display the data.

Ask:

- Was your hypothesis true? If so, what evidence can you point to?
- If a person is about 150 centimeters tall, can you predict about how long their foot is?
- If a person's foot is about 25 centimeters long, can you predict about how tall they are?

Leveled Lesson Resources

Chapter 8 Resource Masters

BL = Below Grade Level   **OL** = On Grade Level   **AL** = Above Grade Level   **ELL** = English Language Learner

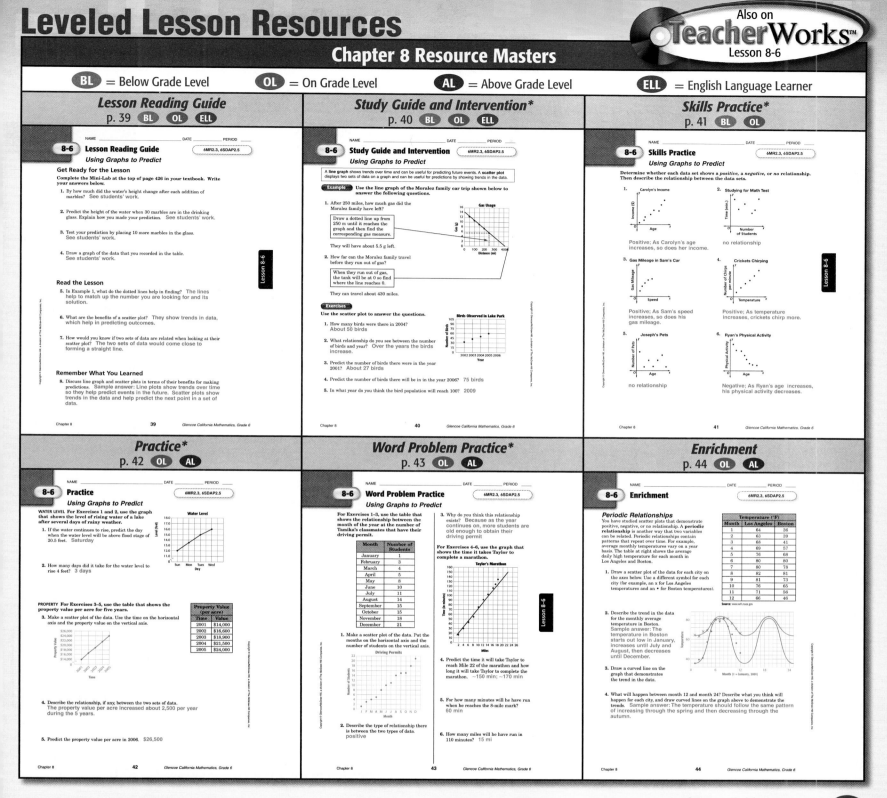

Additional Lesson Resources

Transparencies
- *5-Minute Check Transparency*, Lesson 8-6

Other Print Products
- *Teaching Mathematics with Manipulatives*
- *Noteables™ Interactive Study Notebook with Foldables™*
- *Science and Mathematics Lab Manual*, pp. 33–36

Teacher Tech Tools
- *Interactive Classroom CD-ROM*, Lesson 8-6
- *AssignmentWorks CD-ROM*, Lesson 8-6

Student Tech Tools
ca.gr6math.com
- Extra Examples, Chapter 8, Lesson 6
- Self-Check Quiz, Chapter 8, Lesson 6

* Also available in Spanish **ELL**

 1 Focus

Standards Alignment

Before Lesson 8-6
Identify ordered pairs of data from a graph and interpret the meaning of the data in terms of the situation depicted by the graph
from ◆━ Standard 5SDAP1.4

Lesson 8-6
Estimate unknown quantities graphically. Identify claims based on statistical data from ◆━
Standards 6MR2.3 and 6SDAP2.5

After Lesson 8-6
Represent two numerical variables on a scatterplot and informally describe how the data points are distributed and any apparent relationship that exists between the two variables from Standard 7SDAP1.2

2 Teach

▶ **MINI Lab**

The lab will work best if students use drinking glasses that are cylindrical, or beakers. Plastic is preferable so as to avoid breaking.

Scaffolding Questions

With masking tape, mark heights of 2 feet, 4 feet, 6 feet, and 8 feet on a wall. Show students a tennis ball. Ask for a volunteer to help you. After you ask each question, drop the ball from the given height. Have the volunteer mark the ball's bounce height and measure it. Record the drop and bounce heights in a table on the board.

Ask:
• How high do you think the ball will bounce when I drop it from 2 feet?

Continued at right

8-6 **Using Graphs to Predict**

Main IDEA
Analyze line graphs and scatter plots to make predictions and conclusions.

 Standard 6MR2.3 Estimate unknown quantities graphically and solve for them by using logical reasoning and arithmetic and algebraic techniques. ◆━ **Standard 6SDAP2.5 Identify claims based on statistical data,** and in simple cases, evaluate the validity of the claims.

NEW Vocabulary

line graph
scatter plot

▶ **MINI Lab**

• Pour 1 cup of water into the drinking glass.
• Measure the height of the water, and record it in a table like the one shown.
• Place 5 marbles in the glass. Measure the height of the water. Record.
• Continue adding marbles, 5 at a time, until there are 20 marbles in the glass. After each time, measure and record the height of the water.

Number of Marbles	Height of Water (cm)
0	
5	
10	
15	
20	

1. By how much did the water's height change after each addition of marbles?
2. Predict the height of the water when 30 marbles are in the drinking glass. Explain how you made your prediction.
3. Test your prediction by placing 10 more marbles in the glass.
4. Draw a graph of the data that you recorded in the table.

1–4. See students' work.

You created a line graph in the Mini Lab. **Line graphs** can be useful in predicting future events because they show relationships or trends over time.

EXAMPLES **Use a Line Graph to Predict**

1 **TEMPERATURE** The relationship between temperature readings in °C and °F is shown below. Use the line graph to predict the temperature reading 35°C in °F.

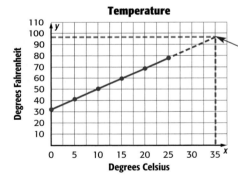

Continue the graph with a dotted line in the same direction until you align vertically with 35°C. Graph a point. Find what value in °F corresponds with the point.

The temperature reading 35°C is equivalent to 95°F.

• How high do you think the ball will drop when I drop it from 4 feet?

• How high do you think the ball will bounce when I drop it from 6 feet?

• How high do you think the ball will bounce when I drop it from 8 feet?

• Is the height from which you drop the ball related to the height the ball bounces?

about 10 days

See margin for graph; about 68 to 0 juice boxes

② **SCHOOL** The graph shows the student enrollment at McDaniel Middle School for the past several years. If the trend continues, what will be the enrollment in 2010?

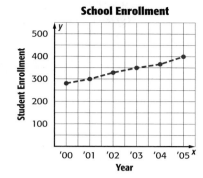

School Enrollment

If the trend continues, the enrollment in 2010 will be about 525 students.

✓ CHECK **Your Progress**

a. **READING** Kerry is reading *The Game of Sunken Places* over summer break. The graph shows the time it has taken her to read the book so far. Predict the time it will take her to read 150 pages.

The Game of Sunken Places

b. **JUICE BOXES** The table shows the number of juice boxes a cafeteria sold in a five-week period. Display the data in a line graph. If the trend continues, how many juice boxes will be sold in week 8?

Juice Box Sales	
Week	Number Sold
1	50
2	52
3	56
4	60
5	62

A **scatter plot** displays two sets of data on the same graph. Like line graphs, scatter plots are useful for making predictions because they show trends in data. If the points on a scatter plot come close to lying on a straight line, the two sets of data are related.

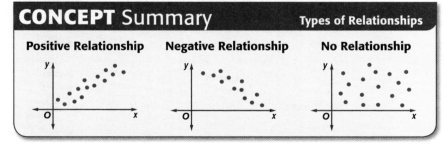

CONCEPT Summary — Types of Relationships

Positive Relationship Negative Relationship No Relationship

Additional Answer

b.

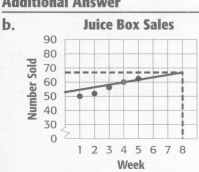

Juice Box Sales

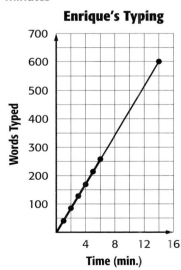

2 TESTS The line graph shows the math test scores of a middle-school student for five chapters. If the trend continues, what do you think her score will be on the next math test? about 86%

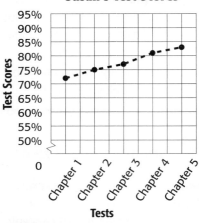

Susan's Test Scores

3 POLLUTION The scatter plot shows the number of days that San Bernardino, California, failed to meet air-quality standards from 1990 to 1998. Predict the number of days of bad air quality in 2004. about 48 days

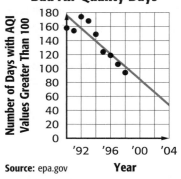

Bad Air Quality Days

Source: epa.gov

Tips for New Teachers

Scatter Plots

You might want to supply pieces of dry spaghetti to students for the scatter plot exercises. They can place a piece of spaghetti on a scatter plot, positioning it to "fit" as many points as possible. Then they can draw the visualized line with their pencils and make their predictions.

READING Math

Scatter Plots Another name for scatter plot is *scattergram*.

EXAMPLE Use a Scatter Plot to Predict

3 SWIMMING The scatter plot shows the winning times for the women's 100-meter butterfly event at the Summer Olympics from 1968 to 2004. Predict a winning time for this event at the 2012 Olympics.

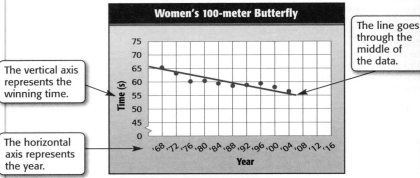

The vertical axis represents the winning time.

The horizontal axis represents the year.

The line goes through the middle of the data.

Women's 100-meter Butterfly

Source: *The World Almanac*

By looking at the pattern, we can predict that the winning time at the 2012 Olympics will be about 54 seconds.

CHECK Your Progress

c. about 52 s

c. SWIMMING Use the scatter plot above to predict a winning time for the Women's 100-meter Butterfly event at the 2016 Olympics.

Online Personal Tutor at ca.gr6math.com

CHECK Your Understanding

Examples 1, 2
(pp. 426–427)

1. Sample answer: The graph shows a negative relationship. That is, as the weeks pass, the time decreases.

TRACK Sierra is training for cross-country try-outs. To make the team, she needs to be able to run 1 mile in under 8 minutes. The graph charts her progress.

1. Describe the relationship between the two sets of data.

2. If the trend continues, will Sierra make the team? Explain.
Yes; she will be able to run 1 mile in less than 8 minutes.

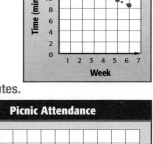

1-Mile Run

Example 3
(p. 428)

3. **PICNICS** The scatter plot shows the number of people who attended a neighborhood picnic each year. How many people should be expected to attend the picnic in 2007?
about 155–160 people

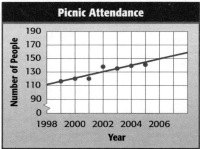

Picnic Attendance

Tips for New Teachers

Predictions

Data that do not lie on a straight line shows a relationship that is not linear. Predictions may be limited to certain intervals. In Example 3, the line that best represents the data would eventually fall below the x-axis, which does not make sense in real life. It may also be helpful to point out to students that predicting too far in the future is not necessarily a good idea because of the many factors that can affect events down the road.

Exercises

HOMEWORK HELP

For Exercises	See Examples
4–5	1, 2
6–7	3

Exercise Levels
: 4–7
: 8–17
: 18–21

MONUMENTS For Exercises 4 and 5, use the graph that shows the time it takes Ciro to climb the Statue of Liberty.

4. Predict the time it will take Ciro to climb 354 steps to reach the top. **about 13 min**

5. How many steps will he have climbed after 14 minutes? **about 400**

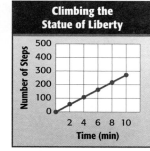

Climbing the Statue of Liberty

SCHOOL For Exercises 6 and 7, use the graph that shows the time students spent studying for a test and their test score.

6. What score should a student who studies for 1 hour be expected to earn? **about 80**

7. If a student scored 90 on the test, about how much time can you assume the student spent studying? **about 95 min**

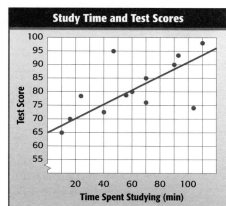

Study Time and Test Scores

SAFETY For Exercises 8–10, use the table that shows the relationship between the speed of a vehicle and the distance required to stop.

8. Make a scatter plot of the data. Use the speed on the horizontal axis and the stopping distance on the vertical axis. **See margin.**

9. Describe the relationship, if any, between the two sets of data.

10. Predict the stopping distance for a car traveling 45 miles per hour. **Sample answer: about 200 ft**

Speed (mph)	Stopping Distance (ft)
55	273
60	312
65	355
70	400
75	447

9. Sample answer: As the speed increases, the distance required to come to a complete stop increases.

11. See Ch. 8 Answer Appendix.

12. Sample answer: about 210 nations

13. Sample answer: In most years, the number of participants increases.

OLYMPICS For Exercises 11–13, use the table that shows the number of nations that participated in the Summer Olympics from 1936 to 2004.

11. Display the data in a scatter plot.

12. Predict the number of nations that will participate in the 2012 Summer Olympics.

13. Describe the trend in the data.

Year	Number of Nations	Year	Number of Nations
1936	49	1976	92
1948	59	1980	80
1952	69	1984	140
1956	72	1988	159
1960	83	1992	169
1964	93	1996	197
1968	112	2000	199
1972	121	2004	201

Lesson 8-6 Using Graphs to Predict **429**

---

3 Practice

Formative Assessment

Use Exercises 1–3 to check for understanding.

Then use the chart at the bottom of this page to customize your assignments for students.

Intervention You may wish to use the Study Guide and Intervention Master on page 40 of the *Chapter 8 Resource Masters* for additional reinforcement.

Odd/Even Assignments

Exercises 4–7 are structured so that students practice the same concepts whether they are assigned odd or even problems.

⚠ Exercise Alert!

Grid Paper Exercises 8–13 require students to make scatter plots. Make sure everyone has grid paper for these exercises.

Additional Answer

8.

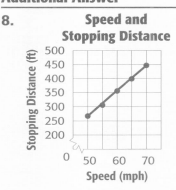

Speed and Stopping Distance

DIFFERENTIATED HOMEWORK OPTIONS

Level	Assignment	Two-Day Option	
BL Basic	4–7, 18, 19, 21–27	5–7 odd, 22, 23	4–6 even, 18, 19, 21, 24–27
OL Core	5, 7, 8–19, 21–27	4–7, 22, 23	8–19, 21, 24–27
AL Advanced/Pre-AP	8–25 (optional: 26, 27)		

SCHOOLS For Exercises 14 and 15, use the graphic that shows public school teachers' average salaries for the past few years.

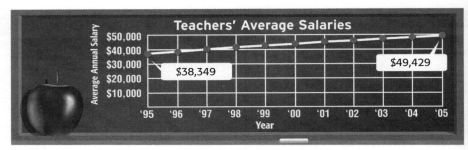

Source: nea.org

14. The two sets of data show a positive relationship. As the years increase, so do the salaries.

14. Describe the relationship, if any, between the two sets of data.

15. If the trend continues, what will be the average annual salary in 2009? about $55,000

16. RESEARCH Use the Internet or another source to find a real-world example of a scatter plot. Write a description of what the graph displays and extend the graph to show where the data will be in the future. **See students' work.**

17. See margin.

17. POPULATION The *multiple line graph* at the right shows the population of Miami-Dade and Broward Counties in Florida from 1950 to 2000. Do you think that the population of Broward County will catch up to the population of Miami-Dade County in the next census in 2010? Write a convincing argument as to why or why not.

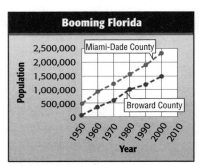

Source: U.S. Census Bureau

H.O.T. Problems

19. mode; the other three are ways to display data.

18. OPEN ENDED Name two sets of data that can be graphed on a scatter plot. **Sample answer: weight of an animal as it gets older**

19. Which One Doesn't Belong? Identify the term that does not have the same characteristic as the other three. Explain your reasoning.

| line plot | mode | bar graph | scatter plot |

20. The data do not appear to fall along a straight line. So, birth month and height do not seem to be related.

20. CHALLENGE What can you conclude about the relationship between birth month and height shown in the scatter plot at the right?

21. **WRITING IN MATH** Explain how a graph can be used to make predictions. **Graphs often show trends over time. If you continue the pattern, you can use it to make a prediction.**

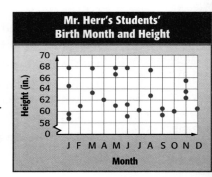

Pre-AP Activity Use after Exercise 21

Have students research two data sets and graph them on a scatter plot. Encourage them *not* to include time as one of the data sets. Have them describe whether their data sets are related and, if so, how.

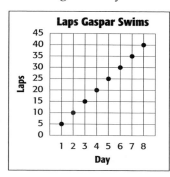
22. The number of laps Gaspar has been swimming each day is shown.

Laps Gaspar Swims

If the trend shown in the graph continues, what is the best prediction for the number of laps he will swim on day 10? **A**

A 50

B 65

C 75

D 100

23. The number of customers at Clothes Palace at different times during the day is shown.

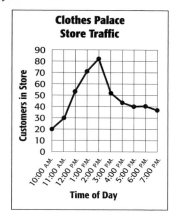

Clothes Palace Store Traffic

If extra workers are needed when the number of customers exceeds 50, between which hours is extra help needed? **F**

F 12:00 P.M.–3:00 P.M.

G 11:00 A.M.–4:00 P.M.

H 1:00 P.M.–4:00 P.M.

J 1:00 P.M.–3:00 P.M.

Spiral Review

24. **SKATING** Use the *use a graph* strategy to compare the number of people who skate in California to the number of people who skate in Texas. (Lesson 8-5)
See margin.

25. **COLORS** Of 57 students, 13 prefer the color red, 16 prefer blue, 20 prefer green, and 8 prefer yellow. Display this data in a bar graph. (Lesson 8-4)
See Ch. 8 Answer Appendix.

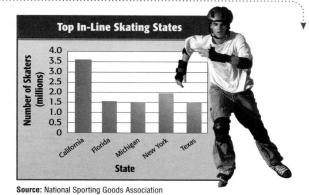

Top In-Line Skating States

Source: National Sporting Goods Association

GET READY for the Next Lesson

PREREQUISITE SKILL Find the mean and median for each set of data. (Lesson 8-2)

26. 89 ft, 90 ft, 74 ft, 81 ft, 68 ft **80.4 ft; 81 ft**   27. 76°, 90°, 88°, 84°, 82°, 78° **83°; 83°**

---

4 Assess

Ticket Out the Door Tell students you are thinking of two sets of data. In the first set of data, the daily high temperatures for Austin, Texas, have been recorded for one month. In the second set of data, the elevations of fifty U.S. cities have been compared to the cities' record low temperatures. Have students write whether they would use a line graph or a scatter plot to show each of the data sets.

FOLDABLES Study Organizer **Foldables™ Follow-Up**

Remind students to record notes about line graphs and scatter plots under the tab for this lesson in their Foldables. Encourage them to draw and label either a line graph or a scatter plot on the front of the tab.

Additional Answer

24. Sample answer: There are more than twice as many people in California who skate than there are in Texas.

1 Focus

Materials

- computers with a spreadsheet program (Microsoft® Excel® is used in this lab)

Teaching Tip

If there are not enough computers for every student in your class, have students work in pairs, sharing the computers.

2 Teach

Activity 1 You might want to have students discuss whether a line graph or a bar graph would be better to show the data. Have them explain their reasoning.

Make sure students understand that the speeds (to be recorded in column A) are not data but intervals of the *x*-axis.

Extend 8-6

Spreadsheet Lab
Multiple-Line and -Bar Graphs

Main IDEA

Use a spreadsheet to make a multiple-line graph and a multiple-bar graph.

 Standard 6SDAP2.3 Analyze data displays and explain why the way in which the question was asked might have influenced the results obtained and why the way in which the results were displayed might have influenced the conclusions reached.
Standard 6MR2.4 Use a variety of methods, such as words, numbers, symbols, charts, **graphs**, tables, diagrams, and models, **to explain mathematical reasoning.**

In Lessons 8-4 and 8-6, you interpreted data in a multiple-bar graph and in a multiple-line graph, respectively. You can use a spreadsheet to make these two types of graphs.

ACTIVITY

1. The stopping distances for a car on dry pavement and on wet pavement are shown in the table at the right.

Speed (mph)	Stopping Distance (ft)	
	Dry Pavement	Wet Pavement
50	200	250
60	271	333
70	342	430
80	422	532

Source: *Continental Teves*

Set up a spreadsheet like the one shown below.

Stopping Distance.xls

◇	A	B	C
1		Stopping Distance (ft)	
2	Speed (mph)	Dry Pavement	Wet Pavement
3	50	200	250
	60	271	333
	70	342	430
	80	422	532
7			

Sheet 1 / Sheet 2 / Sheet 3

In column A, enter the driving speeds.

In columns B and C, enter the stopping distances on dry and wet pavement, respectively.

The next step is to "tell" the spreadsheet to make a double-line graph for the data.

1. Highlight the data in columns B and C, from B2 through C6.
2. Click on the Chart Wizard icon. This tells the spreadsheet to read the data in columns B and C.
3. Choose the line graph and click Next.
4. To set the *x*-axis, choose the Series tab and press the icon next to the Category (X) axis labels.
5. On the spreadsheet, highlight the data in column A, from A3 through A6.
6. Press the icon on the bottom of the Chart Wizard box to automatically paste the information.
7. Click Next and enter the chart title and labels for the *x*- and *y*-axes.
8. Click Next and then Finish.

432 Chapter 8 Statistics: Analyzing Data

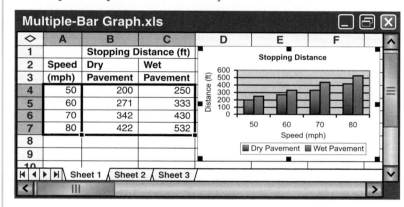

Multiple-Line Graph.xls

◇	A	B	C	D	E	F
1		**Stopping Distance (ft)**				
2	**Speed**	**Dry**	**Wet**			
3	**(mph)**	**Pavement**	**Pavement**			
4	50	200	250			
5	60	271	333			
6	70	342	430			
7	80	422	532			
8						
9						
10						
11						

Sheet 1 / Sheet 2 / Sheet 3

ACTIVITY

2 Use the same data to make a multiple-bar graph.

- Highlight the data in columns B and C, from B2 through C6.
- Click on the Chart Wizard icon.
- Click on Column and Next to choose the vertical bar graph.
- Complete steps 4–8 from Activity 1.

Multiple-Bar Graph.xls

◇	A	B	C	D	E	F
1		**Stopping Distance (ft)**				
2	**Speed**	**Dry**	**Wet**			
3	**(mph)**	**Pavement**	**Pavement**			
4	50	200	250			
5	60	271	333			
6	70	342	430			
7	80	422	532			
8						
9						
10						

Sheet 1 / Sheet 2 / Sheet 3

ANALYZE THE RESULTS   1–2. See margin.

1. Explain the steps you would take to make a multiple-line graph of the stopping distances that include the speeds 55, 65, and 75.

2. **COLLECT THE DATA** Collect two sets of data that represent the number of boys and the number of girls in your class born in the spring, summer, fall, and winter. Use a spreadsheet to make a multiple-line or -bar graph of the data. Justify your selection.

Extend 8-6 Spreadsheet Lab: Multiple-Line and -Bar Graphs **433**

Extend 8-6 Lesson Notes

Activity 2 You might want to have students print both graphs and compare them. Which graph do students think is a better display of the data? Why? Ask students which graph would be more useful for predicting the stopping distances of a car traveling at 47 mph or 72 mph.

3 Assess

Formative Assessment

Use Exercise 1 to determine whether students understand how to use a spreadsheet program to create a multiple-line graph.

From Concrete to Abstract Use students' justifications in Exercise 2 to bridge the gap between using a spreadsheet program to create graphs and understanding which kind of graph is better suited to display different kinds of data.

Extending the Concept You might want to have students include vertical gridlines in their line graphs. Instruct them to click on Chart Options in the Chart menu. Then they can click on Gridlines and one of the boxes for Category (X) axis.

Additional Answers

1. Insert the numbers 55, 65, and 75 in the appropriate places in column A, along with the stopping distances for dry and wet pavement.

2. See students' work.

Using Data to Predict

Preparation for 6SDAP2.2	Identify different ways of selecting a sample (e.g., convenience sampling, responses to a survey, random sampling) and which method makes a sample more representative for a population.
Standard 6SDAP2.5	**Identify claims based on statistical data,** and in simple cases, evaluate the validity of the claims.
PACING:	**Regular:** 1 period, **Block:** 0.5 period

Options for Differentiated Instruction

ELL = English Language Learner   **AL** = Above Grade Level   **SS** = Struggling Students   **SN** = Special Needs

Naturalist Learning ELL SS SN

Use after presenting Examples.

Have students measure the length of each of ten fresh pea pods. Then have them count and record the number of peas in each pod.

Pea Pod	1	2	3	4	5	6	7	8	9	10
Length (in.)										
Number of Peas										

Ask:
- Make a prediction for how many peas are in a 6-inch pea pod.
- How did you make your prediction?

Working in Groups ELL SS SN

Use with Check Your Understanding.

Have students work in small groups. Each student should read a problem to the group and then discuss the information presented. Have part of the group solve the problem using the percent proportion and the other part using the percent equation. Students should share their results within their groups.

Visual Cues SS SN

Use before assigning the Exercises.

Have students create a percent proportion checklist on an index card.

Part of the population $\longrightarrow$ □ = □ $\longleftarrow$ percent

Entire Population $\longrightarrow$ □ $\dfrac{}{100}$

- Fill in the numbers that are given.
- Find the cross products.
- Solve.

Leveled Lesson Resources

Chapter 8 Resource Masters

BL = Below Grade Level   **OL** = On Grade Level   **AL** = Above Grade Level   **ELL** = English Language Learner

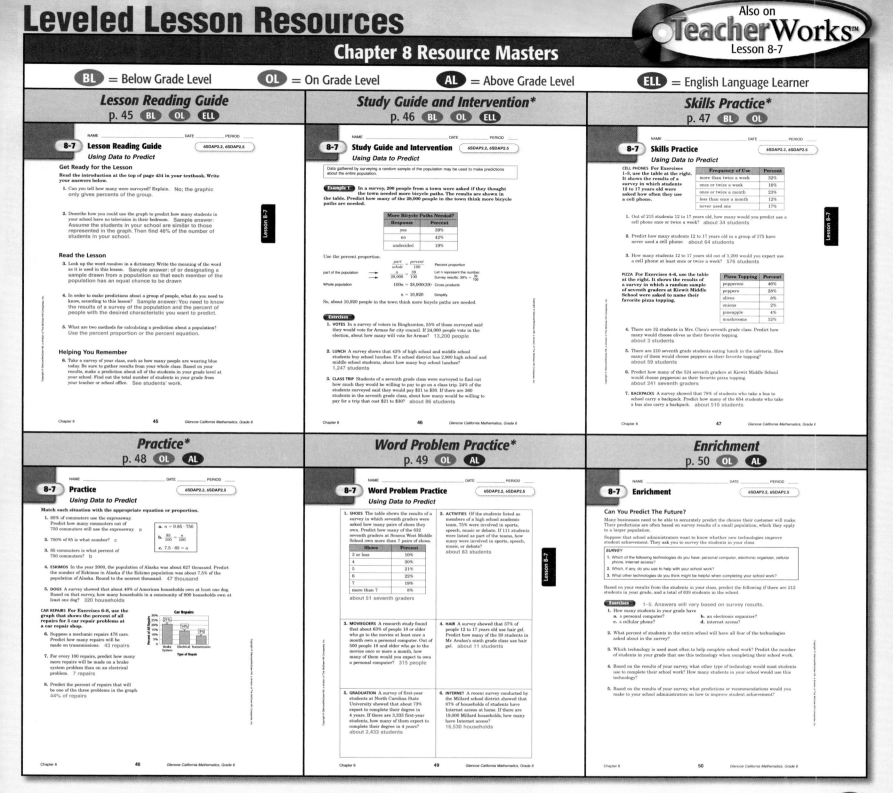

Lesson Reading Guide
p. 45 **BL** **OL** **ELL**

8-7 Lesson Reading Guide   6SDAP2.2, 6SDAP2.5

Using Data to Predict

Get Ready for the Lesson

Read the introduction at the top of page 434 in your textbook. Write your answers below.

1. Can you tell how many were surveyed? Explain. No; the graphic only gives percents of the group.

2. Describe how you could use the graph to predict how many students in your school have no television in their bedroom. Sample answer: Assume the students in your school are similar to those represented in the graph. Then find 46% of the number of students in your school.

Read the Lesson

3. Look up the word *random* in a dictionary. Write the meaning of the word as it is used in this lesson. Sample answer: of or designating a sample drawn from a population so that each member of the population has an equal chance to be drawn

4. In order to make predictions about a group of people, what do you need to know, according to this lesson? Sample answer: You need to know the results of a survey of the population and the percent of people with the desired characteristic you want to predict.

5. What are two methods for calculating a prediction about a population? Use the percent proportion or the percent equation.

Helping You Remember

6. Take a survey of your class, such as how many people are wearing blue today. Be sure to gather results from your whole class. Based on your results, make a prediction about all of the students in your grade level at your school. Find out the total number of students in your grade from your teacher or school office. See students' work.

Chapter 8   45   Glencoe California Mathematics, Grade 6

Study Guide and Intervention*
p. 46 **BL** **OL** **ELL**

8-7 Study Guide and Intervention   6SDAP2.2, 6SDAP2.5

Using Data to Predict

Data gathered by surveying a random sample of the population may be used to make predictions about the entire population.

Example 1 In a survey, 200 people from a town were asked if they thought the town needed more bicycle paths. The results are shown in the table. Predict how many of the 28,000 people in the town think more bicycle paths are needed.

More Bicycle Paths Needed?	
Response	**Percent**
yes	39%
no	42%
undecided	19%

Use the percent proportion.

$$\frac{part}{whole} = \frac{percent}{100}$$ Percent proportion

part of the population → $\frac{n}{28,000} = \frac{39}{100}$ Let n represent the number. Survey result: 39% = $\frac{39}{100}$

Whole population → $100n = 38,000(39)$ Cross products

$n = 10,920$ Simplify.

So, about 10,920 people in the town think more bicycle paths are needed.

Exercises

1. **VOTES** In a survey of voters in Binghamton, 55% of those surveyed said they would vote for Armas for city council. If 24,000 people vote in the election, about how many will vote for Armas? 13,200 people

2. **LUNCH** A survey shows that 43% of high school and middle school students buy school lunches. If a school district has 2,900 high school and middle school students, about how many buy school lunches? 1,247 students

3. **CLASS TRIP** Students of a seventh grade class were surveyed to find out how much they would be willing to pay to go on a class trip. 24% of the students surveyed said they would pay $21 to $30. If there are 360 students in the seventh grade class, about how many would be willing to pay for a trip that cost $21 to $30? about 86 students

Chapter 8   46   Glencoe California Mathematics, Grade 6

Skills Practice*
p. 47 **BL** **OL**

8-7 Skills Practice   6SDAP2.2, 6SDAP2.5

Using Data to Predict

CELL PHONES For Exercises 1–3, use the table at the right. It shows the results of a survey in which students 12 to 17 years old were asked how often they use a cell phone.

Frequency of Use	Percent
more than twice a week	32%
once or twice a week	16%
once or twice a month	23%
less than once a month	12%
never used one	17%

1. Out of 215 students 12 to 17 years old, how many would you predict use a cell phone once or twice a week? about 34 students

2. Predict how many students 12 to 17 years old in a group of 375 have never used a cell phone. about 64 students

3. How many students 12 to 17 years old out of 1,200 would you expect to use a cell phone at least once or twice a week? 576 students

PIZZA For Exercises 4–6, use the table at the right. It shows the results of a survey in which a random sample of seventh graders at Kiewit Middle School were asked to name their favorite pizza topping.

Pizza Topping	Percent
pepperoni	46%
peppers	28%
olives	8%
onions	2%
pineapple	4%
mushrooms	12%

4. There are 32 students in Mrs. Chen's seventh grade class. Predict how many would choose olives as their favorite topping. about 3 students

5. There are 210 seventh grade students eating lunch in the cafeteria. How many of them would choose peppers as their favorite topping? about 59 students

6. Predict how many of the 524 seventh graders at Kiewit Middle School would choose pepperoni as their favorite pizza topping. about 241 seventh graders

7. **BACKPACKS** A survey showed that 78% of students who take a bus to school carry a backpack. Predict how many of the 654 students who take a bus also carry a backpack. about 510 students

Chapter 8   47   Glencoe California Mathematics, Grade 6

Practice*
p. 48 **OL** **AL**

8-7 Practice   6SDAP2.2, 6SDAP2.5

Using Data to Predict

Match each situation with the appropriate equation or proportion.

1. 85% of commuters use the expressway. Predict how many commuters out of 750 commuters will use the expressway. a

2. 750% of 85 is what number? c

3. 85 commuters is what percent of 750 commuters? b

a. $n = 0.85 \cdot 750$

b. $\frac{85}{100} = \frac{n}{100}$

c. $7.5 \cdot 85 = n$

4. **ESKIMOS** In the year 2000, the population of Alaska was about 627 thousand. Predict the number of Eskimos in Alaska if the Eskimo population was about 7.5% of the population of Alaska. Round to the nearest thousand. 47 thousand

5. **DOGS** A survey showed that about 40% of American households own at least one dog. Based on that survey, how many households in a community of 800 households own at least one dog? 320 households

CAR REPAIRS For Exercises 6–8, use the graph that shows the percent of all repairs for 3 car repair problems at a car repair shop.

Car Repairs

6. Suppose a mechanic repairs 478 cars. Predict how many repairs will be made on transmissions. 43 repairs

7. For every 100 repairs, predict how many more repairs will be made on a brake system problem than on an electrical problem. 7 repairs

8. Predict the percent of repairs that will be one of the three problems in the graph. 44% of repairs

Chapter 8   48   Glencoe California Mathematics, Grade 6

Word Problem Practice*
p. 49 **OL** **AL**

8-7 Word Problem Practice   6SDAP2.2, 6SDAP2.5

Using Data to Predict

1. **SHOES** The table shows the results of a survey in which seventh graders were asked how many pairs of shoes they own. Predict how many of the 632 seventh graders at Seneca West Middle School own more than 7 pairs of shoes.

Shoes	Percent
3 or less	10%
4	20%
5	21%
6	22%
7	19%
more than 7	8%

about 51 seventh graders

2. **ACTIVITIES** Of the students listed as members of a high school academic team, 75% were involved in sports, speech, music or debate. If 111 students were listed as part of the teams, how many were involved in sports, speech, music, or debate? about 83 students

3. **MOVIEGOERS** A research study found that about 65% of people 18 or older who go to the movies at least once a month own a personal computer. Out of 500 people 18 and older who go to the movies once or more a month, how many would you expect to own a personal computer? 315 people

4. **HAIR** A survey showed that 37% of people 12 to 17 years old use hair gel. Predict how many of the 30 students in Mr. Avalon's ninth grade class use hair gel. about 11 students

5. **GRADUATION** A survey of first-year students at North Carolina State University showed that about 73% expect to complete their degree in 4 years. If there are 3,333 first-year students, how many of them expect to complete their degree in 4 years? about 2,433 students

6. **INTERNET** A recent survey conducted by the Millard school district showed that 87% of households of students have Internet access at home. If there are 19,000 Millard households, how many have Internet access? 16,530 households

Chapter 8   49   Glencoe California Mathematics, Grade 6

Enrichment
p. 50 **OL** **AL**

8-7 Enrichment   6SDAP2.2, 6SDAP2.5

Using Data to Predict

Can You Predict The Future?

Many businesses need to be able to accurately predict the choices their customer will make. Their predictions are often based on survey results of a small population, which they apply to a larger population.

Suppose that school administrators want to know whether new technologies improve student achievement. They ask you to survey the students in your class.

SURVEY
1. Which of the following technologies do you have: personal computer, electronic organizer, cellular phone, internet access?
2. Which, if any, do you use to help with your school work?
3. What other technologies do you think might be helpful when completing your school work?

Based on your results from the students in your class, predict the following if there are 212 students in your grade, and a total of 639 students in the school.

Exercises 1–5. Answers will vary based on survey results.

1. How many students in your grade have
   a. a personal computer?   b. an electronic organizer?
   c. a cellular phone?   d. internet access?

2. What percent of students in the entire school will have all four of the technologies asked about in the survey?

3. Which technology is used most often to help complete school work? Predict the number of students in your grade that use this technology when completing their school work.

4. Based on the results of your survey, what other type of technology would most students use to complete their school work? How many students in your school would use this technology?

5. Based on the results of your survey, what predictions or recommendations would you make to your school administrators on how to improve student achievement?

Chapter 8   50   Glencoe California Mathematics, Grade 6

Additional Lesson Resources

* Also available in Spanish ELL

Transparencies

- *5-Minute Check Transparency,* Lesson 8-7

Other Print Products

- *Noteables™ Interactive Study Notebook with Foldables™*
- *Science and Mathematics Lab Manual,* pp. 29–32

Teacher Tech Tools

- *Interactive Classroom CD-ROM,* Lesson 8-7
- *AssignmentWorks CD-ROM,* Lesson 8-7

Student Tech Tools

ca.gr6math.com

- Extra Examples, Chapter 7, Lesson 7
- Self-Check Quiz, Chapter 7, Lesson 7

8-7 **Lesson Notes**

1 Focus

Standards Alignment

Before Lesson 8-7
Organize and display single-variable data in appropriate graphs and representations and explain which types of graphs are appropriate for various data sets from Standard 5SDAP1.2

Lesson 8-7
Identify different ways of selecting a sample and which method makes a sample more representative for a population.
from ◆— Standard 6SDAP2.2
Identify claims based on statistical data from ◆— Standard 6SDAP2.5

After Lesson 8-7
Represent two numerical variables on a scatterplot and informally describe how the data points are distributed and any apparent relationship that exists between the two variables from Standard 7SDAP1.2

2 Teach

Scaffolding Questions

Tell students that a nationwide survey was taken about seventh graders' favorite kinds of books: fantasy, romance, sports, mystery.

Ask:
- If 51% of the students surveyed chose fantasy, about how many students in this class do you think would choose fantasy? about half the class

- If 10% of the students surveyed chose mystery, about how many students in this class do you think would choose mystery? about one tenth of the class

- If 24% of the survey students chose sports, about how many students in this class do you think would choose sports? about one quarter of the class

---

 8-7 **Using Data to Predict**

Main IDEA
Predict actions of a larger group by using a sample.

Preparation for 6SDAP2.2 Identify different ways of selecting a sample (e.g., convenience sampling, responses to a survey, random sampling) and which method makes a sample more representative for a population.
◆— **Standard 6SDAP2.5** Identify claims based on statistical data, and in simple cases, evaluate the validity of the claims.

NEW Vocabulary

survey
population

READING in the Content Area

For strategies in reading this lesson, visit ca.gr6math.com.

▶ **GET READY for the Lesson**

TELEPHONE The circle graph shows the results of a survey in which children ages 8 to 12 were asked whether they have a television in their bedroom.

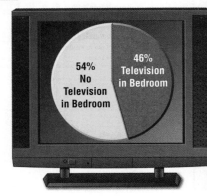

Source: mediafamily.org

1. Can you tell how many were surveyed? Explain.

2. Describe how you could use the graph to predict how many students in your school have television in their bedroom. **See margin.**

1. No; the graphic only gives percents of the group.
A **survey** is designed to collect data about a specific group of people, called the **population**. If a survey is conducted at random, or without preference, you can assume that the survey represents the population. In this lesson, you will use the results of randomly conducted surveys to make predictions about the population.

🌐 **Real-World EXAMPLE**

① **TELEVISION Refer to the graphic above. Predict how many out of 1,250 students would not have a television in their bedroom.**

You can use the percent proportion and the survey results to predict what part p of the 1,250 students have no TV in their bedroom.

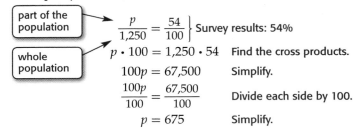

$$\frac{p}{1,250} = \frac{54}{100}\ \Big\} \text{Survey results: 54\%}$$

$p \cdot 100 = 1,250 \cdot 54$ Find the cross products.

$100p = 67,500$ Simplify.

$\dfrac{100p}{100} = \dfrac{67,500}{100}$ Divide each side by 100.

$p = 675$ Simplify.

About 675 students do not have a television in their bedroom.

✓ **CHECK Your Progress**

a. **TELEVISION** Refer to the same graphic. Predict how many out of 1,370 students have a television in their bedrooms. **about 630**

Additional Answer

2. Sample answer: Assume the students in your school are similar to those represented in the graph. Then find 46% of the number of students in your school.

Real-World Link . . . . .
A survey found that 85% of people use buddy icons on their instant messengers.
Source: AOL Research

② **INSTANT MESSAGING** Use the information at the left to predict how many of the 2,450 students at Washington Middle School use buddy icons on their instant messengers.

You need to predict how many of the 2,450 students use buddy icons.

Words	What number of students is 85% of 2,450 students?
Variable	Let n represent the number of students.
Equation	n = 0.85 · 2,450

$n = 0.85 \cdot 2,450$ Write the percent equation.

$n = 2,082.5$ Multiply.

About 2,083 of the students use buddy icons.

CHECK Your Progress

b. INSTANT MESSAGING This same survey found that 59% of people use sound on their instant messengers. Predict how many of the 2,450 students use sound on their instant messengers. **about 1,446**

nline **Personal Tutor at** ca.gr6math.com

★ indicates multi-step problem

CHECK Your Understanding

Example 1
(p. 434)

SPENDING For Exercises 1 and 2, use the circle graph that shows the results of a poll to which 60,000 teens responded.

1. How many of the teens surveyed said that they would save their money?

. 19,800
. 8.96 million

2. Predict how many of the approximately 28 million teens in the United States would buy a music CD if they were given $20.

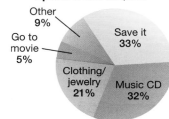

How Would You Spend a Gift of $20?
Other 9%
Go to movie 5%
Clothing/ jewelry 21%
Save it 33%
Music CD 32%

Source: *USA WEEKEND*

Example 2
(p. 435)

TRANSPORTATION For Exercises 3 and 4, use the bar graph that shows the results of a survey in which working adults in America were asked how they get to work.

3. Out of the 143 million working adults in America, predict how many walk or ride a bicycle to work. **5.72 million**

4. Predict how many working adults in America drive to work. **124.41 million**

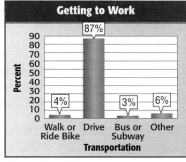

Getting to Work
87%
4%   3%   6%
Walk or Ride Bike   Drive   Bus or Subway   Other
Transportation

Source: Gallup Poll

Math nline **Extra Examples at** ca.gr6math.com

Lesson 8-7 Using Data to Predict **435**

Focus on Mathematical Content

The results of a **random survey** can be used to make predictions about part of the survey's population.

One way to make predictions from survey results is to set up a **percent proportion**.

Another way to make predictions from survey results is to use the **percent equation**.

Formative Assessment

Use the Check Your Progress exercises after each Example to determine students' understanding of concepts.

ADDITIONAL EXAMPLES

① **PETS** The table shows the results of a survey in which people were asked whether their house pets watch television.

Does your pet watch television?	
Response	**Percent**
yes	38%
no	60%
don't know	2%

There are 540 students at McCloskey Middle School who own pets. Predict how many of them would say their pets watch TV.
about 205

② **SUMMER JOBS** According to one survey, 25% of high school students reported that they would not get summer jobs. Predict how many of the 948 students at Mohawk High School will not get summer jobs. 237 students

Additional Examples are also in:
- Noteables™ Interactive Study Notebook with Foldables™
- Interactive Classroom PowerPoint® Presentations

Exercises

3 Practice

3 Practice

Formative Assessment

Use Exercises 1–4 to check for understanding.

Then use the chart at the bottom of this page to customize your assignments for students.

Intervention You may wish to use the Study Guide and Intervention Master on page 46 of the *Chapter 8 Resource Masters* for additional reinforcement.

Odd/Even Assignments

Exercises 5–8 are structured so that students practice the same concepts whether they are assigned odd or even problems.

HOMEWORK HELP

For Exercises	See Examples
5–8	1, 2

Exercise Levels
A: 5–8
B: 9–14
C: 15–18

COMPUTERS For Exercises 5 and 6, use the table that shows the results of a survey in which students were asked how they use a personal computer at home.

PC Use	Percent
Educational programs	93%
Homework	80%
Games	70%
Download music	95%

5. Predict how many of the 1,745 Allegheny Valley Middle School students use a PC for homework. **1,396 students**

6. About how many of the students use a PC for games? **about 1,222 students**

7. **CAMERAS** In a survey, 14% of teens said that they own a digital camera. Predict how many of the 420,000 teens in Arizona own digital cameras. **58,800 teens**

8. **VOLUNTEERING** A survey showed that 90% of teens donate money to a charity during the holidays. Based on that survey, how many teens in a class of 400 will donate money the next holiday season? **360**

Match each situation with the appropriate equation or proportion.

9. 27% of MP3 owners download music weekly. Predict how many MP3 owners out of 238 owners download music weekly. **b.**

10. 27 MP3s is what percent of 238 MP3s? **c.**

11. 238% of 27 is what number? **a.**

    a. $n = 27 \cdot 2.38$

    b. $\frac{27}{100} = \frac{n}{238}$

    c. $\frac{27}{238} = \frac{n}{100}$

CATS For Exercises 12 and 13, use the graph that shows the percent of cat owners who train their cats in each category.

12. Out of 255 cat owners, predict how many owners trained their cat not to climb on furniture. **about 110 people**

★ 13. Out of 316 cat owners, predict how many more cat owners have trained their cat not to claw on furniture than have trained their cat not to fight with other animals. **about 38 people**

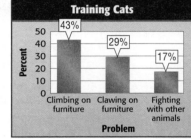

Training Cats

Source: Purina Cat Chow

EXTRA PRACTICE

See pages 700, 722.

Math Online
Self-Check Quiz at
ca.gr6math.com

---

14. **FIND THE DATA** Refer to the California Data File on pages 16–19. Choose some data and write a real-world problem in which you could use the percent proportion or percent equation to make a prediction. **See students' work.**

H.O.T. Problems

15. **CHALLENGE** A survey found that 80% of teens enjoy going to the movies in their free time. Out of 5,200 teens, predict how many said that they do not enjoy going to the movies in their free time. **about 1,040**

16. **OPEN ENDED** Select a newspaper or magazine article that contains a table or graph. Identify the population and explain how you think the results were found. **See students' work.**

DIFFERENTIATED HOMEWORK OPTIONS			
Level	**Assignment**	**Two-Day Option**	
BL Basic	5–8, 16–32	5, 7, 19–21	6, 8, 16–18, 22–32
OL Core	5, 7, 9–14, 16–32	5–8, 19–21	9–14, 16–18, 22–32
AL Advanced/Pre-AP	9–28 (optional: 29–32)		

17. Sample answer: Since large numbers are involved, use a calculator; 0.15 • 5,900,962 = 885,144.3, so about 885,000 people would belong to a fitness center

17. SELECT A TOOL A survey showed that 15% of the people in Tennessee over the age of 16 belong to a fitness center. Predict how many of the 5,900,962 people in Tennessee over the age of 16 belong to a fitness center. Select one or more of the following tools to solve the problem. Justify your selection(s).

make a model	calculator	paper/pencil	real objects

18. **WRITING IN MATH** Explain how to use a sample to predict what a group of people prefer. Then give an example of a situation in which it makes sense to use a sample. **See margin.**

STANDARDS PRACTICE 6SDAP2.2

19. A survey of 80 seventh graders at Lincoln Middle School was taken to find how they get to school each day. The results are shown in the table.

Getting to School	Percent
Take a Bus	33%
Walk	29%
Adult Drives	18%
Other	20%

Of the 423 seventh graders in the school, predict about how many walk to school. **C**

A 23   **C** 123

B 64   **D** 394

20. Yesterday, a bakery baked 54 loaves of bread in 20 minutes. Today, the bakery needs to bake 375 loaves of bread. At this rate, predict how long it will take to bake the bread. **G**

F 1.5 hours   **H** 3.0 hours

G 2.3 hours   **J** 3.75 hours

21. Of the 357 students in a freshman class, about 82% plan to go to college. How many students plan on going to college? **B**

A 224   **C** 314

B 293   **D** 325

Spiral Review

RUNNING For Exercises 22–24, refer to the table that shows the time it took Dale to run each mile of a 5-mile run.
22–23. See margin.

22. Make a scatter plot of the data. (Lesson 8-6)

23. Describe the relationship, if any, between the two sets of data. (Lesson 8-6)

24. Suppose the trend continues. Predict the time it would take Dale to run a sixth mile. (Lesson 8-5) **Sample answer: 5 min 10 s**

Mile	Time
1	4 min 19 s
2	4 min 28 s
3	4 min 39 s
4	4 min 54 s
5	5 min 1 s

Multiply. (Lesson 2-6)

25. -4×6 **−24**   **26.** $5 \times (-8)$ **−40**   **27.** $-6 \times (-9)$ **54**   **28.** 8×3 **24**

GET READY for the Next Lesson

PREREQUISITE SKILL Simplify. (Lesson 1-4)

29. $\frac{10-7}{10}$ $\frac{3}{10}$ or 0.3   **30.** $\frac{50-18}{50}$ $\frac{16}{25}$ or 0.64   **31.** $\frac{22-4}{4}$ $\frac{9}{2}$ or 4.5   **32.** $\frac{39-15}{15}$ $\frac{8}{5}$ or 1.6

Lesson 8-7 Using Data to Predict   **437**

Pre-AP Activity   Use after Exercise 18

Have students research surveying methods on the Internet or in an encyclopedia. Have them describe a random sample of your school's students and a nonrandom sample. Then have them write whether the size of the survey sample matters.

---

4 Assess

Crystal Ball Tell students that tomorrow's lesson is about finding the percent of change in a quantity, such as height or weight. Have students write how they think what they learned today will connect with tomorrow's material.

FOLDABLES Study Organizer **Foldables™ Follow-Up**

Remind students to record how to use survey results to make predictions in their Foldables tables, along with examples.

Formative Assessment

Check for student understanding of concepts in Lessons 8-6 and 8-7.

CRM Quiz 3, p. 68

Additional Answer

18. Sample answer: Randomly select a part of the group to get a sample. Find their preferences, and use the results to find the percent of the total group.

22.

Time it Takes Dale to Run Each Mile of a 5-Mile Run

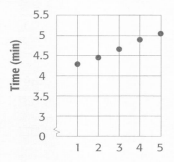

23. It takes Dale a little bit longer to run each successive mile of the 5-mile run.

 **Using Sampling to Predict**

Standard 6SDAP2.1	Compare different samples of a population with the data from the entire population and identify a situation in which it makes sense to use a sample.
Standard 6SDAP2.2	Identify different ways of selecting a sample (e.g., convenience sampling, responses to a survey, random sampling) and which method makes a sample more representative for a population.
Standard 6SDAP2.5	Identify claims based on statistical data and, in simple cases, evaluate the validity of the claims.
PACING:	**Regular:** 2 periods, **Block:** 1 period

Options for Differentiated Instruction

ELL = English Language Learner   **AL** = Above Grade Level   **SS** = Struggling Students   **SN** = Special Needs

Conceptual Understanding **ELL** **SS**

Use after presenting the Concept Summary.

Inform students that whether a sample is unbiased or biased depends in part on the survey. For example, suppose a sample is chosen randomly from customers in a bakery.
- The sample is unbiased if the survey is about the baked goods preferences of persons living near the store.
- The sample is biased if the survey were about favorite television programs or about the baked goods preferences of all Americans.

Gathering Data **AL**

Use before assigning the Exercises.

Have pairs of students use the survey described in *Get Ready for the Lesson* to survey their classmates about the type of ring tones they would use. Have them create a table like the one at the right to help them organize their data.

Ask:
- If you were to survey the whole school, do you think you would get similar results? Explain why or why not.
- How could you use the results of your survey to make predictions about ring tone preferences of all students in the United States?
- Without surveying the whole school, is there a way that you could get more information that could help you determine the ring tone preferences of students in the school? Explain.

| What kind of Musical Ring Tone Do You Prefer? | |
Type	Number of Students
Classical	
Rock	
Rap/Hip-Hop	
Dance	
Other	

Leveled Lesson Resources

Chapter 8 Resource Masters

BL = Below Grade Level   **OL** = On Grade Level   **AL** = Above Grade Level   **ELL** = English Language Learner

---

Reading to Learn
p. 52 **BL** **OL** **ELL**

8-8 Lesson Reading Guide
6SDAP2.1, 6SDAP2.2, 6SDAP2.5

Using Sampling to Predict

Get Ready for the Lesson

Read the introduction at the top of page 438 in your textbook. Write your answers below.

1. Suppose she decides to survey the listeners of a rock radio station. Do you think the results would represent the entire population?
No; listeners of a rock radio station will probably prefer a rock music ring tone more than other ring tones.

2. Suppose she decides to survey a group of people standing in line for a symphony. Do you think the results would represent the entire population?
No; people standing in line for a symphony will probably prefer a classical music ring tone than other ring tones.

3. Suppose she decides to mail a survey to every 100th household in the area. Do you think the results would represent the entire population? Explain.
Yes; people of all ages and backgrounds are more likely to be represented.

Read the Lesson

4. Match the type of sample with its example. Put the correct letter on the line.

simple random sample	c	a. Every 10th person is given a survey.
stratified random sample	e	b. Only those who volunteer take a survey.
systematic random sample	a	c. Names are picked randomly out of a hat.
convenience sample	d	d. A store manager surveys his first 20 customers.
voluntary response sample	b	e. 5 residents are randomly surveyed from each floor of a 25 story apartment building.

Remember What You Learned

5. If you are conducting a survey, explain why it is important to have an unbiased sample.
Only through an unbiased sample can our results be valid.

Chapter 8   52   Glencoe California Mathematics, Grade 6

Study Guide and Intervention*
p. 53 **BL** **OL** **ELL**

8-8 Study Guide and Intervention
6SDAP2.1, 6SDAP2.2, 6SDAP2.5

Using Sampling to Predict

In an **unbiased sample** the whole population is represented. In a **biased sample** one or more parts of the population are favored over the others.

Example 1 Look at the following table to determine the favorite sport of middle school students.

Favorite Sports of Middle School Students

Basketball	Baseball	Football	Soccer
10	5	17	52

Based on the table, it would appear that soccer is the favorite sport of middle school students. However, suppose the data collected for this survey was taken at a World Cup soccer match. It can then be concluded that our sample is **biased** because students who are at a soccer match may be more likely to choose soccer as their favorite sport.

To receive an **unbiased** sample of middle school students, the sports survey could be completed at randomly selected middle schools throughout the country.

Exercises Determine whether the given situations represent a *biased* or *unbiased* sample. Then tell the type of sample.

1. Writers of a popular teen magazine want to write a story about which movies their readers like. The writers decide to interview the first 50 people that walk out of a movie theater.
Biased; convenience sample

2. The student council wanted to raise money for their school by selling homemade cookies during lunch time. To find out the favorite kind of cookie for the majority of their school, they conducted a survey. They gave the survey to 20 randomly selected students from each grade level.
Unbiased; stratified random sample

3. To determine the most frequently used gas station, a researcher randomly selected every 10th person from a drive-through fast food restaurant and asked them where they last filled up with gas.
Unbiased; systematic random sample

Chapter 8   53   Glencoe California Mathematics, Grade 6

Skills Practice*
p. 54 **BL** **OL**

8-8 Skills Practice
6SDAP2.1, 6SDAP2.2, 6SDAP2.5

Using Sampling to Predict

Each word in the box is a vocabulary word from lesson 8-8. Use the words to complete the sentences below. Not all of the words will be used.

unbiased	voluntary response sample	convenience sample
biased	simple random sample	stratified random sample
sampling	systematic random sample	valid

1. A _convenience sample_ is when members of the population are selected because they are easily accessed.

2. The survey is considered _unbiased_ when the entire population is represented.

3. It is called a _simple random sample_ when each person in the population has an equal chance to be selected.

4. When the population is divided into similar, non-overlapping groups and then chosen at random from each group it is said to be _stratified random sample_.

5. If only some members of the population choose to participate in a survey then it would be called a _voluntary response sample_.

6. A sample would be considered _biased_ if one or more parts of he population are favored.

7. If people were selected by a specific time or item interval, such as every 50th person, then this would be a _systematic random sample_.

8. A conclusion can only be considered _valid_ when the information came from an unbiased sample.

Chapter 8   54   Glencoe California Mathematics, Grade 6

Practice*
p. 55 **OL** **AL**

8-8 Practice
6SDAP2.1, 6SDAP2.2, 6SDAP2.5

Using Sampling to Predict

Determine if the sample method is valid (unbiased) and if so, use the results to make predictions. If the sample is not valid (biased), write *not valid* on the line and explain why.

1. A representative from the cable company randomly calls 100 households to determine the number of customers who receive movie channels. Of these, 15% do have movie channel access. If there are 2,300 customers total, how many can be expected to have the movie channels? It is valid, and 345 customers would have movie channels.

2. An electronics store just received a huge shipment of video games. Kenny has been put in charge of making sure the goods are not damaged. There are 350 boxes and 50 games in each box. Kenny decides to take the nearest 5 boxes and check for damages. He finds only 2 damaged games, so what can he predict for the total number of damaged games in the boxes? Kenny's sample is not valid because it is a convenience sample.

3. Taylor was given the following problem:

A researcher, who was trying to link after-school students from 20 different schools around the country. He found that 74% of students were involved in after-school sports. How many students surveyed were involved in sports?

This is how Taylor solved the problem:

50	1000	It's valid because it is
× 20	× 74	a systematic random
1,000	74,000	sample and there were
		74,000 students.

Explain what Taylor did wrong.
Taylor did not multiply 74% as a decimal. If she did, the answer would be 740. Also, it is a stratified random sample.

Chapter 8   55   Glencoe California Mathematics, Grade 6

Word Problem Practice*
p. 56 **OL** **AL**

8-8 Word Problem Practice
6SDAP2.1, 6SDAP2.2, 6SDAP2.5

Using Sampling to Predict

Use the word problem and table to answer the questions below.

Miguel is the manager of a clothing store. He wants to find out what are the most popular styles of men's pants and how many of each to order. He decides to survey every 10th man that walks in over a two-week period. Here are his results.

Pant Style	Number of People
Jeans	52
Khakis	31
Slacks	17

1. What type of sample does Miguel use for his survey?
Systematic random sample

2. What percentage of the customers surveyed prefer khakis?
31%

3. What percentage of the customers surveyed prefer jeans?
52%

4. If Miguel has 1,000 male customers over a two week period, how many pairs of jeans will he predict to sell?
520 pairs of jeans

5. If he has 1,300 customers in a two week period, how many pairs of slacks will he predict to sell?
221 pairs of slacks

6. Why would Miguel's sample not have been valid if he decided to survey only the first ten people to walk in?
This would have been a convenience sample which is biased and not valid.

Chapter 8   56   Glencoe California Mathematics, Grade 6

Enrichment
p. 57 **OL** **AL**

8-8 Enrichment
6SDAP2.1, 6SDAP2.2, 6SDAP2.5

Using Sampling to Predict

According to the bar graph below, sports video game companies are leading in games sold to children and adults throughout the country. If these companies want to continue to lead in sales they will have to make sure they create games with graphics and features that their customers want. One way to do that is through customer surveys.

Video Games Sold

In the space below create your own customer survey for a video game. Make sure to ask questions that will give you information to create the best game possible.

Answers will vary.

Chapter 8   57   Glencoe California Mathematics, Grade 6

Additional Lesson Resources

Also available in Spanish **ELL**

Transparencies
- *5-Minute Check Transparency*, Lesson 8-8

Other Print Products
- *Noteables™ Interactive Study Notebook with Foldables™*

Teacher Tech Tools
- *Interactive Classroom CD-ROM*, Lesson 8-8
- *Answer Key Maker CD-ROM*, Lesson 8-8

Student Tech Tools
ca.gr6math.com
- Extra Examples, Chapter 8, Lesson 8
- Self-Check Quiz, Chapter 8, Lesson 8

 Using Sampling to Predict

1 Focus

 Standards Alignment

Before Lesson 8-8
Identify ordered pairs of data from a graph and interpret the meaning of the data in terms of the situation depicted by the graph from 🔑 Standard 5SDAP1.4

Lesson 8-8
Compare different samples of a population with the data from the entire population and identify a situation in which it makes sense to use a sample. from 🔑 Standard 6SDAP2.1
Identify different ways of selecting a sample and which method makes a sample more representative for a population. from 🔑 Standard 6SDAP2.2
Identify claims based on statistical data and, in simple cases, evaluate the validity of the claims from 🔑 Standard 6SDAP2.5

After Lesson 8-8
Represent two numerical variables on a scatterplot and informally describe how the data points are distributed and any apparent relationship that exists between the two variables from Standard 7SDAP1.2

2 Teach

Scaffolding Questions

Discuss with students ways of choosing a sample of students in their school to survey with this question: *Should the school day be lengthened to allow more time for music and arts courses?*

Ask:
• Would a sample consisting of students who are choir or band members be representative? No; they might be biased in favor of music courses.

Main IDEA
Predict the actions of a larger group by using a sample.

 Standard 6SDAP2.1
Compare different samples of a population with the data from the entire population and identify a situation in which it makes sense to use a sample.
🔑 **Standard 6SDAP2.2**
Identify different ways of selecting a sample (e.g., convenience sampling, responses to a survey, random sampling) and which method makes a sample more representative for a population.
🔑 **Standard 6SDAP2.5**
Identify claims based on statistical data and, in simple cases, evaluate the validity of the claims.

NEW Vocabulary

sample
unbiased sample
simple random sample
biased sample
convenience sample
voluntary response sample

1. No; listeners of a rock radio station will probably prefer a rock music ring tone more than other ring tones.
2. No; people standing in line for a symphony will probably prefer a classical music ring tone than other ring tones.

438 Chapter 8 Statistics: Analyzing Data

▶ **GET READY for the Lesson**

CELL PHONES The manager of a local cell phone company wants to conduct a survey to determine what kind of musical ring tones people typically use.

What Kind of Musical Ring Tone Do You Use?
Classical
Rock
Rap/Hip-Hop
Dance
Other

1. Suppose she decides to survey the listeners of a rock radio station. Do you think the results would represent the entire population? Explain.

2. Suppose she decides to survey a group of people standing in line for a symphony. Do you think the results would represent the entire population? Explain.

3. Suppose she decides to mail a survey to every 100th household in the area. Do you think the results would represent the entire population? Explain.

3. Yes; people of all ages and backgrounds are more likely to be represented.

The manager of the cell phone company cannot survey everyone. A smaller group called a **sample** is chosen. A sample should be representative of the population.

Population	Sample
United States citizens	registered voters
California residents	homeowners
Six Flags Marine World visitors	teenagers

For valid results, a sample must be chosen very carefully. An **unbiased sample** is selected so that it is representative of the entire population. A simple random sample is the most common type of unbiased sample.

CONCEPT Summary — Unbiased Samples

Type	Description	Example
Simple Random Sample	Each item or person in the population is as likely to be chosen as any other.	Each student's name is written on a piece of paper. The names are placed in a bowl, and names are picked without looking.

438 Chapter 8 Statistics: Analyzing Data

• Would a sample consisting of students who ccan receive the survey question as an e-mail at home be representative? No; not every student has internet access at home.

• Would a sample consisting of names drawn from a bag containing the names of all students be representative? Yes; each person has an equal chance of being part of the sample.

Tips for New Teachers **English Language Learners**

A fair amount of reading and writing is required of students during this lesson. For the struggling reader and those students learning English, it may be helpful to pair or group students of differing reading proficiencies together to discuss Examples and Exercises.

In a **biased sample**, one or more parts of the population are favored over others. Two ways to pick a biased sample are listed below.

CONCEPT Summary — Biased Samples

Type	Description	Example
Convenience Sample	A convenience sample includes members of a population that are easily accessed.	To represent all the students attending a school, the principal surveys the students in one math class.
Voluntary Response Sample	A voluntary response sample involves only those who want to participate in the sampling.	Students at a school who wish to express their opinion are asked to complete an online survey.

EXAMPLES — Determine Validity of Conclusions

Determine whether each conclusion is valid. Justify your answer.

1 **To determine what kind of movies people like to watch, every tenth person that walks into a video rental store is surveyed. The store carries all kinds of movies. Out of 180 customers surveyed, 62 stated that they prefer action movies. The store manager concludes that about a third of all customers prefer action movies.**

The conclusion is valid. Since the population is every tenth customer of a video rental store, the sample is an unbiased random sample.

2 **A television program asks its viewers to visit a Web site to indicate their preference for two presidential candidates. 76% of the viewers who responded preferred candidate A, so the television program announced that most people prefer candidate A.**

The conclusion is not valid. The population is restricted to viewers who have Internet access, it is a voluntary response sample, and is biased. The results of a voluntary response sample do not necessarily represent the entire population.

CHECK Your Progress

Determine whether each conclusion is valid. Justify your answer.

a. To determine what people like to do in their leisure time, people at a local mall are surveyed. Of these, 82% said they like to shop. The mall manager concludes that most people like to shop during their leisure time.

b. To determine what kind of sport junior high school students like to watch, 100 students are randomly selected from each of four junior high schools in a city. Of these, 47% like to watch football. The superintendent concludes that about half of all junior high students like to watch football.

 Extra Examples at ca.gr6math.com   **Lesson 8-8** Using Sampling to Predict   **439**

 Focus on Mathematical Content

A **sample** is a smaller group that is representative of a population.

An **unbiased sample** is selected so that it is representative of the entire population.

Formative Assessment

Use the Check Your Progress exercises after each Example to determine students' understanding of concepts.

ADDITIONAL EXAMPLES

Determine whether each conclusion is valid. Justify your answer.

1 A newspaper asks its readers to answer a poll about whether or not an issue should be on the ballot in an upcoming election. 85% of the readers who responded said they wanted the issue on the ballot, so the newspaper printed an article saying that 85% of people want the issue on the ballot. The conclusion is not valid. The population is restricted to readers and it is a voluntary response sample and is biased. The readers of a voluntary response sample do not necessarily represent the entire population.

2 To award prizes at a sold out baseball game, a computer will pick 10 different seat numbers. Abbey concludes that she has as good a chance as everyone else to win one of the prizes. The conclusion is valid. The population is a simple random sample.

Additional Examples are also in:

• Noteables™ Interactive Study Notebook with Foldables™

• Interactive Classroom PowerPoint® Presentations

3 Practice

Formative Assessment

Use Exercises 1–3 to check for understanding.

Then use the chart on the next page to customize your assignments for students.

Intervention You may wish to use the Study Guide and Intervention Master on p. 53 of the *Chapter 8 Resource Masters* for additional reinforcement.

Addtional Answer

1. The conclusion is invalid. This is a biased sample since people in other states might have more umbrellas than those in Arizona. The sample is a convenience sample since all the people are from the same state.

Surveys

Maintain a file of product surveys and opinion polls that you encounter in magazines, on television, and on the Internet. Students can classify the types of surveys, evaluate whether the surveys are biased, use bar graphs or circle graphs to display the results, or use them as models for their own surveys.

In Lesson 8-7, you used the results of a random sampling method to make predictions. In this lesson, you will first determine if a sampling method is valid and if so, use the results to make predictions.

Real-World EXAMPLE

3 **MASCOTS** The Student Council at a new junior high school surveyed 5 students from each of the 10 homerooms to determine what mascot students would prefer. The results of the survey are shown at the right. If there are 375 students at the school, predict how many students prefer a tiger as the school mascot.

Mascot	Number
Tornadoes	15
Tigers	28
Twins	7

The sample is an unbiased random sample since students were randomly selected. Thus, the sample is valid.

$\frac{28}{50}$ or 56% of the students prefer a tiger. So, find 56% of 375.

$0.56 \times 375 = 210$ **56% of 375 = 0.56 × 375**

So, about 210 students would prefer a tiger as the school mascot.

CHECK Your Progress

c. Sample answer: The sample is a convenience sample. Therefore, no valid conclusion can be made.

c. **AIRLINES** During flight, a pilot determined that 20% of the passengers were traveling for business and 80% were traveling for pleasure. If there are 120 passengers on the next flight, how many can be expected to be traveling for pleasure?

Online **Personal Tutor at** ca.gr6math.com

CHECK Your Understanding

Examples 1, 2 (p. 439)

Determine whether each conclusion is valid. Justify your answer.

2. The conclusion is valid. This is an unbiased random sample.
3. This is an unbiased random survey, so the sample is valid; about 102 students.

1. To determine the number of umbrellas the average household in the United States owns, a survey of 100 randomly selected households in Arizona is conducted. Of the households, 24 said that they own 3 or more umbrellas. The researcher concluded that 24% of the households in the United States own 3 or more umbrellas. **See margin.**

2. A researcher randomly surveys ten employees from each floor of a large company to determine the number of employees who carpool to work. Of these, 31% said that they carpool. The researcher concludes that most employees do not carpool.

Example 3 (p. 440)

3. **LUNCH** Jared randomly surveyed some students to determine their lunch habits. The results are shown in the table. If there are 268 students in the school, predict how many bring their lunch from home.

Lunch Habit	Number
Bring Lunch from Home	19
Buy Lunch in the Cafeteria	27
Other	4

440 Chapter 8 Statistics: Analyzing Data

Exercises

HOMEWORK HELP

For Exercises	See Examples
4–9	1, 2
10, 11	3

Exercise Levels
A: 4–11
B: 12–24
C: 25–26

4. The conclusion is valid. This is an unbiased random sample.
5. The conclusion is invalid. This is a biased, voluntary response sample.
7. The conclusion is valid. This is an unbiased random sample.

Real-World Link . . . .
There are more than 600 shapes of pasta produced worldwide.
Source: ilovepasta.org

Determine whether each conclusion is valid. Justify your answer.

4. The principal of a high school randomly selects 50 students to participate in a school improvement survey. Of these, 38 said that more world language courses should be offered. As a result, the principal decides to offer both Japanese and Italian language classes.

5. To evaluate their product, the manufacturer of light bulbs inspects the first 50 light bulbs produced on one day. Of these, 2 are defective. The manufacturer concludes that about 4% of light bulbs produced are defective. **The conclusion is invalid. This is a biased, convenience sample.**

6. To evaluate its service, a restaurant asks its customers to call a number and complete a telephone survey. The majority of those who replied said that they prefer broccoli instead of carrots as the vegetable side dish. As a result, the restaurant decides to offer broccoli instead of carrots.

7. To determine which type of pet is preferred by most customers, the manager of a pet store surveys every 15th customer that enters the store.

8. To determine which school dance theme most students favor, 20 students from each grade level at Lakewood Middle School are surveyed. The results are shown in the table. Based on these results, the student council decides that the dance theme should be *Unforgettable*. **The conclusion is valid. This is an unbiased random sample.**

Theme	Number
Starry Night	23
Unforgettable	26
At the Hop	11

9. To determine whether 15 boxes of porcelain tea sets have not been cracked during shipping, the owner of an antique store examines the first two boxes. None of the tea sets have been cracked, so the owner concludes that none of the tea sets in the remaining boxes are cracked. **The conclusion is invalid. This is a biased, convenience sample.**

10. **LAWNS** A researcher randomly surveyed 100 households in a small community to determine the number of households that use a professional lawn service. Of these, 27% of households use a professional lawn service. If there are 786 households in the community, how many can be expected to use a professional lawn service? **This is an unbiased random sample, so the sample is valid; about 212 households.**

11. **PASTA** A grocery store asked every 20th person entering the store what kind of pasta they preferred. The results are shown in the table. If the store decides to restock their shelves with 450 boxes of pasta, how many boxes of lasagna should they order? **This is an unbiased random sample, so the results are valid; about 132 boxes**

Pasta	Number
Macaroni	38
Spaghetti	56
Rigatoni	12
Lasagna	44

12. **FURNITURE** The manager of a furniture store asks the first 25 customers who enter the store if they prefer dining room tables made of oak, cherry, or mahogany wood. Of these, 17 said they prefer cherry. If the store manager orders 80 dining room tables in the next shipment, how many should be made of cherry wood? **See margin.**

Odd/Even Assignments

Exercises 4–11 are structured so that students practice the same concepts whether they are assigned odd or even problems.

Addtional Answer

12. The sample is a convenience sample. Therefore, no conclusion can be made.

Math Online **Extra Examples at** ca.gr6math.com

DIFFERENTIATED **HOMEWORK OPTIONS**			
Level	**Assignment**	**Two-Day Option**	
BL Basic	4–11, 26–36	5–11 odd, 27, 28	4–10 even, 26, 29–36
OL Core	5–11 odd, 12–24, 26–36	4–11, 27, 28	12–24, 26, 29–36
AL Advanced/Pre-AP	12–34 (optional: 35, 36)		

21. Not necessarily; Sample answer: Different samples may have different results.

23. Sample answer: If the entire population is too large to survey, it will be less time consuming and easier to use a sample.

---

13. This sample is a voluntary response sample. Therefore, no valid conclusion can be made.

14. Sample answer: Pedro could use a random survey, asking every 10th student who enters the school.

16. This is not a valid conclusion. Because the survey is voluntary, not all the forms were returned and the results are biased.

17. Sample answer: This is an unbiased random sample. The time a student spends on the Internet during this week may not be typical of other weeks.

18. Sample answer: This is a voluntary response sample. Parents may not respond.

19. Sample answer: This is a convenience sample. The softball team may not represent the entire student population.

EXTRA**PRACTICE**
See pages 701, 722.
Math**Online**
Self-Check Quiz at
ca.gr6math.com

22. See students' work.

---

13. RADIO A radio station asks its listeners to dial one of two numbers to indicate their preference for one of two candidates in an upcoming election. Of the responses received, 76% favored candidate A. If there are 1,500 registered voters, how many will vote for candidate A?

14. HOBBIES Pedro wants to conduct a survey about the kinds of hobbies that sixth graders enjoy. Describe a valid sampling method he could use.

AMUSEMENT PARKS For Exercises 15 and 16, use the following information.

The manager of an amusement park mailed 2,000 survey forms to households near the park. The results of the survey are shown in the graph at the right.

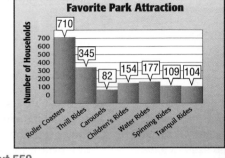

Favorite Park Attraction

15. Assume the survey is valid. If there are 5,000 park visitors, about how many would prefer water rides? **about 550**

16. Based on the survey results, the manager concludes that about 36% of park visitors prefer roller coasters. Is this a valid conclusion? Explain.

INTERNET For Exercises 17–19, use the following information.

A survey is to be conducted to find out how many hours students at a school spend on the Internet each weeknight. Describe the sample and explain why each sampling method might not be valid.

17. Ten randomly selected students from each grade level are asked to keep a log during their winter vacation.

18. Randomly selected parents are mailed a questionnaire and asked to return it.

19. A questionnaire is handed out to all students on the softball team.

COMPARE SAMPLES For Exercises 20–23, use the following information.

Suppose you were asked to determine the approximate percent of students in your school who are left-handed without surveying every student in the school.

20. Describe three different samples of the population that you could use to approximate the percent of students who are left-handed. **See students' work.**

21. Would you expect the percent of left-handed students to be the same in each of these three samples? Explain your reasoning. **See margin.**

22. Describe any additional similarities and differences in your three samples.

23. You could have surveyed every student in your school to determine the percent of students who are left-handed. Describe a situation in which it makes sense to use a sample to describe aspects of a population instead of using the entire population. **See margin.**

24. 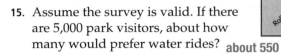 **FIND THE DATA** Refer to the California Data File on pages 16–19. Choose some data and write a real-world problem in which you would make a prediction based on samples. **See students' work.**

25. **CHALLENGE** Is it possible to create an unbiased random sample that is also a convenience sample? Explain and cite an example, if possible. **See margin.**

26. **WRITING IN MATH** Explain why the way in which a survey question is asked might influence the results that are obtained. Cite at least two examples in your explanation. **See margin.**

4 Assess

Ticket Out the Door Have students name one type of biased sample and explain the bias.

STANDARDS PRACTICE 6SDAP2.2, 6SDAP2.5

27. Yolanda wants to conduct a survey to determine what type of salad dressing is preferred by most students at her school. Which of the following methods is the best way for her to choose a random sample of the students at her school? **C**

   A Select students in her math class.

   B Select members of the Spanish Club.

   C Select ten students from each homeroom.

   D Select members of the girls basketball team.

28. The manager of a zoo wanted to know which animals are most popular among visitors. She surveyed every 10th visitor to the reptile exhibit. Of these, she found that 75% like snakes. If there are 860 visitors to the zoo, which of the following claims is valid? **J**

   F About 645 zoo visitors like snakes.

   G The reptile exhibit is the most popular exhibit.

   H 25% of zoo visitors prefer mammals.

   J No valid prediction can be made since the sample is a convenience sample.

Additional Answers

25. Yes; Sample answer: Every 10th person at a basketball game is asked whether they prefer basketball or baseball. This survey is systematic because every 10th person is surveyed. It is also a convenience sample because people attending a basketball game probably prefer basketball.

26. Sample answer: If the question is not worded or asked in a neutral manner, the people might not reveal their true opinion. For example, the question "Why would anyone like to run?" might not get the same answer as the question "What kind of exercise do you prefer to do?" Also, the question, "You don't really like country music, do you?" might not get the same answer as the question "What kind of music do you like?"

Spiral Review

29. **SCHOOL** In a survey of 120 randomly selected students at Jefferson Middle School, 34% stated that science was their favorite class. Predict how many of the 858 students in the school would choose science as their favorite class. (Lesson 8-7) **about 292 students**

30. **HEALTH** Use the scatter plot at the right to predict the height of a 16 year-old. (Lesson 8-6) **about 70 in.**

31. **SHOPPING** Nora bought a pair of running shoes that was discounted 35%. If the original price of the shoes was $89.90, find the discounted price to the nearest cent. (Lesson 7-7) **$58.44**

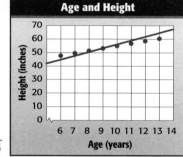
Age and Height

Write each percent as a fraction in simplest form. (Lesson 6-8)

32. 17% $\frac{17}{100}$

33. 62.5% $\frac{5}{8}$

34. 12.8% $\frac{16}{125}$

GET READY for the Next Lesson

PREREQUISITE SKILL Determine whether each statement is *true* **or** *false.* (Lesson 8-6)

35. The vertical scale on a line graph must have equal intervals. **true**

36. You do not need to label the axes of a line graph. **false**

Lesson 8-8 Using Sampling to Predict **443**

Misleading Statistics

Standard 6SDAP2.3 **Analyze data displays and explain** why the way in which the question was asked might have influenced the results obtained and **why the way in which the results were displayed might have influenced the conclusions reached.**

Standard 6SDP2.4 **Identify data that represent sampling errors and explain why the sample (and the display) might be biased.**

PACING: **Regular:** 1 period, **Block:** 0.5 period

Options for Differentiated Instruction

ELL = English Language Learner   **AL** = Above Grade Level   **SS** = Struggling Students   **SN** = Special Needs

Class Discussions ELL AL SS SN

Use after presenting Examples.

Review the examples presented in the lesson, and have a class discussion about the implications of the graphs. After the discussion, have students write in their journals answers to the following questions.

Ask:
- How can you determine if a graph is misleading?
- What should you look for to make sure the graph that you are reading is a true reflection of the data?
- How can you be sure that the graphs that you create accurately represent the data?
- How do you decide the appropriate intervals?

Have students choose one of the misleading graphs in this lesson and create a display that is not misleading to represent the data.

Working in Groups ELL AL SS SN

Use after presenting Examples.

Divide the class into groups of four and have students in each group count off from 1 to 4. Display a graph that has been exaggerated, such as the one shown at the right.

Give each group 30 seconds to discuss how this graph could be used to persuade people. Then randomly call a number from 1 to 4. Students with that number should be polled for their groups' conclusions.

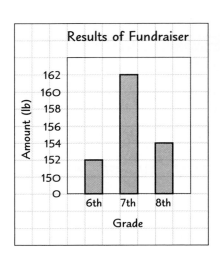

Results of Fundraiser

BL = Below Grade Level   **OL** = On Grade Level   **AL** = Above Grade Level   **ELL** = English Language Learner

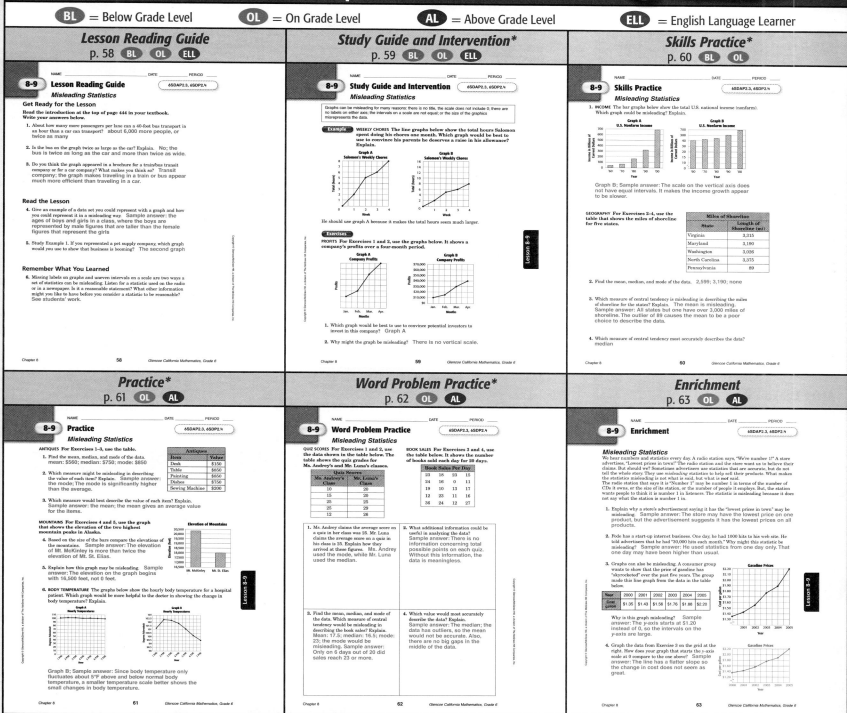

Additional Lesson Resources

* Also available in Spanish **ELL**

Transparencies
- *5-Minute Check Transparency,* Lesson 8-9

Other Print Products
- *Noteables™ Interactive Study Notebook with Foldables™*

Teacher Tech Tools
- *Interactive Classroom CD-ROM,* Lesson 8-9
- *AssignmentWorks CD-ROM,* Lesson 8-9

Student Tech Tools
ca.gr6math.com
- Extra Examples, Chapter 8, Lesson 9
- Self-Check Quiz, Chapter 8, Lesson 9

8-9 **Misleading Statistics**

1 Focus

Standards Alignment

Before Lesson 8-9
Organize and display single-variable data in appropriate graphs and representations and explain which types of graphs are appropriate for various data sets *from Standard 5SDAP1.2*

Lesson 8-9
Analyze data displays and why the way in which the results were displayed might have influenced the conclusions reached. *from* **Standard 6SDAP2.3**
Identify data that represent sampling errors and explain why the sample might be biased *from* **Standard 6SDAP2.4**

After Lesson 8-9
Know various forms of display for data sets, including a stem-and-leaf plot or box-and-whisker plot; use the forms to display a single set of data or to compare two sets of data *from Standard 7SDAP1.1*

2 Teach

Scaffolding Questions

Write the following money amounts on the board: $27, $19, $25, $36, and $28. Tell the class that these are the prices of steak dinners at six restaurants and that you want to display them in a bar graph.

Ask:

• What range should the scale have?
sample answer: $0 to $40

• What intervals should the scale have?
sample answer: $5

• What would the graph look like if the scale had a range from $0 to $100?
The bars would be shorter, and the differences in the bars' heights would be decreased.

Main IDEA
Recognize when statistics and graphs are misleading.

 Standard 6SDAP2.3 Analyze data displays and explain why the way in which the question was asked might have influenced the results obtained and **why the way in which the results were displayed might have influenced the conclusions reached.**
Standard 6SDAP2.4 Identify data that represent sampling errors and explain why the sample (and the display) might be biased.

1. about 6,000 more people, or twice as many
2. No; the bus is twice as long as the car and more than twice as wide.
3. Transit company; the graph makes traveling in a train or bus appear much more efficient than traveling in a car.

STUDY TIP

Changing Scales
To emphasize a change over time, reduce the scale interval on the vertical axis.

▶ **GET READY for the Lesson**

TRANSPORTATION A graph like the one at the right appeared in a brochure describing various modes of transportation.

1. About how many more passengers per lane can a 40-foot bus transport in an hour than a car can transport?

2. Is the bus on the graph twice as large as the car? Explain.

3. Do you think the graph appeared in a brochure for a train/bus transit company or for a car company? What makes you think so?

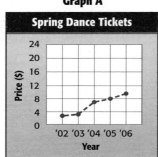

Methods of Travel

Trains

40-foot Buses

Cars

2 4 6 8 10 12 14 16 18 20+
Passenger Capacity Per Lane/Per Hour (thousands)

Graphs let readers analyze and interpret data easily, but are sometimes drawn to influence conclusions by misrepresenting the data. The use of different scales can influence conclusions drawn from graphs.

EXAMPLE **Changing the Interval of Graphs**

1 **SCHOOL DANCES** The graphs show how the price of spring dance tickets increased.

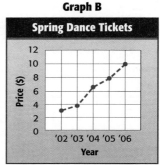

Graph A

Spring Dance Tickets

Price ($)
24
20
16
12
8
4
0
'02 '03 '04 '05 '06
Year

Graph B

Spring Dance Tickets

Price ($)
12
10
8
6
4
2
0
'02 '03 '04 '05 '06
Year

Do the graphs show the same data? If so, explain how they differ.
The graphs show the same data. However, the graphs differ in that Graph A uses an interval of 4, and Graph B uses an interval of 2.

Which graph makes it appear that the prices increased more rapidly?
Graph B makes it appear that the prices increased more rapidly even though the price increase is the same.

• What would the graph look like if the scale had a range from $15 to $40? The differences in the bars' heights would be increased.

Formative Assessment

Use the Check Your Progress exercises after each Example to determine students' understanding of concepts.

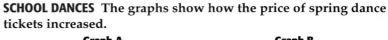

Tips for New Teachers **Scales**

Figures that represent quantities should be drawn to scale. Otherwise, the representations are not accurate, as in the graph in the lesson opener.

Which graph might Student Council use to show that while ticket prices have risen, the increase is not significant? Explain. They might use Graph A. The scale used on the vertical axis of this graph makes the increase appear less significant.

CHECK Your Progress

a. BUSINESS The line graphs show monthly profits of a company from October to March. Which graph suggests that the business is extremely profitable? Is this a valid conclusion? Explain.

 **Personal Tutor at** ca.gr6math.com

Sometimes the data used to create the display comes from a biased sample. In these cases, the data and the display are both biased and should be considered invalid.

EXAMPLE Identify Biased Displays

2 FITNESS The president of a large company mailed a survey to 500 of his employees in order to determine if they use the fitness room at work. The results are shown in the graph. Identify any sampling errors and explain why the sample and the display might be biased.

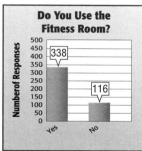

Not all of the surveys were returned since $338 + 116 < 500$. This is a biased, voluntary response sample. The sample is not representative of the entire population since only those who wanted to participate in the survey are involved in the sampling.

The display is biased because the data used to create the display came from a biased sample.

ath **nline Extra Examples at** ca.gr6math.com

Lesson 8-9 Misleading Statistics **445**

Focus on Mathematical Content

Graphs designed to influence decisions may be created in a misleading manner.

Misleading graphs often use **scales and intervals** that make data trends appear greater or lesser.

Statistics cited to influence decisions may be used in a misleading manner.

Misleading statistics often rely on the wrong **measure of central tendency**.

ADDITIONAL EXAMPLE

1 BUSINESS The line graphs below show the last 10 weeks of sales for the Crumby Cookie Bakery.

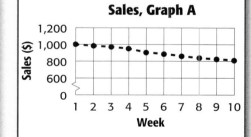

Do the graphs show the same data? If so, explain how the graphs differ. The graphs show the same data, but the scale of Graph A has greater intervals and a greater range.

Which graph makes it appear that the bakery's sales declined only slightly? Graph A

2 **TECHNOLOGY** A Web site e-mailed 1,000 of its members to determine its members' favorite hobbies. The results are shown in the graph below. Identify any sampling errors and explain why the sample and display might be biased.

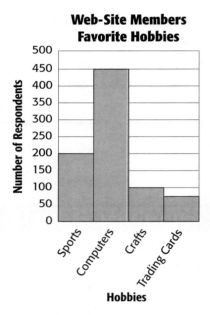

Web-Site Members Favorite Hobbies

The sample is a biased convenience sample. Members of a Web site probably enjoy computers more than other activities. The display is biased because the data used to create the display came from a biased sample.

3 **GRADES** Michael and Melissa both claim to be earning a C average—70% to 79%—in their Latin class. One student is wrong. Which one? Explain how he or she is using a misleading statistic.

Test	Grade (%)	
	Michael	**Melissa**
1	80	88
2	76	83
3	73	75
4	70	70
5	40	60
6	25	65
7	10	62

b. The sample is a biased convenience sample. Customers at a movie theater probably like to watch movies more than other activities. The display is biased because the data used to create the display came from a biased sample.

Real-World Link . . . .
The tallest roller coaster in the world is the Kingda Ka in Jackson, New Jersey, with a height of 456 feet.
Source: ultimaterollercoaster.com

c. See Ch. 8 Answer Appendix.

Additional Examples are also in:

• Noteables™ Interactive Study Notebook with Foldables™

• Interactive Classroom PowerPoint® Presentations

✔ **CHECK** **Your Progress**

b. **MOVIES** The manager of a movie theater asked 100 of his customers what they like to do on a Saturday night. The results are shown in the graph. Identify any sampling errors and explain why the sample and the display might be biased.

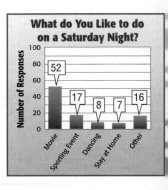

Statistics can also be used to influence conclusions.

EXAMPLE **Misleading Statistics**

3 **MARKETING** Refer to the table that gives the height of roller coasters at an amusement park. The park boasts that the average height of their roller coasters is 170 feet. Explain how this is misleading.

Park Rollercoaster Heights	
Coaster	**Height (ft)**
Viper	109
Monster	135
Red Zip	115
Tornado	365
Riptide	126

mean: $\dfrac{109 + 135 + 115 + 365 + 126}{5} = \dfrac{850}{5}$
$= 170$

median: 109, 115, ⑫⑥, 135, 365

mode: none

The average used by the park was the mean. This measure is much greater than most of the heights listed because of the outlier, 365 feet. So, it is misleading to use this measure to attract visitors.

A more appropriate measure to describe the data would be the median, 126 feet, which is closer to the height of most of the coasters.

✔ **CHECK** **Your Progress**

c. **SALARY** ABC Corporation claims the average salary for its employees is more than $60,000, while the average salary at XYZ Incorporated is only $25,000. Use the table to explain their reasoning and determine where you would prefer to work.

Position	Salary ($)	
	ABC Corp.	**XYZ Inc.**
President	500,000	120,000
1st Vice President	400,000	85,000
2nd Vice President	240,000	75,000
Sales Staff (5)	20,000	40,000
Supporting Staff (2)	15,000	25,000
Catalog Staff (7)	9,000	22,500

Additional Answer (Additional Examples)

3.
	Michael	Melissa
mean	53.4%	71.9%
median	70%	70%

Michael is wrong. He claimed to be earning a C because the median of his test grades was 70%. But his mean, or average, is much less than 70%.

CHECK Your Understanding

Example 1
(pp. 444)

1. BASEBALL Refer to the graphs below. Which graph suggests that Hank Aaron hit four times as many home runs as Willie Mayes? Is this a valid conclusion? Explain. **See margin.**

Graph A

Graph B

Example 2
(p. 445)

2. PHONES The manager of a telephone company mailed a survey to 400 households asking each household how they prefer to pay their monthly bill. The results are shown in the graph at the right. Identify any sampling errors and explain why the sample and the display might be biased.

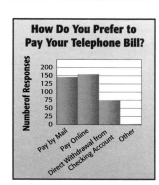

The sample is a biased voluntary response sample. Not all surveys were returned. The display is biased because the data used to create the display came from a biased sample.

Example 3
(p. 446)

3. TUNNELS The table lists the five largest land vehicle tunnels in the U.S. Write a convincing argument for which measure of central tendency you would use to emphasize the average length of the tunnels.

Sample answer: The mean is 8,638 and the median is 8,941. Since the median is greater than the mean, use the median to emphasize the average length.

U.S. Vehicle Tunnels on Land	
Name	**Length (ft)**
Anton Anderson Memorial	13,300
E. Johnson Memorial	8,959
Eisenhower Memorial	8,941
Allegheny	6,072
Liberty Tubes	5,920

Source: Federal Highway Association

Exercises

HOMEWORK HELP

For Exercises	See Examples
4, 8	1
5, 9	2
6, 7	3

Exercise Levels
4–9
10–11
12–13

4. UTILITIES The line graph shows the monthly electric bill for the condominium that Toshiko is interested in renting. Why is the graph misleading?

Sample answer: The graph does not include the very hot summer months or the very cold winter months, which would have higher electricity bills.

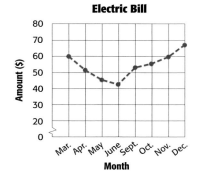

---

3 Practice

✓ Formative Assessment

Use Exercises 1–3 to check for understanding.

Then use the chart at the bottom of this page to customize your assignments for students.

Intervention You may wish to use the Study Guide and Intervention Master on page 59 of the *Chapter 8 Resource Masters* for additional reinforcement.

Odd/Even Assignments

Exercises 4–9 are structured so that students practice the same concepts whether they are assigned odd or even problems.

Additional Answer

1. Graph A; From the length of the bars, it appears that Hank Aaron hit about 4 times as many home runs Willie Mayes. However, Willie Mayes hit about 600 home runs and Hank Aaron hit about 750 home runs. So, the conclusion is not valid.

DIFFERENTIATED HOMEWORK OPTIONS

Level	Assignment	Two-Day Option	
BL Basic	4–9, 11–15	5–9 odd, 14, 15	4–8 even, 11, 16, 17
OL Core	5–9 odd, 11–17,	4–9, 14, 15	10, 11, 13–17
AL Advanced/Pre-AP	10–17		

⚠ Exercise Alert!

Use Grid Paper Exercises 10–11 requires students to draw a graph. You may wish to have students use grid paper for this exercise.

Tips for New Teachers

Using a Scale

Encourage students to always analyze the scale of a graph. Is the range appropriate? Are the intervals equal? Are any intervals missing? Sometimes, it is appropriate to use a broken scale. But a scale with a shorter range will make differences in the data appear greater, just as a scale with a greater range will make differences in the data appear lesser.

Addtional Answer

7. The median or the mode because it is much closer in value to most of the pieces of data.

---

6. 5,580,000; 4,600,000; 4,600,000; The mean because the value of the mean is much higher in value than most of the pieces of data.

8. Graph A; It appears that the stock has not increased or decreased dramatically.

9. The sample is a biased, convenience sample. The first 100 batteries produced may not be representative of all the batteries produced. The display is biased because the data used to create the display came from a biased sample.

10–11. See Ch. 8 Answer Appendix.

EXTRAPRACTICE

See pages 701, 722.

Math Online

Self-Check Quiz at ca.gr6math.com

---

5. **SCHOOL** To determine how often his students are tardy, Mr. Kessler considered his first period class. The results are shown in the graph at the right. Identify any sampling errors and explain why the sample and the display might be biased. **The sample is a biased convenience sample. Mr. Kessler's first period class may not be representative of all his students. The display is biased because the data used to create the display came from a biased sample.**

TRAVEL For Exercises 6 and 7, use the table.

6. Find the mean, median, and mode of the data. Which measure might be misleading in describing the average annual number of visitors that visit these sights? Explain.

7. Which measure would be best if you wanted a value close to the most number of visitors? Explain. **See margin.**

Annual Sight-Seeing Visitors	
Sight	**Visitors***
Cape Cod	4,600,000
Grand Canyon	4,500,000
Lincoln Memorial	4,000,000
Castle Clinton	4,600,000
Smoky Mountains	10,200,000

Source: *The World Almamac*
*Approximation

8. **STOCK** The graphs below show the increases and decreases in the monthly closing prices of Skateboard Depot's stock.

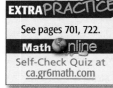

Suppose you are a stockbroker and want to show a customer that the price of the stock has been fairly stable since January. Write a convincing argument as to which graph you should show the customer.

9. **MANUFACTURING** To evaluate their product, the manager of an assembly line inspects the first 100 batteries that are produced out of 30,000 total batteries produced that day. He displays the results in the graph at the right and then releases it to the local newspaper. Identify any sampling errors and explain why the sample and the display might be biased.

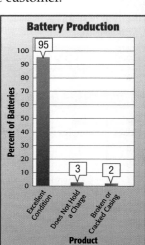

APARTMENTS For Exercises 10 and 11, create a display that would support each argument given the monthly costs to rent an apartment for the last five years are $500, $525, $560, $585, and $605.

10. Rent has remained fairly stable.

11. Rent has increased dramatically.

12. **CHALLENGE** Does adding values that are much greater or much less than the other values in a set of data affect the median of the set? Give an example to support your answer. **See margin.**

13. **WRITING IN MATH** Describe at least two ways in which the display of data can influence the conclusions reached. **See margin.**

STANDARDS PRACTICE 6SDAP2.3, 6SDAP2.4

14. The bar graph shows the average number of hours each week that a group of students attend an extracurricular activity after school.

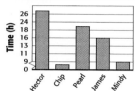

Time Spent on Extracurricular Activities

Which statement best tells why the graph may be misleading if you want to use the graph to compare the number of hours the students attend an extracurricular activity? **C**

A The vertical scale should show days instead of hours.

B The graph does not show which activity each person attended.

C The intervals on the vertical scale are inconsistent.

D The graph's title is misleading.

15. A department store mailed 100 surveys to teenagers about their preferred style of jeans. The graph shows the results.

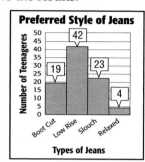

Preferred Style of Jeans

Which of the following is true concerning the sample and the display?

F Both the display and the sample are unbiased. **G**

G The display is biased because the sample is a biased, voluntary response sample.

H The display is biased because the sample is a biased, convenience sample.

J The sample is biased but the display is unbiased.

Spiral Review

16. **CARS** To determine what kind of automobile is preferred by most customers, the owner of an auto dealership surveys every 10th person that enters the dealership. Of these, 54% state that they prefer 4-door sedans. Based on these results, if the dealership stocks 150 cars, about how many of them should be 4-door sedans? (Lesson 8-8) **This is an unbiased, systematic sample, so the sample is valid; about 81 cars.**

17. **MP3 PLAYERS** In a survey, 46% of randomly selected teens said they own an MP3 player. Predict how many of the 850 teens at Harvey Middle School own an MP3 player. (Lesson 8-7) **about 391 teens**

Lesson 8-9 Misleading Statistics **449**

Yesterday's News Remind students that yesterday's lesson was about selecting an appropriate display for a data set. Have them write how yesterday's concepts helped them with today's material.

 Formative Assessment

Check for student understanding of concepts in Lessons 8-8 and 8-9.

 Quiz 4, p. 68

FOLDABLES **Foldables™**
Study Organizer **Follow-Up**

Remind students to record notes about misleading uses of graphs and statistics under the tab for this lesson in their Foldables. Encourage them to draw a misleading graph on the front of the tab, identifying the misleading part.

Additional Answers

12. Not usually; for example, the median of 9, 10, 11, 12, 100 is the same as the median of 9, 10, 11, 12, 13. But the median of 1, 17, 23 is not the same as the median of 1, 17, 23, 400.

13. Sample answer: Outliers may distort measures of central tendency; data shown in graphs may be exaggerated or minimized by manipulating scales and intervals.

CHAPTER 8
Study Guide and Review

Download Vocabulary Review from ca.gr6math.com

FOLDABLES™ Study Organizer

Dinah Zike's Foldables

Have students look through the chapter to make sure they have included examples in their Foldables for each tab.

Suggest that students keep their Foldables handy while completing the Study Guide and Review pages. Point out that their Foldables can serve as a quick review tool for studying for the Chapter Test.

✓ Formative Assessment

Key Vocabulary The page references after each word denote where that term was first introduced. If students have difficulty answering Exercises 1–8, remind them that they can use these page references to refresh their memories about the vocabulary terms.

Math Online ca.gr6math.com

FOLDABLES™ Study Organizer — GET READY to Study

Be sure the following Key Concepts are noted in your Foldable.

8-1 Line Plots

Key Concepts

Mean, Median, and Mode (Lesson 8-2)
- The mean of a set of data is the sum of the data divided by the number of items in the set.
- The median of a set of data is the middle number of the ordered data if there is an odd number of values, or the mean of the middle two numbers if there is an even number of values.
- The mode of a set of data is the number or numbers that occur most often. If there are two or more numbers that occur most often, all of them are modes.

Statistical Displays (Lessons 8-1, 8-3 through 8-9)
- Line plots show how many times each number occurs in a data set.
- Stem-and-leaf plots list all individual numerical data in a condensed form.
- Bar graphs show the data in specific categories.
- Histograms show the frequency of data divided into smaller intervals.
- Circle graphs compare data parts to the whole.
- Line graphs show change over a period of time.
- Scatter plots determine if there is a relationship between two sets of data.

Sampling Methods (Lesson 8-8)
- In a random sample, each item or person in the population is as likely to be chosen as any other.
- A convenience sample includes members of a population that are easily accessed.
- A voluntary response sample involves only those who want to participate in the sampling.

Key Vocabulary

analyze (p. 397)
bar graph (p. 415)
cluster (p. 397)
convenience sample (p. 439)
mean (p. 402)
data (p. 396)
histogram (p. 416)
leaf (p. 410)
line graph (p. 426)
line plot (p. 396)
mean (p. 402)

measures of central tendency (p. 402)
median (p. 403)
mode (p. 403)
outlier (p. 397)
random sample (p. 438)
range (p. 397)
scatter plot (p. 427)
statistics (p. 396)
stem (p. 410)
stem-and-leaf plot (p. 410)
voluntary response sample (p. 439)

Vocabulary Check

State whether each sentence is *true* or *false*. If *false*, replace the underlined word or number to make a true sentence.

1. The range is the difference between the greatest and the least values in a set of data. **true**

2. The mode divides a set of data in half. **false; median**

3. A graph that uses bars to make comparisons is a bar graph. **true**

4. A scatter plot shows two sets of related data. **true**

5. The median is a data value that is quite separated from the rest of the data. **false; outlier**

6. The mean is the arithmetic average of a set of data. **true**

7. The number or item that appears most often in a set of data is the mode. **true**

8. The range is the middle number of the ordered data, or the mean of the middle two numbers. **false; median**

Math Online Vocabulary Review at ca.gr6math.com

Vocabulary PuzzleMaker improves students' mathematics vocabulary using four puzzle formats—crossword, scramble, word search using a word list, and word search using clues. Students can work online or from a printed worksheet.

✓ Summative Assessment

 Vocabulary Test, p. 70

8-1 Line Plots (pp. 396–401)

Display each set of data in a line plot. Identify any clusters, gaps, or outliers.

9. 10°, 12°, 10°, 8°, 13°, 10°, 8°, 12°.

10. 7 ft, 8 ft, 8 ft , 9 ft, 14 ft, 9 ft, 8 ft, 7 ft

11. Number of Calories: 43, 41, 42, 45, 43, 42, 43, 46, 44, 44

9–11. See margin.

Example 1 Display the test scores 72, 75, 72, 74, 73, 68, 73, 74, 74, 75, and 73 in a line plot. Identify any clusters, gaps, or outliers.

Test Scores

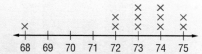

There is a cluster from 72 to 75, a gap between 68 and 72, and an outlier at 68.

8-2 Measures of Central Tendency and Range (pp. 402–408)

Find the mean, median, and mode. Round to the nearest tenth if necessary.

12. Number of siblings: 2, 3, 4, 3, 4, 3, 8, 7, 2 **4; 3; 3**

13. 89°, 76°, 93°, 100°, 72°, 86°, 74° **84.3°, 86°, none**

14. **MONEY** Which measure, mean, median, mode, or range best represents the amount of money students spent on clothing? **median**

Money Spent ($)			
125	108	172	136
121	112	218	172

Example 2 Find the mean, median, and mode for the following college students' ages: 23, 22, 19, 19, and 20.

mean: $\dfrac{23 + 22 + 19 + 19 + 20}{5}$ or 20.6 years

median: 20, the middle value of the ordered set

mode: 19, the data value that occurs most often

8-3 Stem-and-Leaf Plots (pp. 410–414) **15–17. See Ch. 8 Answer Appendix.**

Display each set of data using a stem-and-leaf plot.

15. Hours worked: 29, 54, 31, 26, 38, 46, 23, 21, 32, 37

16. Number of points: 75, 83, 78, 85, 87, 92, 78, 53, 87, 89, 91

17. Birthdates: 9, 5, 12, 21, 18, 7, 16, 24, 11, 10, 3, 14

Example 3 Display the number of pages read 12, 15, 17, 20, 22, 22, 23, 25, 27, and 35 in a stem-and-leaf plot.

The tens digits form the stems, and the ones digits form the leaves.

Pages Read	
Stem	Leaf
1	2 5 7
2	0 2 2 3 5 7
3	5

2|3 = 23 pages

Lesson-by-Lesson Review

Intervention If the given examples are not sufficient to review the topics covered by the questions, remind students that the page references tell them where to review that topic in their textbooks.

Two-Day Option Have students complete the Lesson-by-Lesson Review on pages 451–454. Then you can use ExamView® Assessment Suite to customize another review worksheet that practices all the objectives of this chapter or only the objectives on which your students need more help.

For more information on ExamView® Assessment Suite, see page 392C.

Differentiated Instruction

Super DVD: MindJogger Plus
Use this DVD as an alternative format of review for the test. For more information on this game show format, see page 392D.

Additional Answers

9.

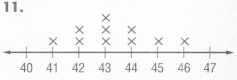

Sample answer: no significant clusters, gaps or outliers.

10.

Sample answer: cluster 7–9; gap 9–14; outlier 14

11.

Sample answer: cluster 42–44; no gaps or outliers

Additional Answer

20. The attendance at the National Zoo is about 3 times the attendance at the Denver Zoo.

8-4 Bar Graphs and Histograms (pp. 415–421)

ATTENDANCE For Exercises 18–20, refer to the graph.

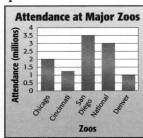

Attendance at Major Zoos

18. Which zoo did the most people attend? **San Diego**

19. About what was the total attendance for all five zoos? **10.75 million**

20. Write a statement comparing the attendance at the National Zoo to the attendance at the Denver Zoo.

20. See margin.

Example 4 The histogram below shows the heights of students in a classroom.

Students' Heights

How many students are 50–59 inches tall?

13 students

Write a statement comparing the 70–79 interval to the 60–69 interval.

The 60–69 interval is three times larger than the 70–70 interval.

8-5 PSI: Use a Graph (pp. 424–425)

STATUES For Exercises 21 and 22, use the graph that shows the heights of free-standing statues in the world.

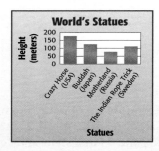

World's Statues

21. Which statue is the tallest? *Crazy Horse*

22. Compare the height of the *Motherland* statue to the height of the *Crazy Horse* statue.

Example 5 The graph shows the results of a survey about favorite vacation places.

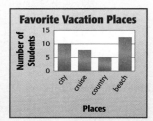

Favorite Vacation Places

Which place was favored by most students?

The beach was favored by 12 students, which was the greatest number.

22. The *Crazy Horse* statue is twice as tall as the *Motherland* statue.

8-6 **Using Graphs to Predict** (pp. 426–431)

PHONE CALLS For Exercises 23 and 24, use the graph showing the number of people in a family and the number of weekly calls.

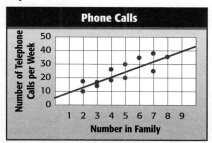

Phone Calls

23. Describe the relationship between the two sets of data. **See margin.**

24. Predict the number of weekly phone calls for a family of 10. **about 40**

Example 6 The scatter plot below shows the keyboarding speeds in words per minute of 12 students.

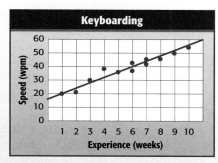

Keyboarding

Describe the relationship between the two sets of data.

The graph shows a positive relationship. That is, as the weeks pass, speed increases.

Additional Answer

23. Sample answer: The graph shows a positives relationship. That is, as the number of people in a family increases, the number of telephone calls per week increases.

8-7 **Using Data to Predict** (pp. 434–437)

CAREERS For Exercises 25 and 26, use the table that shows the results of a university survey of incoming freshman.

Career Goal	Percent
Elementary teacher	5.5%
Engineer	6.4%

25. Predict how many of the 3,775 freshmen would choose a career as an elementary teacher. **about 208**

26. How many of the 3,775 freshmen would you expect to choose a career as an engineer? **about 242**

27. SHOES A survey showed that 72% of teens bought new athletic shoes for the new school year. Based on that survey, how many teens in group of 225 bought new athletic shoes for the new school year? **162 teens**

Example 7 The circle graph shows the results of a survey to which 150 students at McAuliffe Middle School responded. Predict how many of the 644 students at the school have after-school jobs.

Do You Have an After-School Job?

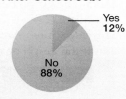

Yes 12%

No 88%

Find 12% of 644.

$n = 0.12 \cdot 644$ Write an equation.

$= 77.28$ Multiply.

So, you could predict that about 77 students at McAuliffe Middle School have after-school jobs.

Chapter 8 Study Guide and Review   **453**

Problem Solving Review

For additional practice in problem solving for Chapter 8, see the Mixed Problem Solving Appendix, page 722 in the Student Handbook section.

Anticipation Guide

Have students complete the Chapter 8 Anticipation Guide and discuss how their responses have changed now that they have completed Chapter 8.

 Anticipation Guide, p. 7

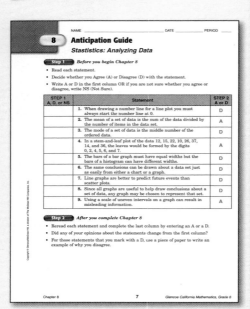

8-8 Using Sampling to Predict (pp. 438–443)

Determine whether each conclusion is valid. Justify your answer.

28. To determine the number of vegetarians in a city, a restaurant owner surveys the first 50 customers who enter the restaurant. Of these, 6 said they are vegetarians, so the owner concludes that about 12% of the city's population are vegetarians.

29. The principal of a junior high school randomly surveys 40 students from each grade level to determine how many students are interested in after-school tutoring. Of these, 88% are interested, so the principal decides to offer after-school tutoring.

30. **BOOKS** The owner of a bookstore surveyed every 10th person that entered the store to determine her customers' preferred type of book. Of these, 32% preferred mysteries. If the owner will order 500 new books, about how many should be mysteries?

Example 8 To determine the preference of her customers, a florist mails surveys to 100 of her customers. The results are shown in the table. Based on these results, the florist decides to stock more roses.

Type of Flower	Number
Roses	45
Tulips	26
Lilacs	17

This conclusion is invalid. This is a biased, voluntary response sample. Not all surveys were returned.

28. The conclusion is invalid. This is a biased, convenience sample.
29. The conclusion is valid. This is an unbiased random sample.
30. This is a simple random survey, so the sample is valid: about 160 mysteries.

8-9 Misleading Statistics (pp. 444–449)

31. **SALES** The graph below shows the monthly CD sales for one year at the Music Madness Warehouse. Why might the graph be misleading?

There are no labels on the vertical scale.

Example 9 The graph shows the pounds of cans recycled in eight weeks. Why might this graph be misleading?

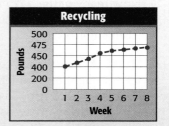

The scale is not divided into equal intervals. It has intervals of 200, 50, and 25.

For Exercises 1 and 2, use the line plot that shows the number of hours students spend listening to the radio per week. **1. See margin.**

Number of Radio Hours

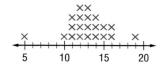

1. Identify any clusters, gaps, or outliers.

2. Describe how the range of data would change if 5 was not part of the data set. **The range would be 9 instead of 14.**

3. **INSECTS** The lengths in inches of several insects are given below. Find the mean, median, and mode of the data set. Round to the nearest tenth if necessary.

0.75, 1.24, 0.95, 2.6, 1.18, 1.3

1.3 in., 1.2 in., no mode

Display each data set in a stem-and-leaf plot.

4. 37°, 59°, 26°, 42°, 57°, 53°, 31°, 58° **See margin.**

5. $461, $422, $430, $425, $425, $467, $429
See Ch. 8 Answer Appendix.

6. **STANDARDS PRACTICE** Refer to the data below. Which of the following statements is true concerning the measures of central tendency? **C**

41, 45, 42, 38, 77, 44, 36, 43

A The mode is most affected by the inclusion of the outlier.

B The median is not affected by the inclusion of the outlier.

C The mean is most affected by the inclusion of the outlier.

D None of the measures of central tendency are affected by the inclusion of the outlier.

7. See Ch. 8 Answer Appendix.

7. **GRADES** Make a histogram for the following French test grades: 95, 76, 82, 90, 83, 76, 79, 82, 95, 85, 93, 81, and 63.

8. **EMPLOYMENT** The line graph shows the percent of women who had jobs outside the home from 1975 to 2000. Use the graph to predict the number of women who will have jobs outside the home in 2010.

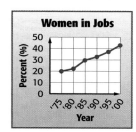 **Sample answer: 55%**

9. **AMUSEMENT PARKS** A researcher asked 250 students at Lake Valley Middle School to dial one of four telephone numbers to indicate their preference for the type of amusement park rides that they enjoy. Of these, 19% said they prefer the Ferris wheel. The researcher concludes that about $\frac{1}{5}$ of the students at Lake Valley Middle School prefer the Ferris wheel.
See Ch. 8 Answer Appendix.

10. **STANDARDS PRACTICE** The line graph shows ship sales at Marvin's Marina in thousands of dollars. Which of the following statements best tells why the graph is misleading? **J**

F The graph's title is misleading.

G The intervals on the horizontal scale are inconsistent.

H The graph does not show any data.

J The vertical axis is not labeled.

Summative Assessment

CRM **Chapter 8 Resource Masters**

Leveled Chapter 8 Tests			
Form	Type	Level	Pages
1	MC	BL	71–72
2A	MC	OL	73–74
2B	MC	OL	75–76
2C	FR	OL	77–78
2D	FR	OL	79–80
3	FR	AL	81–82

MC = multiple-choice questions
FR = free-response questions
BL = below grade level
OL = on grade level
AL = above grade level

- Vocabulary Test, p. 70
- Extended-Response Test, p. 83

ExamView Assessment Suite
Customize and create multiple versions of your chapter test and their answer keys. All of the questions from the leveled chapter tests in the *Chapter 8 Resource Masters* are also available on ExamView® Assessment Suite with the California Standard that each item assesses.

Additional Answers

1. clusters:10–16; gaps: 5–10, 16–19; outlier: 5

4. **Number of Wins**

Stem	Leaf
2	6
3	1 7
4	2
5	3 7 8 9

4|2 = 42

Data-Driven Decision Making	Exercises	Lesson	Standard	**Resources for Review**
Diagnostic Teaching Based on the results of the Chapter 8 Practice Test, use the following to review concepts that students continue to find challenging.	8	8-5	6SDAP2.3	CRM Study Guide and Intervention pp. 35, 40, 46, 53, and 59
	9	8-6	6SDAP2.5	Math Online
	9	8-7	6SDAP2.5	• Extra Examples
	9	8-8	6SDAP2.2	• Personal Tutor
	10	8-9	6SDAP2.4	• Concepts in Motion

TEST-TAKING TIP

Exercise 1 Point out that students can use mental math to estimate the solution and select the correct answer choice. They can add 32 thousand and 4 thousand, and then divide the sum by 6. (Since 36 thousand is an underestimate of the cars' actual total cost, students should realize that the quotient is also an underestimate.)

 Formative Assessment

You can use these two pages to benchmark student progress. The California Standards are listed with each question.

 Chapter 8 Resource Masters

• Standardized Test Practice, pp. 84–86

ExamView
Assessment Suite
Create practice worksheets or tests that align to the California Standards, as well as TIMSS and NAEP tests.

 Read each question. Then fill in the correct answer on the answer document provided by your teacher or on a sheet of paper.

1 Ed's Used Car Lot bought 5 used cars for $32,000. The business later bought another used car for $4,600. What was the mean cost of all of the used cars? **C**

A $3,200.00   C $6,100.00
B $4,600.00   D $8,500.00

2 A fitness club charges a membership fee of $50 plus $25 each month you belong to the club. Which expression could be used to find the total cost of belonging to the club for 10 months? **H**

F $50(10) + 25$

G $50 - 25(10)$

H $50 + 25(10)$

J $50(10) + 25(10)$

3 Sierra has 11.5 yards of fabric. She will use 20% of the fabric to make a flag. How many yards of fabric will she use? **D**

A 9.2 yd   C 4.5 yd
B 8.6 yd   D 2.3 yd

4 Ms. Thompson made 17 liters of punch for a party. The punch contained 5 liters of orange juice. Which equation could be used to find y, the percent of orange juice in the punch? **G**

F $\frac{17}{5} = \frac{y}{100}$

G $\frac{5}{17} = \frac{y}{100}$

H $\frac{5}{17} = \frac{100}{y}$

J $\frac{17}{y} = \frac{100}{5}$

---

5 The number of students in each grade level at Hampton Middle School is shown in the graph below. **B**

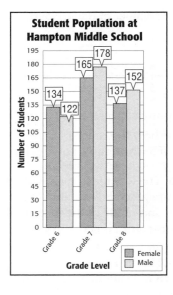

Which statement is true based on this information?

A There are more total students in the 6th grade than there are in the 8th grade.

B The female 7th graders outnumber the male 8th graders.

C The student population decreases by the same amount as each grade level increases.

D There are more female students in each grade level than male students.

6 A football team scored 20, 32, 28, 21, and 24 points in their first five games. How many points should they score in the next game so that the median and mode scores are equal? **G**

F 32   H 21
G 24   J 20

More California Standards Practice
For practice by standard, see pages CA1–CA39.

CHAPTER
8
California Standards Practice

7 Regina priced six MP3 players. The prices are shown below.

$120.00, $90.00, $75.00,
$105.00, $85.00, $150.00

What is the median price? **B**

A $90.00

B $97.50

C $104.17

D $105.00

8 Which of the following is the prime factorization of the lowest common denominator of $\frac{3}{8} + \frac{5}{6}$? **H**

F 2×3

G $2 \times 2 \times 2$

H $2 \times 2 \times 2 \times 3$

J $2 \times 2 \times 2 \times 2 \times 3$

9 If a is a negative number and b is a negative number, which of the following expressions is always negative? **A**

A $a + b$

B $a - b$

C $a \times b$

D $a \div b$

10. The numbers of monthly minutes Gary used on his cell phone for the last eight months are shown below.

400, 550, 450, 620, 550, 600, 475, 425

What is the mode of this data? **F**

F 550   H 450

G 475   J 400

11 Taylor spends between $125 and $200 per month on food. Which is the best estimate of how much she spends on food in 6 months? **B**

A From $1,500 to $2,400

B From $750 to $1,200

C From $250 to $400

D From $125 to $200

12 A store has 2,545 CDs. On Saturday, the store sold $12\frac{1}{2}\%$ of the CDs. What fraction of the CDs were sold on Saturday? **F**

F $\frac{1}{8}$ H $\frac{2}{9}$

G $\frac{3}{25}$ J $\frac{2}{17}$

TEST-TAKING TIP

Question 13 If you find that you cannot answer every part of an open-ended question, do as much as you can. You may earn partial credit.

Pre-AP

Record your answers on a sheet of paper. Show your work.

13 The table shows how values of a painting increased over ten years.

Year	Value	Year	Value
1997	$350	2002	$1,851
1998	$650	2003	$2,151
1999	$950	2004	$2,451
2000	$1,200	2005	$2,752
2001	$1,551	2006	$3,052

a. Make a line graph of the data. **See margin.**

b. Use the graph to predict what the value of the painting will be in 2010.
Sample answer: $4,000

NEED EXTRA HELP?

If You Missed Question...	1	2	3	4	5	6	7	8	9	10	11	12	13
Go to Lesson...	8-2	1-6	7-1	7-2	8-6	8-2	8-2	4-1	2-4	8-2	1-1	6-8	8-6
For Help with Standard...	SDAP1.1	AF1.2	NS1.4	NS1.3	SDAP2.3	SDAP1.2	SDAP1.1	NS1.4	NS2.3	SDAP1.1	MR2.7	NS1.2	SDAP2.3

Answer Sheet Practice

Have students simulate taking a standardized test by recording their answers on a practice recording sheet.

CRM Student Recording Sheet, p. 65

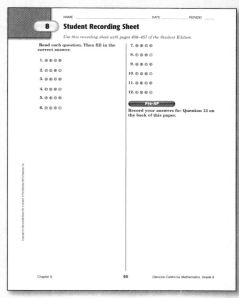

Additional Answer

13a.

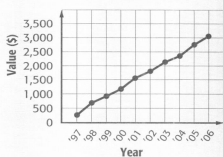

Homework Option

Get Ready for Chapter 9 Assign students the exercises on page 459 as homework to assess whether they possess the prerequisite skills needed for the next chapter.

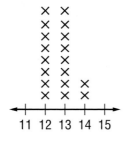

Page 397, Lesson 8-1 (Check Your Progress)

b. Sample answer: The data appear to be clustered around 19 and 21 stories. One gap appers bteween 24 and 30. The number 10 could be considered an outleir. The range is 40 − 10 or 30 stories.

c. Sample answer: The range of the number of stories would remain unchanged at 34.

Pages 398–400, Lesson 8-1

1.   **Cost of Video Games ($)**

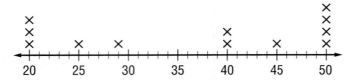

2.   Sizes of Tennis Shoes

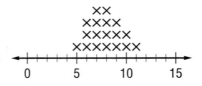

9.   Heights of Desert Cacti (ft)

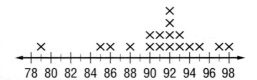

10.   Test Scores (%)

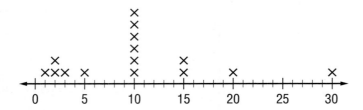

11.   Basketball Scores (pts)

12. Ages of Students (y)

26.   Average Life Spans

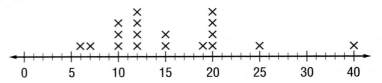

29.   Maximum Life Spans

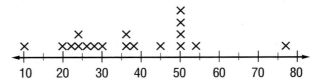

Sample answer: The data are more spread out, with a range of 67 compared with the previous range of 34. There is a cluster from 20 to 30 and a gap between 54 and 77. The piece of data that occurs most frequently is 50, which means that the maximum life span of most animals is 50 years.

Page 409, Extend 8-2

1. Sample answer: Kendrick is using the mean to describe the average number of times a student waited longer than 5 minutes, but the mean is affected by outliers, and two people indicated that they had had to wait longer than 5 minutes 9 times the previous week. That is 4 more times than the next greatest number of times, 5. When you view all of the data on a line plot, it is clear that these two responses are outliers.

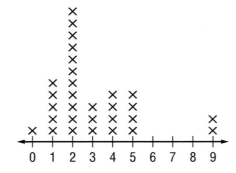

In this instance, the median is more representative of the data. On average, a student waited longer than 5 minutes 2 times in the previous week.

Page 410, Lesson 8-3 (Check Your Progress)

a.
Homework Time

Stem	Leaf
0	0 5
1	
2	3 4
3	0 0 5 9
4	2 5 5 5 7 9
5	1 5 6 8
6	
7	5 5

$4|2 = 42\ min$

Pages 412–413, Lesson 8-3

1.
Height of Trees (ft)

Stem	Leaf
0	8 8
1	0 2 5 5 6 8
2	0 5

$2|0 = 20\ ft$

2.
Cost of Shoes ($)

Stem	Leaf
1	6 9
2	1 3 5 5 9
3	1 3 4 5 9
4	2 7 8

$3|4 = \$34$

6.
Quiz Scores (%)

Stem	Leaf
7	0 2 3 6 7 9
8	0 0
9	0 1 1 3 3 3 5 6

$8|0 = 80\%$

7.
Low Temperatures (°F)

Stem	Leaf
1	3 3 5
2	0 4 8
3	0 1 2 2 5 6 8 8 8

$1|3 = 13°F$

8.
Floats at Annual Parade

Stem	Leaf
10	3
11	1
12	
13	3 4 9
14	2 9
15	1 4 7 8 9

$13|9 = 139$

9.
School Play Attendance

Stem	Leaf
22	5 7 9
23	0
24	3 6
25	
26	7 9 9
27	8 8 8

$26|7 = 267$

25.

Price ($)	Tally	Frequency
20–29	IIII	4
30–39	IIII IIII	10
40–49	IIII	5
50–59	I	1

Price of Jeans ($)

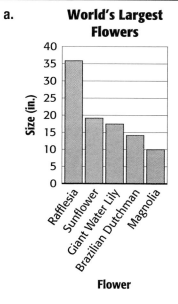

24 26 28 30 32 34 36 38 40 42 44 46 48 50 52 54 56

Price of Jeans

Stem	Leaf
2	4 6 6 8
3	0 2 3 4 5 5 6 6 8 8
4	0 0 0 5 9
5	6

$3|5 = \$35$

All three representations show the frequency of data occurring. The frequency table shows intervals of data and is useful in comparing price ranges. The line plot gives a good picture of the spread of the data. The stem-and-leaf plot shows individual prices as in the line plot, as well as intervals, such as $20s, $30s, and so on. See students' favorites and reasons.

Pages 416–417, Lesson 8-4 (Check Your Progress)

a.
World's Largest Flowers

Chapter 8 Answer Appendix

b.

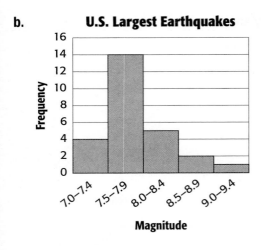

U.S. Largest Earthquakes

Page 418, Lesson 8-4

1.

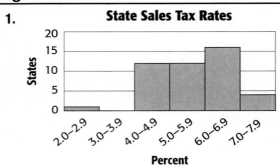

State Sales Tax Rates

5.

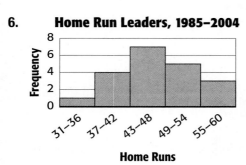

Most Threatened Reptiles

6. **Home Run Leaders, 1985–2004**

7.

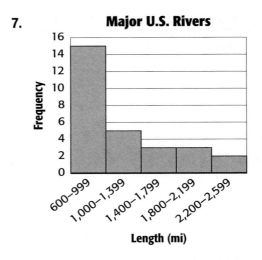

Major U.S. Rivers

8. **City Skyscrapers**

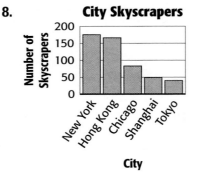

Page 423, Mid-Chapter Quiz

3. Sample answer: cluster 16–18; gap 21–25; outlier 25

6. 7.1 m; 6.9 m; 6.8 m

7.

Speeds	
Stem	**Leaf**
5	9
6	5 5 5 8 8 9 9
7	0 1 1 2 4 4 6

6|5 = 65 mph

Sample answer: Most cars drive about 69 mph.

10. mean; Sample answer: There is no mode of the data set with or without the inclusion of the outlier, so the mode is not affected. The median of the data set is 1.3 without the outlier and 1.4 including the outlier. The mean is approximately 1.43 without the outlier and approximately 1.87 including the outlier. Since 1.87 − 1.43 or 0.44 is greater than 1.4 − 1.3 or 0.1, the mean is the most affected measure.

Page 424, Lesson 8-5

1. Sample answer: Graphs provide a visual representation of a situation involving comparisons. A graphical model can sometimes show conclusively what is often difficult to interpret from looking at lists alone.

Page 429–431, Lesson 8-6

11.

Olympic Participation

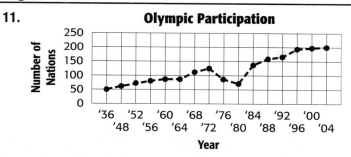

25.

Favorite Color

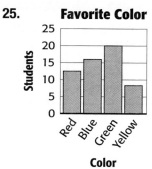

Page 446, Lesson 8-9 (Check Your Progress)

c. Sample answer: ABC Corporation used the mean to represent its average salary. They used the median to represent the average salary at XYZ Inc. Unless you could be a president or vice president, it would be better to work for XYZ Inc. because its 14 lowest-paid employees are all better paid than any of the 14 lowest-paid employees at ABC Corporation.

Page 448, Lesson 8-9

10.

Monthly Cost to Rent an Apartment

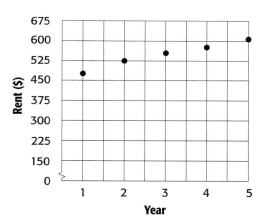

11.

Monthly Cost to Rent an Apartment

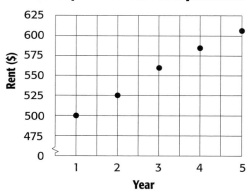

Page 451, Study Guide and Review

15.

Hours Worked

Stem	Leaf
2	1 3 6 9
3	1 2 7 8
4	6
5	4

$3|2 = 32$ hours

16.

Points Scored

Stem	Leaf
5	3
6	
7	5 8 8
8	3 5 7 7 9
9	1 2

$7|5 = 75$ points

17.

Birthdates

Stem	Leaf
0	3 5 7 9
1	0 1 2 4 6 8
2	1 4

$1|2 = 12$

Page 455, Practice Test

5.

Stem	Leaf
42	2 5 5 9
43	0
44	
45	
46	1 7

$43|1 = 431$

7. Sample answer:

French Test Grades

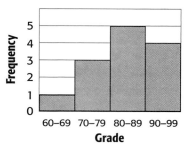

9. The conclusion is valid. The sample is a biased, voluntary response sample.

Chapter Overview

Probability

Standards-Based Lesson Plan	Pacing Your Lessons		
LESSONS AND OBJECTIVES	California Standards	40–50 Minute Periods	90-Minute Periods
9-1 Simple Events (pp. 460–464) • Find the probability of a simple event.	6SDAP3.3	1	0.5
9-2 Sample Spaces (pp. 465–470) • Find sample spaces and probabilities.	6SDAP3.1	1	0.5
9-3 The Fundamental Counting Principle (pp. 471–474) • Use multiplication to count outcomes.	6SDAP3.1	1	0.5
9-4 Permutations (pp. 475–478) • Find the number of permutations of a set of objects.	6SDAP3.1	1	0.5
9-5 Combinations (pp. 480–483) • Find the number of combinations of a set of objects.	6SDAP3.1	1	0.5
9-6 Problem-Solving Investigation: Act It Out (pp. 484–485) • Solve problems by acting it out.	6SDAP3.2 6SDAP2.4	1	0.5
9-7 Theoretical and Experimental Probability (pp. 486–490) • Find and compare experimental and theoretical probabilities. **Extend 9-7 Probability Lab: Simulations** (p. 491) • Investigate experimental probability by conducting a simulation.	6SDAP3.2 6MR1.2	2	1
9-8 Compound Events (pp. 492–497) • Find the probability of independent events.	6SDAP3.4 6SDAP3.5	2	1
REVIEW		1	0.5
ASSESSMENT		1	0.5*
TOTAL		12	6

*The complete **Assessment Planner** for Chapter 9 is provided on page 459.*

* Begin Chapter 10 in the second half of the period.

Professional Development

California Standards Vertical Alignment

Before Chapter 9

Related Topics from Grade 5

- Use fractions and percentages to compare data sets of different sizes Standard 5SDAP1.3

- Add, subtract, multiply, and divide with decimals; add with negative integers; subtract positive integers from negative integers; and verify the reasonableness of the results ⟜ Standard 5NS2.1

Chapter 9

Topics from Grade 6

- Represent probabilities as ratios, proportions, decimals, and percentages and verify that the probabilities computed are reasonable; know that if P is the probability of an event, $1 - P$ is the probability of an event *not* occurring ⟜

- Represent all possible outcomes for compound events in an organized way and express the theoretical probability of each outcome ⟜

- Understand that the probability of either of two disjoint events occurring is the sum of the two individual probabilities and that the probability of one event following another, in independent trials, is the product of the two probabilities

- Understand the difference between independent and dependent events ⟜

See individual lessons for the specific Standards covered.

After Chapter 9

Preparation for Grade 7

- Represent probabilities as ratios, proportions, decimals between 0 and 1, and percentages between 0 and 100 and verify that the probabilities computed are reasonable; know that if P is the probability of an event, $1 - P$ is the probability of an event not occurring ⟜ Standard 6SDP3.3

Back-Mapping

California Mathematics: Concepts, Skills, Problem Solving was conceived and developed with the final result in mind, student success in Algebra I and beyond. The authors, using the California Mathematics Standards as their guide, developed this brand-new series by "back-mapping" from the desired result of student success in Algebra I and beyond. McGraw-Hill's K-7 intervention program, *California Math Triumphs: Intensive Intervention* as well as *California Algebra 1, California Geometry, California Algebra 2,* and *California Algebra Readiness* were developed utilizing the same philosophy.

What the Research Says . . .

According to Shaughnessy and Bergman in "Thinking about Uncertainty: Probability and Statistics," it is important to give students opportunities to investigate probability problems by using a problem-solving approach.

- Each lesson in Chapter 9 contains real-world application problems involving probability.

McGraw Hill Professional Development

Targeted professional development has been articulated throughout the *California Mathematics: Concepts, Skills, and Problem Solving* series. The **McGraw-Hill Professional Development Video Library** provides short videos that support the ⟜ Key Standards. For more information, visit ca.gr6math.com.

| Model Lessons | Instructional Strategies |

Technology Solutions

Teacher Resources

TeacherWorks™ All-in-One Planner and Resource Center

All of the print materials from the Classroom Resource Masters are available on your TeacherWorks™ CD-ROM.

BL = Below Grade Level   **OL** = On Grade Level   **AL** = Above Grade Level   **ELL** = English Language Learner

Chapter Resource Masters				9-1	9-2	9-3	9-4	9-5	9-6	9-7	9-8
BL **OL**		**ELL**	Lesson Reading Guide	9	15	21	27	34		45	52
BL **OL**		**ELL**	Study Guide and Intervention*	10	16	22	28	35	41	46	53
BL **OL**			Skills Practice*	11	17	23	29	36	42	47	54
	OL	**AL**	Practice*	12	18	24	30	37	43	48	55
	OL	**AL**	Word Problem Practice*	13	19	25	31	38	44	49	56
	OL	**AL**	Enrichment	14	20	26	32	39		50	57
	OL	**AL**	Calculator and Spreadsheet Activities				33	40		51	58
	OL	**AL**	Chapter Assessments*	59–80							
BL **OL**		**AL**	5-Minute Check Transparencies	✓	✓	✓	✓	✓	✓	✓	✓
BL **OL**			Teaching Mathematics with Manipulatives				✓	✓		✓	

Also available in Spanish.
Real-World Investigations for Differentiated Instruction, pp. 55–56

AssignmentWorks

Differentiated Assignments, Answers, and Solutions

- Print a customized assignment worksheet using the Student Edition exercises along with an answer key or worked-out solutions.
- Use default lesson assignments as outlined in the Differentiated Homework Options in the Teacher Wraparound Edition.
- Includes modified questions from the Student Edition for students with special needs.

Interactive Classroom

This CD-ROM is a customizable Microsoft® PowerPoint® presentation that includes:

- In-Class Examples
- Your Turn Exercises*
- 5-Minute Check Transparencies*
- Links to Online Study Tools
- Concepts in Motion

compatible with response pad technology

Example 2

Check   Make a diagram in which each person is represented by a point. Draw line segments between two points to represent the games. There are 45 line segments.

Answer: There will be 45 introductions taking place.

End of slide

ExamView®Assessment Suite

- Create, edit, and customize tests and worksheets using QuickTest Wizard
- Create multiple versions of tests and modify them for a desired level of difficulty
- Translate from English to Spanish and vice versa
- Build tests aligned with your state standards
- Track students' progress using the Teacher Management System

Student Tools

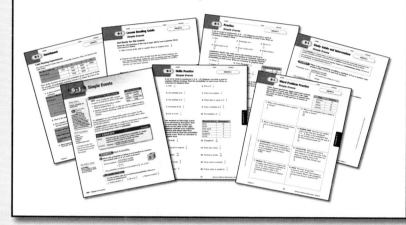
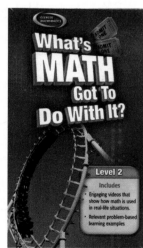
Internet Resources

Math Online ca.gr6math.com

TEACHER	STUDENT	PARENT	**Online Study Tools**
	•	•	Online Student Edition
•	•	•	Multilingual Glossary
			Lesson Resources
	•	•	BrainPOP®
•	•	•	Concepts in Motion
•	•	•	Extra Examples
•			Group Activity Cards
•			Problem of the Week Cards
	•	•	Other Calculator Keystrokes
	•	•	Reading in the Content Area
	•	•	Real-World Careers
	•	•	Self-Check Quizzes
			Chapter Resources
	•	•	Chapter Readiness
	•	•	Chapter Test
	•	•	Family Letters and Activities
	•	•	Standardized Test Practice
	•	•	Vocabulary Review/Chapter Review Activities
			Unit Resources
•	•		Cross-Curricular Internet Project
			Other Resources
•			Dinah Zike's Foldables
•	•		Game Zone Games and Recording Sheets
	•	•	Hotmath Homework Help
•			Key Concepts
•	•	•	Math Skills Maintenance
•	•	•	Meet the Authors
•			NAEP Correlations
	•	•	Personal Tutor
•			Project CRISS℠
	•	•	Scavenger Hunts and Answer Sheets
•			Vocabulary PuzzleMakers

Reading and Writing in Mathematics

Noteables™ Interactive Study Notebook with Foldables™

This workbook is a study organizer that provides helpful steps for students to follow to organize their notes for Chapter 9.

- Students use Noteables to record notes and to complete their Foldables as you present the material for each lesson.
- Noteables correspond to the Examples in the *Teacher Wraparound Edition* and *Interactive Classroom CD-ROM*.

READING in the Content Area

This online worksheet provides strategies for reading and analyzing Lesson 9-3, The Fundamental Counting Principle. Students are guided through questions about the main idea, subject matter, supporting details, conclusion, clarifying details, and vocabulary of the lesson.

ca.gr6math.com

Recommended Outside Reading for Students

Mathematics and Amusement Parks

- *Math Trek: Adventures in the Math Zone* by Ivars Peterson and Nancy Henderson ©1999 [nonfiction]

This book shows students the math of an amusement park. Games and activities are included. "Trek 13: Luck on the Boredwalk" will be of special interest to students after completing their study of probability.

Mathematics and Mystery

- *Conned Again, Watson! Cautionary Tales of Logic, Math, and Probability* by Colin Bruce ©2002 [fiction]

Using the stories of Sherlock Holmes, the author creates mysteries that require mathematical skill to be solved. This book provides interesting insight as probability and statistics are used by Sherlock Holmes to outwit con men.

Project CRISS

STUDY SKILL

Mapping can help students create useful representations of new subject matter to use as study tools. The sample map at the right shows how to find the probability of rolling an even number on a number cube. Have students work in cooperative groups to design maps for lessons of their choosing from Chapter 9. The maps should be designed after each student has carefully read the lesson. Afterward, have each group present their map to the class.

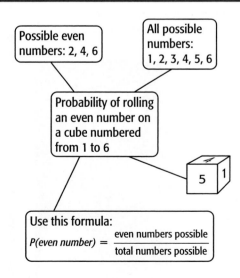

Possible even numbers: 2, 4, 6

All possible numbers: 1, 2, 3, 4, 5, 6

Probability of rolling an even number on a cube numbered from 1 to 6

Use this formula:

$$P(\text{even number}) = \frac{\text{even numbers possible}}{\text{total numbers possible}}$$

CReating **I**ndependence through **S**tudent-owned **S**trategies

Differentiated Instruction

Quick Review Math Handbook*

is Glencoe's mathematical handbook for students and parents.

Hot Words includes a glossary of terms.

Hot Topics consists of two parts:

- explanations of key mathematical concepts
- exercises to check students' understanding.

Lesson	Hot Topics Section	Lesson	Hot Topics Section
9-1	4•6	9-5	4•5
9-2	4•5	9-7	4•6
9-3	4•6	9-8	4•6
9-4	4•5		

Also available in Spanish

Teacher To Teacher

Lizabeth Peters
Mathematics Department Chair
Hal Peterson Middle School
Kerrville, Texas

USE WITH LESSON 9-3

"I offer students an opportunity to bring a take-home (paper) menu from a local restaurant to class. They investigate how many appetizers, main entrees, side items, beverages, and desserts are possible. I ask them to use the Fundamental Counting Principle to determine how many different choices are possible if they order one from each category. I then ask how many years they could eat at that restaurant once a day and never have the same dinner.**"**

Intervention Options

Intensive Intervention

Math Triumphs can provide intensive intervention for students who are at risk of not meeting the California standards addressed in Chapter 9.

Diagnose student readiness with the Quick Check and Quick Review on page 459. Then use *Math Triumphs* to accelerate their achievement.

Algebra: Integers

Prerequisite Skill	Math Triumphs
Multiply whole numbers	Volume 1, Chapter 4
Multiply and simplify fractions	Volume 2, Chapter 3

See chart on page T24 for other *Math Triumphs* lessons that will support the prerequisite skills needed for success in *Glencoe California Mathematics, Grade 6*.

Strategic Intervention

For strategic intervention options, refer to the Diagnostic Assessment table on page 459.

FOLDABLES Study Organizer
Dinah Zike's Foldables

Focus This Foldable is designed to help students organize their thoughts and notes about probability.

Teach Have students make their Foldables and label the tab for each lesson. Explain to students that they will write a descriptive paragraph about each lesson in their Foldables. Were students familiar with some of the material in the lesson? Did the material seem difficult at first? Which parts of the lesson proved most difficult? How did the lesson's material relate to students' everyday lives?

When to Use It At the end of each lesson, remind students to record their thoughts about the lesson in their Foldables.

A version of a completed Foldable is shown on p. 498.

Differentiated Instruction

CRM Student-Built Glossary, p. 1

Students complete the chart by providing the definition of each term and an example as they progress through Chapter 9.

This study tool can be used to review for the chapter test.

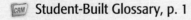

Materials Needed for Chapter 9
• counters (Lesson 9-2)
• markers (Lesson 9-2)
• masking tape (Lesson 9-2)
• index cards (Lesson 9-4)
• number cubes (Lesson 9-7)
• coins (Lesson 9-7)
• grid paper (Lesson 9-7)
• paper bags (Extend 9-7)
• colored cubes (Extend 9-7)

CHAPTER 9 Probability

BIG Idea
• **Standard SDAP3.0** Determine theoretical and experimental probabilities and use these to make predictions about events.

Key Vocabulary
compound event (p. 492)
independent event (p. 492)
probability (p. 460)
sample space (p. 465)

 Real-World Link

GAMES Rolling number cubes allows you to advance forward or backward in many board games. Probability tells you that rolling doubles on a pair of number cubes happens only about 17% of the time.

FOLDABLES Study Organizer

Probability Make this Foldable to help you organize your notes. Begin with five sheets of $8\frac{1}{2}''$ by 11'' paper.

1 Stack five sheets of paper $\frac{3}{4}$ inch apart.

2 Roll up bottom edges so that all tabs are the same size.

3 Crease and staple along the fold.

4 Write the chapter title on the front. Label each tab with a lesson number and title. Label the last tab *Vocabulary*.

GET READY for Chapter 9

Diagnose Readiness You have two options for checking Prerequisite Skills.

Option 1

Take the Quick Check below. Refer to the Quick Review for help.

Option 2

Math Online Take the Online Readiness Quiz at ca.gr6math.com.

QUICK Check

(Used in Lessons 9-3 and 9-4)
Multiply. (Prior Grade)

1. 7×15 **105**
2. 24×6 **144**
3. 13×4 **52**
4. 8×21 **168**
5. 5×32 **160**
6. 30×8 **240**
7. $7 \times 6 \times 5$ **210**
8. $8 \times 7 \times 6$ **336**
360 9. $6 \times 5 \times 4 \times 3$
10. $4 \times 3 \times 2 \times 1$ **24**
11. $10 \times 9 \times 8 \times 7$
5,040
12. $11 \times 10 \times 9$
990

13. **JOBS** If you earn $9 an hour and work 5 hours each day for 7 days, how much have you earned?
(Prior Grade) **$315**

(Used in Lessons 9-1, 9-7, and 9-8)
Write each fraction in simplest form. Write *simplified* **if the fraction is already in simplest form.** (Lesson 4-4)

14. $\frac{8}{12}$ $\frac{2}{3}$
15. $\frac{3}{18}$ $\frac{1}{6}$
16. $\frac{4}{9}$ **simplified**
17. $\frac{5}{15}$ $\frac{1}{3}$

18. **SLEEP** If the average adult gets 8 hours of sleep, what fraction of the day, in simplest form, is spent asleep? (Lesson 4-4) $\frac{1}{3}$

(Used in Lesson 9-5)
Find each value. (Prior Grade)

19. $\frac{6 \times 5}{3 \times 2}$ **5**
20. $\frac{9 \times 8 \times 7}{5 \times 4 \times 3}$ **8.4**
21. $\frac{4 \times 3 \times 2}{3 \times 2 \times 1}$ **4**
22. $\frac{7 \times 6 \times 5 \times 4}{4 \times 3 \times 2 \times 1}$ **35**

QUICK Review

Example 1 Multiply $7 \times 6 \times 5 \times 4$.

$7 \times 6 \times 5 \times 4 = 42 \times 5 \times 4$ Multiply from
$= 210 \times 4$ left to right.
$= 840$

Example 2 Write $\frac{21}{28}$ in simplest form.

$\frac{21}{28} = \frac{3}{4}$ Divide the numerator and denominator by the GCF, 7.

Example 3 Find the value of $\frac{6 \times 5 \times 4}{3 \times 2 \times 1}$.

$\frac{6 \times 5 \times 4}{3 \times 2 \times 1} = \frac{120}{6}$ ← Multiply the numerator.
   ← Multiply the denominator.
$= 20$ Simplify.

Chapter 9 Get Ready for Chapter 9   **459**

Diagnostic Assessment

Exercises	California Standards	Strategic Intervention
1–13	4NS3.2	*Math Skills Maintenance Masters*, pp. 9–10
14–18	6NS2.4	SE Review Lesson 4–4, pp. 192–195
19–22	6NS2.1; 6NS2.2	SE Review Lesson 5–5, pp. 252–257

Formative Assessment

CRM Anticipation Guide, pp. 7–8

Spotting Preconceived Ideas
Students complete this survey to determine prior knowledge about ideas from Chapter 10. Revisit this worksheet after completing the chapter. Also see page 502.

TWE **Lesson Activities**

- Ticket Out the Door, pp. 464, 483, 497
- Crystal Ball, pp. 470, 485
- Name the Math, pp. 474, 490
- Yesterday's News, p. 478

Chapter Checkpoints

SE Mid-Chapter Quiz, p. 479
SE Study Guide and Review, pp. 498–502
SE California Standards Practice, pp. 504–505
CRM Quizzes, pp. 61 and 62
CRM Standardized Test Practice, pp. 78–80

Math Online ca.gr6math.com

- Self-Check Quizzes
- Practice Test
- Standardized Test Practice

Summative Assessment

SE Chapter Practice Test, p. 503
CRM Mid-Chapter Test, p. 63
CRM Vocabulary Test, p. 64
CRM Extended-Response Test, p. 77
CRM Leveled Chapter Tests, pp. 65–76
 ExamView® Assessment Suite

KEY

CRM *Chapter 9 Resource Masters*
SE Student Edition
TWE Teacher Wraparound Edition
CD-ROM

 **9-1**

Simple Events

◆━ **Standard**
6SDAP3.3

Represent probabilities as ratios, proportions, decimals between 0 and 1, and percentages between 0 and 100 and verify that the probabilities computed are reasonable; know that if *P* is the probability of an event, 1 — *P* is the probability of an event *not* occurring.

PACING: **Regular:** 1 period, **Block:** 0.5 period

Options for Differentiated Instruction

ELL = English Language Learner   **AL** = Above Grade Level   **SS** = Struggling Students   **SN** = Special Needs

Class Discussions

Use before presenting Example 1.

Preview the lesson by discussing situations in which probability is used in daily life. Some examples include weather, sports, and games of chance.

Ask:
- What information does probability give you?
- How can knowing probability influence your decisions?

Collecting and Recording Data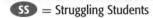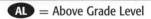

Use after presenting Example 1.

Have each student toss a number cube 30 times and record the results in a table like the one below.

Toss	Even Number	Odd Number
1		
2		
3		
4		
Totals		

Have students compare their results with the predicted results in Example 1. Then collect the results of all the students and compile them into one large data set. Save both the individual results and the compiled data set for review when students are learning about experimental probability.

Creating a Resource Sheet

Use before assigning the Exercises.

The notation of this lesson is often difficult for students because they are not familiar with it. Have students begin a resource sheet that they will add to throughout the chapter. The following should be included in the first entry:
- a description of how to read the notation *P*(event)
- a meaningful example that uses the notation

Leveled Lesson Resources

Chapter 9 Resource Masters

BL = Below Grade Level   **OL** = On Grade Level   **AL** = Above Grade Level   **ELL** = English Language Learner

---

Lesson Reading Guide
p. 9 BL OL ELL

NAME _____ DATE _____ PERIOD _____

9-1 Lesson Reading Guide   6SDAP3.3

Simple Events

Get Ready for the Lesson

Read the introduction at the top of page 460 in your textbook. Write your answers below.

1. What fraction of the taffy is vanilla? Write in simplest form. $\frac{1}{8}$

2. Suppose you take one piece of taffy from the box without looking. Are your chances of picking vanilla the same as picking root beer? Explain. Sample answer: Yes; there is the same number of vanilla pieces as root beer pieces.

Read the Lesson

Use the information from the introduction to answer Exercises 3–5.

3. How do you read P(cherry)? the probability of picking a piece of cherry taffy

4. $P(\text{cherry}) = \frac{6}{48}$; where does the 6 come from? Where does the 48 come from? 6 = the number of pieces of cherry taffy; 48 = the total number of pieces of taffy

5. Probability can be written as a fraction, a decimal, or a percent. Write P(cherry) as a decimal. 0.125

6. If there is a 25% chance that something will happen, what is the chance that it will *not* happen? What are these two events called? 75%; complementary events

Remember What You Learned

7. Write the equation P(A) + P(not A) = 1 in words. What does it mean with respect to event A? Sample answer: The probability of A either happening or not happening is equal to 1; it is certain that event A will either happen or not happen.

Chapter 9   9   Glencoe California Mathematics, Grade 6

Study Guide and Intervention*
p. 10 BL OL ELL

NAME _____ DATE _____ PERIOD _____

9-1 Study Guide and Intervention   6SDAP3.3

Simple Events

The **probability** of a simple event is a ratio that compares the number of favorable outcomes to the number of possible outcomes. Outcomes occur at **random** if each outcome occurs by chance.

Two events that are the only ones that can possibly happen are **complementary events**. The sum of the probabilities of complementary events is 1.

Example 1 What is the probability of rolling a multiple of 3 on a number cube marked with 1, 2, 3, 4, 5, and 6 on its faces.

$P(\text{multiple of 3}) = \frac{\text{multiples of 3 possible}}{\text{total numbers possible}}$

$= \frac{2}{6}$ Two numbers are multiples of 3: 3 and 6.

$= \frac{1}{3}$ Simplify.

The probability of rolling a multiple of 3 is $\frac{1}{3}$ or about 33.3%.

Example 2 What is the probability of *not* rolling a multiple of 3 on a number cube marked with 1, 2, 3, 4, 5, and 6 on its faces?

$P(A) + P(\text{not } A) = 1$

$\frac{1}{3} + P(\text{not } A) = 1$ Substitute $\frac{1}{3}$ for P(A).

$-\frac{1}{3} \qquad -\frac{1}{3}$ Subtract $\frac{1}{3}$ from each side

$P(\text{not } A) = \frac{2}{3}$ Simplify

The probability of not rolling a multiple of 3 is $\frac{2}{3}$ or about 66.7%.

Exercises

A set of 30 cards is numbered 1, 2, 3, ..., 30. Suppose you pick a card at random without looking. Find the probability of each event. Write as a fraction in simplest form.

1. $P(12)$ $\frac{1}{30}$

2. $P(2 \text{ or } 3)$ $\frac{1}{15}$

3. $P(\text{odd number})$ $\frac{1}{2}$

4. $P(\text{a multiple of 5})$ $\frac{1}{5}$

5. $P(\text{not a multiple of 5})$ $\frac{4}{5}$

6. $P(\text{less than or equal to 10})$ $\frac{1}{3}$

Chapter 9   10   Glencoe California Mathematics, Grade 6

Skills Practice*
p. 11 BL OL

NAME _____ DATE _____ PERIOD _____

9-1 Skills Practice   6SDAP3.3

Simple Events

A set of 12 cards is numbered 1, 2, 3, ...12. Suppose you pick a card at random without looking. Find the probability of each event. Write as a fraction in simplest form.

1. $P(5)$ $\frac{1}{12}$

2. $P(6 \text{ or } 8)$ $\frac{1}{6}$

3. $P(\text{a multiple of 3})$ $\frac{1}{3}$

4. $P(\text{an even number})$ $\frac{1}{2}$

5. $P(\text{a multiple of 4})$ $\frac{1}{4}$

6. $P(\text{less than or equal to 8})$ $\frac{2}{3}$

7. $P(\text{a factor of 12})$ $\frac{1}{2}$

8. $P(\text{not a multiple of 4})$ $\frac{3}{4}$

9. $P(1, 3, \text{ or } 11)$ $\frac{1}{4}$

10. $P(\text{a multiple a 5})$ $\frac{1}{6}$

The students at Job's high school were surveyed to determine their favorite foods. The results are shown in the table at the right. Suppose students were randomly selected and asked what their favorite food is. Find the probability of each event. Write as a fraction in simplest form.

Favorite Food	Responses
pizza	19
steak	8
chow mein	5
seafood	4
spaghetti	3
cereal	1

11. $P(\text{steak})$ $\frac{1}{5}$

12. $P(\text{spaghetti})$ $\frac{3}{40}$

13. $P(\text{cereal or seafood})$ $\frac{1}{8}$

14. $P(\text{not chow mein})$ $\frac{7}{8}$

15. $P(\text{pizza})$ $\frac{19}{40}$

16. $P(\text{cereal or steak})$ $\frac{9}{40}$

17. $P(\text{not steak})$ $\frac{4}{5}$

18. $P(\text{not cereal or seafood})$ $\frac{7}{8}$

19. $P(\text{chicken})$ 0

20. $P(\text{chow mein or spaghetti})$ $\frac{1}{5}$

Chapter 9   11   Glencoe California Mathematics, Grade 6

Practice*
p. 12 OL AL

NAME _____ DATE _____ PERIOD _____

9-1 Practice   6SDAP3.3

Simple Events

A set of cards is numbered 1, 2, 3, ... 24. Suppose you pick a card at random without looking. Find the probability of each event. Write as a fraction in simplest form.

1. $P(5)$ $\frac{1}{24}$

2. $P(\text{multiple of 4})$ $\frac{1}{4}$

3. $P(6 \text{ or } 17)$ $\frac{1}{12}$

4. $P(\text{not equal to 15})$ $\frac{23}{24}$

5. $P(\text{not a factor of 6})$ $\frac{5}{6}$

6. $P(\text{odd number})$ $\frac{1}{2}$

COMMUNITY SERVICE The table shows the students involved in community service. Suppose one student is randomly selected to represent the school at a state-wide awards ceremony. Find the probability of each event. Write as a fraction in simplest form.

Community Service	
girls	15
boys	25
6th graders	20
7th graders	8
8th graders	12

7. $P(\text{boy})$ $\frac{5}{8}$

8. $P(\text{not 6th grader})$ $\frac{1}{2}$

9. $P(\text{girl})$ $\frac{3}{8}$

10. $P(\text{8th grader})$ $\frac{3}{10}$

11. $P(\text{boy or girl})$ 1

12. $P(\text{6th or 7th grader})$ $\frac{7}{10}$

13. $P(\text{7th grader})$ $\frac{1}{5}$

14. $P(\text{not a 9th grader})$ 1

MENU A delicatessen serves different menu items, of which 2 are soups, 6 are sandwiches, and 4 are salads. How likely is it for each event to happen if you choose one item at random from the menu? Explain your reasoning.

15. $P(\text{sandwich})$ There are 6 sandwich items of the 12 menu items. $\frac{6}{12} = \frac{1}{2}$

16. $P(\text{not a soup})$ There are 2 soup items. So there are 10 non-soup items of the 12 menu items. $\frac{10}{12} = \frac{5}{6}$

17. $P(\text{salad})$ There are 4 salad items of the 12 menu items. $\frac{4}{12} = \frac{1}{3}$

18. **NUMBER CUBE** What is the probability of rolling an even number or a prime number on a number cube? Write as a fraction in simplest form. $\frac{5}{6}$

19. **CLOSING TIME** At a convenience store there is a 25% chance a customer enters the store within one minute of closing time. Describe the complementary event and find its probability. There is a 75% chance no customer will enter within one minute of closing time.

Chapter 9   12   Glencoe California Mathematics, Grade 6

Word Problem Practice*
p. 13 OL AL

NAME _____ DATE _____ PERIOD _____

9-1 Word Problem Practice   6SDAP3.3

Simple Events

COINS Susan opened her piggy bank and counted the number of each coin. The table at the right shows the results. For Exercises 1–3, assume that the coins are put in a bag and one is chosen at random.

Coin	Number
quarters	15
dimes	21
nickels	22
pennies	32

1. What is the probability that a quarter is chosen? $\frac{1}{6}$

2. What is the probability that a nickel or a dime is chosen? $\frac{43}{90}$

3. What is the probability that the chosen coin is worth more than 5 cents? $\frac{2}{5}$

4. **NUMBER CUBES** Juan has two number cubes, each with faces numbered 1, 2, ...6. What is the probability that he can roll the cubes so that the sum of the faces showing equals 11? $\frac{1}{18}$

5. **SKATEBOARDS** Carlotta bought a new skateboard for which the probability of having a defective wheel is 0.015. What is the probability of not having a defective wheel? 0.985

6. **CALCULATORS** Jake's teacher had 6 calculators for 28 students to use. If the first students to use the calculators are chosen at random, what is the probability that Jake will get one? $\frac{3}{14}$

7. **VEHICLES** The rental car company had 14 sedans and 8 minivans available to rent. If the next customer picks a vehicle at random, what is the probability that a minivan is chosen? $\frac{4}{11}$

8. **MUSIC** Tina has 16 pop CDs, 6 classical, and 2 rock. Tina chooses a CD at random. What is the probability she does not choose a classical CD? $\frac{3}{4}$

Chapter 9   13   Glencoe California Mathematics, Grade 6

Enrichment
p. 14 OL AL

NAME _____ DATE _____ PERIOD _____

9-1 Enrichment   6SDAP3.1

Coin-Tossing Experiments

If a coin is tossed 3 times, there are 8 possible outcomes. They are listed in the table below.

Number of Heads	0	1	2	3
Outcomes	TTT	HTT	HHT	HHH
		THT	THH	
		TTH	HTH	

Once all the outcomes are known, the probability of any event can be found. For example, the probability of getting 2 heads is $\frac{3}{8}$. Notice that this is the same as getting 1 tail.

1. A coin is tossed 4 times. Complete this chart to show the possible outcomes.

Number of Heads	0	1	2	3	4
Outcomes	TTTT	HTTT	HHTT	THHH	HHHH
		THTT	HTHT	HTHH	
		TTHT	HTHT	HTHH	
		TTTH	TTHH	HHHT	
			THTH		
			HTTH		

2. What is the probability of getting all tails? $\frac{1}{16}$

3. Now complete this table. Make charts like the one in Exercise 1 to help find the answers. Look for patterns in the numbers.

Number of Coin Tosses	2	3	4	5	6	7	8
Total Outcomes	4	8	16	32	64	128	256
Probability of Getting All Tails	$\frac{1}{4}$	$\frac{1}{8}$	$\frac{1}{16}$	$\frac{1}{32}$	$\frac{1}{64}$	$\frac{1}{128}$	$\frac{1}{256}$

4. What happens to the number of outcomes? the probability of all tails? Sample answer: It is doubling; it is halving.

Chapter 9   14   Glencoe California Mathematics, Grade 6

Additional Lesson Resources

*** Also available in Spanish ELL**

Transparencies
- *5-Minute Check Transparency,* Lesson 9-1

Other Print Products
- *Noteables™ Interactive Study Notebook with Foldables™*

Teacher Tech Tools
- *Interactive Classroom CD-ROM,* Lesson 9-1
- *AssignmentWorks CD-ROM,* Lesson 9-1

Student Tech Tools
ca.gr6math.com
- Extra Examples, Chapter 9, Lesson 1
- Self-Check Quiz, Chapter 9, Lesson 1

9-1 Simple Events

1 Focus

Standards Alignment

Before Lesson 9-1
Use fractions and percentages to compare data sets of different sizes from Standard 5SDAP1.3

Lesson 9-1
Represent probabilities as ratios, proportions, decimals, and percentages and verify that the probabilities computed are reasonable; know that if P is the probability of an event, $1 - P$ is the probability of an event *not* occurring from Standard 6SDAP3.3

After Lesson 9-1
Understand that the probability of either of two disjoint events occurring is the sum of the two individual probabilities and that the probability of one event following another, in independent trials, is the product of the two probabilities from Standard 6SDAP3.4

2 Teach

Scaffolding Questions

Ask the class to imagine a bag with 10 marbles. Say that 7 of the marbles are green, 2 are red, and 1 is yellow.

Ask:

• If I pick a marble without looking, what color am I most likely to pick?
green

• If I pick a marble without looking, what color am I least likely to pick?
yellow

• Am I likely to pick a red marble? no

• Am I likely to pick a marble that is not red? yes

Main IDEA
Find the probability of a simple event.

 Standard 6SDAP3.3
Represent probabilities as ratios, proportions, decimals between 0 and 1, and percentages between 0 and 100 and verify that the probabilities computed are reasonable; know that if P is the probability of an event, $1 - P$ is the probability of an event *not* occurring.

NEW Vocabulary

outcome
simple event
probability
random
complementary event

2. Sample answer: Yes; there is the same number of vanilla pieces as root beer pieces.

READING Math

Probability
P(even number) is read *the probability of rolling an even number.*

GET READY for the Lesson

Saltwater Taffy Flavors	
peppermint	chocolate
grape	raspberry
root beer	orange creme
cherry	vanilla

TAFFY A box of saltwater taffy contains six pieces of each flavor shown at the right.

1. What fraction of the taffy is vanilla? Write in simplest form. $\frac{1}{8}$

2. Suppose you take one piece of taffy from the box without looking. Are your chances of picking vanilla the same as picking root beer? Explain.

An **outcome** is any one of the possible results of an action. For the action of picking a piece of taffy out of the box described above, there are 48 total outcomes.

A **simple event** is one outcome or a collection of outcomes. For example, picking a piece of vanilla taffy is a simple event. The chance of that event happening is called its **probability**.

KEY CONCEPT — Probability

Words	If all outcomes are equally likely, the probability of a simple event is a ratio that compares the number of favorable outcomes to the number of possible outcomes.
Symbols	$P(\text{event}) = \dfrac{\text{number of favorable outcomes}}{\text{number of possible outcomes}}$

EXAMPLE Find Probability

① What is the probability of rolling an even number on a number cube marked with 1, 2, 3, 4, 5, and 6 on its faces?

$$P(\text{even number}) = \frac{\text{even numbers possible}}{\text{total numbers possible}}$$
$$= \frac{3}{6} \text{ or } \frac{1}{2}$$

The probability of rolling an even number is $\frac{1}{2}$, 0.5, or 50%.

CHECK Your Progress

Use the number cube above to find each probability. Write as a fraction in simplest form.

a. P(odd number) $\frac{1}{2}$ b. P(5 or 6) $\frac{1}{3}$ c. P(prime number) $\frac{1}{2}$

460 Chapter 9 Probability

 Formative Assessment

Use the Check Your Progress exercises after each Example to determine students' understanding of concepts.

Favorable Outcomes

Tips for New Teachers

It may be helpful to explain what *favorable* means, especially to ELL students. Have students brainstorm similar words, such as *favor* and *favorite* and use the meanings of these words to help explain the meaning of the word *favorable* in terms of probability outcomes.

Outcomes occur at **random** if each outcome occurs by chance. For example, rolling a number on a number cube occurs at random.

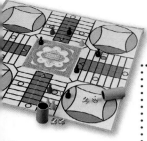

Real-World EXAMPLE

2 **PARCHEESI** Jewel and her three friends are playing Parcheesi. To decide which player goes first, each player rolls a number cube. The player who rolls the lowest number goes first. If her friends rolled a 4, 3, and 5, what is the probability that Jewel will go first?

The possible outcomes of rolling a number cube are 1, 2, 3, 4, 5, and 6. In order for Jewel to go first, she will need to roll a 1 or 2.

Let $P(A)$ be the probability that Jewel will go first.

$P(A) = \dfrac{\text{number of favorable outcomes}}{\text{number of possible outcomes}}$

$\quad = \dfrac{2}{6}$ There are 6 possible outcomes and 2 of them are favorable.

$\quad = \dfrac{1}{3}$ Simplify.

The probability that Jewel will go first is $\dfrac{1}{3}$, $0.\overline{3}$, or about 33%.

Real-World Link . . . .
Parcheesi is derived from the Indian word *pacis*, which means 25.
Source: www.yesterdayland.com

CHECK Your Progress

MUSIC The table at the right shows the numbers of brass instruments in the California Symphony. Suppose one brass instrument musician is randomly selected to be a featured performer. Find the probability of each event. Write as a fraction in simplest form.

California Symphony Brass Instruments	
Horn	3
Trombone	3
Trumpet	2
Tuba	1

d. $P(\text{trumpet})$ $\dfrac{2}{9}$

e. $P(\text{brass})$ **1**

f. $P(\text{flute})$ **0**

g. $P(\text{horn or tuba})$ $\dfrac{4}{9}$

COncepts in MOtion
BrainPOP® ca.gr6math.com

The probability that an event will happen can be any number from 0 to 1, including 0 and 1, as shown on the number line below. Notice that probabilities can be written as fractions, decimals, or percents.

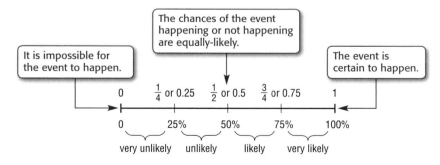

Focus on Mathematical Content

Probability is a measurement of the likelihood that an event will occur. Probability is often written as a ratio or fraction.

The sum of the probability of an event occurring and its **complement**—the probability of it *not* occurring—is always 1.

ADDITIONAL EXAMPLES

1 If the spinner shown below is spun once, what is the probability of its landing on an odd number? $\dfrac{1}{2}$

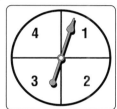

2 **GAMES** A game requires spinning the spinner shown in Additional Example 1. If the number spun is greater than 3, the player wins. What is the probability of winning the game? $\dfrac{1}{4}$

Additional Examples are also in:
• Noteables™ Interactive Study Notebook with Foldables™
• Interactive Classroom PowerPoint® Presentations

Either Jewel will go first or she will *not* go first. These two events are **complementary events**. The sum of the probabilities of an event and its complement is 1 or 100%. In symbols, $P(A) + P(not\ A) = 1$.

STUDY TiP

Complement of an Event The probability that event *A* will not occur is noted as $P(not\ A)$. Since $P(A) + P(not\ A) = 1$, $P(not\ A) = 1 - P(A)$. $P(not\ A)$ is read as *the probability of the complement of A.*

EXAMPLE Complementary Events

3 **PARCHEESI** Refer to Example 2. Find the probability that Jewel will *not* go first.

The probability that Jewel will *not* go first is the complement of the probability that Jewel will go first.

$P(A) + P(not\ A) = 1$	Property of Complementary Events
$\frac{1}{3} + P(not\ A) = 1$	Substitute $\frac{1}{3}$ for $P(A)$.
$\underline{-\frac{1}{3} \qquad\qquad -\frac{1}{3}}$	Subtract $\frac{1}{3}$ from each side.
$P(not\ A) = \frac{2}{3}$	$1 - \frac{1}{3}$ is $\frac{3}{3} - \frac{1}{3}$ or $\frac{2}{3}$

The probability that Jewel will *not* go first is $\frac{2}{3}$, $0.\overline{6}$, or about 67%.

CHECK Your Progress

SCHOOL Ramón's teacher uses a spinner similar to the one shown at the right to determine the order in which each group will make their presentation. Use the spinner to find each probability. Write as a fraction in simplest form.

h. $P(not$ group 4) $\frac{5}{6}$ **i.** $P(not$ group 1 or group 3) $\frac{2}{3}$

online Personal Tutor at ca.gr6math.com

★ indicates multi-step problem

CHECK Your Understanding

Example 1
(p. 460)

Use the spinner to find each probability. Write as a fraction in simplest form.

1. $P(J)$ $\frac{1}{12}$ **2.** $P(E\ or\ H)$ $\frac{1}{6}$ **3.** $P(vowel)$ $\frac{1}{4}$

Examples 2, 3
(pp. 461–462)

MARBLES Robert has a bag that contains 7 blue, 5 purple, 12 red, and 6 orange marbles. Find each probability if he draws one marble at random from the bag. Write as a fraction in simplest form.

4. $P(purple)$ $\frac{1}{6}$ **5.** $P(red\ or\ orange)$ $\frac{3}{5}$ **6.** $P(green)$ 0

7. $P(not$ blue) $\frac{23}{30}$ **8.** $P(not$ red or orange) $\frac{2}{5}$ **9.** $P(not$ yellow) 1

Example 3
(p. 462)

10. **SURVEYS** Shanté asked her classmates how many $\frac{21}{25}$ pets they own. The responses are in the table. If a student in her class is selected at random, what is the probability that the student does *not* own 3 or more pets?

Number of Pets	Response
None	6
1–2	15
3 or more	4

Exercises

HOMEWORK HELP

For Exercises	See Examples
11–14	1
17–22	2
15–16, 23–26	3

Exercise Levels:
A: 11–26
B: 27–30
C: 31–34

A set of 20 cards is numbered 1, 2, 3, . . ., 20. Suppose you pick a card at random without looking. Find the probability of each event. Write as a fraction in simplest form.

11. $P(1)$ $\frac{1}{20}$ 12. $P(3 \text{ or } 13)$ $\frac{1}{10}$ 13. $P(\text{multiple of } 3)$ $\frac{3}{10}$

14. $P(\text{even number})$ $\frac{1}{2}$ 15. $P(\text{not } 20)$ $\frac{19}{20}$ 16. $P(\text{not a factor of } 10)$ $\frac{4}{5}$

STUDENT COUNCIL The table shows the membership of the Student Council at Lincoln Middle School. Suppose one student is randomly selected as the president. Find the probability of each event. Write as a fraction in simplest form.

Student Council	
girls	30
boys	20
8th graders	25
7th graders	15
6th graders	10

17. $P(\text{girl})$ $\frac{3}{5}$ 18. $P(\text{boy})$ $\frac{2}{5}$

19. $P(\text{5th grader})$ 0 20. $P(\text{8th grader})$ $\frac{1}{2}$

21. $P(\text{boy or girl})$ 1 22. $P(\text{6th or 8th grader})$ $\frac{7}{10}$

23. $P(\text{not 6th grader})$ $\frac{4}{5}$ 24. $P(\text{not 7th grader})$ $\frac{7}{10}$

25. **SOUP** A cupboard contains 20 soup cans. Seven are tomato, 4 are cream of mushroom, 5 are chicken, and 4 are vegetable. If one can is chosen at random from the cupboard, what is the probability that it is *neither* cream of mushroom *nor* vegetable soup? Write as a percent. **60%**

26. **VIDEOS** In a drawing, one name is randomly chosen from a jar of 75 names to receive free video rentals for a month. If Enola entered her name 8 times, what is the probability that she is *not* chosen to receive the free rentals? Write as a fraction in simplest form. $\frac{67}{75}$

27. $\frac{1}{11}$; Sample answer: The bar height for $111–160 is low compared to other bar heights, so the probability should be relatively low.

27. **TECHNOLOGY** The graph shows the cost of 22 digital cameras. If one camera is chosen at random, what is the probability that the cost ranges from $111 up to $160? Write as a fraction in simplest form. Explain how you know the answer is reasonable.

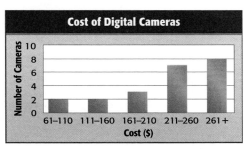

28. **MOVIES** The probability of buying a defective DVD is 0.002. What is the probability of buying a DVD that is *not* defective? **0.998**

29. **WEATHER** The forecast for tomorrow says that there is a 37% chance of rain. ★ Describe the complementary event and predict its probability. **See margin.**

EXTRA PRACTICE

See pages 701, 723.

Math Online
Self-Check Quiz at ca.gr6math.com

30. **FUND-RAISER** The Jefferson Middle School Band is selling raffle tickets for a new computer system. They sold 1,000 tickets at $2 each. Ted's parents spent $200 on tickets. What is the probability they will *not* win? $\frac{9}{10}$

Lesson 9-1 Simple Events   **463**

DIFFERENTIATED HOMEWORK OPTIONS

Level	Assignment	Two-Day Option	
BL Basic	11–26, 31, 33–43	11–25 odd, 35, 36	12–26 even, 31, 33, 34, 37–43
OL Core	11–23 odd, 25–31, 33–43	11–26, 35, 36	27–31, 33–34, 37–43
AL Advanced/Pre-AP	27–38 (optional: 39–43)		

Odd/Even Assignments

Exercises 11–26 are structured so that students practice the same concepts whether they are assigned odd or even problems.

Additional Answer

29. Sample answer: The complementary event is the chance of no rain. Its probability is 63%.

Ticket Out the Door Write a sentence such as "Probability is the likely topic of tomorrow's lesson" on the board. Have students imagine all of the letters of the sentence in a bag. Have them find the probability of randomly picking a vowel from the bag.

 Foldables™
Study Organizer **Follow-Up**

Remind students to write a descriptive paragraph under the tab for this lesson of their Foldables. Encourage them to describe the thoughts and experiences they had while working on the lesson. Do they feel any differently about probability now?

Additional Answers

31a. 1; Sample answer: Since 2032 is a leap year, there will be 29 days in February, making this event certain to happen.

31b. 0; Sample answer: Since 2058 is not a leap year, there will only be 28 days in February, making this event impossible to happen.

32. 3; Sample answer: There are currently $6 + 4 + 8$ or 18 marbles in the bag. A total of $27 - 18$ or 9 marbles should be added to the bag. To do so without changing the probability of randomly selecting one marble of each color, add 3 red marbles, 2 blue marbles, and 4 green marbles. Then, $P(\text{red}) = \frac{9}{27}$ or $\frac{1}{3}$, $P(\text{blue}) = \frac{6}{27}$ or $\frac{2}{9}$, and $P(\text{green}) = \frac{12}{27}$ or $\frac{4}{9}$.

33. 0.65, 0.55 are probabilities that are not complementary because $0.65 + 0.55 \neq 1$. The other sets of probability are complementary.

H.O.T. Problems

31–33. See margin.

34. See Ch. 9 Answer Appendix.

31. REASONING A *leap year* has 366 days and occurs in non-century years that are evenly divisible by 4. The extra day is added as February 29th. Determine whether each probability is 0 or 1. Explain your reasoning.

  a. P(there will be 29 days in February in 2032)

  b. P(there will be 29 days in February in 2058)

32. CHALLENGE A bag contains 6 red marbles, 4 blue marbles, and 8 green marbles. How many marbles of each color should be added so that the total number of marbles is 27, but the probability of randomly selecting one marble of each color remains unchanged? Explain your reasoning.

33. Which One Doesn't Belong? Identify the pair of probabilities that does not represent probabilities of complementary events. Explain your reasoning.

$\frac{5}{8}, \frac{3}{8}$	0.65, 0.55	$\frac{4}{6}, \frac{1}{3}$	0.875, $\frac{1}{8}$

34. **WRITING IN MATH** Marissa has 5 black T-shirts, 2 purple T-shirts, and 1 orange T-shirt. Without calculating, determine whether each of the following probabilities is reasonable if she randomly selects one T-shirt. Explain your reasoning.

  a. $P(\text{black T-shirt}) = \frac{1}{3}$ **b.** $P(\text{orange T-shirt}) = \frac{4}{5}$ **c.** $P(\text{purple T-shirt}) = \frac{1}{4}$

STANDARDS PRACTICE 6SDAP3.3

35. A bag contains 8 blue marbles, 15 red marbles, 10 yellow marbles, and 3 brown marbles. If a marble is randomly selected, what is the probability that it will be brown? **C**

  A 0.27   **C** $0.08\overline{3}$

  B 11%   **D** $\frac{3}{8}$

36. What is the probability of the spinner landing on a number less than 3? **G**

  F 25%   **H** 50%

  G 37.5%   **J** 75%

Spiral Review

37. RAIN The scatter plot shows the relationship between rainfall and lawn growth. Why might the graph be misleading? (Lesson 8-8) **There are no labels on the vertical scale.**

38. PARKS A researcher randomly selected 100 households near a city park. Of these, 26% said they visit the park daily. If there are 500 households near the park, about how many visit it daily? (Lesson 8-8) **about 130 households**

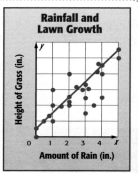

Rainfall and Lawn Growth

▶ **GET READY for the Next Lesson**

PREREQUISITE SKILL Write each fraction in simplest form. (Lesson 4-4)

39. $\frac{2}{6}$ $\frac{1}{3}$ **40.** $\frac{6}{8}$ $\frac{3}{4}$ **41.** $\frac{15}{30}$ $\frac{1}{2}$ **42.** $\frac{6}{16}$ $\frac{3}{8}$ **43.** $\frac{18}{32}$ $\frac{9}{16}$

464 Chapter 9 Probability

Differentiated Instruction

Kinesthetic Learners Separate students into pairs. Give each pair a number cube. Have the members of each pair calculate the probability of an event such as $P(> 4)$, $P(\leq 4)$, or $P(\text{prime number})$. Then have them roll the cube 10 times and record the results. How close were their results to the calculated probability? Finally, have them roll the cube 30 times and record the results. Were their results closer to the calculated probability after 30 rolls than after 10 rolls?

9-2 Sample Spaces

Standard 6SDAP3.1 Represent all possible outcomes for compound events in an organized way (e.g., tables, grids, tree diagrams) and express the theoretical probability of each outcome.

PACING: **Regular:** 1 period, **Block:** 0.5 period

Options for Differentiated Instruction

 = English Language Learner   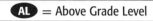 = Above Grade Level   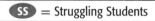 = Struggling Students   = Special Needs

Language Skills

Use before presenting Lesson 9-2.

Before beginning the lesson, prepare an outline of your lecture for the lesson and distribute it to students. This is especially helpful for ELL students, as it allows them to follow the lesson more easily and become more confident in participating in class discussions.

- Avoid correcting ELL students in front of their classmates.
- Allow sufficient time for them to take notes, complete examples, and solve problems.
- Do not pressure them to speak, but rather, encourage them to participate when they are ready.

Understanding the Concept

Use after presenting Example 2.

When dealing with repeated events, having students imagine that the events are occurring one after the other helps them conceptualize the sample space. However, they should understand that events can be simultaneous without affecting the sample space. For example, the tree diagrams below show that the events of tossing a coin twice and tossing two coins at the same time both have the same sample space.

One Coin is Tossed Twice	Two Coins are Tossed at the Same Time
First Toss Second Toss	First Coin Second Coin

```
One Coin is                    Two Coins are Tossed
Tossed Twice                     at the Same Time

First         Second         First         Second
Toss           Toss          Coin           Coin

                    H                             H
        H <                          H <
                    T                             T

                    H                             H
        T <                          T <
                    T                             T
```

Language Skills

Use with the exercises.

- Scaffold the experience of drawing a tree diagram by providing an incomplete diagram that students can fill in for Exercises 5–10. For each exercise, leave more work for the students to fill in than in the previous exercise, until they are ready to create a sample space on their own.

Leveled Lesson Resources

Chapter 9 Resource Masters

BL = Below Grade Level   **OL** = On Grade Level   **AL** = Above Grade Level   **ELL** = English Language Learner

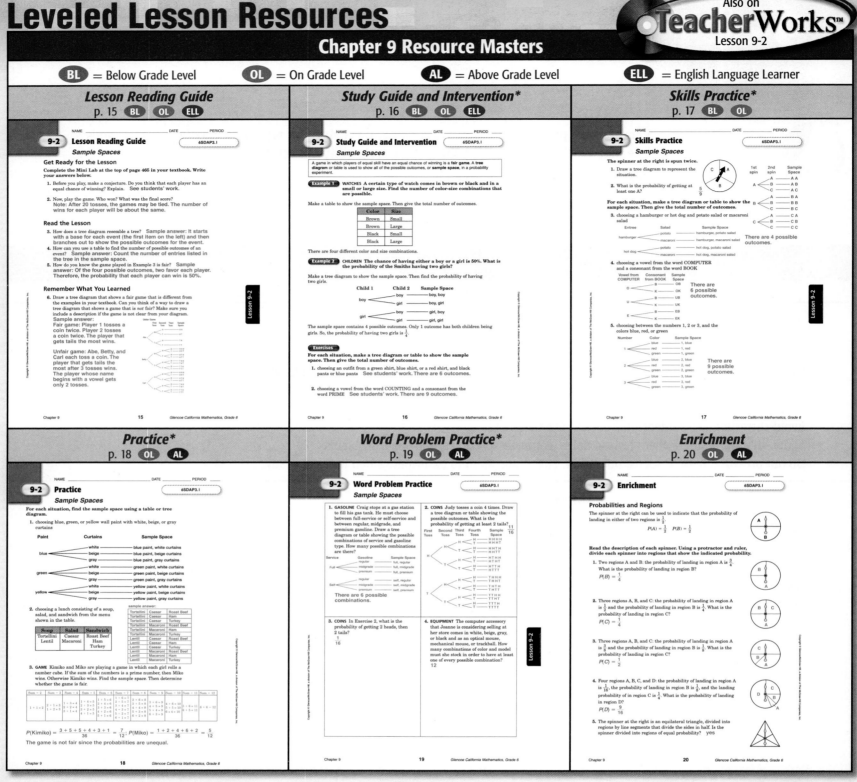

Lesson Reading Guide
p. 15 **BL** **OL** **ELL**

Study Guide and Intervention*
p. 16 **BL** **OL** **ELL**

Skills Practice*
p. 17 **BL** **OL**

Practice*
p. 18 **OL** **AL**

Word Problem Practice*
p. 19 **OL** **AL**

Enrichment
p. 20 **OL** **AL**

Additional Lesson Resources

* Also available in Spanish **ELL**

Transparencies
- *5-Minute Check Transparency,* Lesson 9-2

Other Print Products
- *Noteables™ Interactive Study Notebook with Foldables™*

Teacher Tech Tools
- *Interactive Classroom CD-ROM,* Lesson 9-2
- *AssignmentWorks CD-ROM,* Lesson 9-2

Student Tech Tools
ca.gr6math.com
- Extra Examples, Chapter 9, Lesson 2
- Self-Check Quiz, Chapter 9, Lesson 2

Main IDEA

Find sample spaces and probabilities.

 Standard 6SDAP3.1 **Represent all possible outcomes for compound events in an organized way (e.g., tables, grids, tree diagrams) and express the theoretical probability of each outcome.**

NEW Vocabulary

sample space
tree diagram
fair game

2. Note: After 20 tosses, the games may be tied. The number of wins for each player will be about the same.

STUDY TIP

Making a Table Begin with one choice and list *all* of the outcomes that correspond with that choice before listing the outcomes that correspond with another choice.

a. See Ch. 9 Answer Appendix.

▶ MINI Lab

Here is a probability game that you can play with two counters.

- Mark one side of the first counter A. Mark the other side B. Mark both sides of the second counter A.
- Player 1 tosses the counters. If both sides shown are the same, Player 1 wins a point. If the sides are different, Player 2 wins a point. Record your results.
- Player 2 then tosses the counters and the results are recorded. Continue alternating the tosses until each player has tossed the counters ten times. The player with the most points wins.

1. Before you play, make a conjecture. Do you think that each player has an equal chance of winning? Explain. **See students' work.**

2. Now, play the game. Who won? What was the final score?

The set of all of the possible outcomes in a probability experiment is called the **sample space**. A table or grid can be used to list the outcomes in the sample space.

EXAMPLE Find the Sample Space

1 **ICE CREAM** A vendor sells vanilla and chocolate ice cream. Customers can choose from a waffle or sugar cone and either hot fudge or caramel topping. Find the sample space for all possible orders of one scoop of ice cream in a cone with one topping.

Make a table that shows all of the possible outcomes.

Outcomes		
Vanilla	Waffle	Hot Fudge
Vanilla	Waffle	Caramel
Vanilla	Sugar	Hot Fudge
Vanilla	Sugar	Caramel
Chocolate	Waffle	Hot Fudge
Chocolate	Waffle	Caramel
Chocolate	Sugar	Hot Fudge
Chocolate	Sugar	Caramel

✓ CHECK Your Progress

a. **PETS** The animal shelter has both male and female Labradors in yellow, brown, or black. Find the sample space for all possible Labradors available at the shelter.

 **Personal Tutor at** ca.gr6math.com

1 Focus

 Standards Alignment

Before Lesson 9-2
Represent all possible outcomes for a simple probability situation in an organized way from Standard 4SDAP2.1

Lesson 9-2
Represent all possible outcomes for compound events in an organized way and express the theoretical probability of each outcome from ◆— Standard 6SDAP3.1

After Lesson 9-2
Represent probabilities as ratios, proportions, decimals, and percentages and verify that the probabilities computed are reasonable; know that if *P* is the probability of an event, 1 − *P* is the probability of an event *not* occurring from ◆— Standard 6SDAP3.3

2 Teach

▶ MINI Lab

You may find that the easiest way to mark the counters is to place a piece of masking tape on each side of each counter, and then mark the masking tape. Make sure students make their conjectures before they play.

Scaffolding Questions

As you ask the following questions, write students' answers on the board.

Ask:

- If I toss a coin once, what are the possible outcomes? H, T (H = heads, T = tails)

- If I toss a coin twice, what are the possible outcomes? HH, HT, TH, TT

Tips for New Teachers

Sample Spaces

After students complete the Mini Lab, collect the data from the entire class. Have them find the combined score for Player 1 versus Player 2. Note that the number of wins for each player should be about the same.

- If I toss a coin three times, what are the possible outcomes? HHH, HHT, HTH, HTT, THH, THT, TTH, TTT

1 **CHILDREN** A couple would like to have two children. Find the sample space of the children's genders if having a boy is equally likely as having a girl.

girl	girl
girl	boy
boy	boy
boy	girl

2 **STANDARDS EXAMPLE** Amy was trying to decide what kind of sandwich to make. She had two kinds of bread, wheat and sourdough. And she had three kinds of lunchmeat: ham, turkey, and roast beef. Which list shows all the possible bread-lunchmeat combinations? C

A Outcomes

wheat	ham
sourdough	turkey
wheat	turkey
sourdough	ham

B Outcomes

wheat	ham
wheat	turkey
wheat	roast beef

C Outcomes

wheat	ham
wheat	turkey
wheat	roast beef
sourdough	ham
sourdough	turkey
sourdough	roast beef

D Outcomes

wheat	turkey
sourdough	turkey
wheat	turkey
sourdough	ham
wheat	ham
sourdough	ham

A **tree diagram** can also be used to display the sample space.

STANDARDS EXAMPLE 6SDAP3.1

2 A scooter comes in silver, red, or purple with 125 or 180-millimeter wheel sizes. Which list shows all possible color-wheel size outcomes?

A Outcomes

silver	125 mm
silver	180 mm
red	125 mm
red	180 mm
purple	125 mm
purple	180 mm

C Outcomes

silver	125 mm
red	180 mm
purple	125 mm
silver	180 mm

B Outcomes

silver	125 mm
red	180 mm
purple	125 mm

D Outcomes

silver	125 mm
red	180 mm
purple	125 mm
silver	180 mm
purple	180 mm

Test-Taking Tip

Educated Guess Find out if there is a penalty for incorrect answers. If there is no penalty, making an educated guess can only increase your score, or at worst, leave your score the same.

Read the Item The scooter comes in 3 colors, silver, red, or purple, and 2 wheel sizes, 125 or 180 millimeters. Find all of the color-wheel size combinations.

Solve the Item

Make a tree diagram to show the sample space.

There are 6 different color-wheel size combinations. The answer is A.

Scooter Color	Wheel Size	Sample Space
silver	125 mm	silver, 125 mm
	180 mm	silver, 180 mm
red	125 mm	red, 125 mm
	180 mm	red, 180 mm
purple	125 mm	purple, 125 mm
	180 mm	purple, 180 mm

 CHECK Your Progress

b. For dessert, you can have apple or cherry pie with or without ice cream. Which list shows all the possible outcomes of choosing pie and ice cream? G

F Outcomes

apple	with ice cream
cherry	without ice cream

H Outcomes

apple	without ice cream
cherry	with ice cream

G Outcomes

apple	with ice cream
apple	without ice cream
cherry	with ice cream
cherry	without ice cream

J Outcomes

apple	with ice cream
cherry	with ice cream
apple	without ice cream

Formative Assessment

Use the Check Your Progress exercises after each Example to determine students' understanding of concepts.

Focus on Mathematical Content

A **sample space** contains all the possible outcomes of a probability experiment. **Tables** and **tree diagrams** are good ways to display sample spaces.

You can use a table or a tree diagram to find the probability of an event.

EXAMPLE Find Probability

③ **GAMES** Refer to the Mini Lab at the start of this lesson. Find the sample space. Then find the probability that player 2 wins.

There are 4 equally-likely outcomes with 2 favoring each player. So, the probability that player 2 wins is $\frac{2}{4}$, or $\frac{1}{2}$.

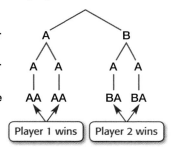

First Counter

Second Counter

Sample Space

Player 1 wins   Player 2 wins

✓ CHECK **Your Progress**

c. **GAMES** Pablo tosses three coins. If all three coins show up heads, Pablo wins. Otherwise, Kara wins. Find the sample space. Then find the probability that Pablo wins. **See Ch. 9 Answer Appendix.**

★ indicates multi-step problem

CHECK **Your Understanding**

Examples 1, 2
(pp. 465–466)

For each situation, find the sample space using a table or tree diagram.

1. A number cube is rolled twice. **1–2. See Ch. 9 Answer Appendix.**

2. A pair of brown or black sandals are available in sizes 7, 8, or 9.

Example 2
(p. 466)
6SDAP3.1

3. **STANDARDS PRACTICE** Sandwiches can be made with ham or turkey on rye, white, or sourdough breads. Which list shows all the possible outcomes? **C**

A

Outcomes	
ham	rye
turkey	white
ham	sourdough
ham	rye
turkey	white
turkey	sourdough

C

Outcomes	
ham	rye
turkey	rye
ham	white
turkey	white
ham	sourdough
turkey	sourdough

B

Outcomes	
ham	rye
turkey	white
turkey	sourdough

D

Outcomes	
ham	rye
turkey	white
ham	sourdough

4. See Ch. 9 Answer Appendix.

Example 3
(p. 467)

4. **GAMES** Brianna spins a spinner with four sections of equal size twice, labeled A, B, C, and D. If letter A is spun at least once, Brianna wins. Otherwise, Odell wins. Find the probability that Odell wins.

ADDITIONAL EXAMPLE

③ **GAMES** Peter and Linda are playing a game in which the spinner below is spun twice. If the sum of the numbers spun is even, Peter wins. If the sum of the numbers is odd, Linda wins. Find the sample space. Then find the probability that Linda wins.

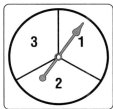

$$1 \begin{cases} 1 \text{—} 1 + 1 = 2 \\ 2 \text{—} 1 + 2 = 3 \\ 3 \text{—} 1 + 3 = 4 \end{cases}$$
$$2 \begin{cases} 1 \text{—} 2 + 1 = 3 \\ 2 \text{—} 2 + 2 = 4 \\ 3 \text{—} 2 + 3 = 5 \end{cases}$$
$$3 \begin{cases} 1 \text{—} 3 + 1 = 4 \\ 2 \text{—} 3 + 2 = 5 \\ 3 \text{—} 3 + 3 = 6 \end{cases}$$

$\frac{4}{9}$

Additional Examples are also in:

• Noteables™ Interactive Study Notebook with Foldables™

• Interactive Classroom PowerPoint® Presentations

③ **Practice**

✓ **Formative Assessment**

Use Exercises 1–4 to check for understanding.

Then use the chart at the bottom of the next page to customize your assignments for students.

Intervention You may wish to use the Study Guide and Intervention Master on page 16 of the *Chapter 9 Resource Masters* for additional reinforcement.

Tips for New Teachers **Tree Diagrams**

Tree diagrams can be made either horizontally, as in Example 2, or vertically, as in Example 3.

Tips for New Teachers **Probability Games**

For games in which number cubes or coins are rolled or tossed simultaneously (such as in Exercise 13), some students will find it easier to conceptualize the game as repeated events—first the quarter is tossed, then the dime, and then the nickel. Make sure students understand that they will find the same sample space whether the coins are tossed simultaneously or one at a time.

Odd/Even Assignments

Exercises 5–14 are structured so that students practice the same concepts whether they are assigned odd or even problems.

Additional Answers

6. Sample answer:

Outcomes	
Circle	Boots
Circle	Gym Shoes
Circle	Dress Shoes
Square	Boots
Square	Gym Shoes
Square	Dress Shoes

7. Sample answer:

Coin	Number Cube	Sample Space

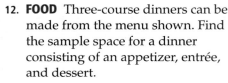

```
          1 ———— H1
          2 ———— H2
          3 ———— H3
    H  <  4 ———— H4
          5 ———— H5
          6 ———— H6

          1 ———— T1
          2 ———— T2
    T  <  3 ———— T3
          4 ———— T4
          5 ———— T5
          6 ———— T6
```

Exercises

HOMEWORK HELP

For Exercises	See Examples
5–12	1, 2
28	2
13–14	3

Exercise Levels
A: 5–14
B: 15–23
C: 24–27

5, 8–12. See Ch. 9 Answer Appendix.

6–7. See margin.

For each situation, find the sample space using a table or tree diagram.

5. choosing a card with a shape and spinning the spinner from the choices at the right

6. choosing a card with a shape and either boots, gym shoes, or dress shoes

7. tossing a coin and rolling a number cube

8. picking a number from 1 to 5 and choosing the color red, white, or blue

9. choosing a purple, green, black, or silver mountain bike having 10, 18, 21, or 24 speeds

10. choosing a letter from the word SPACE and choosing a consonant from the word MATH

11. **CLOTHES** Jerry can buy a school T-shirt with either short sleeves or long sleeves in either gray or white and in small, medium, or large. Find the sample space for all possible T-shirts he can buy.

12. **FOOD** Three-course dinners can be made from the menu shown. Find the sample space for a dinner consisting of an appetizer, entrée, and dessert.

Appetizers	Entrees	Desserts
Soup	Steak	Carrot Cake
Salad	Chicken	Cheesecake
	Fish	

13–14. See Ch. 9 Answer Appendix.

For each game, find the sample space. Then find the indicated probability.

13. Elba tosses a quarter, a dime, and a nickel. If tails comes up at least twice, ★ Steve wins. Otherwise Elba wins. Find P(Elba wins).

14. Ming rolls a number cube, tosses a coin, and chooses a card from two cards ★ marked A and B. If an even number and heads appears, Ming wins, no matter which card is chosen. Otherwise Lashonda wins. Find P(Ming wins).

Real-World Link
The average family size in the United States is 2.59 people.
Source: U.S. Census Bureau

FAMILIES Mr. and Mrs. Romero are expecting triplets. Suppose the chance of each child being a boy is 50% and of being a girl is 50%. Find each probability.

15. P(all three children will be boys) $\frac{1}{8}$ 16. P(at least one boy and one girl) $\frac{3}{4}$

17. P(two boys and one girl) $\frac{3}{8}$ 18. P(at least two girls) $\frac{1}{2}$

19. P(the first two born are boys and the last born is a girl) $\frac{1}{8}$

20. P(Player 1) $= \frac{6}{8}$, or $\frac{3}{4}$; P(Player 2) $= \frac{2}{8}$, or $\frac{1}{4}$

20. **GAMES** The following is a game for two players. Find the probability that each player wins.

   • Three counters are labeled according to the table at the right.

   • Toss the three counters.

   • If exactly 2 counters match, Player 1 scores a point. Otherwise, Player 2 scores a point.

	Side 1	Side 2
Counter 1	A	B
Counter 2	A	C
Counter 3	B	C

468 Chapter 9 Probability

DIFFERENTIATED HOMEWORK OPTIONS

Level	Assignment	Two-Day Option	
BL Basic	5–14, 25–44	5–13 odd, 28	6–14 even, 25–27, 29–44
OL Core	5–19 odd, 20–23, 25–44	5–14, 28	15–23, 25–27, 29–44
AL Advanced/Pre-AP	15–40, (optional: 41–44)		

	Home Jersey	Road Jersey	Practice Jersey	Cap
Green	0	0	2	2
White	1	0	0	0
Gray	0	1	0	0

Linus is a big fan of the Oakland Athletics baseball team and wears a different jersey and cap every time he goes to a game. The table shows the number of different jerseys and caps Linus owns.

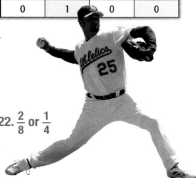

21. How many jersey/cap combinations can Linus wear when he goes to the baseball game to cheer on the Athletics? **8**

22. If Linus picks a jersey/cap combination at random, what is the probability that he will pick a practice jersey with a green cap?

22. $\frac{2}{8}$ or $\frac{1}{4}$

XTRA PRACTICE

See pages 702, 723.

Math Online

Self-Check Quiz at ca.gr6math.com

23. **RESEARCH** Use the Internet or another resource to find the number of jerseys and caps your favorite professional sports team has as part of its uniform. How many jersey/cap combinations are there for the team you picked? **See students' work.**

H.O.T. Problems

24. **CHALLENGE** Refer to Exercise 20. A *fair game* is one in which each player has an equal chance of winning. Adjust the scoring of the game so that it is fair.

25. **SELECT A TOOL** Mei wants to determine the probability of guessing correctly on two true-false questions on her history test. Which of the following tools might Mei use to determine the probability of answering both questions correctly by guessing? Justify your selection(s). Then use the tool(s) to solve the problem. **See margin.**

26. **FIND THE ERROR** Rhonda and Elise are finding all the possible unique outcomes of rolling an even number on a number cube and landing on A or B on the spinner shown. Who is correct? Explain your reasoning.

Rhonda

Outcomes	
Number Cube	**Spinner**
2	A
2	B
4	C
4	A
6	B
6	C

Elise

Outcomes	
Number Cube	**Spinner**
2	A
2	B
4	A
4	B
6	A
6	B

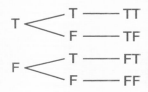

27. **WRITING IN MATH** Describe a game between two players using one coin in which each player has an equal chance of winning.

Lesson 9-2 Sample Spaces **469**

Margin notes (left column):

24. Sample answer: new scoring for a fair game—if exactly 2 counters match, Player 1 scores one point. Otherwise, Player 2 scores three points.

26. Elise; In her list, Rhonda included landing on C on the spinner.

27. Sample game: each player tosses a coin 10 times. If it comes up heads, Player 1 receives 1 point. If it comes up tails, player 2 receives 1 point. The player with the most points at the end of 20 tosses wins.

Margin notes (right column):

⚠ **Exercise Alert!**

Use the Internet Exercise 23 requires research on the Internet or in another source, such as a sports magazine.

⚠ **Exercise Alert!**

Find the Error In Exercise 26, Rhonda incorrectly included landing on C in her spinner outcomes. Remind students to include only favorable outcomes when they are constructing partial sample spaces.

Additional Answer

25. Sample answer: Mei can draw a model of the situation using a tree diagram to show the sample space. Then she can determine the probability. The probability of guessing correctly is $\frac{1}{4}$.

True/ False	True/ False	Sample Space
T	T	TT
	F	TF
F	T	FT
	F	FF

4 Assess

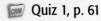

Crystal Ball Tell students that tomorrow's lesson is about using multiplication to find the number of possible outcomes in a sample space. Ask them to write how they think what they learned today will connect with tomorrow's material.

 Formative Assessment

Check for student understanding of concepts in Lessons 9-1 and 9-2.

[CRM] Quiz 1, p. 61

 **Foldables™ Follow-Up**

Remind students to write a descriptive paragraph about sample spaces, tree diagrams, and probability games under the tab for this lesson of their Foldables. Encourage them to describe the thoughts and experiences they had while working on the lesson.

Additional Answers

35. The cost is increasing over time. In about a year's time, the cost has more than tripled.

36. Sample answer: The pattern of the cost tripling each year is not likely to continue.

STANDARDS PRACTICE 6SDAP3.1

28. Mr. Zajac will choose one student from each of the two groups below to present their history reports to the class.**C**

Group 1	Group 2
Julia	Keith
Antoine	Isabel
Greg	

Which set shows all the possible choices?

A {(Julia, Keith), (Antoine, Keith), (Greg, Keith)}

B {(Julia, Antoine), (Antoine, Greg), (Isabel, Keith)}

C {(Julia, Keith), (Antoine, Keith), (Greg, Keith), (Julia, Isabel), (Antoine, Isabel), (Greg, Isabel)}

D {(Isabel, Antoine), (Keith, Greg), (Julia, Isabel), (Keith, Antoine)}

Spiral Review

PROBABILITY A spinner is equally likely to stop on each of its regions numbered 1 to 20. Find each probability as a fraction in simplest form. (Lesson 9-1)

29. a prime number $\frac{2}{5}$

30. GCF(12, 18) $\frac{1}{20}$

31. multiple of 2 or 3 $\frac{13}{20}$

32. *not* a multiple of 4 $\frac{3}{4}$

33. factor of 10 or 6 $\frac{3}{10}$

34. *not* an even number $\frac{1}{2}$

UTILITIES For Exercises 35 and 36, use the graph that shows the prices for natural gas charged by an Illinois natural gas supplier. (Lesson 8-6) **35–36. See margin.**

35. What trend seems to be revealed in the line graph?

36. What problems might there be in using this information to predict future prices of natural gas?

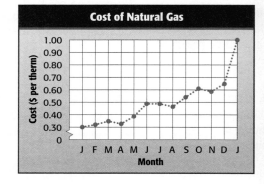

Cost of Natural Gas

37. **INTEREST** If Carlota invests $2,100 in a CD for 5 years at a simple interest rate of 4.75%, how much will the CD be worth after 5 years? (Lesson 7-8) **$2,598.75**

Find each number. Round to the nearest tenth if necessary. (Lesson 7-1)

38. 43% of 266 **114.4**

39. 17% of 92 **15.6**

40. 2.5% of 44 **1.1**

GET READY for the Next Lesson

PREREQUISITE SKILL Multiply.

41. 7 · 22 **154**

42. 11 · 16 **176**

43. 23 · 20 **460**

44. 131 · 4 **524**

The Fundamental Counting Principle

Standard 6SDAP3.1 — **Represent all possible outcomes for compound events in an organized way** (e.g., tables, grids, tree diagrams) **and express the theoretical probability of each outcome.**

PACING: **Regular:** 1 period, **Block:** 0.5 period

Options for Differentiated Instruction

ELL = English Language Learner   **AL** = Above Grade Level   **SS** = Struggling Students   **SN** = Special Needs

Making Relevant Connections

Use before presenting Example 1.

Present the following scenario to students:

The cafeteria is offering breakfast before school. You have a choice of one food item and one beverage, as shown in the table. Make a tree diagram of all the possible food/beverage combinations.

Food	Beverage
bagel	milk
cereal	orange juice
muffin	

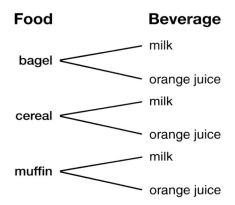

Ask:
- How many different food/beverage combinations are there? 6
- How would the sample space change if another drink were added, such as hot chocolate? There would be 3 more possible combinations, for a total of 9.
- Suppose that instead of adding hot chocolate, another food item were added, such as fruit cup. How would the sample space change from the original? There would be 2 more possible combinations, for a total of 8.
- Is there a way to determine how many combinations there will be without having to make a tree diagram? How? Yes; multiply the number of outcomes in each event.
- Test your conjecture with four food items and four drinks. Make a table or tree diagram to support your answer. See students' work.

Peer Tutoring

Use before assigning the Exercises 1.

Some students may be comfortable with tree diagrams and small numbers but may have difficulty applying the Fundamental Counting Principle to problems with larger numbers. Have students who understand the concept tutor other students and work with them to solve problems with more difficult numbers.

Leveled Lesson Resources

Also on
TeacherWorks™
Lesson 9-3

Chapter 9 Resource Masters

BL = Below Grade Level   **OL** = On Grade Level   **AL** = Above Grade Level   **ELL** = English Language Learner

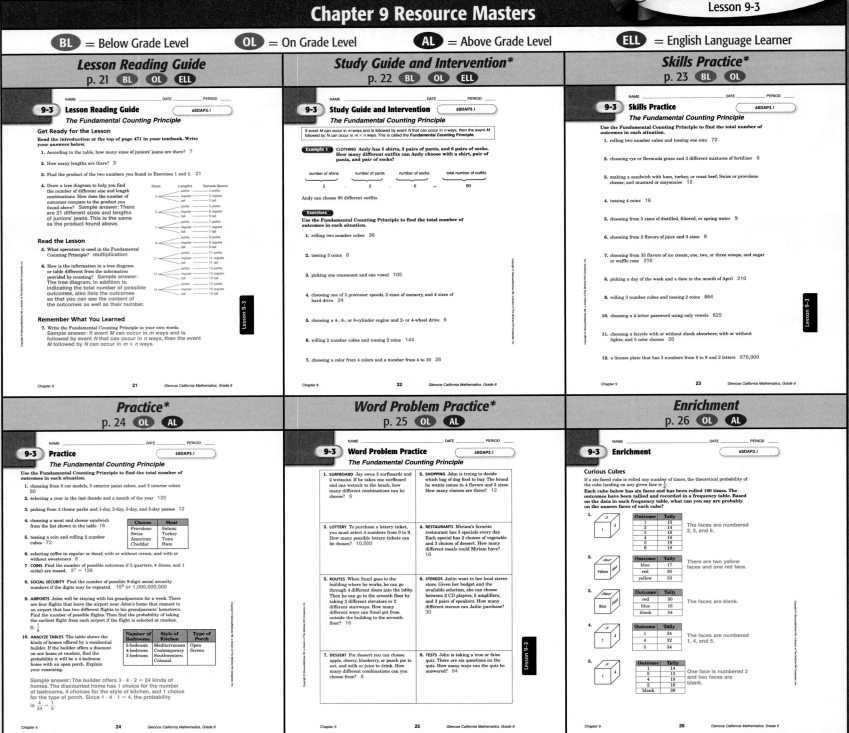

Lesson Reading Guide
p. 21 **BL** **OL** **ELL**

9-3 Lesson Reading Guide (6SDAP3.1)
The Fundamental Counting Principle

Get Ready for the Lesson
Read the introduction at the top of page 471 in your textbook. Write your answers below.

1. According to the table, how many sizes of juniors' jeans are there? 7
2. How many lengths are there? 3
3. Find the product of the two numbers you found in Exercises 1 and 2. 21
4. Draw a tree diagram to help you find the number of different size and length combinations. How does the number of outcomes compare to the product you found above? Sample answer: There are 21 different sizes and lengths of juniors' jeans. This is the same as the product found above.

Read the Lesson

5. What operation is used in the Fundamental Counting Principle? multiplication
6. How is the information in a tree diagram or table different from the information provided by counting? Sample answer: The tree diagram, in addition to indicating the total number of possible outcomes, also lists the outcomes so that you can see the content of the outcomes as well as their number.

Remember What You Learned

7. Write the Fundamental Counting Principle in your own words. Sample answer: If event M can occur in m ways and is followed by event N that can occur in n ways, then the event M followed by N can occur in m × n ways.

Study Guide and Intervention*
p. 22 **BL** **OL** **ELL**

9-3 Study Guide and Intervention (6SDAP3.1)
The Fundamental Counting Principle

If event M can occur in m ways and is followed by event N that can occur in n ways, then the event M followed by N can occur in m × n ways. This is called the **Fundamental Counting Principle**.

Example 1 CLOTHING Andy has 5 shirts, 3 pairs of pants, and 6 pairs of socks. How many different outfits can Andy choose with a shirt, pair of pants, and pair of socks?

number of shirts	number of pants	number of socks	total number of outfits
5	3	6	90

Andy can choose 90 different outfits.

Exercises

Use the Fundamental Counting Principle to find the total number of outcomes in each situation.

1. rolling two number cubes 36
2. tossing 3 coins 8
3. picking one consonant and one vowel 105
4. choosing one of 3 processor speeds, 2 sizes of memory, and 4 sizes of hard drive 24
5. choosing a 4-, 6-, or 8-cylinder engine and 2- or 4-wheel drive 6
6. rolling 2 number cubes and tossing 2 coins 144
7. choosing a color from 4 colors and a number from 4 to 10 28

Skills Practice*
p. 23 **BL** **OL**

9-3 Skills Practice (6SDAP3.1)
The Fundamental Counting Principle

Use the Fundamental Counting Principle to find the total number of outcomes in each situation.

1. rolling two number cubes and tossing one coin 72
2. choosing rye or Bermuda grass and 3 different mixtures of fertilizer 6
3. making a sandwich with ham, turkey, or roast beef; Swiss or provolone cheese; and mustard or mayonaise 12
4. tossing 4 coins 16
5. choosing from 3 sizes of distilled, filtered, or spring water 9
6. choosing from 3 flavors of juice and 3 sizes 9
7. choosing from 35 flavors of ice cream; one, two, or three scoops; and sugar or waffle cone 210
8. picking a day of the week and a date in the month of April 210
9. rolling 3 number cubes and tossing 2 coins 864
10. choosing a 4-letter password using only vowels 625
11. choosing a bicycle with or without shock absorbers; with or without lights; and 5 color choices 20
12. a license plate that has 3 numbers from 0 to 9 and 2 letters 676,000

Practice*
p. 24 **OL** **AL**

9-3 Practice (6SDAP3.1)
The Fundamental Counting Principle

Use the Fundamental Counting Principle to find the total number of outcomes in each situation.

1. choosing from 8 car models, 5 exterior paint colors, and 2 interior colors 80
2. selecting a year in the last decade and a month of the year 120
3. picking from 3 theme parks a 1-day, 2-day, 3-day, and 5-day passes 12
4. choosing a meat and cheese sandwich from the list shown in the table 16

Cheese	Meat
Provolone	Salami
Swiss	Turkey
American	Tuna
Cheddar	Ham

5. tossing a coin and rolling 2 number cubes 72
6. selecting coffee in regular or decaf, with or without cream, and with or without sweeteners 8
7. COINS Find the number of possible outcomes if 2 quarters, 4 dimes, and 1 nickel are tossed. $2^7 = 128$
8. SOCIAL SECURITY Find the number of possible 9-digit social security numbers if the digits may be repeated. 10^9 or 1,000,000,000
9. AIRPORTS JoJon will be staying with his grandparents for a week. There are four flights that leave the airport near JoJon's home that connect to an airport that has two different flights to his grandparents' hometown. Find the number of possible flights. Then find the probability of taking the earliest flight from each airport if the flight is selected at random. 8; $\frac{1}{8}$
10. ANALYZE TABLES The table shows the kinds of homes offered by a residential builder. If the builder offers a discount on one home at random, find the probability that it will be a 4-bedroom home with an open porch. Explain your reasoning.

Number of Bedrooms	Style of Kitchen	Type of Porch
5-bedroom	Mediterranean	Open
4-bedroom	Contemporary	Screen
3-bedroom	Southwestern	
	Colonial	

Sample answer: The builder offers 3 · 4 · 2 = 24 kinds of homes. The discounted home has 1 choice for the number of bedrooms, 4 choices for the style of kitchen, and 1 choice for the type of porch. Since 1 · 4 · 1 = 4, the probability is $\frac{4}{24} = \frac{1}{6}$.

Word Problem Practice*
p. 25 **OL** **AL**

9-3 Word Problem Practice (6SDAP3.1)
The Fundamental Counting Principle

1. SURFBOARD Jay owns 3 surfboards and 2 wetsuits. If he takes one surfboard and one wetsuit to the beach, how many different combinations can he choose? 6
2. SHOPPING John is trying to decide which bag of dog food to buy. The brand he wants comes in 4 flavors and 3 sizes. How many choices are there? 12
3. LOTTERY To purchase a lottery ticket, you must select 4 numbers from 0 to 9. How many possible lottery tickets can be chosen? 10,000
4. RESTAURANTS Miriam's favorite restaurant has 3 specials every day. Each special has 2 choices of vegetable and 3 choices of dessert. How many different meals could Miriam have? 18
5. ROUTES When Sunil goes to the building where he works, he can go through 4 different doors into the lobby. Then he can go to the seventh floor by taking 2 different elevators or 2 different stairways. How many different ways can Sunil get from outside the building to the seventh floor? 16
6. STEREOS Jailin went to her local stereo store. Given her budget and the available selection, she can choose between 2 CD players, 5 amplifiers, and 3 pairs of speakers. How many different stereos can Jailin purchase? 30
7. DESSERT For dessert you can choose apple, cherry, blueberry, or peach pie to eat, and milk or juice to drink. How many different combinations can you choose from? 8
8. TESTS John is taking a true or false quiz. There are six questions on the quiz. How many ways can the quiz be answered? 64

Enrichment
p. 26 **OL** **AL**

9-3 Enrichment (6SDAP3.1)

Curious Cubes

If a six-faced cube is rolled any number of times, the theoretical probability of the cube landing on any given face is $\frac{1}{6}$.

Each cube below has six faces and has been rolled 100 times. The outcomes have been tallied and recorded in a frequency table. Based on the data in each frequency table, what can you say are probably on the unseen faces of each cube?

1.
Outcome	Tally
1	15
2	14
3	18
4	16
5	19
6	18

The faces are numbered 2, 3, and 6.

2.
Outcome	Tally
blue	17
red	30
yellow	53

There are two yellow faces and one red face.

3.
Outcome	Tally
red	30
blue	16
blank	54

The faces are blank.

4.
Outcome	Tally
1	34
4	32
5	34

The faces are numbered 1, 4, and 5.

5.
Outcome	Tally
1	14
3	13
4	18
2	16
blank	39

One face is numbered 2 and two faces are blank.

Additional Lesson Resources

* Also available in Spanish **ELL**

Transparencies
- *5-Minute Check Transparency*, Lesson 9-3

Other Print Products
- *Noteables™ Interactive Study Notebook with Foldables™*

Teacher Tech Tools
- *Interactive Classroom CD-ROM*, Lesson 9-3
- *AssignmentWorks CD-ROM*, Lesson 9-3

Student Tech Tools
ca.gr6math.com
- Extra Examples, Chapter 9, Lesson 3
- Self-Check Quiz, Chapter 9, Lesson 3

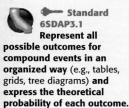

Main IDEA

Use multiplication to count outcomes and find probabilities.

⚷ **Standard 6SDAP3.1** **Represent all possible outcomes for compound events in an organized way** (e.g., tables, grids, tree diagrams) **and express the theoretical probability of each outcome.**

NEW Vocabulary

Fundamental Counting Principle

4. Sample answer; there are 21 different sizes and lengths of junior's jeans. This is the same as the product found in Exercise 3. See Ch. 9 Answer Appendix for diagram.

READING in the Content Area

For strategies in reading this lesson, visit ca.gr6math.com.

▶ GET READY for the Lesson

RETAIL SALES The Jean Factory sells juniors' jeans in different sizes and lengths. The table shows what they have available.

Sizes	Lengths
3	petite
5	regular
7	tall
9	
11	
13	
15	

1. According to the table, how many sizes of juniors' jeans are there? **7**

2. How many lengths are there? **3**

3. Find the product of the two numbers you found in Exercises 1 and 2. **21**

4. Draw a tree diagram to help you find the number of different size and length combinations. How does the number of outcomes compare to the product you found above?

In the activity above, you discovered that multiplication, instead of a tree diagram, can be used to find the number of possible outcomes in a sample space. This is called the **Fundamental Counting Principle**.

KEY **CONCEPT**   Fundamental Counting Principle

Words   If event M has m possible outcomes and event N has n possible outcomes, then event M followed by event N has $m \times n$ possible outcomes.

EXAMPLE   **Find the Number of Outcomes**

① Find the total number of outcomes when a coin is tossed and a number cube is rolled.

number of outcomes on one coin		number of outcomes on one number cube		total number of outcomes	
2	·	6	=	12	Fundamental Counting Principle

There are 12 different outcomes.

Check Draw a tree diagram to show the sample space.

 CHECK Your Progress

a. Find the total number of outcomes when choosing from bike helmets that come in three colors and two styles. **6**

ADDITIONAL EXAMPLE

① Find the total number of outcomes when a number from 0 to 9 is picked randomly, and then when a letter from A to D is picked randomly. **40**

 Formative Assessment

Use the Check Your Progress exercises after each Example to determine students' understanding of concepts.

---

1 Focus

🔑 **Standards Alignment**

Before Lesson 9-3
Add, subtract, multiply, and divide with decimals; add with negative integers; subtract positive integers from negative integers; and verify the reasonableness of the results from ⚷ Standard 5NS2.1

Lesson 9-3
Represent all possible outcomes for compound events in an organized way and express the theoretical probability of each outcome from ⚷ Standard 6SDAP3.1

After Lesson 9-3
Understand that the probability of either of two disjoint events occurring is the sum of the two individual probabilities and that the probability of one event following another, in independent trials, is the product of the two probabilities from Standard 6SDAP3.4

2 Teach

Scaffolding Questions

After you ask each question, give students time to find the sample space and count the outcomes.

Ask:
• If I toss one coin, how many possible outcomes are there? Make a sample space and count the outcomes. 2

• If I toss two coins, how many possible outcomes are there? 4

• If I toss three coins, how many possible outcomes are there? 8

ADDITIONAL EXAMPLE

② CLOTHING The table below shows the shirts, shorts, and shoes in Gerry's wardrobe. How many possible outfits—one shirt, one pair of shorts, and one pair of shoes—can he choose? **24**

Shirts	Shorts	Shoes
red	beige	black
blue	green	brown
white	blue	
yellow		

Additional Examples are also in:

- Noteables™ Interactive Study Notebook with Foldables™
- Interactive Classroom PowerPoint® Presentations

③ Practice

✓ Formative Assessment

Use Exercises 1–4 to check for understanding.

Then use the chart at the bottom of the next page to customize your assignments for students.

Intervention You may wish to use the Study Guide and Intervention Master on page 22 of the *Chapter 9 Resource Masters* for additional reinforcement.

Tips for New Teachers
Foundamental Counting Principle

In Example 2, assume that each choice is equally-likely, that is, assume that the customer randomly selects from each choice of steak, each choice of how the steak is cooked, and each choice of potatoes.

The Fundamental Counting Principle can be used to find the number of possible outcomes and solve probability problems in more complex problems, when there are more than two events.

Real-World EXAMPLE

② FOOD A famous steak house allows customers to create their own steak dinners. The choices are shown at the right. Find the number of steak dinners possible. Then find the probability that a customer randomly selects a well-done ribeye steak and a baked potato.

451 Steakhouse		
Steak	**How Steaks Are Cooked**	**Potatoes**
New York Strip	rare	mashed
Ribeye	medium	baked
Filet	well	twice baked
Porterhouse		au gratin
T-Bone		

number of types of steaks		number of ways steaks can be cooked		number of types of potatoes		total number of steak dinners	
5	·	3	·	4	=	60	Fundamental Counting Principle

There are 60 different ways of choosing a steak dinner. Out of the 60 possible outcomes, only one is favorable. So, the probability of randomly selecting a well-done ribeye steak and a baked potato is $\frac{1}{60}$.

✓ CHECK Your Progress

b. 90 possible dinners; $\frac{1}{90}$

b. FOOD If the chef adds sirloin steak and scalloped potatoes to the menu, find the number of possible steak dinners. Then find the probability of randomly selecting a medium-done sirloin steak and mashed potatoes.

 **Personal Tutor at** ca.gr6math.com

★ indicates multi-step problem

✓ CHECK Your Understanding

Example 1
(p. 471)

Use the Fundamental Counting Principle to find the total number of outcomes in each situation.

1. tossing a quarter, a dime, and a nickel **8**

2. choosing scrambled, sunny-side up, or poached eggs with bacon or sausage and milk or orange juice **12**

3. choosing a card from 20 different cards and spinning the spinner at the right **60**

Example 2
(p. 472)

4. **CLOTHES** Beth has 3 sweaters, 4 blouses, and 6 skirts that coordinate. Find the number of different outfits consisting of a sweater, blouse, and skirt that are possible. Then find the probability of randomly selecting a particular sweater-blouse-skirt outfit. **72; $\frac{1}{72}$**

472 Chapter 9 Probability

Math Online Extra Examples at ca.gr6math.com

Focus on Mathematical Content

Tree diagrams can be used to find the **number of outcomes in a sample space**. But it is quicker to multiply using the Fundamental Counting Principle.

The **Fundamental Counting Principle** is especially useful for finding the number of outcomes in probability situations with more than two events.

The **Fundamental Counting Principle** allows students to easily calculate the two quantities of the probability ratio—number of favorable outcomes, number of possible outcomes.

Exercises

HOMEWORK HELP

For Exercises	See Examples
5–10	1
11–12	2

Exercise Levels
: 5–12
: 13–16
: 17–19

Use the Fundamental Counting Principle to find the total number of outcomes in each situation.

5. choosing a bagel with one type of cream cheese from the list shown in the table **12**

6. choosing a number from 1 to 20 and a color from 7 colors **140**

7. picking a month of the year and a day of the week **84**

8. choosing from a comedy, horror, or action movie each shown in four theaters **12**

9. rolling a number cube and tossing two coins **24**

10. choosing iced tea in regular, raspberry, lemon, or peach flavors; sweetened or unsweetened; and in a glass or a plastic container **16**

Bagels	Cream Cheese
plain	plain
blueberry	chive
cinnamon raisin	sun-dried tomato
garlic	

11. ★ **ROADS** Two roads, Broadway and State, connect the towns of Eastland and Harping. Three roads, Park, Fairview, and Main, connect the towns of Harping and Johnstown. Find the number of possible routes from Eastland to Johnstown that pass through Harping. Then find the probability that State and Fairview will be used if a route is selected at random. **6 possible routes; $\frac{1}{6}$**

12. ★ **APPLES** An orchard makes apple nut bread, apple pumpkin nut bread, and apple buttermilk bread using 6 different varieties of apples, including Fuji. Find the number of possible bread choices. Then find the probability of selecting a Fuji apple buttermilk bread if a customer buys a loaf of bread at random. **18 possible bread choices; $\frac{1}{18}$**

Real-World Link · · · ·
A popular orchard in Placerville, California, grows 7 varieties of apples including Granny Smith and Fuji.
Source: allaboutapples.com

13. **GAMES** Find the number of possible outcomes if five number cubes are rolled at one time during a board game. **7,776**

14. ★ **PASSWORDS** Find the number of possible choices for a 2-digit password that is greater than 19. Then find the number of possible choices for a 4-digit Personal Identification Number (PIN) if the digits *cannot* be repeated. **80; 5,040**

15. **ADVERTISING** The Wake-Up Restaurant advertises that you can have a different pancake breakfast every day of the year. It offers 25 different kinds of pancakes and 14 flavored syrups. If the restaurant is open every day of the year, is its claim valid? Justify your answer.
No; the number of selections is 25 • 14 or 350, which is less than 365.

16. $\frac{1}{12}$; See margin for explanation.

16. **ANALYZE TABLES** The table shows cell phone options offered by a wireless phone company. If a phone with one payment plan and one accessory is given away at random, predict the probability that it will be Brand B and have a headset. Explain your reasoning.

Phone Brands	Payment Plans	Accessories
Brand A	Individual	Leather Case
Brand B	Family	Car Mount
Brand C	Business	Headset
	Government	Travel Charger

EXTRA PRACTICE
See pages 702, 723.

Math Online
Self-Check Quiz at
ca.gr6math.com

Odd/Even Assignments

Exercises 5–12 are structured so that students practice the same concepts whether they are assigned odd or even problems.

Additional Answer

16. Sample answer: There are $3 \times 4 \times 4$ or 48 different possible outcomes of a phone plan. There are $1 \times 4 \times 1$ or 4 different possible outcomes of a phone plan that includes Brand B and has a headset. The probability of randomly selecting this phone plan is $\frac{4}{48}$ or $\frac{1}{12}$.

DIFFERENTIATED HOMEWORK OPTIONS

Level	Assignment	Two-Day Option	
BL Basic	5–12, 18–30	5–11 odd, 20, 21	6–12 even, 18, 19, 22–30
OL Core	5–11 odd, 13–16, 18–30	5–12, 20, 21	13–16, 18, 19, 22–30
AL Advanced/Pre-AP	13–26 (optional: 27–30)		

Name the Math Tell students that you have four kinds of cereal and two kinds of berries to put on the cereal. What are your cereal-berry choices? How many choices do you have? Have students write what mathematical procedures they would use to construct the sample space and to find the number of possible outcomes.

FOLDABLES Study Organizer **Foldables™ Follow-Up**

Remind students to write a descriptive paragraph about the Fundamental Counting Principle under the tab for this lesson of their Foldables. Encourage them to describe the thoughts and experiences they had while working on the lesson.

Additional Answer

19. Sample answer: When there are multiple events, the Fundamental Counting Principle is a much faster method of obtaining the total number of outcomes than drawing a tree diagram. The Fundamental Counting Principle also saves paper space and can often be done mentally. When you need to see what the specific outcomes are, make a tree diagram since the Fundamental Counting Principle only gives the number of outcomes.

H.O.T. Problems

17. 2; 4; 8; 2^n; Sample answer: I used a pattern to determine the number of outcomes for n coins. One coin: 2^1 outcomes, two coins: $2 \cdot 2$ or 2^2 outcomes, three coins: $2 \cdot 2 \cdot 2$ or 2^3 outcomes, n coins: 2^n outcomes.

17. CHALLENGE Determine the number of possible outcomes for tossing one coin, two coins, and three coins. Then determine the number of possible outcomes for tossing n coins. Describe the strategy you used.

18. Which One Doesn't Belong? Identify the choices for event M and N that do *not* result in the same number of outcomes as the other two. Explain your reasoning. **18 hats, 8 sizes have 144 outcomes; the other two have 96 outcomes**

| 12 meats, 8 breads | 18 hats, 8 sizes | 24 teams, 4 sports |

19. WRITING IN MATH Explain when you might choose to use the Fundamental Counting Principle to find the number of possible outcomes and when you might choose to use a tree diagram. **See margin.**

STANDARDS PRACTICE 6SDAP3.1

20. A bakery offers white, chocolate, or yellow cakes with white or chocolate icing. There are also 24 designs that can be applied to a cake. If all orders are equally likely, what is the probability that a customer will order a white cake with white icing in a specific design? **D**

A $\frac{1}{30}$ C $\frac{1}{120}$

B $\frac{1}{64}$ D $\frac{1}{144}$

21. WritePen makes 8 different styles of pens in several colors with 2 types of grips. If the company makes 112 kinds of pens, how many different colors do they make? **F**

F 7 H 16

G 8 J 1,792

Spiral Review

22. SCHOOL Horacio can choose from 2 geography, 3 history, and 2 statistics classes. Find the sample space for all possible schedules. (Lesson 9-2) **See Ch. 9 Answer Appendix.**

PROBABILITY Find the probability that the spinner shown at the right will stop on each of the following. Write as a fraction in simplest form. (Lesson 9-1)

23. an even number $\frac{1}{2}$

24. a multiple of 4 $\frac{1}{4}$

Order each set of numbers from least to greatest. (Lesson 6-8)

25. 27%, $\frac{1}{5}$, 0.22, 20.1 $\frac{1}{5}$, 0.22, 27%, 20.1

26. $\frac{19}{20}$, 88%, 0.85, $\frac{3}{4}$ $\frac{3}{4}$, 0.85, 88%, $\frac{19}{20}$

GET READY for the Next Lesson

PREREQUISITE SKILL Multiply.

27. $3 \cdot 2 \cdot 1$ **6**

28. $9 \cdot 8 \cdot 7$ **504**

29. $5 \cdot 4 \cdot 3 \cdot 2$ **120**

30. $7 \cdot 6 \cdot 5 \cdot 4$ **840**

Pre-AP Activity Use as an Extension

Have students research the names of regular polyhedrons with more than 6 faces, such as an octahedron or a decahedron. Have them describe a probability experiment involving more than one such polyhedron. For example, the polyhedrons might have numbered or colored faces. Have them exchange experiments with a partner. Each student should calculate the number of possible outcomes in his or her partner's experiment.

9-4 Permutations

Standard 6SDAP3.1 Represent all possible outcomes for compound events in an organized way (e.g., tables, grids, tree diagrams) and **express the theoretical probability of each outcome.**

PACING: **Regular:** 1 period, **Block:** 0.5 period

Options for Differentiated Instruction

ELL = English Language Learner   **AL** = Above Grade Level   **SS** = Struggling Students   **SN** = Special Needs

Modeling the Activity ELL SS SN

Use with the Mini Lab.

Model the Mini Lab with students by presenting the following scenario.

> Suppose three students need to give presentations. The task is to find out how many different orders they can give their presentations.
>
> | First Presentation | Second Presentation | Third Presentation |
> | --- | --- | --- |

Pick three students to stand in the front of the class to demonstrate. Have the class record the different ways they get in order, 1st, 2nd, and 3rd. Once students think they have found all the different orders, discuss a way to make an organized list of all the unique orders.

Ask:
- What would happen if there were 4 students or 5 students?
- How would this affect the number of orders?

Use Modeling SS SN

Use with the Examples.

Encourage students to model the simpler permutations presented in this lesson. This could involve standing in different orders and counting those orders. It could also involve using different colored counters to represent different elements. As students see more and more of these patterns represented visually, they will develop a better conceptual understanding of permutations.

Real-World Applications ELL SS SN

Use after presenting Example 1.

Present the following real-world situations to students:
- A baseball team has nine players that come up to bat. How many different batting orders could the team make? 362,880 orders
- Does this surprise you? If so, why? Answers will vary.

Leveled Lesson Resources

Chapter 9 Resource Masters

BL = Below Grade Level **OL** = On Grade Level **AL** = Above Grade Level **ELL** = English Language Learner

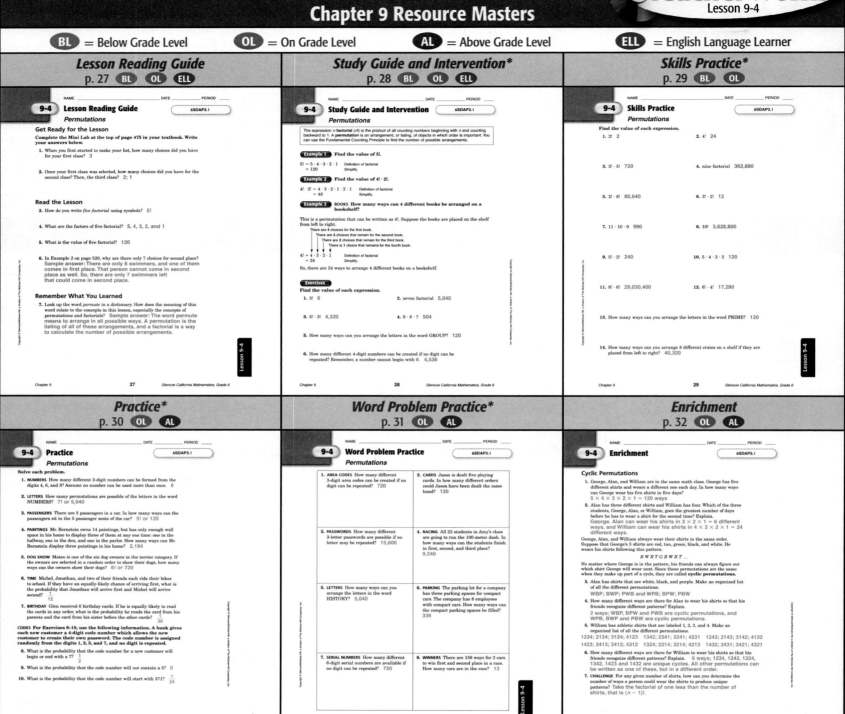

Additional Lesson Resources

* Also available in Spanish **ELL**

Transparencies
- *5-Minute Check Transparency*, Lesson 9-4

Other Print Products
- *Teaching Mathematics with Manipulatives*
- *Noteables™ Interactive Study Notebook with Foldables™*

Teacher Tech Tools
- *Interactive Classroom CD-ROM*, Lesson 9-4
- *AssignmentWorks CD-ROM*, Lesson 9-4

Student Tech Tools
ca.gr6math.com
- Extra Examples, Chapter 9, Lesson 4
- Self-Check Quiz, Chapter 9, Lesson 4

Main IDEA

Find the number of permutations of a set of objects and find probabilities.

Standard 6SDAP3.1 Represent all possible outcomes for compound events in an organized way (e.g., tables, grids, tree diagrams) and express the theoretical probability of each outcome.

EW Vocabulary

ermutation

MINI Lab

How many different ways are there to arrange your first 3 classes if they are math, science, and language arts?

STEP 1 Write math, science, and language arts on the index cards.

MATH	SCIENCE	LANGUAGE ARTS

STEP 2 Find and record all arrangements of classes by changing the order of the index cards. **See margin.**

1. When you first started to make your list, how many choices did you have for your first class? **3**

2. Once your first class was selected, how many choices did you have for the second class? Then, the third class? **2; 1**

A **permutation** is an arrangement, or listing, of objects in which order is important. In the example above, the arrangement Science, Math, Language Arts is a permutation of Math, Science, Language Arts because the order of the classes is different. You can use the Fundamental Counting Principle to find the number of possible permutations.

EXAMPLE Find a Permutation

1. **SCHEDULES** Find the number of possible arrangements of classes in the Mini-Lab above using the Fundamental Counting Principle.

There are **3** choices for the first class.
There are **2** choices that remain for the second class.
There is **1** choice that remains for the third class.

3 · 2 · 1 = 6 ◄——— The number of permutations of 3 classes

There are 6 possible arrangements, or permutations, of the 3 classes.

CHECK Your Progress

a. **VOLLEYBALL** In how many ways can the starting six players of a volleyball team stand in a row for a picture? **720**

Math Online Extra Examples at ca.gr6math.com

Additional Answer

Step 2

Math	Science	Language Arts
Math	Language Arts	Science
Science	Math	Language Arts
Science	Language Arts	Math
Language Arts	Math	Science
Language Arts	Science	Math

• If I *do not* replace the marble I picked, and then pick again, what is the number of possible outcomes? 3

Formative Assessment

Use the Check Your Progress exercises after each Example to determine students' understanding of concepts.

1 Focus

Standards Alignment

Before Lesson 9-4
Add, subtract, multiply, and divide with decimals; add with negative integers; subtract positive integers from negative integers; and verify the reasonableness of the results from Standard 5NS2.1

Lesson 9-4
Express the theoretical probability of each outcome from Standard 6SDAP3.1

After Lesson 9-4
Understand that the probability of either of two disjoint events occurring is the sum of the two individual probabilities and that the probability of one event following another, in independent trials, is the product of the two probabilities from Standard 6SDAP3.4

2 Teach

MINI Lab

You might also want to have students construct the sample space by drawing a tree diagram or making a table.

Scaffolding Questions

Have students imagine a bag with four colored marbles: red, green, blue, and white.

Ask:
• If I pick a marble without looking, what is the number of possible outcomes? 4

• If I replace the marble I picked, and then pick again, what is the number of possible outcomes? 4

3 Practice

You can use a permutation to find the probability of an event.

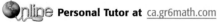

Real-World EXAMPLE **Find Probability**

2 **SWIMMING** The finals of the Northwest Swimming League features 8 swimmers. If each swimmer has an equally likely chance of finishing in the top two, what is the probability that Yumii will be in first place and Paquita in second place?

Northwest League Finalists	
Octavia	Eden
Natasha	Paquita
Calista	Samantha
Yumii	Lorena

There are **8** swimmers for first place.

There are **7** swimmers that remain for second place.

$8 \cdot 7 = 56$ ◄——— The number of permutations of the swimmers for the 2 places

There are 56 possible arrangements, or permutations, of the swimmers for the 2 places.

Since there is only one way of having Yumii come in first and Paquita second, the probability of this event is $\frac{1}{56}$.

CHECK Your Progress

b. **LETTERS** Two different letters are randomly selected from the letters in the word *math*. What is the probability that the first letter selected is *m* and the second letter is *h*? $\frac{1}{12}$

Online Personal Tutor at ca.gr6math.com

★ indicates multi-step problem

CHECK Your Understanding

Example 1 (p. 475)

1. **TRANSPORTATION** In how many ways can the 7 students shown waiting at the bus stop board the bus when it arrives? **5,040**

2. **COMMITTEES** In how many ways can a president, vice-president, and secretary be randomly selected from a class of 25 students? **13,800**

Example 2 (p. 476)

3. **DVD** You have five seasons of your favorite TV show on DVD. If you randomly select two of them from a shelf, what is the probability that you will select season one first and season two second? $\frac{1}{20}$

4. **PASSWORDS** A password consists of four letters, of which none are repeated. What is the probability that a person could guess the entire password by randomly selecting the four letters? $\frac{1}{358,800}$

476 Chapter 9 Probability

Exercises

HOMEWORK HELP

For Exercises	See Examples
5–8	1
9–12	2

Exercise Levels
: 5–12
: 13–15
: 16–17

5. **CONTESTS** In the Battle of the Bands contest, in how many ways can the four participating bands be ordered? **24**

6. **ZIP CODES** How many different 5-digit zip codes are there if no digit is repeated? **30,240**

7. **LETTERS** How many permutations are possible of the letters in the word *friend*? **720**

8. **NUMBERS** How many different 3-digit numbers can be formed using the digits 9, 3, 4, 7, and 6? Assume no number can be used more than once. **60**

9. **CAPTAINS** The members of the Evergreen Junior High Quiz Bowl team are listed at the right. If a captain and an assistant captain are chosen at random, what is the probability that Walter is selected as captain and Mi-Ling as co-captain? **$\frac{1}{90}$**

Evergreen Junior High Quiz Bowl Team	
Jamil	Luanda
Savannah	Mi-Ling
Tucker	Booker
Ferdinand	Nina
Walter	Meghan

10. **BASEBALL** Adriano, Julián and three of their friends will sit in a row of five seats at a baseball game. If each friend is equally-likely to sit in any seat, what is the probability that Adriano will sit in the first seat and Julián will sit in the second seat? **$\frac{1}{20}$**

11. **GAMES** Alex, Aiden, Dexter, and Dion are playing a video game. If they each have an equally-likely chance of getting the highest score, what is the probability that Dion will get the highest score and Alex the second highest? **$\frac{1}{12}$**

12. **BLOCKS** A child has wooden blocks with the letters *G*, *R*, *T*, *I*, and *E*. Find the probability that the child randomly arranges the letters in the order *TIGER*. **$\frac{1}{120}$**

Real-World Link . . . . .
: the 2005 estminster Kennel ub Dog Show, *arlee, a German northaired Pointer* om the Sporting roup, won the Best Show Trophy.
ource: *Westminster ennel Club*

13. **SELECT A TOOL** Refer to the information in the table. The best dog in each breed competes to win one of four top ribbons in the group. Which of the following tools might you use to find the number of ways a ribbon can be awarded to a dog in the Working group? Justify your selection(s). Then use your tool(s) to solve the problem. **See margin.**

Westminster Kennel Club Dog Show Attendance 2005	
Group	**Number of Breeds**
Herding	19
Hounds	25
Non-Sporting	18
Sporting	28
Terriers	28
Toy	23
Working	24

| calculator | mental math | estimation |

Lesson 9-4 Permutations **477**

Odd/Even Assignments

Exercises 5–12 are structured so that students practice the same concepts whether they are assigned odd or even problems.

Additional Answer

13. Sample answer: Calculator; An exact answer is required. 24 × 23 × 22 × 21 = 255,024

DIFFERENTIATED HOMEWORK OPTIONS

Level	Assignment	Two-Day Option	
BL Basic	5–12, 17–29	5–11 odd, 18, 19	6–12 even, 17, 20–29
OL Core	5–11 odd, 13–15, 17–29	5–12, 18, 19	13–15, 17, 20–29
AL Advanced/Pre-AP	13–25 (optional: 26–29)		

Yesterday's News Remind students that yesterday's lesson was about using the Fundamental Counting Principle to find the number of possible outcomes in a sample space. Have students write how yesterday's concepts helped them with today's material.

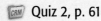 **Formative Assessment**

Check for student understanding of concepts in Lessons 9-3 and 9-4.

CRM Quiz 2, p. 61

 **Foldables™ Follow-Up**

Remind students to write a descriptive paragraph about the permutations and the Fundamental Counting Principle under the tab for this lesson of their Foldables. Encourage them to describe the thoughts and experiences they had while working on the lesson.

16. 12 students; Since 12 • 11 • 10 = 1,320, there must be 12 students on the debate team.

14. **PHOTOGRAPHY** A family discovered they can stand in a row for their portrait in 720 different ways. How many members are in the family? 6

15. **STUDENT ID** Hamilton Middle School assigns a four-digit identification number to each student. The number is made from the digits 1, 2, 3, and 4, and no digit is repeated. If assigned randomly, what is the probability that an ID number will end with a 3? $\frac{1}{4}$

H.O.T. Problems

16. **CHALLENGE** There are 1,320 ways for three students to win first, second, and third place during a debate match. How many students are there on the debate team? Explain your reasoning.

17. **WRITING IN MATH** Describe a real-world situation that has 6 permutations. Justify your answer. **Sample answer: The number of ways you can order 3 books on a shelf is 3 • 2 • 1 or 6.**

STANDARDS PRACTICE 6SDAP3.1

18. The five finalists in a random drawing are shown. Find the probability that Sean is awarded first prize and Teresa is awarded second prize. **D**

A $\frac{1}{5}$

B $\frac{1}{10}$

C $\frac{2}{5}$

D $\frac{1}{20}$

Finalists
Cesar
Teresa
Sean
Nikita
Alfonso

19. A baseball coach is deciding on the batting order for his nine starting players with the pitcher batting last. How many batting orders are possible? **H**

F 8

G 72

H 40,320

J 362,880

Spiral Review

20. **BREAKFAST** Find the total number of outcomes if you can choose from 8 kinds of bagels, 3 toppings, and 4 beverages. (Lesson 9-3) **96**

21. **LUNCH** Make a tree diagram showing different ways to make a sandwich with turkey, ham, or salami and either cheddar or Swiss cheese. (Lesson 9-2) **See Ch. 9 Answer Appendix.**

22. **PROBABILITY** What is the probability of rolling a number greater than four on a number cube? (Lesson 9-1) $\frac{1}{3}$

Find each product. Write in simplest form. (Lesson 5-5)

23. $\frac{4}{5} \times 2\frac{1}{3}$ $1\frac{13}{15}$

24. $11\frac{1}{8} \times \frac{1}{2}$ $5\frac{9}{16}$

25. $4\frac{5}{6} \times \frac{7}{8}$ $4\frac{11}{48}$

GET READY for the Next Lesson

PREREQUISITE SKILL Find each value. (Lesson 1-4)

26. $\frac{5 \cdot 4}{2 \cdot 1}$ 10

27. $\frac{8 \cdot 7 \cdot 6}{3 \cdot 2 \cdot 1}$ 56

28. $\frac{5 \cdot 4 \cdot 3}{4 \cdot 3 \cdot 2}$ 2.5

29. $\frac{10 \cdot 9 \cdot 8 \cdot 7}{8 \cdot 7 \cdot 6 \cdot 5}$ 3

Pre-AP Activity Use as an Extension

When 3-digit area codes for telephone numbers were first developed, the following rules applied: the first digit could not be 0 or 1; the second digit must be 0 or 1; and the third digit could be any digit, 0 to 9. How many possible area codes were there under this system? 160

Mid-Chapter Quiz

Lessons 9-1 through 9-4

A number cube is rolled. Find each probability. Write as a fraction in simplest form. (Lesson 9-1)

1. P(an odd number) $\frac{1}{2}$

2. P(a number not greater than 4) $\frac{2}{3}$

3. P(a number less than 6) $\frac{5}{6}$

4. P(a multiple of 2) $\frac{1}{2}$

5. **DVDS** Andrés has 2 action, 3 comedy, and 5 drama DVDs. If he randomly picks a DVD to watch, what is the probability that he will *not* pick a comedy? Write as a percent. (Lesson 9-1) **70%**

6. See margin.

For each situation, find the sample space using a table or tree diagram. (Lesson 9-2)

6. Two coins are tossed.

7. The spinner shown is spun, and a digit is randomly selected from the number 803.
See Ch. 9 Answer Appendix.

8. **STANDARDS PRACTICE** At a diner, a customer can choose from eggs or pancakes as an entrée and from ham or sausage as a side. Which set shows all the possible choices of one entrée and one side? (Lesson 9-2) **B**

   A {(eggs, pancakes), (ham, sausage)}

   B {(eggs, ham), (eggs, sausage), (pancakes, ham), (pancakes, sausage)}

   C {(eggs, ham), (eggs, pancakes), (sausage, pancakes)}

   D {(eggs, ham), (pancakes, sausage)}

9. See Ch. 9 Answer Appendix.

9. **GAMES** Abbey rolls a number cube and chooses a card from among cards marked A, B, and C. If an odd number and a vowel turn up, Abbey wins. Otherwise Benny wins. Find the sample space. Then find the probability that Benny wins. (Lesson 9-2)

For Exercises 10 and 11, use the Fundamental Counting Principle to find the total number of possible outcomes in each situation. (Lesson 9-3)

10. A customer chooses a paper color, size, and binding style for some copies.

Color	Size	Binding
white	8.5" x 11"	paper clip
yellow	8.5" x 14"	binder clip
green	8.5" x 17"	staple

27 outcomes

11. A number cube is rolled and three coins are tossed. **48 outcomes**

12. **CARS** A certain car model comes in the colors in the table and either automatic or manual transmission. Find the probability that a randomly selected car will have a black exterior, tan interior, and manual transmission if all combinations are equally likely. (Lesson 9-3) $\frac{1}{16}$

Exterior	Interior
Black	Gray
White	Tan
Red	
Silver	

13. **STUDENT COUNCIL** In how many ways can a president, treasurer, and a secretary be chosen from among 8 candidates? (Lesson 9-4) **336 ways**

14. **STANDARDS PRACTICE** Noriko packed five different sweaters for her weekend vacation. If she randomly selects one sweater to wear each day, what is the probability that she will select the brown sweater on Friday, the orange sweater on Saturday, and the pink sweater on Sunday? She will not wear each sweater more than once. (Lesson 9-4) **F**

   F $\frac{1}{60}$

   G $\frac{1}{120}$

   H $\frac{3}{5}$

   J $\frac{1}{5}$

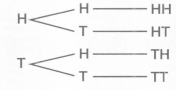
Data-Driven Decision Making	Exercises	Lesson	Standard	Resources for Review
Diagnostic Teaching Based on the results of the Chapter 9 Mid-Chapter Quiz, use the following to review concepts that students continue to find challenging.	1–5	9–1	6SDAP3.3	CRM Study Guide and Intervention pp. 10, 16, 22, and 28 **Math Online** • Extra Examples • Personal Tutor • Concepts in Motion
	6–9	9–2	6SDAP3.1	
	10–12	9–3	6SDAP3.1	
	13, 14	9–4	6SDAP3.1	

9-5 Combinations

Standard 6SDAP3.1 Represent all possible outcomes for compound events in an organized way (e.g., tables, grids, tree diagrams) and **express the theoretical probability of each outcome.**

PACING: **Regular:** 1 period, **Block:** 0.5 period

Options for Differentiated Instruction

ELL = English Language Learner   **AL** = Above Grade Level   **SS** = Struggling Students   **SN** = Special Needs

Vocabulary Tools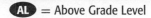

Use after presenting the Examples.

Some students might mistakenly think that a *combination* indicates a situation where order matters, such as a combination lock. Provide the following clues to help students remember the definitions.

permutation	The word comes from Latin words meaning *thoroughly changed.*
combination	The word means a collection of items that have been brought together.

Discuss with students ways to use these clues to help them distinguish permutations from combinations. Sample answer: In a permutation, the order of items *thoroughly changes* the permutation. In a combination, items can be combined or *brought together* in any order.

Using Patterns

Use after students complete Lesson 9-5.

Have students complete the following table.

Situation	Number of Combinations
Choose 2 students from a group of 5.	10
Choose 2 students from a group of 6.	15
Choose 2 students from a group of 7.	21
Choose 2 students from a group of 8.	28
Choose 2 students from a group of 9.	36

Ask:

- Do you notice a pattern? If so, describe it. Yes; as the groups increase in size, the number of combinations increases by a greater amount each time.
- How would the pattern change if 3 students are chosen from the groups instead of 2? Explain how you determined your answer. For each group, the number of combinations is greater than before; as the groups increase in size, the number of combinations increases by an even greater amount each time than previously.

Leveled Lesson Resources

Chapter 9 Resource Masters

BL = Below Grade Level   **OL** = On Grade Level   **AL** = Above Grade Level   **ELL** = English Language Learner

---

Lesson Reading Guide
p. 34 BL OL ELL

NAME ___ DATE ___ PERIOD ___

9-5 Lesson Reading Guide   6SDAP3.I

Combinations

Get Ready for the Lesson

Read the introduction at the top of page 480 in your textbook. Write your answers below.

1. Use the first letter of each name to list all of the permutations of co-captains. How many are there? JB, JO, JD, BJ, BO, BD, OJ, OB, OD, DJ, DB, DO; 12

2. Cross out any arrangement that contains the same letters as another one in the list. How many are there now? 6

3. Explain the difference between the two lists above. The list in Exercise 1 is a permutation where order is important. The list in Exercise 2 does not take order into account.

Read the Lesson

4. How can you find the number of combinations of objects in a set?
Sample answer: Divide the number of permutations of the entire set by the number of ways each smaller set can be arranged.

5. Why might it be easier to calculate the number of combinations of a set of objects using a permutation rather than making a list? Sample answer: A list could be quite lengthy, depending on the number of objects in the set and the number of them being chosen.

For Exercises 6 and 7, refer to Example 2 on page 525 in your textbook.

6. In the diagram, how many points are there? How many line segments connect to any one point? 8; 7

7. How does your answer to Exercise 6 above correspond to Example 2 in your book? There are 8 · 7 ways to choose 2 people.

Remember What You Learned

8. Work with a partner. Take turns thinking of situations in which a selection from a group must have some order or is not ordered. Tell each other which situations are permutations and which are combinations. Solve each problem and show your work. See students' work.

Chapter 9   34   Glencoe California Mathematics, Grade 6

Study Guide and Intervention*
p. 35 BL OL ELL

NAME ___ DATE ___ PERIOD ___

9-5 Study Guide and Intervention   6SDAP3.I

Combinations

An arrangement, or listing, of objects in which order is *not* important is called a **combination**. You can find the number of combinations of objects by dividing the number of permutations of the entire set by the number of ways each smaller set can be arranged.

Example 1 Jill was asked by her teacher to choose 3 topics from the 8 topics given to her. How many different three-topic groups could she choose?

There are 8 · 7 · 6 permutations of three-topic groups chosen from eight. There are 3! ways to arrange the groups.

$$\frac{8 \cdot 7 \cdot 6}{3!} = \frac{336}{6} = 56$$

So, there are 56 different three-topic groups.

Tell whether each situation represents a *permutation* or *combination*. Then solve the problem.

Example 2 On a quiz, you are allowed to answer any 4 out of the 6 questions. How many ways can you choose the questions?

This is a combination because the order of the 4 questions is not important. So, there are 6 · 5 · 4 · 3 permutations of four questions chosen from six. There are 4! or 4 · 3 · 2 · 1 orders in which these questions can be chosen.

$$\frac{6 \cdot 5 \cdot 4 \cdot 3}{4!} = \frac{360}{24} = 15$$

So, there are 15 ways to choose the questions.

Example 3 Five different cars enter a parking lot with only 3 empty spaces. How many ways can these cars be filled?

This is a permutation because each arrangement of the same 3 cars counts as a distinct arrrangement. So, there are 5 · 4 · 3 or 60 ways the spaces can be filled.

Exercises

Tell whether each situation represents a *permutation* or *combination*. Then solve the problem.

1. How many ways can 4 people be chosen from a group of 11? combination; 330

2. How many ways can 3 people sit in 4 chairs? permutation; 24

3. How many ways can 2 goldfish be chosen from a tank containing 15 goldfish? combination; 105

Chapter 9   35   Glencoe California Mathematics, Grade 6

Skills Practice*
p. 36 BL OL

NAME ___ DATE ___ PERIOD ___

9-5 Skills Practice   6SDAP3.I

Combinations

Tell whether each situation represents a *permutation* or *combination*. Then solve the problem.

1. You are allowed to omit two out of 12 questions on a quiz. How many ways can you select the questions to omit? combination; 66

2. Six students are to be chosen from a class of 18 to represent the class at a math contest. How many ways can the six students be chosen? combination; 18,564

3. How many different 5-digit zip codes are possible if no digits are repeated? permutation; 30,240

4. In a race with six runners, how many ways can the runners finish first, second, or third? permutation; 120

5. How many ways can two names be chosen from 76 in a raffle if only one entry per person is allowed? combination; 2,850

6. How many ways can six students be arranged in a lunch line? permutation; 720

7. A family has a bike rack that fits seven bikes but they only have five bikes. How many ways can the bikes fit in the bike rack? permutation; 2,520

8. How many ways can you select three sheriff deputies from eight candidates? combination; 56

9. How many ways can four finalists be selected from 50 contestants? combination; 230,300

10. How many 4-digit pin numbers are available if no number is repeated? permutation; 5,040

11. How many handshakes can occur between five people if everyone shakes hands? combination; 10

Chapter 9   36   Glencoe California Mathematics, Grade 6

Practice*
p. 37 OL AL

NAME ___ DATE ___ PERIOD ___

9-5 Practice   6SDAP3.I

Combinations

Solve each problem.

1. BASKETBALL In how many ways can a coach select 5 players from a team of 10 players? 252

2. BOOKS In how many ways can 3 books be selected from a shelf of 25 books? 2,300

3. CAFETERIA In how many ways can you choose 2 side dishes from 15 items? 105

4. CHORES Of 8 household chores, in how many ways can you do three-fourths of them? 28

5. ELDERLY Latanya volunteers to bake and deliver pastries to elderly people in her neighborhood. In how many different ways can Latanya deliver to 2 of the 6 elderly people in her neighborhood? 15

6. DELI A deli makes potato, macaroni, three bean, Caesar, 7-layer, and Greek salads. The deli randomly makes only four salads each day. What is the probability that the four salads made one day are 7-layer, macaroni, Greek, and potato? $\frac{1}{15}$

7. AUTOGRAPHS A sports memorabilia enthusiast collected autographed baseballs from the players in the table. The enthusiast is giving one autographed baseball to each of his three grandchildren. If the baseballs are selected at random, what is the probability that the Hank Aaron, Alex Rodriquez, and Mickey Mantle autographed baseballs are given to his grandchildren? $\frac{1}{10}$

Player
Cal Ripkin
Hank Aaron
Barry Bonds
Alex Rodriquez
Mickey Mantle

For Exercises 8-10, tell whether each problem represents a *permutation* or a *combination*. Then solve the problem.

8. LOCKS In how many ways can three different numbers be selected from 10 numbers to open a keypad lock? permutation; 720

9. MOVIES How many ways can 10 DVDs be placed on a shelf? permutation; 10! or 3,628,800

10. TRANSPORTATION Eight people need transportation to the concert. How many different groups of 6 people can ride with Mrs. Johnson? combination; 28

Chapter 9   37   Glencoe California Mathematics, Grade 6

Word Problem Practice*
p. 38 OL AL

NAME ___ DATE ___ PERIOD ___

9-5 Word Problem Practice   6SDAP3.I

Combinations

1. SNACKS A vending machine can display six snacks. If there are eight different kinds of snacks available, how many different groups of six different snacks can be displayed? 28

2. MUSIC Each month, Jose purchases two CDs from a selection of 20 bestselling CDs. How many different pairs of CDs can Jose choose if he chooses two different CDs? 190

3. TESTS On a math test, you can choose any 20 out of 23 questions. How many different groups of 20 questions can you choose? 1,771

4. RESTAURANTS The dinner special at a local pizza parlor gives you the choice of two toppings from a selection of six toppings. How many different choices are possible if two different toppings are chosen? 15

5. TESTING In a science fair experiment, two units are selected for testing from every 500 units produced. How many ways can these two units be selected? 124,750

6. MEETINGS Linda's teacher divided the class into groups of five and required each member of a group to meet with every other member of that group. How many meetings will each group have? 10

7. BASEBALL A baseball coach has 13 players to fill nine positions. How many different teams could he put together? 715

8. GEOMETRY Ten points are marked on a circle. How many different triangles can be drawn between any three points? 120

Chapter 9   38   Glencoe California Mathematics, Grade 6

Enrichment
p. 39 OL AL

NAME ___ DATE ___ PERIOD ___

9-5 Enrichment   6SDAP3.I

From Impossible to Certain Events

A probability is often expressed as a fraction. As you know, an event that is impossible is given a probability of 0 and an event that is certain is given a probability of 1. Events that are neither impossible nor certain are given a probability somewhere between 0 and 1. The probability line below shows relative probabilities.

```
          not so          pretty
impossible likely equally likely likely  certain
    0       1/4      1/2       3/4     1
```

Determine the probability of an event by considering its place on the diagram above. Answers will vary. Accept logical responses.

1. Medical research will find a cure for all diseases.

2. There will be a personal computer in each home by the year 2010.

3. One day, people will live in space or under the sea.

4. Wildlife will disappear as Earth's human population increases.

5. There will be a fifty-first state in the United States.

6. The sun will rise tomorrow morning.

7. Most electricity will be generated by nuclear power by the year 2010.

8. The fuel efficiency of automobiles will increase as the supply of gasoline decreases.

9. Astronauts will land on Mars.

10. The percent of high school students who graduate and enter college will increase.

11. Global warming problems will be solved.

12. All people in the United States will exercise regularly within the near future.

Chapter 9   39   Glencoe California Mathematics, Grade 6

Additional Lesson Resources

* Also available in Spanish ELL

Transparencies
- *5-Minute Check Transparency, Lesson 9-5*

Other Print Products
- *Teaching Mathematics with Manipulatives*
- *Noteables™ Interactive Study Notebook with Foldables™*

Teacher Tech Tools
- *Interactive Classroom CD-ROM, Lesson 9-5*
- *AssignmentWorks CD-ROM, Lesson 9-5*

Student Tech Tools
ca.gr6math.com
- Extra Examples, Chapter 9, Lesson 5
- Self-Check Quiz, Chapter 9, Lesson 5

9-5 Combinations

1 Focus

 Standards Alignment

Before Lesson 9-5
Add, subtract, multiply, and divide with decimals; add with negative integers; subtract positive integers from negative integers; and verify the reasonableness of the results from Standard 5NS2.1

Lesson 9-5
Express the theoretical probability of each outcome from Standard 6SDAP3.1

After Lesson 9-5
Understand that the probability of either of two disjoint events occurring is the sum of the two individual probabilities and that the probability of one event following another, in independent trials, is the product of the two probabilities from Standard 6SDAP3.4

2 Teach

Scaffolding Questions

Ask:

- If I select two pizza toppings randomly from a menu, does the order matter? no

- If I write the five digits of a zip code on an envelope, does the order matter? yes

- If I want to know the probability of my brother winning first prize in a raffle and my sister winning second prize, does the order matter? yes

- If I want to know the probability of picking two green marbles from a bag of marbles, does the order matter? no

Formative Assessment

Use the Check Your Progress exercises after each Example to determine students' understanding of concepts.

480 Chapter 9 Probability

Main IDEA
Find the number of combinations of a set of objects and find probabilities.

Standard 6SDAP3.1 Represent all possible outcomes for compound events in an organized way (e.g., tables, grids, tree diagrams) and **express the theoretical probability of each outcome.**

NEW Vocabulary

combination

 Vocabulary Link . . . . .
Combination
Everyday Use the result of putting objects together, as in a combination of ingredients

Math Use an arrangement of objects in which order is not important

---

1. JB, JO, JD, BJ, BO, BD, OJ, OB, OD, DJ, DB, DO; 12

> **GET READY for the Lesson**

BASKETBALL Coach Chávez wants to select co-captains for her basketball team. She will select two girls from the four oldest members on the team: Jenna, Bailey, Oleta, and Danielle.

1. Use the first letter of each name to list all of the permutations of co-captains. How many are there?

2. Cross out any arrangement that contains the same letters as another one in the list. How many are there now? 6

3. Explain the difference between the two lists. See margin.

An arrangement, or listing, of objects in which order is not important is called a **combination**. In the activity above, choosing Jenna and Bailey is the same as choosing Bailey and Jenna.

Permutations and combinations are related. You can find the number of combinations of objects by dividing the number of permutations of the entire set by the number of ways the smaller set can be arranged.

> **EXAMPLE** Find the Number of Combinations

① **FOOD** Terrence's Pizza Parlor is offering the special shown in the table. How many different two-topping pizzas are possible?

This is a combination problem because the order of the toppings on the pizza is not important.

Today's Special:
Large two-topping pizza
for $14.99

Toppings
Pepperoni
Sausage
Green Peppers
Onions
Mushrooms

METHOD 1 Make a list.

Use the first letter of each topping to list all of the permutations of the toppings taken two at a time. Then cross out the pizzas that are the same as another one.

p, s	s̶,̶ ̶p̶	g̶,̶ ̶p̶	o̶,̶ ̶p̶	m̶,̶ ̶p̶
p, o	s, o	g̶,̶ ̶s̶	o̶,̶ ̶s̶	m̶,̶ ̶s̶
p, m	s, m	g̶,̶ ̶o̶	o, m	m̶,̶ ̶o̶
p, g	s, g	g̶,̶ ̶m̶	o, g	m, g

So, there are 10 different two-topping pizzas.

480 Chapter 9 Probability

> **ADDITIONAL EXAMPLE**

① **DECORATING** Ada can select from seven paint colors for her room. She wants to choose two colors to paint stripes on her walls. How many different pairs of colors can she choose? 21 pairs

Additional Answer

3. The list in Exercise 1 is a permutation where order is important. The list in Exercise 2 does not take order into account.

METHOD 2 Use permutations.

Step 1 Find the number of permutations of the entire set.
$5 \cdot 4 = 20$ A permutation of 5 toppings, taken 2 at time

Step 2 Find the number of permutations of the smaller set.
$2 \cdot 1 = 2$ Number of ways to arrange 2 toppings

Step 3 Find the number of combinations.
$\frac{20}{2}$ or 10   Divide the number of permutations of the entire set by the number of permutations of each smaller set.

So, there are 10 different two-topping pizzas.

 **CHOOSE Your Method**

a. **FOOD** How many different three-topping pizzas are possible if Terrence adds ham and anchovies to the topping choices? **35**

🌐 **Online** Personal Tutor at ca.gr6math.com

Real-World Link . . . .
Checkers is played on an 8-by-8 board in the U.S., England, Australia, and Ireland. People in eastern Europe play on a 10-by-10 board.
Source: about.com

Real-World EXAMPLES

2 **CHECKERS** A checkers tournament features each of the top 8 regional players playing every opponent one time. The 2 players with the best records will then play in a final championship round. How many matches will be played if there are no ties?

Find the number of ways 2 players can be chosen from a group of 8.

There are $8 \cdot 7$ ways to choose 2 people. → $\frac{8 \cdot 7}{2 \cdot 1} = \frac{56}{2}$ or 28
There are $2 \cdot 1$ ways to arrange 2 people.

There are 28 matches plus 1 final match to determine the champion. So, there will be 29 matches played.

Check Make a diagram in which each person is represented by a point. Draw a line segment between each pair of points to represent all the matches. This produces 28 line segments, or 28 matches. Then add the final-round match to make a total of 29 matches.

3 If the players in Example 2 are selected at random, what is the probability that player 2 will play player 7 in the first match?

There are 28 possible combinations of players for the first match and only one favorable outcome. So, the probability is $\frac{1}{28}$.

CHECK Your Progress   b. $\frac{1}{120}$

b. **CHECKERS** What is the probability that player 2 will play player 16 in the first match if the top 16 regional players are invited to play in the tournament?

Math 🌐 **Online** Extra Examples at ca.gr6math.com

Lesson 9-5 Combinations   **481**

Differentiated Instruction

Interpersonal Learners Separate students into groups of four. Have them find the number of different ways they could sit in a row in a movie theater. Encourage them to act the problem out and then check their answers by calculating the permutations. Next, have them find the number of ways that two of them could be chosen, say, to go buy popcorn. Again, encourage them to act the problem out and then check their answers by calculating the combinations.

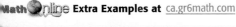

Use Exercises 1–4 to check for understanding.

Then use the chart at the bottom of this page to customize your assignments for students.

Intervention You may wish to use the Study Guide and Intervention Master on page 35 of the *Chapter 9 Resource Masters* for additional reinforcement.

Odd/Even Assignments

Exercises 5–10 are structured so that students practice the same concepts whether they are assigned odd or even problems.

 CHECK Your Understanding

Example 1
(p. 480–481)

1. **PUPPIES** In how many ways can you pick 2 puppies from a litter of 7? **21 ways**

2. **SCIENCE FAIR** In how many ways can 3 out of 10 students be chosen to present their projects at a science fair? **120 ways**

Examples 2, 3
(p. 481)

PAINTING For Exercises 3 and 4, use the information below.

Jade is going to paint her room two different colors from among white, gray, sage, or yellow. **4. $\frac{1}{6}$**

3. How many combinations of two paint colors are there? **6**

4. Find the probability that two colors chosen randomly will be white and sage.

Exercises

HOMEWORK HELP

For Exercises	See Examples
5–8	1, 2
9–10	3

Exercise Levels
A: 5–10
B: 11–14
C: 15–17

5. **ESSAYS** In how many ways can you select 4 essay questions out of 10? **210**

6. **ART** In how many ways can four paintings out of 15 be chosen for display? **1,365**

7. **INTERNET** Of 12 Web sites, in how many ways can you choose to visit 6? **924**

8. **SPORTS** On an 8-member volleyball team, how many different 6-player starting teams are possible? **28**

9. **STUDENT COUNCIL** The students listed are members of Student Council. Three will be chosen at random to form a committee. Find the probability that the three students chosen will be Placido, Maddie, and Akira. $\frac{1}{20}$

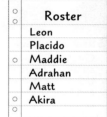

Roster
Leon
Placido
Maddie
Adrahan
Matt
Akira

10. **FOOD** At a hot dog stand, customers can select three toppings from among chili, onions, cheese, mustard, or relish. What is the probability that three toppings selected at random will include onions, mustard, and relish? $\frac{1}{10}$

11. **MUSIC** Marissa practiced the five pieces listed at the right for a recital. Find the number of different ways that three pieces will be randomly chosen for her to play. Then find the probability that all three were composed by Beethoven. **10; $\frac{1}{10}$**

Recital Piece	Composer
Fur Elise	Ludwig van Beethoven
First Piano Sonata	Sergei Rachmaninoff
The Four Seasons	Antonio Vivaldi
Cappricio	Ludwig van Beethoven
Moonlight Sonata	Ludwig van Beethoven

Tell whether each problem represents a *permutation* or a *combination*. Then solve the problem.

EXTRA PRACTICE
See page 703, 723.

Math Online
Self-Check Quiz at
ca.gr6math.com

12. Six children remain in a game of musical chairs. If two chairs are removed, how many different groups of four children can remain? **combination; 15**

13. How many ways can first and second chair positions be awarded in a band that has 10 flute players? **permutation; 90**

14. How many ways can 12 books be stacked in a single pile? **14. permutation; 479,001,600**

DIFFERENTIATED	HOMEWORK OPTIONS		
Level	**Assignment**	**Two-Day Option**	
BL Basic	5–10, 16–25	5–9 odd, 18, 19	6–10 even, 16, 17, 20–25
OL Core	5–13 odd, 16–25	5–10, 18, 19	11–14, 16, 17, 20–25
AL Advanced/Pre-AP	11–23 (optional: 24–25)		

15. CHALLENGE How many people were at a party if each person shook hands exactly once with every other person and there were 105 handshakes? **15**

16. FIND THE ERROR Allison and Francisca are calculating the number of ways that a 3-member committee can be chosen from a 7-member club. Who is correct? Explain your reasoning.

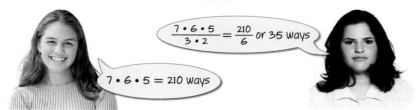

Allison: $7 \cdot 6 \cdot 5 = 210$ ways

Francisca: $\dfrac{7 \cdot 6 \cdot 5}{3 \cdot 2} = \dfrac{210}{6}$ or 35 ways

17. WRITING IN MATH Write about a real-world situation that can be solved using a combination. Then solve the problem. **See margin.**

STANDARDS PRACTICE 6SDAP3.1

18. Three cheerleaders will be randomly selected to represent the squad at a game. If there are 12 cheerleaders, find the probability that the three members chosen are Kameko, Lynn, and Tory.

A $\dfrac{1}{220}$ C $\dfrac{1}{4}$ **A**

B $\dfrac{3}{110}$ D $\dfrac{1}{3}$

19. Four students are to be chosen from a roster of 9 students to attend a science camp. In how many ways can these 4 students be chosen? **H**

F 5   H 126

G 36   J 3,024

Spiral Review

20. SAILING Six sailboats are entered in a race. In how many different ways can the race be completed? Assume there are no ties. (Lesson 9-4) **720 ways**

21. CARS A certain brand of car has the choices listed in the table. How many different cars are possible? (Lesson 9-3) **72**

Engine	Extras	Seats	Color
2.5 L	DVD-player	Cloth	Silver
3.1 L	CD-player	Leather	Green
4.0 L	CD-changer		Red
			White

Estimate. (Lesson 5-2) **22–23. See margin.**

22. $\dfrac{1}{10} + \dfrac{7}{8}$

23. $\dfrac{5}{12} - \dfrac{1}{9}$

GET READY for the Next Lesson

PREREQUISITE SKILL For Exercises 24 and 25, use the graph. (Lesson 8-5)

24. How many students were surveyed? **50**

25. Find the probability that a student's favorite picnic game is sack racing. $\dfrac{1}{5}$

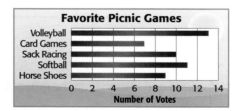

Favorite Picnic Games

⚠️ **Exercise Alert!**

Find the Error In Exercise 16, Allison forgot to divide by the number of ways that three members can be arranged. Remind students that a combination is the number of permutations of a set, divided by the number of permutations of the chosen subset.

4 Assess

Ticket Out the Door Tell students that a bag has the following numbers of colored marbles: 4 blue, 3 red, 2 green, and 1 yellow. Have them find the number of ways of picking at least one green marble if two marbles are randomly picked from the bag. **4**

FOLDABLES Study Organizer **Foldables™ Follow-Up**

Remind students to write a descriptive paragraph about combinations under the tab for this lesson of their Foldables. Encourage them to describe the thoughts and experiences they had while working on the lesson.

Additional Answers

17. The number of ways you can choose three CDs from a collection of ten CDs is 120 ways.

22. Sample answer: $0 + 1 = 1$

23. Sample answer: $\dfrac{1}{2} - 0 = \dfrac{1}{2}$

9-6 Problem-Solving Investigation
ACT IT OUT

Standard 6SDAP3.2 **Use data to estimate the probability of future events** (e.g., batting averages or number of accidents per mile driven).

Standard 6SDAP2.4 **Use a variety of methods, such as words,** numbers, symbols, charts, **graphs,** tables, **diagrams, and models, to explain mathematical reasoning.**

PACING: **Regular:** 1 period, **Block:** 0.5 period

Options for Differentiated Instruction

ELL = English Language Learner **AL** = Above Grade Level **SS** = Struggling Students **SN** = Special Needs

Additional Practice **ELL** **SS**

Use after presenting the Lesson Opener.

Have students add the strategy of acting it out to their problem-solving booklets. Then have them use the strategy to solve the following problem.

> There are eight figure skaters participating in a competition. The skaters placing in the top 2 spots will go on to the next level of competition. In how many ways can the skaters go on to the next level? 28 ways

Ask students to describe how they acted out the problem.

Acting It Out **SS** **SN**

Use after presenting the Examples.

When you group students together to discuss problems to solve, try placing students with different interests in each group. Students will naturally choose *act it out* strategies based on their own experiences. Mixing students interested in sports, music, and photography, for example, will enrich students' visions of possible *act it out* strategies.

Choosing a Strategy **ELL** **SS** **SN**

Use before assigning the Exercises.

Prior to assigning Exercises 7–11, read each problem aloud and discuss with the group which strategy might be best to solve the problem.

Possible discussion questions:
- What question do you need to answer?
- What information is given?
- Is this like any problems you have done in the past?
- What strategy would be most effective to solve the problem?
- How could you check your answer to make sure it is reasonable?

Make sure that all students have chosen a strategy for each of the problems so they can complete the assignment independently.

Leveled Lesson Resources

Chapter 9 Resource Masters

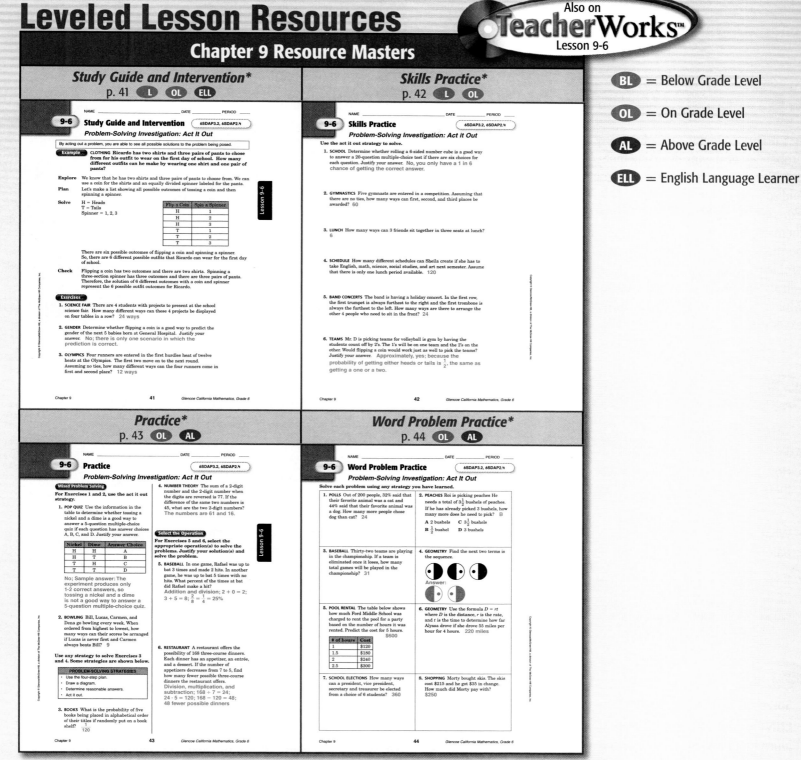

BL = Below Grade Level

OL = On Grade Level

AL = Above Grade Level

ELL = English Language Learner

* Also available in Spanish **ELL**

Additional Lesson Resources

Transparencies
- *5-Minute Check Transparency,* 9-6

Other Print Products
- *Noteables™ Interactive Study Notebook with Foldables™*

Teacher Tech Tools
- *Interactive Classroom CD-ROM,* Lesson 9-6
- *AssignmentWorks CD-ROM,* Lesson 9-6

Student Tech Tools
ca.gr6math.com
- Extra Examples, Chapter 9, Lesson 6
- Self-Check Quiz, Chapter 9, Lesson 6

9-6 Lesson Notes

1 Focus

Act It Out Students can solve many probability problems by acting them out. They can use number cubes, coins, and spinners to perform probability experiments, and they can even use themselves and their classmates to solve permutation and combination problems. This problem-solving strategy will also prove useful in Lesson 9-7, when students compare theoretical and experimental probabilities.

2 Teach

Scaffolding Questions

Ask:

• How many possible outcomes are there for rolling two number cubes? 36

• What is the probability of rolling a pair of 1s with two number cubes? $\frac{1}{36}$

• If you rolled two number cubes 36 times, how many pairs of 1s would you expect? about 1

ADDITIONAL EXAMPLE

Solve. Use the act-it-out strategy.

LUNCH Salvador is looking for his lunch money, which he put in one of the pockets of his backpack this morning. If the backpack has six pockets, what is the probability that he will find the money in the first pocket that he checks? $\frac{1}{6}$; Check students' experiments to see whether they accurately represented the situation.

9-6 Problem-Solving Investigation

MAIN IDEA: Solve problems by acting it out.

Standard 6SDAP3.2 Use data to estimate the probability of future events (e.g., batting averages or number of accidents per mile driven). **Standard 6MR2.4** Use a variety of methods, such as words, numbers, symbols, charts, **graphs**, tables, **diagrams**, and models, to explain mathematical reasoning.

P.S.I. TEAM +

e-Mail: ACT IT OUT

YOUR MISSION: Solve the problem by acting it out.

THE PROBLEM: Determine the probability that Eddie makes two free-throws in a row.

> **Eddie:** I make an average of 3 out of every 4 free-throws I try.

EXPLORE	You know that Eddie makes an average of 3 out of every 4 free throws. You could have Eddie actually make free throws, but that requires a basketball hoop. You could also act it out with a spinner.
PLAN	Spin a spinner, numbered 1 to 4, two times. If the spinner lands on 1, 2, or 3, he makes the free-throw. If the spinner lands on 4, he doesn't make it. Repeat the experiment of 10 times.
SOLVE	Spin the spinner and make a table of the results.

Trials	1	2	3	4	5	6	7	8	9	10
First Spin	4	1	4	3	1	2	2	1	3	2
Second Spin	2	3	3	2	1	4	1	4	3	3

	The highlighted columns show that six out of the 10 trials resulted in two free-throws in a row. So the probability is 60%.
CHECK	Repeat the experiment several times to see whether the results agree.

Analyze The Strategy

1. Explain whether the results of the experiment would be the same if it were repeated. **Sample answer: Results would vary slightly.**

2. **WRITING IN MATH** Write a problem that can be solved by acting it out. Then solve the problem by acting it out. **See margin.**

484 Chapter 9 Probability

Tips for New Teachers

Probability Experiments

Make sure students understand that the results of repeated probability experiments will vary. Ask them to imagine tossing a coin ten times, and then repeating the experiment. Point out that the number of heads tossed for each experiment can change (and will not necessarily be 5).

Additional Answer

2. Sample answer: In how many different ways can a four people be seated in a car if there are 2 front seats and 2 back seats and only 3 of the four people are able to drive? There are 18 possible ways.

For Exercises 3–6, use the *act it out* strategy.

3. **POP QUIZ** Determine whether using a spinner with four equal sections is a good way to answer a 5-question multiple-choice quiz if each question has choices A, B, C, and D. Justify your answer. **See margin.**

4. **PHOTOGRAPHS** Samuel is taking a photo of the Spanish Club's five officers. The president will always stand on the left, and the vice-president will always stand on the right. How many different ways can he arrange the officers for the photo? **6**

5. **RUNNING** Six runners are entered in a race. Assuming no ties, in how many different ways can first and second places be awarded? **30**

6. **MOVIES** In how many different ways can four friends sit in a row of four seats at the movies if two of the friends insist on sitting next to each other? **12**

Use any strategy to solve Exercises 7–11. Some strategies are shown below.

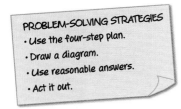

PROBLEM-SOLVING STRATEGIES
• Use the four-step plan.
• Draw a diagram.
• Use reasonable answers.
• Act it out.

7. **SEASONS** Refer to the graph. In a middle school of 800 students, would about 150, 250, or 350 be a reasonable answer for the number of students that prefer autumn? Justify your solution.

Seasons of Change

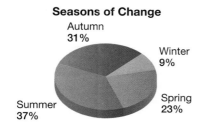

Autumn 31%
Winter 9%
Spring 23%
Summer 37%

250 is a reasonable answer since 31% of 800 is 248.

8. **SPACE SCIENCE** A 21-kilogram sample of rocks from the Moon is composed of 40% oxygen and 19.2% silicon. How many kilograms more is the oxygen than the silicon mass? **about 4.368 kg more**

9. **ALGEBRA** The pattern below is known as Pascal's Triangle. Would 1, 6, 10, 10, 6, 1 be a reasonable conjecture for the numbers in the 6th row? Justify your answer. **See margin.**

1st Row					1				
2nd Row				1		1			
3rd Row			1		2		1		
4th Row		1		3		3		1	
5th Row	1		4		6		4		1

10. **SOCCER** Sixteen teams are playing in a soccer tournament. If a team loses one game, it is eliminated. How many total games will be played in the tournament? **15**

11. **SCHOOL** Suppose rolling an even number on a number cube corresponds to an answer of *true* and rolling an odd number corresponds to an answer of *false*. Determine whether rolling this number cube is a good way to answer a 5-question true-false quiz. Justify your answer. **See margin.**

Select the Operation

For Exercises 12–14, select the appropriate operation(s) to solve the problem. Justify your selection(s) and solve the problem.

12. **TRANSPORTATION** A taxi charges $3.25 for the first 0.4 mile and $0.75 for each additional 0.4 mile. Find the cost of a 4-mile taxi ride. **See margin.**

13. **MOUNTAINS** The mountain Mauna Kea in Hawaii is about 1.38×10^4 feet tall while Everest is about 29,000 feet tall. About how many feet taller is Mt. Everest? **subtraction; $29{,}000 - 1.38 \times 10^4 = 15{,}200$ ft**

14. **MONEY** Lola purchased a $35 book bag at a sale price of $27.50. What was the approximate percent of decrease from the original price to the sale price? **See margin.**

---

3 Practice

Using the Exercises

Exercises 1 and 2 can be used to check for understanding.

Exercises 3–6 give students an opportunity to practice the act it out strategy.

Exercises 7–11 are structured so that students have the opportunity to practice many different problem-solving strategies. You may wish to review some of the strategies they have studied.

• Use the four-step plan (p. 25)
• Draw a diagram (p. 314)
• Determine reasonable answers (p. 366)
• Act it out (p. 484)

Exercises 12–14 require students to select the operation to solve problems. Have students analyze each problem and its wording, asking themselves what kind of information is needed. Which operation(s) must be performed to get the information?

4 Assess

Crystal Ball Tell students that tomorrow's lesson is about comparing experimental and theoretical probabilities. Ask students to write how they think what they learned today will connect with tomorrow's material.

Formative Assessment

Check for student understanding of concepts in Lessons 9-5 and 9-6.

CRM Quiz 3, p. 62

14. Subtraction followed by division; $35 − $27.50 = $7.50; $7.50 ÷ $35 ≈ 0.214, or 21.4%

Additional Answers

3. No; Sample answer: the experiment produces about 1–2 correct answers, so using a spinner with 4 sections is not a good way to answer a 5-question multiple-choice quiz.

9. No, the 6th row should have the numbers 1, 5, 10, 10, 5, 1.

11. No; Sample answer: the experiment produces about 2-3 correct answers, so using a number cube is not a good way to answer a 5-question true-false quiz.

12. Subtraction followed by division followed by multiplication followed by addition; 4 − 0.4 = 3.6; 3.6 ÷ 0.4 = 9; 9 × $0.75 = $6.75; $6.75 + $3.25 = $10

Theoretical and Experimental Probability

Standard 6SDAP3.2   **Use data to estimate the probability of future events** (e.g., batting averages or number of accidents per mile driven).

PACING: **Regular:** 2 periods, **Block:** 1 period

Options for Differentiated Instruction

ELL = English Language Learner   **AL** = Above Grade Level   **SS** = Struggling Students   **SN** = Special Needs

Collecting and Organizing Data **SS** **SN**

Use before beginning Lesson 9-7.

Step 1: Create a set of class data.
- Have each student roll a number cube 12 times and record the results.
- Discuss that the theoretical probability of rolling a given number on the number cube is $\frac{1}{6}$. So, theoretically, they should get each number twice.

Step 2: Compile the data.
- Draw a line plot on the board.
- Have students add their results to the line plot one at a time.
- As more and more data points are added, discuss what is happening in the line plot.

Conducting a Survey **ELL** **AL** **SS** **SN**

Use after presenting the Examples.

Have students work in small groups to create surveys. Questions should have either yes/no answers or multiple-choice answers. Each group should conduct its survey with the other students in the class. Students should use the results to predict how many students from the entire grade or school could be expected to have the same answers.

Study Tools **ELL** **SS** **SN**

Use before assigning the Exercises.

Have students add the definitions of theoretical and experimental probability to their resource sheets. Provide the following template as a guide.

Term	Definition	How to Find	Example
theoretical probability	probability based on what *should* happen during a probability experiment	Apply a formula.	rolling a 1: $\frac{6}{36} = \frac{1}{6}$
experimental probability	probability based on what *actually* happens during a probability experiment	Collect data.	rolling a 1: $\frac{n}{36}$, where n is the number of 1s rolled in 36 rolls

Leveled Lesson Resources

Chapter 9 Resource Masters

BL = Below Grade Level   **OL** = On Grade Level   **AL** = Above Grade Level   **ELL** = English Language Learner

---

Lesson Reading Guide
p. 45 **BL** **OL** **ELL**

9-7 Lesson Reading Guide   6SDAP3.2
Theoretical and Experimental Probability

Get Ready for the Lesson
Complete the Mini Lab at the top of page 486 in your textbook. Write your answers below.

1. Compare the number of times you *expected* to roll a sum of 7 with the number of times you *actually* rolled a sum of 7. Then compare your result to the results of other groups. See students' work.

2. Write the probability of rolling a sum of 7 out of 36 rolls using the number of times you *expected* to roll a 7 from Step 1. Then write the probability of rolling a sum of 7 out of 36 rolls using the number of times you *actually* rolled a sum of 7 from Step 2. See students' work.

Read the Lesson
3. Look up the word *experimental* in a dictionary. Write the meaning for the word as used in the lesson. Sample answer: based on experience rather than on theory

4. How does theoretical probability differ from experimental probability? Sample answer: Theoretical probability is the expected probability of an event happening. Experimental probability is based on something you actually try (for example, an experiment or game).

5. Complete the sentence: Experimental probability can be based on past performances and can be used to make predictions about future events.

Remember What You Learned
6. Work with a partner. Design an experiment that you can use to express the experimental probability of an event. Compare your findings with those of others in your class. See students' work.

Chapter 9   45   Glencoe California Mathematics, Grade 6

Study Guide and Intervention*
p. 46 **BL** **OL** **ELL**

9-7 Study Guide and Intervention   6SDAP3.2
Theoretical and Experimental Probability

Experimental probability is found using frequencies obtained in an experiment or game. Theoretical probability is the expected probability of an event occurring.

Example 1 The graph shows the results of an experiment in which a number cube was rolled 100 times. Find the experimental probability of rolling a 3 for this experiment.

$P(3) = \frac{\text{number of times 3 occurs}}{\text{number of possible outcomes}}$

$= \frac{16}{100}$ or $\frac{4}{25}$

The experimental probability of rolling a 3 is $\frac{4}{25}$, which is close to its theoretical probability of $\frac{1}{6}$.

Example 2 In a telephone poll, 225 people were asked for whom they planned to vote in the race for mayor. What is the experimental probability of Juarez being elected?

Candidate	Number of People
Juarez	75
Davis	67
Abramson	83

Of the 225 people polled, 75 planned to vote for Juarez.
So, the experimental probability is $\frac{75}{225}$ or $\frac{1}{3}$.

Example 3 Suppose 5,700 people vote in the election. How many can be expected to vote for Juarez?

$\frac{1}{3} \cdot 5,700 = 1,900$

About 1,900 will vote for Juarez.

Exercises
For Exercises 1–3, use the graph of a survey of 150 students asked whether they prefer cats or dogs.

1. What is the probability of a student preferring dogs? $\frac{22}{25}$

2. Suppose 100 students were surveyed. How many can be expected to prefer dogs? 88

3. Suppose 300 students were surveyed. How many can be expected to prefer cats? 36

Chapter 9   46   Glencoe California Mathematics, Grade 6

Skills Practice*
p. 47 **BL** **OL**

9-7 Skills Practice   6SDAP3.2
Theoretical and Experimental Probability

For Exercises 1–5, a number cube is rolled 50 times and the results are shown in the graph below.

1. Find the experimental probability of rolling a 2. $\frac{4}{25}$

2. What is the theoretical probability of rolling a 2? $\frac{1}{6}$

3. Find the experimental probability of *not* rolling a 2. $\frac{21}{25}$

4. What is the theoretical probability of *not* rolling a 2? $\frac{5}{6}$

5. Find the experimental probability of rolling a 1. $\frac{1}{5}$

For Exercises 6–9, use the results of the survey at the right.

What is your favorite season of the year?
Spring 13%
Summer 39%
Fall 25%
Winter 13%
None, I like them all 10%

6. What is the probability that a person's favorite season is fall? Write the probability as a fraction. $\frac{1}{4}$

7. Out of 300 people, how many would you expect to say that fall is their favorite season? 75

8. Out of 20 people, how many would you expect to say that they like all the seasons? 2

9. Out of 650 people, how many more would you expect to say that they like summer than say that they like winter? 169

Chapter 9   47   Glencoe California Mathematics, Grade 6

Practice*
p. 48 **OL** **AL**

9-7 Practice   6SDAP3.2
Theoretical and Experimental Probability

For Exercises 1–4, a number cube is rolled 24 times and lands on 2 four times and on 6 three times.

1. Find the experimental probability of landing on a 2. $\frac{1}{6}$

2. Find the experimental probability of *not* landing on a 6. $\frac{7}{8}$

3. Compare the experimental probability you found in Exercise 1 to its theoretical probability. The theoretical probability of landing on a 2, $\frac{1}{6}$, is the same as the experimental probability.

4. Compare the experimental probability you found in Exercise 2 to its theoretical probability. The theoretical probability of *not* landing on a 6, $\frac{5}{6}$, is fairly close to the experimental probability.

ENTERTAINMENT For Exercises 5–7, use the results of the survey in the table shown.

Best Entertainment Value	
Type of Entertainment	Percent
Playing Interactive Games	48%
Reading Books	22%
Renting Movies	10%
Going to Movie Theaters	10%
Surfing the Internet	9%
Watching Television	1%

5. What is the probability that someone in the survey considered reading books or surfing the Internet as the best entertainment value? Write the probability as a fraction. $\frac{31}{100}$

6. Out of 500 people surveyed, how many would you expect considered reading books or surfing the Internet as the best entertainment value? 155

7. Out of 300 people surveyed, is it reasonable to expect that 30 considered watching television as the best entertainment value? Why or why not? No; 1% of 300 = 3, not 30.

For Exercises 8–10, a spinner marked with four sections blue, green, yellow, and red was spun 100 times. The results are shown in the table.

Section	Frequency
Blue	14
Green	10
Yellow	8
Red	68

8. Find the experimental probability of landing on green. $\frac{1}{10}$

9. Find the experimental probability of landing on red. $\frac{17}{25}$

10. If the spinner is spun 50 more times, how many of these times would you expect the pointer to land on blue? 7

Chapter 9   48   Glencoe California Mathematics, Grade 6

Word Problem Practice*
p. 49 **OL** **AL**

9-7 Word Problem Practice   6SDAP3.2
Theoretical and Experimental Probability

HOBBIES For Exercises 1–3, use the graph of a survey of 24 seventh grade students asked to name their favorite hobby.

What is your favorite hobby?
Singing
Hanging with friends
Building things
Bike riding
T.V.
Computer
Roller skating
Sports

WINTER ACTIVITIES For Exercises 5 and 6, use the graph of a survey with 104 responses in which respondents were asked about their favorite winter activities.

What is your favorite winter activity?
Building a snowman
Snowboarding/skiing
Sledding

1. What is the probability that a student's favorite hobby is roller skating? $\frac{1}{8}$

2. Suppose 200 seventh grade students were surveyed. How many can be expected to say that roller skating is their favorite hobby? 25

3. Suppose 60 seventh grade students were surveyed. How many can be expected to say that bike riding is their favorite hobby? 5

4. **MARBLES** A bag contains 5 blue, 4 red, 9 white, and 6 green marbles. If a marble is drawn at random and replaced 100 times, how many times would you expect to draw a green marble? 25

5. What is the probability that someone's favorite winter activity is building a snowman? Write the probability as a fraction. $\frac{7}{52}$

6. If 500 people had responded, how many would have been expected to list sledding as their favorite winter activity? Round to the nearest whole person. 101

Chapter 9   49   Glencoe California Mathematics, Grade 6

Enrichment
p. 50 **OL** **AL**

9-7 Enrichment   6SDAP3.2

Rolling a Dodecahedron
A dodecahedron is a solid. It has twelve faces, and each face is a pentagon.

At the right, you see a dodecahedron whose faces are marked with the integers from 1 through 12. You can roll this dodecahedron just as you roll a number cube. With the dodecahedron, however, there are *twelve* equally likely outcomes.

Refer to the dodecahedron shown at the right. Find the probability of each event.

1. $P(5)$ $\frac{1}{12}$
2. $P(\text{odd})$ $\frac{1}{2}$
3. $P(\text{prime})$ $\frac{5}{12}$
4. $P(\text{divisible by 5})$ $\frac{1}{6}$
5. $P(\text{less than 4})$ $\frac{1}{4}$
6. $P(\text{fraction})$ 0

You can make your own dodecahedron by cutting out the pattern at the right. Fold along each of the solid lines. Then use tape to join the faces together so that your dodecahedron looks like the one shown above.

7. Roll your dodecahedron 100 times. Record your results on a separate sheet of paper, using a table like this.

Outcome	Tally	Frequency
1		
2		

Answers will vary.

8. Use your results from Exercise 7. Find the experimental probability for each of the events described in Exercises 1–6. Answers will vary.

Chapter 9   50   Glencoe California Mathematics, Grade 6

Additional Lesson Resources

Transparencies
• *5-Minute Check Transparency,* Lesson 9-7

Other Print Products
• *Teaching Mathematics with Manipulatives*
• *Noteables™ Interactive Study Notebook with Foldables™*

Teacher Tech Tools
• *Interactive Classroom CD-ROM,* Lesson 9-7
• *AssignmentWorks CD-ROM,* Lesson 9-7

Student Tech Tools
ca.gr6math.com
• Extra Examples, Chapter 9, Lesson 7
• Self-Check Quiz, Chapter 9, Lesson 7

1 Focus

Standards Alignment

Before Lesson 9-7
Represent probabilities as ratios, proportions, decimals, and percentages and verify that the probabilities computed are reasonable; know that if P is the probability of an event, $1 - P$ is the probability of an event *not* occurring from ⊙━━ Standard 6SDAP3.3

Lesson 9-7
Use data to estimate the probability of future events from Standard 6SDAP3.2

After Lesson 9-7
Understand that the probability of either of two disjoint events occurring is the sum of the two individual probabilities and that the probability of one event following another, in independent trials, is the product of the two probabilities from Standard 6SDAP3.4

2 Teach

▶ MINI Lab

Suggest that one student in each pair roll the number cubes while the other student keeps a tally of the number of sums of 7 rolled and the total number of rolls. You may wish to supply grid paper for students to make the addition tables.

Scaffolding Questions

Tell students that a book club raised money by selling 100 raffle tickets for an encyclopedia. Say that you bought 10 tickets, and a friend bought 2 tickets. Your friend won the encyclopedia.

Main IDEA
Find and compare experimental and theoretical probabilities.

 Standard 6SDAP3.2 Use data to estimate the probability of future events (e.g., batting averages or number of accidents per mile driven).

NEW Vocabulary
theoretical probability
experimental probability

REVIEW Vocabulary
sample space a list of all possible outcomes (Lesson 9-2)

1. See students' work. Sample answer: The number of times a sum of 7 is expected on 36 tosses is 6. Students' experiments may vary slightly.

2. See students' work. Sample answer: The expected probability of rolling a sum of 7 is $\frac{6}{36}$, or $\frac{1}{6}$. Students' experimental probabilities may vary slightly.

▶ GET READY for the Lesson

Follow the steps to determine how many times a sum of 7 is expected to turn up when two number cubes are rolled.

Step 1 Use an addition table from 1 to 6 to help you find the expected number of times the sum of 7 should come up after rolling two number cubes 36 times. The top row represents one number cube, and the left column represents the other number cube. A partial addition table is shown below.

+	1	2	3	4	5	6
1	2	3	4	5	6	7
2	3	4	5	6	7	8

Step 2 Roll two number cubes 36 times. Record the number of times the sum of the number cubes is 7.

1. Compare the number of times you *expected* to roll a sum of 7 with the number of times you *actually* rolled a sum of 7. Then compare your result to the results of other groups.

2. Write the probability of rolling a sum of 7 out of 36 rolls using the number of times you *expected* to roll a 7 from Step 1. Then write the probability of rolling a sum of 7 out of 36 rolls using the number of times you *actually* rolled a sum of 7 from Step 2.

In the Mini-Lab above, you found both the theoretical probability and the experimental probability of rolling a sum of 7 using two number cubes. **Theoretical probability** is based on what *should* happen when conducting a probability experiment. This is the probability you have been using since Lesson 10-1. **Experimental probability** is based on what *actually* occurred during such an experiment.

Theoretical Probability

$\frac{6}{36}$ ← 6 rolls *should* occur
 ← total number of rolls

Experimental Probability

$\frac{n}{36}$ ← *n* rolls *actually* occurred
 ← total number of rolls

The theoretical probability and the experimental probability of an event may or may not be the same. As the number of times an experiment is conducted increases, the theoretical probability and the experimental probability should become closer in value.

Ask:
- What was my probability of winning the encyclopedia? $\frac{1}{10}$
- What fraction of my tickets won? $\frac{0}{10}$
- What was my friend's probability of winning? $\frac{1}{50}$
- What fraction of her tickets won? $\frac{1}{2}$

 Tips for New Teachers

Theoretical and Experimental Probability

Combine the class data from the Mini Lab to see if the experimental and theoretical probabilities become closer in value than by comparing those probabilities within each group alone.

EXAMPLE Experimental Probability

1 Two number cubes are rolled 75 times, and a sum of 9 is rolled 10 times. What is the experimental probability of rolling a sum of 9?

$$P(9) = \frac{\text{number of these times a sum of 9 occurs}}{\text{total number of rolls}}$$

$$= \frac{10}{75} \text{ or } \frac{2}{15}$$

The experimental probability of rolling a sum of 9 is $\frac{2}{15}$.

✓ CHECK Your Progress

a. In the above experiment, what is the experimental probability of rolling a sum that is *not* 9? $\frac{13}{15}$

b. In the above experiment, what is the experimental probability of rolling a sum that is *not* six if a sum of six was rolled 18 times? $\frac{19}{25}$

STUDY TIP

Trials A *trial* is one experiment in a series of successive experiments.

EXAMPLES Experimental and Theoretical Probability

2 The graph shows the results of an experiment in which a coin was tossed thirty times. Find the experimental probability of getting tails in this experiment.

The frequency graph indicates that the coin landed on heads 12 times and tails 18 times.

$$P(\text{tails}) = \frac{\text{number of times tails occurs}}{\text{total number of tosses}}$$

$$= \frac{18}{30} \text{ or } \frac{3}{5}$$

The experimental probability of getting tails was $\frac{3}{5}$.

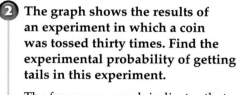

3 Compare the experimental probability you found in Example 2 to its theoretical probability.

The coin has two equally likely outcomes, heads or tails. So, the theoretical probability of tossing tails is $\frac{1}{2}$. Since $\frac{3}{5} \approx \frac{1}{2}$, the experimental probability is close to the theoretical probability.

d. The experimental probability is slightly greater than the theoretical probability of $\frac{1}{2}$. Since $\frac{1}{2} = \frac{4}{8}$ and $\frac{5}{8} > \frac{4}{8}$.

✓ CHECK Your Progress

c. Refer to Example 2. If the coin was tossed 2 more times and landed on tails each time, predict the experimental probability of tossing heads for this experiment. $\frac{5}{8}$

d. Compare the experimental probability you found in Exercise c to its theoretical probability.

 Personal Tutor at ca.gr6math.com

Lesson 9-7 Theoretical and Experimental Probability **487**

✓ Formative Assessment

Use the Check Your Progress exercises after each Example to determine students' understanding of concepts.

ADDITIONAL EXAMPLES

1 A spinner is spun 50 times, and it lands on the color blue 15 times. What is the experimental probability of spinning blue? $P(\text{blue}) = \frac{15}{50} = \frac{3}{10}$

2 The graph below shows the results of an experiment in which a number cube is rolled 30 times. Find the experimental probability of rolling a 5. $\frac{2}{15}$

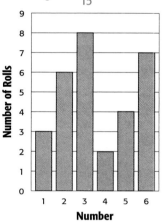

3 Compare the experimental probability you found in Additional Example 2 to its theoretical probability. The theoretical probability $\left(\frac{1}{6}\right)$ is close to the experimental probability.

Focus on Mathematical Content

The **theoretical probability** of an experiment or situation can be calculated. It is the ratio of the number of favorable outcomes to the number of possible outcomes.

Experimental probability is the ratio of actual favorable outcomes in an experiment or situation to the actual number of trials.

The **more times an experiment is repeated**, the closer the experimental probability will approach the theoretical probability.

Experimental probability can be used to make **inferences** about the subject data and/or **predictions** about future events.

Experimental probability can be used to make predictions about future events.

Real-World EXAMPLES Predict Future Events

4. **FOOD** In a survey, 100 people in a city were asked to name their favorite Independence Day side dishes. What is the experimental probability that macaroni salad was someone's favorite side dish?

Side Dish	Number of People
potato salad	55
green salad or vegetables	25
macaroni salad	12
coleslaw	8

There were 100 people surveyed and 12 chose macaroni salad. So, the experimental probability is $\frac{12}{100}$, or $\frac{3}{25}$.

5. Suppose 2,500 people attend the city's Independence Day barbecue. Based on the survey results how many can be expected to choose macaroni salad as their favorite side dish?

$$\frac{3}{25} = \frac{x}{2,500} \quad \text{Write a proportion.}$$

$3 \cdot 2,500 = 25 \cdot x \quad$ Find the cross products.

$\quad 7,500 = 25x \quad$ Multiply.

$\quad\quad 300 = x \quad$ Divide each side by 25.

About 300 will choose macaroni salad.

CHECK Your Progress

e. What is the experimental probability of potato salad being someone's favorite dish? $\frac{11}{20}$

f. About how many people can be expected to choose potato salad as their favorite dish if 400 attend the barbecue? 220

Real-World Career . . . .
How Does a Chef Use Math? In addition to cooking, chefs order enough food and supplies based on customers' preferences and recent sales.

Math Online
For more information, go to ca.gr6math.com.

CHECK Your Understanding

Examples 1–3
(p. 487)

For Exercises 1–3, a coin is tossed 50 times, and it lands on heads 28 times.

1. Find the experimental probability of the coin landing heads. $\frac{14}{25}$

2. Find the theoretical probability of the coin landing heads. $\frac{1}{2}$

3. Compare the probabilities in Exercises 1 and 2.

Example 4
(p. 488)

TRAFFIC For Exercises 4 and 5, use the table of the types of vehicles that drove through an intersection between 3:00 and 4:00 P.M. one Saturday.

Vehicle	Number of Vehicles
sedan	11
truck	15
sports car	6

4. Based on this information, what is the probability that a vehicle that drives through the intersection is a sports car? $\frac{3}{16}$

Example 5
(p. 488)

5. If 128 vehicles drove through the intersection, about how many would you expect to be sports cars? 24

488   Chapter 9 Probability

 Math Online Extra Examples at ca.gr6math.com

Exercises

HOMEWORK HELP

For Exercises	See Examples
6–7	1–3
8–9	4
10–11	5

Exercise Levels
A: 6–11
B: 12–17
C: 18–20

For Exercises 6 and 7, a number cube is rolled 20 times and lands on 1 two times and on 5 four times. 6, 7. See margin for comparisons.

6. Find the experimental probability of landing on 5. Compare the experimental probability to the theoretical probability. $\frac{1}{5}$

7. Find the experimental probability of *not* landing on 1. Compare the experimental probability to the theoretical probability. $\frac{9}{10}$

X GAMES For Exercises 8–11, use the graph of a survey of 50 students asked to name their favorite X Game sport.

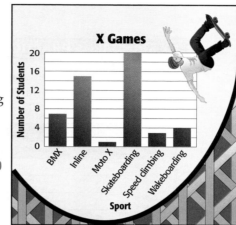

8. What is the probability of Moto X being someone's favorite sport? $\frac{1}{50}$

9. What is the probability of skateboarding being someone's favorite sport? $\frac{2}{5}$

10. Suppose 500 students attend the X Games. Predict how many will choose inline as their favorite sport. **150**

11. Suppose 850 students attend. Predict how many will choose speed climbing as their favorite sport. **51**

For Exercises 12–14, a spinner with three equal-sized sections marked A, B, and C was spun 100 times. The results are shown in the table.

Section	Frequency
A	24
B	50
C	26

12. What is the experimental probability of landing on A? Of landing on C? $\frac{6}{25}, \frac{13}{50}$

13. If this spinner is spun 20 more times, predict how many of these times the pointer will land on B. **10**

14. Make a drawing of what the spinner might look like based on its experimental probabilities. Explain your reasoning. **See margin.**

GIFTS For Exercises 15–17, use the graph at the right.

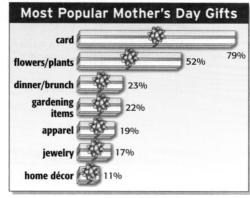

Most Popular Mother's Day Gifts

- card 79%
- flowers/plants 52%
- dinner/brunch 23%
- gardening items 22%
- apparel 19%
- jewelry 17%
- home décor 11%

Source: Carlton Cards

15. What is the probability that a mother will receive a gift of flowers or plants? Write the probability as a fraction. $\frac{13}{25}$

16. Out of 400 mothers that receive gifts, predict how many will receive flowers or plants. **208**

17. Out of 750 mothers that receive gifts, is it reasonable to expect 250 mothers to receive jewelry? Why or why not? **See margin.**

EXTRA PRACTICE

See page 703, 723.

Math Online
Self-Check Quiz at
ca.gr6math.com

Lesson 9-7 Theoretical and Experimental Probability **489**

Odd/Even Assignments

Exercises 6–11 are structured so that students practice the same concepts whether they are assigned odd or even problems.

Additional Answers

6. The experimental probability, $\frac{1}{5}$ or 20%, is close to its theoretical probability of $\frac{1}{6}$ or about 17%.

7. The experimental probability, $\frac{9}{10}$ or 90%, is close to its theoretical probability of $\frac{5}{6}$ or about 83%.

14.

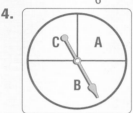

The experimental probability of landing on section A is $\frac{6}{25}$, or about $\frac{1}{4}$. The experimental probability of landing on section B is $\frac{50}{100}$, or $\frac{1}{2}$. The experimental probability of landing on section C is $\frac{13}{50}$, or about $\frac{1}{4}$. So, section B should be one-half of the spinner and sections A and C should each be one-fourth of the spinner.

17. No. The experimental probability that a mother will receive jewelry is $\frac{17}{100}$. Out of 750 mothers that receive gifts, only about 128 can expect to receive jewelry not 250.

DIFFERENTIATED HOMEWORK OPTIONS			
Level	**Assignment**	**Two-Day Option**	
BL Basic	6–11, 19–29	7–11 odd, 21, 22	6–10 even, 19, 20, 23–29
OL Core	7–17 odd, 19–29	6–11, 21, 22	12–17, 19, 20, 23–29
AL Advanced/Pre-AP	12–25 (optional: 26–29)		

490 Chapter 9 Probability

18. CHALLENGE The experimental probability of a coin landing on heads is $\frac{7}{12}$. If the coin landed on tails 30 times, find the number of tosses. **72**

19. REASONING Twenty sharpened pencils are placed in a box containing an unknown number of unsharpened pencils. Suppose 15 pencils are taken out at random, of which five are sharpened. Based on this, is it reasonable to assume that the number of unsharpened pencils was 40? Explain your reasoning. **See Ch. 9 Answer Appendix.**

20. WRITING IN MATH Compare and contrast experimental probability and theoretical probability. **See margin.**

STANDARDS PRACTICE 6SDAP3.2

21. The frequency table shows Mitch's record for the last thirty par-3 holes he has played.

Mitch's Golf Results	
Score	Number of Holes
2	4
3	14
4	9
5	3

Based on this record, what is the probability that Mitch will score a 2 or 3 on the next par-3 hole? **B**

A $\frac{7}{9}$ C $\frac{3}{10}$

B $\frac{3}{5}$ D $\frac{9}{50}$

22. J.R. tossed a coin 100 times and graphed the results.

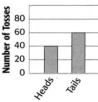

Tossing a Coin

Based on this information, what is the experimental probability of tossing tails on the next toss? **H**

F $\frac{1}{5}$ H $\frac{3}{5}$

G $\frac{2}{3}$ J $\frac{4}{5}$

Spiral Review

23. SPINNERS In how many ways could the colors in the spinner shown be arranged so that red and blue remain in the same places? (Lesson 9-6)
6

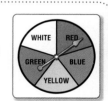

24. BASEBALL How many ways can a baseball coach select four starting pitchers from a pitching staff of eight? (Lesson 9-5) **70**

25. CLOTHES A pair of jeans comes in 4 different styles, 3 different colors, and 5 different sizes. How many unique outcomes are possible? (Lesson 9-3) **60**

▶ GET READY for the Next Lesson

PREREQUISITE SKILL Write each fraction as a percent. (Lesson 6-8)

26. $\frac{4}{5}$ **80%**   **27.** $\frac{11}{20}$ **55%**   **28.** $\frac{7}{8}$ **87.5%**   **29.** $\frac{39}{50}$ **78%**

---

4 Assess

Name the Math Have students describe a theoretical probability and an experiment to test it. You might need to give them some ideas, such as: *How many boys and girls would you expect in a class with 30 students? What color socks are in your dresser drawer?*

FOLDABLES Study Organizer Foldables™ Follow-Up

Remind students to write a descriptive paragraph comparing experimental probability and theoretical probability under the tab for this lesson in their Foldables. Encourage them to describe the thoughts and experiences they had while working on the lesson.

Differentiated Instruction

Bodily/Kinesthetic Learners In Exercise 23, encourage students to use the *act it out* problem-solving strategy they learned in Lesson 9-6. Have them brainstorm ways in which they could use this strategy if a spinner similar to the one shown was not available.
Sample answer: Use five index cards to represent each of the colored sections in the spinner. Label the index cards white, red, blue, yellow, and green, respectively. Arrange the index cards in a circle so that the cards labeled red and blue are in the same place. Record this arrangement. Then find and record all possible arrangements.

Additional Answer

20. Sample answer: Both probabilities are ratios that compare the number of favorable outcomes to the total number of outcomes. Experimental probability is the result of an experiment. Theoretical probability is what is expected to happen.

Pre-AP Activity   Use as an Extension

Tell students that a bag has 10 colored marbles. The task is to guess the colors of the marbles without looking in the bag. Only one marble can be taken out at a time, then it must be returned. Have students describe a probability experiment to infer the colors of the marbles in the bag. Make sure students state how many events the experiment should have.

Main IDEA

Investigate experimental probability by conducting a simulation.

Standard 6SDAP3.2 Use data to estimate the probability of future events (e.g., batting averages or number of accidents per mile driven).
Standard 6MR1.2 Formulate and justify mathematical conjectures based on a general description of the mathematical question or problem posed.

STUDY TIP

Assumption This simulation assumes that each prize is equally likely to appear in each box of cereal.

2. The theoretical probability of getting each prize is $\frac{1}{4}$.

3. The theoretical and experimental probabilities will likely not be the same because of the small number of trials.

7. Sample answer: For each trial, toss 5 coins and record the results.

8. See students' work. The probability should be close to $\frac{1}{32}$ or about 3.1%.

A *simulation* is a way of acting out a problem situation. Simulations often use models to act out events that would be difficult or impractical to perform. In this lab, you will simulate purchasing a box of cereal and getting one of four possible prizes inside.

ACTIVITY

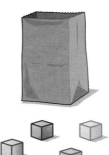

STEP 1 Place four different colored cubes into a paper bag.

STEP 2 Without looking, draw a cube from the bag, record its color, and then place the cube back in the bag.

STEP 3 Repeat steps 1 and 2 until you have drawn a cube from the bag a total of four times.

ANALYZE THE RESULTS

1. Based on your results, predict the probability of getting each prize. **See students' work.**

2. What is the theoretical probability of getting each prize?

3. How do your probabilities in Exercises 1 and 2 compare?

4. **MAKE A PREDICTION** Predict the probability of selecting all four prizes in four boxes of cereal. **See students' work.**

5. Repeat the simulation above 20 times. Use this data to predict the probability of selecting all four prizes in four boxes of cereal. **See students' work.**

6. Calculate the experimental probability described in Exercise 5 using the combined data of five different groups. How does this probability compare with your prediction? **See students' work.**

7. Describe a simulation that could be used to predict the probability of taking a five question true/false test and getting all five questions correct by guessing. Choose from among two-sided counters, number cubes, coins, or spinners as your model.

8. **COLLECT THE DATA** Conduct 50 trials of the experiment you described in Exercise 7. Then calculate the experimental probability of getting all five questions correct by guessing.

Extend 9-7 Probability Lab: Simulations   **491**

1 Focus

Materials
- colored cubes
- paper bags

2 Teach

Working in Cooperative Groups
You might want to have students work in pairs, with one student drawing the cubes and the other student recording the colors.

Activity Have students discuss why the simulation requires that each drawn cube be replaced in the bag. Make sure everyone understands that, for a consumer, the probability of picking any one kind of prize is $\frac{1}{4}$ (given the simulation's assumption), so replacing the drawn cubes makes the simulation accurate.

3 Assess

 Formative Assessment

Use Exercises 5 and 6 to determine whether students understand how to find an experimental probability by conducting a simulation.

From Concrete to Abstract Use Exercise 7 to bridge the gap between conducting a given simulation to find an experimental probability and devising a new simulation to find an experimental probability.

Differentiated Instruction

Interpersonal Learners To complete Exercise 8, the class could be divided into groups. Depending on the size of each group and the class time alloted, it is possible that more than 50 trials could be conducted. As the number of trials increases, the experimental probability of getting all five questions correct by guessing should become closer to $\frac{1}{32}$, or about 3.1%

9-8 Compound Events

Standard 6SDAP3.4 **Understand that the probability of either of two disjoint events occurring is the sum of the two individual probabilities and that the probability of one event following another, in independent trials, is the product of the two probabilities.**

 Standard 6SDAP3.5 **Understand the difference between independent and dependent events.**

PACING: **Regular:** 2 periods, **Block:** 1 period

Options for Differentiated Instruction

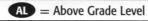 = English Language Learner    = Above Grade Level   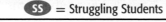 = Struggling Students   = Special Needs

Organizing Student Work and Thinking

Use after presenting the Examples.

Have students add compound events and independent events to their resource sheet. They should include the following:

- a description of each term in their own words,
- examples of each term, and
- an explanation of what the notation $P(A \text{ and } B)$ means and how to read it.

Logical Learners

Use before assigning the Exercises.

Place the names of all the students in the class in a hat. Explain that you are going to divide the class into two groups by drawing names from the hat.

- Ask students to predict the gender composition of each group.
- Before each draw, have students compute the probability that a boy will be chosen and the probability that a girl will be chosen. (Remind them that the sum of the two probabilities must equal 1.)
- Ask them to notice how the probabilities change as names are removed from the hat.

Extending the Concept

Use after students complete Lesson 9-8.

Present the following problem to students.

> The probability of a compound event is $\frac{1}{12}$. What can be said about the two independent events? Describe two possible scenarios that would yield that probability.

Sample answers: The probability of the events could be $\frac{1}{3}$ and $\frac{1}{4}$, respectively. Spinning one spinner with 3 colors and another spinner with 4 colors would yield that probability. Or, choosing one marble from a bag that has 3 different colored marbles and another from a bag that has 4 different colored marbles would also yield a probability of $\frac{1}{12}$.

Leveled Lesson Resources

Chapter 9 Resource Masters

BL = Below Grade Level   **OL** = On Grade Level   **AL** = Above Grade Level   **ELL** = English Language Learner

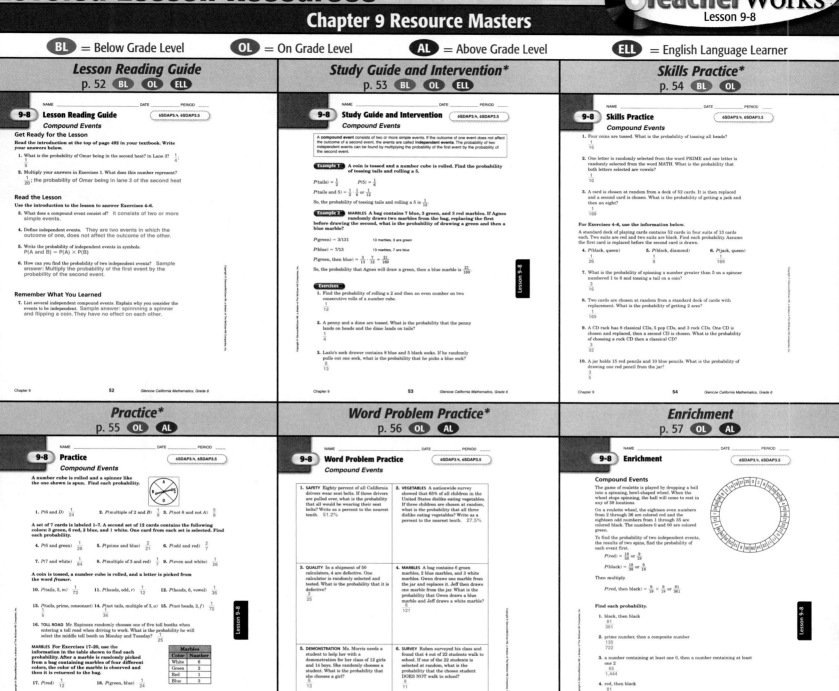

Lesson Reading Guide
p. 52 BL OL ELL

9-8 Lesson Reading Guide   6SDAP3.4, 6SDAP3.5
Compound Events

Get Ready for the Lesson
Read the introduction at the top of page 492 in your textbook. Write your answers below.

1. What is the probability of Omar being in the second heat? in Lane 3? $\frac{1}{5}$; $\frac{1}{4}$

2. Multiply your answers in Exercises 1. What does this number represent? $\frac{1}{20}$; the probability of Omar being in lane 3 of the second heat

Read the Lesson
Use the introduction to the lesson to answer Exercises 4–6.

3. What does a compound event consist of? It consists of two or more simple events.

4. Define independent events. They are two events in which the outcome of one, does not affect the outcome of the other.

5. Write the probability of independent events in symbols. P(A and B) = P(A) × P(B)

6. How can you find the probability of two independent events? Sample answer: Multiply the probability of the first event by the probability of the second event.

Remember What You Learned

7. List several independent compound events. Explain why you consider the events to be independent. Sample answer: spinning a spinner and flipping a coin. They have no effect on each other.

Chapter 9   52   Glencoe California Mathematics, Grade 6

Study Guide and Intervention*
p. 53 BL OL ELL

9-8 Study Guide and Intervention   6SDAP3.4, 6SDAP3.5
Compound Events

A **compound event** consists of two or more simple events. If the outcome of one event does not affect the outcome of a second event, the events are called **independent events**. The probability of two independent events can be found by multiplying the probability of the first event by the probability of the second event.

Example 1 A coin is tossed and a number cube is rolled. Find the probability of tossing tails and rolling a 5.

$P(\text{tails}) = \frac{1}{2}$ $P(5) = \frac{1}{6}$

$P(\text{tails and } 5) = \frac{1}{2} \cdot \frac{1}{6}$ or $\frac{1}{12}$

So, the probability of tossing tails and rolling a 5 is $\frac{1}{12}$.

Example 2 MARBLES A bag contains 7 blue, 3 green, and 3 red marbles. If Agnes randomly draws two marbles from the bag, replacing the first before drawing the second, what is the probability of drawing a green and then a blue marble?

$P(\text{green}) = 3/131$ 13 marbles, 3 are green

$P(\text{blue}) = 7/13$ 13 marbles, 7 are blue

$P(\text{green, then blue}) = \frac{3}{13} \cdot \frac{7}{13} = \frac{21}{169}$

So, the probability that Agnes will draw a green, then a blue marble is $\frac{21}{169}$.

Exercises

1. Find the probability of rolling a 2 and then an even number on two consecutive rolls of a number cube. $\frac{1}{12}$

2. A penny and a dime are tossed. What is the probability that the penny lands on heads and the dime lands on tails? $\frac{1}{4}$

3. Lazlo's sock drawer contains 8 blue and 5 black socks. If he randomly pulls out one sock, what is the probability that he picks a blue sock? $\frac{8}{13}$

Chapter 9   53   Glencoe California Mathematics, Grade 6

Skills Practice*
p. 54 BL OL

9-8 Skills Practice   6SDAP3.4, 6SDAP3.5
Compound Events

1. Four coins are tossed. What is the probability of tossing all heads? $\frac{1}{16}$

2. One letter is randomly selected from the word PRIME and one letter is randomly selected from the word MATH. What is the probability that both letters selected are vowels? $\frac{1}{10}$

3. A card is chosen at random from a deck of 52 cards. It is then replaced and a second card is chosen. What is the probability of getting a jack and then an eight? $\frac{1}{169}$

For Exercises 4–6, use the information below.
A standard deck of playing cards contains 52 cards in four suits of 13 cards each. Two suits are red and two suits are black. Find each probability. Assume the first card is replaced before the second card is drawn.

4. P(black, queen) $\frac{1}{26}$ 5. P(black, diamond) 0   6. P(jack, queen) $\frac{1}{169}$

7. What is the probability of spinning a number greater than 5 on a spinner numbered 1 to 8 and tossing a tail on a coin? $\frac{3}{16}$

8. Two cards are chosen at random from a standard deck of cards with replacement. What is the probability of getting 2 aces? $\frac{1}{169}$

9. A CD rack has 8 classical CDs, 5 pop CDs, and 3 rock CDs. One CD is chosen and replaced, then a second CD is chosen. What is the probability of choosing a rock CD then a classical CD? $\frac{3}{32}$

10. A jar holds 15 red pencils and 10 blue pencils. What is the probability of drawing one red pencil from the jar? $\frac{3}{5}$

Chapter 9   54   Glencoe California Mathematics, Grade 6

Practice*
p. 55 OL AL

9-8 Practice   6SDAP3.4, 6SDAP3.5
Compound Events

A number cube is rolled and a spinner like the one shown is spun. Find each probability.

1. P(6 and D) $\frac{1}{24}$ 2. P(multiple of 2 and B) $\frac{1}{8}$ 3. P(not 6 and not A) $\frac{5}{8}$

A set of 7 cards is labeled 1–7. A second set of 12 cards contains the following colors: 3 green, 6 red, 2 blue, and 1 white. One card from each set is selected. Find each probability.

4. P(6 and green) $\frac{1}{28}$ 5. P(prime and blue) $\frac{2}{21}$ 6. P(odd and red) $\frac{2}{7}$

7. P(7 and white) $\frac{1}{84}$ 8. P(multiple of 3 and red) $\frac{1}{7}$ 9. P(even and white) $\frac{1}{28}$

A coin is tossed, a number cube is rolled, and a letter is picked from the word *framer*.

10. P(tails, 5, m) $\frac{1}{72}$ 11. P(heads, odd, r) $\frac{1}{12}$ 12. P(heads, 6, vowel) $\frac{1}{36}$

13. P(tails, prime, consonant) $\frac{1}{6}$ 14. P(not tails, multiple of 3, a) $\frac{1}{36}$ 15. P(not heads, 2, f) $\frac{1}{72}$

16. TOLL ROAD Mr. Espinoza randomly chooses one of five toll booths when entering a toll road when driving to work. What is the probability he will select the middle toll booth on Monday and Tuesday? $\frac{1}{25}$

MARBLES For Exercises 17–20, use the information in the table shown to find each probability. After a marble is randomly picked from a bag containing marbles of four different colors, the color of the marble is observed and then it is returned to the bag.

Marbles	
Color	Number
White	6
Green	2
Red	1
Blue	3

17. P(red) $\frac{1}{12}$ 18. P(green, blue) $\frac{1}{24}$

19. P(red, white, blue) $\frac{1}{96}$ 20. P(blue, blue, blue) $\frac{1}{64}$

Chapter 9   55   Glencoe California Mathematics, Grade 6

Word Problem Practice*
p. 56 OL AL

9-8 Word Problem Practice   6SDAP3.4, 6SDAP3.5
Compound Events

1. SAFETY Eighty percent of all California drivers wear seat belts. If three drivers are pulled over, what is the probability that all would be wearing their seat belts? Write as a percent to the nearest tenth. 51.2%

2. VEGETABLES A nationwide survey showed that 65% of all children in the United States dislike eating vegetables. If three children are chosen at random, what is the probability that all three dislike eating vegetables? Write as a percent to the nearest tenth. 27.5%

3. QUALITY In a shipment of 50 calculators, 4 are defective. One calculator is randomly selected and tested. What is the probability that it is defective? $\frac{2}{25}$

4. MARBLES A bag contains 6 green marbles, 2 blue marbles, and 3 white marbles. Gwen draws one marble from the jar and replaces it. Jeff then draws one marble from the jar. What is the probability that Gwen draws a blue marble and Jeff draws a white marble? $\frac{6}{121}$

5. DEMONSTRATION Ms. Morris needs a student to help her with a demonstration for her class of 12 girls and 14 boys. She randomly chooses a student. What is the probability that she chooses a girl? $\frac{6}{13}$

6. SURVEY Ruben surveyed his class and found that 4 out of 22 students walk to school. If one of the 22 students is selected at random, what is the probability that the chosen student DOES NOT walk to school? $\frac{9}{11}$

Chapter 9   56   Glencoe California Mathematics, Grade 6

Enrichment
p. 57 OL AL

9-8 Enrichment   6SDAP3.4, 6SDAP3.5
Compound Events

Compound Events
The game of roulette is played by dropping a ball into a spinning, bowl-shaped wheel. When the wheel stops spinning, the ball will come to rest in any of 38 locations.

On a roulette wheel, the eighteen even numbers from 2 through 36 are colored red and the eighteen odd numbers from 1 through 35 are colored black. The numbers 0 and 00 are colored green.

To find the probability of two independent events, the results of two spins, find the probability of each event first.

$P(\text{red}) = \frac{18}{38}$ or $\frac{9}{19}$

$P(\text{black}) = \frac{18}{38}$ or $\frac{9}{19}$

Then multiply.

$P(\text{red, then black}) = \frac{9}{19} \times \frac{9}{19}$ or $\frac{81}{361}$

Find each probability.

1. black, then black $\frac{81}{361}$

2. prime number, then a composite number $\frac{135}{722}$

3. a number containing at least one 0, then a number containing at least one 2 $\frac{65}{1,444}$

4. red, then black $\frac{81}{361}$

5. the numbers representing your age, month of birth, and then day of birth $\frac{1}{54,872}$

Chapter 9   57   Glencoe California Mathematics, Grade 6

Additional Lesson Resources

*** Also available in Spanish** ELL

Transparencies
- *5-Minute Check Transparency,* Lesson 9-8

Other Print Products
- *Noteables™ Interactive Study Notebook with Foldables™*
- *Science and Mathematics Lab Manual,* pp. 87–92

Teacher Tech Tools
- *Interactive Classroom CD-ROM,* Lesson 9-8
- *AssignmentWorks CD-ROM,* Lesson 9-8

Student Tech Tools
ca.gr6math.com
- Extra Examples, Chapter 9, Lesson 8
- Self-Check Quiz, Chapter 9, Lesson 8

1 Focus

 Standards Alignment

Before Lesson 9-8
Represent all possible outcomes for compound events in an organized way (e.g., tables, grids, tree diagrams) and express the theoretical probability of each outcome from ◆── Standard 6SDAP3.1

Lesson 9-8
Understand that the probability of either of two disjoint events occurring is the sum of the two individual probabilities and that the probability of one event following another, in independent trials, is the product of the two probabilities. Understand the difference between independent and dependent events from ◆── Standards 6SDAP3.4 and 6SDAP3.5

After Lesson 9-8
Develop generalizations of the results obtained and the strategies used and apply them in new problem situations from Standard 6MR3.3

2 Teach

Scaffolding Questions

Tell students that you have a bag containing 4 blue marbles and 6 red marbles. Say that you have picked a marble from the bag, and it is blue.

Ask:

• If I replace the blue marble and pick another marble, what is the probability that the second marble will be blue? $\frac{2}{5}$

• If I *do not* replace the blue marble, and then pick another marble, what is the probability that the second marble will be blue? $\frac{1}{3}$

9-8 Compound Events

Main IDEA

Find the probability of independent and dependent events.

 Standard 6SDAP3.4 Understand that the probability of either of two disjoint events occurring is the sum of the two individual probabilities and that the probability of one event following another, in independent trials, is the product of the two probabilities. **Standard 6SDAP3.5** Understand the difference between independent and dependent events.

NEW Vocabulary

compound event
independent events
dependent events
disjoint events

2. $\frac{1}{20}$; the probability of Omar being in lane 3 of the second heat

READING Math

Probability Notation
$P(A, B)$ is read *the probability of A followed by B.*

Heat Number   Lane Number

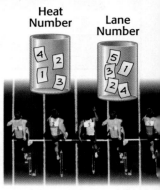

▶ **GET READY for the Lesson**

TRACK AND FIELD The 100-meter dash features 20 runners competing in a preliminary round of 4 heats. The winner of each heat advances to the final race. Before the race, each runner chooses a number from jar 1 to determine the heat in which he runs and a number from jar 2 to determine one of five lanes he occupies. Omar is the first runner to choose from the jars.   1. $\frac{1}{4}$; $\frac{1}{5}$

1. What is the probability of Omar being in the second heat? in lane 3?

2. Multiply your answers in Exercise 1. What does this number represent?

In the example above, choosing the heat and the lane is a compound event. A **compound event** consists of two or more simple events. Since choosing the heat number does not affect choosing the lane number, the two events are called **independent events**. The outcome of one event does not affect the outcome of the other event.

EXAMPLE Independent Events

① **A coin is tossed, and the spinner shown is spun. Find the probability of tossing heads and spinning a consonant.**

List the sample space. Use H for heads and T for tails.

| H, A | H, B | H, C |
| T, A | T, B | T, C |

$P(\text{H and a consonant}) = \dfrac{\text{number of times heads and a consonant occurs}}{\text{number of possible outcomes}}$

$P(\text{H and a consonant}) = \dfrac{2}{6}$ or $\dfrac{1}{3}$

So, the probability is $\frac{1}{3}$ or about 33%.

✓ **CHECK Your Progress**

A number cube is rolled, and the spinner in Example 1 is spun. Find each probability.

a. $P(4 \text{ and a consonant})$ $\frac{1}{9}$ b. $P(\text{odd and a } B)$ $\frac{1}{6}$

✏ Formative Assessment

Use the Check Your Progress exercises after each Example to determine students' understanding of concepts.

ADDITIONAL EXAMPLE

① The spinner below is spun and a number cube is tossed. Find the probability of spinning a C and rolling a number less than 5. $\frac{2}{9}$

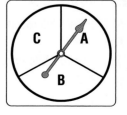

The probability in Example 1 can also be found by multiplying the probabilities of each event. $P(H) = \frac{1}{2}$ and $P(\text{consonant}) = \frac{2}{3}$ and so $P(H \text{ and consonant}) = \frac{1}{2} \cdot \frac{2}{3}$ or $\frac{1}{3}$. This leads to the following.

KEY **CONCEPT**   Probability of Independent Events

Words	The probability of two independent events can be found by multiplying the probability of the first event by the probability of the second event.
Symbols	$P(A \text{ and } B) = P(A) \cdot P(B)$

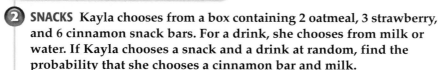 **Real-World EXAMPLE**

2 **SNACKS** Kayla chooses from a box containing 2 oatmeal, 3 strawberry, and 6 cinnamon snack bars. For a drink, she chooses from milk or water. If Kayla chooses a snack and a drink at random, find the probability that she chooses a cinnamon bar and milk.

$P(\text{cinnamon and milk}) = P(\text{cinnamon}) \cdot P(\text{milk})$

$$= \frac{6}{11} \cdot \frac{1}{2} \qquad \text{6 out of 11 bars are cinnamon.}$$
$$\text{1 out of 2 drink choices is milk.}$$

$$= \frac{\overset{3}{\cancel{6}}}{11} \cdot \frac{1}{\underset{1}{\cancel{2}}} \text{ or } \frac{3}{11} \qquad \text{Simplify.}$$

So, the probability is $\frac{3}{11}$ or about 27%.

Reasonable Answer You can check your answer in Example 2 by listing the sample space or by making a tree diagram.

✔ CHECK **Your Progress**

c. **SNACKS** If tea and juice are added to Kayla's drink choices, find the probability that she chooses an oatmeal bar and water. $\frac{1}{22}$

 **Personal Tutor at** ca.gr6math.com

If the outcome of one event affects the outcome of a second event, the events are called **dependent events**. Just as in independent events, the probabilities of dependent events can be found by multiplying the probabilities of each event. However, now the probability of the second event depends on the fact that the first event has already occurred.

KEY **CONCEPT**   Probability of Dependent Events

Words	If two events, A and B, are dependent, then the probability of both events occurring is the product of the probability of A and the probability of B after A occurs.
Symbols	$P(A \text{ and } B) = P(A) \cdot P(B \text{ following } A)$

    **Lesson 9-8** Compound Events   **493**

🔍 **Focus on Mathematical Content**

In a probability experiment (or situation), a **compound (or composite) event** has more than one simple event.

In a compound event, if one event does not affect another event, they are **independent events**.

In a compound event, if one event affects another event, they are **dependent events**.

One way to find the probability of a compound event is to **construct the sample space**.

If a compound event is made up of independent events, its probability can be found by **multiplying the probability of each event**.

ADDITIONAL EXAMPLE

2 **LUNCH** For lunch, Jessica may choose a turkey sandwich, a tuna sandwich, a salad, or a soup. For a drink, she can choose juice, milk, or water. If she chooses a lunch and a drink at random, what is the probability that she will choose a sandwich and juice? $\frac{1}{6}$

Additional Examples are also in:

- Noteables™ Interactive Study Notebook with Foldables™
- Interactive Classroom PowerPoint® Presentations

Focus on Mathematical Content

In a compound event, if one event affects the outcome of another event, the events are **dependent**.

Disjoint events are events that cannot occur at the same time. Disjoint events are also called **mutually exclusive events**.

EXAMPLE Dependent Events

③ There are 2 red, 5 green, and 8 yellow marbles in a jar. Martina randomly selects two marbles without replacing the first marble. What is the probability that she selects two green marbles?

Since the first marble is not replaced, the first event affects the second event. These are dependent events.

$P(\text{first marble is green}) = \dfrac{5}{15}$ ← number of green marbles ← total number of marbles

$P(\text{second marble is green}) = \dfrac{4}{14}$ ← number of green marbles after one green marble is removed ← total number of marbles after one green marble is removed

$P(\text{two green marbles}) = \dfrac{\overset{1}{\cancel{5}}}{\underset{3}{\cancel{15}}} \cdot \dfrac{\overset{2}{\cancel{4}}}{\underset{7}{\cancel{14}}}$ or $\dfrac{2}{21}$

So, the probability of selecting two green marbles is $\dfrac{2}{21}$, or about 9.5%.

CHECK Your Progress   d. $\dfrac{1}{11}$

d. There are 4 blueberry, 6 raisin, and 2 plain bagels in a bag. Javier randomly selects two bagels without replacing the first bagel. Find the probability that he selects a raisin bagel and then a plain bagel.

Sometimes two events cannot happen at the same time. For example, when a coin is tossed, the outcome of heads cannot happen at the same time as tails. Either heads *or* tails will turn up. Tossing heads and tossing tails are examples of **disjoint events**, or events that cannot happen at the same time. Disjoint events are also called *mutually exclusive events*.

STUDY TIP

Disjoint Events When finding the probabilities of disjoint events, the word *or* is usually used.

EXAMPLE Disjoint Events

④ A number cube is rolled. What is the probability of rolling an odd number or a 6?

These are disjoint events since it is impossible to roll an odd number and a 6 at the same time.

$P(\text{odd number or 6}) = \dfrac{4}{6}$ ← There are four favorable outcomes: 1, 3, 5, or 6. ← There are 6 total possible outcomes.

So, the probability of rolling an odd number or a 6 is $\dfrac{4}{6}$, or $\dfrac{2}{3}$.

CHECK Your Progress

e. Twenty-six cards are labeled, each with a letter of the alphabet, and placed in a box. A single card is randomly selected. What is the probability that the card selected will be labeled with the letter M or the letter T? $\dfrac{2}{26}$ or $\dfrac{1}{13}$

STUDY TIP

Probability
The probability of two disjoint events is the *sum* of the two individual probabilities. The probability of two independent events is the *product* of the two individual probabilities.

Notice that the probability in Example 4 can also be found by adding the probabilities of each event.

KEY CONCEPT   **Probability of Disjoint Events**

Words	If two events, *A* and *B*, are disjoint, then the probability that either *A* or *B* occurs is the sum of their probabilities.
Symbols	$P(A \text{ or } B) = P(A) + P(B)$

CHECK Your Understanding

Example 1
(p. 492)

A number cube is rolled, and the spinner is spun. Find each probability.

1. $P(5 \text{ and } E)$ $\frac{1}{30}$
2. $P(2 \text{ and vowel})$ $\frac{1}{15}$
3. $P(3 \text{ and a consonant})$ $\frac{1}{10}$
4. $P(\text{factor of 6 and } D)$ $\frac{2}{15}$

Example 2
(p. 493)

5. **CLOTHES** Loretta has 2 pairs of black jeans, 3 pairs of blue jeans, and 1 pair of tan jeans. She also has 4 white and 2 red T-shirts. If Loretta chooses a pair of jeans and a T-shirt at random, what is the probability that she will choose a pair of black jeans and a white T-shirt? $\frac{2}{9}$

6. **MARBLES** A jar contains 12 marbles. Four are red, 3 are white, and 5 are blue. A marble is randomly selected, its color recorded, and then the marble is returned to the jar. A second marble is randomly selected. Find the probability that both marbles selected are blue. $\frac{25}{144}$

Example 3
(p. 494)

7. The digits 0–9 are each written on a slip of paper and placed in a hat. Two slips of paper are randomly selected, without replacing the first. What is the probability that the number 0 is drawn first and then a 7 is drawn? $\frac{1}{90}$

Example 4
(p. 494)

A number cube is rolled. Find each probability.

8. $P(4 \text{ or } 5)$ $\frac{1}{3}$
9. $P(3 \text{ or even number})$ $\frac{2}{3}$
10. $P(1 \text{ or multiple of } 2)$ $\frac{2}{3}$
11. $P(6 \text{ or number less than } 3)$ $\frac{1}{2}$

Exercises

HOMEWORK HELP

For Exercises	See Examples
12–17	1
18–19	2
20–21	3
22–25	4

A coin is tossed, and a number cube is rolled. Find each probability.

12. $P(\text{heads and } 1)$ $\frac{1}{12}$
13. $P(\text{tails and multiple of } 3)$ $\frac{1}{6}$

A set of five cards is labeled 1–5. A second set of ten cards contains the following colors: 2 red, 3 purple, and 5 green. One card from each set is selected. Find each probability.

14. $P(5 \text{ and green})$ $\frac{1}{10}$
15. $P(\text{odd and red})$ $\frac{3}{25}$
16. $P(\text{prime and purple})$ $\frac{9}{50}$
17. $P(\text{even and yellow})$ 0

Lesson 9-8 Compound Events   **495**

 Practice

Formative Assessment

Use Exercises 1–11 to check for understanding.

Then use the chart at the bottom of this page to customize your assignments for students.

Intervention You may wish to use the Study Guide and Intervention Master on page 53 of the *Chapter 9 Resource Masters* for additional reinforcement.

Odd/Even Assignments

Exercises 12–25 are structured so that students practice the same concepts whether they are assigned odd or even problems.

DIFFERENTIATED HOMEWORK OPTIONS

Level	Assignment	Two-Day Option	
BL Basic	12–25, 37–45	13–25 odd, 38, 39	12–24 even, 37, 40–45
OL Core	13–33 odd, 34, 37–45	12–25, 38, 39	26–34, 37, 40–45
AL Advanced/Pre-AP	26–45		

Additional Answer

30.

Number of Children	P(all boys)
1	$\frac{1}{2}$
2	$\frac{1}{2} \cdot \frac{1}{2}$ or $\frac{1}{4}$
3	$\frac{1}{2} \cdot \frac{1}{2} \cdot \frac{1}{2}$ or $\frac{1}{8}$
4	$\frac{1}{2} \cdot \frac{1}{2} \cdot \frac{1}{2} \cdot \frac{1}{2}$ or $\frac{1}{16}$
5	$\frac{1}{2} \cdot \frac{1}{2} \cdot \frac{1}{2} \cdot \frac{1}{2} \cdot \frac{1}{2}$ or $\frac{1}{32}$

⚠ Exercise Alert!

Use the Internet Exercise 34 requires students to use the Internet or another source to research the 48 contiguous states.

The contiguous states ending with the letter A or O are:

Alabama, Arizona, California, Colorado, Idaho, Indiana, Iowa, Louisiana, Minnesota, Montana, Nebraska, Nevada, New Mexico, North Carolina, North Dakota, Ohio, Oklahoma, Pennsylvania, South Carolina, South Dakota, Virginia, West Virginia

Exercise Levels
A: 12–25
B: 26–34
C: 35–37

18. **MUSIC** Denzel is listening to a CD that contains 12 songs. If he presses the random button on his CD player, what is the probability that the first two songs played will be the first two songs listed on the album? $\frac{1}{144}$

19. **JUICE POPS** Lakita has two boxes of juice pops with an equal number of pops in each flavor. Find the probability of randomly selecting a grape juice pop from the first box and randomly selecting a juice pop from the second box that is *not* grape. $\frac{3}{16}$

20. **FRUIT** Francesca randomly selects two pieces of fruit from a basket containing 8 oranges and 4 apples without replacing the first fruit. Find the probability that she selects two oranges. $\frac{14}{33}$

21. **SCHOOL** The names of 24 students, of which 14 are girls and 10 are boys, in Mr. Santiago's science class are written on cards and placed in a jar. Mr. Santiago randomly selects two cards without replacing the first to determine which students will present their lab reports today. Find the probability that two boys are selected. $\frac{15}{92}$

A day of the week is randomly selected. Find each probability. 23. $\frac{3}{7}$

22. P(Monday or Tuesday) $\frac{2}{7}$

23. P(a day beginning with T or Friday)

24. P(a weekday or Saturday) $\frac{6}{7}$

25. P(Wednesday or a day with 6 letters) $\frac{4}{7}$

A coin is tossed twice, and a letter is randomly picked from the word *event*. **Find each probability.**

26. P(two heads and T) $\frac{1}{20}$

27. P(tails, not tails, consonant) $\frac{3}{20}$

28. P(heads, tails, not V) $\frac{1}{5}$

29. P(two tails and vowel) $\frac{1}{10}$

FAMILY For Exercises 30–32, use the fact that the probability for a boy or a girl is each $\frac{1}{2}$.

30. Copy and complete the table that gives the probability that all the children in a family are boys given the number of children in the family. **See margin.**

31. Predict the probability that, in a family of ten children, all ten are boys. $\frac{1}{1,024}$

32. Predict the probability that, in a family of n children, all n are boys. $\frac{1}{2^n}$

Number of Children	P(all boys)
1	$\frac{1}{2}$
2	$\frac{1}{2} \cdot \frac{1}{2}$ or $\frac{1}{4}$
3	■
4	■
5	■

33. **TRAFFIC** Two consecutive traffic signals on a street operate independently of each other. The first signal is green 45% of the time, and the second signal is yellow 10% of the time and red 40% of the time. What is the probability of a person driving down the street making both green lights? Write as a percent. **22.5%**

34. **RESEARCH** The *contiguous* United States consists of all states excluding Alaska and Hawaii. If one of these contiguous states is chosen at random, what is the probability that it will end with the letter A or O? Write as a percent. **50%**

CHALLENGE For Exercises 35 and 36, use the spinner.

35. Use a tree diagram to construct the sample space of all the possible outcomes of three successive spins.

36. Suppose the spinner is designed so that for each spin there is a 40% probability of spinning red and a 20% chance of spinning blue. What is the probability of spinning two reds and then one blue? **0.032**

37. **WRITING IN MATH** A shelf has books A, B, and C on it. You pick a book at random, place it on a table, and then pick a second book. Explain why the probability that you picked books A and B is *not* $\frac{1}{9}$. **See margin.**

STANDARDS PRACTICE 6SDAP3.4, 6SDAP3.5

38. A jar contains 8 white marbles, 4 green marbles, and 2 purple marbles. If Darla picks one marble from the jar without looking, what is the probability that it will be either white or purple? **A**

A $\frac{5}{7}$ C $\frac{2}{7}$

B $\frac{4}{7}$ D $\frac{1}{7}$

39. What is the probability of spinning a red, the number 1, and the letter A on the three spinners below? **G**

F $\frac{1}{3}$ G $\frac{1}{32}$ H $\frac{1}{12}$ J $\frac{1}{64}$

Spiral Review

40. **PROBABILITY** Paz performed a probability experiment by spinning a spinner 20 times. The results are shown in the table. If the spinner is divided into four equal sections, how many sections would you expect to be blue? (Lesson 9-7) **1**

Color	Frequency
red	IIII
green	IIII IIII
blue	IIII

41. **CHORES** This weekend, Brennen needs to do laundry, mow the lawn, and clean his room. How many different ways can he do these three chores? (Lesson 9-6) **6**

ALGEBRA Evaluate each expression if $a = 6$, $b = -4$, and $c = -3$. (Lesson 2-7)

42. $9c$ **−27**   43. $-8a$ **−48**   44. $2bc$ **24**   45. $5b^2$ **80**

Cross-Curricular Project

Math and Recreation

Step Right Up and Win a Prize It's time to complete your project. Use the information and data you have gathered about carnival games to prepare a Web page or poster. Be sure to include a scale drawing of the game you design with your project.

Math Online Cross-Curricular Project at ca.gr6math.com

Ticket Out the Door Tell students that someone tossed a coin 5 times, and it landed tails each time. Have them write the probability on a piece of paper. $\frac{1}{32}$

Formative Assessment

Check for student understanding of concepts in Lessons 9-7 and 9-8.

CRM Quiz 4, p. 62

FOLDABLES **Foldables™**
Study Organizer **Follow-Up**

Remind students to write a descriptive paragraph about finding the probability of compound events under the tab for this lesson of their Foldables. Encourage them to describe the thoughts and experiences they had while working on the lesson.

Additional Answer

37. These events are dependent, not independent. Selecting one book and not returning it to the shelf limits your choices for the next pick to 2 books not 3, as on the first pick.

CHAPTER 9
Study Guide and Review

STUDY TO GO Download Vocabulary Review from ca.gr6math.com

FOLDABLES™ Study Organizer
Dinah Zike's Foldables

Have students look through the chapter to make sure they have included paragraphs about the key concepts of each lesson in their Foldables.

Encourage students to refer to their Foldables while completing the Study Guide and Review and while preparing for the Chapter Test.

Formative Assessment

Key Vocabulary The page references after each word denote where that term was first introduced. If students have difficulty answering Exercises 1–7, remind them that they can use these page references to refresh their memories about the vocabulary terms.

Math Online ca.gr6math.com

Vocabulary PuzzleMaker improves students' mathematics vocabulary using four puzzle formats—crossword, scramble, word search using a word list, and word search using clues. Students can work online or from a printed worksheet.

Summative Assessment

 Vocabulary Test, p. 64

498 Chapter 9 Probability

FOLDABLES™ Study Organizer
GET READY to Study

Be sure the following Key Concepts are noted in your Foldable.

Key Concepts

Probability (Lesson 9-1)
- The probability of a simple event is a ratio that compares the number of favorable outcomes to the number of possible outcomes.

Fundamental Counting Principle (Lesson 9-3)
- If event M has m possible outcomes and is followed by event N that has n possible outcomes, then the event M followed by N has $m \times n$ possible outcomes.

Theoretical and Experimental Probability (Lesson 9-7)
- Theoretical probability is based on what *should* happen when conducting a probability experiment.
- Experimental probability is based on what *actually occurred* during a probability experiment.

Independent Events (Lesson 9-8)
- The probability of two independent events can be found by multiplying the probability of the first event by the probability of the second event.

Dependent Events (Lesson 9-8)
- If two events, A and B, are dependent, then the probability of both events occurring is the product of the probability of A and the probability of B after A occurs.

Disjoint Events (Lesson 9-8)
- If two events are disjoint, then the probability that either event will occur is the sum of their individual probabilities.

Key Vocabulary

combination (p. 480)
complementary events (p. 462)
compound event (p. 492)
dependent events (p. 493)
disjoint events (p. 494)
experimental probability (p. 486)
Fundamental Counting Principle (p. 471)

independent events (p. 492)
outcome (p. 460)
permutation (p. 465)
probability (p. 460)
random (p. 461)
sample space (p. 465)
simple event (p. 460)
theoretical probability (p. 486)
tree diagram (p. 466)

4. false; multiplication
5. false; independent events
6. false; complement

Vocabulary Check

State whether each sentence is *true* or *false*. If *false*, replace the underlined word or number to make a true sentence.

1. <u>Compound events</u> consists of two or more simple events. **true**

2. A <u>random</u> outcome is an outcome that occurs by chance. **true**

3. $P(\text{not } A)$ is read the <u>permutation</u> of the complement of A. **false; probability**

4. The Fundamental Counting Principle counts the number of possible outcomes using the operation of <u>addition</u>.

5. Events in which the outcome of the first event does not affect the outcome of the other event(s) are <u>simple events</u>.

6. The <u>sample space</u> of an event is the set of outcomes not included in the event.

7. Events that cannot occur at the same time are called <u>dependent</u> events. **false; disjoint**

Math Online Vocabulary Review at ca.gr6math.com

Lesson-by-Lesson Exercises and Examples

9-1 Simple Events (pp. 460–464)

A bag contains 6 red, 3 pink, and 3 white bows. Suppose you draw a bow at random. Find the probability of each event. Write as a fraction in simplest form.

8. $P(\text{red})$ $\frac{1}{2}$

9. $P(\text{white})$ $\frac{1}{4}$

10. $P(\text{red or pink})$ $\frac{3}{4}$

11. $P(not \text{ pink})$ $\frac{3}{4}$

12. $P(\text{red, white, or pink})$ **1**

13. **ARRIVALS** The probability that a plane **8%** will arrive at the airport on time is $\frac{23}{25}$. Find the probability that the plane will *not* arrive on time. Write as a percent.

Example 1 What is the probability of rolling an odd number on a number cube?

$$P(\text{odd}) = \frac{\text{number of odd outcomes}}{\text{total number of possible outcomes}}$$

$$= \frac{3}{6} \quad \text{Three numbers are odd: 1, 3, and 5.}$$

$$= \frac{1}{2} \quad \text{Simplify.}$$

Therefore, $P(\text{odd}) = \frac{1}{2}$.

9-2 Sample Spaces (pp. 465–470) 15–16. See Ch. 9 Answer Appendix.

For each situation, find the sample space using a table or tree diagram. **See margin.**

14. rolling a number cube and tossing a coin

15. choosing from white, wheat, or rye bread and turkey, ham, or salami to make a sandwich

16. **GAMES** Eliza and Zeke are playing a game in which Zeke spins the spinner shown and rolls a number cube. If the sum of the numbers is less than six, Eliza wins. Otherwise Zeke wins. Find the sample space. Then find the probability that Zeke wins.

Example 2 Ginger and Micah are playing a game in which a coin is tossed twice. If heads comes up exactly once, Ginger wins. Otherwise Micah wins. Find the sample space. Then find the probability that Ginger wins.

Make a tree diagram.

First Toss	Second Toss	Sample Space	
H	H	HH	Micah wins
	T	HT	Ginger wins
T	H	TH	Ginger wins
	T	TT	Micah wins

There are four equally-likely outcomes with 2 favoring each player. The probability that Ginger wins is $\frac{2}{4}$ or $\frac{1}{2}$.

Lesson-by-Lesson Review

Intervention If the given examples are not sufficient to review the topics covered by the questions, remind students that the page references tell them where to review that topic in their textbooks.

Two-Day Option Have students complete the Lesson-by-Lesson on pages 499–502. Then you can use ExamView® Assessment Suite to customize another review worksheet that practices all the objectives of this chapter or only the objectives on which your students need more help.

For more information on ExamView® Assessment Suite, see page 458C.

Differentiated Instruction

Super DVD: MindJogger Plus Use this DVD as an alternative format of review for the test. For more information on this game show format, see page 458D.

Additional Answer

14. Sample answer:

Number Cube	Coin	Sample Space
1	H	1H
	T	1T
2	H	2H
	T	2T
3	H	3H
	T	3T
4	H	4H
	T	4T
5	H	5H
	T	5T
6	H	6H
	T	6T

9-3 **The Fundamental Counting Principle** (pp. 471–474)

Use the Fundamental Counting Principle to find the total number of outcomes in each situation.

17. rolling two number cubes **36**

18. making an ice cream sundae selecting from 5 flavors of ice cream and 4 different toppings **20**

19. **SHOPPING** A catalog offers a jogging suit in three colors, gray, pink, and black. It comes in sizes S, M, L, XL, and XXL and is available with a hood or without a hood. If a jogging suit is selected at random, what is the probability that it will be a pink hooded suit in size medium? $\frac{1}{30}$

Example 3 Use the Fundamental Counting Principle to find the total number of outcomes for the genders of the children in a family that has four children.

There are 2 possible outcomes, a boy or a girl, each time a child is born. For a family with four children, there are $2 \cdot 2 \cdot 2 \cdot 2$, or 16 outcomes.

Example 4 Find the probability that, in a family of four children, all four children are girls.

There are 16 outcomes. There is one possible outcome resulting in four girls. So, the probability that all four children are girls is $\frac{1}{16}$.

9-4 **Permutations** (pp. 475–478)

20. **BASKETBALL** In how many ways can five basketball players be placed in three positions: center, forward, and guard? **60**

21. **LETTERS** How many permutations are there of the letters in the word *computer*? **40,320**

22. **RUNNING** Jacinda and Raul are entered in a race with 5 other runners. If each runner is equally likely to win, what is the probability that Jacinda will finish first and Raul will finish second? $\frac{1}{42}$

Example 5 Nathaniel needs to choose two of the chores shown to do after school. If he is equally likely to choose the chores, what is the probability that he will walk the dog first and rake the leaves second?

Chores
Walk the Dog
Do Homework
Clean the Kitchen
Rake the Leaves

There are $4 \cdot 3$, or 12, arrangements in which Nathaniel can complete the chores.

There is one way in which he will walk the dog first and rake the leaves second. So, the probability that he will walk the dog first and rake the leaves second is $\frac{1}{12}$.

Mixed Problem Solving
For mixed problem-solving practice,
see page 723.

CHAPTER
9 **Study Guide and Review**

9-5 **Combinations** (pp. 480–483)

23. PIZZA How many three-topping pizzas are possible given eight different toppings? **56**

24. KITTENS How many groups of three kittens are possible from a litter of six? **20**

25. GAMES In how many ways can Rondell select two board games from the ten games that his family owns? **45**

26. QUIZ Frances must answer 3 of the 5 questions on a quiz, numbered 1–5. What is the probability that Frances will answer questions 2, 3, and 4? $\frac{1}{10}$

Example 6 Caitlin and Román are playing a game in which Román chooses four different numbers from 1–15. What is the probability that Caitlin will guess all four numbers correctly?

There are $15 \cdot 14 \cdot 13 \cdot 12$ permutations of four numbers chosen from 15 numbers. There are $4 \cdot 3 \cdot 2 \cdot 1$ ways to arrange the 4 numbers.

$$\frac{15 \cdot 14 \cdot 13 \cdot 12}{4 \cdot 3 \cdot 2 \cdot 1} = \frac{32{,}760}{24} \text{ or } 1{,}365$$

There are 1,365 ways to choose four numbers from 15 numbers. There is one way to guess all four numbers correctly, so the probability that Caitlin will guess all four numbers correctly is $\frac{1}{1{,}365}$.

9-6 **PSI: Act it Out** (pp. 484–485)

Solve each problem. Use the *act it out* strategy.

27. QUIZ Determine whether tossing a coin is a good way to answer a 6-question true-false quiz. Justify your answer. **See margin.**

28. FAMILY PORTRAIT In how many ways can the Maxwell family pose for a portrait if Mr. and Mrs. Maxwell are sitting in the middle and their three children are standing behind them? **12**

29. AMUSEMENT PARK In how many ways can 4 friends be seated in 2 rows of 2 seats each on a roller coaster if Judy and Harold must ride together? **8**

Example 7 In how many ways can three females and two males sit in a row of five seats at a concert if the females must sit in the first three seats?

Place five desks or chairs in a row. Have three females and two males sit in any of the seats as long as the females sit in the first three seats. Continue rearranging until you find all the possibilities. Record the results.

F_1 F_2 F_3 M_1 M_2 F_2 F_3 F_1 M_1 M_2
F_1 F_2 F_3 M_2 M_1 F_2 F_3 F_1 M_2 M_1
F_1 F_3 F_2 M_1 M_2 F_3 F_2 F_1 M_1 M_2
F_1 F_3 F_2 M_2 M_1 F_3 F_2 F_1 M_2 M_1
F_2 F_1 F_3 M_1 M_2 F_3 F_1 F_2 M_1 M_2
F_2 F_1 F_3 M_2 M_1 F_3 F_1 F_2 M_2 M_1

There are 12 possible arrangements.

Additional Answer

27. No; Sample answer: the experiment produces about 3 correct answers, so tossing a coin is not a good way to answer a 6-question true-false quiz.

CHAPTER 9 Study Guide and Review

Problem Solving Review

For additional practice in problem solving for Chapter 9, see the Mixed Problem Solving Appendix, page 723 in the Student Handbook section.

Anticipation Guide

Have students complete the Chapter 9 Anticipation Guide and discuss how their responses have changed now that they have completed Chapter 9.

[CRM] Anticipation Guide, p. 7

Additional Answer (p. 503)

5. Sample answer:

Outcomes		
1st Toss	2nd Toss	3rd Toss
H	H	H
H	T	H
H	H	T
H	T	T
T	T	T
T	H	T
T	T	H
T	H	H

9-7 **Theoretical and Experimental Probability** (pp. 486–490)

The results of spinning a spinner labeled A–E fifty times are given. Find the experimental probability of each event.

Letter	Frequency
A	8
B	17
C	9
D	6
E	10

30. $P(A)$ $\frac{4}{25}$ **31.** $P(D)$ $\frac{3}{25}$ **32.** $P(E)$ $\frac{1}{5}$

33. $P(A \text{ or } B)$ $\frac{1}{2}$ **34.** $P(not\ C)$ **35.** $P(B \text{ or } D)$

34. $\frac{41}{50}$

35. $\frac{23}{50}$

36. If the spinner is equally likely to land on each section, what is the theoretical probability of landing on B? $\frac{1}{5}$

Example 8 A coin is tossed 75 times, and it lands on tails 55 times. What is the experimental probability of the coin landing on heads?

The coin landed on heads 20 times.

$$P(\text{heads}) = \frac{\text{number of times heads occurs}}{\text{total number of possible outcomes}}$$

$$= \frac{20}{75} \text{ or } \frac{4}{15}$$

So, the experimental probability of the coin landing on heads is $\frac{4}{15}$ or about 27%.

9-8 **Compound Events** (pp. 492–497)

A bag contains 6 green, 8 white, and 2 blue counters. Two counters are randomly drawn. Find each probability if the first counter is replaced before the second counter is drawn. Then find each probability if the first counter is not replaced.

37. $P(\text{green, blue})$ $\frac{3}{64}; \frac{1}{20}$

38. $P(2 \text{ white})$ $\frac{1}{4}; \frac{7}{30}$

39. $P(\text{blue, not white})$ $\frac{1}{16}; \frac{7}{120}$

40. $P(\text{not white, green})$ $\frac{3}{16}; \frac{1}{5}$

41. **PROBABILITY** A coin is tossed and a number cube is rolled. Find the probability that tails and a number less than 5 comes up. $\frac{1}{3}$

42. **COMPUTERS** A computer randomly generates a digit from 0–9. Find the probability that an odd number or the number 8 is generated. $\frac{3}{5}$

Example 9 A box contains 12 solid, 14 striped, and 10 spotted marbles. Find the probability of choosing a striped marble, replacing it, and then choosing a spotted marble.

$$P(\text{striped}) = \frac{14}{36}$$

$$P(\text{spotted, after replacing the striped}) = \frac{10}{36}$$

$$\frac{14}{36} \cdot \frac{10}{36} = \frac{140}{1,296} \text{ or } \frac{35}{324}$$

So, the probability of choosing a striped marble, replacing it, and then choosing a spotted marble is $\frac{35}{324}$, or about 11%.

The spinner shown has an equal chance of landing on each number. Find each probability.

1. P(odd number) $\frac{1}{2}$

2. P(1 or 7) $\frac{1}{4}$

3. P(*not* a prime number) $\frac{1}{2}$

4. P(number greater than 1) $\frac{7}{8}$

For each situation, use a table or a tree diagram to find the sample space.

5. A coin is tossed three times. **See margin.**

6. A letter is chosen from the word *MATH* and then a digit from the number 123.
6–7. See Ch. 9 Answer Appendix.

7. **GAMES** Randall and Lucy are playing a game in which Lucy rolls a number cube and selects a card from the cards A and B. If a number less than 4 and a consonant comes up, Lucy wins. Otherwise Randall wins. Find the sample space. Then find the probability that Lucy wins.

Use the Fundamental Counting Principle to find the total number of outcomes in each situation. **1,000 outcomes**

8. A 3-digit security code is chosen.

9. A number cube is rolled four times. **1,296 outcomes**

10. **STANDARDS PRACTICE** A cooler contains 8 grape juice boxes, 12 orange juice boxes, and 4 apple juice boxes. If a juice box is selected at random, what is the probability that it will be grape? **B**

A 50%

B $\frac{1}{3}$

C $0.1\overline{6}$

D $\frac{5}{6}$

11. **PARADES** If there are 50 floats in a parade, how many ways can a first place and a second place trophy be awarded? **2,450 ways**

12. **STANDARDS PRACTICE** A brand of yogurt has 15 different flavors. Which of the following gives the number of ways in which you can choose three flavors? **G**

F 2,730

G 455

H 45

J 5

13. **CAMPING** Four campers are chosen from nine to pitch the tents. If Sandy, Jarrod, Dyami, and Clara are among the nine campers, find the probability that they are chosen. $\frac{1}{126}$

14. **SCHOOL** Determine whether spinning a spinner with five equal sections would be a good way to answer a 5-question multiple-choice quiz if each question has answer choices A, B, C, D, and E. Justify your answer. **See Ch. 9 Answer Appendix.**

15. **SURVEY** Two hundred fifty teenagers were asked what type of pet they owned. The results of the survey are in the table. What is the experimental probability that a teenager owns a pet? Write as a percent. **94%**

Pet	Number of Teenage Pet Owners
fish	26
cat	65
dog	86
bird	20
other	38
no pet	15

16. **POPCORN** Two variety bags of popcorn each contain 100 pieces of regular popcorn, 60 pieces of cheese popcorn, and 40 pieces of caramel popcorn. Peter picks one piece of popcorn from each bag. What is the probability that he picks caramel from the first bag and regular from the second bag? $\frac{1}{10}$

Summative Assessment

CRM *Chapter 9 Resource Masters*

Leveled Chapter 9 Tests

Form	Type	Level	Pages
1	MC	BL	65–66
2A	MC	OL	67–68
2B	MC	OL	69–70
2C	FR	OL	71–72
2D	FR	OL	73–74
3	FR	AL	75–76

MC = multiple-choice questions
FR = free-response questions
BL = below grade level
OL = on grade level
AL = above grade level

- Vocabulary Test, p. 64
- Extended-Response Test, p. 77
- Unit 4 Test, pp. 81–82

ExamView Assessment Suite — Customize and create multiple versions of your chapter test and the answer key. All of the questions from the leveled chapter tests in the *Chapter 9 Resource Masters* are also available on ExamView Assessment Suite with the California Standard that each item assesses.

Data-Driven Decision Making	Exercises	Lesson	Standard	Resources for Review
Diagnostic Teaching Based on the results of the Chapter 9 Practice Test, use the following to review concepts that students continue to find challenging.	12, 13	9–5	6SDAP3.1	**CRM** Study Guide and Intervention pp. 35, 41, 46, and 53 Math Online • Extra Examples • Personal Tutor • Concepts in Motion
	14	9–6	6SDAP3.2	
	15	9–7	6SDAP3.2	
	16	9–8	6SDAP3.5	

Formative Assessment

You can use these two pages to benchmark student progress. The California Standards are listed with each question.

CRM *Chapter 9 Resource Masters*
- Standardized Test Practice, pp. 78–80

ExamView
Assessment Suite
Create practice worksheets or tests that align to the California Standards, as well as TIMSS and NAEP tests.

Read each question. Then fill in the correct answer on the answer document provided by your teacher or on a sheet of paper.

1 Jessica played a game where she spun each of the spinners shown below once. If she spins an even number on Spinner 1, red or yellow on Spinner 2, and a B on Spinner 3, how many possible unique combinations are there? **B**

Spinner 1   Spinner 2   Spinner 3

A 4   **C** 10
B 8   **D** 16

2 Mr. Campos bought 40 pencils priced at 8 for $0.99 and 3 dozen notebooks priced at 4 for $2.49. Find the total amount, not including tax, Mr. Campos spent on pencils and notebooks. **G**

F $28.86   **H** $17.88
G $27.36   **J** $15.96

3 In a movie theatre there are 168 seats. If 75% of the theatre is filled, how many people are sitting in the movie theatre? **D**

A 156   **C** 134
B 148   **D** 126

4 Mr. Blackwell gave his math students a pop quiz. The students' scores are listed below. What is the median quiz score? **G**

23	19	18	12	21	24	25

F 12   **H** 24
G 21   **J** 25

---

5 The results of an election for student body president showed that Trey received 250 votes, Marta 100 votes, and Ed 50 votes. Which of the following correctly displays the election results? **C**

A
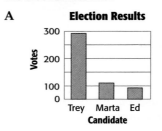

B
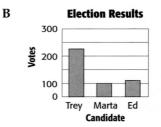

C
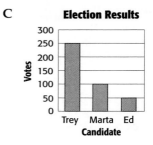

D
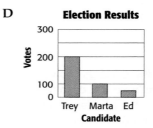

6 What is $4 \div \frac{1}{3}$? **J**

F $\frac{1}{12}$ **H** 7
G $\frac{4}{3}$ **J** 12

---

504 Chapter 9 Probability

 **California Standards Practice at** <u>ca.gr6math.com</u>

More California Standards Practice
For practice by standard, see pages CA1–CA39.

CHAPTER
9 California Standards Practice

7 Hanako spins each spinner shown below once. Find the total possible letter/number combinations that could have resulted from Hanako's spins. **C**

| First Spinner | Second Spinner |

A 3

B 6

C 9

D 12

8 Juan rolled a number cube four times. Each time, the number 3 appeared. If Juan rolls the number cube one more time, what is the probability that the number 3 will appear? **H**

F $\frac{2}{3}$ **H** $\frac{1}{6}$

G $\frac{1}{2}$ **J** $\frac{5}{6}$

9 The owner of a fruit stand has x pounds of apples on display. She sells 30 pounds and then adds $4y$ pounds of apples to the display. Which of the following expressions represents the weight in pounds of the apples that are now on the display? **B**

A $x + 30 + 4y$

B $x - 30 + 4y$

C $x + 30 - 4y$

D $x - 30 - 4y$

10 A building is 182 meters tall. About how tall is the building in feet and inches? (1 meter ≈ 39 inches) **J**

F 56 ft 0 in.   **H** 591 ft 5 in.

G 546 ft 5 in.   **J** 591 ft 6 in.

11 Wilson has 7 different pieces of fruit in his refrigerator. If he randomly selects 3 pieces of fruit, how many possible unique combinations are there? **D**

A 7   **C** 21

B 14   **D** 35

TEST-TAKING TIP

Question 11 You may want to find your own answer before looking at the answer choices. Doing so keeps you from being tempted by wrong answer choices that look correct, but are still wrong.

Pre-AP

Record your answers on a sheet of paper. Show your work.

12 Paula has a 5-disc CD player. She has jazz, country, rap, pop, and R&B CDs in the player. She listens to the CDs on random mode on both Friday and Saturday night.

  a. Make a tree diagram that shows all of the possible outcomes.

  b. What is the probability that Paula will hear a country song first on Friday night? $\frac{1}{5}$

  c. What is the probability that Paula will hear a rap song first on Friday night and a jazz song first on Saturday night? $\frac{1}{25}$

12a. See Ch. 9 Answer Appendix.

NEED EXTRA HELP?												
If You Missed Question...	1	2	3	4	5	6	7	8	9	10	11	12
Go to Lesson...	9-2	1-1	7-1	8-2	8-4	5-7	9-2	9-8	3-1	6-4	9-2	9-8
For Help with Standard...	SDAP3.1	MR1.1	NS1.4	SDAP1.1	SDAP2.3	NS2.1	SDAP3.1	SDAP3.5	AF1.1	AF2.1	SDAP3.1	SDAP3.5

Homework Option

Get Ready for Chapter 10   Assign students the exercises on page 509 as homework to assess whether they possess the prerequisite skills needed for the next chapter.

Page 464, Lesson 9-1

34a. No; Sample answer: There are many more black T-shirts than any other type of T-shirt. The probability of selecting a black T-shirt should be relatively high.

34b. No; Sample answer: There is only one orange T-shirt and many other types of T-shirts. The probability of selecting an orange T-shirt should be relatively low.

34c. Yes; Sample answer: There are only two purple T-shirts and many other types of T-shirts. the probability of selecting a purple T-shirt should be relatively low.

Page 465, Lesson 9-2 (Check Your Progress)

a. Sample answer:

Outcomes	
Male	Yellow Lab
Female	Yellow Lab
Male	Brown Lab
Female	Brown Lab
Male	Black Lab
Female	Black Lab

Page 467, Lesson 9-2 (Check Your Progress)

c.

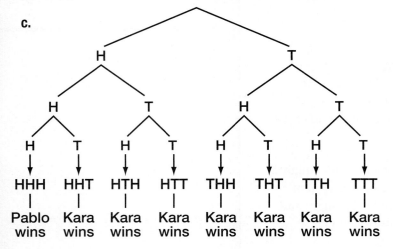

There are eight equally-likely outcomes with one favoring Pablo. So, the probability that Pablo wins is $\frac{1}{2}$.

Page 467, Lesson 9-2 (Check Your Understanding)

1. Sample answer:

Outcomes						
	1	2	3	4	5	6
1	1, 1	1, 2	1, 3	1, 4	1, 5	1, 6
2	2, 1	2, 2	2, 3	2, 4	2, 5	2, 6
3	3, 1	3, 2	3, 3	3, 4	3, 5	3, 6
4	4, 1	4, 2	4, 3	4, 4	4, 5	4, 6
5	5, 1	5, 2	5, 3	5, 4	5, 5	5, 6
6	6, 1	6, 2	6, 3	6, 4	6, 5	6, 6

2. Sample answer:

Outcomes	
Brown	7
Brown	8
Brown	9
Black	7
Black	8
Black	9

4. Sample answer:

1st Spin	2nd Spin	Sample Space	
A	A	AA	Brianna wins
	B	AB	Brianna wins
	C	AC	Brianna wins
	D	AD	Brianna wins
B	A	BA	Brianna wins
	B	BB	Odell wins
	C	BC	Odell wins
	D	BD	Odell wins
C	A	CA	Brianna wins
	B	CB	Odell wins
	C	CC	Odell wins
	D	CD	Odell wins
D	A	DA	Brianna wins
	B	DB	Odell wins
	C	DC	Odell wins
	D	DD	Odell wins

There are 16 equally-likely outcomes with 9 favoring Odell. So, the probability that Odell wins is $\frac{9}{16}$.

Page 468, Lesson 9-2

5. Sample answer:

Shape	Color	Sample Space
square	orange	square, orange
	blue	square, blue
	yellow	square, yellow
	red	square, red
	green	square, green
circle	orange	circle, orange
	blue	circle, blue
	yellow	circle, yellow
	red	circle, red
	green	circle, green

8. Sample answer:

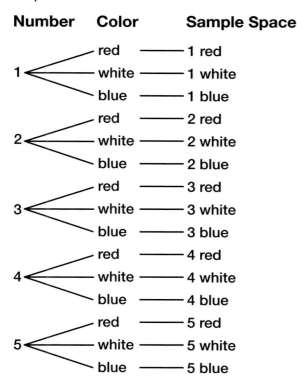

Number	Color	Sample Space
1	red	1 red
1	white	1 white
1	blue	1 blue
2	red	2 red
2	white	2 white
2	blue	2 blue
3	red	3 red
3	white	3 white
3	blue	3 blue
4	red	4 red
4	white	4 white
4	blue	4 blue
5	red	5 red
5	white	5 white
5	blue	5 blue

9. Sample answer:

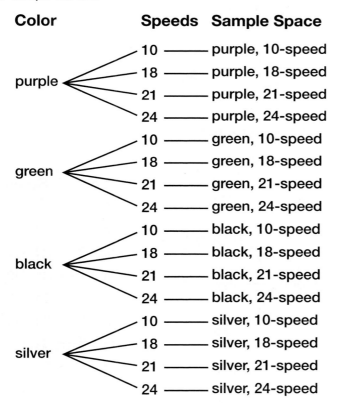

Color	Speeds	Sample Space
purple	10	purple, 10-speed
purple	18	purple, 18-speed
purple	21	purple, 21-speed
purple	24	purple, 24-speed
green	10	green, 10-speed
green	18	green, 18-speed
green	21	green, 21-speed
green	24	green, 24-speed
black	10	black, 10-speed
black	18	black, 18-speed
black	21	black, 21-speed
black	24	black, 24-speed
silver	10	silver, 10-speed
silver	18	silver, 18-speed
silver	21	silver, 21-speed
silver	24	silver, 24-speed

10. Sample answer:

SPACE	MATH	Sample Space
S	M	SM
S	T	ST
S	H	SH
P	M	PM
P	T	PT
P	H	PH
A	M	AM
A	T	AT
A	H	AH
C	M	CM
C	T	CT
C	H	CH
E	M	EM
E	T	ET
E	H	EH

11. Sample answer:

Outcomes		
Short Sleeve	Gray	Small
Short Sleeve	Gray	Medium
Short Sleeve	Gray	Large
Short Sleeve	White	Small
Short Sleeve	White	Medium
Short Sleeve	White	Large
Long Sleeve	Gray	Small
Long Sleeve	Gray	Medium
Long Sleeve	Gray	Large
Long Sleeve	White	Small
Long Sleeve	White	Medium
Long Sleeve	White	Large

12. Sample answer:

Outcomes		
Soup	Steak	Carrot Cake
Soup	Steak	Cheese Cake
Soup	Chicken	Carrot Cake
Soup	Chicken	Cheese Cake
Soup	Fish	Carrot Cake
Soup	Fish	Cheese Cake
Salad	Steak	Carrot Cake
Salad	Steak	Cheese Cake
Salad	Chicken	Carrot Cake
Salad	Chicken	Cheese Cake
Salad	Fish	Carrot Cake
Salad	Fish	Cheese Cake

13. Sample answer:

Quarter	Dime	Nickel	Sample Space	

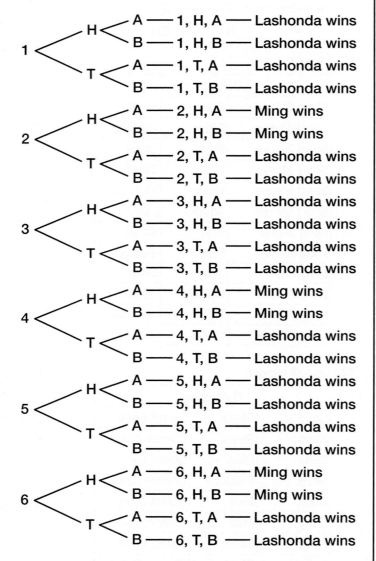

```
              H ── HHH ── Elba wins
        H <
              T ── HHT ── Elba wins
   H <
              H ── HTH ── Elba wins
        T <
              T ── HTT ── Steve wins
              H ── THH ── Elba wins
        H <
              T ── THT ── Steve wins
   T <
              H ── TTH ── Steve wins
        T <
              T ── TTT ── Steve wins
```

There are 8 equally-likely outcomes with 4 favoring Elba. So, the probability that Elba wins is $\frac{4}{8}$ or $\frac{1}{2}$.

14.

Number Cube   Coin   Card   Sample Space

```
              A ── 1, H, A ── Lashonda wins
        H <
              B ── 1, H, B ── Lashonda wins
   1 <
              A ── 1, T, A ── Lashonda wins
        T <
              B ── 1, T, B ── Lashonda wins
              A ── 2, H, A ── Ming wins
        H <
              B ── 2, H, B ── Ming wins
   2 <
              A ── 2, T, A ── Lashonda wins
        T <
              B ── 2, T, B ── Lashonda wins
              A ── 3, H, A ── Lashonda wins
        H <
              B ── 3, H, B ── Lashonda wins
   3 <
              A ── 3, T, A ── Lashonda wins
        T <
              B ── 3, T, B ── Lashonda wins
              A ── 4, H, A ── Ming wins
        H <
              B ── 4, H, B ── Ming wins
   4 <
              A ── 4, T, A ── Lashonda wins
        T <
              B ── 4, T, B ── Lashonda wins
              A ── 5, H, A ── Lashonda wins
        H <
              B ── 5, H, B ── Lashonda wins
   5 <
              A ── 5, T, A ── Lashonda wins
        T <
              B ── 5, T, B ── Lashonda wins
              A ── 6, H, A ── Ming wins
        H <
              B ── 6, H, B ── Ming wins
   6 <
              A ── 6, T, A ── Lashonda wins
        T <
              B ── 6, T, B ── Lashonda wins
```

There are 24 equally-likely outcomes with 6 favoring Ming. So, the probability that Ming wins is $\frac{6}{24}$ or $\frac{1}{4}$.

Page 471, Lesson 9-3 (Get Ready for the Lesson)

4.

Size   Length   Sample Space

```
           petite ── 3, petite
   3 <     regular ── 3, regular
           tall ──── 3, tall

           petite ── 5, petite
   5 <     regular ── 5, regular
           tall ──── 5, tall

           petite ── 7, petite
   7 <     regular ── 7, regular
           tall ──── 7, tall

           petite ── 9, petite
   9 <     regular ── 9, regular
           tall ──── 9, tall

           petite ── 11, petite
  11 <     regular ── 11, regular
           tall ──── 11, tall

           petite ── 13, petite
  13 <     regular ── 13, regular
           tall ──── 13, tall

           petite ── 15, petite
  15 <     regular ── 15, regular
           tall ──── 15, tall
```

Page 474, Lesson 9-3

22. Sample answer:

Geography Class   History Class   Statistics Class   Sample Space

```
                      History 1 < Statistics 1 ── G1, H1, S1
                                  Statistics 2 ── G1, H1, S2
   Geography 1 <
                      History 2 < Statistics 1 ── G1, H2, S1
                                  Statistics 2 ── G1, H2, S2
                      History 3 < Statistics 1 ── G1, H3, S1
                                  Statistics 2 ── G1, H3, S2

                      History 1 < Statistics 1 ── G2, H1, S1
                                  Statistics 2 ── G2, H1, S2
   Geography 2 <
                      History 2 < Statistics 1 ── G2, H2, S1
                                  Statistics 2 ── G2, H2, S2
                      History 3 < Statistics 1 ── G2, H3, S1
                                  Statistics 2 ── G2, H3, S2
```

Page 478, Lesson 9-4

21.

Meat	Cheese	Outcomes
turkey	cheddar	turkey, cheddar
	Swiss	turkey, Swiss
ham	cheddar	ham, cheddar
	Swiss	ham, Swiss
salami	cheddar	salami, cheddar
	Swiss	salami, Swiss

Page 479, Mid-Chapter Quiz

7. Sample answer:

Outcomes	
A	8
A	0
A	3
B	8
B	0
B	3
C	8
C	0
C	3
D	8
D	0
D	3

9.

Outcomes		
1	A	Abbey Wins
1	B	Benny Wins
1	C	Benny Wins
2	A	Benny Wins
2	B	Benny Wins
2	C	Benny Wins
3	A	Abbey Wins
3	B	Benny Wins
3	C	Benny Wins
4	A	Benny Wins
4	B	Benny Wins
4	C	Benny Wins
5	A	Abbey Wins
5	B	Benny Wins
5	C	Benny Wins
6	A	Benny Wins
6	B	Benny Wins
6	C	Benny Wins

There are 18 equally-likely outcomes with 15 favoring Benny.
So, the probability that Benny wins is $\frac{15}{18}$, or $\frac{5}{6}$.

Page 490, Lesson 9-7

19. Yes; Sample answer: If there are 40 unsharpened pencils in the box, then there are twice as many unsharpened pencils as there are sharpened pencils. If there are five sharpened pencils in the sample that was taken out, then there should be ten unsharpened pencils which would give a total of 15 pencils in the sample, which was the size of the sample. It is important to note that this was only one sample. To be sure that the sample represents the population, other samples should be taken and compared to the first sample.

Page 497, Lesson 9-8

35.

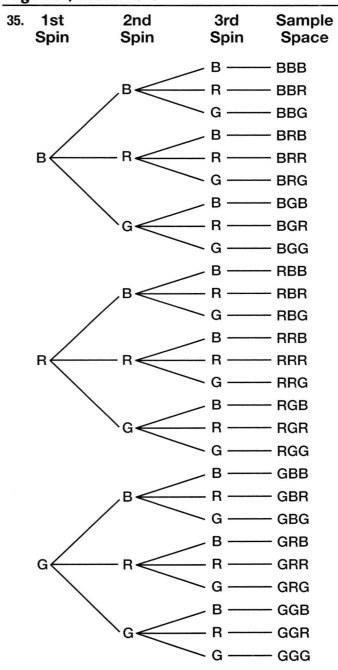

Chapter 9 Answer Appendix

15. Sample answer:

Outcomes	
White	Turkey
White	Ham
White	Salami
Wheat	Turkey
Wheat	Ham
Wheat	Salami
Rye	Turkey
Rye	Ham
Rye	Salami

16. Sample answer:

Outcomes		
1	1	Eliza wins
1	2	Eliza wins
1	3	Eliza wins
1	4	Eliza wins
1	5	Zeke wins
1	6	Zeke wins
2	1	Eliza wins
2	2	Eliza wins
2	3	Eliza wins
2	4	Zeke wins
2	5	Zeke wins
2	6	Zeke wins
3	1	Eliza wins
3	2	Eliza wins
3	3	Zeke wins
3	4	Zeke wins
3	5	Zeke wins
3	6	Zeke wins
4	1	Eliza wins
4	2	Zeke wins
4	3	Zeke wins
4	4	Zeke wins
4	5	Zeke wins
4	6	Zeke wins

There are 24 equally-likely outcomes with 14 favoring Zeke. So, the probability that Zeke will win is $\frac{14}{24}$, or $\frac{7}{12}$.

6. Sample answer:

Letter	Number	Sample Space
M	1	M1
	2	M2
	3	M3
A	1	A1
	2	A2
	3	A3
T	1	T1
	2	T2
	3	T3
H	1	H1
	2	H2
	3	H3

7.

Outcomes		
1	A	Randall wins
2	A	Randall wins
3	A	Randall wins
4	A	Randall wins
5	A	Randall wins
6	A	Randall wins
1	B	Lucy wins
2	B	Lucy wins
3	B	Lucy wins
4	B	Randall wins
5	B	Randall wins
6	B	Randall wins

There are 12 equally-likely outcomes with 3 favoring Lucy. So, the probability that Lucy will win is $\frac{3}{12}$, or $\frac{1}{4}$.

14. Sample answer: The experiment produces about 2 or 3 correct answers, so using a spinner with five equal sections is not a good way to answer a 5-question multiple-choice quiz.

Page 505, California Standards Practice

12a.

First Song on Friday	First Song on Saturday	Sample Space
jazz	jazz	jazz, jazz
	country	jazz, country
	rap	jazz, rap
	pop	jazz, pop
	R & B	jazz, R & B
country	jazz	country, jazz
	country	country, country
	rap	country, rap
	pop	country, pop
	R & B	country, R & B
rap	jazz	rap, jazz
	country	rap, country
	rap	rap, rap
	pop	rap, pop
	R & B	rap, R & B
pop	jazz	pop, jazz
	country	pop, country
	rap	pop, rap
	pop	pop, pop
	R & B	pop, R & B
R & B	jazz	R & B, jazz
	country	R & B, country
	rap	R & B, rap
	pop	R & B, pop
	R & B	R & B, R & B

Unit 5
Notes

Introduction

In this unit, students will explore the geometry and measurement of two- and three-dimensional figures. They will learn to classify angles based on their measurements and then will apply their knowledge of angles to similar figures, the classification of polygons, and tessellations. Students will also translate and reflect two-dimensional figures on a coordinate plane.

Students then will find the area of parallelograms, triangles, and trapezoids. They will explore the area of circles and complex figures and find the volume and surface area of three-dimensional figures. Finally, they will investigate square roots and the Pythagorean Theorem.

Assessment Options

Unit 5 Test Pages 61–62 of the *Chapter 12 Resource Masters* may be used as a test or a review for Unit 5. This assessment contains both multiple-choice and short-response items.

ExamView®
Assessment Suite

Create additional customized Unit Tests and review worksheets for differentiated instruction.

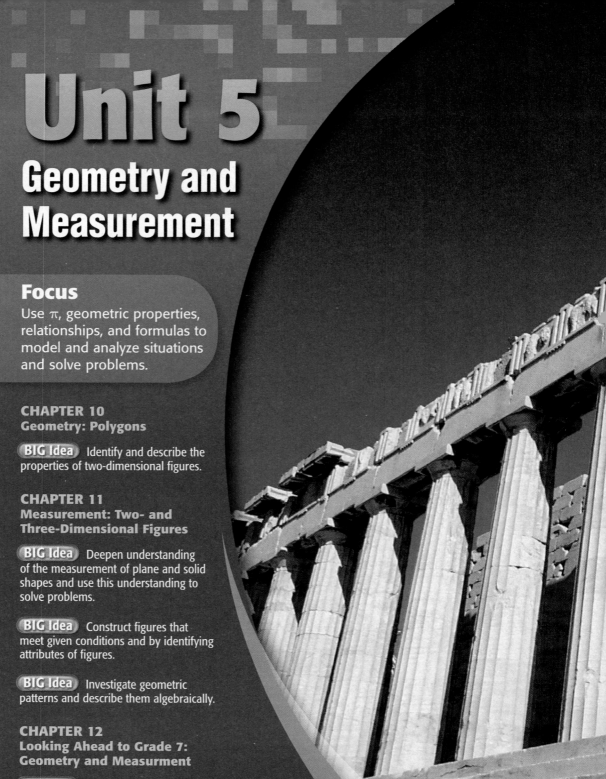

Unit 5
Geometry and Measurement

Focus

Use π, geometric properties, relationships, and formulas to model and analyze situations and solve problems.

CHAPTER 10
Geometry: Polygons

BIG Idea Identify and describe the properties of two-dimensional figures.

CHAPTER 11
Measurement: Two- and Three-Dimensional Figures

BIG Idea Deepen understanding of the measurement of plane and solid shapes and use this understanding to solve problems.

BIG Idea Construct figures that meet given conditions and by identifying attributes of figures.

BIG Idea Investigate geometric patterns and describe them algebraically.

CHAPTER 12
Looking Ahead to Grade 7: Geometry and Measurment

BIG Idea Know the Pythagorean Theorem and deepen the understanding of plane and solid geometric shapes.

506

Real-Life Math Videos engage students, showing them how math is used in everyday situations. Use Video 5 with this unit to discuss how polygons and area are used in construction and sports. (also available on one Super DVD combined with MindJogger Videoquizzes)

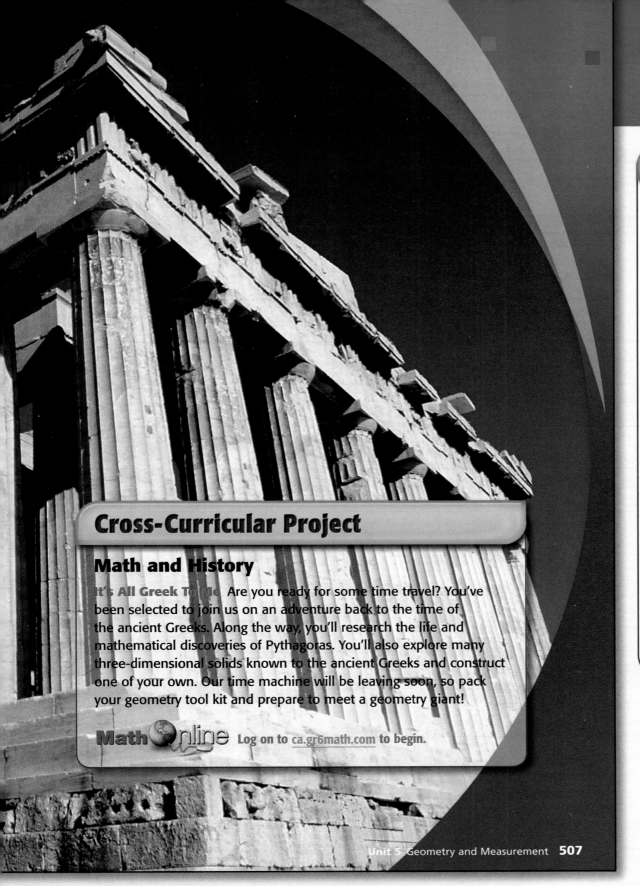

Math and History

It's All Greek To Me
This Cross-Curricular Project is an online project in which students do research on the Internet, gather data, and make presentations using word processing, graphing, page-making, or presentation software. In each chapter, students advance to the next step in their project. At the end of Chapter 12, the project culminates with a presentation of their findings.

Math **nline**
ca.gr6math.com Log on for teaching suggestions and sample answers for this project.

Team Teaching You can use this Cross-Curricular Project with your students' social studies teacher to make the connection from mathematics to the history your students are studying.

Cross-Curricular Project

Math and History

It's All Greek To Me Are you ready for some time travel? You've been selected to join us on an adventure back to the time of the ancient Greeks. Along the way, you'll research the life and mathematical discoveries of Pythagoras. You'll also explore many three-dimensional solids known to the ancient Greeks and construct one of your own. Our time machine will be leaving soon, so pack your geometry tool kit and prepare to meet a geometry giant!

Math **nline** Log on to ca.gr6math.com to begin.

More Cross-Curricular Connections

You may wish to share these suggestions with your students' other teachers.

Math and Art
Research the art and architecture of the ancient Greeks. Investigate the two- and three-dimensional shapes favored by the Greeks. Make a poster or diorama depicting examples of shapes you found in art works and buildings.

Math and Language Arts
Read about Plato (427–347 B.C.) and his views on ideal beauty and mathematics. What are the platonic solids, in particular the dodecahedron, and how do they exemplify Plato's vision of the universe?

Chapter Overview

Geometry: Polygons

Standards-Based Lesson Plan		Pacing Your Lessons	
LESSONS AND OBJECTIVES	**California Standards**	**45–50 Minute Periods**	**90-Minute Periods**
10-1 Angle Relationships (pp. 510–513) • Classify angles.	6MG2.1	1	0.5
10-2 Complementary and Supplementary Angles (pp. 514–517) • Identify complementary and supplementary angles.	6MG2.1 6MG2.2	1	0.5
10-3 Statistics: Display Data in a Circle Graph (pp. 518–523) • Construct and interpret circle graphs.	5SDAP1.2	1	0.5
10-4 Triangles (pp. 524–529) • Identify and classify triangles.	6MG2.2 6MG2.3	1	0.5
10-5 Problem-Solving Investigation: Use Logical Reasoning (pp. 530–531) • Solve problems by using logical reasoning.	6MR1.2 6MG2.3	1	0.5
Explore 10-6 Geometry Lab: Investigating Quadrilaterals (p. 532) • Investigate the properties of special quadrilaterals. **10-6 Quadrilaterals** (pp. 533–538) • Identify and classify quadrilaterals.	6MR1.1 6MG2.3	1	0.5
10-7 Similar Figures (pp. 540–545) • Determine whether figures are similar and find a missing length in a pair of similar figures.	6NS1.3	2	1
10-8 Polygons and Tessellations (pp. 546–551) • Classify polygons and determine which polygons can form a tessellation. **Extend 10-8 Geometry Lab: Tessellations** (p. 552) • Create tessellations using translations.	6MR2.2 6AF3.2 7MG3.4	2	1
10-9 Translations (pp. 553–557) • Graph translations of polygons on a coordinate plane.	7MG3.2	1	0.5
10-10 Reflections (pp. 558–562) • Identify figures with line symmetry and graph reflections on a coordinate plane.	7MG3.2	1	0.5
REVIEW		1	0.5
ASSESSMENT		1	0.5*
TOTAL		14	7

*The complete **Assessment Planner** for Chapter 10 is provided on page 509.*

* Begin Chapter 11 in the second half of the period.

Professional Development

California Standards Vertical Alignment

Before Chapter 10

Related Topics from Grade 5

- Measure, identify, and draw angles, perpendicular and parallel lines, rectangles, and triangles by using appropriate tools ➤ Standard 5MG2.1

- Know that the sum of the angles of any triangle is 180° and the sum of the angles of any quadrilateral is 360° and use this information to solve problems ➤ Standard 5MG2.2

- Identify and graph ordered pairs in the four quadrants of the coordinate plane ➤ Standard 5AF1.4

Chapter 10

Topics from Grade 6

- Identify angles as vertical, adjacent, complementary, or supplementary and provide descriptions of these terms

- Use the properties of complementary and supplementary angles and the sum of the angles of a triangle to solve problems involving an unknown angle ➤

- Use proportions to solve problems. Use cross-multiplication as a method for solving such problems ➤

- Use coordinate graphs to plot simple figures, determine lengths and areas related to them, and determine their image under translations and reflections

See individual lessons for the specific Standards covered.

After Chapter 10

Preparation for Grade 7

- Identify and construct basic elements of geometric figures by using a compass and straightedge Standard 7MG3.1

- Use formulas routinely for finding the perimeter and area of basic two-dimensional figures and the surface area and volume of basic three-dimensional figures Standard 7MG3.1

- Demonstrate an understanding of conditions that indicate two geometrical figures are congruent ➤ Standard 7MG3.4

Back-Mapping

California Mathematics: *Concepts, Skills, Problem Solving* was conceived and developed with the final result in mind, student success in Algebra I and beyond. The authors, using the California Mathematics Standards as their guide, developed this brand-new series by "back-mapping" from the desired result of student success in Algebra I and beyond. McGraw-Hill's K-7 intervention program, *California Math Triumphs: Intensive Intervention* as well as *California Algebra 1, California Geometry, California Algebra 2,* and *California Algebra Readiness* were developed utilizing the same philosophy.

What the Research Says . . .

According to "The van Hiele Model of Thinking in Geometry among Adolescents," which appeared in Journal for Research in Mathematics Education, it is important to distinguish between the common and mathematical usage of geometry vocabulary.

- The Reading Math features throughout the chapter help students understand the mathematical meaning by relating them to the everyday use.

Professional Development

Targeted professional development has been articulated throughout the *California Mathematics: Concepts, Skills, and Problem Solving* series. The **McGraw-Hill Professional Development Video Library** provides short videos that support the ➤ Key Standards. For more information, visit ca.gr6math.com.

| Model Lessons | Instructional Strategies |

TeacherWorks™ All-in-One Planner and Resource Center

All of the print materials from the Classroom Resource Masters are available on your TeacherWorks™ CD-ROM.

BL = Below Grade Level **OL** = On Grade Level **AL** = Above Grade Level **ELL** = English Language Learner

Chapter Resource Masters		10-1	10-2	10-3	10-4	10-5	10-6	10-7	10-8	10-9	10-10
BL **OL** **ELL**	Lesson Reading Guide	9	15	21	28		38	44	50	57	64
BL **OL** **ELL**	Study Guide and Intervention*	10	16	22	29	34	39	45	51	58	65
BL **OL**	Skills Practice*	11	17	23	30	35	40	46	52	59	66
OL **AL**	Practice*	12	18	24	31	36	41	47	53	60	67
OL **AL**	Word Problem Practice*	13	19	25	32	37	42	48	54	61	68
OL **AL**	Enrichment	14	20	26	33		43	49	55	62	69
OL **AL**	Calculator and Spreadsheet Activities			27					56	63	70
OL **AL**	Chapter Assessments*	71–92									
BL **OL** **AL**	5-Minute Check Transparencies	✓	✓	✓	✓	✓	✓	✓	✓	✓	✓
BL **OL**	Teaching Mathematics with Manipulatives	✓	✓			✓		✓			

Also available in Spanish.
Real-World Investigations for Differentiated Instruction, pp. 63, 65–66, 67

AssignmentWorks

Differentiated Assignments, Answers, and Solutions

- Print a customized assignment worksheet using the Student Edition exercises along with an answer key or worked-out solutions.
- Use default lesson assignments as outlined in the Differentiated Homework Options in the Teacher Wraparound Edition.
- Includes modified questions from the Student Edition for students with special needs.

Interactive Classroom

This CD-ROM is a customizable Microsoft® PowerPoint® presentation that includes:

- In-Class Examples
- Your Turn Exercises*
- 5-Minute Check Transparencies*
- Links to Online Study Tools
- Concepts in Motion

compatible with response pad technology

ExamView®Assessment Suite

- Create, edit, and customize tests and worksheets using QuickTest Wizard
- Create multiple versions of tests and modify them for a desired level of difficulty
- Translate from English to Spanish and vice versa
- Build tests aligned with your state standards
- Track students' progress using the Teacher Management System

Student Tools

StudentWorks™ Plus

Textbook, Audio, Workbooks, and more

This CD-ROM is a valuable resource for students to access content online and use online resources to continue learning Chapter 10 concepts. Includes:

- Complete Student Editions in both English and Spanish
- English audio integrated throughout the text
- Links to Concepts in Motion, Personal Tutor, and other online resources
- Access to all student worksheets
- Daily Assignments and Grade Log

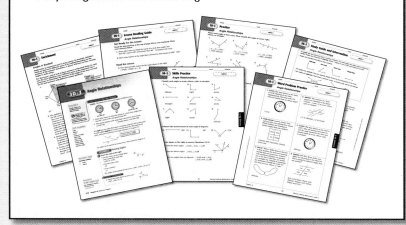

Super DVD

The Super DVD contains two Glencoe multimedia products.

MindJogger Plus An alternative review of concepts in which students work as teams in a game show format to gain points for correct answers.

What's Math Got to Do With It?
Real-Life Math Videos
Engaging video that shows students how math is used in everyday situations.

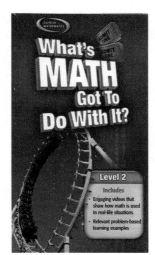

Internet Resources

Math Online ca.gr6math.com

TEACHER	STUDENT	PARENT	Online Study Tools
	●	●	Online Student Edition
●	●	●	Multilingual Glossary
			Lesson Resources
	●	●	BrainPOP®
●	●	●	Concepts in Motion
●	●	●	Extra Examples
●			Group Activity Cards
●			Problem of the Week Cards
	●	●	Other Calculator Keystrokes
	●	●	Reading in the Content Area
	●	●	Real-World Careers
	●	●	Self-Check Quizzes
			Chapter Resources
	●	●	Chapter Readiness
	●	●	Chapter Test
	●	●	Family Letters and Activities
	●		Standardized Test Practice
	●	●	Vocabulary Review/Chapter Review Activities
			Unit Resources
●	●		Cross-Curricular Internet Project
			Other Resources
●			Dinah Zike's Foldables
●	●		Game Zone Games and Recording Sheets
	●	●	Hotmath Homework Help
●			Key Concepts
●	●	●	Math Skills Maintenance
●	●	●	Meet the Authors
●			NAEP Correlations
	●	●	Personal Tutor
●			Project CRISS^SM
	●	●	Scavenger Hunts and Answer Sheets
●			Vocabulary PuzzleMakers

Noteables™ Interactive Study Notebook with Foldables™

This workbook is a study organizer that provides helpful steps for students to follow to organize their notes for Chapter 10.

- Students use Noteables to record notes and to complete their Foldables as you present the material for each lesson.
- Noteables correspond to the Examples in the *Teacher Wraparound Edition* and *Interactive Classroom CD-ROM.*

READING in the Content Area

This online worksheet provides strategies for reading and analyzing Lesson 10-1, Angle Relationships. Students are guided through questions about the main idea, subject matter, supporting details, conclusion, clarifying details, and vocabulary of the lesson.

ca.gr6math.com

Recommended Outside Reading for Students

Mathematics and Careers

- *Geometry for Dummies* by Wendy Arnone ©2001 [nonfiction]

This book is an easy-to-read introduction to geometry. It contains material on vocabulary and terms, angles, and angle relationships, and career connections with geometry.

Mathematics and Adventure

- *Sir Cumference and the Great Knight of Angleland: A Math Adventure* by Cindy Neuschwander; illustrated by Wayne Geehan ©2001 [fiction]

This is the third book in the Sir Cumference series. In this adventure, Radius needs to earn his knighthood by completing tasks, examining every angle along the way. Students will be able to apply their knowledge of angles and shapes when reading this book.

STUDY SKILL

Concept maps can be developed as part of a class discussion to help students understand newly introduced mathematical relationships. After students have read Lesson 10-1, write "Types of Angles" on the chalkboard, as shown in the sample map at the right. Allow students to complete the concept map. Encourage them to make drawings to accompany their descriptions. Students can develop similar concept maps as part of class discussions about "Types of Triangles" and "Types of Quadrilaterals."

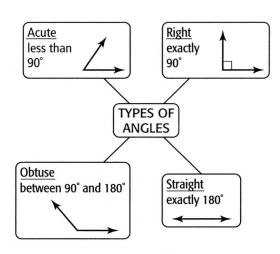

C Reating **I**ndependence through **S**tudent-owned **S**trategies

Differentiated Instruction

Quick Review Math Handbook*

is Glencoe's mathematical handbook for students and parents.

Hot Words includes a glossary of terms.

Hot Topics consists of two parts:

- explanations of key mathematical concepts
- exercises to check students' understanding.

Lesson	Hot Topics Section	Lesson	Hot Topics Section
10-1	7•1, 9•3	10-7	6•5
10-3	7•8	10-8	6•7, 7•2
10-4	7•1, 9•3	10-9	6•7, 7•3, 9•4
10-6	7•2	10-10	6•7, 7•3

*Also available in Spanish

Teacher to Teacher

Judy Lecocq
Murphysboro Middle School
Murphysboro, IL

USE WITH LESSON 10-2

❝I teach definitions of complementary and supplementary angles by considering the *p* in each word as a backward 9. Therefore, one *p* in *complementary* represents one 9, or 90 degrees. The two *p*'s in *supplementary* represent two 9's, or 180 degrees.❞

Intervention Options

Intensive Intervention

Math Triumphs can provide intensive intervention for students who are at risk of not meeting the California standards addressed in Chapter 10.

Diagnose student readiness with the Quick Check and Quick Review on page 509. Then use *Math Triumphs* to accelerate their achievement.

Algebra: Integers

Prerequisite Skill	*Math Triumphs*
Multiply and divide decimals 5NS2.1	Volume 2, Chapter 4
Solve equations 5AF1.2	Volume 4, Chapter 3

See chart on page T24 for other *Math Triumphs* lessons that will support the prerequisite skills needed for success in *Glencoe California Mathematics, Grade 6*.

Strategic Intervention

For strategic intervention options, refer to the Diagnostic Assessment table on page 509.

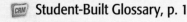

Dinah Zike's Foldables

Focus This Foldable is designed to help students organize their notes about polygons.

Teach Have students make their Foldables and label the three columns. Explain to students that they should take notes, define terms, and show examples in the appropriate columns of their Foldables tables.

When to Use It Prior to beginning Lesson 10-1, have students complete the first column in their Foldable chart (What I Know About Polygons). As students complete Lessons 10-4, 10-5, 10-7, 10-8, 10-9, and 10-10, have them complete the second and third columns (What I Need to Know and What I've Learned).

A version of a completed Foldable is shown on p. 563.

Differentiated Instruction

📋 Student-Built Glossary, p. 1

Students complete the chart by providing a definition for each term and an example as they progress through Chapter 10.

This study tool can be used to review for the chapter test.

CHAPTER 10

Geometry: Polygons

 BIG Idea

- **Standard 6MG2.0** Identify and describe the properties of two-dimensional figures.

Key Vocabulary

complementary angles (p. 514)
line of symmetry (p. 558)
similar figures (p. 540)
supplementary angles (p. 514)

🌐 **Real-World Link**

Tigers Geometry is used to explain how the face of a tiger shows a line of vertical reflection symmetry.

FOLDABLES **Study Organizer**

Geometry: Polygons Make this Foldable to help you organize your notes. Begin with a piece of 11" by 17" paper.

1 **Fold** a 2" tab along the long side of the paper.

2 **Unfold** the paper and fold in thirds widthwise.

3 **Open** and draw lines along the folds. Label the head of each column as shown. Label the front of the folded table with the chapter title.

508 **Chapter 10** Geometry: Polygons

Materials Needed for Chapter 10

- compasses (Lesson 10-3) (optional)
- protractors (Lessons 10-3, 10-7, and Explore 10-6)
- straightedges (Lesson 10-4)
- scissors (Lesson 10-4 and Extend 10-8)
- rulers (Explore 10-6)
- dot paper (Lesson 10-7)
- index cards (Extend 10-8)
- tape (Extend 10-8)
- grid paper (Lesson 10-9 and Explore 10-6)
- pattern blocks (Lesson 10-9)
- geomirrors (Lesson 10-10)

GET READY for Chapter 10

Diagnose Readiness You have two options for checking Prerequisite Skills.

ASSESSMENT PLANNER

Option

Option 2

Math Online Take the Online Readiness Quiz at ca.gr6math.com.

Take the Quick Check below. Refer to the Quick Review for help.

QUICKCheck

(Used in Lesson 10-2)
Multiply or divide. Round to the nearest hundredth if necessary.
(Prior Grade)

1. 360×0.85 **306**
2. $48 \div 191$ **0.25**
3. $24 \div 156$ **0.15**
4. 0.37×360 **133.2**
5. $33 \div 307$ **0.11**
6. 0.69×360 **248.4**

(Used in Lessons 10-3, and 10-4)
Solve each equation. (Lesson 3-2)

7. $122 + x + 14 = 180$ **44**

8. $45 + 139 + k + 17 = 360$ **159**

9. **SCHOOL** There are 180 school days at Lee Middle School. If school has been in session for 62 days and there are 13 days until winter break, how many school days are after the break? (Lesson 3-2)
105

(Used in Lesson 10-6)
Solve each proportion. (Lesson 6-5)

10. $\frac{4}{a} = \frac{3}{9}$ **12**
11. $\frac{7}{16} = \frac{h}{32}$ **14**
12. $\frac{5}{8} = \frac{15}{y}$ **24**
13. $\frac{t}{42} = \frac{6}{7}$ **36**

14. **READING** Sandra can read 28 pages of a novel in 45 minutes. At this rate, how many pages can she read in 135 minutes? (Lesson 6-5) **84**

QUICKReview

Example 1
Find 0.92×360.

$$
\begin{array}{r}
360 \\
\times\ 0.92 \quad \leftarrow \text{ Two decimal places} \\
\hline
720 \\
+\ 32400 \\
\hline
331.20 \quad \leftarrow \text{ Two decimal places}
\end{array}
$$

So, $0.92 \times 360 = 331.2$.

Example 2
Solve the equation.
$46 + 90 + p = 180$.

$46 + 90 + p = 180$ Write the equation.
$136 + p = 180$ Add 46 and 90.
$\underline{-136 \qquad -136}$ Subtract 136 from
$p = 44$ each side.

The solution to the equation $46 + 90 + p = 180$ is $p = 44$.

Example 3
Solve the proportion $\frac{3}{8} = \frac{g}{48}$.

$\frac{3}{8} = \frac{g}{48}$ Write a proportion.

$\frac{3}{8} = \frac{18}{48}$ Since $8 \times 6 = 48$, multiply 3 by 6 to find g.

So, $g = 18$.

Chapter 10 Get Ready for Chapter 10   **509**

Diagnostic Assessment

Exercises	California Standards	Strategic Intervention
1–6	5NS2.1, 5NS2.2	SE Prerequisite Skills, pp. 674 and 676
7–9	6AF1.1	SE Review Lesson 3-2, pp. 136–141
10–14	6NS1.3	SE Review Lesson 6-5, pp. 306–311

Formative Assessment

CRM Anticipation Guide, pp. 7–8
Spotting Preconceived Ideas
Students complete this survey to determine prior knowledge about ideas from Chapter 10. Revisit this worksheet after completing the chapter. Also see page 566.

TWE **Lesson Activities**
- Ticket Out the Door, pp. 517, 545, 562
- Crystal Ball, p. 513, 557
- Name the Math, pp. 529, 531, 551
- Yesterday's News, pp. 523, 538

Chapter Checkpoints

SE Mid-Chapter Quiz, p. 539
SE Study Guide and Review, pp. 563–566
SE California Standards Practice, pp. 568–569
CRM Quizzes, pp. 73 and 74
CRM Standardized Test Practice, pp. 90–92

Math Online ca.gr6math.com
- Self-Check Quizzes
- Practice Test
- Standardized Test Practice

Summative Assessment

SE Chapter Practice Test, p. 567
CRM Mid-Chapter Test, p. 75
CRM Vocabulary Test, p. 76
CRM Extended Response Test, p. 89
CRM Leveled Chapter Tests, pp. 77–88
ExamView Pro® Assessment Suite

KEY
CRM *Chapter 10 Resource Masters*
SE Student Edition
TWE Teacher Wraparound Edition
CD-ROM

10-1 Angle Relationships

Standard 6MG2.1   **Identify angles as vertical, adjacent,** complementary, or supplementary **and provide descriptions of these terms.**

PACING: **Regular:** 1 period, **Block:** 0.5 period

Options for Differentiated Instruction

ELL = English Language Learner   **AL** = Above Grade Level   **SS** = Struggling Students   **SN** = Special Needs

Vocabulary Development   **ELL** **SS** **SN**

Use while presenting Lesson 10-1.

Since the vocabulary is so extensive, it may be helpful to have students create a *vocabulary booklet* for this chapter.

• With construction paper as a cover, have students staple together notebook paper to make a booklet.
• Have students decorate their own covers.
• Have them create a table of contents on the first page.
• Have them add vocabulary words, diagrams, and examples, updating the table of contents as necessary.

Mathematical Displays   **SS** **SN**

Use before presenting Example 2.

Have students work in small groups to create a poster displaying the different types of angles. The poster should include the following:

• pictures and/or drawings of objects in everyday life that are acute angles, obtuse angles, right angles, and straight angles,
• an estimate of the measure of each angle that is drawn, and
• the classification of each angle as *acute*, *obtuse*, *right*, or *straight*.

Leveled Lesson Resources

Also on TeacherWorks™ Lesson 10-1

Chapter 10 Resource Masters

BL = Below Grade Level **OL** = On Grade Level **AL** = Above Grade Level **ELL** = English Language Learner

Lesson Reading Guide
p. 9 **BL** **OL** **ELL**

Study Guide and Intervention*
p. 10 **BL** **OL** **ELL**

Skills Practice*
p. 11 **BL** **OL**

Practice*
p. 12 **OL** **AL**

Word Problem Practice*
p. 13 **OL** **AL**

Enrichment
p. 14 **OL** **AL**

Additional Lesson Resources

* Also available in Spanish **ELL**

Transparencies
- *5-Minute Check Transparency,* Lesson 10–1

Other Print Products
- *Noteables™ Interactive Study Notebook with Foldables™*
- *Science and Mathematics Lab Manual,* pp. 37–40

Teacher Tech Tools
- *Interactive Classroom CD-ROM,* Lesson 10-1
- *AssignmentWorks CD-ROM,* Lesson 10-1

Student Tech Tools
ca.gr6math.com
- Extra Examples, Chapter 10, Lesson 1
- Self-Check Quiz, Chapter 10, Lesson 1

Lesson 10-1 Angle Relationships **510b**

10-1 **Angle Relationships**

1 Focus

Standards Alignment

Before Lesson 10-1
Measure, identify, and draw angles, perpendicular and parallel lines, rectangles, and triangles by using appropriate tools from ⌐ Standard 5MG2.1

Lesson 10-1
Identify angles as vertical, adjacent, and provide descriptions of these terms from Standard 6MG2.1

After Lesson 10-1
Identify and construct basic elements of geometric figures by using a compass and straightedge from Standard 7MG3.1

2 Teach

Scaffolding Questions

Ask:

• What are some examples in the classroom of angles with measures less than 90°? Sample answer: yardstick leaning against wall

• What are some examples in the classroom of angles with measures greater than 90°? Sample answer: front and back covers of open book

• What are some examples of objects in the classroom that have edges that form right angles? Sample answer: side and top of a door

• How many right angles do you see in a doorway? 4

• What is another name for the shape of a doorway? rectangle

• What is the sum of the measures of the angles in a doorway? 360 degrees

---

Main IDEA

Classify angles and identify vertical and adjacent angles.

Standard 6MG2.1 **Identify angles as vertical, adjacent,** complementary, or supplementary **and provide descriptions of these terms.**

NEW Vocabulary

angle
degrees
vertex
congruent angles
right angle
acute angle
obtuse angle
straight angle
vertical angles
adjacent angles

READING Math

Geometry symbols
∠   angle
°   degree

READING in the Content Area

For strategies in reading this lesson, visit ca.gr6math.com.

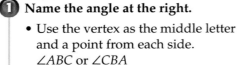
CLOCKS The hands of a clock form angles of different sizes.

3:10
less than 90°

3:00
90°

3:40
greater than 90°

1. Name other times in which the hands of a clock form angles less than 90°, equal to 90°, and greater than 90°.

2. How many degrees is the angle that is formed by clock hands at 6:00? **180°**   1. Sample answer: 7:45, 9:00, 2:50

An **angle** has two sides that share a common endpoint and is measured in units called **degrees**. If a circle were divided into 360 equal-sized parts, each part would have an angle measure of 1 degree (1°).

The point where the sides meet is called the **vertex**.

An angle can be named in several ways. The symbol for angle is ∠.

EXAMPLE **Naming Angles**

1 Name the angle at the right.

• Use the vertex as the middle letter and a point from each side.
∠ABC or ∠CBA

• Use the vertex only.
∠B

• Use a number.
∠1

The angle can be named in four ways: ∠ABC, ∠CBA, ∠B, or ∠1.

CHECK Your Progress

a. Name the angle shown in four ways.
∠RST, ∠TSR, ∠S, ∠2

Tips for New Teachers

Naming Angles

If more than one angle share a vertex, the angles cannot be named by their vertex alone. Also, angles do not have to be both numbered and lettered as in Example 1. Often, angles are labeled with either numbers or letters, not both.

Angles are classified according to their measure. Two angles that have the same measure are said to be **congruent**.

KEY **CONCEPT**
Types of Angles

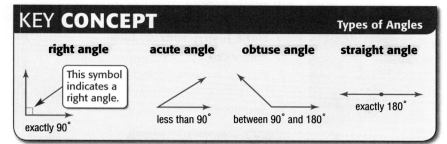

right angle   acute angle   obtuse angle   straight angle

This symbol indicates a right angle.

exactly 90°   less than 90°   between 90° and 180°   exactly 180°

EXAMPLES Classify Angles

Classify each angle as *acute, obtuse, right,* or *straight.*

 **2**

The angle is less than 90°, so it is an acute angle.

3

The angle is between 90° and 180°, so it is an obtuse angle.

✓ CHECK Your Progress

Classify each angle as *acute, obtuse, right,* or *straight.*

b.

right

c.

obtuse

d.

straight

Some angle pairs share a special relationship.

KEY **CONCEPT**
Vertical Angles

Words	Two angles are **vertical** if they are opposite angles formed by the intersection of two lines.
Examples	∠1 and ∠3 are vertical angles. ∠2 and ∠4 are vertical angles.

Adjacent Angles

Words	Two angles are **adjacent** if they share a common vertex, a common side, and do not overlap.
Examples	Adjacent angle pairs are ∠1 and ∠2, ∠2 and ∠3, ∠3 and ∠4, and ∠4 and ∠1.
	∠5 and ∠6 are adjacent angles.

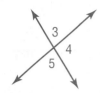
3 Practice

✓ Formative Assessment

Use Exercises 1–3 to check for understanding.

Then use the chart at the bottom of this page to customize your assignments for students.

Intervention You may wish to use the Study Guide and Intervention Master on page 10 of the *Chapter 10 Resource Masters* for additional reinforcement.

Odd/Even Assignments

Exercises 4–17 are structured so that students practice the same concepts whether they are assigned odd or even problems.

 Tips for New Teachers **Classifying Angles** Point out that students can classify angles by mentally comparing them with a right angle nearby, such as the corner of a page or index card.

Additional Answers

e. ∠1 and ∠3 Sample answer: Since ∠1 and ∠3 are opposite angles formed by the intersection of two lines, they are vertical angles.

f. ∠2 and ∠3 Sample answer: Since ∠2 and ∠3 share a common vertex, a common side, and do not overlap, they are adjacent angles.

512 Chapter 10 Geometry: Polygons

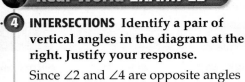

④ **INTERSECTIONS** Identify a pair of vertical angles in the diagram at the right. Justify your response.

Since ∠2 and ∠4 are opposite angles formed by the intersection of two lines, they are vertical angles. Similarly, ∠1 and ∠3 are also vertical angles.

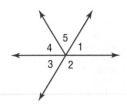

Real-World Link · · · ·
The United States has a total of 6,407,637 kilometers of roadways. Of these, 4,164,637 kilometers are paved.
Source: Central Intelligence Agency

✓ CHECK Your Progress e, f. See margin.

Refer to the diagram at the right. Identify each of the following. Justify your response.

e. a pair of vertical angles

f. a pair of adjacent angles

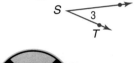

🖥 **Personal Tutor at** ca.gr6math.com

✓ CHECK Your Understanding

Examples 1–3
(pp. 510–511)

Name each angle in four ways. Then classify the angle as *acute*, *right*, *obtuse*, or *straight*.

1. ∠MNP, ∠PNM, ∠N, ∠1; obtuse

2. ∠RST, ∠TSR, ∠S, ∠3; acute

Example 4
(p. 512)

1.

2.

3. ∠1 and ∠3; Sample answer: Since ∠1 and ∠3 are opposite angles formed by the intersection of two lines, they are vertical angles.

3. **RAILROADS** Identify a pair of vertical angles on the railroad crossing sign. Justify your response.

Exercises

HOMEWORK HELP

For Exercises	See Examples
4–9	1–3
10–17	4

Exercise Levels
A: 4–17
C: 18–20

Name each angle in four ways. Then classify the angle as *acute*, *right*, *obtuse*, or *straight*. 4–9. See margin.

4.

5.

6.

7.

8.

9.

512 Chapter 10 Geometry: Polygons

DIFFERENTIATED HOMEWORK OPTIONS			
Level	**Assignment**	**Two-Day Option**	
BL Basic	4–17, 20–30	5–17 odd, 21, 22	4–16 even, 20, 23–30
OL Core	5–17 odd, 20, 21–26	4–17, 21, 22	20, 21, 23–30
AL Advanced/Pre-AP	20–26 (optional: 27–30)		

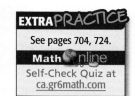
EXTRA PRACTICE

See pages 704, 724.

Math online

Self-Check Quiz at
ca.gr6math.com

For Exercises 10–15, refer to the diagram at the right.
Identify each angle pair as *adjacent*, *vertical*, or *neither*.

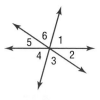

vertical
10. ∠2 and ∠5

neither
11. ∠4 and ∠6

adjacent
12. ∠3 and ∠4

13. ∠5 and ∠6
adjacent

14. ∠1 and ∠3
neither

15. ∠1 and ∠4
vertical

GEOGRAPHY For Exercises 16 and 17, use the diagram at the right and the following information.   16–17. See margin.

The corner where the states of Utah, Arizona, New Mexico, and Colorado meet is called the Four Corners.

16. Identify a pair of vertical angles. Justify your response.

17. Identify a pair of adjacent angles. Justify your response.

H.O.T. Problems

CHALLENGE For Exercises 18 and 19, determine whether each statement is *true* or *false*. If the statement is true, provide a diagram to support it. If the statement is false, explain why.

18. A pair of obtuse angles can also be vertical angles.   18–20. See margin.

19. A pair of straight angles can also be adjacent angles.

20. **WRITING IN MATH** Describe the differences between vertical and adjacent angles. **See margin.**

STANDARDS PRACTICE 6MG2.1

21. Which word best describes the angle marked in the figure?

angle

YIELD

A

A acute

B obtuse

C right

D straight

22. Which of the following is true in the diagram? **G**

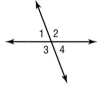

F ∠1 and ∠4 are adjacent angles.

G ∠2 and ∠3 are vertical angles.

H ∠3 and ∠4 are vertical angles.

J ∠2 and ∠3 are adjacent angles.

Spiral Review

A coin is tossed twice and a number cube is rolled. Find each probability.
(Lesson 9-8)

23. P(2 heads and 6) $\frac{1}{24}$ **24.** P(1 head, 1 tail, and a 3) $\frac{1}{24}$ **25.** P(2 tails and *not* 4) $\frac{5}{24}$

26. **PROBABILITY** Anica spins a spinner fifty times, and it lands on 3 fifteen times. What is the experimental probability of *not* landing on 3? (Lesson 9-7) $\frac{7}{10}$

GET READY for the Next Lesson

ALGEBRA Solve each equation. Check your solution. (Lesson 3-2)

27. $44 + x = 90$ **46**   **28.** $117 + x = 180$ **63**   **29.** $90 = 36 + x$ **54**   **30.** $180 = 75 + x$ **105**

Pre-AP Activity   Use as an Extension

Have students think of the minute hand and hour hand of the classroom clock as the sides of angles. Have them find the measure of the angles formed by the hands at 1:00, 2:00, and 3:00. How many degrees does the minute hand travel in one hour? In one half hour? In one quarter hour? 30°, 60°, and 90°; 360°; 180°; 90°

4 Assess

Crystal Ball Draw two intersecting lines that form a 60° angle. What are the measures of the other three angles formed by the lines? 60°, 120°, 120° What is the sum of all four angles? 360° Is this always the same sum of four angles formed by two intersecting lines?

yes

Additional Answers

4. ∠ABC, ∠CBA, ∠B, ∠4; acute

5. ∠DEF, ∠FED, ∠E, ∠5; right

6. ∠XYZ, ∠ZYX, ∠Y, ∠6; obtuse

7. ∠MNP, ∠PNM, ∠N, ∠7; straight

8. ∠HKI, ∠IKH, ∠K, ∠8; obtuse

9. ∠RTS, ∠STR, ∠T, ∠9; acute

16. ∠1 and ∠3; Sample answer: Since ∠1 and ∠3 are opposite angles formed by the intersection of two lines, they are vertical angles.

17. ∠1 and ∠2; Sample answer: Since ∠1 and ∠2 share a common vertex, a common side, and do not overlap, they are adjacent angles.

18. True; Sample answer:

19. True; Sample answer:

20. Sample answer: Vertical angles are opposite angles formed by the intersection of two lines, share a common vertex, and do not share a common side. Adjacent angles can be formed by the intersection of two lines but must share a common side and a common vertex.

Complementary and Supplementary Angles

Standard 6MG2.1 : Identify angles as vertical, adjacent, **complementary, or supplementary and provide descriptions of these terms.**

Standard 6MG2.2 : Use the properties of complementary and supplementary angles and the sum of the angles of a triangle to solve problems involving an unknown angle.

PACING: **Regular:** 1 period, **Block:** 0.5 period

Options for Differentiated Instruction

ELL = English Language Learner   **AL** = Above Grade Level   **SS** = Struggling Students   **SN** = Special Needs

Real-World Connection   **ELL** **SS** **SN**

Use while presenting the lesson.

Ask students to bring in pictures from newspapers or magazines that show things in the world that create complementary or supplementary angles. Have pairs of students examine each picture and tell whether the angles are complementary or supplementary and explain why.

Vocabulary Development   **ELL** **SS** **SN**

Use after presenting the Examples.

Have strudents write a summary about the differences and similariies between complementary and supplementary angles. Have them include sketches of complementary and supplementary angles so that they have a visual as well as a written representation of the angles.

Mathematical Displays   **SN**

Use after presenting the Examples.

Open the classroom door so that it forms a right angle with the wall. Use masking tape on the floor to mark the door's position. Then have pairs of students move the door to a new position and mark this new position with masking tape. Have each pair of students measure one of the new angles with a large classrom protractor and then determine the missing angle measure.

Leveled Lesson Resources

Chapter 10 Resource Masters

BL = Below Grade Level   **OL** = On Grade Level   **AL** = Above Grade Level   **ELL** = English Language Learner

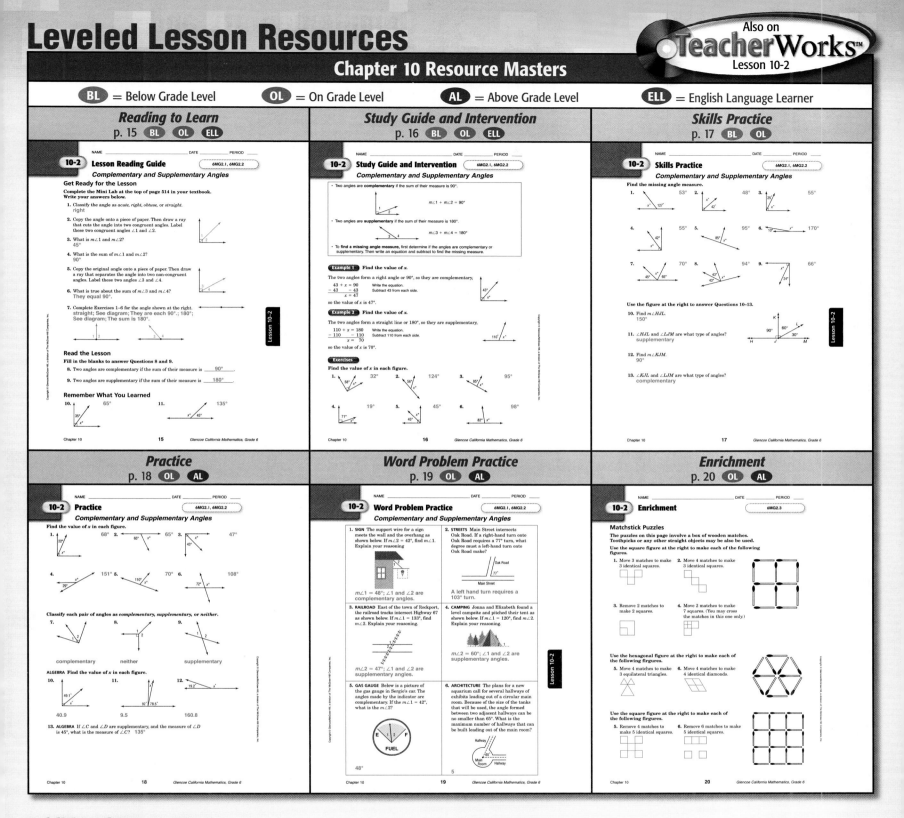

Reading to Learn
p. 15 **BL** **OL** **ELL**

Study Guide and Intervention
p. 16 **BL** **OL** **ELL**

Skills Practice
p. 17 **BL** **OL**

Practice
p. 18 **OL** **AL**

Word Problem Practice
p. 19 **OL** **AL**

Enrichment
p. 20 **OL** **AL**

Additional Lesson Resources

Transparencies
- *5-Minute Check Transparency,* Lesson 10-2

Other Print Products
- *Noteables™ Interactive Study Notebook with Foldables™*

Teacher Tech Tools
- *Interactive Classroom CD-ROM,* Lesson 10-2
- *AssignmentWorks CD-ROM,* Lesson 10-2

Student Tech Tools
ca.gr6math.com
- Extra Examples, Chapter 10, Lesson 2
- Self-Check Quiz, Chapter 10, Lesson 2

10-2 Complementary and Supplementary Angles

10-2 Complementary and Supplementary Angles

1 Focus

Standards Alignment

Before Lesson 10-2
Measure, identify, and draw angles, perpendicular and parallel lines, rectangles, and triangles by using appropriate tools from
🔑 Standard 5MG2.1

Lesson 10-2
Identify angles as complementary or supplementary and provide descriptions of these terms. Use the properties of complementary and supplementary angles to solve problems involving an unknown angle from 🔑 Standard 6MG2.1 and 6MG2.2

After Lesson 10-2
Identify and construct basic elements of geometric figures by using a compass and straightedge from Standard 7MG3.1

2 Teach

Scaffolding Questions

Ask:

• What is the everyday meaning of complementary? Sample answer: a pair of contrasting colors

• What is the everyday meaning of supplementary? Sample answer: something in addition

• What do you think these words might mean with respect to angles? Sample answer: Complementary—angles that complete each other Supplementary—angles that complete or make an addition

Main IDEA
Identify complementary and supplementary angles and find missing angle measures.

 Standard 6MG2.1 Identify angles as vertical, adjacent, **complementary, or supplementary and provide descriptions of these terms.** **Standard 6MG2.2** **Use the properties of complementary and supplementary angles** and the sum of the angles of a triangle **to solve problems involving an unknown angle.**

NEW Vocabulary

complementary angles
supplementary angles

READING Math

Angle Measure The notation $m\angle 1$ is read *the measure of angle 1.*

▶ MINI Lab

GEOMETRY Refer to $\angle A$ shown at the right.

1. Classify it as *acute, right, obtuse,* or *straight.* **right**

2. Copy the angle onto a piece of paper. Then draw a ray that separates the angle into two congruent angles. Label these angles $\angle 1$ and $\angle 2$.

3. What is $m\angle 1$ and $m\angle 2$?

4. What is the sum of $m\angle 1$ and $m\angle 2$?

5. Copy the original angle onto a piece of paper. Then draw a ray that separates the angle into two non-congruent angles. Label these angles $\angle 3$ and $\angle 4$.

6. What is true about the sum of $m\angle 3$ and $m\angle 4$?

7. Complete Exercises 1–6 for $\angle B$ shown at the right. **2–7. See margin.**

A special relationship exists between two angles whose sum is 90°. A special relationship also exists between two angles whose sum is 180°.

KEY CONCEPTS   Complementary Angles

Words	Two angles are **complementary** if the sum of their measures is 90°.
Examples	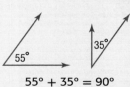

$m\angle 1 + m\angle 2 = 90°$ \qquad $55° + 35° = 90°$

Supplementary Angles

Words	Two angles are **supplementary** if the sum of their measures is 180°.
Examples	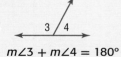

$m\angle 3 + m\angle 4 = 180°$ \qquad $40° + 140° = 180°$

You can use these relationships to identify complementary and supplementary angles.

Additional Answers

2.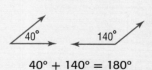

3. They are each 45°.

4. 90°

5. Sample answer: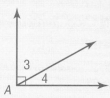

6. The sum is 90°.

Identify each pair of angles as *complementary*, *supplementary*, or *neither*.

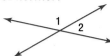
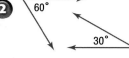

∠1 and ∠2 form a straight angle. So, the angles are supplementary.

60° + 30° = 90°
The angles are complementary.

 CHECK Your Progress

Identify each pair of angles as *complementary*, *supplementary*, or *neither*.

a. neither
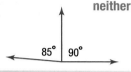
85° 90°

b. complementary

75°
15°

You can use angle relationships to find missing measures.

EXAMPLE Find a Missing Angle Measure

3 ALGEBRA Find the value of *x*.

Since the two angles form a right angle, they are complementary.

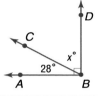

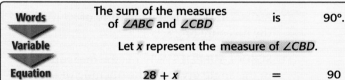

Words	The sum of the measures of ∠ABC and ∠CBD	is	90°.
Variable	Let *x* represent the measure of ∠CBD.		
Equation	28 + x	=	90

$$28 + x = 90 \quad \text{Write the equation.}$$
$$-28 \qquad -28 \quad \text{Subtract 28 from each side.}$$
$$x = 62$$

So, value of *x* is 62.

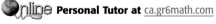 CHECK Your Progress

c. **ALGEBRA** Find the value of *x*. 134

46° x°

d. **ALGEBRA** If ∠J and ∠K are complementary and the measure of ∠K is 65°, what is the measure of ∠J? **25°**

 Personal Tutor at ca.gr6math.com

Lesson 10-2 Complementary and Supplementary Angles **515**

Additional Answer

7. straight; See diagram; They are each 90°.;
   180°; Sample answer:

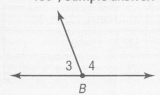

The sum is 180°.

Focus on Mathematical Content

If the sum of the measures of two angles is 90°, the angles are **complementary**.

If the sum of the measures of two angles is 180°, the angles are **supplementary**.

Students can use what they know about angle relationships to find missing angle measures by **solving algebraic equations**.

Formative Assessment

Use the Check Your Progress exercises after each example to determine students' understanding of concepts.

ADDITIONAL EXAMPLES

Classify each pair of angles as *complementary*, *supplementary*, or *neither*.

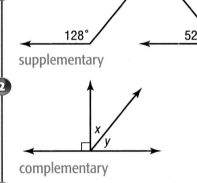

1 128° 52°
   supplementary

2 x y
   complementary

3 **ALGEBRA** Angles *PQS* and *RQS* are supplementary. If *m*∠*PQS* = 56°, find *m*∠*RQS*. 124°

Angle Relationships

Point out to students that complementary and supplementary angles may or may not be adjacent angles.

3 Practice

Formative Assessment

Use Exercises 1–3 to check for understanding.

Then use the chart at the bottom of this page to customize your assignments for students.

Intervention You may wish to use the Study Guide and Intervention master on page 16 of the *Chapter 10 Resource Masters* for additional reinforcement.

Odd/Even Assignments

Exercises 4–11 are structured so that students practice the same concepts whether they are assigned odd or even problems.

Additional Answers

14. Sample answer: ∠*IJK*, ∠*KJG*

15. Sample answer: ∠*CGK*, ∠*KJG*

16. Sample answer: ∠*AKB*, ∠*JKG*

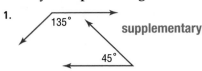

CHECK Your Understanding

Examples 1, 2 (p. 515) Identify each pair of angles as *complementary, supplementary,* or *neither.*

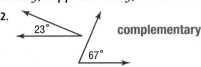

1. supplementary   2. complementary

Example 3 (p. 515)

3. **ALGEBRA** Find the value of *x*. 135

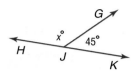

Exercises

HOMEWORK HELP

For Exercises	See Examples
4–9	1, 2
10–11	3

Exercise Levels
A: 4–11
B: 12–20
C: 21–23

Identify each pair of angles as *complementary, supplementary,* or *neither.*

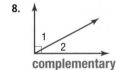

4. neither   5. supplementary   6. supplementary

7. supplementary   8. complementary   9. neither

10. **ALGEBRA** If ∠*A* and ∠*B* are complementary and the measure of ∠*B* is 67°, what is the measure of ∠*A*? **23°**

11. **ALGEBRA** What is the measure of ∠*J* if ∠*J* and ∠*K* are supplementary and the measure of ∠*K* is 115°? **65°**

12. **SCHOOL SUPPLIES** What is the measure of the angle given by the opening of the scissors, *x*? **64**

13. **BASKETBALL** Beatriz makes a bounce pass to Tyrone. Find the value of *x* so that Beatriz's pass hits Tyrone's hands. **84**

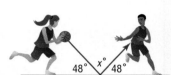

14–16.
See margin.

EXTRA PRACTICE

See pages 704, 724.

Math Online

Self-Check Quiz at ca.gr6math.com

Use the figure at the right to name the following.

14. a pair of supplementary angles

15. a pair of complementary angles

16. a pair of vertical angles

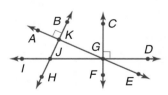

516 Chapter 10 Geometry: Polygons

DIFFERENTIATED HOMEWORK OPTIONS

Level	Assignment	Two-Day Option	
BL Basic	4–11, 22–30	5–11 odd, 23, 24	4–10 even, 22, 25–30
OL Core	5–11 odd, 12–20, 23–30	4–11, 23, 24	12–20, 25–30
AL Advanced/Pre-AP	12–26 (optional: 27–30)		

17. adjacent; adjacent; vertical

18. $m\angle 1 + m\angle 2 = 180°$; $m\angle 2 + m\angle 3 = 180°$

19. $m\angle 1 = 180° - m\angle 2$; $m\angle 3 = 180° - m\angle 2$; Sample answer: $m\angle 1$ and $m\angle 3$ are equal.

H.O.T. Problems

GEOMETRY For Exercises 17–20, use the figure at the right.

17. Are $\angle 1$ and $\angle 2$ vertical angles, adjacent angles, or neither? $\angle 2$ and $\angle 3$? $\angle 1$ and $\angle 3$?

18. Write an equation representing the sum of $m\angle 1$ and $m\angle 2$. Then write an equation representing the sum of $m\angle 2$ and $m\angle 3$.

19. Solve the equations you wrote in Exercise 18 for $m\angle 1$ and $m\angle 3$, respectively. What do you notice?

20. MAKE A CONJECTURE Use your answer to Exercise 19 to make a conjecture as to the relationship between vertical angles.
Sample answer: Vertical angles are congruent.

21. CHALLENGE Angles E and F are complementary. If $m\angle E = x - 10$ and $m\angle F = x + 2$, find the measure of each angle. $m\angle E = 39°$, $m\angle F = 51°$

22. WRITING IN MATH Describe a strategy for determining whether two angles are *complementary*, *supplementary*, or *neither* without knowing or measuring each angle using a protractor. **See margin.**

Ticket Out the Door Tell students that angles 1 and 2 are complementary, and that angle 2 measures $x°$. Have students write an algebraic equation for the measure of angle 1.

Additional Answer

22. Sample answer: You could align the angles at their vertices so that they share a common side. Use a corner of a book, a right angle, to determine if the angles are complementary and use the edge of a book, a straight line, to determine if the angles are supplementary. If the sides of the angles that are not shared align with the corner of the book, they are complementary. If the sides of angles that are not shared align with the edge of the book, they are supplementary. Otherwise, the angles are neither complementary nor supplementary.

STANDARDS PRACTICE 6MG2.1, 6MG2.2

23. In the figure below, $m\angle YXZ = 35°$ and $m\angle WXV = 40°$. What is $m\angle ZXW$? **B**

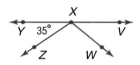

A 180°   **C** 75°

B 105°   **D** 15°

24. Which is a true statement about angles 1 and 2 shown below? **H**

F $\angle 1$ is complementary to $\angle 2$.

G $\angle 1$ and $\angle 2$ are vertical angles.

H $\angle 1$ is supplementary to $\angle 2$.

J Both angles are obtuse.

Spiral Review

25. Name the angle at the right in four ways. Then classify it as *acute, right, obtuse,* or *straight*. (Lesson 10-1)
$\angle P, \angle 1, \angle RPQ, \angle QPR$; acute

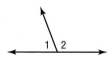

26. MEASUREMENT A house for sale has a rectangular lot with a length of 250 feet and a width of 120 feet. What is the area of the lot? (Lesson 3-6) **30,000 ft²**

GET READY for the Next Lesson

PREREQUISITE SKILL Multiply or divide. Round to the nearest hundredth if necessary. (p. 674 and p. 676)

27. $0.62 \cdot 360$ **223.2**   **28.** $360 \cdot 0.25$ **90**   **29.** $17 \div 146$ **0.12**   **30.** $63 \div 199$ **0.32**

10-3 Statistics: Display Data in a Circle Graph

Reinforcement of Standard 5SDAP1.2

Organize and display single-variable data in appropriate graphs and representations (e.g., histogram, **circle graphs**) and explain which types of graphs are appropriate for various data sets.

PACING:

Regular: 1 period, **Block:** 0.5 period

Options for Differentiated Instruction

ELL = English Language Learner **AL** = Above Grade Level **SS** = Struggling Students **SN** = Special Needs

Using Tools SS SN

Use before beginning Lesson 10-3.

Many students have difficulty using a protractor. In particular, they have difficulty determining which set of numbers to use. By encouraging students to determine whether an angle is acute or obtuse before measuring, they should be able to determine which number on the protractor is correct for that angle.

Have students work in pairs to draw an angle having each measure.

1. 90°   **2.** 160°   **3.** 35°   **4.** 100°   **5.** 74°

Creating a Survey ELL AL SS SN

Use after presenting the Examples.

Have students write a survey question and pass it out to their classmates. They should use a multiple-choice format with four or five responses. A sample question is shown below.

> What is your favorite subject in school?
> **A** science   **B** math   **C** history   **D** English   **E** other

Be sure to review the questions for content and format before they are distributed. After the questions are answered, have students create a circle graph to display their results.

Using Templates ELL AL SS SN

Use with the Exercises.

Distributing circle graph templates like the one shown at the right may be helpful for students with fine motor issues. This would allow them to construct circle graphs for the independent exercises without having to use a protractor.

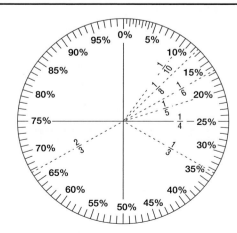

Chapter 10 Resource Masters

BL = Below Grade Level **OL** = On Grade Level **AL** = Above Grade Level **ELL** = English Language Learner

Lesson Reading Guide	Study Guide and Intervention*	Skills Practice*
p. 21 **BL** **OL** **ELL**	p. 22 **BL** **OL** **ELL**	p. 23 **BL** **OL**

10-3 Lesson Reading Guide
Statistics: Display Data in a Circle Graph

Get Ready for the Lesson
Read the introduction at the top of page 518 in your textbook.
Write your answers below.

1. Explain how you know that each person surveyed chose only one shade of blue. Sample answer: The percents add up to 100.

2. If 500 people took part in the survey, how many preferred aquamarine? 85

Read the Lesson

3. In the following circle graph, what is the percent represented by section C? How do you know?

62.5%; The percents must add up to 100.

4. As stated in Example 2 on page 519, when you construct a circle graph, you can check your work by measuring the last section of a circle graph to verify that the angles have the correct measure. Why will this work as a check? Sample answer: If the graph is accurate then the last section will have a measurement corresponding to the percent remaining to be graphed on the circle.

Remember What You Learned

5. If you are given the results of a survey and the results are given in percents, how do you draw a circle graph to represent the results of the survey? Describe each step.
Sample answer:
a. Find the degrees for each part.
b. Use a compass to draw a circle. Then draw a radius.
c. Use a protractor to draw the angle that corresponds to each percent.
d. Label each section of the graph.

10-3 Study Guide and Intervention
Statistics: Display Data in a Circle Graph

A graph that shows data as parts of a whole circle is called a *circle graph*. In a circle graph, the percents add up to 100. When percents are not given, you must first determine what part of the whole each item represents.

Example 1 ENERGY Make a circle graph of the data in the table.

Nuclear Reactors in Operation, 2001	
Country	Number of Reactors
United States	104
France	59
Japan	54
Other Countries	222

Step 1 Find the total number of reactors: 104 + 59 + 54 + 222 = 439.
Step 2 Find the ratio that compares each number with the total. Write the ratio as a decimal rounded to the nearest hundredth.
United States: $\frac{104}{439} \approx 0.24$ Japan: $\frac{54}{439} \approx 0.12$
France: $\frac{59}{439} \approx 0.13$ Other: $\frac{222}{439} \approx 0.51$
Step 3 Find the number of degrees for each section of the graph.
United States: $0.24 \cdot 360° \approx 86°$ Japan: $0.12 \cdot 360° \approx 43°$
France: $0.13 \cdot 360° \approx 47°$ Other: $0.51 \cdot 360° \approx 183°$
Step 4 Use a compass to construct a circle and draw a radius. Then use a protractor to draw an 86° angle. This represents the percent of nuclear reactors in the United States.
Step 5 From the new radius, draw a 47° angle for France. Repeat this step for the other two sections. Label each section and give the graph a title.

Exercises

1. SWIMMING The table shows the number of members of the swim team who competed at the swim meet. Each competed in only one event. Make a circle graph of the data.

Swim Team Member Participation	
Event	Number
Freestyle	18
Breaststroke	7
Backstroke	5
Butterfly	2

10-3 Skills Practice
Statistics: Display Data in a Circle Graph

For each table, find the number of degrees in each section of a circle graph. Then make a circle graph of the data.

1.
United States Energy Usage, 2001	
Category	Percent
Commercial and Industrial	52%
Residential	20%
Transportation	27%
Other	1%

Commercial and Industrial: 187°; Residential: 72°; Transportation: 97°; Other: 4°

2.
Family Members Students Confide In	
Family Member	Percent
Mom	52%
Dad	17%
Brother/Sister	16%
Grandparent/Other	15%

Mom: 187°; Dad: 61°; Brother/Sister: 58°; Grandparent/Other: 54°

3.
Successful Space Launches, 2001	
Country	Number
India	2
United States	23
European Space Agency	11
China	1

India: 22°; United States: 251°; European Space Agency: 76°; China: 11°

4.
United States Coastline	
Coast	Length (mi)
Atlantic	2,100
Pacific	7,600
Gulf	1,600
Arctic	1,100

Atlantic: 61°; Pacific: 221°; Gulf: 47°; Arctic: 32°

Practice*	Word Problem Practice*	Enrichment
p. 24 **OL** **AL**	p. 25 **OL** **AL**	p. 26 **OL** **AL**

10-3 Practice
Statistics: Display Data in a Circle Graph

Display each set of data in a circle graph.

1.
Volume of World's Oceans	
Ocean	Percent
Pacific	49%
Atlantic	26%
Indian	21%
Arctic	4%
Source: peacecorps.gov

2.
America's Energy Sources	
Type	Percent
Petroleum	40%
Natural Gas	23%
Coal	22%
Nuclear	8%
Other	7%
Source: conocophillips.com

EXPORTS For Exercises 3 and 4, use the circle graph that shows the percent of Persian Gulf petroleum exports by country for the year 2003.

3. Which country has the most petroleum exports? Saudi Arabia

4. How many times more exports does Iran have than Qatar? 3 times

DATA SENSE For each graph, find the missing values.

5. Recycled Products 10%
6. Time Management 100°

10-3 Word Problem Practice
Statistics: Display Data in a Circle Graph

LANGUAGES For Exercises 1 and 2, use the table that shows the number of people that speak the five languages that are spoken by the most people in the world.

Languages Spoken by the Most People	
Language	Speakers (millions)
Chinese, Mandarin	874
Hindi	366
English	341
Spanish	322
Bengali	207

1. Find the degrees for each part of a circle graph that shows the data. Chinese, Mandarin: 151°; Hindi: 61°; English: 58°; Spanish: 54°; Bengali: 36°

2. Make a circle graph of the data. Which three languages account for 41% of the total?

MILITARY For Exercises 3 and 4, use the table that shows the number of people active in the United States military in 2002.

United States Military, Active Duty, 2002	
Branch	Personnel (thousands)
Army	486
Navy	385
Marine Corps	174
Air Force	368
Coast Guard	38

3. Make a circle graph of the data.

4. Which two branches taken together account for almost half of the total? Air Force and Navy

10-3 Enrichment

Relative Frequency and Circle Graphs

The **relative frequency** tells how the frequency of one item compares to the total of all the frequencies. Relative frequencies are written as fractions, decimals, or percents.

For example, in Exercise 1 below, the total of all the frequencies is 50. So, the relative frequency of the grade A is 8 ÷ 50, or 0.16.

The circle at the right is divided into 20 equal parts. You can trace this circle and then use relative frequencies to make circle graphs.

Complete each chart to show the relative frequencies. Then sketch a circle graph for the data. Use decimals rounded to the nearest hundredth.

1. History Grades for 50 Students

Grade	Frequency	Relative Frequency
A	8	0.16
B	16	0.32
C	18	0.36
D	6	0.12
F	2	0.04

2. Steve's Budget

Item	Amount Spent	Relative Spending
Telephone	$26	0.13
Movies	$46	0.23
Books	$24	0.12
Car	$38	0.19
Other	$66	0.33

Additional Lesson Resources

* Also available in Spanish ELL

Transparencies
- *5-Minute Check Transparency,* Lesson 10-3

Other Print Products
- *Teaching Mathematics with Manipulatives*
- *Noteables™ Interactive Study Notebook with Foldables™*

Teacher Tech Tools
- *Interactive Classroom CD-ROM,* Lesson 10-3
- *AssignmentWorks CD-ROM,* Lesson 10-3

Student Tech Tools
ca.gr6math.com
- Extra Examples, Chapter 10, Lesson 3
- Self-Check Quiz, Chapter 10, Lesson 3

1 Focus

Standards Alignment

Before Lesson 10-3
Interpret one- and two-variable data graphs to answer questions about a situation from Standard 4SDAP1.3

Lesson 10-3
Organize and display single-variable data in appropriate graphs and representations from Standard 5SDAP1.2

After Lesson 10-3
Know various forms of display for data sets, use the forms to display a single set of data or to compare two sets of data from Standard 7SDAP1.1

2 Teach

Scaffolding Questions

Draw the *x*-axis and *y*-axis on the board intersecting to meet at the origin.

Ask:
- What is the measure of the angle between the *x*- and the *y*-axes in each Quadrant? 90°
- What is the sum of the angles formed in each Quadrant? 360°
- What percent of the entire coordinate plane is located in each Quadrant? 25%

Draw a line passing through Quadrants I and III through the origin that is equidistant from the *x*- and *y*-axes. (This line is the line $y = x$)

Ask:
- What is the measure of the angle between the *x*-axis and the line in Quadrant I? 45°
- What fraction of the entire coordinate

plane is formed by this angle? $\frac{1}{8}$

- What percent of the entire coordinate plane is formed by this angle? 12.5%

10-3 Statistics: Display Data in a Circle Graph

Main IDEA
Construct and interpret circle graphs.

Reinforcement of Standard 5SDAP1.2 Organize and display single-variable data in appropriate graphs and representations (e.g., histogram, **circle graphs**) and explain which types of graphs are appropriate for various data sets.

NEW Vocabulary
circle graph

1. Sample answer: The percents add up to 100.

▶ GET READY for the Lesson

COLORS In a recent survey, people ages 13–20 were asked to choose their favorite shade of blue. The results are shown in the table.

1. Explain how you know that each person surveyed chose only one shade of blue.

2. If 500 people took part in the survey, how many preferred aquamarine? 85

Favorite Shade of Blue for People Ages 13–20	
Shade	**Percent**
Navy	35%
Sky/Light Blue	30%
Aquamarine	17%
Other	18%

Source: *Amercian Demographics*

A graph that shows data as parts of a whole is called a **circle graph**. In a circle graph, the percents add up to 100.

EXAMPLE Display Data in a Circle Graph

1 COLORS Display the data above in a circle graph.

- There are 360° in a circle. Find the degrees for each part.

  35% of 360° = 0.35 · 360° or 126°   **Round to the nearest whole degree.**

  30% of 360° = 0.30 · 360° or 108°

  17% of 360° = 0.17 · 360° or about 61°

  18% of 360° = 0.18 · 360° or about 65°

- Draw a circle with a radius as shown. Then use a protractor to draw the first angle, in this case 126°. Repeat this step for each section or *sector*.

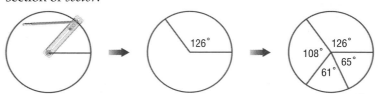

- Label each section of the graph with the category and percent it represents. Give the graph a title.

Check To draw an accurate circle graph, make sure the sum of the angle measures is equal to, or is approximately equal to, 360°.

Favorite Shade of Blue for People Ages 13–20

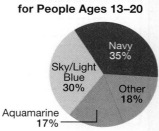

Circle Graphs

Remind students that there are 360° in a circle. When constructing a circle graph, students can begin at any point on the circle. Check to see if the percents add up to 100. If students have rounded, the sum of the percents may not be exactly equal to 100 but it should be close.

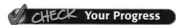

a. SCIENCE The table shows the present composition of Earth's atmosphere. Display the data in a circle graph.
See Ch. 10 Answer Appendix.

Composition of Earth's Atmosphere	
Element	**Percent**
Nitrogen	78%
Oxygen	21%
Other gases	1%

Source: www.nasa.gov

When constructing a circle graph, you may need to first convert the data to ratios and decimals and then to degrees and percents.

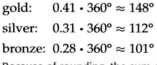 **EXAMPLE** Construct a Circle Graph

2 **OLYMPICS** The table shows the number of each type of medal won by the United States during the Summer Olympics from 1896 to 2004. Make a circle graph of the data.

U.S. Summer Olympic Medals	
Type	**Number**
Gold	907
Silver	697
Bronze	615

Source: infoplease.com

- Find the total number of medals:
  $907 + 697 + 615$ or $2,219$.

- Find the ratio that compares each number with the total. Write the ratio as a decimal rounded to the nearest hundredth.

  gold: $\frac{907}{2,219} \approx 0.41$ silver: $\frac{697}{2,219} \approx 0.31$ bronze: $\frac{615}{2,219} \approx 0.28$

- Find the number of degrees for each section of the graph.

  gold: $0.41 \cdot 360° \approx 148°$

  silver: $0.31 \cdot 360° \approx 112°$

  bronze: $0.28 \cdot 360° \approx 101°$

  Because of rounding, the sum of the degrees is 361°.

U.S. Summer Olympic Medals

Gold 41%
Silver 31%
Bronze 28%

- Draw the circle graph.
  $0.41 = 41\%, 0.31 = 31\%, 0.28 = 28\%$

Check After drawing the first two sections, you can measure the last section of a circle graph to verify that the angles have the correct measures.

Real-World Link · · · ·
The United States has won 2,219 Summer Olympic medals through 2004, the most for any country.
Source: infoplease.com

CHECK Your Progress

b. OLYMPICS The number of Winter Olympic medals won by the U.S. from 1924 to 2002 is shown in the table. Display the data in a circle graph.
See Ch. 10 Answer Appendix.

U.S. Winter Olympic Medals	
Type	**Number**
Gold	69
Silver	72
Bronze	52

Source: answers.com

Tips for New Teachers

Comparing Circle Graphs

After students have constructed a circle graph for Check Your Progress b, have them compare the percent of medals won, by type, in the Summer Olympics to the percent of medals won, by type, in the Winter Olympics. Point out to students that constructing a circle graph to display the data is a useful way to compare the two sets of data. Sample answer: The U.S. won a greater percent of gold medals in the Summer Olympics than in the Winter Olympics but a greater percent of silver medals in the Winter Olympics than in the Summer Olympics.

Focus on Mathematical Content

Students can use what they know about **angle measures** to create **circle graphs**. Circle graphs can be used to analyze data and to make predictions about larger data sets.

A circle has 360°; a circle graph shows 100% of a data set. So, to find the number of degrees in a sector of the graph, multiply the percent of that data (written as a decimal) by 360°.

If the total number of data in a circle graph is known, **the percent equation** can be used to find the number of data in each sector.

Formative Assessment

Use the Check Your Progress exercises after each Example to determine students' understanding of concepts.

ADDITIONAL EXAMPLE

1 **SPORTS** In a survey, a group of middle-school students was asked to name their favorite sport. The results are shown in the table. Make a circle graph of the data.

Sport	Percent
football	30%
basketball	25%
baseball	22%
tennis	8%
other	15%

Favorite Sport

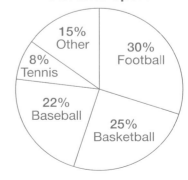

15% Other
30% Football
8% Tennis
22% Baseball
25% Basketball

2 **MOVIES** Gina has the following types of movies in her DVD collection. Make a circle graph of the data.

Type of Movie	Number
action	24
comedy	15
science fiction	7

Movies

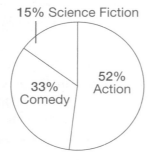

15% Science Fiction

33% Comedy

52% Action

VOTING The circle graph below shows the percent of voters in a town who are registered with a political party.

Party Registration

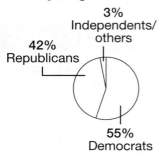

3% Independents/ others

42% Republicans

55% Democrats

3 Which party has the most registered voters? Democrats

4 If the town has 3,400 registered Republicans, about how many voters are registered in all? 8,095

EXAMPLES Analyze a Circle Graph

AUTOMOBILES The graph shows the percent of automobiles registered in the western United States in a recent year.

U.S. Registered Automobiles in West

Washington 13%
Oregon 6%
Nevada 3%
California 78%

Source: Bureau of Transportation Statistics

3 Which state had the most registered automobiles?

The largest section of the circle is the one representing California. So, California has the most registered automobiles.

4 If 24.0 million automobiles were registered in these states, how many more automobiles were registered in California than Oregon?

California: 78% of 24.0 million → 0.78 × 24.0, or 18.72 million

Oregon: 6% of 24.0 million → 0.06 × 24.0, or 1.44 million

There were 18.72 million − 1.44 million, or 17.28 million more registered automobiles in California than in Oregon.

CHECK Your Progress

c. Nevada; Sample answer: the smallest section of the circle is the one representing Nevada.

c. Which state had the least number of registered automobiles? Explain.

d. What was the total number of registered automobiles in Washington and Oregon? **4.56 million**

Personal Tutor at ca.gr6math.com

CHECK Your Understanding

Examples 1, 2 (pp. 518–519)

Display each set of data in a circle graph. 1–2. See margin.

1.

Blood Types in the U.S.	
Blood Type	**Percent**
O	44%
A	42%
B	10%
AB	4%

Source: Stanford School of Medicine

2.

Population of U.S. by Region	
Region	**Population (millions)**
Northeast	54
Midwest	65
South	104
West	66

Source: U.S. Census Bureau, 2004

Examples 3, 4 (p. 520)

COLORS For Exercises 3 and 4, use the graph that shows the results of a survey.

3. What color is most favored? **Blue**

4. If 400 people were surveyed, how many more people favored purple than red? **20**

Favorite Color

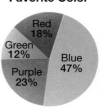

Red 18%
Green 12%
Blue 47%
Purple 23%

Additional Answers

1. **Blood Types in U.S.**

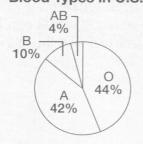

AB 4%
B 10%
A 42%
O 44%

2. **Population of U.S. Regions**

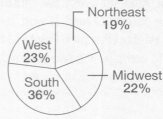

Northeast 19%
West 23%
South 36%
Midwest 22%

Exercises

HOMEWORK HELP

For Exercises	See Examples
5–6	1
7–8	2
9–14	3,4

Exercise Levels
A: 5–14
B: 15–24
C: 25–27

6–8. See Ch. 10 Answer Appendix.

9. grades 1–8
10. about twice as many

Display each set of data in a circle graph.   5. See margin.

5.

U.S. Steel Roller Coasters	
Type	**Percent**
Sit down	86%
Inverted	8%
Other	6%

Source: rcdb.com

6.

New York City Commuters	
Transportation	**Percent**
Driving Alone	24%
Carpool/Other	23%
Public Transit	53%

Source: *Time Almanac*

7.

Endangered Species in U.S.	
Species	**Number of Species**
Mammals	68
Birds	77
Reptiles	14
Amphibians	11

Source: U.S. Fish and Wildlife Service

8.

Speed Limits in U.S.	
Speed Limit (mph)	**Number of States**
60	1
65	20
70	16
75	13

Source: *The World Almanac*

EDUCATION For Exercises 9–11, use the circle graph that shows the percent of students by grade level in U.S. schools.

9. In which grades are most students?

10. About how many times more students are there in grades 1–8 than in grades 9–12?

11. There are about 75 million students in U.S. schools. How many students are in grades 9–12? **about 16.5 million**

Grade Level of U.S. Students

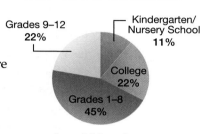

Grades 9–12 22%
Kindergarten/Nursery School 11%
College 22%
Grades 1–8 45%

Source: U.S. Census Bureau

MONEY For Exercises 12–14, use the graph that shows the results of a survey about a common currency for North America.

Do Americans Favor Common North American Currency?

No 53%
Yes 43%
Don't Know 4%

Source: Coinstar

12. 43%
13–14. See margin.

12. What percent of Americans favor a common North American currency?

13. Based on these results, about how many of the approximately 298 million Americans would say "Don't Know" in response to this survey?

14. About how many more Americans oppose a common currency than favor it?

✏️ **Formative Assessment**

Use Exercises 1–4 to check for understanding.

Then use the chart at the bottom of this page to customize your assignments for students.

Intervention You may wish to use the Study Guide and Intervention Master on page 22 of the *Chapter 10 Resource Masters* for additional reinforcement.

Odd/Even Assignments

Exercises 5–14 are structured so that students practice the same concepts whether they are assigned odd or even problems.

Tips for New Teachers   **Drawing Circles**
Students can use a compass to draw circles for their circle graphs. Or they can trace a round object such as the base of a glass or cup.

⚠️ **Exercise Alert!**

Use a Protractor Exercises 1, 2, and 5–8 require students to display data in a circle graph. Have students use a protractor for these problems.

Additional Answer

5. **U.S. Steel Roller Coasters**

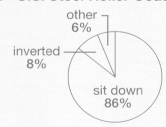

other 6%
inverted 8%
sit down 86%

13. about 12 million
14. about 30 million

DIFFERENTIATED HOMEWORK OPTIONS

Level	Assignment	Two-Day Option	
BL Basic	5–14, 26–34	5–13 odd, 28	6–14 even, 26, 27, 29–34
OL Core	5–7 odd, 9–14, 15–17 odd, 19–24, 26–34	5–14, 28	15–24, 26, 27, 29–34
AL Advanced/Pre-AP	15–30 (optional: 31–34)		

Additional Answers

17. **Birthplaces of Presidents**

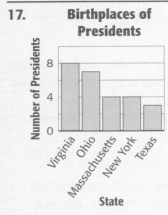

18. **Tanya's Day**

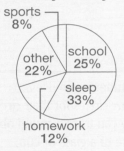

19. **Sizes of U.S Great Lakes**

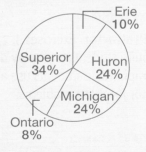

23. No; a 50% increase in 126 students is 189 and 189 is not equal to 366. So, it is not reasonable to say that 50% more students said they could make a difference. Since 300% of 126 is 378, it is reasonable to say that 300% more students said they could make a difference than those who said they cannot make a difference.

DATA SENSE For each graph, find the missing values.

15. **Dog Expenses**

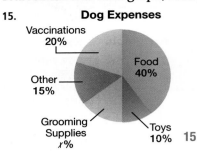

15

16. **Family Budget**

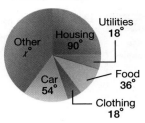

144

Select an appropriate type of graph to display each set of data: line graph, bar graph, or circle graph. Then display the data using the graph.

17–18. See margin for graphs.

17.

Top 5 Presidential Birth States	
Place	**Presidents**
Virginia	8
Ohio	7
Massachusetts	4
New York	4
Texas	3

Source: *The World Book of Facts*
bar graph

18.

Tanya's Day	
Activity	**Percent**
School	25%
Sleep	33%
Homework	12%
Sports	8%
Other	22%

circle graph

GEOGRAPHY For Exercises 19–21, use the table.

19. See margin.
20. Lake Huron and Lake Erie or Lake Michigan and Lake Erie
21. Lake Ontario is one-third the size of Lake Michigan.
23. See margin.
24. See students' work.

19. Display the data in a circle graph.

20. Use your graph to find which two lakes equal the size of Lake Superior.

21. Compare the size of Lake Ontario to the size of Lake Michigan.

Sizes of U.S. Great Lakes	
Lake	**Size (sq mi)**
Erie	9,930
Huron	23,010
Michigan	22,400
Ontario	7,520
Superior	31,820

POLITICS For Exercises 22 and 23, use the graph and information below.

A group of students were asked whether people their age could make a difference in the political decisions of elected officials.

22. How many students participated in the survey? 502

23. Write a convincing argument explaining whether or not it is reasonable to say that 50% more students said they could make a difference than those who said they could not make a difference.

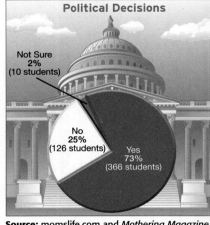

Political Decisions

Source: *momslife.com* and *Mothering Magazine*

24.  **FIND THE DATA** Refer to the California Data File on pages 16–19. Choose some data that can be displayed in a circle graph. Then display the data in a circle graph and write one statement analyzing the data.

Differentiated Instruction

Interpersonal Learners Separate students into groups of three or four. Have each group research data on the Internet or in another source such as a news magazine. Instruct the groups to find data that show parts of a whole. Finally, have each group create a circle graph of their data and present it to the class.

25. **CHALLENGE** The graph shows the results of a survey about students' favorite school subject. About what percent of those surveyed said that math was their favorite subject? Explain your reasoning.

Favorite Subject

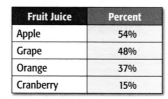

26. **COLLECT THE DATA** Collect some data from your classmates that can be represented in a circle graph. Then create the circle graph and write one statement analyzing the data. **See students' work.**

27. **WRITING IN MATH** The table shows the percent of people that like each type of fruit juice. Can the data be represented in a circle graph? Justify your answer.

Fruit Juice	Percent
Apple	54%
Grape	48%
Orange	37%
Cranberry	15%

27. Sample answer: No; the sum of the percents is greater than 100. The people surveyed must have been able to choose more than one fruit juice.

STANDARDS PRACTICE 5SDAP1.2

28. The graph shows the type of vehicles that used Highway 82 during one month.

A

Types of Vehicles

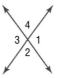

Which statement is true according to the circle graph shown?

A More cars used the highway than RVs and trucks combined.

B More than half the vehicles that used the highway were cars.

C More RVs used the highway than trucks.

D More trucks used the highway than cars.

Spiral Review

29. **GEOMETRY** Refer to the diagram at the right. Identify a pair of vertical angles. (Lesson 10-1) **Sample answer: ∠1 and ∠3**

30. **ALGEBRA** ∠A and ∠B are complementary. If $m\angle A = 15°$, find $m\angle B$. (Lesson 10-2) **75°**

GET READY for the Next Lesson

PREREQUISITE SKILL Solve each equation. (Lesson 3-2) **31. 68 32. 130 33. 101 34. 55**

31. $x + 112 = 180$ 32. $50 + t = 180$ 33. $180 = 79 + y$ 34. $180 = h + 125$

Lesson 10-3 Statistics: Display Data in a Circle Graph   **523**

⚠ **Exercise Alert!**

Use a Protractor Exercise 26 requires students to display data in a circle graph. Have students use a protractor for this problem.

4 **Assess**

Yesterday's News Remind students that yesterday's lesson was about the measure and classification of angles. Have students write how yesterday's concepts helped them with today's material.

✓ **Formative Assessment**

Check for student understanding of concepts in Lessons 10-1 through 10-3.

CRM Quiz 1, p. 67

 **Triangles**

Standard 6MG2.2 **Use** the properties of complementary and supplementary angles **and the sum of the angles of a triangle to solve problems involving an unknown angle.**

Standard 6MG2.3 **Draw** quadrilaterals and **triangles from given information about them** (e.g., a quadrilateral having equal sides but no right angles, **a right isosceles triangle.**)

PACING: **Regular:** 1 period, **Block:** 0.5 period

Options for Differentiated Instruction

ELL = English Language Learner **AL** = Above Grade Level **SS** = Struggling Students **SN** = Special Needs

Previewing Material **SS** **SN**

Use before beginning Lesson 10-4.

Before beginning the lesson, have students make a table like the one shown below.

Triangle	Angle Measures			
	∠1	∠2	∠3	∠1 + ∠2 + ∠3
1				
2				
3				

Then have them do the following:
- Draw several triangles with a ruler and measure and each of the angles. Record the measures in the table.
- Find the sum of the three angles in each triangle and record the values in the table.
- Compare your results with your classmates. What can you conclude about the three angles of a triangle?

Peer Teaching **ELL** **AL** **SS** **SN**

Use after presenting the Examples.

Try to group students who understand the quantitative relationships among angles with those who are good at modeling and drawing angles. Encourage each student to teach one aspect of an activity to the other group members. Examples of possible teaching duties are shown below:
- Demonstrate the algebraic method for finding the missing angle measure of a triangle.
- Demonstrate how to classify a triangle using angles and using sides.

Extensions and Challenges **AL**

Use after presenting Lesson 10-4.

Display the triangle on the board or overhead.

Ask:
- What is the value of *x*? 40
- Find the measure of all three angles. Explain or show how you determined your answer. 50°; 60°; 70°; (*x* + 20) + (*x* + 10) + (*x* + 30) = 180

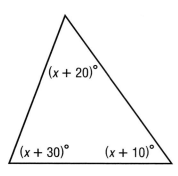

Leveled Lesson Resources

Chapter 10 Resource Masters

BL = Below Grade Level   **OL** = On Grade Level   **AL** = Above Grade Level   **ELL** = English Language Learner

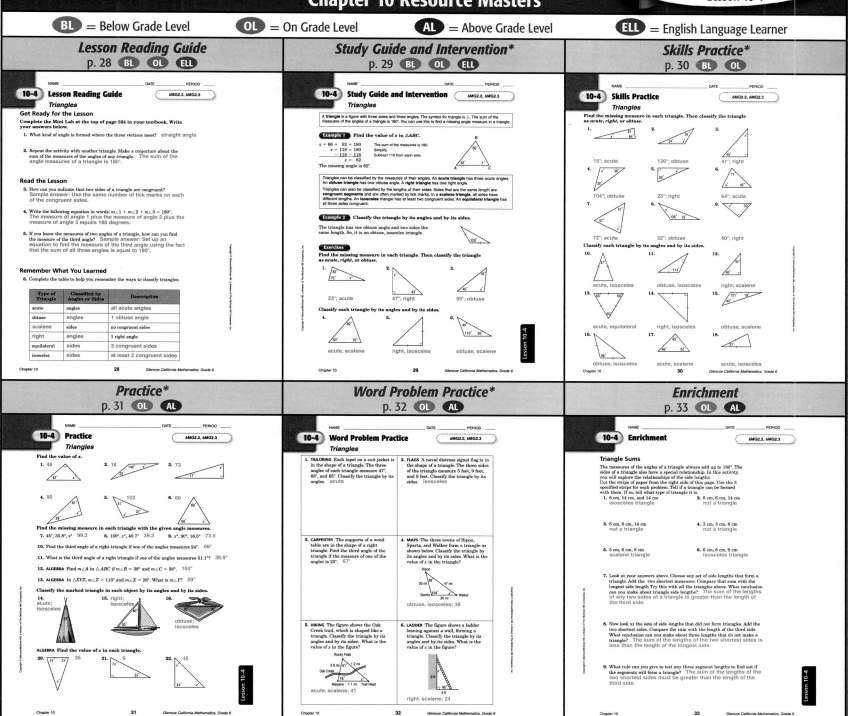

Additional Lesson Resources

Transparencies
- *5-Minute Check Transparency,* Lesson 10-4

Other Print Products
- *Noteables™ Interactive Study Notebook with Foldables™*

Teacher Tech Tools
- *Interactive Classroom CD-ROM,* Lesson 10-4
- *AssignmentWorks CD-ROM,* Lesson 10-4

Student Tech Tools
ca.gr6math.com
- Extra Examples, Chapter 10, Lesson 4
- Self-Check Quiz, Chapter 10, Lesson 4

* Also available in Spanish **ELL**

10-4 Triangles

1 Focus

Standards Alignment

Before Lesson 10-4
Know that the sum of the angles of any triangle is 180° and the sum of the angles of any quadrilateral is 360° and use this information to solve problems from Standard 5MG2.2

Lesson 10-4
Use the sum of the angles of a triangle to solve problems involving an unknown angle. Draw triangles from given information from Standard 6MG2.2 and Standard 6MG2.3

After Lesson 10-4
Use formulas routinely for finding the perimeter and area of basic two-dimensional figures and the surface area and volume of basic three-dimensional figures from Standard 7MG2.1

2 Teach

MINI Lab

Make sure students understand that the initial fold Step 2 must be parallel to the base of the triangle.

Scaffolding Questions

Place students into groups of 3–4 and give each group an assortment of polygons, including acute, right, obtuse, scalene, isosceles, and equilateral triangles. Groups should create their own categories to classify these shapes according to their geometric properties. Have groups construct a Venn diagram displaying their results.

Main IDEA

Identify and classify triangles.

 Standard 6MG2.2 Use the properties of complementary and supplementary angles **and the sum of the angles of a triangle to solve problems involving an unknown angle.** **Standard 6MG2.3 Draw** quadrilaterals and **triangles from given information about them** (e.g., a quadrilateral having equal sides but no right angles, **a right isosceles triangle.**)

NEW Vocabulary

triangle
congruent segments
acute triangle
right triangle
obtuse triangle
scalene triangle
isosceles triangle
equilateral triangle

READING Math

Angle Measure The symbol *m*, used just before the name of an angle, refers to the measure of that angle.

MINI Lab

STEP 1 Use a straightedge to draw a triangle with three acute angles. Label the angles *A*, *B*, and *C*. Cut out the triangle.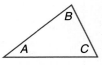

STEP 2 Fold ∠*A*, ∠*B*, and ∠*C* so the vertices meet on the line between angles *A* and *C*.
straight angle

1. What kind of angle is formed where the three vertices meet?

2. Repeat the activity with another triangle. Make a conjecture about the sum of the measures of the angles of any triangle.

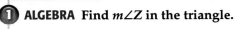 2. The sum of the measures of a triangle is 180°.

A **triangle** is a figure with three sides and three angles. The symbol for triangle is △. There is a relationship among the three angles in a triangle.

KEY CONCEPT   Angles of a Triangle

		Model
Words	The sum of the measures of the angles of a triangle is 180°.	
Algebra	$x + y + z = 180$	

EXAMPLE   Find a Missing Measure

1 **ALGEBRA** Find $m\angle Z$ in the triangle.

Since the sum of the angle measures in a triangle is 180°, $m\angle Z + 43° + 119° =$ 180°.

$$m\angle Z + 43° + 119° = 180° \quad \text{Write the equation.}$$
$$m\angle Z + 162° = 180° \quad \text{Simplify.}$$
$$\underline{-162° = -162°} \quad \text{Subtract 162° from each side.}$$
$$m\angle Z = 18°$$

So, $m\angle Z$ is 18°.

CHECK Your Progress   47°

a. **ALGEBRA** In △*ABC*, if $m\angle A = 25°$ and $m\angle B = 108°$, what is $m\angle C$?

524   Chapter 10 Geometry: Polygons

Ask: Answers will vary.
- How many categories did you use?

- What geometric properties did you use?

- Did you find shapes that did not fit into a category? Where did you place these shapes?

- Did you find shapes that belonged to more than one category? Where did you place these shapes?

- Could you organize your Venn diagram differently? How?

2 A kite is constructed with two triangles as shown. What is the missing measure of the kite?

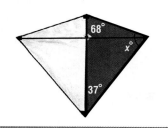

A 45°   C 75°

B 52°   D 80°

Read the Item

To find the missing measure, write and solve an equation.

Solve the Item

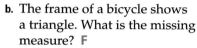

$x + 68 + 37 =$ 180   The sum of the measures is 180.

$x + 105 =$ 180   Simplify.

$\underline{-105 = -105}$ Subtract 105 from each side.

$x =$ 75

The answer is C.

CHECK Your Progress

b. The frame of a bicycle shows a triangle. What is the missing measure? F

F 31°   H 45°

G 40°   J 50°

Online Personal Tutor at ca.gr6math.com

Every triangle has at least two acute angles. One way you can classify a triangle is by using the third angle. Another way to classify triangles is by their sides. Sides with the same length are **congruent segments**.

KEY CONCEPT

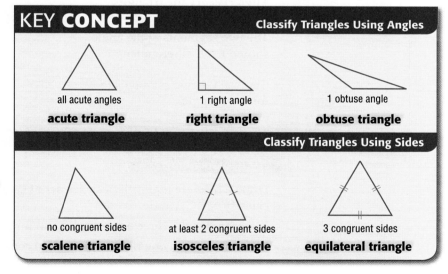

Classify Triangles Using Angles

all acute angles — **acute triangle**

1 right angle — **right triangle**

1 obtuse angle — **obtuse triangle**

Classify Triangles Using Sides

no congruent sides — **scalene triangle**

at least 2 congruent sides — **isosceles triangle**

3 congruent sides — **equilateral triangle**

Math Online Extra Examples at ca.gr6math.com

Lesson 10-4 Triangles   **525**

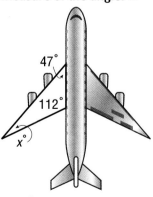

Classify the marked triangle on each object by its angles and by its sides.

3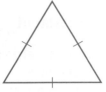

right, scalene

4 **DRAWING TRIANGLES** Draw a triangle with three acute angles and three congruent sides. Then classify the triangle. Sample answer: acute equilateral

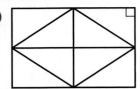

5 **DRAWING TRIANGLES** Draw a triangle with two acute angles and two congruent sides. Sample answer: acute isosceles

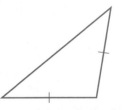

It may be helpful to point out to students that the phrase *isosceles right triangle* refers to a triangle that is both an isosceles triangle and a right triangle. That is, the triangle has at least two congruent sides and exactly one right angle. Likewise, it may be helpful to point out to students that the phrase *obtuse scalene triangle* refers to a triangle that is both an obtuse triangle and a scalene triangle. That is, the triangle has one obtuse angle and no congruent sides.

Real-World Link · · · ·
There are two main types of roofs—flat and pitched. Most houses have pitched, or sloped, roofs. A pitched roof generally lasts 15 to 20 years.
Source: National Association of Certified Home Inspectors

e. Sample answer:

; acute equilateral

f. Sample answer:

; right scalene

Real-World EXAMPLE

3 Classify the marked triangle at the right by its angles and by its sides.

The triangle on the side of a house has one obtuse angle and two congruent sides. So, it is an obtuse, isosceles triangle.

CHECK Your Progress   c. right, isosceles
                                 d. right, scalene

c.   d.

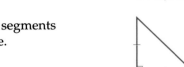

EXAMPLES **Draw Triangles**

4 Draw a triangle with one right angle and two congruent sides. Then classify the triangle.

Draw a right angle. The two segments should be congruent.

Connect the two segments to form a triangle.

The triangle is a right isosceles triangle.

5 Draw a triangle with one obtuse angle and no congruent sides. Then classify the triangle.

Draw an obtuse angle. The two segments of the angle should have different lengths.

Connect the two segments to form a triangle.

The triangle is an obtuse scalene triangle.

CHECK Your Progress

Draw a triangle that satisfies each set of conditions below. Then classify each triangle.

e. a triangle with three acute angles and three congruent sides

f. a triangle with one right angle and no congruent sides

★ indicates multi-step problem

CHECK Your Understanding

Example 1
(p. 524)

Find the value of x.

1.

44

2.

134

3.

45

4. **ALGEBRA** Find $m\angle T$ in $\triangle RST$ if $m\angle R = 37°$ and $m\angle S = 55°$. **88°**

Example 2
(p. 525)
6MG2.2

5. **STANDARDS PRACTICE** A triangle is used in the game of pool to rack the pool balls. Find the missing measure of the triangle. **C**

A 30°   C 60°
B 40°   D 75°

Example 3
(p. 526)

FLAGS Classify the marked triangle in each flag by its angles and by its sides.

6. acute, equilateral
7. obtuse, scalene
8. right, isosceles

6.

Puerto Rico

7.
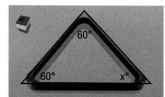
Seychelles Islands

8.

Bosnia-Herzegovina

Examples 4, 5
(p. 526)

DRAWING TRIANGLES For Exercises 9 and 10, draw a triangle that satisfies each set of conditions. Then classify each triangle. See margin for drawings.

9. a triangle with three acute angles and two congruent sides **acute isosceles**

10. a triangle with one obtuse angle and two congruent sides **obtuse isosceles**

Exercises

HOMEWORK HELP	
For Exercises	**See Examples**
11–18, 47, 48	1–2
19–26	3
27–30	4, 5

Exercise Levels
A: 11–30
B: 31–41
C: 42–46

Find the value of x.

11.
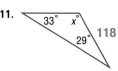
118

12.
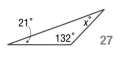
60

13.
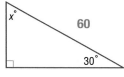
27

14.

65

15.
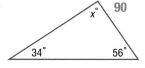
90

16.
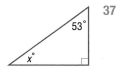
37

17. **ALGEBRA** Find $m\angle Q$ in $\triangle QRS$ if $m\angle R = 25°$ and $m\angle S = 102°$. **53°**

18. **ALGEBRA** In $\triangle EFG$, $m\angle F = 46°$ and $m\angle G = 34°$. What is $m\angle E$? **100°**

Lesson 10-4 Triangles **527**

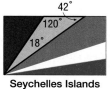
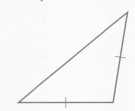

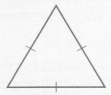
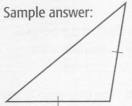

19. acute, equilateral
20. obtuse, scalene
21. right, isosceles
22. right, scalene
23. acute, scalene
24. acute, isosceles

Classify the marked triangle in each object by its angles and by its sides.

19.  60° 60° 60°

20. 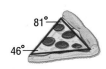 30° 53°

21. 45°

22.  50° 40°

23. 81° 46°

24. 32°

25. ART The sculpture at the right is entitled *Texas Triangles*. It is located in Lincoln, Massachusetts. What type of triangle is shown: *acute*, *right*, or *obtuse*? **right**

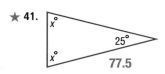

Source: DeCordova Museum and Sculpture Park

26. ARCHITECTURE Use the photo at the left to classify the side view of the Transamerica building by its angles and by its sides. **acute, isosceles**

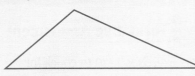

Real-World Link · · · ·
The Transamerica building in San Francisco is 853 feet tall.
Source: transamerica.com

DRAWING TRIANGLES For Exercises 27–30, draw a triangle that satisfies each set of conditions. Then classify each triangle. **27–30. See margin for drawings.**

27. a triangle with three acute angles and no congruent sides **acute scalene**

28. a triangle with one obtuse angle and two congruent sides **obtuse isosceles**

29. a triangle with three acute angles and three congruent sides **acute equilateral**

30. a triangle with one right angle and no congruent sides **right scalene**

Find the missing measure in each triangle with the given angle measures.

31. 80°, 20.5°, $x°$ **79.5**
32. 75°, $x°$, 50.2° **54.8**
33. $x°$, 10.8°, 90° **79.2**
34. 45.5°, $x°$, 105.6° **28.9**
35. $x°$, 140.1°, 18.6° **21.3**
36. 110.2°, $x°$, 35.6° **34.2**

37. ALGEBRA Find the third angle measure of a right triangle if one of the angles measures 10°. **80°**

38. ALGEBRA What is the third angle measure of a right triangle if one of the angle measures is 45.8°? **44.2°**

ALGEBRA Find the value of x in each triangle.

39. ★ $x°$ $x°$ $x°$ 60

40. ★ $x°$ $x°$ $2x°$ 30

41. ★ $x°$ $x°$ 25° 77.5

42. CHALLENGE Apply what you know about triangles to find the missing angle measures in the figure.
$a = 55$; $b = 65$; $c = 60$; $d = 30$

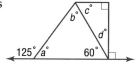

43. OPEN ENDED Draw an acute scalene triangle. Describe the angles and sides of the triangle.

REASONING Determine whether each statement is *sometimes*, *always*, or *never* true. Justify your answer. 44–46. See margin.

44. It is possible for a triangle to have two right angles.

45. It is possible for a triangle to have two obtuse angles.

46. **WRITING IN MATH** An equilateral triangle not only has three congruent sides, but also has three congruent angles. Based on this, explain why it is impossible to draw an equilateral triangle that is either right or obtuse.

STANDARDS PRACTICE 6MG2.2

47. How would you find $m\angle R$? **B**

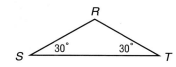

A Add 30° to 180°.

B Subtract 60° from 180°.

C Subtract 30° from 90°.

D Subtract 180° from 60°.

48. Which of the following is an acute triangle? **J**

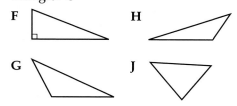

Spiral Review

49. STATISTICS A circle graph shows that 41% of birdwatchers live in the Northeast region of the U.S. What is the measure of the angle of the Northeast section of the graph? (Lesson 10-3) **147.6°**

Classify each pair of angles as *complementary*, *supplementary*, or *neither*. (Lesson 10-2)

50.

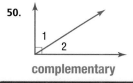

complementary

51.

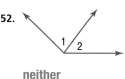

supplementary

52.

neither

GET READY for the Next Lesson

53. PREREQUISITE SKILL If Jade buys 5 notebooks at $1.75 each, what will be the total cost of the notebooks; about $6, $7, or $9? (Lesson 7-4) **about $9**

Lesson 10-4 Triangles **529**

Lesson 10-4 Triangles **529**

Problem-Solving Investigation
USE LOGICAL REASONING

Standard 6MR1.2	**Formulate and justify mathematical conjectures based on a general description of the mathematical question or problem posed.**
Standard 6MG2.3	**Draw quadrilaterals and triangles from given information about them** (e.g., a quadrilateral having equal sides but no right angles, a right isosceles triangle.)
PACING:	**Regular:** 1 period, **Block:** 0.5 period

Options for Differentiated Instruction

ELL = English Language Learner   **AL** = Above Grade Level   **SS** = Struggling Students   **SN** = Special Needs

Multiple Strategies **ELL** **SN**

Use with the P.S.I. Team +.

Make sure ELL students understand the differences among the various problem-solving strategies they have learned. Explain that many problems are solved more easily if multiple strategies in various combinations are used.

For example, in the P.S.I. Team +, Dion drew the following figures to look for a pattern.

   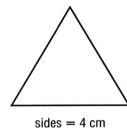

sides = 1 cm   sides = 2 cm   sides = 3 cm   sides = 4 cm

He then used logical reasoning to solve the problem.

Choosing the Best Strategy **ELL** **SS** **SN**

Use before assigning the Exercises.

Discuss with the class which strategy might be best to solve each problem.

Ask:
- What is the question asking?
- What information is given?
- What strategy would be most effective to solve the problem?

Make sure that all students have chosen a strategy for each of the problems so that they can complete the assignment independently.

Cooperative Learning **ELL** **AL** **SN**

Use after students complete Lesson 10-5.

Separate the class into groups of three or four students. Each group should write a word problem that can be solved using logical reasoning. Have the groups exchange problems and solve them.

Leveled Lesson Resources

Chapter 10 Resource Masters

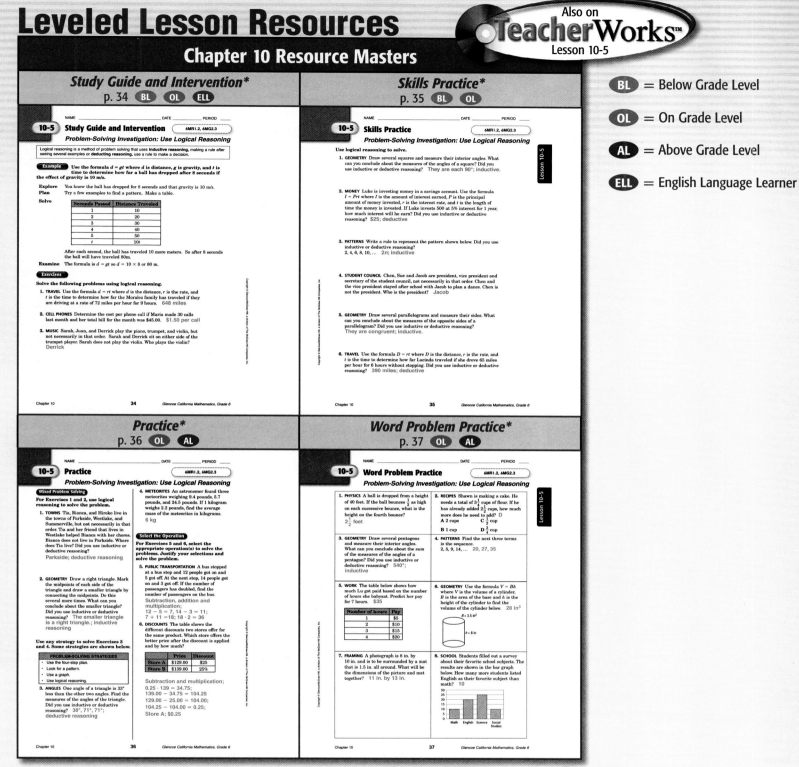

Study Guide and Intervention*
p. 34 BL OL ELL

10-5 Study Guide and Intervention (6MR1.2, 6MG2.3)

Problem-Solving Investigation: Use Logical Reasoning

Logical reasoning is a method of problem solving that uses **inductive reasoning**, making a rule after seeing several examples or **deducting reasoning**, use a rule to make a decision.

Example Use the formula $d = gt$ where d is distance, g is gravity, and t is time to determine how far a ball has dropped after 8 seconds if the effect of gravity is 10 m/s.

Explore You know the ball has dropped for 8 seconds and that gravity is 10 m/s.

Plan Try a few examples to find a pattern. Make a table.

Solve

Seconds Passed	Distance Traveled
1	10
2	20
3	30
4	40
5	50
t	$10t$

After each second, the ball has traveled 10 more meters. So after 8 seconds the ball will have traveled 80m.

Examine The formula is $d = gt$ so $d = 10 \times 8$ or 80 m.

Exercises

Solve the following problems using logical reasoning.

1. **TRAVEL** Use the formula $d = rt$ where d is the distance, r is the rate, and t is the time to determine how far the Morales family has traveled if they are driving at a rate of 72 miles per hour for 9 hours. 648 miles

2. **CELL PHONES** Determine the cost per phone call if Maria made 30 calls last month and her total bill for the month was $45.00. $1.50 per call

3. **MUSIC** Sarah, Juan, and Derrick play the piano, trumpet, and violin, but not necessarily in that order. Sarah and Derrick sit on either side of the trumpet player. Sarah does not play the violin. Who plays the violin? Derrick

Chapter 10   34   Glencoe California Mathematics, Grade 6

Skills Practice*
p. 35 BL OL

10-5 Skills Practice (6MR1.2, 6MG2.3)

Problem-Solving Investigation: Use Logical Reasoning

Use logical reasoning to solve.

1. **GEOMETRY** Draw several squares and measure their interior angles. What can you conclude about the measure of the angles of a square? Did you use inductive or deductive reasoning? They are each 90°; inductive.

2. **MONEY** Luke is investing money in a savings account. Use the formula $I = Prt$ where I is the amount of interest earned, P is the principal amount of money invested, r is the interest rate, and t is the length of time the money is invested. If Luke invests 500 at 5% interest for 1 year, how much interest will he earn? Did you use inductive or deductive reasoning? $25; deductive

3. **PATTERNS** Write a rule to represent the pattern shown below. Did you use inductive or deductive reasoning?
2, 4, 6, 8, 10, ... $2n$; inductive

4. **STUDENT COUNCIL** Chen, Sue and Jacob are president, vice president and secretary of the student council, not necessarily in that order. Chen and the vice president stayed after school with Jacob to plan a dance. Chen is not the president. Who is the president? Jacob

5. **GEOMETRY** Draw several parallelograms and measure their sides. What can you conclude about the measures of the opposite sides of a parallelogram? Did you use inductive or deductive reasoning? They are congruent; inductive.

6. **TRAVEL** Use the formula $D = rt$ where D is the distance, r is the rate, and t is the time to determine how far Lucinda traveled if she drove 65 miles per hour for 6 hours without stopping. Did you use inductive or deductive reasoning? 390 miles; deductive

Chapter 10   35   Glencoe California Mathematics, Grade 6

Practice*
p. 36 OL AL

10-5 Practice (6MR1.2, 6MG2.3)

Problem-Solving Investigation: Use Logical Reasoning

Mixed Problem Solving

For Exercises 1 and 2, use logical reasoning to solve the problem.

1. **TOWNS** Tia, Bianca, and Hiroko live in the towns of Parkside, Westlake, and Summerville, but not necessarily in that order. Tia and her friend that lives in Westlake helped Bianca with her chores. Bianca does not live in Parkside. Where does Tia live? Did you use inductive or deductive reasoning?
Parkside; deductive reasoning

2. **GEOMETRY** Draw a right triangle. Mark the midpoints of each side of the triangle and draw a smaller triangle by connecting the midpoints. Do this several more times. What can you conclude about the smaller triangle? Did you use inductive or deductive reasoning? The smaller triangle is a right triangle; inductive reasoning

Use any strategy to solve Exercises 3 and 4. Some strategies are shown below.

PROBLEM-SOLVING STRATEGIES
• Use the four-step plan.
• Look for a pattern.
• Use a graph.
• Use logical reasoning.

3. **ANGLES** One angle of a triangle is 33° less than the other two angles. Find the measures of the angles of the triangle. Did you use inductive or deductive reasoning? 38°, 71°, 71°; deductive reasoning

4. **METEORITES** An astronomer found three meteorites weighing 9.4 pounds, 5.7 pounds, and 24.5 pounds. If 1 kilogram weighs 2.2 pounds, find the average mass of the meteorites in kilograms. 6 kg

Select the Operation

For Exercises 5 and 6, select the appropriate operation(s) to solve the problems. Justify your selections and solve the problem.

5. **PUBLIC TRANSPORTATION** A bus stopped at a bus stop and 12 people got on and 5 got off. At the next stop, 14 people got on and 3 got off. If the number of passengers has doubled, find the number of passengers on the bus. Subtraction, addition and multiplication;
$12 − 5 = 7, 14 − 3 = 11;$
$7 + 11 = 18; 18 \cdot 2 = 36$

6. **DISCOUNTS** The table shows the different discounts two stores offer for the same product. Which store offers the better price after the discount is applied and by how much?

	Price	Discount
Store A	$129.00	$25
Store B	$139.00	25%

Subtraction and multiplication;
$0.25 \cdot 139 = 34.75;$
$139.00 − 34.75 = 104.25$
$129.00 − 25.00 = 104.00;$
$104.25 − 104.00 = 0.25;$
Store A; $0.25

Chapter 10   36   Glencoe California Mathematics, Grade 6

Word Problem Practice*
p. 37 OL AL

10-5 Word Problem Practice (6MR1.2, 6MG2.3)

Problem-Solving Investigation: Use Logical Reasoning

1. **PHYSICS** A ball is dropped from a height of 40 feet. If the ball bounces $\frac{1}{2}$ as high on each successive bounce, what is the height on the fourth bounce? $2\frac{1}{2}$ feet

2. **RECIPES** Shawn is making a cake. He needs a total of $3\frac{1}{2}$ cups of flour. If he has already added $2\frac{1}{2}$ cups, how much more does he need to add? D
A 2 cups   C $\frac{1}{2}$ cup
B 1 cup   D $\frac{3}{4}$ cup

3. **GEOMETRY** Draw several pentagons and measure their interior angles. What can you conclude about the sum of the measures of the angles of a pentagon? Did you use inductive or deductive reasoning? 540°; inductive

4. **PATTERNS** Find the next three terms in the sequence.
2, 5, 9, 14, ... 20, 27, 35

5. **WORK** The table below shows how much Lu got paid based on the number of hours she babysat. Predict her pay for 7 hours. $35

Number of hours	Pay
1	$5
2	$10
3	$15
4	$20

6. **GEOMETRY** Use the formula $V = Bh$ where V is the volume of a cylinder, B is the area of the base and h is the height of the cylinder to find the volume of the cylinder below. 28 in³
$B = 3.5 \text{ in}^2$
$h = 8 \text{ in}$

7. **FRAMING** A photograph is 8 in. by 10 in. and is to be surrounded by a mat that is 1.5 in. all around. What will be the dimensions of the picture and mat together? 11 in. by 13 in.

8. **SCHOOL** Students filled out a survey about their favorite school subjects. The results are shown in the bar graph below. How many more students listed English as their favorite subject than math? 10

Chapter 10   37   Glencoe California Mathematics, Grade 6

* Also available in Spanish ELL

Additional Lesson Resources

Transparencies
• *5-Minute Check Transparency*, 10-5

Other Print Products
• *Noteables™ Interactive Study Notebook with Foldables™*

Teacher Tech Tools
• *Interactive Classroom CD-ROM*, Lesson 10-5
• *AssignmentWorks CD-ROM*, Lesson 10-5

Student Tech Tools
ca.gr6math.com
• Extra Examples, Chapter 10, Lesson 5
• Self-Check Quiz, Chapter 10, Lesson 5

1 Focus

Use Logical Reasoning

Students have used logical reasoning to solve mathematical problems throughout the year. For example, they used deductive reasoning to classify triangles in Lesson 10-4. Because geometry is based on rules and relationships that are often visually apparent, it is an especially good field for students to practice their deductive and inductive reasoning skills.

2 Teach

Scaffolding Questions

Ask:

- Can a triangle have more than 3 sides? no

- Can a triangle have two obtuse angles? no

- Can the sum of the measures of a triangle be 179°? no

- Can a scalene triangle be equilateral? no

ADDITIONAL EXAMPLE

1 NUMBER BALL Solve. Use logical reasoning.

Draw an isosceles triangle. How can you confirm that it is isosceles? Drawings will vary. Sample response: I measured the sides and found that two (or three) of them have the same length.

Additional Examples are also in:

- Noteables™ Interactive Study Notebook with Foldables™
- Interactive Classroom PowerPoint® Presentations

10-5 Problem-Solving Investigation

MAIN IDEA: Solve problems by using logical reasoning.

Standard 6MR1.2 Formulate and justify mathematical conjectures based on a general description of the mathematical question or problem posed. **Standard 6MG2.3** Draw quadrilaterals and triangles from given information about them (e.g., a quadrilateral having equal sides but no right angles, a right isosceles triangle).

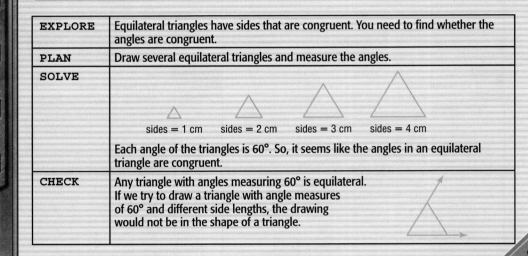

P.S.I. TEAM +

e-Mail: USE LOGICAL REASONING

YOUR MISSION: Use logical reasoning to solve the problem.

THE PROBLEM: Do the angles in an equilateral triangle have a special relationship?

> **Dion:** It looks like the angles in an equilateral triangle are congruent. Is that true?

EXPLORE	Equilateral triangles have sides that are congruent. You need to find whether the angles are congruent.
PLAN	Draw several equilateral triangles and measure the angles.
SOLVE	sides = 1 cm sides = 2 cm sides = 3 cm sides = 4 cm Each angle of the triangles is 60°. So, it seems like the angles in an equilateral triangle are congruent.
CHECK	Any triangle with angles measuring 60° is equilateral. If we try to draw a triangle with angle measures of 60° and different side lengths, the drawing would not be in the shape of a triangle.

Analyze The Strategy 1–2. See margin.

1. When you use *inductive reasoning*, you make a rule after seeing several examples. When you use *deductive reasoning*, you use a rule to make a decision. What type of reasoning did Dion use to solve the problem? Explain your reasoning.

2. Explain how the *look for a pattern* strategy is similar to inductive reasoning.

530 Chapter 10 Geometry: Polygons

Additional Answers

1. Sample answer: They used inductive reasoning because they made a rule after seeing four examples.

2. Sample answer: Both strategies base a conclusion on a pattern.

For Exercises 3–5, use logical reasoning to solve the problem. Justify your response.

3. **GEOMETRY** Draw several isosceles triangles and measure their angles. What do you notice about the measures of the angles of an isosceles triangle? **See margin.**

4. **BASKETBALL** Placido, Dexter, and Scott play guard, forward, and center on a team, but not necessarily in that order. Placido and the center drove Scott to practice on Saturday. Placido does not play guard. Who is the guard? **4–5. See Ch. 10 Answer Appendix.**

5. **ALGEBRA** Hannah was finding the relationship between the time it took a yo-yo to swing back and forth and its length. Predict the length of a yo-yo if it takes 5 seconds to swing back and forth.

Time (seconds)	Length (units)
1	1
2	4
3	9
4	16

Use any strategy to solve Exercises 6–10. Some strategies are shown below.

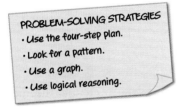

PROBLEM-SOLVING STRATEGIES
· Use the four-step plan.
· Look for a pattern.
· Use a graph.
· Use logical reasoning.

6. **GEOMETRY** Draw several rectangles and measure their diagonals. Find a relationship between the diagonals of a rectangle. **They are congruent.**

7. **TRAVEL** Mrs. Petricca drove at an average speed of 55 miles per hour for three hours. After stopping for lunch, she drove at an average speed of 40 miles for 2.5 hours. How far did she drive? **265 mi**

8. **ALGEBRA** Find the next three numbers in the pattern below. **43, 36, 29**

71, 64, 57, 50, ▪, ▪, ▪

9. **MEASUREMENT** The large ★ square has been divided into 9 squares. The lengths of the squares are given. Find the area of the entire square. **196 sq units**

10. **SHOES** What can you conclude about the number of boys who favor brand C and the number of boys who prefer brand D?

Favorite Athletic Shoes

The number of boys who favor brand D is twice as many boys who prefer brand C.

Select the Operation

For Exercises 11–13, select the appropriate operation(s) to solve the problem. Justify your selection(s) and solve the problem.

11. **MEASUREMENT**
★ Shelby wants to build a fence around her garden with the dimensions shown. How much fencing will she need? **See margin.**

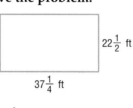

$22\frac{1}{2}$ ft

$37\frac{1}{4}$ ft

12. **MEASUREMENT** Suppose you enlarge a ★ drawing to 120% of its original size on the copy machine. If the drawing is 2 inches long and 3 inches wide, what are the dimensions of the copy? **See margin.**

13. **STATISTICS** David has earned scores of 73, 85, ★ 91 and 82 on the first four out of five math tests for the grading period. He would like to finish the grading period with a test average of at least 82. What is the minimum score David needs to earn on the fifth test in order to achieve his goal? **See margin.**

Lesson 10-5 Problem-Solving Investigation: Use Logical Reasoning **531**

Additional Answers

3. See students' work; Two angles are congruent.

11. Sample answer: addition;
$22\frac{1}{2} + 22\frac{1}{2} + 37\frac{1}{4} + 37\frac{1}{4} = 119\frac{1}{2}$ ft

12. Sample answer: multiplication;
120% of 2 = 2.4 and 120% of 3 = 3.6 so the dimensions of the copy will be 2.4 inches by 3.6 inches.

13. Sample answer: addition and division; Find the score that when added to the others, the total sum divided by the number of scores, 5, is equal to 82. The answer is 79.

Using the Exercises

Exercises 1 and 2 can be used to check students' understanding of the logical reasoning strategy.

Exercises 3–5 give students an opportunity to practice the logical reasoning strategy.

Exercises 6–10 give students the opportunity to practice many different problem-solving strategies. You may wish to have students review some of the strategies they have studied:

- Use the four-step plan (p. 25)
- Look for a pattern (p. 112)
- Use a graph (p. 424)
- Use logical reasoning (p. 530)

Exercises 11–13 require students to select an operation to solve a problem. Have students analyze each problem and its wording, asking themselves what kind of information is needed. Which operation(s) must be performed to get the information?

4 Assess

Name the Math Have students tell what mathematical procedures they used to solve Exercise 10.

Formative Assessment

Check for student understanding of concepts in Lessons 10-4 and 10-5.

Quiz 2, p. 73

Differentiated Instruction

Verbal/Linguistic Learners Have students write a short story in which the hero, a mathematical private investigator, solves a mystery by inductive or deductive reasoning. What is the mystery? What are the clues? How did the investigator solve the mystery? Encourage students to use their imaginations.

1 Focus

Materials

- grid paper
- rulers
- protractors

Easy-to-Make Manipulatives

Teaching Mathematics with Manipulatives, Templates for:

- Quarter-Inch Grid p. 14

Teaching Tip

If your students use centimeter grid paper, have them use centimeter rulers; if they use quarter-inch grid paper, have them use 12-inch rulers.

2 Teach

Activity Students should realize that they won't need to use their rulers to measure many of the sides; rather, they can count squares on the grid paper. You may need to show students how to extend the sides of the quadrilaterals so that they can measure the angles with their protractors.

3 Assess

✓ Formative Assessment

Use Exercises 1 and 2 to determine whether students understand how to find properties of quadrilaterals by examining drawings of them.

From Concrete to Abstract Use Exercise 3 to bridge the gap between using drawings to find quadrilaterals' properties and classifying the quadrilaterals according to those properties.

Geometry Lab
Investigating Quadrilaterals

Main IDEA

Investigate the properties of special quadrilaterals.

Standard 6MR1.1 Analyze problems by identifying relationships, distinguishing relevant from irrelevant information, identifying missing information, sequencing and prioritizing information, **and observing patterns.**
Standard 6MG2.3 Draw quadrilaterals and triangles from given information about them (e.g., a quadrilateral having equal sides but no right angles, a right isosceles triangle.)

Four-sided figures are called *quadrilaterals*. In this lab, you will explore the properties of different types of quadrilaterals.

ACTIVITY

STEP 1 Draw the quadrilaterals shown on grid paper.

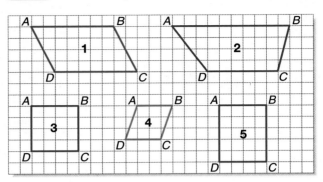

STEP 2 Use a ruler and a protractor to measure the sides and angles of each quadrilateral. Record your results in a table.

Quadrilateral	m∠A	m∠B	m∠C	m∠D	AB	BC	CD	DA
1								
2								

ANALYZE THE RESULTS   3–5. See Ch. 10 Answer Appendix.

1. Describe any similarities or patterns in the angle measurements.

2. Describe any similarities or patterns in the side measurements.

3. **MAKE A VENN DIAGRAM** Cut out the quadrilaterals you drew in the activity. Then sort them into categories according to their similarities and differences. Arrange and record your categories in a two-circled Venn diagram. Be sure to label each circle with its category.

4. Create two other Venn diagrams illustrating two different ways of categorizing these quadrilaterals.

5. **WRITING IN MATH** Did you find shapes that did not fit a category? Where did you place these shapes? Did any shapes have properties allowing them to belong to more than one category? Could you arrange these quadrilaterals into a three-circled Venn diagram? If so, how?

1. Sample answer; the sum of the angle measures in each quadrilateral is 360°. Angles that are opposite each other are congruent and angles that are adjacent to each other are supplementary, except in figure 2.
2. Sample answer; sides that are opposite are congruent, except in figure 2.

532 Chapter 10 Geometry: Polygons

Focus on Mathematical Content

Rhombi In the Activity, Quadrilateral 4 approximates a rhombus but not precisely a rhombus. For the purposes of this activity, you may wish to have students measure the side measures of each quadrilateral to the nearest centimeter.

 **Quadrilaterals**

Standard 6MG2.3 **Draw quadrilaterals** and triangles **from given information about them** **(e.g., a quadrilateral having equal sides but no right angles,** a right isosceles triangle.)

PACING: **Regular:** 1 period, **Block:** 0.5 period

Options for Differentiated Instruction

ELL = English Language Learner   **AL** = Above Grade Level   **SS** = Struggling Students   **SN** = Special Needs

Discovery Through Drawings   **ELL** **AL** **SS** **SN**

Use before presenting the Examples.

In pairs, have students draw several of the quadrilaterals shown below.

square	rectangle	parallelogram	trapezoid

For each figure, have students measure the four angles and find the sum of the measures. 360°

Then have students draw the two diagonals for each figure and measure the diagonals and the angles that they form.

Ask:

What can you conclude about the diagonals of each figure? Sample answer: Students may discover that the diagonals of a parallelogram bisect each other. The diagonals of a rectangle are congruent and bisect each other. The diagonals of a square are congruent, bisect each other and are perpendicular.

Verbal Descriptions   **SS** **SN**

Use after presenting Examples 1 and 2.

Have students write a description of one of the quadrilaterals presented in Lesson 11-5. Then have students exchange descriptions. The students should read the descriptions and then draw a sketch of the quadrilateral that is described.

Ask:
- Did your drawing match the description?
- Should the description have included more details? Explain.

Verbal Descriptions   **ELL** **AL** **SS** **SN**

Use after presenting Lesson 10-6.

Have students update their vocabulary booklets to include the new terms presented in Lesson 10-6. They should include a diagram of each quadrilateral and an explanation of the markings and what they mean. Suggest that they color code the parallel sides of the figures.

Leveled Lesson Resources

Chapter 10 Resource Masters

BL = Below Grade Level   **OL** = On Grade Level   **AL** = Above Grade Level   **ELL** = English Language Learner

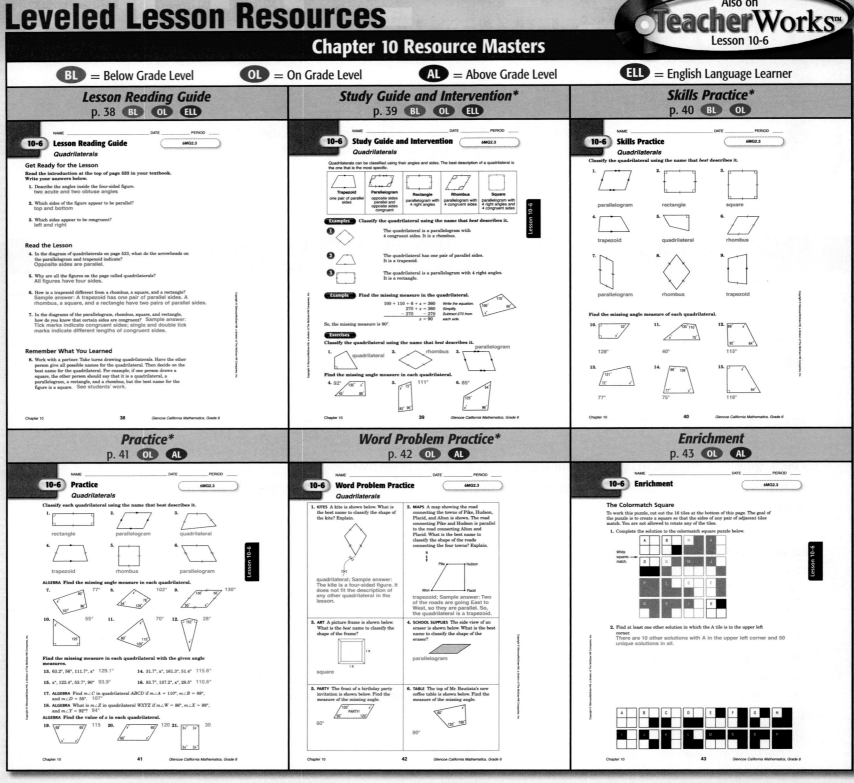

Lesson Reading Guide
p. 38 **BL** **OL** **ELL**

Study Guide and Intervention*
p. 39 **BL** **OL** **ELL**

Skills Practice*
p. 40 **BL** **OL**

Practice*
p. 41 **OL** **AL**

Word Problem Practice*
p. 42 **OL** **AL**

Enrichment
p. 43 **OL** **AL**

Additional Lesson Resources

Also available in Spanish **ELL**

Transparencies
- *5-Minute Check Transparency,* Lesson 10-6

Other Print Products
- *Teaching Mathematics with Manipulatives*
- *Noteables™ Interactive Study Notebook with Foldables™*

Teacher Tech Tools
- *Interactive Classroom CD-ROM,* Lesson 10-6
- *AssignmentWorks CD-ROM,* Lesson 10-6

Student Tech Tools
ca.gr6math.com
- Extra Examples, Chapter 10, Lesson 6
- Self-Check Quiz, Chapter 10, Lesson 6

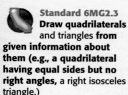

Main IDEA

Identify and classify quadrilaterals.

Standard 6MG2.3 **Draw quadrilaterals and triangles from given information about them (e.g., a quadrilateral having equal sides but no right angles,** a right isosceles triangle.)

NEW Vocabulary

quadrilateral
parallelogram
trapezoid
rhombus

. two acute and two obtuse angles
. top and bottom
. left and right

STUDY TIP

Parallel Lines
The sides with matching arrows are parallel.

GET READY for the Lesson

VIDEO GAMES The general shape of a video game controller is shown.

1. Describe the angles inside the four-sided figure.

2. Which sides of the figure appear to be parallel?

3. Which sides appear to be congruent?

A **quadrilateral** is a closed figure with four sides and four angles. Quadrilaterals are named based on their sides and angles. The diagram shows how quadrilaterals are related. Notice how it goes from the most general to the most specific.

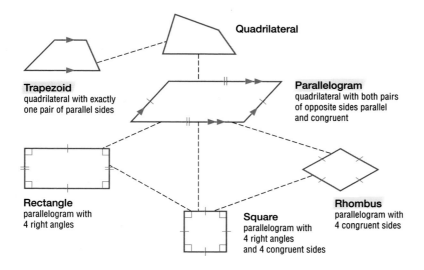

Quadrilateral

Trapezoid
quadrilateral with exactly one pair of parallel sides

Parallelogram
quadrilateral with both pairs of opposite sides parallel and congruent

Rectangle
parallelogram with 4 right angles

Square
parallelogram with 4 right angles and 4 congruent sides

Rhombus
parallelogram with 4 congruent sides

The name that *best* describes a quadrilateral is the one that is most specific.

- If a quadrilateral has all the properties of a parallelogram and a rhombus, then the *best* description of the quadrilateral is a rhombus.

- If a quadrilateral has all the properties of a parallelogram, rhombus, rectangle, and square, then the *best* description of the quadrilateral is a square.

Lesson 10-6 Quadrilaterals **533**

Tips for New Teachers

Quadrilaterals

Make sure students understand the relationship between the figures in the diagram. You might want to emphasize the relationships. For example, you could say: *A rhombus is a* kind *of parallelogram because both its pairs of opposite sides are parallel and congruent; A square is a* kind *of rhombus because it is a parallelogram with four congruent sides; and so on.*

1 Focus

Standards Alignment

Before Lesson 10-6
Measure, identify, and draw angles, perpendicular and parallel lines, rectangles, and triangles by using appropriate tools Key Know that the sum of the angles of any triangle is 180° and the sum of the angles of any quadrilateral is 360° and use this information to solve problems from ⚷ Standards 5MG2.1 and 5MG2.2

Lesson 10-6
Draw quadrilaterals from given information from Standard 6MG2.3

After Lesson 10-6
Use formulas routinely for finding the perimeter and area of basic two-dimensional figures and the surface area and volume of basic three-dimensional figures from Standard 7MG2.1

2 Teach

Scaffolding Questions

Ask:
- What are some examples of classroom objects with edges that form a rectangle? Sample answers: door, desktop, chalkboard

- What are some examples of classroom objects with edges that form a square? Sample answers: box, window, floor tile

- What is the difference between a rectangle and a square? The pairs of opposite sides of a rectangle are congruent, while all four sides of a square are congruent.

534 **Chapter 10** Geometry: Polygons

 Focus on Mathematical Content

If the measures of three angles of a quadrilateral are known, the measure of the fourth angle can be calculated using an algebraic equation.

Quadrilaterals are classified according to their sides and angles. To classify a quadrilateral, determine which, if any, of its sides are parallel and/or congruent, and whether its four angles are right angles.

✓ **Formative Assessment**

Use the Check Your Progress exercises after each Example to determine students' understanding of concepts.

ADDITIONAL EXAMPLES

Classify the quadrilateral using the name that best describes it.

①

rectangle

②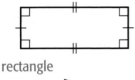

trapezoid

③ **ALGEBRA** Find the value of *x* in the quadrilateral shown. 120°

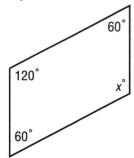

Additional Examples are also in:

• Noteables™ Interactive Study Notebook with Foldables™

• Interactive Classroom PowerPoint® Presentations

STUDY TIP

Check for Reasonableness Use a ruler and a protractor to measure the sides and angles to verify that your drawing satisfies the given conditions.

a. Sample answer:

; trapezoid

b. Sample answer:

; rhombus

EXAMPLES Draw and Classify Quadrilaterals

Draw a quadrilateral that satisfies each set of conditions. Then classify each quadrilateral with the name that best describes it.

① **a parallellogram with four right angles and four congruent sides**

Draw one right angle. The two segments should be congruent.

Draw a second right angle that shares one of the congruent segments. The third segment drawn should be congruent to the first two segments drawn.

Connect the fourth side of the quadrilateral. All four angles should be right angles, and all four sides should be congruent.

The figure is a square.

② **a quadrilateral with opposite sides parallel**

Draw two parallel sides of equal length.

Connect the endpoints of these two sides so that two new parallel sides are drawn.

The figure is a parallelogram.

✓ **CHECK Your Progress**

Draw a quadrilateral that satisfies each set of conditions. Then classify each quadrilateral with the name that best describes it.

a. a quadrilateral with exactly one pair of parallel sides

b. a parallelogram with four congruent sides

A quadrilateral can be separated into two triangles, *A* and *B*. Since the sum of the angle measures of each triangle is 180°, the sum of the angle measures of the quadrilateral is 2 · 180, or 360°.

KEY **CONCEPT**		Angles of a Quadrilateral
Words	The sum of the measures of the angles of a quadrilateral is 360°.	**Model**
Algebra	$w + x + y + z = 360$	

3 **ALGEBRA** Find the value of *x* in the quadrilateral shown.

Write and solve an equation.

Words	The sum of the measures is 360°.
Variable	Let *x* represent the missing measure.
Equation	$85 + 73 + 59 + x = 360$

$$85 + 73 + 59 + x = 360 \quad \text{Write the equation.}$$
$$217 + x = 360 \quad \text{Simplify.}$$
$$\underline{-217 \qquad = -217} \quad \text{Subtract 217 from each side.}$$
$$x = 143$$

So, the missing angle measure is 143°.

✓ **CHECK Your Progress**

c. **ALGEBRA** Find the value of *x* in the quadrilateral shown. **100**

🌐 **Personal Tutor at** ca.gr6math.com

✓ **CHECK Your Understanding**

Examples 1, 2
(p. 534)

Classify each quadrilateral with the name that best describes it.

1. 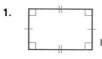 **rectangle**

2. quadrilateral

3. **parallelogram**

4. **BOATS** The photo shows a sailboat called a schooner. What type of quadrilateral does the indicated sail best represent? **trapezoid**

Example 3
(p. 535)

5. **ALGEBRA** In quadrilateral *DEFG*, $m\angle D = 57°$, $m\angle E = 78°$, $m\angle G = 105°$. What is $m\angle F$? **120°**

ALGEBRA Find the missing angle measure in each quadrilateral.

6.

7.

8.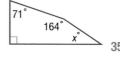

Lesson 10-6 Quadrilaterals **535**

---

3 **Practice**

✏️ **Formative Assessment**

Use Exercises 1–8 to check for understanding.

Then use the chart at the bottom of this page to customize your assignments for students.

Intervention You may wish to use the Study Guide and Intervention Master on page 39 of the *Chapter 10 Resource Masters* for additional reinforcement.

DIFFERENTIATED HOMEWORK OPTIONS			
Level	**Assignment**	**Two-Day Option**	
BL Basic	9–24, 38–60	9–23 odd, 46, 47	10–24 even, 38–45, 49–60
OL Core	9–19 odd, 21–24, 25–35 odd, 40–60	9–24, 46, 47	25–37, 40–45, 49–60
AL Advanced/Pre-AP	24–55 (optional: 56–60)		

Odd/Even Assignments

Exercises 9–24 are structured so that students practice the same concepts whether they are assigned odd or even problems.

Classify each quadrilateral with the name that best describes it.

9. 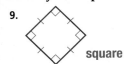 square

10.  trapezoid

11.  quadrilateral

12. 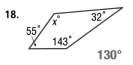 rhombus

13.  trapezoid

14. 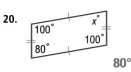 parallelogram

ALGEBRA Find the missing angle measure in each quadrilateral.

15.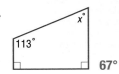

16.

17.

18.

19.

20.

24. 65°; 73°; 17°; 138°; Sample answer: The sum of the measures of ∠b and ∠c is 180° — 90° or 90° since these angles are complementary. The measure of ∠a is 360° — 115° — 90° or 65° since these angles form a quadrilateral. The measure of ∠b is 180° — 42° — 65° or 73° since these angles form a triangle. The measure of ∠c is 90° — 73° or 17° since ∠b and ∠c are complementary. The measure of ∠d is 180° — 42° or 138° since these angles are supplementary.

21. **ALGEBRA** Find $m\angle B$ in quadrilateral $ABCD$ if $m\angle A = 87°$, $m\angle C = 135°$, and $m\angle D = 22°$. **116°**

22. **ALGEBRA** What is $m\angle X$ in quadrilateral $WXYZ$ if $m\angle W = 45°$, $m\angle Y = 128°$, and $\angle Z$ is a right angle? **97°**

23. **LANDSCAPE** Identify the shapes of the bricks used in the design at the right. Use the names that *best* describe the bricks.
Bricks A, B, and D are rectangles and brick C is a square.

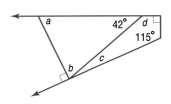

24. **MEASUREMENT** Find each of the missing angle measures $a, b, c,$ and d in the figure at the right. Justify your answers.

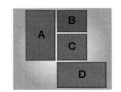

Find the missing measure in each quadrilateral with the given angle measures.

25. 37.5°, 78°, 115.4°, $x°$ **129.1°**

26. $x°$, 108.3°, 49.8°, 100° **101.9°**

27. 25.5°, $x°$, 165.9°, 36.8° **131.8°**

28. 79.1°, 120.8°, $x°$, 65.7° **94.4°**

29. trapezoids, squares, scalene triangles, equilateral triangles
30. rectangles, squares, right isosceles triangles
31. right isosceles triangles, squares, trapezoids

ART For Exercises 29–31, identify the types of triangles and quadrilaterals used in each quilt block pattern. Use the names that *best* describe the figures.

29.

30.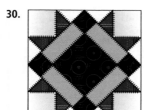

31.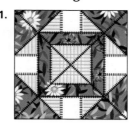

DRAWING QUADRILATERALS Determine whether each figure described below can be drawn. If the figure can be drawn, draw it. If not, explain why not.

32. a quadrilateral that is both a rhombus and a rectangle 32–34. See margin.

33. a trapezoid with three right angles

34. a trapezoid with two congruent sides

EXTRA PRACTICE
See page 705, 724.

Math Online
Self-Check Quiz at
ca.gr6math.com

ALGEBRA Find the value of x in each quadrilateral.

35.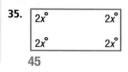
45

36.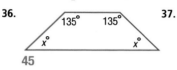
45

37.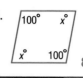
80

H.O.T. Problems

CHALLENGE For Exercises 38 and 39, refer to the table that gives the properties of several parallelograms. Property A states that both pairs of opposite sides are parallel and congruent.

Parallelogram	Properties
1	A, C
2	A, B, C
3	A, B

38. If property C states that all four sides are congruent, classify parallelograms 1–3. Justify your response.

39. If parallelogram 3 is a rectangle, describe Property B. Justify your response.
38–39. See margin.

REASONING Determine whether each statement is *sometimes*, *always*, or *never* true. Explain your reasoning. 40, 41, 43. See margin.

40. A quadrilateral is a trapezoid.
41. A trapezoid is a parallelogram.
42. A square is a rectangle.
43. A rhombus is a square.

42. Always; Sample answer: A square has all the properties of a rectangle.

44. Justin; Isabelle did not mention the 4 congruent sides of a square.

44. **FIND THE ERROR** Isabelle and Justin are describing a square. Who is more accurate? Explain.

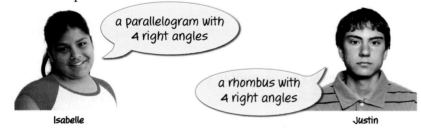

a parallelogram with 4 right angles

a rhombus with 4 right angles

Isabelle

Justin

45. **WRITING IN MATH** The diagonals of a rectangle are congruent, and the diagonals of a rhombus are perpendicular. Based on this information, what can you conclude about the diagonals of a square? of a parallelogram? Explain your reasoning. See margin.

45. Since a square has all the properties of a rectangle and a rhombus, the diagonals of a square must be congruent and perpendicular. Nothing can be concluded about the diagonals of a parallelogram unless more information is provided. If a quadrilateral is a parallelogram, it is not necessarily a rectangle or a rhombus. So, it would not necessarily have the properties of a rectangle or a rhombus.

Additional Answers

32. Yes; a square is a rhombus and a rectangle.

33. No; a quadrilateral with three right angles will have both pairs of opposite sides parallel. So, it cannot be a trapezoid.

34. Yes; one pair of opposite sides are parallel, while the other pair of opposite sides are congruent.

38. rhombus, square, rectangle; Sample answer: Since parallelogram 1 has all 4 sides congruent and no other properties other than A, it must be a rhombus. Since parallelogram 2 has property A, all 4 sides congruent and an additional property not shared with the rhombus, it must be a square. Since parallelogram 3 has property A and this additional property is not shared with the rhombus, it must be a rectangle.

39. Property B states that there are 4 right angles; Sample answer: A rectangle has 4 right angles in addition to property A. So, property B must state that there are 4 right angles.

40. Sometimes; Sample answer: A quadrilateral can also be a rectangle.

41. Never; Sample answer: A trapezoid has only one pair of parallel sides. A parallelogram has 2 pairs of parallel sides.

43. Sometimes; Sample Answer; A rhombus is only a square if all 4 angles are right angles.

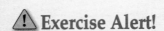

 **Exercise Alert!**

Find the Error In Exercise 44, Isabelle forgot to mention that a square has four congruent sides (so her description includes rectangles). Remind students that when describing a quadrilateral or other polygon, they should be as specific as possible.

4 Assess

Yesterday's News Remind students that yesterday's lesson was about using logical reasoning to solve problems. Have them write how yesterday's concepts helped them with today's material.

FOLDABLES **Foldables™**
Study Organizer **Follow-Up**

Remind students to complete the second and third columns in their Foldable about the classifications and properties of quadrilaterals.

 STANDARDS PRACTICE 6MG2.3

46. Identify the name that does *not* describe the quadrilateral shown. **D**

  A square

  B rectangle

  C rhombus

  D trapezoid

47. Which statement is always true about a rhombus? **J**

  F It has 4 right angles.

  G The sum of the measures of the angles is 180°.

  H It has exactly one pair of parallel sides.

  J It has 4 congruent sides.

48. Which of the following is a correct drawing of a quadrilateral with both pairs of opposite sides parallel and congruent and with four right angles? **C**

  A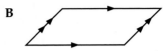

  B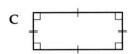

  C

  D

Spiral Review

49. REASONING Neva, Sophie, and Seth have a turtle, a dog, and a hamster for a pet, but not in that order. Sophie's pet lives in a glass aquarium and does not have fur. Neva never has to give her pet a bath. Who has what pet? Use the *logical reasoning* strategy. (Lesson 10-5) **Neva: hamster, Sophie: turtle, Seth: dog**

Classify each triangle by its angles and by its sides. (Lesson 10-4)

50.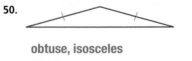

    obtuse, isosceles

51.

    right, scalene

52.

    acute, equilateral

53. LETTERS How many permutations are possible of the letters in the word *Fresno?* (Lesson 9-4) **720**

Find the sales tax or discount to the nearest cent. (Lesson 7-7)

54. $54 jacket; 7% sales tax **$3.78**   **55.** $23 hat; 15% discount **$3.45**

GET READY for the Next Lesson

PREREQUISITE SKILL Solve each proportion. (Lesson 6-4)

56. $\frac{3}{5} = \frac{x}{75}$ **45**   **57.** $\frac{a}{7} = \frac{18}{42}$ **3**   **58.** $\frac{7}{9} = \frac{28}{m}$ **36**   **59.** $\frac{3.5}{t} = \frac{16}{32}$ **7**   **60.** $\frac{3}{6} = \frac{c}{5}$ **2.5**

Name each angle in four ways. Then classify each angle as *acute, obtuse, right,* **or** *straight.* (Lesson 10-1) **1.** ∠EFG, ∠GFE, ∠F, ∠1; right

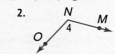

2. ∠MNO, ∠ONM, ∠N, ∠4; obtuse

3. **STANDARDS PRACTICE** Which angle is complementary to ∠CBD? (Lesson 10-2) **A**

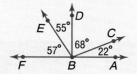

A ∠ABC   **C** ∠DBE

B ∠FBC   **D** ∠EBF

4. **STATISTICS** Display the data in a circle graph. (Lesson 10-3) **See margin.**

Injuries of High School Girls' Soccer Players	
Position	**Percent**
Halfbacks	37%
Fullbacks	23%
Forward Line	28%
Goalkeepers	12%

Source: National Athletic Trainers' Association

STATISTICS For Exercises 5 and 6, use the graph that shows the results of a survey. (Lesson 10-3)

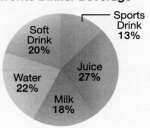

Favorite Dinner Beverage

5. What beverage is liked most by students? **juice**

6. About how many more students drink juice than sport drinks with dinner? **about 2 times**

ALGEBRA Find the value of x. (Lesson 10-4)

7.

8.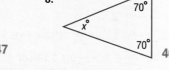

9. **STANDARDS PRACTICE** In triangle ABC, m∠A = 62° and m∠C = 44°. What is m∠B? (Lesson 10-4) **G**

F 90°   **H** 64°

G 74°   **J** 42°

10. ★ **RACES** Norberto, Isabel, Fiona, Brock, and Elizabeth were the first five finishers of a race. From the given clues, find the order in which they finished. Use the *logical reasoning* strategy. (Lesson 10-5) **See margin.**

- Norberto passed Fiona just before the finish line.
- Elizabeth finished 5 seconds ahead of Norberto.
- Isabel crossed the finish line after Fiona.
- Brock was fifth at the finish line.

Classify the quadrilateral with the name that best describes it. (Lesson 10-6)

11.

parallelogram

12.

trapezoid

ALGEBRA Find the value of x in each quadrilateral. (Lesson 10-6)

13.

14.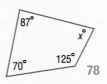

15. **ALGEBRA** What is m∠A in quadrilateral ABCD if m∠B = 36°, m∠C = 74°, and ∠D is a right angle? (Lesson 10-6) **160°**

CHAPTER 10 Mid-Chapter Quiz

Formative Assessment

Use the Mid-Chapter Quiz to assess students' progress in the first half of the chapter.

Have students review the lesson indicated for the problems they answered incorrectly.

Summative Assessment

CRM Mid-Chapter Test, p. 75

ExamView Assessment Suite — Customize and create multiple versions of your Mid-Chapter Test and their answer keys.

FOLDABLES Study Organizer — **Dinah Zike's Foldables**

Before students complete the Mid-Chapter Quiz, encourage them to review the notes they recorded about triangles, and quadrilaterals in the second and third columns of their Foldable.

Additional Answers

4.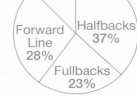

Soccer Injuries

10. 1st, Elizabeth; 2nd, Norberto; 3rd, Fiona; 4th, Isabel; 5th, Brock

Data-Driven Decision Making	Exercises	Lesson	Standard	Resources for Review
Diagnostic Teaching Based on the results of the Chapter 10 Mid-Chapter Quiz, use the following to review concepts that students continue to find challenging.	1, 2	10–1	6MG2.1	**CRM** Study Guide and Intervention pp. 10, 16, 22, 29, 34, and 39
	3	10–2	🔑 6MG2.2	**Math Online**
	4–6	10–3	Reinforcement of 5SDAP1.2	• Extra Examples
	7–9	10–4	🔑 6MG2.2	• Personal Tutor
	10	10–5	6MR1.2	• Concepts in Motion
	11–15	10–6	6MG2.3	

10-7 Similar Figures

Standard
6NS1.3

Use proportions to solve problems (**e.g.** determine the value of n if $\frac{4}{7} = \frac{N}{21}$, **find the length of a side of a polygon similar to a known polygon). Use cross-multiplication as a method for solving such problems,** understanding it as the multiplication of both sides of an equation by a multiplicative inverse.

PACING: **Regular:** 2 periods, **Block:** 1 period

Options for Differentiated Instruction

ELL = English Language Learner   **AL** = Above Grade Level   **SS** = Struggling Students   **SN** = Special Needs

Reviewing Concepts   ELL AL SS SN

Use before beginning Lesson 10-7.

Review with students the steps used to solve a proportion.

Example   Solve $\frac{n}{28} = \frac{5}{8}$.

$\frac{n}{28} = \frac{5}{8}$ Write the proportion.

$n \cdot 8 = 28 \cdot 5$ Find the cross products.

$8n = 140$ Multiply.

$\frac{8n}{8} = \frac{140}{8}$ Divide each side by 8.

$n = 17.5$ Simplify.

Have students complete the following practice problems so that they can feel more confident with the skills needed to be successful with the material presented in this lesson.

Solve each proportion.

1. $\frac{3}{2} = \frac{a}{12}$ 18   2. $\frac{4}{n} = \frac{5}{7}$ 5.6   3. $\frac{2}{13} = \frac{10}{x}$ 65   4. $\frac{r}{22} = \frac{9}{4}$ 49.5

Naturalist Learners   ELL AL SS SN

Use after presenting the Examples.

Have students determine the heights of trees or other objects by using similar triangles. Sketch one example problem for them on the board or overhead. (Refer them to Exercise 4 on page 543 for another example.) Then tell students to follow this procedure for two other natural objects. They should sketch the problem, indicate the measurements, and calculate the unknown height.

Study Tools   ELL SS SN

Use before assigning the Exercises.

Have students update their vocabulary booklets. Suggest that they include the following:
- the symbols for *similar*, and how to write a similarity statement,
- an example showing how to determine whether two figures are similar, and
- an example showing how to use a proportion to find the missing side of a similar figure.

Leveled Lesson Resources

Chapter 10 Resource Masters

BL = Below Grade Level   **OL** = On Grade Level   **AL** = Above Grade Level   **ELL** = English Language Learner

Lesson Reading Guide
p. 44 **BL** **OL** **ELL**

Study Guide and Intervention*
p. 45 **BL** **OL** **ELL**

Skills Practice*
p. 46 **BL** **OL**

Practice*
p. 47 **OL** **AL**

Word Problem Practice*
p. 48 **OL** **AL**

Enrichment
p. 49 **OL** **AL**

Additional Lesson Resources

* Also available in Spanish ELL

Transparencies
- *5-Minute Check Transparency,* Lesson 10-7

Other Print Products
- *Teaching Mathematics with Manipulatives*
- *Noteables™ Interactive Study Notebook with Foldables™*

Teacher Tech Tools
- *Interactive Classroom CD-ROM,* Lesson 10-7
- *AssignmentWorks CD-ROM,* Lesson 10-7

Student Tech Tools
ca.gr6math.com
- Extra Examples, Chapter 10, Lesson 7
- Self-Check Quiz, Chapter 10, Lesson 7

10-7 Similar Figures

Standards Alignment

Before Lesson 10-7
Measure, identify, and draw angles, perpendicular and parallel lines, rectangles, and triangles by using appropriate tools from ← Standard 5MG2.1

Lesson 10-7
Use proportions to solve problems. Use cross-multiplication as a method for solving such problems from ← Standard 6NS1.3

After Lesson 10-7
Demonstrate an understanding of conditions that indicate two geometric figures are congruent and what congruence means about the relationship between the sides and angles of the two figures from ← Standard 7MG3.4

2 Teach

MINI Lab

You might need to show students how to extend the sides of the triangles so that they can measure the angles with their protractors. Make sure students understand that "matching" sides and "matching" angles correspond; that is, they have the same position in each figure.

Scaffolding Questions

Draw two squares and two rectangles such as the following on the board.

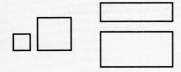

Ask:
• Are the squares the same shape? yes

Main IDEA

Determine whether figures are similar and find a missing length in a pair of similar figures.

 Standard 6NS1.3 Use proportions to solve problems (e.g. determine the value of n if $\frac{4}{7} = \frac{n}{21}$, **find the length of a side of a polygon similar to a known polygon). Use cross-multiplication as a method for solving such problems,** understanding it as the multiplication of both sides of an equation by a multiplicative inverse.

NEW Vocabulary

similar figures
corresponding sides
corresponding angles
indirect measurement

1. $\overline{AB}$ and $\overline{EF}$, $\overline{BC}$ and $\overline{FG}$, $\overline{CD}$ and $\overline{GH}$, $\overline{DA}$ and $\overline{HE}$; $\overline{RT}$ and $\overline{XZ}$, $\overline{ST}$ and $\overline{YZ}$, $\overline{RS}$ and $\overline{XY}$
3. They are equal.
4. ∠A and ∠E, ∠B and ∠F, ∠C and ∠G, ∠D and ∠H; ∠R and ∠X, ∠T and ∠Z, ∠S and ∠Y; They are equal.
5. Sample answer: Similar figures have corresponding sides that form equal ratios and their corresponding angles are congruent.

MINI Lab

The figures in each pair below have the same shape but different sizes. Copy each pair onto dot paper. Then find the measure of each angle using a protractor and the measure of each side using a centimeter ruler.

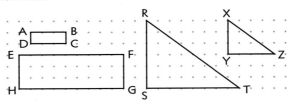

1. $\overline{AB}$ on the smaller rectangle matches $\overline{EF}$ on the larger rectangle. Name all pairs of matching sides in each pair of figures.
   The notation $\overline{AB}$ means the segment with endpoints at A and B.

2. Write each ratio in simplest form.
   The notation AB means the *measure* of segment AB.
   a. $\frac{AB}{EF}$, $\frac{BC}{FG}$, $\frac{DC}{HG}$, $\frac{AD}{EH}$ $\frac{1}{3}$, $\frac{1}{3}$, $\frac{1}{3}$, $\frac{1}{3}$ b. $\frac{RS}{XY}$, $\frac{ST}{YZ}$, $\frac{RT}{XZ}$ 2; 2; 2

3. What do you notice about the ratios of matching sides?

4. Name all pairs of matching angles in the figures above. What do you notice about the measure of these angles?

5. **MAKE A CONJECTURE** about figures that have the same shape but not necessarily the same size.

Figures that have the same shape but not necessarily the same size are **similar figures**. In the figures below, triangle RST is similar to triangle XYZ. We write this as $\triangle RST \sim \triangle XYZ$.

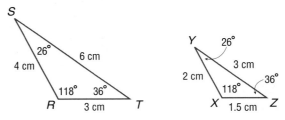

The matching sides are $\overline{ST}$ and $\overline{YZ}$, $\overline{SR}$ and $\overline{YX}$, and $\overline{RT}$ and $\overline{XZ}$. The sides of similar figures that "match" are called **corresponding sides**.

The matching angles are ∠S and ∠Y, ∠R and ∠X, and ∠T and ∠Z. The angles of similar figures that "match" are called **corresponding angles**.

• Are the squares the same size? no

• Are the rectangles the same shape? no

• Are the rectangles the same size? No; they have the same length but different widths.

The Mini Lab illustrates the following statements.

KEY CONCEPT   Similar Figures

Words	If two figures are similar, then • the corresponding sides are proportional, and • the corresponding angles are congruent.
Models	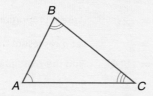 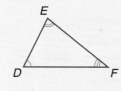

Symbols $\triangle ABC \sim \triangle DEF$ The symbol ~, means *is similar to*.

corresponding sides: $\dfrac{AB}{DE} = \dfrac{BC}{EF} = \dfrac{AC}{DF}$

corresponding angles: $\angle A \cong \angle D;\ \angle B \cong \angle E;\ \angle C \cong \angle F$

READING Math

Geometry Symbols
~ is similar to
≅ is congruent to

Focus on Mathematical Content

If two figures are **similar**, the corresponding sides are proportional. So, to find the missing length of a side in one of the figures, write and solve a **proportion**.

The proportionality of similar figures makes it possible to use **indirect measurement** to find missing dimensions of real-world objects.

EXAMPLE Identify Similar Figures

1. Which trapezoid below is similar to trapezoid *DEFG*?

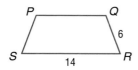 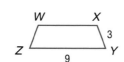 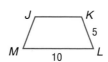

Find the ratios of the corresponding sides to see if they form a constant ratio.

Trapezoid *PQRS* **Trapezoid *WXYZ*** **Trapezoid *JKLM***

$\dfrac{EF}{QR} = \dfrac{4}{6}$ or $\dfrac{2}{3}$ $\dfrac{EF}{XY} = \dfrac{4}{3}$ $\dfrac{EF}{KL} = \dfrac{4}{5}$

$\dfrac{FG}{RS} = \dfrac{12}{14}$ or $\dfrac{6}{7}$ $\dfrac{FG}{YZ} = \dfrac{12}{9}$ or $\dfrac{4}{3}$ $\dfrac{FG}{LM} = \dfrac{12}{10}$ or $\dfrac{6}{5}$

Not similar   Similar   Not similar

So, trapezoid *WXYZ* is similar to trapezoid *DEFG*.

CHECK Your Progress

a. Which triangle below is similar to triangle *DEF*? triangle *XYZ*

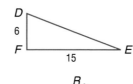

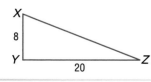 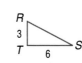

Formative Assessment

Use the Check Your Progress exercises after each Example to determine students' understanding of concepts.

ADDITIONAL EXAMPLE

1. Which rectangle in the bottom margin is similar to rectangle *FGHI*? rectangle *ABCD*

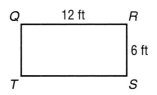

Additional Examples are also in:
• Noteables™ Interactive Study Notebook with Foldables™
• Interactive Classroom PowerPoint® Presentations

Differentiated Instruction

Verbal/Linguistic Learners After completing Check Your Progress a, have students write a paragraph explaining how they determined which triangle was similar to triangle *DEF*. Their explanation should include the critical attributes of similarity presented in the Key Concept box with specific numerical calculations related to the figures in Check Your Progress a. See students' work.

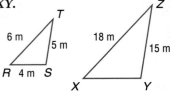

EXAMPLE **Find Side Measures of Similar Triangles**

2 If △RST ~ △XYZ, find the length of $\overline{XY}$.

Since the two triangles are similar, the ratios of their corresponding sides are equal. Write and solve a proportion to find XY.

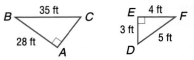

$\dfrac{RT}{XZ} = \dfrac{RS}{XY}$ Write a proportion.

$\dfrac{6}{18} = \dfrac{4}{n}$ Let *n* represent the length of $\overline{XY}$. Then substitute.

$6n = 18(4)$ Find the cross products.

$6n = 72$ Simplify.

$n = 12$ Divide each side by 6.   The length of $\overline{XY}$ is 12 meters.

CHECK Your Progress

b. If △ABC ~ △EFD, find the length of $\overline{AC}$. **21 ft**

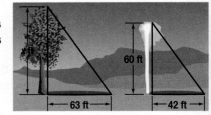

Indirect measurement uses similar figures to find the length, width, or height of objects that are too difficult to measure directly.

Real-World EXAMPLE

3 **GEYSERS** Old Faithful in Yellowstone National Park shoots water 60 feet into the air that casts a shadow of 42 feet. What is the height of a nearby tree that casts a shadow 63 feet long? Assume the triangles are similar.

Tree   Old Faithful

$\dfrac{x}{63} = \dfrac{60}{42}$ ← height
                ← shadow

$42x = 60(63)$ Find the cross products.

$42x = 3{,}780$ Simplify.

$x = 90$ Divide each side by 42.

The tree is 90 feet tall.

CHECK Your Progress

c. **PHOTOGRAPHY** Destiny wants to resize a 4-inch wide by 5-inch long photograph for the school newspaper. It is to fit in a space that is 2 inches wide. What is the length of the resized photograph? **2.5 in.**

Online **Personal Tutor at** ca.gr6math.com

CHECK Your Understanding

Example 1
(p. 541)

1. Which rectangle below is similar to rectangle *ABCD*? **rectangle *PQRS***

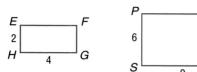

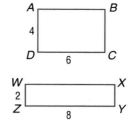

Use Exercises 1–4 to check for understanding.

Then use the chart at the bottom of this page to customize your assignments for students.

Intervention You may wish to use the Study Guide and Intervention Master on page 45 of the *Chapter 10 Resource Masters* for additional reinforcement.

Example 2
(p. 542)

ALGEBRA Find the value of *x* in each pair of similar figures.

2.

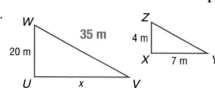

3.

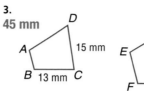

Example 3
(p. 542)

4. **TREES** A certain tree casts a 40-foot shadow. At the same time, Roberto who is 6 feet tall, casts a 5-foot shadow. What is the height of the tree? Assume the triangles are similar. **48 ft**

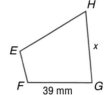

Odd/Even Assignments

Exercises 5–12 are structured so that students practice the same concepts whether they are assigned odd or even problems.

Exercises

HOMEWORK HELP

For Exercises	See Examples
5–6	1
7–10	2
11–12	3

Exercise Levels
A: 5–12
B: 13–17
C: 18–20

5. Which triangle below is similar to triangle *FGH*? **triangle *CAB***

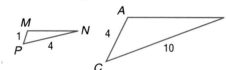

6. Which parallelogram below is similar to parallelogram *HJKM*? **parallelogram *RSTU***

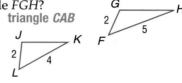
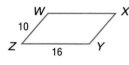
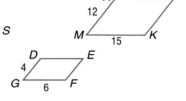

ALGEBRA Find the value of *x* in each pair of similar figures.

7.

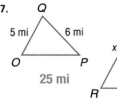
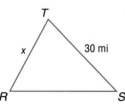

8.

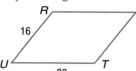
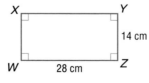

Lesson 10-7 Similar Figures **543**

DIFFERENTIATED HOMEWORK OPTIONS

Level	Assignment	Two-Day Option	
BL Basic	5–12, 20–31	5–11 odd, 21–23	6–12 even, 20, 24–31
OL Core	5–9 odd, 11–13, 15–17, 20–31	5–12, 21–23	13–17, 20, 24–31
AL Advanced/Pre-AP	13–27 (optional: 28–31)		

Draw a Diagram Strategy

If students have difficulties with word problems such as Exercises 15–17, encourage them to draw diagrams, showing the known measurements and the missing measurement.

ALGEBRA Find the value of *x* in each pair of similar figures.

9.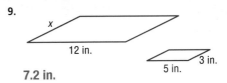
7.2 in.

10.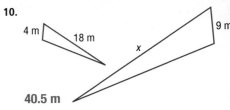

11. **PARKS** Ruth is at the park standing next to a slide. Ruth is 5 feet tall, and her shadow is 4 feet long. If the shadow of the slide is 4.8 feet long, what is the height of the slide? Assume the triangles are similar. **6 ft**

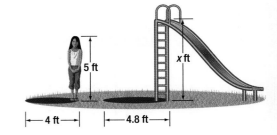

12. **FURNITURE** A child's desk is made so that it is a replica of a full-sized adult desk. Suppose the top of the full-size desk measures 54 inches long by 36 inches wide. If the top of a child's desk is 24 inches wide and is similar to the full-size desk, what is the length? **36 in.**

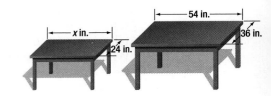

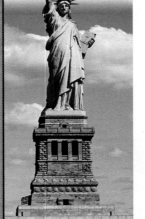

ALGEBRA Find the value of *x* in each pair of similar figures.

13.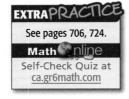
29.4 m
14 m
25.2 m **12 m**

14. 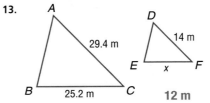 **10.2 mm**
7.2 mm x

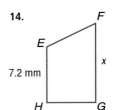
5.1 mm   3.6 mm

STATUES For Exercises 15 and 16 use the information below and at the left.

Alyssa has a miniature replica of the Statue of Liberty. The replica is 9 inches tall, and the length of the statue's right arm holding the torch is $1\frac{1}{4}$ inches.

15. About how long is the actual Statue of Liberty's right arm? **about 42 ft**

16. Alyssa's friend has a smaller replica in which the length of the statue's right arm is $\frac{3}{4}$ inch. How tall is the smaller statue? **about $5\frac{2}{5}$ in.**

120 m

17. **MEASUREMENT** The ratio of the length of square *A* to the length of square *B* is 3:5. If the length of square *A* is 18 meters, what is the perimeter of square *B*?

H.O.T. Problems

CHALLENGE For Exercises 18 and 19, use the following information.

Two rectangles are similar. The ratio of their corresponding sides is 1:4.

18. Find the ratio of their perimeters. **1:4**

19. What is the ratio of their areas? **1:16**

20. **WRITING IN MATH** Write a problem about a real-world situation that could be solved using proportions and the concept of similarity. Then use what you have learned in this lesson to solve the problem.

See students' work.

STANDARDS PRACTICE 6NS1.3

21. Which rectangle is similar to the rectangle shown? **B**

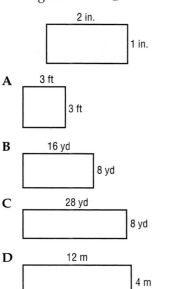

2 in.

1 in.

A 3 ft

3 ft

B 16 yd

8 yd

C 28 yd

8 yd

D 12 m

4 m

22. Which of the following equations is a correct use of cross-multiplication in solving the proportion $\frac{12}{15} = \frac{m}{6}$? **G**

F $12 \cdot m = 15 \cdot 6$

G $12 \cdot 6 = m \cdot 15$

H $12 \cdot 15 = m \cdot 6$

J $12 \div 6 = m \div 15$

23. Horatio is 6 feet tall and casts a shadow of 3 feet long. What is the height of a nearby tower if it casts a shadow 25 feet long at the same time? **C**

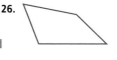

h

6 ft

|←25 ft→| ←|3 ft|→

A 25 feet   **C** 50 feet

B 45 feet   **D** 75 feet

Spiral Review

GEOMETRY Classify the quadrilateral using the name that *best* describes it. (Lesson 10-6)

24.   **25.**   **26.**

square   trapezoid   quadrilateral

27. MEASUREMENT A triangular-shaped sail has angle measures of 44° and 67°. Find the measure of the third angle. (Lesson 10-4)   **69°**

GET READY for the Next Lesson

PREREQUISITE SKILL Solve each equation. (Lesson 3-3)

28. $5a = 120$ **24**   **29.** $360 = 4x$ **90**   **30.** $940 = 8n$ **117.5** **31.** $6t = 720$ **120**

Differentiated Instruction

Bodily/Kinesthetic Learners If the day is sunny, separate students into groups of three or four. Distribute a tape measure or yardstick to each group. Have them go outside and use what they know about similarity to find the height of a tree, flagpole, or other tall object. Make sure each student in each group draws a diagram of the problem, writes the proportion, and finds the missing height.

4 Assess

Ticket Out the Door Tell students that a Big Boy steam locomotive was 132 feet long and its engineer was 6 feet tall. Say that a model of the Big Boy is 2 feet long. Have students write how tall a model of the engineer should be.

FOLDABLES Foldables™
Study Organizer Follow-Up

Remind students to complete the second and third columns in their Foldable about similar figures and their proportionality.

10-8 Polygons and Tessellations

Standard 6MR2.2   Apply strategies and results from simpler problems to more complex problems.

Standard 6AF3.2   Express in symbolic form simple relationships arising from geometry.

PACING: Regular: 2 periods, Block: 1 period

Options for Differentiated Instruction

ELL = English Language Learner   **AL** = Above Grade Level   **SS** = Struggling Students   **SN** = Special Needs

Building Vocabulary ELL SN

Use after presenting the Examples.

Have students update their vocabulary booklets to include the following:
- definitions and diagrams of the polygons presented in lesson
- definitions of the prefixes *pent-*, *hex-*, *hept-*, *oct-*, *non-*, and *dec-*

Making Predictions AL

Use after presenting Example 3.

Display the following figures on the board or overhead.

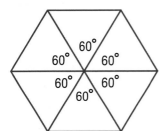 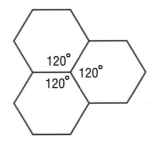 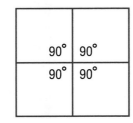

Ask:
- What do you notice about the sum of the angles labeled in each figure? They equal 360°.
- Could two squares and two equilateral triangles be arranged to fit together like the figures above, with no overlaps or holes? Explain. No; the sum of the angles would be 300°, and it needs to equal 360°.

Kinesthetic Learners ELL SS SN

Use after completing Lesson 10-8.

Have each student choose a shape that can tessellate and cut it out of cardboard. Then have them trace it multiple times to make a tessellation. Have them color their design. As an additional challenge, encourage students to try to create a tessellation of two or three different shapes.

Leveled Lesson Resources

Chapter 10 Resource Masters

BL = Below Grade Level   **OL** = On Grade Level   **AL** = Above Grade Level   **ELL** = English Language Learner

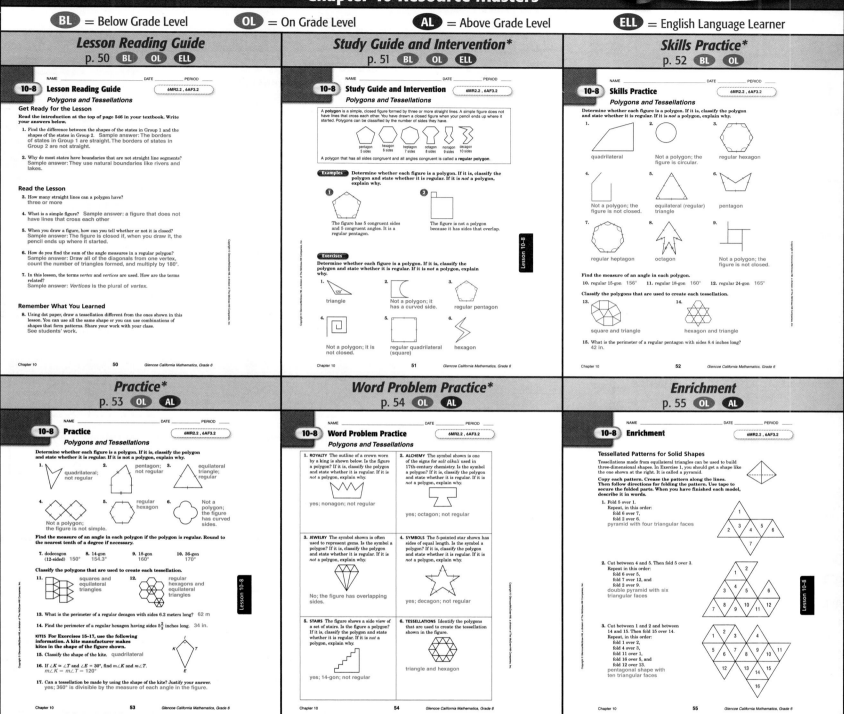

Additional Lesson Resources

* Also available in Spanish **ELL**

Transparencies
- _5-Minute Check Transparency, Lesson 10-8_

Other Print Products
- _Teaching Mathematics with Manipulatives_
- _Noteables™ Interactive Study Notebook with Foldables™_

Teacher Tech Tools
- _Interactive Classroom CD-ROM, Lesson 10-8_
- _AssignmentWorks CD-ROM, Lesson 10-8_

Student Tech Tools
ca.gr6math.com
- Extra Examples, Chapter 10, Lesson 8
- Self-Check Quiz, Chapter 10, Lesson 8

1 Focus

Standards Alignment

Before Lesson 10-8
Measure, identify, and draw angles, perpendicular and parallel lines, rectangles, and triangles by using appropriate tools from Standard 5MG2.1

Lesson 10-8
Apply strategies and results from simpler problems to more complex problems. Express in symbolic form simple relationships arising from geometry from Standards 6MR2.2 and 6AF3.2

After Lesson 10-8
Identify and construct basic elements of geometric figures by using a compass and straightedge from Standard 7MG3.1

2 Teach

Scaffolding Questions

Before you ask the following questions, draw a trapezoid on the chalkboard.

Ask:
- How many sides does a trapezoid have? 4

- What are the sides of a trapezoid? line segments

- Can a line segment be curved? no

- Where do the sides of a trapezoid meet? at the endpoints of the line segments, or at the vertices

Tips for New Teachers
Polygons
After completing the lesson opener, tell students that the states listed in Group 1 are examples of polygons.

10-8 Polygons and Tessellations

Main IDEA
Classify polygons and determine which polygons can form a tessellation.

Standard 6MR2.2 Apply strategies and results from simpler problems to more complex problems. **Standard 6AF3.2** Express in symbolic form simple relationships arising from geometry.

NEW Vocabulary
polygon
pentagon
hexagon
heptagon
octagon
nonagon
decagon
regular polygon
tessellation

READING Math

Polygons The polygons shown at the right have special names. Most other polygons are named using a number. For example, a polygon with 11 sides is an 11-gon.

▶ GET READY for the Lesson

GEOGRAPHY The size and shape of each state in the United States is different. Analyze the shapes of the states in both groups at the right.

1. Find the difference between the shapes of the states in Group 1 (blue states) and the shapes of the states in Group 2 (green states). 1–2. See margin.

2. Why do most states have boundaries that are not straight line segments?

Group 1	Group 2
Utah	Kentucky
Wyoming	Michigan
New Mexico	Mississippi
Colorado	Texas

A **polygon** is a simple, closed figure formed by three or more straight line segments. A *simple figure* does not have lines that cross each other. You have drawn a *closed figure* when your pencil ends up where it started.

Polygons	Not Polygons
• Line segments are called sides. • Sides meet only at their endpoints. • Points of intersection are called vertices.	• Figures with sides that cross each other. • Figures that are open. • Figures that have curved sides.

A polygon can be classified by the number of sides it has.

Words	pentagon	hexagon	heptagon	octagon	nonagon	decagon
Number of Sides	5	6	7	8	9	10
Models						

A **regular polygon** has all sides congruent and all angles congruent. Equilateral triangles and squares are examples of regular polygons.

546 Chapter 10 Geometry: Polygons

Additional Answers

1. Sample answer: The borders of states in Group 1 are straight. The borders of states in Group 2 are not straight.

2. Sample answer: They use natural boundaries like rivers and lakes.

Tips for New Teachers
Classifying Polygons

Most polygons with sides greater than 10 are classified using a number. For example, a polygon with 30 sides is a 30-gon. However, there are exceptions. A polygon with 12 sides is a duodecagon and a polygon with 20 sides is a dodecagon.

EXAMPLES Classify Polygons

READING Math

Regular Polygons Since regular polygons have *equal–sized angles*, they are also called *equiangular*.

Determine whether each figure is a polygon. If it is, classify the polygon and state whether it is regular. If it is not a polygon, explain why.

1

The figure has 6 congruent sides and 6 congruent angles. It is a regular hexagon.

2

The figure is not a polygon since it has a curved side.

CHECK Your Progress

Determine whether each figure is a polygon. If it is, classify the polygon and state whether it is regular. If it is *not* a polygon, explain why.

a. not a polygon; it is not a closed figure

b. pentagon; not regular

The sum of the measures of the angles of a triangle is 180°. You can use this relationship to find the measures of the angles of regular polygons.

EXAMPLE Angle Measures of a Polygon

STUDY TIP

Angle Measures The number of triangles formed is 2 less than the number of sides in the polygon. The equation $(n - 2) \times 180 = s$ gives the sum s of angle measures in a polygon with n sides.

3 **ALGEBRA** Find the measure of each angle of a regular pentagon.

- Draw all of the diagonals from one vertex as shown and count the number of triangles formed.
- Find the sum of the angle measures in the polygon.

number of triangles formed × 180° = sum of angle measures in polygon
$$3 \times 180° = 540°$$

- Find the measure of each angle of the polygon. Let n represent the measure of one angle in the pentagon.

$5n = 540$ There are five congruent angles.

$n = 108$ Divide each side by 5.

The measure of each angle in a regular pentagon is 108°.

CHECK Your Progress

Find the measure of an angle in each polygon.

c. regular octagon   135°
d. equilateral triangle   60°

Math Online Extra Examples at ca.gr6math.com   **Lesson 10-8** Polygons and Tessellations   **547**

Focus on Mathematical Content

Polygons are classified according to their **number of sides**. The sides of a **regular polygon** are congruent, as are its angles.

By **separating a polygon into triangles**, the sum of the measures of its angles can be calculated.

To find whether a regular polygon can be used to create a **tessellation**, find whether the measure of one angle divides evenly into 360°.

Formative Assessment

Use the Check Your Progress exercises after each Example to determine students' understanding of concepts.

ADDITIONAL EXAMPLES

Determine whether each figure is a polygon. If it is, classify the polygon and state whether it is regular. If it is not a polygon, explain why.

1

not a polygon; curved side

2

hexagon; not regular

3 **ALGEBRA** Find the measure of each angle of a regular heptagon. Round to the nearest tenth of a degree. 128.6°

Additional Examples are also in:
- Noteables™ Interactive Study Notebook with Foldables™
- Interactive Classroom PowerPoint® Presentations

Lesson 10-8 Polygons and Tessellations   **547**

COncepts in MOtion
Interactive Lab ca.gr6math.com

A repetitive pattern of polygons that fit together with no overlaps or holes is called a **tessellation**. The surface of a chessboard is an example of a tessellation of squares.

The sum of the measures of the angles where the vertices meet in a tessellation is 360°.

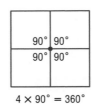

$4 \times 90° = 360°$

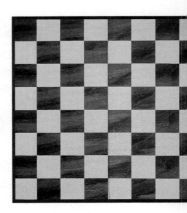

Real-World EXAMPLE

④ **LANDSCAPING** Mr. Brooks bought pentagonal-shaped bricks to create a patio. Can Mr. Brooks make a tessellation using the bricks?

The measure of each angle in a regular pentagon is 108°.

The sum of the measures of the angles where the vertices meet must be 360°. So, solve $108n = 360$.

$108n = 360$ — Write the equation.

$\dfrac{108n}{108} = \dfrac{360}{108}$ — Divide each side by 108.

$n = 3.\overline{3}$ — Use a calculator.

Since 108° does not divide evenly into 360°, the sum of the measures of the angles where the vertices meet is not 360°. So, Mr. Brooks cannot make a tessellation using the bricks.

Check

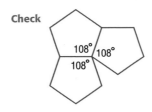

Real-World Career. . .
How Does a Landscape Architect Use Math?
A landscape architect uses math when arranging bricks to create a patio.

Math Online
For more information, go to ca.gr6math.com.

e. Yes; the measure of each angle in a regular triangle is 60°. Since 360° is divisible by 60°, the stones tessellate.

CHECK Your Progress

e. **LANDSCAPING** Can Mr. Brooks use stones that are equilateral triangles to pave the patio? Explain.

Online Personal Tutor at ca.gr6math.com

548 Chapter 10 Geometry: Polygons

Pre-AP Activity Use after the Examples

Have students describe the pattern between the number of sides of a polygon and the sum of the measures of its angles. Suggest that they draw a function table and write the function rule. Then have them use the rule to find the sum of the measures of the angles of a 100-gon.

number of sides	3	4	5	6	n
sum of angle measures	180°	360°	540°	720°	$(n-2) \cdot 180°$

sum of measures of angles of 100-gon = 17,640°

CHECK Your Understanding

Examples 1, 2 (p. 547)
Determine whether each figure is a polygon. If it is, classify the polygon and state whether it is regular. If it is *not* a polygon, explain why.

1. 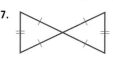 decagon; not regular

2. not a polygon; it is not closed.

3.  hexagon; regular

Example 3 (p. 547)
Find the measure of an angle in each polygon if the polygon is regular. Round to the nearest tenth of a degree if necessary.

4. hexagon 120°

5. heptagon 128.6°

Example 4 (p. 548)
6. **ART** In art class, Trisha traced and then cut several regular octagons out of tissue paper. Can she use the figures to create a tessellation? Explain.
No; the measure of each angle in a regular octagon is 135°. Since 360° is not divisible by 135°, the figures do not tessellate.

Exercises

HOMEWORK HELP	
For Exercises	**See Examples**
7–12	1,2
13–16	3
17–18	4

Exercise Levels
A: 7–18
B: 19–29
C: 30–33

7. not a polygon; the figure is not simple

17–18. See margin.

Determine whether each figure is a polygon. If it is, classify the polygon and state whether it is regular. If it is *not* a polygon, explain why.

7.

8. regular octagon

9. isosceles right triangle; not regular

10. Not a polygon; the figure has a curved side.

11. 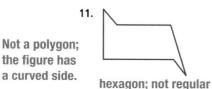 hexagon; not regular

12. regular decagon

Find the measure of an angle in each polygon if the polygon is regular. Round to the nearest tenth of a degree if necessary.

13. decagon 144°
14. nonagon 140°
15. quadrilateral 90°
16. 11-gon 147.3°

17. **TOYS** Marty used his magnetic building set to build the regular decagon at the right. Assume he has enough building parts to create several of these shapes. Can the figures be arranged in a tessellation? Explain.

18. **COASTERS** Paper coasters are placed under a beverage glass to protect the table surface. The coasters are shaped like regular heptagons. Can the coasters be arranged in a tessellation? Explain your reasoning.

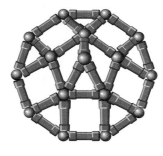

Lesson 10-8 Polygons and Tessellations **549**

 Practice

Formative Assessment

Use Exercises 1–6 to check for understanding.

Then use the chart at the bottom of this page to customize your assignments for students.

Intervention You may wish to use the Study Guide and Intervention Master on page 51 of the *Chapter 10 Resource Masters* for additional reinforcement.

Odd/Even Assignments

Exercises 7–18 are structured so that students practice the same concepts whether they are assigned odd or even problems.

Additional Answers

17. No; the figure is a decagon. Each angle of a decagon measures 144°. Since 144° does not divide evenly into 360°, a decagon cannot make a tessellation.

18. No; Each angle of a regular heptagon measures about 130°. Since 130° does not go into 360°, the polygon cannot make a tessellation.

DIFFERENTIATED HOMEWORK OPTIONS

Level	Assignment	Two-Day Option	
BL Basic	7–18, 30, 31, 33–47	7–17 odd, 34, 35	8–18 even, 30, 31, 33, 36–47
OL Core	7–15 odd, 17–19, 21–31, 33–47	7–18, 34, 35	19–31, 33, 36–47
AL Advanced/Pre-AP	19–43 (optional: 44–47)		

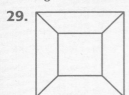

19. hexagon and triangle
20. hexagon, square, and triangle
21. octagon and square
24. triangle, trapezoid, and hexagon

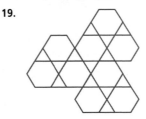

Real-World Link · · · ·
All stop signs have the same shape and meaning. In Spanish-speaking countries, the signs read "ALTO" (halt) or "PARE" (stop).

EXTRAPRACTICE

See pages 706, 724.

Math Online
Self-Check Quiz at
ca.gr6math.com

H.O.T. Problems

32. Yes; the sum of the measures of angles of any triangle is 180°; See students' drawings

Classify the polygons that are used to create each tessellation.

19.
20.
21.

22. What is the perimeter of a regular nonagon with sides 4.8 centimeters? **43.2 c**

23. Find the perimeter of a regular pentagon having sides $7\frac{1}{4}$ yards long. **$36\frac{1}{4}$ yd**

24. ART The mosaic shown is decorated with handmade tiles from Pakistan. Name the polygons used in the tessellation.

··**25. SIGNS** Refer to the photo at the left. Stop signs are made from large sheets of steel. Suppose one sheet of steel is large enough to cut nine signs. Can all nine signs be arranged on the sheet so that none of the steel goes to waste? Explain. **See margin.**

26. RESEARCH Use the Internet or another source to find the shape of other road signs. Name the type of sign, its shape, and state whether or not it is regular. **See students' work.**

SCHOOL For Exercises 27–29, use the information below and the graphic of the cafeteria tray shown.

A company designs cafeteria trays so that four students can place their trays around a square table without bumping corners. The top and bottom sides of the tray are parallel.

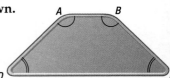

27. Classify the shape of the tray. **trapezoid**

28. If $\angle A \cong \angle B$, $\angle C \cong \angle D$, and $m\angle A = 135°$, find $m\angle B$, $m\angle C$, and $m\angle D$. **135°, 45°, 45°**

29. Name the polygon formed by the outside of four trays when they are placed around the table with their sides touching. Justify your answer. **square; See margin.**

30. REASONING *True* or *False?* Only a regular polygon can tessellate a plane. **false**

31. OPEN ENDED Draw examples of a pentagon and a hexagon that represent real-world objects. **pentagon: the Pentagon; hexagon: section of honeycomb; See margin for drawings.**

32. CHALLENGE You can make a tessellation with equilateral triangles. Can you make a tessellation with any isosceles or scalene triangles? If so, explain your reasoning and make a drawing.

33. **WRITING IN MATH** Analyze the parallelogram at the right and then explain how you know the parallelogram can be used by itself to make a tessellation.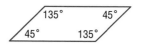
Sample answer; A copy of the parallelogram can fit next to it since $45° + 135° = 180°$ and above or below it since $135° + 45° = 180°$.

STANDARDS PRACTICE 6MR2.2

34. What is the measure of $\angle 1$? **A**

A 60°
B 90°
C 120°
D 150°

35. Which statement is *not* true about polygons? **G**

F A polygon is classified by the number of sides it has.

G The sides of a polygon overlap.

H A polygons is formed by 3 or more line segments.

J The sides of a polygon meet only at its endpoints.

Formative Assessment

Check for student understanding of concepts in Lessons 10-6 through 10-8.

[CRM] Quiz 3, p. 74

FOLDABLES **Foldables™**
Study Organizer **Follow-Up**

Remind students to complete the second and third columns in their Foldable about polygons and tessellations.

Spiral Review

For Exercises 36 and 37, use the figures at the right.

36. **ALGEBRA** The quadrilaterals are similar. Find the value of x. (Lesson 10-7) **8 m**

37. **GEOMETRY** Classify figure $ABCD$. (Lesson 10-6) **trapezoid**

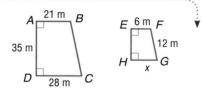

Additional Answers

44–47.

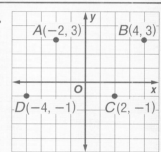

38. **PROBABILITY** Two students will be randomly selected from a group of seven to present their reports. If Carla and Pedro are in the group of 7, what is the probability that Carla will be selected first and Pedro selected second? (Lesson 9-4) $\frac{1}{42}$

39. **MEASUREMENT** How many $\frac{1}{2}$-cup servings of ice cream are there in a gallon of chocolate ice cream? (Lesson 6-3) **32 servings**

Add or subtract. Write each sum or difference in simplest form. (Lesson 5-3)

40. $3\frac{2}{9} + 5\frac{4}{9}$ $8\frac{2}{3}$
41. $5\frac{1}{3} - 2\frac{1}{6}$ $3\frac{1}{6}$
42. $1\frac{3}{7} + 6\frac{1}{4}$ $7\frac{19}{28}$
43. $9\frac{4}{5} - 4\frac{7}{8}$ $4\frac{37}{40}$

GET READY for the Next Lesson

PREREQUISITE SKILL Graph and label each point on the same coordinate plane. (Lesson 2-3) **44–47. See margin.**

44. $A(-2, 3)$
45. $B(4, 3)$
46. $C(2, -1)$
47. $D(-4, -1)$

1 Focus

Materials
- index cards
- scissors
- tape

2 Teach

Activity You may wish to have students discuss the meaning of *translate* in Step 2. They should realize that *translate* indicates a sliding motion along a straight line, without flips or rotations. You may also wish to have students discuss the angle measures of the figures in their pattern—and what can be determined about those angle measures if the figures form a tessellation.

3 Assess

 Formative Assessment

Use Exercises a–c to determine whether students understand how to create tessellations by translating figures.

From Concrete to Abstract Use Exercise 2 to bridge the gap between translating figures to create tessellations and understanding the requirements for creating tessellations.

Extend 10-8

Geometry Lab
Tessellations

Main IDEA

Create tessellations.

 Preparation for Standard 7MG3.4 Demonstrate an understanding of conditions that indicate two geometrical figures are congruent and **what congruence means about the relationships between the sides and angles of the two figures.** **Standard 6MR2.2 Apply strategies and results from simpler problems to more complex problems.**

a–c. See Ch. 10 Answer Appendix.

1. See students' work.
2. Sample answer: Since each figure of a tessellation is made using an identical copy of the original figure, each figure copied is congruent to the original figure and fits together exactly.

In this lab, you will create tessellations.

ACTIVITY

STEP 1 Draw a square on the back of an index card. Then draw a triangle on the inside of the square and a trapezoid on the bottom of the square as shown.

STEP 2 Cut out the square. Then cut out the triangle and slide it from the right side of the square to the left side of the square. Cut out the trapezoid and slide it from the bottom to the top of the square.

STEP 3 Tape the figures together to form a pattern.

STEP 4 Trace this pattern onto a sheet of paper as shown to create a tessellation.

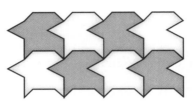

 **Your Progress** Create a tessellation using each pattern.

a.   b.   c.

ANALYZE THE RESULTS

1. Design and describe your own tessellation pattern.
2. **MAKE A CONJECTURE** *Congruent figures* have corresponding sides of equal length and corresponding angles of equal measure. Explain how congruent figures are used in your tessellation.

10-9 Translations

Preparation for 7MG3.2 **Understand and use coordinate graphs to plot simple figures,** determine lengths and areas related to them, **and determine their image under translations** and reflections.

PACING: **Regular:** 1 period, **Block:** 0.5 period

Options for Differentiated Instruction

ELL = English Language Learner   **AL** = Above Grade Level   **SS** = Struggling Students   **SN** = Special Needs

Reusable Coordinate Planes **SS** **SN**

Use with the Examples.

Copy a large coordinate plane and place it in a clear sheet protector for students. They can plot the points of polygons and graph transformations on the plane as you present the examples. The coordinate plane will also be useful to them as they complete the Exercises.

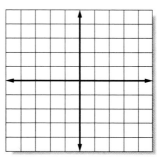

Working in Groups **ELL** **AL** **SS** **SN**

Use after presenting the Examples.

Have students work in groups of three or four. One student should describe the translation of a figure while other students draw the translation. The students can then compare results and assist each other in completing the translation corrections.

Extensions and Challenges **AL**

Use after presenting Lesson 10-9.

Display the square with vertices $A(2, 2)$, $B(2, -2)$, $C(-2, -2)$, and $D(-2, 2)$ on the board or overhead.

Ask:

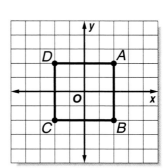

*   After the square is translated, one of the new points is $(-5, 3)$. What are possible coordinates for the other points? Sample answer: If D' is at $(-5, 3)$, then the other points are $A'(-1, 3)$, $B'(-1, -1)$, and $C'(-5, -1)$.
*   Are there any other possibilities? Explain. Yes, there are three other possibilities: If A' is at $(-5, 3)$: $B'(-5, -1)$, $C'(-9, -1)$, $D'(-9, 3)$; if B' is at $(-5, 3)$: $A'(-5, 7)$, $C'(-9, 3)$, $D'(-9, 7)$; if C' is at $(-5, 3)$: $A'(-1, 7)$, $B'(-1, 3)$, $D'(-5, 7)$.

Leveled Lesson Resources

BL = Below Grade Level   **OL** = On Grade Level   **AL** = Above Grade Level   **ELL** = English Language Learner

Lesson Reading Guide
p. 57 BL OL ELL

10-9 Lesson Reading Guide
Translations

Get Ready for the Lesson

Complete the Mini Lab at the top of page 553 in your textbook. Write your answers below.

1. Trace the horizontal and vertical path between corresponding vertices. What do you notice? They have the same path, 5 units to the right and 2 units down.

2. Subtract 5 from each x-coordinate of the vertices of the original figure. Then subtract 2 from each y-coordinate of the vertices of the original figure. What do you notice? The result is the coordinates of the vertices of the figure in its new position.

Read the Lesson

3. When translating a figure, what do you know about every point of the original figure? Sample answer: It moves the same distance and in the same direction.

4. Can a figure be turned in a translation? Explain. no; Sample answer: When a figure is turned, every point does not move in the same direction.

5. What notation is used to indicate the vertices of a translated figure? Sample answer: Prime symbols are used with the vertices of the translated image.

6. Which figure is a translation of Figure 1—Figure 2 or Figure 3? Explain why one figure is a translation and why the other figure is not a translation. Figure 3 is a translation of Figure 1; Sample answer: Each point in Figure 1 moves 4 units down and 4 units to the left (−4, −4). Figure 2 is not a translation of Figure 1. Each point in Figure 1 does not move the same distance and in the same direction to create Figure 2.

Remember What You Learned

7. Describe the translation given by the ordered pair (−7, 3). Think of a way to remember which direction to translate when the x-coordinate of the ordered pair describing the translation is negative. Translate 7 units left and 3 units up. See students' work.

Study Guide and Intervention*
p. 58 BL OL ELL

10-9 Study Guide and Intervention
Translations

A **translation** is the movement of a geometric figure in some direction without turning the figure. When translating a figure, every point of the original figure is moved the same distance and in the same direction. To graph a translation of a figure, move each vertex of the figure in the given direction. Then connect the new vertices.

Example Triangle ABC has vertices A(−4, −2), B(−2, 0), and C(−1, −3). Find the vertices of triangle A'B'C' after a translation of 5 units right and 2 units up.

Add 5 to each x-coordinate.   Add 2 to each y-coordinate.

Vertices of △ABC	(x + 5, y + 2)	Vertices of △A'B'C'
A(−4, −2)	(−4 + 5, −2 + 2)	A'(1, 0)
B(−2, 0)	(−2 + 5, 0 + 2)	B'(3, 2)
C(−1, −3)	(−1 + 5, −3 + 2)	C'(4, −1)

The coordinates of the vertices of △A'B'C' are A'(1, 0), B'(3, 2), and C'(4, −1).

Exercises

1. Translate △GHI 1 unit left and 5 units down.

2. Translate rectangle LMNO 4 units right and 3 units up.

Triangle RST has vertices R(3, 2), S(4, −2), and T(1, −1). Find the vertices of R'S'T' after each translation. Then graph the figure and its translated image.

3. 5 units left, 1 unit up   R'(−2, 3), S'(−1, −1), T'(−4, 0)

4. 3 units left, 2 units down   R'(0, 0), S'(1, −4), T'(−2, −3)

Skills Practice*
p. 59 BL OL

10-9 Skills Practice
Translations

1. Translate △ABC 5 units left.

2. Translate rectangle RSTU 2 units right and 5 units up.

3. Translate △DEF 4 units left and 4 units down.

4. Translate trapezoid LMNO 5 units right and 3 units down.

Triangle XYZ has vertices X(−4, 5), Y(−1, 3), and Z(−2, 0). Find the vertices of X'Y'Z' after each translation. Then graph the translated image.

5. 5 units down   X'(−4, 0), Y'(−1, −2), Z'(−2, −5)

6. 4 units right, 3 units down   X'(0, 2), Y'(3, 0), Z'(2, −3)

Parallelogram RSTU has vertices R(−1, −3), S(0, −1), T(4, −1), and U(3, −3). Find the vertices of R'S'T'U' after each translation. Then graph the figure and its translated image.

7. 3 units left, 3 units up   R'(−4, 0), S'(−3, 2), T'(1, 2), U'(0, 0)

8. 1 unit right, 5 units up   R'(0, 2), S'(1, 4), T'(5, 4), U'(4, 2)

Practice*
p. 60 OL AL

10-9 Practice
Translations

1. Translate rectangle ABCD 3 units right and 4 units down. Graph rectangle A'B'C'D'.

2. Triangle PQR is translated 3 units left and 3 units down. Then the translated figure is translated 6 units right. Graph the resulting triangle.

Triangle EFG has vertices E(1, 1), F(4, −3), and G(−2, 0). Find the vertices of E'F'G' after each translation. Then graph the figure and its translated image.

3. 3 units left, 2 units down   E'(−2, −1), F'(1, −5), G'(−5, −2)

4. 4 units up   E'(1, 5), F'(4, 1), G'(−2, 4)

5. **SEATS** Jatin was given a new seating assignment in science class. The diagram shows his old seat and his new seat. Describe this translation in words and as an ordered pair. 3 units right, 2 units down; (3, −2)

Front of Classroom

REASONING The coordinates of a point and its image after a translation are given. Describe the translation in words and as an ordered pair.

6. A(1, −2) → A'(3, 4) 2 units right and 6 units up; (2, 6)

7. H(3, 3) → H'(−4, 0) 7 units left and 3 units down; (−7, −3)

8. Z(−2, −4) → Z'(1, −5) 3 units right and 1 unit down; (3, −1)

Word Problem Practice*
p. 61 OL AL

10-9 Word Problem Practice
Translations

MAPS For Exercises 1–4, use the map at the right.

1. Stanley's school is located at the corner of Center and Elmwood. The library is located at the corner of Dodge and Delaware. Describe Stanley's walk from school to the library as an ordered pair of the number of blocks. (1, 2)

2. After he goes to the library, Stanley goes to his Aunt Jeanne's house at the corner of California and Harrison. Describe Stanley's walk from the library to his aunt's house as an ordered pair of the number of blocks. (3, −3)

3. If a bus picks up passengers at the corner of New York and Maple and drives 2 blocks south and 3 blocks west, where does the bus end up? the corner of Elmwood and Dodge

4. Organizers of a walkathon want to map out a route that will lead people from the corner of Center and Kensington to the corner of California and Maple. Write a coordinate pair that describes the most direct route. (5, 4)

5. **GEOMETRY** The figure shows an octagon plotted on a coordinate system. The figure is to be translated by 5 units left and 5 units down. Graph the translated image of the figure.

6. **BANKS** Clarissa is waiting in line at the bank. There are several people in line in front of her. Describe the path Clarissa must take to get to the front of the line if each time she moves up in line by one position is considered one unit. 1 unit right, 1 unit up, 3 units left

Enrichment
p. 62 OL AL

10-9 Enrichment
Chess Moves

In the game of chess, a knight can move several different ways. It can move two spaces vertically or horizontally, then one space at a 90° angle. It can also move two spaces vertically or horizontally, then two spaces at a 90° angle. Several examples of a knight's moves are indicated on the grid at the right.

1. Use the diagram at the right. Place a knight or other piece in the square marked 1. Move the knight so that it lands on each of the remaining white squares only once. Mark each square in which the knight lands with 2, then 3, and so on. Sample answer given. Other answers are possible.

1	6	3
4		8
7	2	5

2. Use the diagram below. Place a knight or other piece in the square marked 1. Move the knight so that it lands on each of the remaining squares only once. Mark each square in which the knight lands with 2, then 3, and so on.

29	20	25	10	5	14
26	9	28	13	24	11
19	30	21	6	15	4
8	27	2	17	12	23
1	18	7	22	3	16

Sample answer given. Other answers are possible.

Additional Lesson Resources

***** Also available in Spanish **ELL**

Transparencies
- *5-Minute Check Transparency*, Lesson 10-9

Other Print Products
- *Noteables™ Interactive Study Notebook with Foldables™*

Teacher Tech Tools
- *Interactive Classroom CD-ROM*, Lesson 10-9
- *AssignmentWorks CD-ROM*, Lesson 10-9

Student Tech Tools
ca.gr6math.com
- Extra Examples, Chapter 10, Lesson 9
- Self-Check Quiz, Chapter 10, Lesson 9

Main IDEA

Graph translations of polygons on a coordinate plane.

Preparation for Standard 7MG3.2 Understand and use coordinate graphs to plot simple figures, **determine lengths and areas related to them, and determine their image under translations and reflections.**

NEW Vocabulary

transformation
translation
congruent figures

1. They have the same path, 5 units to the right and 2 units down.
2. The result is the coordinates of the vertices of the figure in its new position.

READING Math

Prime Symbols Use prime symbols for vertices in transformed image.

$A \to A'$
$B \to B'$
$C \to C'$
A' is read A prime.

a. $H'(0, 0)$, $I'(1, 3)$, $J'(5, 2)$ $K'(3, 0)$, See Ch. 10 Answer Appendix for graph.

MINI Lab

CONcepts in MOtion
Interactive Lab ca.gr6math.com

STEP 1 Trace a parallelogram-shaped pattern block onto a coordinate grid. Label the vertices *ABCD*.

STEP 2 Slide the pattern block over 5 units to the right and 2 units down.

STEP 3 Trace the figure in its new position. Label the vertices *A′*, *B′*, *C′*, and *D′*.

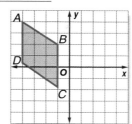

1. Trace the horizontal and vertical path between corresponding vertices. What do you notice?

2. Add 5 to each *x*-coordinate of the vertices of the original figure. Then subtract 2 from each *y*-coordinate of the vertices of the original figure. What do you notice?

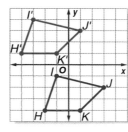

A **transformation** maps one figure onto another. When you move the figure without turning it, the motion is called a **translation**.

When translating a figure, every point of the original figure is moved the same distance and in the same direction.

EXAMPLE Graph a Translation

① Translate quadrilateral *HIJK* 2 units left and 5 units up. Graph quadrilateral *H′ I′ J′ K′*.

- Move each vertex of the figure 2 units left and 5 units up. Label the new vertices *H′*, *I′*, *J′*, and *K′*.

- Connect the vertices to draw the trapezoid. The coordinates of the vertices of the new figure are $H'(-4, 1)$, $I'(-3, 4)$, $J'(1, 3)$, and $K'(-1, 1)$.

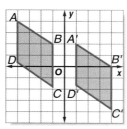

CHECK Your Progress

a. Translate quadrilateral *HIJK* 4 units up and 2 units right. Graph quadrilateral *H′ I′ J′ K′*.

Lesson 10-9 Translations **553**

1 Focus

Standards Alignment

Before Lesson 10-9
Identify and graph ordered pairs in the four quadrants of the coordinate plane from ➤ Standard 5AF1.4

Lesson 10-9
Use coordinate graphs to plot simple figures and determine their image under translations and reflections from Standard 7MG3.2

After Lesson 10-9
Demonstrate an understanding of conditions that indicate two geometrical figures are congruent and what congruence means about the relationships between the sides and angles of the two figures from ➤ Standard 7MG3.4

2 Teach

MINI Lab

If you don't have enough parallelogram pattern blocks for all of your students, they can use square and/or trapezoid pattern blocks. Make sure students remember that the first number of an ordered pair is the *x*-coordinate and the second number is the *y*-coordinate.

Scaffolding Questions

Draw an 8 × 8 coordinate grid on the chalkboard. As you ask the following questions, point to the given point but don't name it.

Ask:
- What are the coordinates of this point? $(-3, -1)$

- What are the coordinates of this point? $(4, -3)$

- How can you describe the movement from point $(-3, -1)$ to point $(4, -3)$? It is seven units to the right and two units down.

- What are the coordinates of this point? $(-1, 2)$

- What are the coordinates of this point? $(2, 0)$

- How can you describe the movement from point $(-1, 2)$ to point $(2, 0)$? It is three units to the right and two units down.

continued at the left

The figure before the transformations is called the *pre-image*. After the transformation, the figure is called the *image*.

Focus on Mathematical Content

In a **translation**, or **slide**, all points of a figure are moved the same distance in the same direction. On a coordinate grid, the movement itself can be written as an **ordered pair**, such as (2, –3).

The vertices of a translated figure can be found by **adding each integer of the translation's ordered pair** (describing the movement) to the vertices of the original figure.

A translated figure is **congruent** to the original figure.

Formative Assessment

Use the Check Your Progress exercises after each Example to determine students' understanding of concepts.

ADDITIONAL EXAMPLE

1 Translate △ABC 5 units left and 1 unit up.

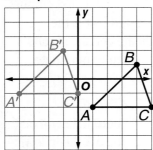

Additional Examples are also in:
- Noteables™ Interactive Study Notebook with Foldables™
- Interactive Classroom PowerPoint® Presentations

When a figure has been translated, the original figure and the translated figure, or *image*, are congruent. **Congruent figures** have the same size and same shape, and the corresponding sides and angles have equal measures.

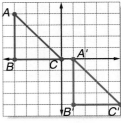

△ABC ≅ △A'B'C'

You can increase or decrease the coordinates of the vertices of a figure by a fixed amount to find the coordinates of the translated vertices.

A *positive* integer describes a translation right or up on a coordinate plane. A *negative* integer describes a translation left or down.

EXAMPLE   Find Coordinates of a Translation

2 Triangle *LMN* has vertices *L*(−1, −2), *M*(6, −3), and *N*(2, −5). Find the vertices of △*L'M'N'* after a translation of 6 units left and 4 units up. Then graph the figure and its translated image.

The vertices can be found by adding −6 to the *x*-coordinates and 4 to the *y*-coordinates.

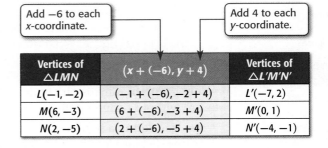

Add −6 to each x-coordinate.   Add 4 to each y-coordinate.

Vertices of △*LMN*	$(x + (-6), y + 4)$	Vertices of △*L'M'N'*
L(−1, −2)	(−1 + (−6), −2 + 4)	*L'*(−7, 2)
M(6, −3)	(6 + (−6), −3 + 4)	*M'*(0, 1)
N(2, −5)	(2 + (−6), −5 + 4)	*N'*(−4, −1)

Use the vertices of △*LMN* and of △*L'M'N'* to graph each triangle.

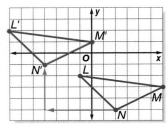

CHECK Your Progress   See margin.

b. Triangle *TUV* has vertices *T*(6, −3), *U*(−2, 0), and *V*(−1, 2). Find the vertices of △*T'U'V'* after a translation of 3 units right and 4 units down. Then graph the figure and its translated image.

Online **Personal Tutor** at ca.gr6math.com

In Example 2, △*LMN* was translated 6 units left and 4 units up. This translation can be described using the ordered pair (−6, 4). In Check Your Progress b., △*TUV* was translated 3 units right and 4 units down. This translation can be described using the ordered pair (3, −4).

Math Online **Extra Examples at** ca.gr6math.com

Tips for New Teachers

Translations

Make sure students understand that translating a figure horizontally and then vertically is the same as translating it once, diagonally.

Additional Answer

b. *T'*(9, −7), *U'*(1, −4), *V'*(2, −2)

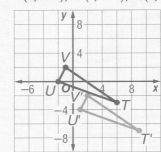

★ indicates multi-step problem

✓ CHECK Your Understanding

Example 1
(p. 553)

1. Translate △ABC 3 units left and 3 units down. Graph △A'B'C'. **See margin.**

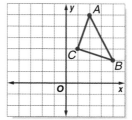

Example 2
(p. 554)

Quadrilateral DEFG has vertices D(1, 0), E(−2, −2), F(2, 4), and G(6, −3). Find the vertices of D'E'F'G' after each translation. Then graph the figure and its translated image.

2. *D′*(5, −5), *E′*(2, −7), *F′*(6, −1), *G′*(10, −8)

2. 4 units right, 5 units down   3. 6 units right
2–3. See Ch. 10 Answer Appendix for graphs.

3. *D′*(7, 0), *E′*(4, −2), *F′*(8, 4), *G′*(12, −3)

4. **GAMES** When playing chess, the rook can only move vertically or horizontally across a chessboard. The chessboard at the right shows the movement of a rook after two turns. Describe this translation in words and as an ordered pair. **5 units left and 3 units up; (−5, 3)**

Exercises

HOMEWORK HELP	
For Exercises	**See Examples**
5–6	1
7–12	2

Exercise Levels
A: 5–12
B: 13–21
C: 22–24

5–6. See Ch. 10 Answer Appendix.

7. *P′*(6, 5), *Q′*(11, 3), *R′*(3, 11),
8. *P′*(−8, −1), *Q′*(−3, −3), *R′*(−11, 5)

11. right 2, down 3; (2, −3)

12. left 2, up 3; (−2, 3)

5. Translate △HIJ 2 units right and 6 units down. Graph △H'I'J'.

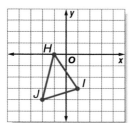

6. Translate rectangle KLMN 1 unit left and 3 units up. Graph rectangle K'L'M'N'.

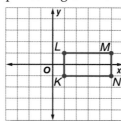

Triangle PQR has vertices P(0, 0), Q(5, −2), and R(−3, 6). Find the vertices of P'Q'R' after each translation. Then graph the figure and its translated image. 7–10. See Ch. 10 Answer Appendix for graphs.

7. 6 units right, 5 units up   8. 8 units left, 1 unit down

9. 3 units left   10. 9 units down
9. *P′*(−3, 0), *Q′*(2, −2), *R′*(−6, 6)   10. *P′*(0, −9), *Q′*(5, −11), *R′*(−3, −3)

MAPS Payat lives at the corner of Wabash and Ohio. His school is located at Huron and Dearborn. Describe each of the following as a translation and as an ordered pair of the number of blocks.

11. Payat's walk from school to home

12. Payat's walk from home to school

Lesson 10-9 Translations **555**

ADDITIONAL EXAMPLE

2. Trapezoid *GHIJ* has vertices *G*(−4, 1), *H*(−4, 3), *I*(−2, 3), and *J*(−1, 1). Find the vertices of trapezoid *G'H'I'J'* after a translation of 5 units right and 3 units down. Then graph the figure and its translated image. *G′*(1, −2), *H′*(1, 0), *I′*(3, 0), *J′*(4, −2)

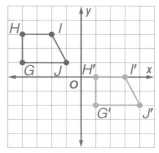

3 Practice

✓ Formative Assessment

Use Exercises 1–4 to check for understanding.

Then use the chart at the bottom of this page to customize your assignments for students.

Intervention You may wish to use the Study Guide and Intervention Master on page 58 of the *Chapter 10 Resource Masters* for additional reinforcement.

Odd/Even Assignments

Exercises 5–12 are structured so that students practice the same concepts whether they are assigned odd or even problems.

Additional Answer

1.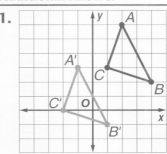

DIFFERENTIATED HOMEWORK OPTIONS

Level	Assignment	Two-Day Option	
BL Basic	5–12, 23–41	5–11 odd, 25, 26	6–12 even, 23, 24, 27–41
OL Core	5–9 odd, 11–13, 15–17, 19, 21, 24–41	5–12, 25, 26	13–21, 23, 24, 27–41
AL Advanced/Pre-AP	13–37 (optional: 38–41)		

Additional Answers

13.

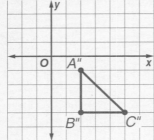

14.

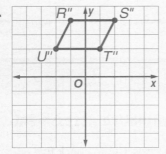

15. Sample answer: There are two main images, the brown horseman and the yellow horeseman. Both main horsemen are translated to different parts of the picture. These translations allow for the tessellation of both horsemen.

17.

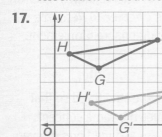

24. The final image is 3 units left and 3 units up from the original figure.

13–14. See margin.

13. ★ Triangle *ABC* is translated 2 units left and 3 units down. Then the translated figure is translated 3 units right. Graph the resulting triangle.

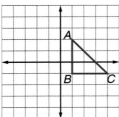

14. ★ Parallelogram *RSTU* is translated 3 units right and 5 units up. Then the translated figure is translated 2 units left. Graph the resulting parallelogram.

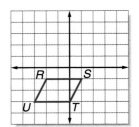

15. ART Explain how translations and tessellations were used in *Horsemen*, created by M.C. Escher at the right. See margin.

16. RESEARCH Use the Internet or another source to find other pieces of art that contain tessellations of translations. Describe how the artists incorporated both ideas into their work. **See students' work.**

17. Triangle *FGH* has vertices *F*(7, 6), *G*(3, 4), *H*(1, 5).Find the coordinates of △*F'G'H'* after a translation $1\frac{1}{2}$ units right and $3\frac{1}{2}$ units down. Then graph the figure and its translated image.

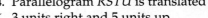

17. $F'\left(8\frac{1}{2}, 2\frac{1}{2}\right)$, $G'\left(4\frac{1}{2}, \frac{1}{2}\right)$, $H'\left(2\frac{1}{2}, 1\frac{1}{2}\right)$;

See margin for graph.

EXTRA PRACTICE
See pages 707, 724.
Math Online
Self-Check Quiz at
ca.gr6math.com

H.O.T. Problems

18. 2 units right and 5 units up; (2, 5)
19. 5 units left and 3 units down; (−5, −3)
23. Transformation A is not a translation; the others are translations.

REASONING The coordinates of a point and its image after a translation are given. Describe the translation in words and as an ordered pair.

18. $N(0, -3) \rightarrow N'(2, 2)$

19. $M(2, 4) \rightarrow M'(-3, 1)$

20. $P(-2, -1) \rightarrow P'(3, -2)$
5 units right and 1 unit down; (5, −1)

21. $Q(-4, 0) \rightarrow Q'(1, 4)$
5 units right and 4 units up; (5, 4)

22. CHALLENGE Is it possible to make a tessellation with translations of an equilateral triangle? Explain your reasoning.
No; the triangle has to be flipped in order to make a tessellation.

23. Which One Doesn't Belong? Identify the transformation that is not the same as the other three. Explain your reasoning.

24. WRITING IN MATH Triangle *ABC* is translated 4 units right and 2 units down. Then the translated image is translated again 7 units left and 5 units up. Describe the final translated image in words. **See margin.**

Pre-AP Activity Use after Exercises 18–21

Write two points such as (x, y) and $(v - 1, w + 2)$ on the board. Tell students to translate both points 5 units right and 2 units down. Have them write the coordinates of the translated points.
$(x + 5, y - 2), (v + 4, w)$

25. Which graph shows a translation of the letter Z? **B**

A

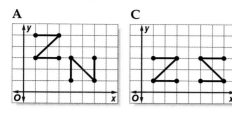

C

B

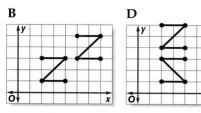

D

26. If point A is translated 4 units left and 3 units up, what will be the coordinates of point A in its new position? **G**

F $(4, 4)$

G $(-5, 5)$

H $(-5, -1)$

J $(-4, 3)$

Spiral Review

27. GEOMETRY What is the name of a polygon with eight sides? (Lesson 10-8) **octagon**

28. GEOMETRY The triangles at the right are similar. What is the measure of $\angle F$? (Lesson 10-7) **30°**

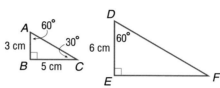

29. FOOD For dinner, you can choose one of two appetizers, one of four entrées, and one of three desserts. How many possible unique dinners can you choose? (Lesson 9-3) **2 × 4 × 3 or 24 dinners**

For each set of data, describe how the range would change if the value 15 was added to the data set. (Lesson 8-1) **30–33. See margin.**

30. $\{8, 17, 32\}$ **31.** $\{22, 38, 41, 77\}$ **32.** $\{10, 10, 19\}$ **33.** $\{7, 11, 13\}$

Write each percent as a decimal. (Lesson 4-7)

34. 83.8% **0.838**   **35.** 56.7% **0.567**   **36.** 3.8% **0.038**   **37.** 102.6% **1.026**

GET READY for the Next Lesson

PREREQUISITE SKILL Determine whether each figure can be folded in half so that one side matches the other. Write *yes* or *no*.

38.
yes

39.
no

40.
no

41.
yes

Crystal Ball Tell students that tomorrow's lesson is about another kind of transformation: reflections. Have students write how they think what they learned today will connect with tomorrow's material.

FOLDABLES Study Organizer **Foldables™ Follow-Up**

Remind students to complete the second and third columns in their Foldable about translations of polygons.

Additional Answers

30. The range would remain unchanged.

31. The range would be 62 instead of 55.

32. The range would remain unchanged.

33. The range would be 8 instead of 6.

10-10 Reflections

Preparation for 7MG3.2 **Understand and use coordinate graphs to plot simple figures,** determine lengths and areas related to them, **and determine their image under** translations and **reflections.**

PACING: **Regular:** 1 period, **Block:** 0.5 period

Options for Differentiated Instruction

ELL = English Language Learner **AL** = Above Grade Level **SS** = Struggling Students **SN** = Special Needs

Using Tables **SS** **SN**

Use with Examples 4 and 5.

Students may be confused as to which coordinate changes when reflecting a figure over an axis. Provide tables like the ones below as you present Examples 4 and 5.

Example 4

Vertices of △ ABC	Distance from x-axis	Vertices of △ A'B'C'
A(5, 2)	2	A'(5, −2)
B(1, 3)	3	B'(1, −3)
C(−1, 1)	1	C'(−1, −1)

Example 5

Vertices of quad KLMN	Distance from y-axis	Vertices of quad K'L'M'N'
K(2, 3)	2	K'(−2, 3)
L(5, 1)	5	L'(−5, 1)
M(4, −2)	4	M'(−4, −2)
N(1, −1)	1	N'(−1, −1)

Point out the following:

- A reflection across the x-axis requires a change in the y-coordinates, with the x-coordinates remaining constant.
- A reflection across the y-axis requires a change in the x-coordinates, with the y-coordinates remaining constant.

Homework Help Sheets **SS** **SN**

Use with the Exercises.

Create homework help sheets that have coordinate grids with different quadrants, like the ones shown below. Students can use these to help them complete the exercises that require graphing.

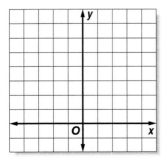 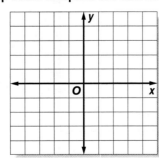 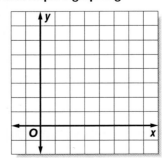

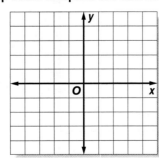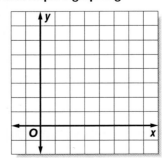

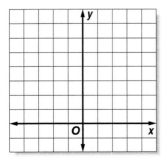

Leveled Lesson Resources

Also on **TeacherWorks™** Lesson 10-10

Chapter 10 Resource Masters

BL = Below Grade Level   OL = On Grade Level   AL = Above Grade Level   ELL = English Language Learner

Lesson Reading Guide
p. 64 BL OL ELL

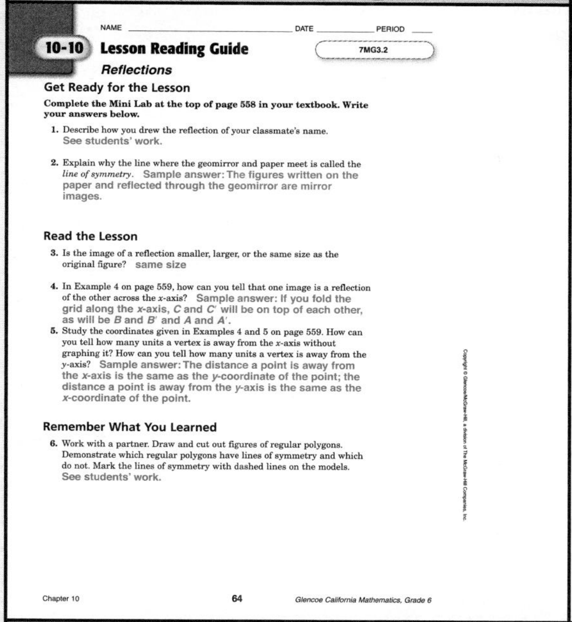
NAME ____ DATE ____ PERIOD ____

10-10 Lesson Reading Guide 7MG3.2
Reflections

Get Ready for the Lesson
Complete the Mini Lab at the top of page 558 in your textbook. Write your answers below.
1. Describe how you drew the reflection of your classmate's name. See students' work.
2. Explain why the line where the geomirror and paper meet is called the *line of symmetry*. Sample answer: The figures written on the paper and reflected through the geomirror are mirror images.

Read the Lesson
3. Is the image of a reflection smaller, larger, or the same size as the original figure? same size
4. In Example 4 on page 559, how can you tell that one image is a reflection of the other across the *x*-axis? Sample answer: If you fold the grid along the *x*-axis, *C* and *C'* will be on top of each other, as will be *B* and *B'* and *A* and *A'*.
5. Study the coordinates given in Examples 4 and 5 on page 559. How can you tell how many units a vertex is away from the *x*-axis without graphing it? How can you tell how many units a vertex is away from the *y*-axis? Sample answer: The distance a point is away from the *x*-axis is the same as the *y*-coordinate of the point; the distance a point is away from the *y*-axis is the same as the *x*-coordinate of the point.

Remember What You Learned
6. Work with a partner. Draw and cut out figures of regular polygons. Demonstrate which regular polygons have lines of symmetry and which do not. Mark the lines of symmetry with dashed lines on the models. See students' work.

Chapter 10 64 Glencoe California Mathematics, Grade 6

*Study Guide and Intervention**
p. 65 BL OL ELL

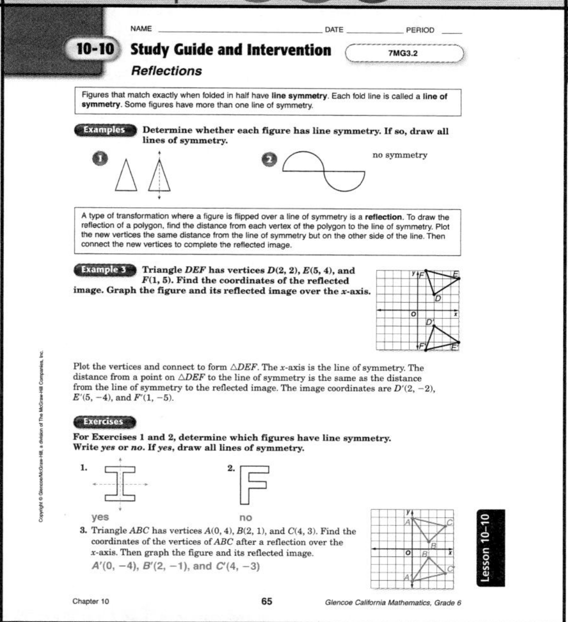
NAME ____ DATE ____ PERIOD ____

10-10 Study Guide and Intervention 7MG3.2
Reflections

Figures that match exactly when folded in half have **line symmetry**. Each fold line is called a **line of symmetry**. Some figures have more than one line of symmetry.

Examples Determine whether each figure has line symmetry. If so, draw all lines of symmetry.

1 2 no symmetry

A type of transformation where a figure is flipped over a line of symmetry is a **reflection**. To draw the reflection of a polygon, find the distance from each vertex of the polygon to the line of symmetry. Plot the new vertices the same distance from the line of symmetry but on the other side of the line. Then connect the new vertices to complete the reflected image.

Example 3 Triangle *DEF* has vertices *D*(2, 2), *E*(5, 4), and *F*(1, 5). Find the coordinates of the reflected image. Graph the figure and its reflected image over the *x*-axis.

Plot the vertices and connect to form △*DEF*. The *x*-axis is the line of symmetry. The distance from a point on △*DEF* to the line of symmetry is the same as the distance from the line of symmetry to the reflected image. The image coordinates are *D'*(2, −2), *E'*(5, −4), and *F'*(1, −5).

Exercises
For Exercises 1 and 2, determine which figures have line symmetry. If yes, draw all lines of symmetry.
1. yes 2. no
3. Triangle *ABC* has vertices *A*(0, 4), *B*(2, 1), and *C*(4, 3). Find the coordinates of the vertices of *ABC* after a reflection over the *x*-axis. Then graph the figure and its reflected image. *A'*(0, −4), *B'*(2, −1), and *C'*(4, −3)

Lesson 10-10

Chapter 10 65 Glencoe California Mathematics, Grade 6

*Skills Practice**
p. 66 BL OL

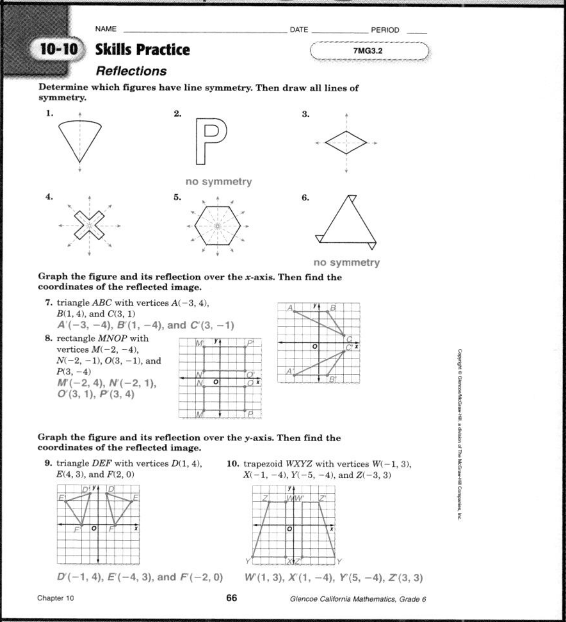
NAME ____ DATE ____ PERIOD ____

10-10 Skills Practice 7MG3.2
Reflections

Determine which figures have line symmetry. Then draw all lines of symmetry.
1. 2. no symmetry 3.
4. 5. 6. no symmetry

Graph the figure and its reflection over the *x*-axis. Then find the coordinates of the reflected image.
7. triangle *ABC* with vertices *A*(−3, 4), *B*(1, 4), and *C*(3, 1) *A'*(−3, −4), *B'*(1, −4), and *C'*(3, −1)
8. rectangle *MNOP* with vertices *M*(−2, −4), *N*(−2, −1), *O*(3, −1), and *P*(3, −4) *M'*(−2, 4), *N'*(−2, 1), *O'*(3, 1), *P'*(3, 4)

Graph the figure and its reflection over the *y*-axis. Then find the coordinates of the reflected image.
9. triangle *DEF* with vertices *D*(1, 4), *E*(4, 3), and *F*(2, 0) *D'*(−1, 4), *E'*(−4, 3), and *F'*(−2, 0)
10. trapezoid *WXYZ* with vertices *W*(−1, 3), *X*(−1, −4), *Y*(−5, −4), and *Z*(−3, 3) *W'*(1, 3), *X'*(1, −4), *Y'*(5, −4), *Z'*(3, 3)

Chapter 10 66 Glencoe California Mathematics, Grade 6

*Practice**
p. 67 OL AL

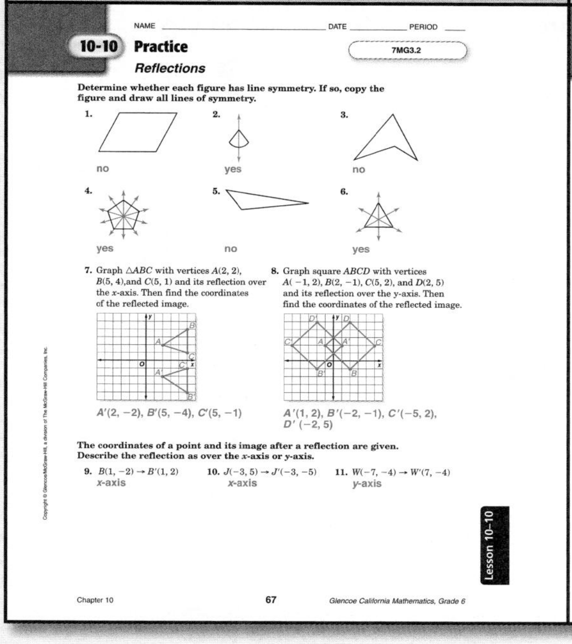
NAME ____ DATE ____ PERIOD ____

10-10 Practice 7MG3.2
Reflections

Determine whether each figure has line symmetry. If so, copy the figure and draw all lines of symmetry.
1. no 2. yes 3. no
4. yes 5. no 6. yes

7. Graph △*ABC* with vertices *A*(2, 2), *B*(5, 4), and *C*(5, 1) and its reflection over the *x*-axis. Then find the coordinates of the reflected image. *A'*(2, −2), *B'*(5, −4), *C'*(5, −1)
8. Graph square *ABCD* with vertices *A*(−1, 2), *B*(2, −1), *C*(5, 2), and *D*(2, 5) and its reflection over the *y*-axis. Then find the coordinates of the reflected image. *A'*(1, 2), *B'*(−2, −1), *C'*(−5, 2), *D'*(−2, 5)

The coordinates of a point and its image after a reflection are given. Describe the reflection as over the *x*-axis or *y*-axis.
9. *B*(1, −2) → *B'*(1, 2) *x*-axis
10. *J*(−3, 5) → *J'*(−3, −5) *x*-axis
11. *W*(−7, −4) → *W'*(7, −4) *y*-axis

Lesson 10-10

Chapter 10 67 Glencoe California Mathematics, Grade 6

*Word Problem Practice**
p. 68 OL AL

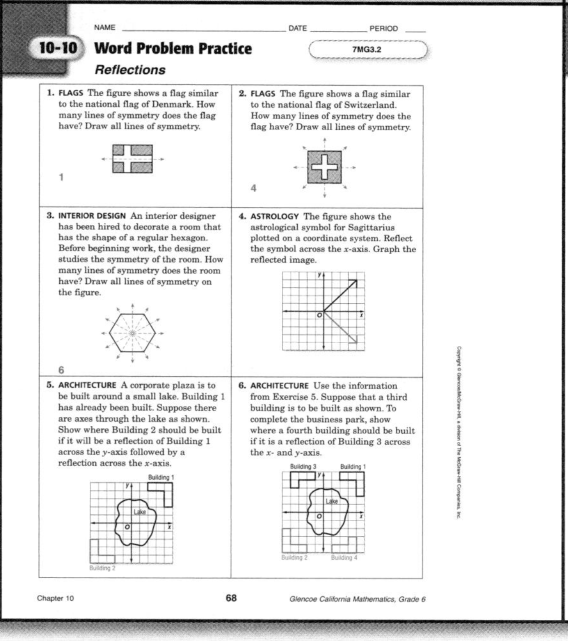
NAME ____ DATE ____ PERIOD ____

10-10 Word Problem Practice 7MG3.2
Reflections

1. FLAGS The figure shows a flag similar to the national flag of Denmark. How many lines of symmetry does the flag have? Draw all lines of symmetry. 1
2. FLAGS The figure shows a flag similar to the national flag of Switzerland. How many lines of symmetry does the flag have? Draw all lines of symmetry. 4
3. INTERIOR DESIGN An interior designer has been hired to decorate a room that has the shape of a regular hexagon. Before beginning work, the designer studies the symmetry of the room. How many lines of symmetry does the room have? Draw all lines of symmetry on the figure. 6
4. ASTROLOGY The figure shows the astrological symbol for Sagittarius plotted on a coordinate system. Reflect the symbol across the *x*-axis. Graph the reflected image.
5. ARCHITECTURE A corporate plaza is to be built around a small lake. Building 1 has already been built. Suppose there are axes through the lake as shown. Show where Building 2 should be built if it will be a reflection of Building 1 across the *y*-axis followed by a reflection across the *x*-axis.
6. ARCHITECTURE Use the information from Exercise 5. Suppose that a third building is to be built as shown. To complete the business park, show where a fourth building should be built if it is a reflection of Building 3 across the *x*- and *y*-axis.

Chapter 10 68 Glencoe California Mathematics, Grade 6

Enrichment
p. 69 OL AL

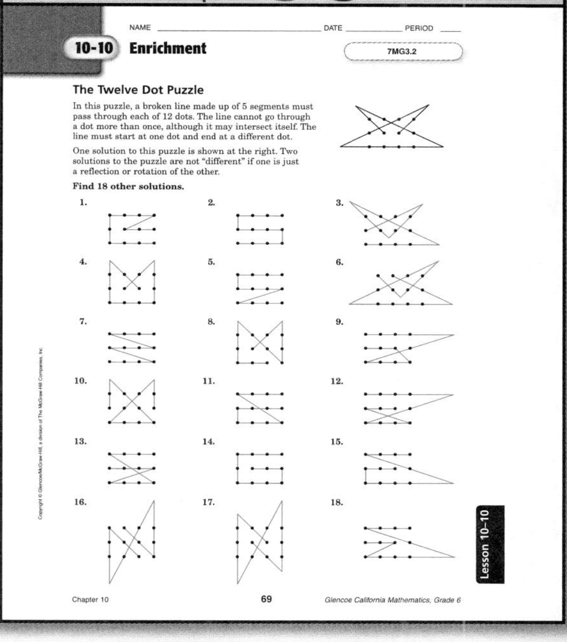
NAME ____ DATE ____ PERIOD ____

10-10 Enrichment 7MG3.2

The Twelve Dot Puzzle
In this puzzle, a broken line made up of 5 segments must pass through each of 12 dots. The line cannot go through a dot more than once, although it may intersect itself. The line must start at one dot and end at a different dot.
One solution to this puzzle is shown at the right. Two solutions to the puzzle are not "different" if one is just a reflection or rotation of the other.
Find 18 other solutions.
1. 2. 3. 4. 5. 6. 7. 8. 9. 10. 11. 12. 13. 14. 15. 16. 17. 18.

Lesson 10-10

Chapter 10 69 Glencoe California Mathematics, Grade 6

Additional Lesson Resources

** Also available in Spanish* ELL

Transparencies
- *5-Minute Check Transparency,* Lesson 10-10

Other Print Products
- *Teaching Mathematics with Manipulatives*
- *Noteables™ Interactive Study Notebook with Foldables™*

Teacher Tech Tools
- *Interactive Classroom CD-ROM,* Lesson 10-10
- *AssignmentWorks CD-ROM,* Lesson 10-10

Student Tech Tools
ca.gr6math.com
- Extra Examples, Chapter 10, Lesson 10
- Self-Check Quiz, Chapter 10, Lesson 10

1 Focus

 Standards Alignment

Before Lesson 10-10
Identify and graph ordered pairs in the four quadrants of the coordinate plane from Standard 5AF1.4

Lesson 10-10
Use coordinate graphs to plot simple figures and determine their image under translations and reflections from Standard 7MG3.2

After Lesson 10-10
Demonstrate an understanding of conditions that indicate two geometrical figures are congruent and what congruence means about the relationships between the sides and angles of the two figures from Standard 7MG3.4

2 Teach

▶ **MINI Lab**

Make sure students print their names and their classmates' names in block, upper-case letters.

Scaffolding Questions

Have students imagine they are looking at their reflections in a mirror.

Ask:

• On which side of your reflection does your left arm appear? right side

• On which side of your reflection does your right arm appear? left side

• Is your reflection the same size and shape as your body? yes

---

10-10 Reflections

Main IDEA

Identify figures with line symmetry and graph reflections on a coordinate plane.

 Preparation for Standard 7MG3.2
Understand and use coordinate graphs to plot simple figures, determine lengths and areas related to them, **and determine their image under translations and reflections.**

NEW Vocabulary

line symmetry
line of symmetry
reflection
line of reflection

1. See students' work.
2. Sample answer: The figures written on the paper and reflected through the geomirror are mirror images.

▶ **MINI Lab**

• Write your first name in capital letters on a sheet of paper.

• Use the geomirror to trace the reflection of the letters in your name.

• Write a classmate's name. Draw the reflection of the letters without using the geomirror.

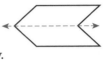

1. Describe how you drew the reflection of your classmate's name.

2. Explain why the line where the geomirror and paper meet is called the *line of symmetry*.

Figures that match exactly when folded in half have **line symmetry**. The figures at the right have line symmetry.

Each fold line is called a **line of symmetry**.

▶ **Real-World EXAMPLES**

GRAPHIC DESIGN Determine whether each figure has line symmetry. If so, copy the figure and draw all lines of symmetry.

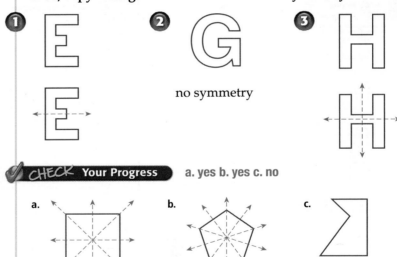

① E

② G   no symmetry

③ H

✓ **CHECK Your Progress**   a. yes b. yes c. no

a.   b.   c.

✓ **Formative Assessment**

Use the Check Your Progress exercises after each Example to determine students' understanding of concepts.

A **reflection** is a mirror image of the original figure. It is the result of a transformation of a figure over a line called a **line of reflection**.

EXAMPLE Reflect a Figure Over the *x*-axis

④ Triangle *ABC* has vertices *A*(5, 2), *B*(1, 3), and *C*(−1, 1). Graph the figure and its reflected image over the *x*-axis. Then find the coordinates of the vertices of the reflected image.

The *x*-axis is the line of reflection. So, plot each vertex of *A′B′C′* the same distance from the *x*-axis as its corresponding vertex on *ABC*.

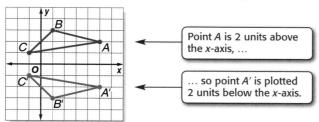

Point *A* is 2 units above the *x*-axis, …

… so point *A′* is plotted 2 units below the *x*-axis.

The coordinates are *A′*(5, −2), *B′*(1, −3), and *C′*(−1, −1).

CHECK Your Progress d. See margin.

d. Rectangle *GHIJ* has vertices *G*(3, −4), *H*(3, −1), *I*(−2, −1), and *J*(−2, −4). Graph the figure and its image after a reflection over the *x*-axis. Then find the coordinates of the reflected image.

Online Personal Tutor at ca.gr6math.com

EXAMPLE Reflect a Figure Over the *y*-axis

⑤ Quadrilateral *KLMN* has vertices *K*(2, 3), *L*(5, 1), *M*(4, −2), and *N*(1, −1). Graph the figure and its reflected image over the *y*-axis. Then find the coordinates of the vertices of the reflected image.

The *y*-axis is the line of reflection. So, plot each vertex of *K′L′M′N′* the same distance from the *y*-axis as its corresponding vertex on *KLMN*.

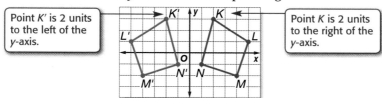

Point *K′* is 2 units to the left of the *y*-axis.

Point *K* is 2 units to the right of the *y*-axis.

The coordinates are *K′*(−2, 3), *L′*(−5, 1), *M′*(−4, −2), and *N′*(−1, −1).

CHECK Your Progress

e. Triangle *PQR* has vertices *P*(1, 5), *Q*(3, 7), and *R*(5, −1). Graph the figure and its reflection over the *y*-axis. Then find the coordinates of the reflected image. See margin.

Additional Answers

d. 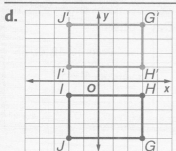 *G′*(3, 4), *H′*(3, 1), *I′*(−2, 1), and *J′*(−2, 4)

e. 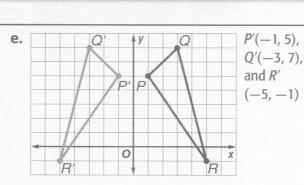 *P′*(−1, 5), *Q′*(−3, 7), and *R′* (−5, −1)

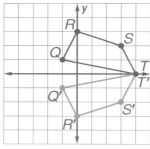
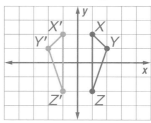

Formative Assessment

Use Exercises 1–8 to check for understanding.

Then use the chart at the bottom of this page to customize your assignments for students.

Intervention You may wish to use the Study Guide and Intervention Master on page 65 of the *Chapter 10 Resource Masters* for additional reinforcement.

Odd/Even Assignments

Exercises 9–24 are structured so that students practice the same concepts whether they are assigned odd or even problems.

Additional Answers

2.

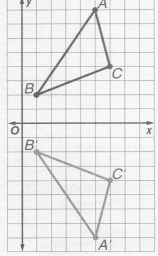

3.

5.

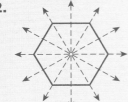

CHECK Your Understanding

Examples 1–3 (p. 558)

Determine whether each figure has line symmetry. If so, copy the figure and draw all lines of symmetry. 2–3. See margin for drawings.

1. no   2. yes   3. yes

4. **INSECTS** Identify the number of lines of symmetry in the photo of the butterfly at the right. 1

Example 4 (p. 559)

5. *A'*(5, −8), *B'*(1, −2), and *C'*(6, −4); See margin for graph.

Graph each figure and its reflection over the *x*-axis. Then find the coordinates of the reflected image.

5. △*ABC* with vertices *A*(5, 8), *B*(1, 2), and *C*(6, 4)

6. quadrilateral *DEFG* with vertices *D*(−3, 6), *E*(−2, −3), *F*(2, 2), and *G*(4, 9)
   D'(−3, −6), *E'*(−2, 3), *F'*(2, −2), and *G'*(4, −9)

Example 5 (p. 559)

6–8. See Ch. 10 Answer Appendix for graphs.

Graph each figure and its reflection over the *y*-axis. Then find the coordinates of the reflected image. *Q'*(−2, −5), *R'*(−4, −5), and *S'*(−2, 3)

7. △*QRS* with vertices *Q*(2, −5), *R*(4, −5), and *S*(2, 3)

8. parallelogram *WXYZ* with vertices *W*(−4, −2), *X*(−4, 3), *Y*(−2, 4), and *Z*(−2, −1) *W'*(4, −2), *X'*(4, 3), *Y'*(2, 4), and *Z'*(2, −1)

Exercises

HOMEWORK HELP	
For Exercises	**See Examples**
9–14 23–24	1, 3
15–18	4
19–22	5

Exercise Levels
A: 9–24
B: 25–35
C: 36–38

Determine whether each figure has line symmetry. If so, copy the figure and draw all lines of symmetry. 9–14. See Ch. 10 Answer Appendix for drawings.

9. 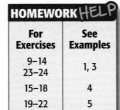 yes   10.  no   11.  yes

12. 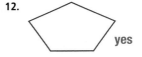 yes   13.  yes   14.  no

Graph each figure and its reflection over the *x*-axis. Then find the coordinates of the reflected image. 15–18. See Ch. 10 Answer Appendix.

15. △*TUV* with vertices *T*(−6, −1), *U*(−2, −3), and *V*(5, −4)

16. △*MNP* with vertices *M*(2, 1), *N*(−3, 1), and *P*(−1, 4)

17. square *ABCD* with vertices *A*(2, 4), *B*(−2, 4), *C*(−2, 8), and *D*(2, 8)

18. trapezoid *WXYZ* with vertices *W*(−1, −1), *X*(4, 1), *Y*(4, 5), and *Z*(1, 7)

DIFFERENTIATED HOMEWORK OPTIONS			
Level	**Assignment**	**Two-Day Option**	
BL Basic	9–24, 36, 38–45	9–23 odd, 39, 40	10–24 even, 36, 38, 41–45
OL Core	9–23 odd, 24, 25, 27–35 odd, 36, 38–45	9–24, 39, 40	26–36, 38, 41–45
AL Advanced/Pre-AP	25–45		

Graph each figure and its reflection over the *y*-axis. Then find the coordinates of the reflected image. **19–22. See margin for graphs.**

19. △RST with vertices R(−5, 3), S(−4, −2), and T(−2, 3) **R′(5, 3), S′(4, −2), T′(2, 3)**

20. G′(−4, 2), H′(−3, −4), J′(−1, 1)

20. △GHJ with vertices G(4, 2), H(3, −4), and J(1, 1)

21. H′(1, 3), I′(1, −1), J′(−2, −2), and K′(−2, 2)

21. parallelogram HIJK with vertices H(−1, 3), I(−1, −1), J(2, −2), and K(2, 2)

22. quadrilateral DEFG with vertices D(1, 0), E(1, −5), F(4, −1), and G(3, 2) **D′(−1, 0), E′(−1, −5), F′(−4, −1), G′(−3, 2)**

23–24. See Ch. 10 Answer Appendix.

23. **BUILDINGS** Describe the location of the line(s) of symmetry in the photograph of the Taj Mahal, which is in India.

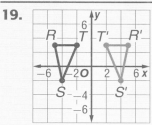

24. **SIGNAL FLAGS** International Marine Signal Flags are used by sailors to send messages at sea. The signal flags shown spell out the word *MATH*. Which flags have line symmetry? Draw all lines of symmetry.

M   A   T   H

25. **MUSIC** Use the photo at the left to determine how many lines of symmetry the body of a violin has. **1**

Real-World Link . . . .
A violin is usually around 14 inches long.

For Exercises 26–29, use the graph shown at the right.

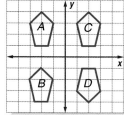

26. Identify the pair(s) of figures for which the *x*-axis is the line of reflection. **figures C and D**

27. For which pair(s) of figures is the line of reflection the *y*-axis? **figures A and C**

28. What type of transformation do figures B and C represent? **translation**

29–31. See Ch. 10 Answer Appendix.

29. Describe the possible transformation(s) required to move figure A onto figure D.

★ 30. △RST is reflected over the *x*-axis and then translated 3 units to the left and 2 units down. Graph the resulting triangle.

★ 31. △MNP is translated 2 units right and 3 units up. Then the translated figure is reflected over the *y*-axis. Graph the resulting triangle.

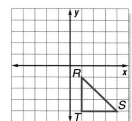 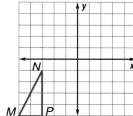

EXTRA PRACTICE
See pages 707, 724.

Math Online
Self-Check Quiz at ca.gr6math.com

Lesson 10-10 Reflections **561**

Tips for New Teachers

Transformations
You may wish to tell students that the vertices of a figure that has been transformed twice (as in Exercises 30, 31 and 37) are written with double prime symbols (″). For example, point *R* in Exercise 30 would be written *R″* after being reflected and translated.

Additional Answers

19.

20.

21.

22.
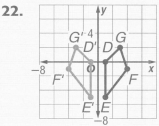
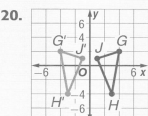
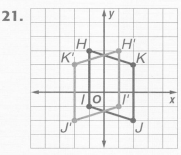

Ticket Out the Door Have students draw a real-world object that has line symmetry (or near line symmetry). Make sure they show the line(s) of symmetry. Many buildings and manufactured products have line symmetry. Do any plants, animals, or minerals show line symmetry?

 Formative Assessment

Check for student understanding of concepts in Lessons 10–9 and 10–10.

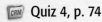 Quiz 4, p. 74

FOLDABLES™ Follow-Up

Remind students to complete the second and third columns in their Foldable about line symmetry and reflections of polygons.

Additional Answers

38. Sample answer:

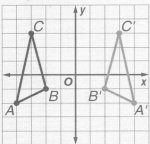

the *x*- and *y*-coordinates of the reflected figure are the same distance from the *y*-axis as the *x*- and *y*-coordinates of the original figure.

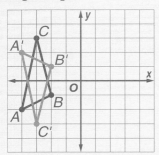

The coordinates of a point and its image after a reflection are given. Describe the reflection as over the *x*-axis or *y*-axis.

32. $A(-3, 5) \rightarrow A'(3, 5)$ *y*-axis

33. $M(3, 3) \rightarrow M'(3, -3)$ *x*-axis

34. $X(-1, -4) \rightarrow X'(-1, 4)$ *x*-axis

35. $W(-4, 0) \rightarrow W'(4, 0)$ *y*-axis

H.O.T. Problems

36. OPEN ENDED Make a tessellation using a combination of translations and reflections of polygons. Explain your method. **See students' work.**

37. $J''(7, -4)$, $K''(-7, -1)$, and $L''(-2, 2)$

37. CHALLENGE Triangle *JKL* has vertices $J(-7, 4)$, $K(7, 1)$, and $L(2, -2)$. Without graphing, find the new coordinates of the vertices of the triangle after a reflection first over the *x*-axis and then over the *y*-axis.

38. WRITING IN MATH Draw a figure on a coordinate plane and its reflection over the *y*-axis. Explain how the *x*- and *y*-coordinates of the reflected figure relate to the *x*- and *y*-coordinates of the original figure. Then repeat, this time reflecting the figure over the *x*-axis. **See margin.**

STANDARDS PRACTICE   7MG3.2

39. The figure shown was transformed from quadrant II to quadrant III.

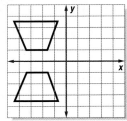

This transformation best represents which of the following? **C**

A translation   **C** reflection

B tessellation   **D** rotation

40. If *ABCD* is reflected over the *x*-axis and translated 5 units to the right, which is the resulting image of point *B*? **F**

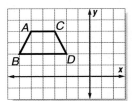

F $(-1, -2)$ **H** $(-1, 2)$

G $(-11, 2)$ **J** $(11, 2)$

Spiral Review

41. GEOMETRY Triangle *FGH* has vertices $F(-3, 7)$, $G(-1, 5)$, and $H(-2, 2)$. Graph the figure and its image after a translation 4 units right and 1 unit down. Write the ordered pairs for the vertices of the image. (Lesson 10-9)
$F'(1, 6)$, $G'(3, 4)$, $H'(2, 1)$; **See margin for graph.**

42. GEOMETRY Melissa wishes to construct a tessellation for a wall hanging made only from regular decagons. Is this possible? Explain. (Lesson 10-8)
No, the measure of one angle is 144°, which is not a factor of 360°.

Estimate. (Lesson 5-1) **43–45. Sample answers are given.**

43. $\frac{4}{9} + 8\frac{1}{9}$ $\frac{1}{2} + 8 = 8\frac{1}{2}$ **44.** $\frac{1}{9} \times \frac{2}{5}$ $0 \times \frac{1}{2} = 0$ **45.** $12\frac{1}{4} \div 5\frac{6}{7}$ $12 \div 6 = 2$

the *x*- and *y*-coordinates of the reflected figure are the same distance from the *x*-axis as the *x*- and *y*-coordinates of the original figure.

41.

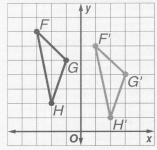

CHAPTER 10 Study Guide and Review

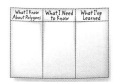

FOLDABLES™
Study Organizer

GET READY to Study

Be sure the following Key Concepts are noted in your Foldable.

What I Know About Polygons	What I Need to Know	What I've Learned

Key Concepts

Angles (Lessons 10-1 and 10-2)
- Two angles are adjacent if they have the same vertex, share a common side, and do not overlap.
- Two angles are vertical if they are opposite angles formed by the intersection of two lines.
- Two angles are complementary if the sum of their measures is 90°.
- Two angles are supplementary if the sum of their measures is 180°.

Triangles (Lesson 10-4)
- The sum of the measures of the angles of a triangle is 180°.

Quadrilaterals (Lesson 10-6)
- The sum of the measures of the angles of a quadrilateral is 360°.

Similar Figures (Lesson 10-7)
- If two figures are similar then the corresponding sides are proportional and the corresponding angles are congruent.

Transformations (Lessons 10-9 and 10-10)
- When translating a figure, every point in the original figure is moved the same distance in the same direction.
- When reflecting a figure, every point in the original figure is the same distance from the line of reflection as its corresponding point on the original figure.

Key Vocabulary

acute angle (p. 511)

angle (p. 510)

circle graph (p. 518)

complementary angles (p. 514)

congruent angles (p. 511)

congruent figures (p. 554)

degrees (p. 510)

hexagon (p. 546)

indirect measurement (p. 542)

line of symmetry (p. 558)

line symmetry (p. 558)

obtuse angle (p. 511)

octagon (p. 546)

parallelogram (p. 533)

pentagon (p. 546)

polygon (p. 546)

quadrilateral (p. 533)

reflection (p. 559)

regular polygon (p. 546)

rhombus (p. 533)

right angle (p. 511)

similar figures (p. 540)

straight angle (p. 511)

supplementary angles (p. 514)

tessellation (p. 548)

transformation (p. 553)

translation (p. 553)

trapezoid (p. 533)

triangle (p. 524)

vertex (p. 510)

1. false; supplementary angles

Vocabulary Check

State whether each sentence is *true* or *false*. If *false*, replace the underlined word or number to make a true sentence.

1. Two angles whose measures add to 180° are called <u>complementary angles</u>.

2. A <u>hexagon</u> is a polygon with 6 sides. **true**

3. An angle whose measure is less than 90° is called a <u>right angle</u>. **false; acute angle**

4. The <u>vertex</u> is where the sides of angle meet. **true**

5. The point (3, −2) when translated up 3 units and to the left 5 units becomes <u>(6, −7)</u>. **false; (−2, 1)**

6. A <u>trapezoid</u> has both pairs of opposite sides parallel. **false; parallelogram**

FOLDABLES™
Study Organizer

Dinah Zike's Foldables

Have students look through the chapter to make sure they have included notes and examples about the key concepts of each lesson in their Foldables.

Encourage students to refer to their Foldables while completing the Study Guide and Review and while preparing for the Chapter Test.

What I Know About Polygons	What I Need to Know	What I've Learned
2-dimensional figures. Triangles, squares, rectangles, and trapezoids are polygons. Similar polygons are the same shape but not necessarily the same size.	Triangles can be classified by angles: acute, right, obtuse or by sides: scalene, isosceles, equilateral. If two figures are similar then corresponding sides are proportional and corresponding angles are congruent. Translation - every point of the original figure is moved the same distance in the same direction. Reflection - a figure is flipped over a line of symmetry.	The sum of the measures of the angles of a triangle is 180°. The sum of the measures of the angles of a quadrilateral is 360°. A regular polygon has all sides congruent and all angles congruent.

✓ Formative Assessment

Key Vocabulary The page references after each word denote where that term was first introduced. If students have difficulty answering Exercises 1–6, remind them that they can use these page references to refresh their memories about the vocabulary terms.

 **Math Online** ca.gr6math.com

Vocabulary PuzzleMaker improves students' mathematics vocabulary using four puzzle formats—crossword, scramble, word search using a word list, and word search using clues. Students can work online or from a printed worksheet.

✓ Summative Assessment

 Vocabulary Test, p. 76

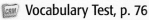

Lesson-by-Lesson Review

Intervention If the given examples are not sufficient to review the topics covered by the questions, remind students that the page references tell them where to review that topic in their textbook.

Two-Day Option Have students complete the Lesson-by-Lesson Review on pages 564–566. Then you can use ExamView Assessment Suite to customize another review worksheet that practices all the objectives of this chapter or only the objectives on which your students need more help.

For more information on ExamView® Assessment Suite, see page 508C.

Differentiated Instruction

Super DVD: MindJogger Plus
Use this DVD as an alternative format of review for the test. For more information on this game show format, see page 508D.

Additional Answers

8. ∠1 and ∠4; Sample answer: Since ∠1 and ∠4 are opposite angles formed by the intersection of two lines, they are vertical angles.

9. Sample answer: ∠1 and ∠2; Since they share a common vertex, a common side, and do not overlap, they are adjacent angles.

12. Favorite Soft Drinks

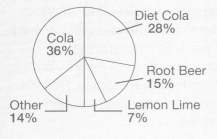

Lesson-by-Lesson Review

10-1 **Angle Relationships** (pp. 510–513) **7.** ∠FGH, ∠HGF, ∠G, or ∠1; obtuse

7. Name the angle shown in four ways. Then classify the angle as *acute, right, obtuse,* or *straight.*

Example 1 Name the angle in four ways.

The angle can be named as ∠JKL, ∠LKJ, ∠K, or ∠5.

For Exercises 8 and 9, refer to the figure at the right to identify each pair of angles. Justify your response.

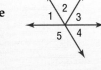

8. a pair of vertical angles

9. a pair of adjacent angles

Example 2 Refer to the figure below. Identify a pair of vertical angles.

∠1 and ∠4 are opposite angles formed by the intersection of two lines.

∠1 and ∠4 are vertical angles.

8–9. See margin.

10-2 **Complementary and Supplementary Angles** (pp. 514–517)

Classify each pair of angles as *complementary, supplementary,* or *neither.*

10.

11.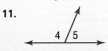

neither   supplementary

Example 3 Find the value of *x*.

$$x + 27 = 90$$
$$-27 = -27$$
$$x = 63$$

10-3 **Statistics: Display Data in a Circle Graph** (pp. 518–523)

12. SOFT DRINKS The table shows favorite soft drinks. Display the set of data in a circle graph. **See margin.**

Soft Drink	Percent
Cola	36%
Diet Cola	28%
Root Beer	15%
Lemon Lime	7%
Other	14%

Example 3 Which season was chosen by about twice as many who chose fall?

Spring, since 40% is about twice as much as 22%.

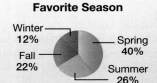

Favorite Season
Winter 12%
Spring 40%
Fall 22%
Summer 26%

10-4 **Triangles** (pp. 564–568)

ALGEBRA Find the value of *x*.

13. 55

14. 45° 45

Example 4 Find the value of *x*.

$$x + 64 + 67 = 180$$
$$x + 131 = 180$$
$$-131 = -131$$
$$x = 49$$

Mixed Problem Solving
For mixed problem-solving practice,
see page 724.

CHAPTER 10 Study Guide and Review

10-5 **PSI: Logical Reasoning** (pp. 530–531)

15. **SPORTS** Donnie, Jenna, Milo, and Barbara play volleyball, field hockey, golf, and soccer but not in that order. Use the clues given below to find the sport each person plays. **See margin.**

- Donnie does not like golf, volleyball, or soccer.
- Neither Milo nor Jenna likes golf.
- Milo does not like soccer.

16. **FOOD** Angelo's Pizza Parlor makes square pizzas. After baking, the pizzas are cut along one diagonal into two triangles. Classify the triangles made.

16. right, isosceles

Example 5 Todd, Virginia, Elaine, and Peter are siblings. Todd was born after Peter, but before Virginia. Elaine is the oldest. Who is the youngest in the family?

Use logical reasoning to determine the youngest of the family.

You know that Elaine is the oldest, so she is first on the list. Todd was born after Peter, but before Virginia. So, Peter was second and then Todd was born. Virginia is the youngest of the family.

Additional Answer

15. Donnie, field hockey; Barbara, golf; Milo, volleyball; Jenna, soccer

10-6 **Quadrilaterals** (pp. 533–539)

Classify the quadrilateral with the name that best describes it.

17.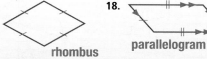

18.

rhombus   parallelogram

19. **GEOMETRY** What quadrilateral does not have opposite sides congruent?

trapezoid

Example 6 Classify the quadrilateral using the name that *best* describes it.

The quadrilateral is a parallelogram with 4 right angles and 4 congruent sides. It is a square.

10-7 **Similar Figures** (pp. 540–545)

Find the value of x in each pair of similar figures.

20.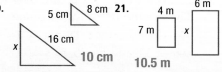
5 cm 8 cm
16 cm
x
10 cm

21.
4 m   6 m
7 m x
10.5 m

22. **FLAGPOLES** Hiroshi is 1.6 meters tall and casts a shadow 0.53 meter in length. How tall is a flagpole if it casts a shadow 2.65 meters in length? 8 m

Example 7

Find the value of x in the pair of similar figures.

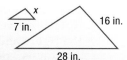
x
7 in.   16 in.
28 in.

$\dfrac{7}{28} = \dfrac{x}{16}$ Write a proportion.

$28 \cdot x = 7 \cdot 16$ Find the cross products.

$28x = 112$ Simplify.

$\dfrac{28x}{28} = \dfrac{112}{28}$ Divide each side by 28.

$x = 4$ Simplify.

So, the value of x is 4.

Problem Solving Review

For additional practice in problem solving for Chapter 10, see the Mixed Problem Solving Appendix, page 724 in the Student Handbook section.

Anticipation Guide

Have students complete the Chapter 10 Anticipation Guide and discuss how their responses have changed now that they have completed Chapter 10.

CRM Anticipation Guide, p. 7

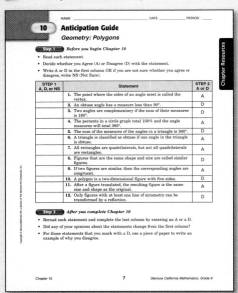

Additional Answer

26. $P'(-2, 1)$, $Q'(-8, 0)$, and $R'(-7, 9)$

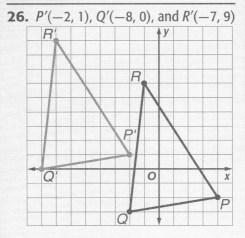

10-8 **Polygons and Tessellations** (pp. 546–551)

Determine whether each figure is a polygon. If it is, classify the polygon and state whether it is regular. If it is *not* a polygon, explain why.

23. nonagon; regular

24. heptagon; not regular

25. **ALGEBRA** Find the measure of each angle of a regular 12-gon. **150°**

Example 8 Determine whether the figure is a polygon. If it is, classify the polygon and state whether it is regular. If it is *not* a polygon, explain why.

Since the polygon has 5 congruent sides and 5 congruent angles, it is a regular pentagon.

10-9 **Translations** (pp. 553–557) **27–29. See Ch. 10 Answer Appendix.**

Triangle PQR has coordinates $P(4, -2)$, $Q(-2, -3)$, and $R(-1, 6)$. Find the coordinates of $P'Q'R'$ after each translation. Then graph each translation.

26. 6 units left, 3 units up **See margin.**

27. 4 units right, 1 unit down

28. 3 units left

29. 7 units down

Example 9 Find the coordinates of $\triangle G'H'I'$ after a translation of 2 units left and 4 units up.

The vertices of $\triangle G'H'I'$ are $G'(-2, 7)$, $H'(2, 3)$, and $I'(-4, 1)$.

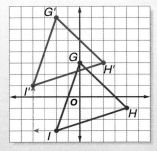

32. $E'(4, -2)$, $F'(-2, -2)$, $G'(-2, 5)$, $H'(4, 5)$; See Ch. 10 Answer Appendix for graph.

10-10 **Reflections** (pp. 558–562) **30–32. See Ch. 10 Answer Appendix.**

Find the coordinates of each figure after a reflection over the given axis. Then graph the figure and its reflected image.

30. $\triangle RST$ with coordinates $R(-1, 3)$, $S(2, 6)$, and $T(6, 1)$; x-axis

31. parallelogram $ABCD$ with coordinates $A(1, 3)$, $B(2, -1)$, $C(5, -1)$, and $D(4, 3)$; y-axis

32. rectangle $EFGH$ with coordinates $E(4, 2)$, $F(-2, 2)$, $G(-2, -5)$, and $H(4, -5)$; x-axis

Example 10 Find the coordinates of $\triangle C'D'E'$ after a reflection over the y-axis. Then graph its reflected image.

The vertices of $\triangle C'D'E'$ are $C'(-3, 4)$, $D'(-2, 1)$, and $E'(-5, 3)$.

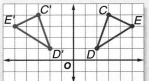

566 Chapter 10 Geometry: Polygons

Name each angle in four ways. Then classify each angle as *acute, obtuse, right,* **or** *straight.*

1.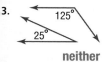
∠ABC, ∠CBA,
∠B, ∠2; **obtuse**

2.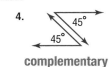
∠ZYX, ∠XYZ,
∠Y, ∠1; **acute**

Classify each pair of angles as *complementary,* *supplementary,* **or** *neither.*

3.
neither

4.
complementary

5. **GEOMETRY** Classify the angle pair at the right as *vertical,* *adjacent,* or *neither.* **adjacent**

6. **STANDARDS PRACTICE** The table shows the results of a survey. The results are to be displayed in a circle graph. Which statement about the graph is *not* true? **D**

Favorite Type of Books	
Type	**Students**
mystery	24
science fiction	8
sports	26
romance	30

A The science fiction section on the graph will have an angle measure of about 33°.
B Romance books were preferred more than any other type of book.
C About 30% of students chose sports books as their favorite.
D The mystery and sports sections on the circle graph are supplementary angles.

ALGEBRA Find the missing measure in each triangle with the given angle measures.

7. 75°, 25.5°, x° **79.5**

8. 23.5°, x°, 109.5° **47**

Math Online Chapter Test at ca.gr6math.com

9. **ALGEBRA** Numbers ending in zero or five are divisible by five. Are the numbers 25, 893, and 690 divisible by 5? Use the *logical reasoning* strategy. **See margin.**

ALGEBRA Find the value of *x* **in each quadrilateral.**

10.
84° **62**
92°
122° x°

11. **142**
x° 70°
58°

12. **GEOGRAPHY** A map is drawn so that it is similar to a map in an atlas. The map in the atlas is 7 inches long and 10 inches wide. If the hand-drawn map has a length of 17.5 inches, what is its width? **25 in.**

13. **GEOMETRY** Can a regular heptagon, with angle measures that total 900°, be used by itself to make a tessellation? Explain. **See margin.**

14. **STANDARDS PRACTICE** Which quadrilateral does *not* have opposite sides congruent? **H**

F parallelogram   H trapezoid
G square   J rectangle

15. **ALGEBRA** Square *ABCD* is shown. What are the vertices of *A'B'C'D'* after a translation 2 units right and 2 units down? Graph the translated image.

A'(4, 2), B'(8, 2),
C'(4, −2),
D'(8, −2),
see margin for graph.

16. **GEOMETRY** Draw a figure with one line of symmetry. Then draw a figure with no lines of symmetry. **See students' work.**

CHAPTER 10 Practice Test

Summative Assessment

CRM *Chapter 10 Resource Masters*

Leveled Chapter 10 Tests			
Form	**Type**	**Level**	**Pages**
1	MC	**BL**	77–78
2A	MC	**OL**	79–80
2B	MC	**OL**	81–82
2C	FR	**OL**	83–84
2D	FR	**OL**	85–86
3	FR	**AL**	87–88

MC = *multiple-choice questions*
FR = *free-response questions*
BL = *below grade level*
OL = *on grade level*
AL = *above grade level*

• Vocabulary Test, p. 76
• Extended-Response Test, p. 89

ExamView Assessment Suite — Customize and create multiple versions of your chapter test and the answer key. All of the questions from the leveled chapter tests in the *Chapter 10 Resource Masters* are also available on Exam View Assessment Suite with the California Standard that each item assesses.

Additional Answers

9. 25 and 690 are divisible by 5. 893 is not divisible by 5 since 893 does not end in a 0 or 5.

For Exercises 13 and 15, see Ch. 10 Answer Appendix.

Data-Driven Decision Making	Exercises	Lesson	Standard	Resources for Review
Diagnostic Teaching Based on the results of the Chapter 10 Practice Test, use the following to review concepts that students continue to find challenging.	12	10–7	🔑 6NS1.3	**CRM** Study Guide and Intervention pp. 45, 51, 58, and 65 Math Online • Extra Examples • Personal Tutor • Concepts in Motion
	13	10–8	6MR2.2	
	15	10–9	Preparation for 7MG3.2	
	16	10–10	Preparation for 7MG3.2	

TEST-TAKING TIP

Exercise 2 Many students will be able to select the correct answer choice by visualizing the large square and its 9 constituent squares. For other students, drawing a diagram of the problem will allow them to see that answer choices F, G, and J can be eliminated.

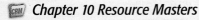 **Formative Assessment**

You can use these two pages to benchmark student progress. The California Standards are listed with each question.

Chapter 10 Resource Masters
• Standardized Test Practice, pp. 90–92

 **ExamView**
Assessment Suite

Create practice worksheets or tests that align to the California Standards, as well as TIMSS and NAEP tests.

 Read each question. Then fill in the correct answer on the answer document provided by your teacher or on a sheet of paper.

1 Which of the following two angles are complementary? **B**

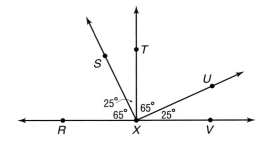

A ∠RXS and ∠TXU
B ∠SXT and ∠TXU
C ∠RXS and ∠SXV
D ∠SXR and ∠SXV

2 A square is divided into 9 congruent squares. Which of the following methods can be used to find the area of the larger square, given the area of one of the smaller squares? **H**

F Multiply the area of the larger square by 9.
G Add 9 to the area of one of the smaller squares.
H Multiply the area of one of the smaller squares by 9.
J Add the area of the larger square to the sum of the areas of each of the 9 smaller squares. **745**

---

3 Which of the following groups does *not* contain equivalent fractions, decimals, and percents? **D**

A $\frac{9}{20}$, 0.45, 45%

B $\frac{3}{10}$, 0.3, 30%

C $\frac{7}{8}$, 0.875, 87.5%

D $\frac{1}{100}$, 0.1, 1%

4 The table below shows all the possible outcomes when tossing two fair coins at the same time.

1st Coin	2nd Coin
H	H
H	T
T	H
T	T

Which of the following must be true? **G**

F The probability that both coins have the same outcome is $\frac{1}{4}$.

G The probability of getting at least one tail is higher than the probability of getting two heads.

H The probability that exactly one coin will turn up heads is $\frac{3}{4}$.

J The probability of getting at least one tail is lower than the probability of getting two tails.

5 Seth has $858.60 in his savings account. He plans to spend 15% of his savings on a bicycle. Which of the following represents the amount Seth plans to spend on the bicycle? **A**

A $128.79   **C** $182.79

B $171.72   **D** $122.79

 California Standards Practice at ca.gr6math.com

6 A manager took an employee to lunch. If the lunch was $48 and she left a 20% tip, how much money did she spend on lunch? **G**

    F $68.00

    G $57.60

    H $55.80

    J $38.40

7 What is the measure of ∠1 in the figure below? **D**

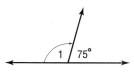

    A 15°   **C** 100°

    B 25°   **D** 105°

8 Natasha wants to take a survey to determine which type of music is most popular at her school. Which of the following methods is the best way for her to choose a random sample of the students at her school? **H**

    F select members of the football team

    G select members of the chess club

    H select 20 students at random from each grade level

    J select students who enjoy rap music

TEST-TAKING TIP

Question 9 Sometimes, it is not necessary to perform any calculations in order to answer the question correctly. In Question 9, you can use number sense to eliminate certain answer choices. Not having to perform calculations can help save time during a test.

9 Josiah found the mean and median of the following list of numbers.

11, 17, 17

If the number 25 is added to this list, then which of the following statements would be true? **A**

    A The mean would increase.

    B The mean would decrease.

    C The median would increase.

    D The median would decrease.

Pre-AP

Record your answers on a sheet of paper. Show your work.

10 Edmundo plotted the polygon *JKLM* on the coordinate plane to the right.

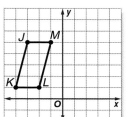

    a. Classify ∠*J*. **obtuse**

    b. Classify ∠*M*. **acute**

    c. Classify the polygon *JKLM* using the name that *best* describes it. **parallelogram**

    d. Can polygon *JKLM* be used by itself to make a tessellation? Explain your reasoning. **d–f. See margin.**

    e. If polygon *JKLM* is translated 2 units right and 5 units down, what are the coordinates of the new figure?

    f. If polygon *JKLM* is reflected over the *x*-axis, what are the coordinates of the new figure?

More California Standards Practice
For practice by standard, see pages CA1–CA39.

Answer Sheet Practice

Have students simulate taking a standardized test by recording their answers on a practice recording sheet.

CRM Student Recording Sheet, p. 71

Additional Answers

10d. Yes; the sum of the angles where the vertices meet is 360°

10e. *J*′(−1, 0), *K*′(−2, −4), *L*′(0, −4), *M*′(1, 0)

10f. *J*′(−3, −5), *K*′(−4, −1), *L*′(−2, −1), *M*′(−1, −5)

NEED EXTRA HELP?

If You Missed Question...	1	2	3	4	5	6	7	8	9	10
Go to Lesson...	10-1	10-5	6-8	9-1	7-1	7-4	10-2	8-8	8-2	10-5
For Help with Standard...	MG2.1	MG2.3	NS1.1	SDAP3.1	NS1.4	NS1.4	MG2.2	SDAP2.2	SDAP1.2	MG2.3

Homework Option

Get Ready for Chapter 11 Assign students the exercises on page 571 as homework to assess whether they possess the prerequisite skills needed for the next chapter.

Page 519, Lesson 10-3 (Check Your Progress)

a.

Compositions of Earth's Atmosphere

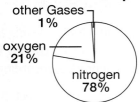

other Gases 1%
oxygen 21%
nitrogen 78%

b. U.S. Winter Olympic Medals, 1924 to 2002

silver 37%
gold 36%
bronze 27%

Page 521, Lesson 10-3

6. NYC Commuters

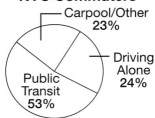

Carpool/Other 23%
Driving Alone 24%
Public Transit 53%

7. Endangered Species in U.S.

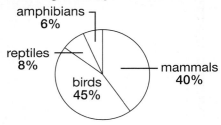

amphibians 6%
reptiles 8%
birds 45%
mammals 40%

8. Speed Limits in U.S.

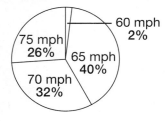

60 mph 2%
75 mph 26%
65 mph 40%
70 mph 32%

Page 531, Lesson 10-5

4. Scott; Sample answer: Since Placido and the center drove Scott to practice, neither Placido nor Scott can be the center. This leaves Dexter as the center. Since Placido does not play guard, he must be the forward. This leaves Scott as the guard.

5. 25 units; Sample answer: The pattern in the table shows that the length in units is the square of the time in seconds. So, the length of the yo-yo if it takes 5 seconds to swing back and forth is 5^2 or 25 units.

Page 532, Explore 10-6

3. See students' work; Sample answer:

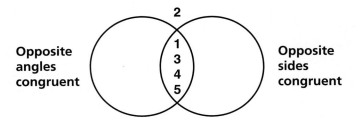

Opposite angles congruent

2
1 3 4 5

Opposite sides congruent

4. See students' work; Sample answer:

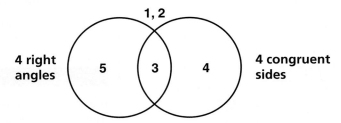

1, 2

4 right angles

5 3 4

4 congruent sides

5. Sample answer; Yes, outside the Venn diagram; Yes, create a three-circled Venn diagram using the categories 4 right angles, 4 congruent sides, and opposite sides parallel.

Page 552, Extend 10-8

a.

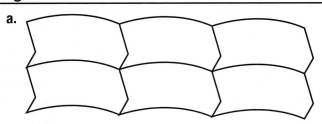

b.

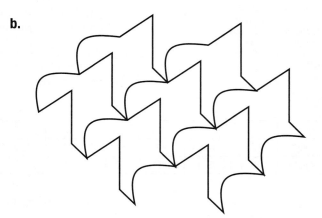

c.

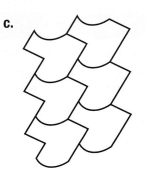

Page 553, Lesson 10-9 (Check Your Progress)

a.

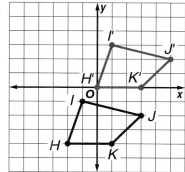

Page 555, Lesson 10-9

2.

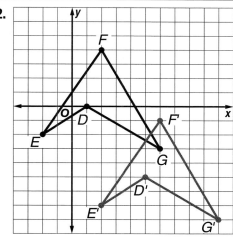

3.

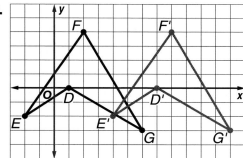

5.

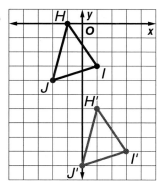

6.

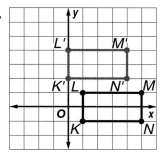

7.

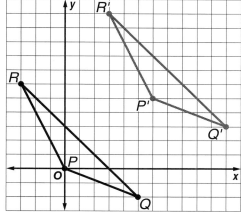

8.

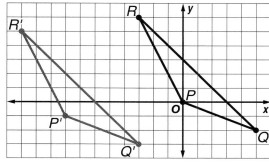

9.

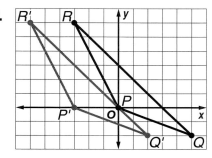

10.

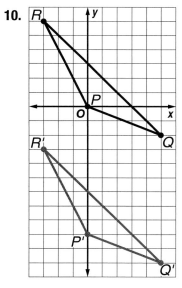

6.

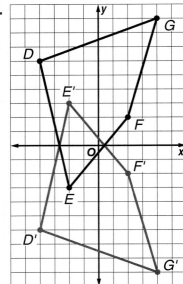

7.

12.

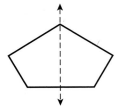

13.

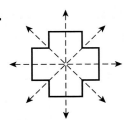

15.

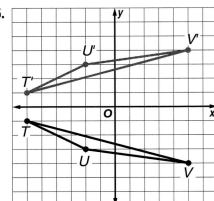

; $T'(-6, 1)$, $U'(-2, 3)$, and $V'(5, 4)$

8.

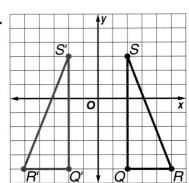

16.

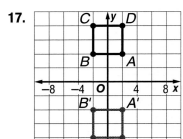

; $M'(2, -1)$, $N'(-3, -1)$, and $P'(-1, -4)$

17.

; $A'(2, -4)$, $B'(-2, -4)$, $C'(-2, -8)$, and $D'(2, -8)$

9.

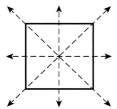

11.

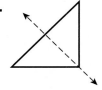

18.

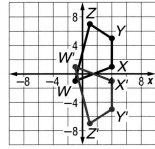

; $W'(-1, 1)$, $X'(4, -1)$, $Y'(4, -5)$, and $Z'(1, -7)$

Page 561, Lesson 10-10

23. Sample answer: One is vertically down the center of the picture. The other is horizontally with the reflection of the water.

24. All four flags have line symmetry.

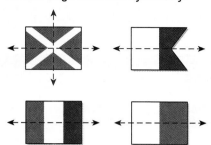

29. Sample answer; A reflection over the *y*-axis followed by a reflection over the *x*-axis.

30.
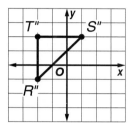

31.
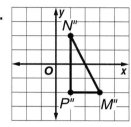

Page 566, Chapter 10 Study Guide and Review

27. *P*′(8, −3), *Q*′(2, −4), and *R*′(3, 5)

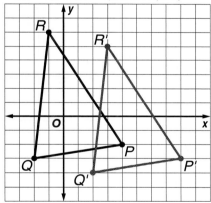

28. *P*′(1, −2), *Q*′(−5, −3), and *R*′(−4, 6)

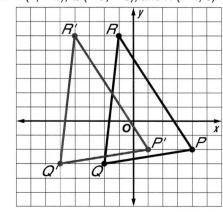

29. *P*′(4, −9), *Q*′(−2, −10), and *R*′(−1, −1)

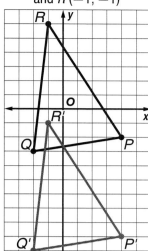

30. *R*′(−1, −3), *S*′(2, −6), and *T*′(6, −1)

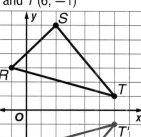

31. *A*′(−1, 3), *B*′(−2, −1), *C*′(−5, −1), *D*′(−4, 3)

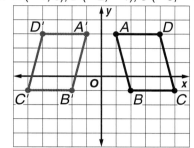

32.
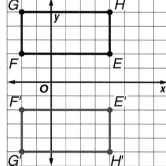

Page 567, Practice Test

13. No: since each angle is about 128.6°, 128.6 cannot divide into 360 evenly.

15.
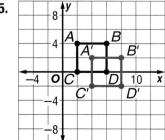

Chapter Overview

Measurement: Two- and Three-Dimensional Figures

Standards-Based Lesson Plan		Pacing Your Lessons	
LESSONS AND OBJECTIVES	California Standards	40–50 Minute Periods	90-Minute Periods
11-1 Area of Parallelograms (pp. 572–576) • Find the area of parallelograms.	6AF3.1 6AF3.2	1	0.5
Explore 11-2 Measurement Lab: Triangles and Trapezoids (p. 577) **11-2 Area of Triangles and Trapezoids** (pp. 578–582) • Find the areas of triangles and trapezoids.	6MR3.3 6AF3.1 6AF3.2	1	0.5
Explore 11-3 Measurement Lab: Circumference of Circles (p. 583) **11-3 Circles and Circumference** (pp. 584–588) • Find the circumference of circles.	6MR3.3 6MG1.1 6MG1.2	1	0.5
11-4 Area of Circles (pp. 589–593) • Find the areas of circles.	6MG1.1 6MG1.2	1	0.5
11-5 Problem-Solving Investigation: Solve a Simpler Problem (pp. 594–595) • Solve problems by solving a simpler problem.	6MR1.3 6MR2.2 6NS2.1	1	0.5
11-6 Area of Complex Figures (pp. 596–599) • Find the areas of complex figures. **Extend 11-6 Measurement Lab: Nets and Surface Area** (pp. 600–601)	6AF3.1 6AF3.2 7MG3.5 6MR3.3	2	1
11-7 Three-Dimensional Figures (pp. 603–606) • Classify three-dimensional figures.	7MG3.6	1	0.5
Explore 11-8 Geometry Lab: Building Three-Dimensional Figures (p. 607) **11-8 Drawing Three-Dimensional Figures** (pp. 608–612) • Draw a three-dimensional figure given the top, side, and front views.	7MG3.6 6MR2.4 5MG2.3 6MR2.4	2	1
11-9 Volume of Prisms (pp. 613–618) • Find the volumes of rectangular and triangular prisms.	6MG1.3	1	0.5
11-10 Volume of Cylinders (pp. 619–623) • Find the volumes of cylinders. **Extend 11-10 Graphing Calculator Lab: Graphing Geometric Relationships** (pp. 624–625)	6MG1.3 6AF3.2 6MR1.2	2	1
REVIEW		1	0.5
ASSESSMENT		1	0.5
TOTAL		15	7.5

*The complete **Assessment Planner** for*
Chapter 11 is provided on page 571.

Professional Development

California Standards Vertical Alignment

Before Chapter 11

Related Topics from Grade 5

- Use formulas for the area of a triangle and of a parallelogram
  — Standard 5MG1.1

- Differentiate between and use appropriate units of measures for two- and three-dimensional objects Standard 5MG1.4

- Visualize and draw two-dimensional views of three-dimensional objects Standard 5MG2.3

Chapter 11

Topics from Grade 6

- Use variables in expressions describing geometric quantities

- Express in symbolic form simple relationships arising from geometry

- Understand the concept of a constant such as π; know the formulas for the circumference and area of a circle
  —

- Know common estimates of π and use these values to estimate and calculate the circumference and area of circles

- Use a variety of methods to explain mathematical reasoning

- Know and use the formulas for the volume of triangular prisms and cylinders

See individual lessons for the specific Standards covered.

After Chapter 11

Preparation for Grade 7

- Use formulas for perimeter, area, surface area, and volume Standard 7MG2.1

- Estimate and compute the area of more complex or irregular two- and three-dimensional figures Standard 7MG2.2

- Students compute volumes and surface areas Standard G9.0

- Construct two-dimensional patterns for three-dimensional models Standard 7MG3.5

Back-Mapping

California Mathematics: Concepts, Skills, Problem Solving was conceived and developed with the final result in mind, student success in Algebra I and beyond. The authors, using the California Mathematics Standards as their guide, developed this brand-new series by "back-mapping" from the desired result of student success in Algebra I and beyond. McGraw-Hill's K-7 intervention program, *California Math Triumphs: Intensive Intervention* as well as *California Algebra 1, California Geometry, California Algebra 2,* and *California Algebra Readiness* were developed utilizing the same philosophy.

What the Research Says . . .

According to Lehrer in "Developing Understanding of Measurement," one conceptual foundation of measurement is the following.

The sum of the measures of two parts that make up the whole equals the measure of the whole (Additivity).

- In Lessons 11-5 and 11-6, students find the area of composite figures by subdividing them.

 Professional Development

Targeted professional development has been articulated throughout the *California Mathematics: Concepts, Skills, and Problem Solving* series. The **McGraw-Hill Professional Development Video Library** provides short videos that support the — Key Standards. For more information, visit ca.gr6math.com.

| Model Lessons | Instructional Strategies |

Technology Solutions

Teacher Resources

TeacherWorks™ All-in-One Planner and Resource Center

All of the print materials from the Classroom Resource Masters are available on your TeacherWorks™ CD-ROM.

BL = Below Grade Level **OL** = On Grade Level **AL** = Above Grade Level **ELL** = English Language Learner

Chapter Resource Masters				11-1	11-2	11-3	11-4	11-5	11-6	11-7	11-8	11-9	11-10
BL **OL**		**ELL**	Lesson Reading Guide	9	16	22	30		40	46	52	58	65
BL **OL**		**ELL**	Study Guide and Intervention*	10	17	23	31	36	41	47	53	59	66
BL **OL**			Skills Practice*	11	18	24	32	37	42	48	54	60	67
	OL **AL**		Practice*	12	19	25	33	38	43	49	55	61	68
	OL **AL**		Word Problem Practice*	13	20	26	34	39	44	50	56	62	69
	OL **AL**		Enrichment	14	21	27	35		45	51	57	63	70
	OL **AL**		Calculator and Spreadsheet Activities	15		28–29						64	
	OL **AL**		Chapter Assessments*	71–92									
BL **OL** **AL**			5-Minute Check Transparencies	✓	✓	✓	✓	✓	✓	✓	✓	✓	✓
BL **OL**			Teaching Mathematics with Manipulatives	✓	✓	✓	✓		✓		✓		

*Also available in Spanish.
Real-World Investigations for Differentiated Instructions, pp. 59, 69–70

AssignmentWorks

Differentiated Assignments, Answers, and Solutions

- Print a customized assignment worksheet using the Student Edition exercises along with an answer key or worked-out solutions.
- Use default lesson assignments as outlined in the Differentiated Homework Options in the Teacher Wraparound Edition.
- Includes modified questions from the Student Edition for students with special needs.

Interactive Classroom

This CD-ROM is a customizable Microsoft® PowerPoint® presentation that includes:

- In-Class Examples
- Your Turn Exercises*
- 5-Minute Check Transparencies*
- Links to Online Study Tools
- Concepts in Motion

compatible with response pad technology

> **Your Turn**
>
> DRIVEWAY The diagram below shows the dimensions of a new driveway. Find the area of the driveway. Round to the nearest tenth.
>
> 21 ft
> 9 ft
>
> Answer: about 220.8 ft²
>
> End of slide

ExamView®Assessment Suite

ExamView®
Assessment Suite

- Create, edit, and customize tests and worksheets using QuickTest Wizard
- Create multiple versions of tests and modify them for a desired level of difficulty
- Translate from English to Spanish and vice versa
- Build tests aligned with your state standards
- Track students' progress using the Teacher Management System

Student Tools

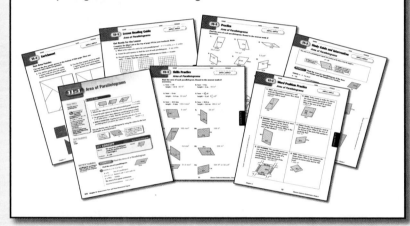
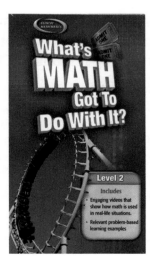
Internet Resources

TEACHER	STUDENT	PARENT	**Online Study Tools**
	•	•	Online Student Edition
•	•	•	Multilingual Glossary
			Lesson Resources
	•	•	BrainPOP®
•	•	•	Concepts in Motion
•	•	•	Extra Examples
•			Group Activity Cards
•			Problem of the Week Cards
	•	•	Other Calculator Keystrokes
	•	•	Reading in the Content Area
	•		Real-World Careers
	•	•	Self-Check Quizzes
			Chapter Resources
	•	•	Chapter Readiness
	•	•	Chapter Test
	•	•	Family Letters and Activities
	•	•	Standardized Test Practice
	•	•	Vocabulary Review/Chapter Review Activities
			Unit Resources
•	•		Cross-Curricular Internet Project
			Other Resources
•			Dinah Zike's Foldables
•	•		Game Zone Games and Recording Sheets
	•	•	Hotmath Homework Help
•			Key Concepts
•	•	•	Math Skills Maintenance
•	•	•	Meet the Authors
•			NAEP Correlations
	•	•	Personal Tutor
•			Project CRISS℠
	•	•	Scavenger Hunts and Answer Sheets
•			Vocabulary PuzzleMakers

Noteables™ Interactive Study Notebook with Foldables™

This workbook is a study organizer that provides helpful steps for students to follow to organize their notes for Chapter 11.

- Students use Noteables to record notes and to complete their Foldables as you present the material for each lesson.
- Noteables correspond to the Examples in the *Teacher Wraparound Edition* and *Interactive Classroom CD-ROM*.

READING in the Content Area

This online worksheet provides strategies for reading and analyzing Lesson 11-9, Volume of Prisms. Students are guided through questions about the main idea, subject matter, supporting details, conclusion, clarifying details, and vocabulary of the lesson.

ca.gr6math.com

Recommended Outside Reading for Students

Mathematics and Activities

- *Janice Vancleave's Geometry for Every Kid: Easy Activities That Make Learning Geometry Fun* by Janice Pratt Vancleave ©1994 [nonfiction]

This book from the Science for Every Kid series presents geometry concepts through fun activities. Students can use the activities to reinforce what they learn in this chapter about areas of parallelograms, triangles, trapezoids, and circles.

Mathematics and Adventure

- *Sir Cumference and the Great Knight of Angleland: A Math Adventure* by Cindy Neuschwander ©2001 [fiction]

In this story, Sir Cumference's son, Radius, must complete a quest. Students will enjoy reading this fanciful tale about the geometric figures they study in this chapter.

Project CRISS℠

STUDY SKILL

Producing an accurate, detailed written summary can help students' understanding of new material. Demonstrate the summarization process using the example at the right for Lesson 11-1. Begin by having students notice lesson titles, boldfaced vocabulary words, and illustrations. Next, have them read the lesson, then summarize it on the chalkboard, as shown. Finally, students should write a summary, in their own words, based on the notes. Have students work through this process individually or in cooperative groups for the remaining lessons in Chapter 11.

Lesson 11-1

- To find the area of a parallelogram, multiply its base and height. The formula is $A = bh$.
- Any side of a parallelogram can be its base.
- The height of a parallelogram is the distance from the base to the opposite side.

CReating **I**ndependence through **S**tudent-owned **S**trategies

---

Differentiated Instruction

Quick Review Math Handbook*

is Glencoe's mathematical handbook for students and parents.

Hot Words includes a glossary of terms.

Hot Topics consists of two parts:

- explanations of key mathematical concepts
- exercises to check students' understanding.

Lesson	Hot Topics Section	Lesson	Hot Topics Section
11-1	7•5, 8•3	11-6	7•5, 8•3
11-2	7•5, 8•3	11-8	7•2
11-3	7•8	11-9	7•7, 8•6, 9•4
11-4	7•8, 8•3	11-10	7•7

Also available in Spanish

Teacher To Teacher

Barbara Van Den Berg
Woodrow Wilson
Middle School
Clifton, NJ

USE WITH LESSON 11-2

"When moving from the area of a triangle to discovering the area of a trapezoid, have students fold a triangle in half vertically and cut on the fold to form a smaller triangle and a trapezoid. To find the area of the trapezoid, use the formula for the area of a triangle, substituting $(b_1 + b_2)$ for b, since the trapezoid has two bases. This helps students remember the formula for the area of a trapezoid because they know how it developed."

Intervention Options

Intensive Intervention

Math Triumphs can provide intensive intervention for students who are at risk of not meeting the California standards addressed in Chapter 11.

Diagnose student readiness with the Quick Check and Quick Review on page 571. Then use *Math Triumphs* to accelerate their achievement.

Algebra: Integers

Prerequisite Skill	*Math Triumphs*
Multiply rational numbers 5NS2.5	Volume 2, Chapters 3 and 4
Evaluate exponents 4NS4.1	Volume 1, Chapter 4

See chart on page T24 for other *Math Triumphs* lessons that will support the prerequisite skills needed for success in *Glencoe California Mathematics, Grade 6*.

Strategic Intervention

For strategic intervention options, refer to the Diagnostic Assessment table on page 571.

FOLDABLES™ Study Organizer

Dinah Zike's Foldables

Focus This Foldable is designed to help students organize their notes about measuring two- and three-dimensional figures.

Teach Have students make their Foldables and label the tabs. Explain to students that they should record formulas, key concepts, and procedures under the appropriate tabs of the Foldable. Encourage students also to give their own examples of the key concepts presented in each lesson.

When to Use It Use the appropriate tab as students cover each lesson in this chapter.

A version of a completed Foldable is shown on p. 626.

Differentiated Instruction

CRM Student-Built Glossary, p. 1

Students complete the chart by providing the definition of each term and an example as they progress through Chapter 11.

This study tool can be used to review for the chapter test.

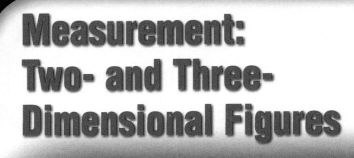
CHAPTER 11
Measurement: Two- and Three-Dimensional Figures

BIG Idea

- **Standard 6MG1.0** Deepen understanding of the measurement of plane and solid shapes and use this understanding to solve problems.

Key Vocabulary

circumference (p. 584)

cylinder (p. 604)

pyramid (p. 603)

volume (p. 613)

🌐 Real-World Link

Architecture If you visit the Transamerica Pyramid building in San Francisco, you will see examples of three-dimensional figures used in architecture.

FOLDABLES™ Study Organizer

Measurement: Two- and Three-Dimensional Figures Make this Foldable to help you organize your notes. Begin with a sheet of $8\frac{1}{2}$" by 11" construction paper and two sheets of notebook paper.

1 **Fold** the construction paper in half lengthwise. Label the chapter title on the outside.

2 **Fold** the sheets of notebook paper in half lengthwise. Then fold top to bottom twice.

3 **Open** the notebook paper. Cut along the second folds to make four tabs.

4 **Glue** the uncut notebook paper side by side onto the construction paper. Label each tab as shown.

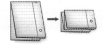
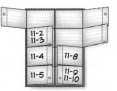

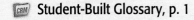

Materials Needed for Chapter 11

- grid paper (Lessons 11-1, 11-2, and Explore 11-3)
- centimeter grid paper (Explore 11-2, Extend 11-10, 11-9, and 11-10)
- masking tape (Explore 11-2, Lesson 11-9, and Lesson 11-10)

- soup cans (Lesson 11-10)
- centimeter rulers (Lesson 11-10)
- cardboard boxes (Extend 11-6)
- poster paper (Extend 11-6)
- graphing calculators (Extend 11-10)

- measuring tapes (Explore 11-3)
- circular objects (Explore 11-3)
- paper plates (Lesson 11-4)
- centimeter cubes (Explore 11-8 and 11-9)
- isometric dot paper (Lesson 11-8)

GET READY for Chapter 11

Diagnose Readiness You have two options for checking Prerequisite Skills.

Option 1

Take the Quick Check below. Refer to the Quick Review for help.

Option 2

Math Online Take the Online Readiness Quiz at ca.gr6math.com.

QUICK Check

(Used in Lessons 11-1, 11-2, and 11-9)
Evaluate each expression. (Prior Grade)

1. 8×17 **136**
2. 5.6×9.8 **54.88**
3. $12 \times 4 \times 26$ **1,248**
4. $4.5 \times 3.2 \times 1.7$ **24.48**
5. $\left(\frac{1}{2}\right)(11)(14)$ **77**
6. $\left(\frac{1}{2}\right)(8.8)(2.3)$ **10.12**

7. **SHOPPING** Margo bought 3 sweaters that originally cost $27.78 each. If they were on sale for half the price, what was the total cost of the sweaters, not including tax? (Prior Grade) **$41.67**

(Used in Lessons 11-4, 11-9, and 11-10)
Evaluate each expression. (Lesson 1-2)

8. 3^2 **9**
9. 11 squared **121**
10. 5 to the third power **125**
11. 6 to the second power **36**
12. **CHESS** If a chessboard has 8^2 squares, how many squares is this? (Lesson 1-2) **64**

(Used in Lessons 11-3 and 11-4)
Evaluate each expression. Use 3.14 for π. Round to the nearest tenth.
(Prior Grade)

13. $\pi \times 4$ **12.6**
14. $\pi \times 13.8$ **43.3**
15. $(2)(\pi)(5)$ **31.4**
16. $(2)(\pi)(1.7)$ **10.7**
17. $\pi \times 9^2$ **254.3**
18. $\pi \times 6^2$ **113.0**

QUICK Review

Example 1 Find $1.2 \cdot 3.4$.

$$
\begin{array}{r}
1.2 \quad \leftarrow \quad \text{1 decimal place} \\
\times\, 3.4 \quad \leftarrow \quad \text{+1 decimal place} \\
\hline
48 \\
36 \\
\hline
4.08 \quad \leftarrow \quad \text{2 decimal places}
\end{array}
$$

Example 2 Find $\left(\frac{1}{2}\right)(26)(19)$.

$\left(\frac{1}{2}\right)(26)(19) = (13)(19)$ Multiply $\frac{1}{2}$ by 26.

$\qquad\qquad\qquad = 247$ Multiply 13 by 19.

Example 3 Evaluate 7^3.

$7^3 = 7 \cdot 7 \cdot 7$ or 343

Example 4 Evaluate 2 to the fourth power.

2 to the fourth power is written 2^4.

$2^4 = 2 \cdot 2 \cdot 2 \cdot 2$ or 16

Example 5 Evaluate $\pi \times 5^2$. Use 3.14 for π. Round to the nearest tenth.

$\pi \cdot 5^2 = \pi \cdot 25$ $5^2 = 25$

$\qquad\quad = 78.5$ Multiply π by 25.

Chapter 11 Get Ready for Chapter 11 **571**

✓ Diagnostic Assessment

Exercises	California Standards	Strategic Intervention
1–7	5NS2.1	SE Prerequisite Skill p. 674
8–12	5NS1.3	SE Review Lesson 1-2, pp. 30–33
13–18	5NS1.1	*Math Skills Maintenance Masters* pp. 52–53

ASSESSMENT PLANNER   CHAPTER 11

✓ Formative Assessment

CRM Anticipation Guide, pp. 7–8
Spotting Preconceived Ideas
Students complete this survey to determine prior knowledge about ideas from Chapter 11. Revisit this worksheet after completing the chapter. Also see page 630.

TWE Lesson Activities
- Ticket Out the Door, pp. 576, 599, 606, 623
- Crystal Ball, pp. 588, 595, 612, 618
- Name the Math, p. 593
- Yesterday's News, p. 582

Chapter Checkpoints

SE Mid-Chapter Quiz, p. 602
SE Study Guide and Review, pp. 626–630
SE California Standards Practice, pp. 632–633
CRM Quizzes, pp. 73 and 74
CRM Standardized Test Practice, pp. 90–92

Math Online ca.gr6math.com
- Self-Check Quizzes
- Practice Test
- Standardized Test Practice

✓ Summative Assessment

SE Chapter Practice Test, p. 631
CRM Mid-Chapter Test, p. 75
CRM Vocabulary Test, p. 76
CRM Extended-Response Test, p. 89
CRM Leveled Chapter Tests, pp. 77–88
CD ExamView® Assessment Suite

KEY
CRM *Chapter 11 Resource Masters*
SE Student Edition
TWE Teacher Wraparound Edition
CD CD-ROM

11-1   Area of Parallelograms

Standard 6AF3.1:   **Use variables in expressions describing geometric quantities** (e.g., $P = 2w + 2\ell$, $A = \frac{1}{2} bh$, $C = \pi d$–the formulas for the perimeter of a rectangle, the area of a triangle, and the circumference of a circle, respectively).

Standard 6AF3.2:   **Express in symbolic form simple relationships arising from geometry.**

PACING: **Regular:** 1 period,   **Block:** 0.5 period

Options for Differentiated Instruction

ELL = English Language Learner   **AL** = Above Grade Level   **SS** = Struggling Students   **SN** = Special Needs

Kinesthetic Learning   **ELL** **SS** **SN**

Use before beginning Lesson 11-1.

Give each student a drawing of a parallelogram. Have them trace and cut out several copies, leaving the original intact. Their task is to cut up the parallelogram and rearrange the pieces to form a rectangle. No pieces should be overlapping and all the pieces need to be used.

Ask:

- What cut(s) did you make in order to make the rectangle?
- Could you have done it in one cut? How?
- How do the dimensions of the rectangle compare to the dimensions of the original parallelogram?
- How do you find the area of a rectangle?
- How can that help you find the formula for the area of a parallelogram?

Preventing Errors   **SS** **SN**

Use after presenting the Mini Lab.

Be sure students do *not* think of a parallelogram as a collapsed rectangle. This may cause them to calculate the area as the length of a base multiplied by the length of a side. Remind them that if a parallelogram does not have four right angles, its height and width can not have the same measure.

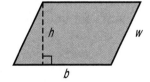

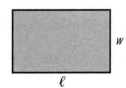

Study Tools   **SS** **SN**

Use after presenting Example 1.

Have students use index cards to make flash cards of the geometry formulas presented in this chapter:

- On the top left corner, write the page number where the formula is introduced. On the top right corner, write the lesson number.
- Write the title of the formula and the formula itself. Also include a drawing if appropriate.
- On the reverse side of the index card, include an example of the formula.

Have students punch a hole in each card and place them on a ring.

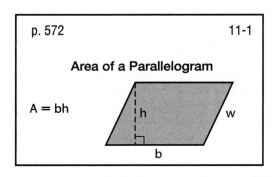

p. 572   11-1

Area of a Parallelogram

$A = bh$

Leveled Lesson Resources

Chapter 11 Resource Masters

BL = Below Grade Level **OL** = On Grade Level **AL** = Above Grade Level **ELL** = English Language Learner

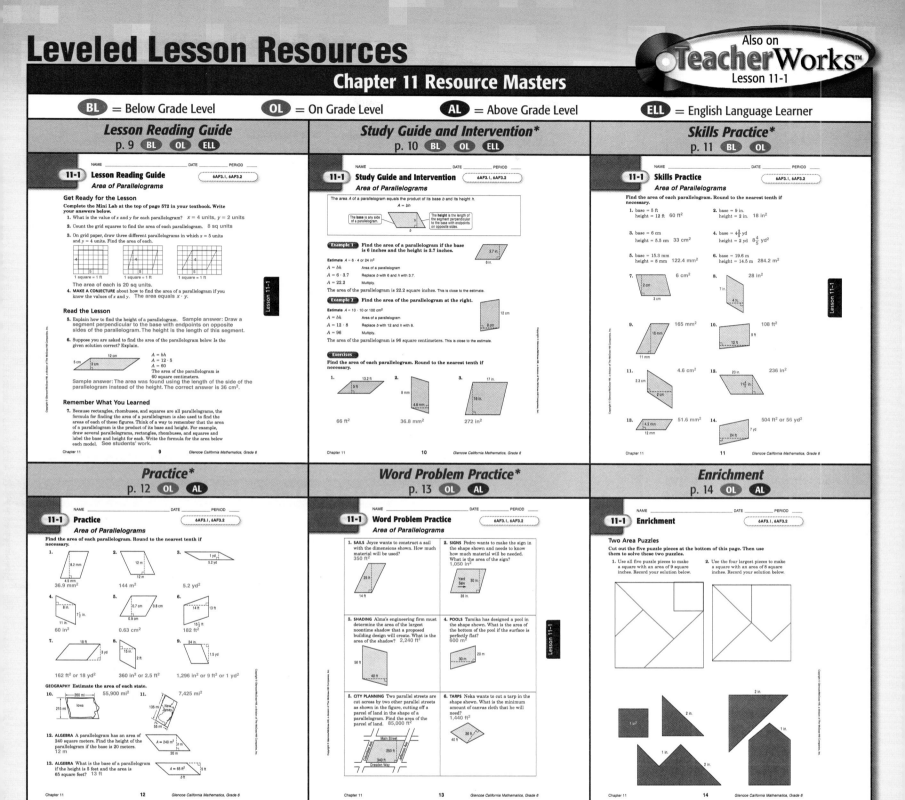

Lesson Reading Guide
p. 9 **BL** **OL** **ELL**

Study Guide and Intervention*
p. 10 **BL** **OL** **ELL**

Skills Practice*
p. 11 **BL** **OL**

Practice*
p. 12 **OL** **AL**

Word Problem Practice*
p. 13 **OL** **AL**

Enrichment
p. 14 **OL** **AL**

Additional Lesson Resources

Transparencies
• *5-Minute Check Transparency,* Lesson 11-1

Other Print Products
• *Teaching Mathematics with Manipulatives*
• *Noteables™ Interactive Study Notebook with Foldables™*

Teacher Tech Tools
• *Interactive Classroom CD-ROM,* Lesson 11-1
• *AssignmentWorks,* Lesson 11-1

Student Tech Tools
ca.gr6math.com
• Extra Examples, Chapter 11, Lesson 1
• Self-Check Quiz, Chapter 11, Lesson 1

11-1 Area of Parallelograms

❶ Focus

Standards Alignment

Before Lesson 11-1
Derive and use the formula for the area of a triangle and of a parallelogram by comparing it with the formula for the area of a rectangle from ⚷— Standard 5MG1.1

Lesson 11-1
Use variables in expressions describing geometric quantities Express in symbolic form simple relationships arising from geometry from Standards 6AF3.1 and 6AF3.2

After Lesson 11-1
Use formulas routinely for finding the perimeter and area of basic two-dimensional figures and the surface area and volume of basic three-dimensional figures from Standard 7MG2.1

❷ Teach

▶ MINI Lab

Some students may have difficulty counting the grid squares of the second and third parallelograms. Point out that they can visualize a right triangle on the left and right sides of each parallelogram. Have students mentally combine the two triangles to form a rectangle.

Scaffolding Questions

Ask:
- Is a rectangle a parallelogram? yes
- What is the formula for the area of a rectangle? area = length × width

Main IDEA
Find the areas of parallelograms.

 Standard 6AF3.1 Use variables in expressions describing geometric quantities (e.g., $P = 2w + 2\ell$, $A = \frac{1}{2}bh$, $C = \pi d$—the formulas for the perimeter of a rectangle, the area of a triangle, and the circumference of a circle, respectively). **Standard 6AF3.2 Express in symbolic form simple relationships arising from geometry.**

NEW Vocabulary

base
height

REVIEW Vocabulary

parallelogram quadrilateral with both pairs of opposite sides parallel and congruent (Lesson 10-5)

▶ MINI Lab

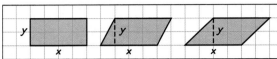

1. What is the value of x and y for each parallelogram? *x* = 4 units, *y* = 2 units
2. 8 sq units
2. Count the grid squares to find the area of each parallelogram.
3. On grid paper, draw three different parallelograms in which $x = 5$ units and $y = 4$ units. Find the area of each. 20 sq units
4. **MAKE A CONJECTURE** Explain how to find the area of a parallelogram if you know the values of x and y. The area equals $x \cdot y$.

You can find the area of a parallelogram by using the values for the base and height, as described below.

The **base** is any side of a parallelogram. 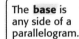 The **height** is the length of the segment perpendicular to the base with endpoints on opposite sides.

KEY CONCEPT   Area of a Parallelogram

Words The area A of a parallelogram equals the product of its base b and height h.

Model

Symbols $A = bh$

EXAMPLES Find the Area of a Parallelogram

Find the area of a parallelogram.

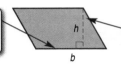

❶ Estimate $A = 13 \cdot 6$ or 78 cm²

$A = bh$ Area of a parallelogram

$A = 13 \cdot 5.8$ Replace b with 13 and h with 5.8.

$A = 75.4$ Multiply.

The area is 75.4 square centimeters.

Check for Reasonableness $75.4 \approx 78$ ✔

ADDITIONAL EXAMPLE

❶ Find the area of the parallelogram. 48 cm²

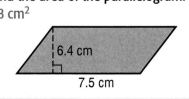

✓ Formative Assessment

Use the Check Your Progress exercises after each Example to determine students' understanding of concepts.

2 **Find the area of the parallelogram.**

The base is 11 inches, and the height is 9 inches.

11 in.

9 in. $9\frac{1}{2}$ in.

Estimate $A = 10 \cdot 10$ or 100 in^2

$A = bh$ Area of a parallelogram

$A = 11 \cdot 9$ Replace b with 11 and h with 9.

$A = 99$ Multiply.

The area of the parallelogram is 99 square inches.

Check for Reasonableness $99 \approx 100$ ✔

CHECK Your Progress

Find the area of each parallelogram.

a.

10.2 ft

7 ft   **71.4 ft²**

b.

$5\frac{1}{4}$ yd   **21 yd²**

4 yd

Online **Personal Tutor at** ca.gr6math.com

Real-World EXAMPLE

3 **WEATHER** The map shows the region of a state that is under a tornado warning. What is the area of this region?

KNOX   27.5 mi   ADAMS

LAKE
30.6 mi
FOX   LUCAS

Estimate $A = 30 \cdot 30$ or 900 mi^2

$A = bh$ Area of a parallelogram

$A = 27.5 \cdot 30.6$ Replace b with 27.5 and h with 30.6.

$A = 841.5$ Multiply.

The area of the region is 841.5 square miles.

Check for Reasonableness $841.5 \approx 900$ ✔

CHECK Your Progress   **193.75 ft²**

c. **SAFETY** A street department painted the pavement markings shown at the right on the surface of a highway to reduce traffic speeds and crashes. What is the area inside one of the markings?

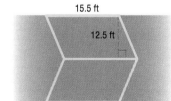

15.5 ft

12.5 ft

Math Online **Extra Examples at** ca.gr6math.com

Lesson 11-1 Area of Parallelograms   **573**

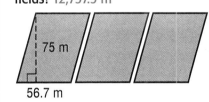

3 Practice

Formative Assessment

Use Exercises 1–5 to check for understanding.

Then use the chart at the bottom of this page to customize your assignments for students.

Intervention You may wish to use the Study Guide and Intervention Master on page 10 of the *Chapter 11 Resource Masters* for additional reinforcement.

Odd/Even Assignments

Exercises 6–15 are structured so that students practice the same concepts whether they are assigned odd or even problems.

CHECK Your Understanding

Example 1
(pp. 572)

Find the area of each parallelogram. Round to the nearest tenth if necessary.

1. 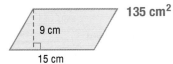 135 cm²
9 cm
15 cm

2. 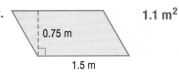 1.1 m²
0.75 m
1.5 m

Example 2
(p. 573)

3. 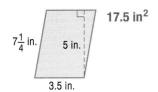 17.5 in²
$7\frac{1}{4}$ in. 5 in.
3.5 in.

4. 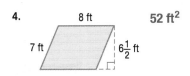 52 ft²
8 ft
7 ft $6\frac{1}{2}$ ft

Example 3
(p. 573)

5. **ART** Martina designs uniquely-shaped ceramic wall tiles. What is the area of the tile shown? **32 in²**

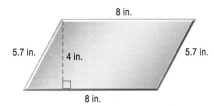
8 in.
5.7 in. 4 in. 5.7 in.
8 in.

Exercises

HOMEWORK HELP	
For Exercises	**See Examples**
6–9, 12–13	1
10–11	2
14–15	3

Exercise Levels
A: 6–15
B: 16–25
C: 26–28

12. $75\frac{1}{4}$ yd²

Find the area of each parallelogram. Round to the nearest tenth if necessary.

6.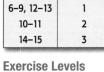
16 ft
16 ft
256 ft²

7.
4 cm
15 cm
60 cm²

8.
21 mm
20.4 mm
428.4 mm²

9.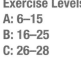
0.3 cm
0.2 cm² 0.5 cm

10.
12 in. 14 in.
$17\frac{1}{4}$ in. **207 in²**

11.
49.5 yd²
9 yd
10 yd $5\frac{1}{2}$ yd

12. What is the area of a parallelogram with base $10\frac{3}{4}$ yards and height 7 yards?

13. Find the area of a parallelogram with base 12.5 meters and height 15.25 meters. **190.625 m²**

★ 14. **WALLPAPER** The design of the wallpaper border at the right contains parallelograms. How much space on the border is covered by the parallelograms? **125 in²**

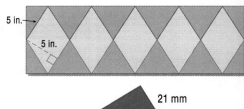
5 in.
5 in.

15. **PATTERN BLOCKS** What is the area of the parallelogram-shaped pattern block shown at the right? **525 mm²**
21 mm
25 mm

DIFFERENTIATED HOMEWORK OPTIONS

Level	Assignment	Two-Day Option	
BL Basic	6–15, 26, 28–38	7–15 odd, 29, 30	6–14 even, 26, 28, 31–38
OL Core	7–13 odd, 14–16, 17–21 odd, 22–26, 28–38	6–15, 29, 30	16–26, 28, 31–38
AL Advanced/Pre-AP	16–34 (optional: 35–38)		

16. PARKING SPACES A city ordinance requires that each parking space has
★ a minimum area of 162 square feet. Do the measurements of the parking
spaces shown below meet the requirements? Explain.

16. Yes; since
$18 \cdot 9 = 162$, the
measurements
meet the
requirements.

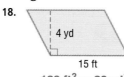

Find the area of each parallelogram. Round to the nearest tenth if necessary.

17.

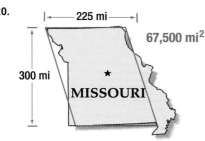

18 in.

1 ft

216 in² or 1.5 ft²

18.

4 yd

15 ft

180 ft² or 20 yd²

19.

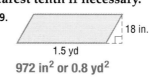

18 in.

1.5 yd

972 in² or 0.8 yd²

GEOGRAPHY Estimate the area of each state.

20.

225 mi

300 mi

67,500 mi²

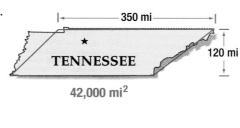

MISSOURI

21.

350 mi

120 mi

TENNESSEE

42,000 mi²

22. ALGEBRA A parallelogram has an
area of 75 square feet. Find the
base of the parallelogram if the
height is 3 feet. **25 ft**

$A = 75$ ft²   3 ft

b ft

23. ALGEBRA What is the height of a
parallelogram if the base is 24 inches
and the area is 360 square inches? **15 in.**

h in.

$A = 360$ in²

24 in.

QUILTING For Exercises 24 and 25, use the four quilt blocks shown and
following information.

Each quilt block uses eight parallelogram-shaped pieces of fabric that have a
height of $3\frac{1}{3}$ inches and a base of $3\frac{3}{4}$ inches.

First Block   Second Block   Third Block   Fourth Block

25. $16\frac{2}{3}$ ft²

24. Find the amount of fabric in square inches needed to make the
★ parallelogram-shaped pieces for one quilt block. **100 in²**

25. How much fabric is needed to make the parallelogram pieces for a quilt
★ that is made using 24 blocks? Write in square feet. (*Hint:* 144 in² = 1 ft²)

**Tips
for New
Teachers**

**Height of a
Parallelogram**

You may wish to point out to students
that the height of a parallelogram is
simply the perpendicular distance
between two opposite sides. Since the
sides are parallel, the height can be
shown outside the parallelogram, as in
Exercises 4, 9, 16, 19, and 20–22.

Ticket Out the Door Tell students that a parallelogram has a base of $x + 1$ feet and a height of 2 feet. Have students find the area of the parallelogram and write it on a slip of paper. $2x + 2$ feet

Foldables™
Study Organizer **Follow-Up**

Remind students to take notes about parallelograms in the Lesson 11-1 section of their Foldables. Encourage them to give an example, drawing and labeling the parts of a parallelogram.

Additional Answers

26.

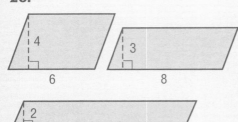

28. Sample answer: The area formula for a rectangle is $A = lw$ where l and w are the sides of the rectangle. The area formula for a parallelogram is $A = bh$ where b is the base (or one side of the parallelogram) and h is the height of the parallelogram perpendicular to the base. The height of the parallelogram is not necessarily one of the sides in a parallelogram as it is in a rectangle.

31.

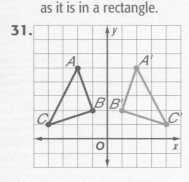

H.O.T. Problems ......
26. OPEN ENDED Draw three different parallelograms, each with an area of 24 square units. **See margin.**

27. CHALLENGE *True* or *False*? The area of a parallelogram doubles if you double the base and the height. Explain or give a counterexample to support your answer. **False; if the base and height are each doubled, then the area is $2b \times 2h = 4bh$, or 4 times greater.**

28. WRITING IN MATH Compare and contrast the formula for the area of a rectangle and a parallelogram. **See margin.**

STANDARDS PRACTICE 6AF3.1

29. A scale drawing of a piece of land is shown below.

What is the actual area of the land if the scale on the drawing is 10 km = 1 cm? **D**

A 67.5 cm² **C** 675 km²

B 67.5 km² **D** 6,750 km²

30. Ms. Cruz painted one wall in her living room. She did not paint the window.

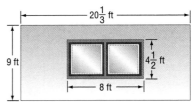

Which of the following is closest to the painted area of the wall in square feet? **G**

F 180 ft² **H** 120 ft²

G 150 ft² **J** 34 ft²

Spiral Review 31. See margin for graph.

For Exercises 31 and 32, refer to △ABC at the right. Find the vertices of △A′B′C′ after each transformation. Then graph the triangle and its reflected or translated image.

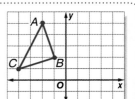

31. △ABC reflected over the *y*-axis (Lesson 10-9) *A′*(2, 5), *B′*(1, 2), *C′*(4, 1)

32. △ABC translated 5 units right and 1 unit up (Lesson 10-8)
A′(3, 6), *B′*(4, 3), *C′*(1, 2); See Ch. 11 Answer Appendix for graphs.

33. GEOMETRY Explain how to determine whether a regular octagon tessellates the plane. (Lesson 10-7)
See Ch. 11 Answer Appendix.

34. FRUIT If 2 out of every 3 pieces of fruit in a fruit basket are oranges, how many oranges are there if the fruit basket has 18 pieces of fruit?
(Lesson 6-5) **12**

▶ **GET READY for the Next Lesson**

PREREQUISITE SKILL Find each value. (Lesson 1-4)

35. $6(4 + 10)$ **84** **36.** $\frac{1}{2}(8)(8)$ **32** **37.** $\frac{1}{2}(24 + 15)$ **19.5** **38.** $\frac{1}{2}(5)(13 + 22)$ **87.5**

Pre-AP Activity Use after Exercise 26

Draw the two parallelograms on the board. Have students find the area of the shaded border region and explain the steps they took. **$3xy$; subtract the area of the small parallelogram from the area of the large parallelogram**

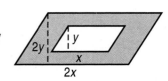

Main IDEA

Find the areas of parallelograms.

Standard 6AF3.2 Express in symbolic form simple relationships arising from geometry.
Standard 6MR3.3 Develop generalizations of the results obtained and the strategies used and apply them in new problem situations.

ACTIVITY

STEP 1 On grid paper, draw a triangle with a base of 6 units and a height of 3 units. Label the base *b* and the height *h* as shown.

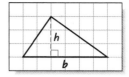

STEP 2 Fold the grid paper in half and cut out the triangle through both sheets so that you have two congruent triangles.

STEP 3 Turn the second triangle upside down and tape it to the first triangle.

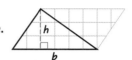

2. $A = bh$; 18 sq units

3. 9 sq units; Each triangle makes up half the parallelogram, so it has half the area.

5. The area of the triangle equals one half the area of the parallelogram.

ANALYZE THE RESULTS

1. What figure is formed by the two triangles? **parallelogram**

2. Write the formula for the area of the figure. Then find the area.

3. What is the area of each of the triangles? How do you know?

4. Repeat the activity above, drawing a different triangle in Step 1. Then find the area of each triangle. **See students' work.**

5. Compare the area of a triangle to the area of a parallelogram with the same base and height.

6. **MAKE A CONJECTURE** Write a formula for the area of a triangle with base *b* and height *h*. $A = \frac{1}{2}bh$

For Exercises 7–10, refer to the information below.

On grid paper, cut out two identical trapezoids. Label the bases b_1 and b_2, respectively, and label the heights *h*. Then turn one trapezoid upside down and tape it to the other trapezoid as shown.

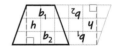

7. $b_1 + b_2$

8. $A = (b_1 + b_2)h$

7. Write an expression to represent the base of the parallelogram.

8. Write a formula for the area *A* of the parallelogram using b_1, b_2, and *h*.

9. How does the area of each trapezoid compare to the area of the parallelogram? **Sample answer: The area of each trapezoid is one-half the area of the parallelogram.**

10. **MAKE A CONJECTURE** Write a formula for the area *A* of a trapezoid with bases b_1 and b_2, and height *h*. $A = \frac{1}{2}(b_1 + b_2)h$

Explore 11-2 Measurement Lab: Triangles and Trapezoids 577

1 Focus

logo Materials
- centimeter grid paper
- straightedges
- scissors
- tape

Easy-to-Make Manipulatives

Teaching Mathematics with Manipulatives, templates for:

- centimeter grid, p. 15

2 Teach

Activity You might want to encourage students to draw different triangles with bases of 6 units and heights of 3 units (by moving the vertex opposite the base left or right). If so, have students who made different triangles compare their results. Did the different triangles have the same area? Did students write the same formula for the area of a triangle? Make sure students realize that the base and the height of a triangle—not its shape—determine its area.

Students can make congruent trapezoids the same way that they made congruent triangles—by drawing a trapezoid on grid paper, folding the paper in half, and cutting through both sheets of the paper.

3 Assess

Formative Assessment

Use Exercises 3 and 4 to determine whether students understand how to find the area of triangles using models of parallelograms.

Moving from Models to Abstract Thought Use Exercises 6 and 10 to bridge the gap between using models to find the areas of triangles and trapezoids and using the formulas for area.

Extending the Concept Have students predict whether any side of a triangle can be used as its base. Then have them draw a right triangle and find its area twice, first using one leg as the base and next using the other leg as the base.

 **Area of Triangles and Trapezoids**

Standard 6AF3.1: Use variables in expressions describing geometric quantities (e.g., $P = 2w + 2\ell$, $A = \frac{1}{2}bh$, $C = \pi d$–the formulas for the perimeter of a rectangle, **the area of a triangle,** and the circumference of a circle, respectively).

Standard 6AF3.2: **Express in symbolic form simple relationships arising from geometry.**

PACING: **Regular:** 1 period, **Block:** 0.5 period

Options for Differentiated Instruction

ELL = English Language Learner   **AL** = Above Grade Level   **SS** = Struggling Students   **SN** = Special Needs

Visualizing Substitutions **ELL** **SN**

Use before assigning the Exercises.

To help students identify which values should be substituted for the variables in the formula for the area of a trapezoid, suggest that they use different color highlighters to organize the information.

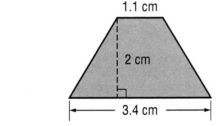

$h = 2$ cm, $b_1 = 1.1$ cm $b_2 = 3.4$ cm $\rightarrow$ A $= \frac{1}{2}h(b_1 + b_2)$

Making Artwork **SS** **SN**

Use after presenting Lesson 11-2.

Give groups of students colored paper, rulers, and scissors. Have each group make a mosaic design using triangles and trapezoids. Have them determine the area of each shape and the total area of the design. You may want to attach the designs to poster board and hang them on the wall.

Additional Practice **AL**

Use after students complete Lesson 11-2.

Have students draw and label the figure described below. Then have them find the area.

> an isosceles triangle with a height greater than 6 inches and an area greater than 20 square inches

Sample answer:

28 in²

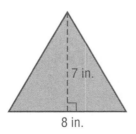

Leveled Lesson Resources

Chapter 11 Resource Masters

BL = Below Grade Level **OL** = On Grade Level **AL** = Above Grade Level **ELL** = English Language Learner

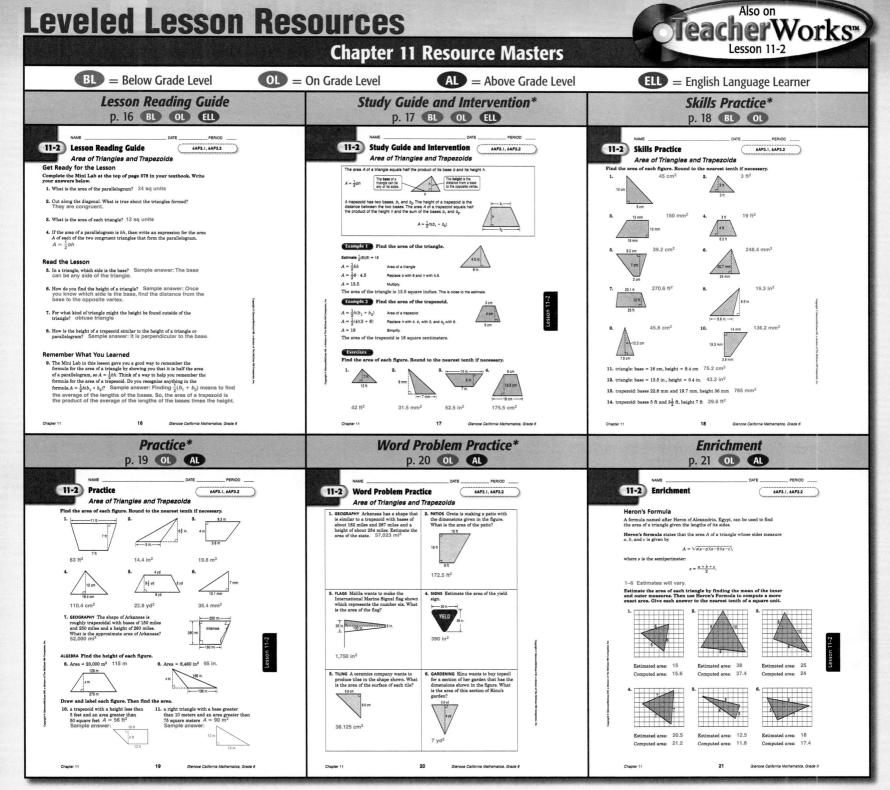

Additional Lesson Resources

* Also available in Spanish **ELL**

Transparencies
- *5-Minute Check Transparency*, Lesson 11-2

Other Print Products
- *Teaching Mathematics with Manipulatives*
- *Noteables™ Interactive Study Notebook with Foldables™*

Teacher Tech Tools
- *Interactive Classroom CD-ROM*, Lesson 11-2
- *AssignmentWorks*, Lesson 11-2

Student Tech Tools
ca.gr6math.com
- Extra Examples, Chapter 11, Lesson 2
- Self-Check Quiz, Chapter 11, Lesson 2

 11-2 **Area of Triangles and Trapezoids**

1 Focus

 Standards Alignment

Before Lesson 11-2
Derive and use the formula for the area of a triangle and of a parallelogram by comparing it with the formula for the area of a rectangle from ⚷— Standard 5MG1.1

Lesson 11-2
Use variables in expressions describing geometric quantities (e.g., $A = \frac{1}{2}bh$—the formula for the area of a triangle. Express in symbolic form simple relationships arising from geometry from Standards 6AF3.1 and 6AF3.2

After Lesson 11-2
Use formulas routinely for finding the perimeter and area of basic two-dimensional figures and the surface area and volume of basic three-dimensional figures from Standard 7MG2.1

2 Teach

▶ **MINI Lab**

Make sure students realize that the two triangles are congruent. Have them flip one of the triangles twice (horizontally and vertically) and compare them.

Scaffolding Questions

Draw the square and the rectangle shown below on the board. Draw the diagonals and label the sides.

 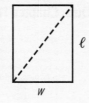

Ask:
- What kind of triangle is formed by the diagonals? right triangle
- What is the area of the square? s^2
- What is the area of one of the triangles formed by the square's diagonal? $\frac{1}{2}s^2$

continued at the right

- What is the area of the rectangle? ℓw
- What is the area of one of the triangles formed by the rectangle's diagonal? $\frac{1}{2}\ell w$

Main IDEA

Find the areas of triangles and trapezoids.

Standard 6AF3.1 Use variables in expressions describing geometric quantities (e.g., $P = 2w + 2\ell$, $A = \frac{1}{2}bh$, $C = \pi d$—the **formulas for** the perimeter of a rectangle, **the area of a triangle**, and the circumference of a circle, respectively).
Standard 6AF3.2 Express in symbolic form simple relationships arising from geometry.

REVIEW Vocabulary

perpendicular lines lines that intersect at right angles (Lesson 10-1)

▶ **MINI Lab**

1. 24 sq units
2. They are congruent.

- Draw a parallelogram with a base of 6 units and a height of 4 units.
- Draw a diagonal as shown.
- Cut out the parallelogram.

1. What is the area of the parallelogram?
2. Cut along the diagonal. What is true about the triangles formed?
3. What is the area of each triangle? 12 sq units
4. If the area of a parallelogram is bh, then write an expression for the area A of each of the two congruent triangles that form the parallelogram. $A = \frac{1}{2}bh$

You can find the area of a triangle by using the base and height.

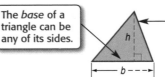

| The *base* of a triangle can be any of its sides. | The *height* is the perpendicular distance from the vertex opposite the base to the line containing the base. |

KEY CONCEPT   Area of a Triangle

| Words | The area A of a triangle equals half the product of its base b and height h. | Model |
| Symbols | $A = \frac{1}{2}bh$ | |

EXAMPLE   Find the Area of a Triangle

1. Find the area of the triangle below.
Estimate $A = \frac{1}{2}(10)(7)$ or 35

$A = \frac{1}{2}bh$ Area of a triangle

$A = \frac{1}{2}(10)(6.5)$ Replace b with 10 and h with 6.5.

$A = 32.5$ Multiply.

The area of the triangle is 32.5 square meters.

Check for Reasonableness $32.5 \approx 35$ ✔

✓ CHECK Your Progress

Find the area of each triangle. Round to the nearest tenth if necessary.

a. 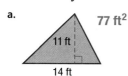 77 ft²

11 ft
14 ft

b. 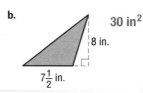 30 in²

8 in.
$7\frac{1}{2}$ in.

A trapezoid has two bases, b_1 and b_2. The bases are always the two sides that are parallel. The height of a trapezoid is the perpendicular distance between the bases.

Concepts in MOtion
Interactive Lab ca.gr6math.com

> ### KEY CONCEPT Area of a Trapezoid
>
> **Words** The area A of a trapezoid equals half the product of the height h and the sum of the bases $b_1 + b_2$.
>
> **Model**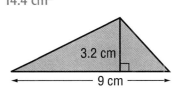
>
> **Symbols** $A = \frac{1}{2}h(b_1 + b_2)$

EXAMPLE Find the Area of a Trapezoid

READING Math

Subscripts Read b_1 as b sub 1. Read b_2 as b sub 2. The subscripts mean that b_1 and b_2 represent different variables.

2 **Find the area of the trapezoid.**

The bases are 5 inches and 12 inches.
The height is 7 inches.

5 in.
7 in.
12 in.

$A = \frac{1}{2}h(b_1 + b_2)$ Area of a trapezoid

$A = \frac{1}{2}(7)(5 + 12)$ Replace h with 7, b_1 with 5, and b_2 with 12.

$A = \frac{1}{2}(7)(17)$ Add 5 and 12.

$A = 59.5$ Multiply.

The area of the trapezoid is 59.5 square inches.

✓ CHECK Your Progress

Find the area of each trapezoid. Round to the nearest tenth if necessary.

c. 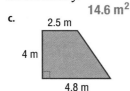 14.6 m²

2.5 m
4 m
4.8 m

d. 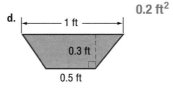 0.2 ft²

1 ft
0.3 ft
0.5 ft

Online **Personal Tutor at** ca.gr6math.com

Math **Online** **Extra Examples at** ca.gr6math.com   **Lesson 11-2** Area of Triangles and Trapezoids **579**

Focus on Mathematical Content

To calculate the area of a triangle, find the length of a **base** and the **height** to that base. Then substitute them in the formula.

To calculate the area of trapezoid, find the length of both **bases** and the **height**. Then substitute them in the formula.

Estimation is a good way to check an area calculation.

✓ **Formative Assessment**

Use the Check Your Progress exercises after each Example to determine students' understanding of concepts.

ADDITIONAL EXAMPLES

1 Find the area of the triangle below. 14.4 cm²

3.2 cm
9 cm

2 Find the area of the trapezoid below. 17.4 m²

4 m
3 m
7.6 m

Additional Examples are also in:

• Noteables™ Interactive Study Notebook with Foldables™

• Interactive Classroom PowerPoint® Presentations

③ GEOGRAPHY The shape of the state of Montana resembles a trapezoid. Find the approximate area of Montana.

about 145,493 mi²

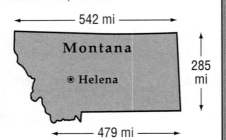

Montana
⊛ Helena

542 mi · 285 mi · 479 mi

Real-World Link · · · · ·
Kern County, larger than Massachusetts, New Jersey, and Hawaii combined, is home to the wild and scenic Kern River which offers rapids, fishing, and camping.
Source: visitkern.com

③ GEOGRAPHY The shape of Kern County resembles a trapezoid. Find the approximate area of this county.

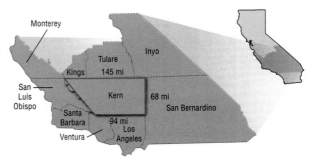

$A = \frac{1}{2}h(b_1 + b_2)$ · · · · Area of a trapezoid

$A = \frac{1}{2}(68)(94 + 145)$ · · · · Replace h with 68, b_1 with 94, and b_2 with 145.

$A = \frac{1}{2}(68)(239)$ · · · · Add 94 and 145.

$A = 8{,}126$ · · · · Multiply.

The area of Kern County is approximately 8,126 square miles.

CHECK Your Progress

e. GEOGRAPHY The shape of the state of Arkansas resembles a trapezoid. Find the approximate area of Arkansas.

about 57,575 mi²

280 mi
235 mi · **ARKANSAS** ⊛ Little Rock
210 mi

★ indicates multi-step problem

CHECK Your Understanding

Examples 1, 2
(pp. 578–579)

Find the area of each figure. Round to the nearest tenth if necessary.

1. 6 in²

3 in.
4 in.

2. 105.6 m²

16.5 m
12.8 m

3. 90.4 ft² 7 ft

8 ft
15.6 ft

Example 3
(p. 580)

4. **GEOGRAPHY** Nevada has a shape that looks like a trapezoid, as shown at the right. Find the approximate area of Nevada.

about 108,756 mi²

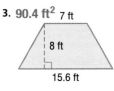

318 mi
206 mi · **NEVADA** ⊛ Carson City
478 mi

Exercises

HOMEWORK HELP

For Exercises	See Examples
5, 6, 9	1
7, 8, 10	2
11, 12	3

Exercise Levels
A: 5–12
B: 13–20
C: 21–23

Find the area of each figure. Round to the nearest tenth if necessary.

5. 147 in²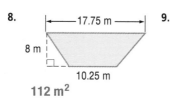
14 in.
21 in.

6. 38.4 mm²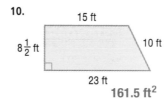
8 mm
9.6 mm

7. 4.5 cm²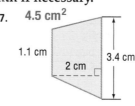
1.1 cm
2 cm
3.4 cm

8.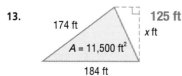
17.75 m
8 m
10.25 m
112 m²

9. 183.7 in²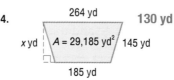
22 in.
16.7 in.

10.
15 ft
$8\frac{1}{2}$ ft
10 ft
23 ft
161.5 ft²

11. **GEOGRAPHY** The shape of Idaho is roughly triangular with a base of 380 miles and a height of 500 miles. Find the approximate area of Idaho. **about 95,000 mi²**

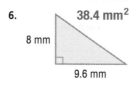
500 mi
★ IDAHO
380 mi

12. **ALGEBRA** Find the area of a trapezoid with bases 13 inches and 15 inches and a height of 7 inches. **98 in²**

ALGEBRA Find the height of each figure.

13.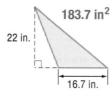
174 ft
125 ft
x ft
$A = 11,500$ ft²
184 ft

14.
264 yd
130 yd
x yd $A = 29,185$ yd² 145 yd
185 yd

Draw and label each figure. Then find the area. **15–17. See margin.**

15. a triangle with no right angles and an area less than 12 square centimeters

16. a trapezoid with a right angle and an area greater than 40 square meters

17. a trapezoid with no right angles and an area less than 25 square feet

★ 18. **ARCHITECTURE** The blueprints for a patio are shown at the right. If the cost of the patio is $4.50 per square foot, what will be the total cost of the patio? **$1,417.50**

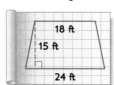
18 ft
15 ft
24 ft

LANDSCAPING For Exercises 19 and 20, use the diagram that shows the lawn that surrounds an office building.

EXTRA PRACTICE

See pages 708, 725.

Math Online
Self-Check Quiz at
ca.gr6math.com

19. What is the area of the lawn? **6,500 ft²**

★ 20. If one bag of grass seed covers 2,000 square feet, how many bags are needed to seed the lawn? **4 bags**

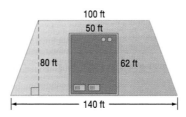
100 ft
50 ft
80 ft 62 ft
140 ft

Lesson 11-2 Area of Triangles and Trapezoids **581**

3 Practice

✓ Formative Assessment

Use Exercises 1–4 to check for understanding.

Then use the chart at the bottom of this page to customize your assignments for students.

Intervention You may wish to use the Study Guide and Intervention Master on page 17 of the *Chapter 11 Resource Masters* for additional reinforcement.

Odd/Even Assignments

Exercises 5–12 are structured so that students practice the same concepts whether they are assigned odd or even problems.

Tips for New Teachers

Measuring Height

You may wish to point out to students that the height of a triangle or trapezoid can be shown outside the figure, as in Exercises 2, 8, 9, 13, and 14.

Additional Answers

15. Sample answer:
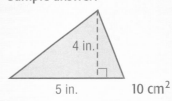
4 in.
5 in. 10 cm²

16. Sample answer:
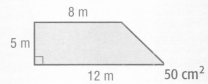
8 m
5 m
12 m 50 cm²

17. Sample answer:
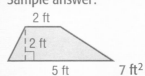
2 ft
2 ft
5 ft 7 ft²

DIFFERENTIATED HOMEWORK OPTIONS

Level	Assignment	Two-Day Option	
BL Basic	5–12, 22–35	5–11 odd, 24, 25	6–12 even, 22, 23, 26–35
OL Core	5–17 odd, 18–20, 22–35	5–12, 24, 25	13–20, 22, 23, 26–35
AL Advanced/Pre-AP	13–31 (optional: 32–35)		

Lesson 11-2 Area of Triangles and Trapezoids **581**

4 Assess

Yesterday's News Remind students that yesterday's lesson was about finding the area of parallelograms. Have them write how yesterday's concepts helped them with today's material.

FOLDABLES™ **Foldables™ Follow-Up**
Study Organizer

Remind students to take notes about triangles and trapezoids in the Lesson 11-2 section of their Foldables. Encourage them to give examples, drawing and labeling the parts of the figures.

Additional Answers

22. Sample answer: The lengths of the bases can be rounded to 20 in. and 30 in., respectively. The area can be rounded to 250 in². Divide 250 by $\frac{1}{2}$ (20 + 30) or 25. The height h is about 10 in.

27.

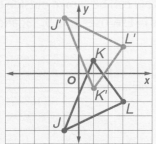

$J'(-1, 4), L'(1, -1), K'(3, 2)$

H.O.T. Problems

23. The area of a triangle is half the area of a parallelogram with the same base and height, because two of these triangles make up the parallelogram.

21. CHALLENGE A triangle has height h. Its base is 4. Create an algebraic equation for the area of the triangle in terms of h. **$A = 2h$**

22. REASONING Apply what you know about rounding to explain how to estimate the height h of the trapezoid shown if the area is 235.5 in². **See margin.**

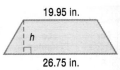

23. WRITING IN MATH Describe the relationship between the area of a parallelogram and the area of a triangle with the same height and base.

STANDARDS PRACTICE   6AF3.1

24. $\triangle FGH$ and $\triangle JKM$ are similar.

Which choice shows the equations that can be used to find the area of $\triangle FGH$? **C**

A $\frac{18}{24} = \frac{12}{x}$ and then $\frac{1}{2}(18x)$

B $\frac{18}{24} = \frac{x}{12}$ and then $18x$

C $\frac{18}{24} = \frac{x}{12}$ and then $\frac{1}{2}(18x)$

D $\frac{18}{24} = \frac{12}{x}$ and then $18x$

25. Randy was hired to put in sod on a piece of land shaped like a trapezoid as shown. How many square feet of sod are needed? **G**

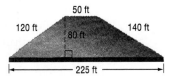

F 4000 ft²

G 11,000 ft²

H 20,400 ft²

J 32,000 ft²

Spiral Review

26. MEASUREMENT Find the area of a parallelogram having a base of 2.3 inches and a height of 1.6 inches. Round to the nearest tenth. (Lesson 11-1) **3.7 in²**

★ **27. GEOMETRY** Graph $\triangle JLK$ with vertices $J(-1, -4)$, $K(1, 1)$, and $L(3, -2)$ and its reflection over the x-axis. Write the ordered pairs for the vertices of the new figure. (Lesson 10-9) **See margin.**

Find each number. Round to the nearest tenth if necessary. (Lesson 7-5)

28. What number is 56% of 600? **336**

29. 24.5 is what percent of 98? **25%**

30. 72 is 45% of what number? **160**

31. 62.5% of 250 is what number? **156.3**

GET READY for the Next Lesson

PREREQUISITE SKILL Find each product to the nearest tenth. Use 3.14 for π. (Lesson 1-4)

32. $\pi \cdot 13$ **40.8**

33. $\pi \cdot 29$ **91.1**

34. $\pi \cdot 16^2$ **803.8**

35. $\pi \cdot 4.8^2$ **72.3**

Differentiated Instruction

Visual/Spatial Learners Separate students into groups of two or three. Distribute colored paper, rulers, and scissors to each group. Have each group design a mosaic using triangles, trapezoids, and parallelograms. Have each group determine the area of each shape and the total area of its design. You may wish to hang the designs on a classroom wall.

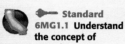

Main IDEA

Find a relationship between circumference and diameter.

🔑 **Standard 6MG1.1** Understand the concept of a constant such as π; know the formulas for the circumference and area of a circle.
Standard 6MR3.3 Develop generalizations of the results obtained and the strategies used and apply them in new problem situations.

In this lab, you will investigate how the *circumference*, or the distance around a circle, is related to its *diameter*, or the distance across a circle through its center.

ACTIVITY

STEP 1 Use a ruler to measure the diameter of a circular object. Record the length in a table like the one shown below.

Object	Diameter (cm)	Circumference (cm)

STEP 2 Make a small mark at the edge of the circular object. Place a measuring tape on a flat surface. Place the mark you made on the circular object at the beginning of the measuring tape. Roll the object along the tape for one revolution, until you reach the mark again.

STEP 3 Record the length in the table. This is the circumference.

STEP 4 Repeat this activity with circular objects of various sizes.

ANALYZE THE RESULTS

1. For each object, divide the circumference by the diameter. Add another column to your table and record the results. Round to the nearest tenth if necessary. **See students' work.**

2. What do you notice about the ratio of each circumference to each diameter? **They are slightly greater than 3.**

3. See students' graphs. All points lie on a diagonal line.

3. Graph the ordered pair (diameter, circumference) on a coordinate plane for each object. What do you notice?

4. Use the graph to predict the circumference of a circular object that has a diameter of 18 centimeters. **Sample answer: about 56.5 cm**

5. **MAKE A CONJECTURE** Write a rule describing how you would find the circumference C of a circle if you know the diameter d.
Sample answer: $C \approx 3.1d$

6. Sample answer: about 45 × 3.1 or 139.5 cm

6. Use your rule to approximate the circumference of a circular object that has a diameter of 45 centimeters.

1 Focus

logo Materials

- rulers
- measuring tapes
- circular objects

2 Teach

Activity You may want to bring to class several circular objects, such as cans, plastic cups, bowls, and buttons. Otherwise, have students find circular objects in classroom. You may wish to have students work in pairs. Depending on the object and the measuring tape, students may find it difficult to measure the circumference with the measuring tape. Suggest that they measure the object's circumference indirectly—by laying a string around the object, marking the string, and then measuring the distance between marks on the string with a ruler.

3 Assess

✔️ **Formative Assessment**

Use Exercise 2 to determine whether students understand that the ratio of any circle's circumference to its diameter is the same number (approximately 3.14).

Moving from Models to Abstract Thought Use Exercise 5 to bridge the gap between measuring to find the circumference of an object and using the object's diameter and π to calculate the circumference.

11-3 Circles and Circumference

Standard 6MG1.1: Understand the concept of a constant such as π; know the formulas for the **circumference** and area of a circle.

Standard 6MG1.2: Know common estimates of π (3.14, $\frac{22}{7}$) and use these values to estimate and calculate the **circumference** and area **of circles; compare with actual measurements.**

PACING: **Regular:** 1 period, **Block:** 0.5 period

Options for Differentiated Instruction

ELL = English Language Learner   **AL** = Above Grade Level   **SS** = Struggling Students   **SN** = Special Needs

Additional Activity   ELL AL SS SN

Use before presenting Lesson 11-3.

Cut different lengths of string and give each student a piece. Have them measure the string in centimeters and record the length. Then have them make the best circle they can with their string, without overlapping the ends. Tell them to measure and record the distance across the circle that goes through the center of the circle (diameter).

After everyone has recorded both measures, have them use a calculator to find the ratio shown at the right. Have each person write their ratio on the board.

> **Ratio**
>
> $$\frac{\text{the total length of the string}}{\text{the distance across the circle}}$$

Ask:

- What value are most of the ratios closest to? 3.14 or pi
- How could this have happened if everyone has different lengths of string? The lengths are different, but so are the distances across the circles, so the ratios are the same.
- Do you think that no matter how big the circle is, the same thing will happen? Answers will vary.
- Which is easier to measure: the distance around a circle or the distance across a circle? distance across a circle
- How could you use the information from this activity to find the distance around a circle? Sample answer: Measure the distance across the circle and use the value of the ratio, 3.14, to find the distance around the circle.

Symbols   AL

Use before presenting Example 1.

Students sometimes mistakenly believe that pi (π) is a variable since measurements are often written as 2π, 3.4π, and so on. Write the following pairs of values on the board.

$$12\pi \text{ cm and } 12 \text{ cm} \qquad\qquad 5x \text{ and } 5\pi$$

Ask:

- What is the different between 12π cm and 12 cm? 12π cm is about 3.14 times 12 cm.
- What is the difference between $5x$ and 5π? x is a variable and can represent any number, so the value of $5x$ is unknown. π is a constant approximately equal to 3.14, so 5π is about 15.7.

Leveled Lesson Resources

Chapter 11 Resource Masters

BL = Below Grade Level   **OL** = On Grade Level   **AL** = Above Grade Level   **ELL** = English Language Learner

Lesson Reading Guide
p. 22 **BL** **OL** **ELL**

11-3 Lesson Reading Guide   6MG1.1, 6MG1.2
Circles and Circumference

Get Ready for the Lesson
Read the introduction at the top of page 584 in your textbook. Write your answers below.

1. Which point appears to be the center of the Ferris wheel? G

2. Is the distance from G to F greater than, less than, or equal to the distance from G to J? equal to

3. What can you say about the distance from G to H and the distance from F to J? It is half of F to J.

Read the Lesson

4. The Greek letter π represents a nonterminating and nonrepeating number. What does this mean? Sample answer: The number that π represents (3.1415926...) is a decimal number whose digits to the right of the decimal point do not end or have any repeating pattern.

5. When is the symbol ≈ used when finding the circumference of a circle? Why is this symbol used? Sample answer: The symbol ≈ is used when a number is substituted for π in the formula for the circumference of a circle. When you use a number in place of π, that number is only an approximation of π, so the value of the circumference will also only be an approximation.

6. What two numbers are used in this lesson as approximations for π? 3.14 and $\frac{22}{7}$

Remember What You Learned

7. The word *diameter* comes from two Greek words that mean "a measure (*metron*) through (*dia*)." What is the diameter of a circle? Sample answer: the distance through the center of a circle from one side to the other

8. One of the definitions given for *radius* is *semidiameter*. Think of the relationship between radius and diameter. What do you think *semidiameter* means? Sample answer: half of a diameter

Chapter 11   22   Glencoe California Mathematics, Grade 6

Study Guide and Intervention*
p. 23 **BL** **OL** **ELL**

11-3 Study Guide and Intervention   6MG1.1, 6MG1.2
Circles and Circumference

A **circle** is the set of all points in a plane that are the same distance from a given point, called the **center**. The **diameter** d is the distance across the circle through its center. The **radius** r is the distance from the center to any point on the circle. The **circumference** C is the distance around the circle. The circumference C of a circle is equal to its diameter d times π, or 2 times its radius r times π.

Example 1 Find the circumference of a circle with a diameter of 7.5 centimeters.

$C = \pi d$ Circumference of a circle.
$C \approx 3.14 \times 7.5$ Replace π with 3.14 and d with 7.5.
$C \approx 23.55$ The circumference of the circle is about 23.55 centimeters.

Example 2 If the radius of a circle is 14 inches, what is its circumference?

$C = 2\pi r$
$C \approx 2 \times 3.14 \times 14$ Replace π with 3.14 and r with 14.
$C \approx 88$ The circumference of the circle is about 88 inches.

Exercises
Find the circumference of each circle. Use 3.14 for π. Round to the nearest tenth if necessary.

1. 37.7 ft   2. 62.8 cm   3. 31.4 m   4. 23.6 in.

5. diameter = 15 cm   47.1 km   6. radius = 21 mi   131.9 mi   7. radius = 50 m   314 m

8. diameter = 600 ft   1,884 ft   9. radius = 62 mm   389.4 mm   10. diameter = 7 km   22.0 km

11. radius = 95 in.   596.6 in.   12. diameter = 6.3 m   19.8 m   13. diameter = $5\frac{1}{4}$ cm   16.5 cm

Chapter 11   23   Glencoe California Mathematics, Grade 6

Skills Practice*
p. 24 **BL** **OL**

11-3 Skills Practice   6MG1.1, 6MG1.2
Circles and Circumference

Find the circumference of each circle. Use 3.14 for π. Round to the nearest tenth if necessary.

1. 4 in.   25.1 in.   2. 15 cm   47.1 cm

3. 8 ft   50.2 ft   4. 21 m   65.9 m

5. 16 km   100.5 km   6. 37 mm   116.2 mm

7. radius = 3 km   18.8 km   8. radius = 46 cm   288.9 cm

9. diameter = 30 in.   94.2 in.   10. diameter = 25 m   78.5 m

11. radius = 5 ft   31.4 ft   12. diameter = $9\frac{1}{2}$ in.   29.8 in.

13. radius = $3\frac{1}{2}$ ft   22.0 ft   14. radius = 9.7 mm   30.5 mm

15. radius = 5.2 km   32.7 km   16. radius = 12 m   37.7 m

17. radius = 22 ft   138.2 ft   18. radius = 9.4 in.   29.5 in.

19. radius = 100 m   628 m   20. radius = 65 mi   408.2 mi

21. diameter = $10\frac{1}{2}$ in.   33.0 in.   22. diameter = 8.5 cm   26.7 cm

Chapter 11   24   Glencoe California Mathematics, Grade 6

Practice*
p. 25 **OL** **AL**

11-3 Practice   6MG1.1, 6MG1.2
Circles and Circumference

Find the circumference of each circle. Use 3.14 for π. Round to the nearest tenth if necessary.

1. 2.4 cm   15.1 cm   2. 28 ft   87.9 ft   3. 1.5 yd   4.7 yd

4. 4.2 mm   26.4 mm   5. 12 m   75.4 m   6. 7 in.   22 in.

7. radius = $2\frac{1}{3}$ ft   14.7 ft   8. radius = 11.9 m   74.7 m   9. diameter = $5\frac{5}{6}$ mi   18.3 mi

10. radius = $6\frac{1}{8}$ in.   38.5 in.   11. diameter = $17\frac{1}{2}$ ft   55 ft   12. radius = 9.2 km   57.8 km

Estimate to find the approximate circumference of each circle. Explain which approximation of π you used.

13. $5\frac{1}{8}$ ft   14. 4.1 cm   15. 59 in.

Sample answer: $5\frac{1}{8}$ is about 5 and $\frac{22}{7}$ is about 3 so, 5 × 3 or 15 ft

Sample answer: 4.1 is about 4 and 3.14 is about 3 so, 4 × 2 × 3 or 24 m

Sample answer: 59 is about 60 and 3.14 is about 3 so, 60 × 3 or 180 in.

ALGEBRA Find the diameter or radius of each circle. Use 3.14 for π. Round to the nearest tenth if necessary.

16. C = 32 m, diameter = ___   10.2 m   17. C = 55 mi, radius = ___   8.8 mi

18. **HELICOPTERS** The landing circle for helicopters on the roof of a hospital has a radius of 20 yards. To the nearest yard, find its circumference. 126 yd

19. **SPA** A circular spa has a diameter of 12 feet. The spa is decorated with 4-inch porcelain tiles around the rim. How many tiles surround the rim of the spa? Round to the nearest whole number. 113 tiles

Chapter 11   25   Glencoe California Mathematics, Grade 6

Word Problem Practice*
p. 26 **OL** **AL**

11-3 Word Problem Practice   6MG1.1, 6MG1.2
Circles and Circumference

1. **PLATES** A manufacturing company is producing dinner plates with a diameter of 12 inches. They plan to put a gold edge on each plate. Determine how much edging they need for each plate by finding the circumference of each plate. Round to the nearest tenth. 37.7 in.

2. **MONEY** A dime has a radius of $8\frac{1}{2}$ millimeters. Find the circumference of a dime to the nearest tenth. 53.4 mm

3. **MERRY-GO-ROUND** Mr. Osterhout is putting trim around the edge of a circular merry-go-round that has a diameter of 15 feet. How much trim does he need to buy to the nearest tenth? 47.1 ft

4. **PIZZA** Find the circumference of a pizza with a diameter of 10 inches. Round to the nearest tenth. 31.4 in.

5. **RACING** A circular racetrack has a diameter of $\frac{1}{2}$ mile. How far does a car travel in one lap around the track? Round to the nearest tenth. 1.6 mi

6. **TIRE** A bicycle tire has a radius of 15 inches. What is the circumference of the tire? Round to the nearest tenth. 94.2 in.

7. **EQUATOR** Earth's diameter at the equator is 7,926 miles. Find the distance around Earth at its equator to the nearest tenth. 24,887.6 mi

8. **SATURN** The ring system around Saturn has a diameter of 170,000 miles. Find the circumference of the ring system. 533,800 mi

Chapter 11   26   Glencoe California Mathematics, Grade 6

Enrichment
p. 27 **OL** **AL**

11-3 Enrichment   6MG1.1, 6MG1.2

Finding the Length of an Arc

Recall that the circumference is the measure of the distance around a circle. A portion of the circumference is called an arc. An arc is named by the endpoints of the radii that create it. To find the measure of an arc, you can use a proportion. The ratio of the arc length to the circumference is equal to the ratio of the central angle of the arc to 360°.

To find the measure of AB, first set up the ratio: $\frac{mAB}{2\pi r} = \frac{m\angle ACB}{360°}$

Next, fill in the known values. $\frac{mAB}{4\pi} = \frac{x}{360°}$

Simplify the fraction. $\frac{mAB}{4\pi} = \frac{1}{9}$

Then solve for mAB. $mAB = \frac{4\pi}{9} \approx 1.40$ cm

Solve the following problems.

1. A circle has a circumference of 48 centimeters. Find the length of an arc that has a central angle of 90°. $\frac{mAB}{48} = \frac{90°}{360°}$ 12 cm

2. A circle has a circumference of 112 meters. The length of DF is 14 meters. Find the measure of the central angle of DF. $\frac{14}{112} = \frac{x}{360°}$ 45°

3. A circle has a radius of 5 inches. Find the length of an arc that has a central angle of 72°. $\frac{mAB}{10\pi} = \frac{72°}{360°}$ 6.28 in.

4. Two arcs in a circle have central angles of 135° and 45°. Find the ratio of the arcs' lengths. $\frac{135°}{45°}$ 3:1

5. AB has a central angle of 50° in a circle whose diameter is 12 feet, while DEF has a central angle of 150° in a circle whose diameter is 3 feet. Which of these two arcs is longer? Explain. $\frac{mAB}{12\pi} = \frac{50°}{360°}, \frac{mDEF}{3\pi} = \frac{150°}{360°}$; AB is 5.23 feet long, and DEF is 3.93 feet long

Chapter 11   27   Glencoe California Mathematics, Grade 6

Also available in Spanish **ELL**

Additional Lesson Resources

Transparencies
- *5-Minute Check Transparency*, Lesson 11-3

Other Print Products
- *Teaching Mathematics with Manipulatives*
- *Noteables™ Interactive Study Notebook with Foldables™*

Teacher Tech Tools
- *Interactive Classroom CD-ROM*, Lesson 11-3
- *AssignmentWorks*, Lesson 11-3

Student Tech Tools
ca.gr6math.com
- Extra Examples, Chapter 11, Lesson 3
- Self-Check Quiz, Chapter 11, Lesson 3

11-3 Circles and Circumference

1 Focus

Standards Alignment

Before Lesson 11-3
Differentiate between and use appropriate units of measures for two- and three-dimensional objects from Standard 5MG1.4

Lesson 11-3
Understand the concept of a constant such as π; know the formula for the circumference of a circle. Know common esti mates of π and use these values to estimate and calculate the circumference of circles; compare with actual measurements from Standards 6MG1.1 and 6MG1.2

After Lesson 11-3
Use formulas routinely for finding the perimeter and area of basic two-dimensional figures and the surface area and volume of basic three-dimensional figures from Standard 7MG2.1

2 Teach

Scaffolding Questions

Ask:
- What is the distance around a triangle called? perimeter

- What is the distance around a rectangle called? perimeter

- How can you find the perimeter of a polygon such as a triangle or rectangle? either add the lengths of the sides or use a formula such as $P = 2(\ell + w)$

- How might you find the distance around a circle? Sample answer: place a string around the circle and then measure length of the string

Main IDEA
Find the circumference of circles.

 Standard **6MG1.1** **Understand the concept of a constant such as π; know the formulas for the circumference** and area **of a circle.** **Standard MG1.2** **Know common estimates of π (3.14, $\frac{22}{7}$) and use these** values to estimate and calculate the circumference and area **of circles; compare with actual measurements.**

NEW Vocabulary

circle
center
diameter
circumference
radius
π (pi)

▶ GET READY for the Lesson

FERRIS WHEELS The London Eye Ferris wheel, in London, England, measures 450 feet across.

1. Which point appears to be the center of the Ferris wheel? **G**

2. Is the distance from G to F greater than, less than, or equal to the distance from G to J? **equal to**

3. How does the distance from G to H compare to the distance from F to J?

4. Find the distance from G to F. **225 ft**

The distance from G to H is half of F to J.

A **circle** is the set of all points in a plane that are the same distance from a given point, called the **center**.

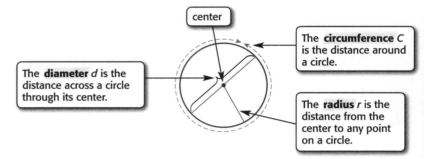

center

The **circumference** C is the distance around a circle.

The **diameter** d is the distance across a circle through its center.

The **radius** r is the distance from the center to any point on a circle.

The diameter of a circle is 2 times the radius, or $d = 2r$. Another relationship that is true of all circles is $\frac{C}{d} = 3.1415926\dots$. This nonterminating and nonrepeating number is represented by the Greek letter π **(pi)**. An approximation often used for π is 3.14.

KEY **CONCEPT**   Circumference of a Circle

Words	The circumference C of a circle is equal to its diameter d times π, or 2 times its radius r times π.
Symbols	$C = \pi d$ or $C = 2\pi r$

When finding the circumference of a circle, it is necessary to use an approximation of π since its exact value cannot be determined.

Real-World EXAMPLE Find Circumference

1 FERRIS WHEELS Refer to the lesson opener. Find the circumference of the London Eye Ferris wheel.

Estimate $C = 3 \cdot 450$ or 1,350 ft

$C = \pi d$	Circumference of a circle
$C \approx 3.14(450)$	Replace π with 3.14 and d with 450.
$C \approx 1,413$	Multiply.

So, the distance around the Ferris wheel is about 1,413 feet.

Check for Reasonableness $1,413 \approx 1,350$ ✔

CHECK Your Progress

Find the circumference of each circle. Use 3.14 for π. Round to the nearest tenth if necessary.

a.   25.1 ft

b.   197.8 in.

🌐 **Personal Tutor at** ca.gr6math.com

Another approximation for π is $\frac{22}{7}$. Use this value when the radius or diameter is a multiple of 7 or has a multiple of 7 in its numerator if the radius is a fraction.

EXAMPLE Find Circumference

2 Find the circumference of a circle with a radius of 21 inches.

Since 21 is a multiple of 7, use $\frac{22}{7}$ for π.

$C = 2\pi r$	Circumference of a circle
$C \approx 2 \cdot \frac{22}{7} \cdot 21$	Replace π with $\frac{22}{7}$ and r with 21.
$C \approx 2 \cdot \frac{22}{\overset{}{7}_1} \cdot \frac{\overset{3}{21}}{1}$	Divide by the GCF, 7.
$C \approx 132$	Simplify.

The circumference of the circle is about 132 inches.

CHECK Your Progress

Find the circumference of each circle. Use $\frac{22}{7}$ for π. Round to the nearest tenth if necessary.

c.   220 in.

d. $5\frac{1}{2}$ ft

Formative Assessment

Use Exercises 1–5 to check for understanding.

Then use the chart at the bottom of this page to customize your assignments for students.

Intervention You may wish to use the Study Guide and Intervention Master on page 23 of the *Chapter 11 Resource Masters* for additional reinforcement.

Odd/Even Assignments

Exercises 6–21 are structured so that students practice the same concepts whether they are assigned odd or even problems.

★ indicates multi-step problem

CHECK Your Understanding

Examples 1, 2
(p. 585)

Find the circumference of each circle. Use 3.14 or $\frac{22}{7}$ for π. Round to the nearest tenth if necessary.

1. 31.4 ft
    5 ft

2. 36.7 m
    11.7 m

3. 44 m
    14 m

4. 264 in.
    42 in.

5. **CLOCKS** To the nearest tenth, how many centimeters does the tip of the minute hand of the clock shown travel each hour? **67.2 cm**
    21.4 cm

Exercises

HOMEWORK HELP	
For Exercises	**See Examples**
6–9, 14–15, 20–21	1
10–13, 16–19	2

Exercise Levels
A: 6–21
B: 22–35
C: 36–40

Find the circumference of each circle. Use 3.14 or $\frac{22}{7}$ for π. Round to the nearest tenth if necessary.

6. 16 m **50.2 m**

7. 8 ft **50.2 ft**

8. 5.8 km **36.4 km**

9. 7.2 cm **22.6 cm**

10. 7 yd **44 yd**

11. 21 ft **66 ft**

12. radius = $1\frac{3}{4}$ in. **11 in.**

13. diameter = $10\frac{1}{2}$ in. **33 in.**

14. diameter = 15.1 m **47.4 m**

15. diameter = 10.8 km **33.9 km**

16. radius = $2\frac{5}{8}$ in. **$16\frac{1}{2}$ in.**

17. diameter = $12\frac{1}{4}$ mi **$38\frac{1}{2}$ mi**

18. **SPORTS** A flying disc has a diameter of $9\frac{5}{8}$ inches. Find its circumference. **$30\frac{1}{4}$ in.**

19. **WHEELS** A hamster wheel has a radius of $4\frac{1}{2}$ inches. How far will the wheel turn in one revolution? **$28\frac{2}{7}$ in.**

20. **PATCHES** A National Guard military patch has a diameter of 2.5 inches. What is its circumference to the nearest tenth? **7.9 in.**

21. **POOLS** The Cole family owns an above-ground circular swimming pool that has walls made of aluminum. Find the length ℓ of aluminum surrounding the pool as shown if the radius is 15 feet. Round to the nearest tenth. **94.2 ft**

DIFFERENTIATED HOMEWORK OPTIONS

Level	Assignment	Two-Day Option	
BL Basic	6–21, 36, 37, 40–51	7–21 odd, 41–43	6–20 even, 36, 37, 40, 44–51
OL Core	7–31 odd, 32–37, 40–51	6–21, 41–43	22–37, 40, 44–51
AL Advanced/Pre-AP	22–47 (optional: 48–51)		

LABELS Determine the length of each can's label.

22.
10 cm
TUNA
31.4 cm

23. 1.75 in.
11.0 in.
Chicken Soup

24. $5\frac{1}{4}$ in. $16\frac{1}{2}$ in.

PAINT

MEASUREMENT For Exercises 25–28, perform each of the following steps.
25-28. See students' work.

a. Use a centimeter ruler to measure the diameter of each circular object listed.

b. Estimate to find the approximate circumference of each circle. State which approximation of π you used.

c. Calculate the circumference of each circle. Use 3.14 for π.

d. Cut a piece of string the length of the circumference of each circle. Use a centimeter ruler to measure the length of the string to the nearest tenth of a centimeter. Compare this actual length to the calculated length.

25. soup can lid
26. quarter
27. CD or DVD
28. button

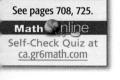

ALGEBRA Find the diameter or radius of each circle. Use 3.14 for π. Round to the nearest tenth if necessary.

29. $C = 25$ ft, diameter = ▦ ft **8.0 ft**
30. $C = 54$ cm, diameter = ▦ cm **17.2 cm**
31. $C = 30$ yd, radius = ▦ yd **4.8 yd**
32. $C = 48$ km, radius = ▦ km **7.6 km**

33. **UNICYCLES** A unicycle wheel has a radius of 10 inches. How many feet will ★ the unicycle travel in 5 revolutions? Explain how you solved this problem.
See margin.

34. **CROPS** The crop circle shown was ★ created in England in a single night by an unknown source. About how many strides would it take for a person to walk around the circle if each stride is 3 feet?
about 262 strides

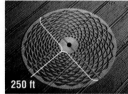
250 ft

35. **FIND THE DATA** Refer to the California Data File on pages 16–19. Choose some data and write a real-world problem in which you would find the circumference of a circle. **See students' work.**

36. **OPEN ENDED** Select a real-world situation in which finding the circumference of a circle would be useful.
Sample answer: sewing fringe on a circular tablecloth

37. **FIND THE ERROR** Aidan and Mya are finding the circumference of a circle with a radius of 5 inches. Who is correct? Explain.

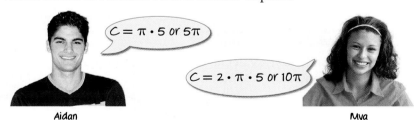

$C = \pi \cdot 5$ or 5π
Aidan

$C = 2 \cdot \pi \cdot 5$ or 10π
Mya

Lesson 11-3 Circles and Circumference **587**

Formative Assessment

Check for student understanding of concepts in Lessons 11-1 through 11-3.

CRM Quiz 1, p.73

 **Foldables™ Follow-Up**

Remind students to take notes about circles in their Foldables. Encourage them to give an example, drawing and labeling the parts of a circle and showing how to calculate the circumference.

Additional Answers

39. Both will be doubled. If the value of x is doubled, the diameter will be $2x$ instead of x. The circumference will increase from $2\pi x$ to $2\pi(2x)$ or $4\pi x$.

40. π is a constant; Sample answer: The formula for the circumference of a circle is $C = \pi \times d$. Both C and d are variables. The Greek letter π is not a variable; it is a constant. π does not change in value.

CHALLENGE For Exercises 38 and 39, use the circle at the right.

38. How many lengths x will fit on the circle's circumference?
2π or about 6.28

39. If the value of x is doubled, what effect will this have on the diameter? on the circumference? Explain your reasoning. **See margin.**

40. **WRITING IN MATH** A *constant* is a quantity whose value never changes. In the formula for the circumference of a circle, identify any constants. Justify your response. **See margin.**

STANDARDS PRACTICE 6AF3.1, 6MG1.1, 6MG1.2

41. Malik's bike tire has a radius of 8 inches. Which equation could be used to find the circumference of the tire in inches? **C**

   A $C = \pi \cdot 4$ **C** $C = \pi \cdot 16$

   B $C = \pi \cdot 16 \times 2$ **D** $C = \pi \cdot 8$

42. Each wheel on Nina's car has a diameter of 18 inches. Which expression could be used to find the circumference of the wheel? **F**

   F $2 \times 9 \times \pi$ **H** $9 \times 9 \times \pi$

   G $2 \times 18 \times \pi$ **J** $18 \times 18 \times \pi$

43. The distance around a tree trunk is the girth of the tree. Which measure is *closest* to the girth of the cross-section of the tree shown below? **B**

22 in.

   A 34.5 in.   **C** 138.2 in.

   B 69.1 in.   **D** 380.0 in.

Spiral Review

MEASUREMENT Find the area of each figure. Round to the nearest tenth if necessary. (Lesson 11-2)

44. 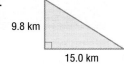   73.5 km²

9.8 km

15.0 km

45. 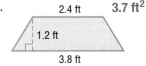   3.7 ft²

2.4 ft

1.2 ft

3.8 ft

46. **MEASUREMENT** Find the area of a parallelogram with base 6.5 meters and height 7.0 meters. (Lesson 11-1) **45.5 m²**

47. **PROBABILITY** Jorge rolled a number cube several times and recorded the results in the table shown. Find the experimental probability that an odd number turned up. (Lesson 9-7) $\frac{15}{27}$ or $\frac{5}{9}$

Outcome	Frequency
1	卌 l
2	lll
3	卌 ll
4	卌
5	ll
6	llll

GET READY for the Next Lesson

PREREQUISITE SKILL Use a calculator to find each product to the nearest tenth. Use 3.14 for π. (Lesson 1-4)

48. $\pi \cdot 5^2$ 78.5   **49.** $\pi \cdot 7^2$ 153.9   **50.** $\pi \cdot (2.4)^2$ 18.1   **51.** $\pi \cdot (4.5)^2$ 63.6

11-4 Area of Circles

Standard 6MG1.1: Understand the concept of a constant such as π; know the formulas for the circumference and **area of a circle.**

Standard 6MG1.2: **Know common estimates of** π (3.14, $\frac{22}{7}$) **and use these values to estimate and calculate the** circumference and **area of circles; compare with actual measurements.**

PACING: **Regular:** 1.5 periods, **Block:** 1 period

Options for Differentiated Instruction

ELL = English Language Learner **AL** = Above Grade Level **SS** = Struggling Students **SN** = Special Needs

Study Tools **SS** **SN**

Use after presenting the Examples.

Have students add the formula for the area of a circle to their flash card rings. Have them include examples when the radius is given, and when the diameter is given.

- On the top left corner, write the page number where the formula is introduced in the textbook.
- On the top right corner, write the lesson number.
- Write the title of the formula and the formula itself. Also include a drawing if appropriate.
- On the reverse side of the index card, include an example of the formula, how you used it in a homework problem, or how you used it in a word problem.

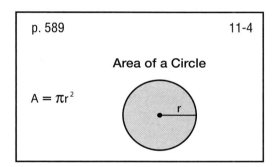

p. 589   11-4

Area of a Circle

$A = \pi r^2$

Challenge Problems **AL**

Use after students complete Lesson 11-4.

While some students may require more time mastering the skills required in Lesson 11-4, more advanced students may use the extra time to work on more advanced problems, such as those given below.

1. Draw a circle that has an area of less than 10 square units. Label the radius. Sample answer:
2. Which is larger, a triangle with a base of 50 feet and a height of 50 feet or a circle with diameter of 50 feet? Justify your answer. circle; triangle: 1,250 ft²; circle: 1,962.5 ft²
3. Which equation below could be used to find the area in square yards of a circle with a diameter of 6 yards? Justify your answer.

   $A = 3 \cdot \pi$ $A = \pi \cdot 6^2$ $A = 6 \cdot \pi$ $A = 3^2 \cdot \pi$

   $A = 3^2 \cdot \pi$; Since the diameter is 6 yards, the radius is 6 ÷ 2 or 3 yards.

1 unit

Leveled Lesson Resources

Chapter 11 Resource Masters

BL = Below Grade Level   **OL** = On Grade Level   **AL** = Above Grade Level   **ELL** = English Language Learner

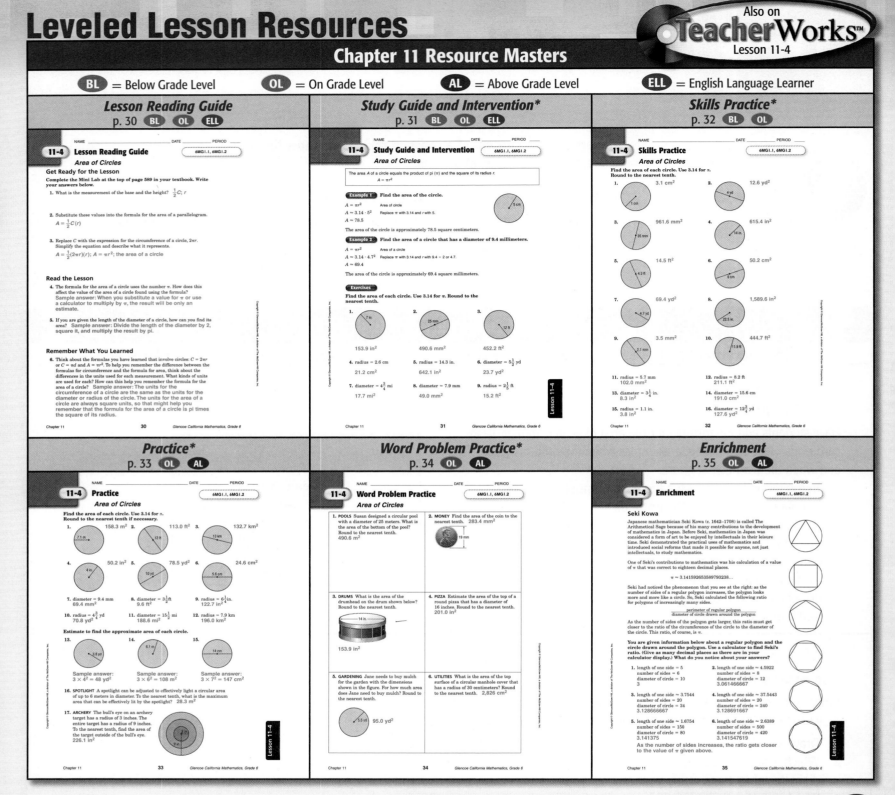

Lesson Reading Guide
p. 30 **BL** **OL** **ELL**

Study Guide and Intervention*
p. 31 **BL** **OL** **ELL**

Skills Practice*
p. 32 **BL** **OL**

Practice*
p. 33 **OL** **AL**

Word Problem Practice*
p. 34 **OL** **AL**

Enrichment
p. 35 **OL** **AL**

Additional Lesson Resources

* Also available in Spanish **ELL**

Transparencies
- *5-Minute Check Transparency, Lesson 11-4*

Other Print Products
- *Teaching Mathematics with Manipulatives*
- *Noteables™ Interactive Study Notebook with Foldables™*

Teacher Tech Tools
- *Interactive Classroom CD-ROM*, Lesson 11-4
- *AssignmentWorks*, Lesson 11-4

Student Tech Tools
ca.gr6math.com
- Extra Examples, Chapter 11, Lesson 4
- Self-Check Quiz, Chapter 11, Lesson 4

Main IDEA

Find the areas of circles.

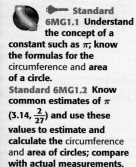

Standard 6MG1.1 Understand the concept of a constant such as π; know the formulas for the circumference and **area of a circle.**
Standard 6MG1.2 Know common estimates of π (3.14, $\frac{2}{27}$) and use these values to estimate and **calculate the** circumference and area of circles; compare with actual measurements.

3. $A = \frac{1}{2}(2\pi r)(r)$;
4. $A = \pi r^2$; the area of a circle

MINI Lab

- Fold a paper plate in half four times to divide it into 16 equal-sized sections.
- Label the radius r as shown. Let C represent the circumference of the circle.
- Cut out each section; reassemble to form a parallelogram-shaped figure.

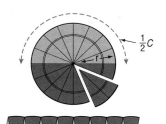

1. What is the measurement of the base and the height? $\frac{1}{2}C$; r

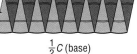
r (height)
$\frac{1}{2}C$ (base)

2. Substitute these values into the formula for the area of a parallelogram. $A = \frac{1}{2}C(r)$

3. Replace C with the expression for the circumference of a circle, $2\pi r$. Simplify the equation and describe what it represents.

In the Mini Lab, the formula for the area of a parallelogram was used to develop a formula for the area of a circle.

KEY CONCEPT   Area of a Circle

Words   The area A of a circle equals the   **Model**
             product of π and the square of
             its radius r.

Symbols $A = \pi r^2$

EXAMPLE   Find the Area of a Circle

① Find the area of the circle.

$A = \pi r^2$ Area of a circle

$A = \pi \cdot 2^2$ Replace π with 3.14 and r with 2.

$A \approx 12.6$ Multiply.

2 in.

The area of the circle is approximately 12.6 square inches.

CHECK Your Progress

a. Find the area of a circle with a radius of 3.2 centimeters. Round to the nearest tenth. **32.2 cm²**

Lesson 11-4 Area of Circles **589**

1 Focus

Standards Alignment

Before Lesson 11-4
Differentiate between and use appropriate units of measures for, two- and three-dimensional objects from Standard 5MG1.4

Lesson 11-4
Understand the concept of a constant such as π; know the formula for the area of a circle. Know common estimates of π and use these values to estimate and calculate the area of circles; compare with actual measurements from Standards 6MG1.1 and 6MG1.2

After Lesson 11-4
Use formulas routinely for finding the perimeter and area of basic two-dimensional figures and the surface area and volume of basic three-dimensional figures from Standard 7MG2.1

2 Teach

MINI Lab

If students do not remember the formula for the area of a parallelogram, have them look in their Foldables. Some students may point out that the figure is not exactly a parallelogram, since two of its sides aren't straight. Have them visualize "stretching" the sides so that they become line segments.

Scaffolding Questions

As you ask the following questions, draw a circle on the board and point to the appropriate parts.

Ask:
- What is the distance around a circle called?
  circumference

- What is the distance across a circle, through its center? diameter

- What is the distance from the center to a point on the circle? radius

- What is the ratio of a circle's circumference to its diameter? π

- What are the approximations of π that you can use to solve an equation? 3.14 and $\frac{22}{7}$

Focus on Mathematical Content

If a circle's radius (or diameter) is known, its **area** can be calculated.

To **estimate the area** of a circle, round π down to 3 and calculate mentally.

✔ Formative Assessment

Use the Check Your Progress exercises after each Example to determine students' understanding of concepts.

ADDITIONAL EXAMPLES

1 Find the area of the circle shown below. about 50.2 cm²

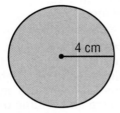

4 cm

2 **KOI** Find the area of the koi pond shown. about 10.2 m²

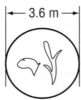

├─ 3.6 m ─┤

3 **TEST EXAMPLE** Mr. McGowan made an apple pie with a diameter of 10 inches. He cut the pie into 6 equal slices. Find the approximate area of each slice. B

A 3 in²
B 13 in²
C 16 in²
D 52 in²

Additional Examples are also in:

- Noteables™ Interactive Study Notebook with Foldables™
- Interactive Classroom PowerPoint® Presentations

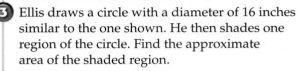

2 **COINS** Find the area of the face of the California quarter shown.

The diameter of the quarter is 24 millimeters, so the radius is $\frac{1}{2}(24)$ or 12 millimeters.

$A = \pi r^2$ Area of a circle

$A = \pi \cdot 12^2$ Replace π with 3.14 and r with 12.

$A \approx 452.2$ Multiply.

The area is approximately 452.2 square millimeters.

── 24 mm ──

✔ CHECK Your Progress   b. 706.5 ft²

b. **POOLS** The bottom of a circular swimming pool with diameter 30 feet is painted blue. How many square feet are blue?

◆ STANDARDS EXAMPLE   6MG1.1

3 Ellis draws a circle with a diameter of 16 inches similar to the one shown. He then shades one region of the circle. Find the approximate area of the shaded region.

A 100 in²
C 402 in²
B 201 in²
D 804 in²

16 in.

Read the Item

Since the segment in the figure is a diameter, you know that the shaded region represents half of the area of the circle. To find the area of the shaded region, you can find the total area of the circle and then divide by 2.

Solve the Item

$A = \pi r^2$ Area of a circle

$A = \pi \cdot 8^2$ Replace r with 16 ÷ 2 or 8.

$A \approx 200$ Multiply. Use 3.14 for π.

Half of the total area is approximately $\frac{1}{2}(200)$ or 100 square inches. The answer is A.

✔ CHECK Your Progress

c. Ray drew one circle with a radius of 7 centimeters and another circle with a radius of 10 centimeters. Find the approximate difference between the areas of the circles. H

F 28 cm²   **G** 40 cm²   **H** 160 cm²   **J** 254 cm²

 Personal Tutor at ca.gr6math.com

Test-Taking Tip

Identifying What is Given Before finding area, be sure to read the question carefully and identify if the radius or diameter is given.

590   **Chapter 11** Measurement: Two- and Three-Dimensional Figures

---

Differentiated Instruction

Verbal/Linguistic Learners After presenting Examples 1–3, have students write a summary comparing the formulas for the circumference of a circle and the area of a circle. In their summary, they should include a drawing of a circle with the length of the radius labeled, a description of how each formula is generated from the circle, the similarities and differences between the formulas, and a calculation for the circumference and area of the circle, with appropriate units. See students' work.

★ indicates multi-step problem

CHECK Your Understanding

Find the area of each circle. Round to the nearest tenth.

1. 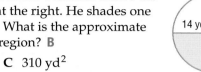 78.5 cm²   2. 254.3 in²

3. diameter = 16 m   201 m²

4. diameter = 13 ft   132.7 ft²

Example 3
(p. 590)
6MG1.1

5. **STANDARDS PRACTICE** Kenneth draws the circle shown at the right. He shades one region of the circle. What is the approximate area of the shaded region? **B**

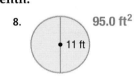

14 yd

A 88 yd²   **C** 310 yd²

B 154 yd²   **D** 615 yd²

---

3 Practice

Formative Assessment

Use Exercises 1–5 to check for understanding.

Then use the chart at the bottom of this page to customize your assignments for students.

Intervention You may wish to use the Study Guide and Intervention Master on page 31 of the *Chapter 11 Resource Masters* for additional reinforcement.

Odd/Even Assignments

Exercises 6–19 are structured so that students practice the same concepts whether they are assigned odd or even problems.

Exercises

Find the area of each circle. Round to the nearest tenth.

For Exercises	See Examples
6–7, 10–11, 14–15, 19	1
8–9, 12–13, 16–18	2
36–37	3

HOMEWORK HELP

Exercise Levels
A: 6–19
B: 20–30
C: 31–35

6. 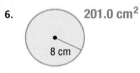 201.0 cm²   7. 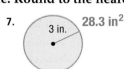 28.3 in²   8.  95.0 ft²

9.  226.9 cm²   10. 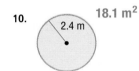 18.1 m²   11.  32.2 mm²

12. diameter = 8.4 m
55.4 m²

13. diameter = 12.6 cm
124.6 cm²

14. radius = $4\frac{1}{2}$ in.
63.6 in²

15. radius = $3\frac{3}{4}$ ft
44.2 ft²

16. diameter = $9\frac{1}{4}$ mi
67.2 mi²

17. diameter = $20\frac{3}{4}$ yd
338.0 yd²

18. **PATCHES** Find the area of the Girl Scout patch shown if the diameter is 1.25 inches. Round to the nearest tenth. **1.2 in²**

19. **TOOLS** A sprinkler that sprays water in a circular area can be adjusted to spray up to 30 feet. To the nearest tenth, what is the maximum area of lawn that can be watered by the sprinkler? **2,826 ft²**

ESTIMATION Estimate to find the approximate area of each circle.

20. 8 cm
Sample answer:
$3 \times 4^2 =$
48 cm²

21. 5.9 ft
Sample answer:
$3 \times 6^2 =$
108 ft²

22. 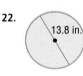 13.8 in.
Sample answer:
$3 \times 7^2 =$
147 in²

DIFFERENTIATED HOMEWORK OPTIONS

Level	Assignment	Two-Day Option	
BL Basic	6–19, 34–47	7–19 odd, 36–38	6–18 even, 34, 35, 39–47
OL Core	7–27 odd, 28–30, 34–47	6–19, 36–38	20–30, 34, 35, 39–47
AL Advanced/Pre-AP	20–43 (optional: 44–47)		

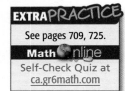

Exercise Alert!

Find the Error In Exercise 34, Domingo substituted the circle's diameter, rather than its radius, in the formula for area. Remind students to check which measurement is given in a problem and, if the diameter is given, to find the radius before using the formula for area.

Real-World Math · · · ·
The Roman Pantheon has a diameter of 142 feet.
Source: Great Building Online

25. about 50.3 cm²
26. Sample answer: They are relatively close in value to each other.

EXTRA PRACTICE
See pages 709, 725.
Math Online
Self-Check Quiz at
ca.gr6math.com

H.O.T. Problems · · ·

34. Bradley; Domingo incorrectly squared the diameter rather than the radius.
35. Sample answer: If the radius of a circular garden is 6 feet, how much room is there for gardening? about 113.1 ft²

For Exercises 23–26, use a compass to draw the circle shown on centimeter grid paper.

23. Count the number of squares that lie completely within the circle. Then count the number of squares that lie completely within or contain the circle. **32; 60**

24. Estimate the area of the circle by finding the mean of the two values you found in Exercise 23. **46 cm²**

25. Find the area of the circle by using the area formula.

26. How do the areas you found in Exercises 24 and 25 compare to one another?

27. A *semicircle* is half a circle. Find the area of the
   ★ semicircle to the nearest tenth. **29.0 m²**
   ←8.6 m→

28. Which has a greater area, a triangle with a base
   ★ of 100 feet and a height of 100 feet or a circle with diameter of 100 feet? Justify your selection.
   triangle: 5,000 ft²; circle: 7,850 ft²; the circle is larger

29. **ARCHITECTURE** The Roman Pantheon is a circular structure that was
   ★ completed about 126 A.D. Use the information at the left to find the approximate area of the floor in square yards. (*Hint:* 1 sq ft ≈ 0.1 sq yd)
   $\pi \cdot 71^2 \approx 15{,}828.7$ ft² and $15{,}828.7 \times 0.1 = 1{,}582.9$ yd²

30. **LANDSCAPE DESIGN** A circular stone path is to
   ★ be installed around a birdbath with radius 1.5 feet, as shown. What is the area of the path? (*Hint:* Find the area of the large circle minus the area of the small circle.) **43.2 ft²**

1 square = 1 ft

CHALLENGE Find the area of the shaded region in each figure. Round to the nearest tenth.

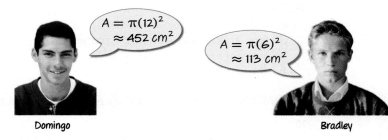

31. **62.8 m²** 8 m 12 m
32. **6 in²** 5.25 in.
33. **103.5 cm²** 3.5 cm 12.5 cm

34. **FIND THE ERROR** Domingo and Bradley are finding the area of a circle that has a diameter of 12 centimeters. Who is correct? Explain.

Domingo: $A = \pi(12)^2 \approx 452$ cm²

Bradley: $A = \pi(6)^2 \approx 113$ cm²

35. **WRITING IN MATH** Write and solve a real-world problem in which you would solve the problem by finding the area of a circle.

Pre-AP Activity Use after Exercise 33

Tell students that in a series of circles, each circle's diameter is twice as long as the diameter of the preceding circle. Have students find the pattern in the areas of the circles. Each circle's area is four times greater than the previous circle's area.

36. The radius of the half dollar in centimeters is given below. **A**

← 1.95 cm →

Which of the following is closest to the area of the face of the half dollar?

A 12 cm²   **C** 28 cm²

B 15 cm²   **D** 735 cm²

37. Which equation could be used to find the area in square inches of a circle with a radius of 12 inches? **J**

F $A = 6 \times \pi$ **H** $A = 12 \times \pi$

G $A = \pi \times 6^2$ **J** $A = \pi \times 12^2$

38. Which two figures have the same area? **A**

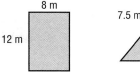

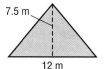

Figure I   Figure II

Figure III   Figure IV

A Figure I and Figure IV

B Figure I and Figure II

C Figure II and Figure IV

D Figure II and Figure III

4 Assess

Name the Math Tell students you have a circular rug in your living room. Say you want to have the rug cleaned, and the cleaner charges by the square foot. Have students write what mathematical procedures they would use to find the area of the rug.

FOLDABLES Study Organizer **Foldables™ Follow-Up**

Remind students to take notes about circles in the Lesson 11-4 section of their Foldables. Encourage them to give an example, drawing and labeling the parts of a circle and showing how to calculate its area.

Spiral Review

39. **MEASUREMENT** What is the circumference of a circle that has a radius of 8 yards? Use 3.14 for π and round to the nearest tenth if necessary. **50.2 yd** (Lesson 11-3)

40. **MEASUREMENT** Find the area of a triangle with a base of 21 meters and a height of 27 meters. (Lesson 11-2) **283.5 m²**

Find the area of each parallelogram. Round to the nearest tenth if necessary.
(Lesson 11-1)

41.
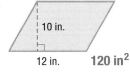
10 in.
12 in.   **120 in²**

42.
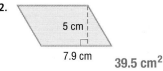
5 cm
7.9 cm   **39.5 cm²**

43.
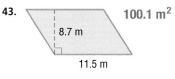
100.1 m²
8.7 m
11.5 m

GET READY for the Next Lesson

PREREQUISITE SKILL Simplify each expression. (Lessons 1-2, 1-3, and 1-4)

44. 8.5^2 **72.25**   45. $3.14 \cdot 6^2$ **113.04**   46. $\frac{1}{2} \cdot 5.4^2 + 11$ **25.58**   47. $\frac{1}{2} \cdot 7^2 + (9)(14)$ **150.5**

Problem-Solving Investigation
SOLVE A SIMPLER PROBLEM

Standard 6MR1.3:   Determine when and how to break a problem into simpler parts.

Standard 6MR2.2:   Apply strategies and results from simpler problems to more complex problems.

Standard 6NS2.1:   Solve problems involving addition, subtraction, multiplication, and division **of positive fractions and explain why a particular operation was used for a given situation.**

PACING: **Regular:** 1.5 periods, **Block:** 1 period

Options for Differentiated Instruction

ELL = English Language Learner   **AL** = Above Grade Level   **SS** = Struggling Students   **SN** = Special Needs

Choosing the Best Strategy **ELL** **SS** **SN**
Use before assigning the Exercises.

Prior to assigning Exercises 6–9, read each exercise aloud and discuss with the class which strategy might be best to solve each problem. Possible discussion questions are listed below.
- What is the question asking?
- Have you seen problems like this before?
- What would be the best strategy to try?

Make sure that all students have chosen a strategy for each of the problems so that they can complete the assignment independently.

Writing Out the Steps **SS** **SN**
Use with Exercises 4 and 5.

Have students write out the steps to solve Exercises 4 and 5 before they actually complete the exercises. Have them draw pictures or diagrams to help break down the problem into simpler problems.

A sample diagram for Exercise 4 is shown.

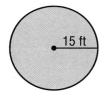

Extra Practice **ELL** **AL**
Use after students complete Lesson 11-5.

Provide the following exercises for students who finish the lesson early or for those who need extra practice with problem solving.
1. **WATER** One hose is adding water to a tank at a rate of 25 gallons per minute. Another hose is draining water from the same tank at a rate of 5 gallons per minute. At this rate, how long will it take to fill a 6,500-gallon tank? 5 h 25 min
2. **EARTH SCIENCE** Earth's atmosphere exerts a pressure of 14.7 pounds per square inch at the ocean's surface. The pressure increases by 12.7 pounds per square inch for every 6 feet that you descend. Find the pressure at 18 feet below the surface. 52.8 lb/in²

Leveled Lesson Resources

Chapter 11 Resource Masters

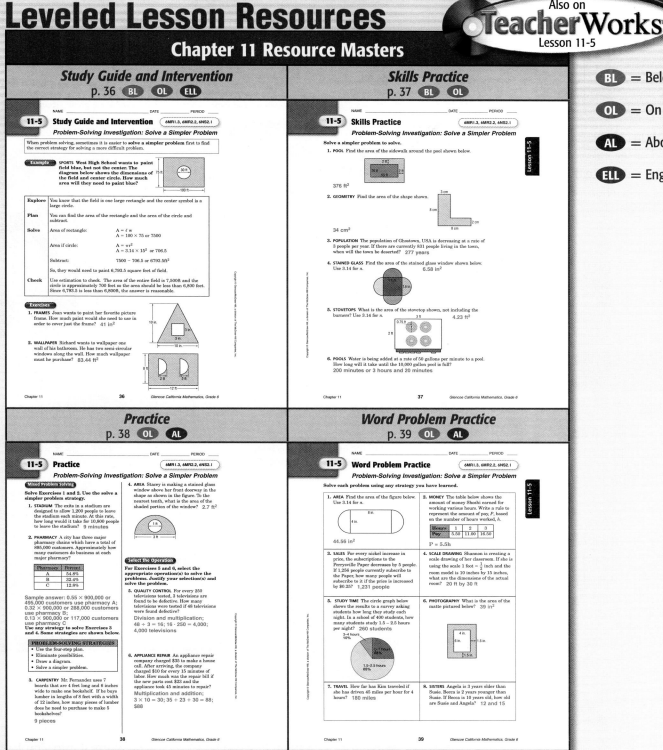

Study Guide and Intervention
p. 36 BL OL ELL

Skills Practice
p. 37 BL OL

Practice
p. 38 OL AL

Word Problem Practice
p. 39 OL AL

BL = Below Grade Level

OL = On Grade Level

AL = Above Grade Level

ELL = English Language Learner

* Also available in Spanish **ELL**

Additional Lesson Resources

Transparencies
- *5-Minute Check Transparency,* Lesson 11-5

Other Print Products
- *Noteables™ Interactive Study Notebook with Foldables™*

Teacher Tech Tools
- *Interactive Classroom CD-ROM,* Lesson 11-5
- *AssignmentWorks,* Lesson 11-5

Student Tech Tools
ca.gr6math.com
- Extra Examples, Chapter 11, Lesson 5
- Self-Check Quiz, Chapter 11, Lesson 5

11-5 **Problem-Solving Investigation**

1 Focus

Solve a Simpler Problem Many problems are composed of several connected problems. This can make the original problem appear difficult or complex. By breaking such problems into parts, students can solve them more easily. This problem-solving strategy will be especially useful in Lesson 11-6, in which students learn to find the area of complex figures.

2 Teach

Scaffolding Questions

Draw the diagram below on the board.

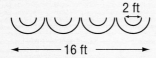
2 ft

← 16 ft →

Ask:

• How can you use the *solve a simpler problem* strategy to find how much ribbon is needed to make this wall decoration? Combine the semicircles to form 2 large and 2 small circles.

• What is the diameter of one of the large circles? 4 ft

ADDITIONAL EXAMPLE

Solve. Use the solve a simpler problem strategy.

PAINT Ben and Sheila are going to paint the wall of a room as shown in the diagram at the bottom of this page. What is the area that will be painted? 67 ft²

Additional Examples are also in:

• Noteables™ Interactive Study Notebook with Foldables™

• Interactive Classroom PowerPoint® Presentations

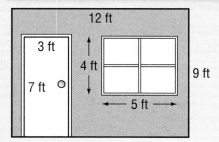
12 ft

3 ft

4 ft

7 ft ○

5 ft

9 ft

MAIN IDEA: Solve problems by solving a simpler problem.

Standard 6MR1.3 Determine when and how to break a problem into simpler parts. **Standard 6MR2.2** Apply strategies and results from simpler problems to more complex problems. **Standard 6NS2.1** Solve problems involving addition, ... multiplication, ... of positive fractions and explain why ... , was used for a given situation.

P.S.I. TEAM +

e-Mail: SOLVE A SIMPLER PROBLEM

YOUR MISSION: Solve the problem by solving a simpler problem.

> Liam: The diagram shows the backdrop for our fall play. We need to find the total area of the backdrop.

THE PROBLEM: How much wallpaper is needed to cover the entire front of the backdrop?

EXPLORE	You know that the backdrop is made of one large rectangle and two semicircles, which equal an entire circle.	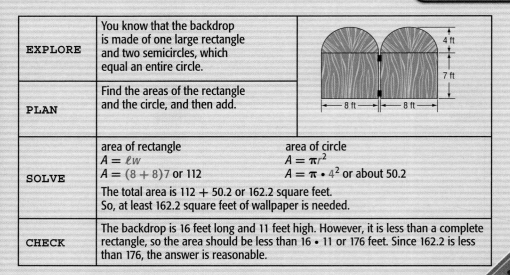
PLAN	Find the areas of the rectangle and the circle, and then add.	

SOLVE	area of rectangle $A = \ell w$ $A = (8 + 8)7$ or 112	area of circle $A = \pi r^2$ $A = \pi \cdot 4^2$ or about 50.2
	The total area is $112 + 50.2$ or 162.2 square feet. So, at least 162.2 square feet of wallpaper is needed.	
CHECK	The backdrop is 16 feet long and 11 feet high. However, it is less than a complete rectangle, so the area should be less than $16 \cdot 11$ or 176 feet. Since 162.2 is less than 176, the answer is reasonable.	

Analyze The Strategy 1–3. See Ch. 11 Answer Appendix.

1. Why is breaking this problem into simpler parts a good strategy to solve it?

2. Describe another way that the problem could have been solved by breaking it into simpler parts.

3. **WRITING IN MATH** Write a problem that can be solved by breaking it into simpler parts. Solve the problem and explain your answer.

594 Chapter 11 Measurement: Two- and Three-Dimensional Figures

---

Solve Exercises 4–5. Use the *solve a simpler problem* strategy.

4. **MEASUREMENT** Mr. James is installing a circular sidewalk around a flower bed, as shown. What is the area, in square feet, of the sidewalk? Use 3.14 for π. **326.56 ft²**

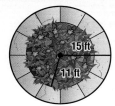

5. **COMMUNICATION** According to a recent report, one city has 2,945,000 phone lines assigned to three different area codes. Approximately how many of the phone lines are assigned to each area code? **See margin.**

Area Code	Percent
888	44.3%
777	23.7%
555	31.5%

Use any strategy to solve Exercises 6–9. Some strategies are shown below.

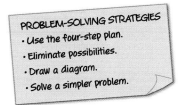

PROBLEM-SOLVING STRATEGIES
- Use the four-step plan.
- Eliminate possibilities.
- Draw a diagram.
- Solve a simpler problem.

6. **SALES** Dee needs to sell $3,000 in ads for the school newspaper. The prices of the ads and the number of ads that she has sold are shown in the table. Which is the smallest single ad she could sell in order to meet her quota? **full-page ad**

Ad Size	Cost per Ad	Number Sold
quarter-page	$75	15
half-page	$125	8
full-page	$175	4

7. **MEASUREMENT** Morgan is painting one wall ★ in her room, as shown by the shaded region below. What is the area that she is painting?

A   92 ft²

B   94 ft²

C   96 ft²

D   100 ft²

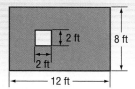

8. **MUSIC** On Mondays, you practice piano for ★ 45 minutes. For each successive day of the week, you practice $\frac{1}{3}$ hour more than the day before. How many hours and minutes do you practice the piano on Saturdays? **2 hours 25 minutes**

9. **TELEVISION** The graph shows the results of a survey in which 365,750 people were asked to name their favorite television programs. About how many people chose sitcoms as their favorite?

Sample answer: $\frac{1}{3} \times 360,000$ or **120,000 people**

Favorite TV Shows

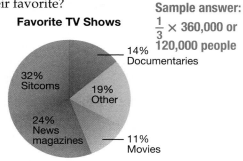

14% Documentaries
32% Sitcoms
19% Other
24% News magazines
11% Movies

Select the Operation

For Exercises 10 and 11, select the appropriate operation(s) to solve the problem. Justify your selection(s) and solve the problem.

10. **THEATER** Mr. Marquez is purchasing new ★ fabric for curtains for a theatrical company. The front of the stage is $15\frac{1}{2}$ yards wide and $5\frac{3}{4}$ yards high. The fabric is sold on bolts that are 60 inches wide and 20 yards long. How many bolts are needed to make the curtains? **10–11. See Ch. 11 Answer Appendix.**

11. **WORK** For every 150 hours Clark works, he receives 10 hours of vacation time. How many hours has he worked if he has 108 vacation hours?

Lesson 11-5 Problem-Solving Investigation: Solve a Simpler Problem   **595**

Additional Answer

5. Sample answer: 0.44 × 3,000,000 or 1,320,000 phone lines have 888 area code; 0.24 × 3,000,000 or 720,000 phone lines have 777 area code; 0.32 × 3,000,000 or 960,000 phone lines have 555 area code.

 Formative Assessment

Check for student understanding of concepts in Lessons 11-4 and 11-5.

Quiz 2, p. 73

Tips for New Teachers

Strategies

Encourage students to write the steps needed to solve a problem that has been broken into simpler parts. Also encourage them to number the steps, showing the order in which they should be solved.

3 Practice

Using the Exercises

Exercises 1–3 can be used to check students' understanding of the solve a simpler problem strategy.

Exercises 4 and 5 give students an opportunity to practice the solve a simpler problem strategy.

Exercises 6–9 are structured so that students have the opportunity to practice many different problem-solving strategies. You may wish to review some of the strategies they have studied.

- use the four-step plan (p. 25)
- eliminate possibilities (p. 248)
- draw a diagram (p. 314)
- solve a simpler problem (p. 594)

Exercises 10 and 11 require students to choose the appropriate operation to solve the problem. Have students analyze each problem and its wording, asking themselves what kind of information is needed. Which operation(s) must be performed to get the information?

4 Assess

Crystal Ball Tell students that tomorrow's lesson is about finding the area of complex figures. Have them write how they think what they learned today will connect with tomorrow's material.

11-6 Area of Complex Figures

Standard 6AF3.1: Use variables in expressions describing geometric quantities (e.g., $P = 2w + 2\ell$, $A = \frac{1}{2}bh$, $C = \pi d$–the formulas for the perimeter of a rectangle, **the area of a triangle, and the circumference of a circle, respectively**).

Standard 6AF3.2: Express in symbolic form simple relationships arising from geometry.

PACING: **Regular:** 2 periods, **Block:** 1 period

Options for Differentiated Instruction

ELL = English Language Learner   **AL** = Above Grade Level   **SS** = Struggling Students   **SN** = Special Needs

Creating Figures **AL**

Use after presenting Lesson 11-6.

Have students create two complex figures that have different shapes but the same area:
- **Figure 1:** made up of a rectangle and a trapezoid
- **Figure 2:** made up of a parallelogram and a triangle

Students should prove that the figures have the same area by showing all their calculations.

Naturalist Learning **SN**

Use after presenting Lesson 11-6.

Have students measure and sketch grassy areas and flowerbeds around the school, or find maps of local, irregularly shaped parks. Then have them calculate the areas by separating the complex figures into simpler figures.

Modifying Assignments **SS** **SN**

Use before assigning the Exercises.

For students with visual or spatial difficulties, it may be helpful to provide an enlarged photocopy of the assignment so that they can write or draw directly on the figures. Suggest that they highlight certain shapes and keep track of the all the dimensions.

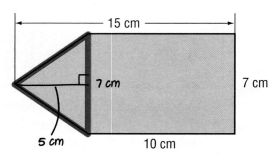

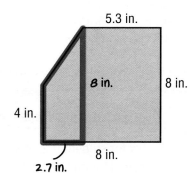

Leveled Lesson Resources

Chapter 11 Resource Masters

BL = Below Grade Level **OL** = On Grade Level **AL** = Above Grade Level **ELL** = English Language Learner

Lesson Reading Guide
p. 40 **BL** **OL** **ELL**

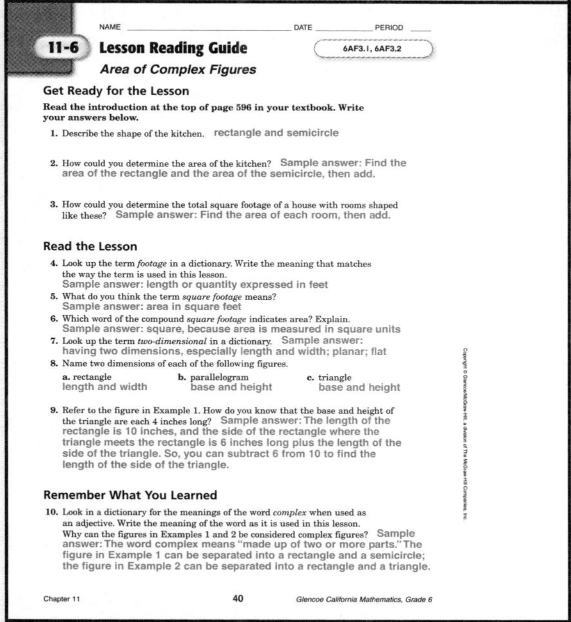

NAME _____ DATE _____ PERIOD _____

11-6 **Lesson Reading Guide**   6AF3.1, 6AF3.2

Area of Complex Figures

Get Ready for the Lesson

Read the introduction at the top of page 596 in your textbook. Write your answers below.

1. Describe the shape of the kitchen. rectangle and semicircle

2. How could you determine the area of the kitchen? Sample answer: Find the area of the rectangle and the area of the semicircle, then add.

3. How could you determine the total square footage of a house with rooms shaped like these? Sample answer: Find the area of each room, then add.

Read the Lesson

4. Look up the term *footage* in a dictionary. Write the meaning that matches the way the term is used in this lesson. Sample answer: length or quantity expressed in feet

5. What do you think the term *square footage* means? Sample answer: area in square feet

6. Which word of the compound *square footage* indicates area? Explain. Sample answer: square, because area is measured in square units

7. Look up the term *two-dimensional* in a dictionary. Sample answer: having two dimensions, especially length and width; planar; flat

8. Name two dimensions of each of the following figures.
   a. rectangle   b. parallelogram   c. triangle
   length and width   base and height   base and height

9. Refer to the figure in Example 1. How do you know that the base and height of the triangle are each 4 inches long? Sample answer: The length of the rectangle is 10 inches, and the side of the rectangle where the rectangle meets the triangle is 6 inches long plus the length of the side of the triangle. So, you can subtract 6 from 10 to find the length of the side of the triangle.

Remember What You Learned

10. Look in a dictionary for the meanings of the word *complex* when used as an adjective. Write the meaning of the word as it is used in this lesson. Why can the figures in Examples 1 and 2 be considered complex figures? Sample answer: The word complex means "made up of two or more parts." The figure in Example 1 can be separated into a rectangle and a semicircle; the figure in Example 2 can be separated into a rectangle and a triangle.

Chapter 11   40   Glencoe California Mathematics, Grade 6

Study Guide and Intervention*
p. 41 **BL** **OL** **ELL**

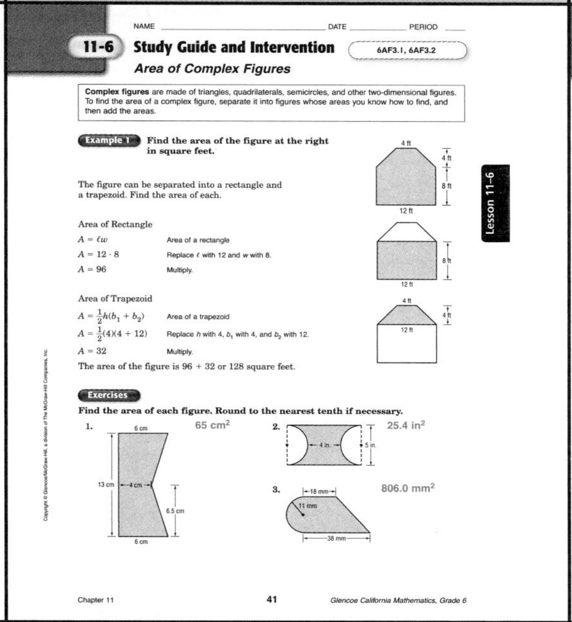

NAME _____ DATE _____ PERIOD _____

11-6 **Study Guide and Intervention**   6AF3.1, 6AF3.2

Area of Complex Figures

Complex figures are made of triangles, quadrilaterals, semicircles, and other two-dimensional figures. To find the area of a complex figure, separate it into figures whose areas you know how to find, and then add the areas.

Example 1 Find the area of the figure at the right in square feet.

The figure can be separated into a rectangle and a trapezoid. Find the area of each.

Area of Rectangle
$A = \ell w$ Area of a rectangle
$A = 12 \cdot 8$ Replace ℓ with 12 and w with 8.
$A = 96$ Multiply.

Area of Trapezoid
$A = \frac{1}{2}h(b_1 + b_2)$ Area of a trapezoid
$A = \frac{1}{2}(4)(4 + 12)$ Replace h with 4, b with 4, and b_2 with 12.
$A = 32$ Multiply.
The area of the figure is 96 + 32 or 128 square feet.

Exercises

Find the area of each figure. Round to the nearest tenth if necessary.

1. 65 cm²   2. 25.4 in²   3. 806.0 mm²

Chapter 11   41   Glencoe California Mathematics, Grade 6

Skills Practice*
p. 42 **BL** **OL**

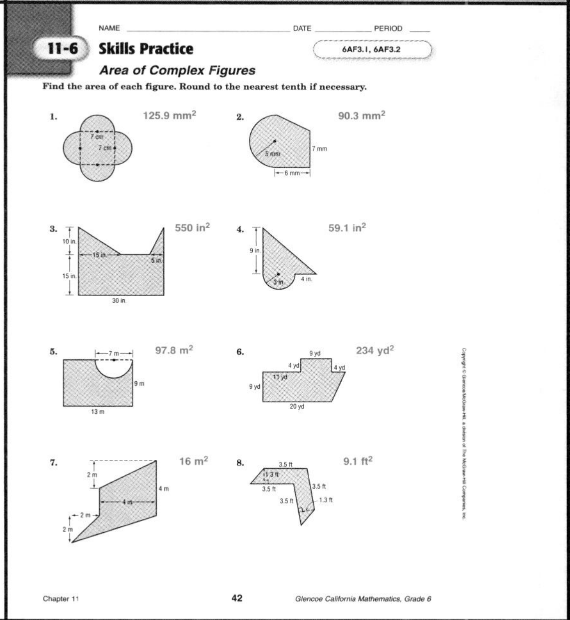

NAME _____ DATE _____ PERIOD _____

11-6 **Skills Practice**   6AF3.1, 6AF3.2

Area of Complex Figures

Find the area of each figure. Round to the nearest tenth if necessary.

1. 125.9 mm²   2. 90.3 mm²
3. 550 in²   4. 59.1 in²
5. 97.8 m²   6. 234 yd²
7. 16 m²   8. 9.1 ft²

Chapter 11   42   Glencoe California Mathematics, Grade 6

Practice*
p. 43 **OL** **AL**

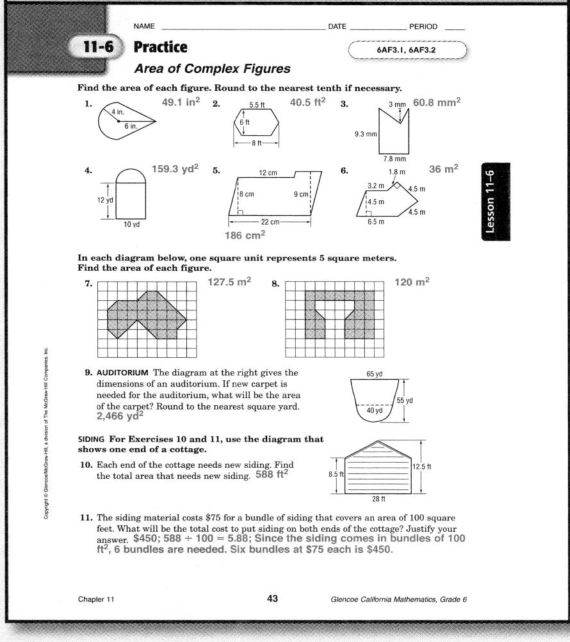

NAME _____ DATE _____ PERIOD _____

11-6 **Practice**   6AF3.1, 6AF3.2

Area of Complex Figures

Find the area of each figure. Round to the nearest tenth if necessary.

1. 49.1 in²   2. 40.5 ft²   3. 60.8 mm²
4. 159.3 yd²   5. 186 cm²   6. 36 m²

In each diagram below, one square unit represents 5 square meters. Find the area of each figure.

7. 127.5 m²   8. 120 m²

9. **AUDITORIUM** The diagram at the right gives the dimensions of an auditorium. If new carpet is needed for the auditorium, what will be the area of the carpet? Round to the nearest square yard. 2,466 yd²

SIDING For Exercises 10 and 11, use the diagram that shows one end of a cottage.

10. Each end of the cottage needs new siding. Find the total area that needs new siding. 588 ft²

11. The siding material costs $75 for a bundle of siding that covers an area of 100 square feet. What will be the total cost to put siding on both ends of the cottage? Justify your answer. $450; 588 ÷ 100 = 5.88; Since the siding comes in bundles of 100 ft², 6 bundles are needed. Six bundles at $75 each is $450.

Chapter 11   43   Glencoe California Mathematics, Grade 6

Word Problem Practice*
p. 44 **OL** **AL**

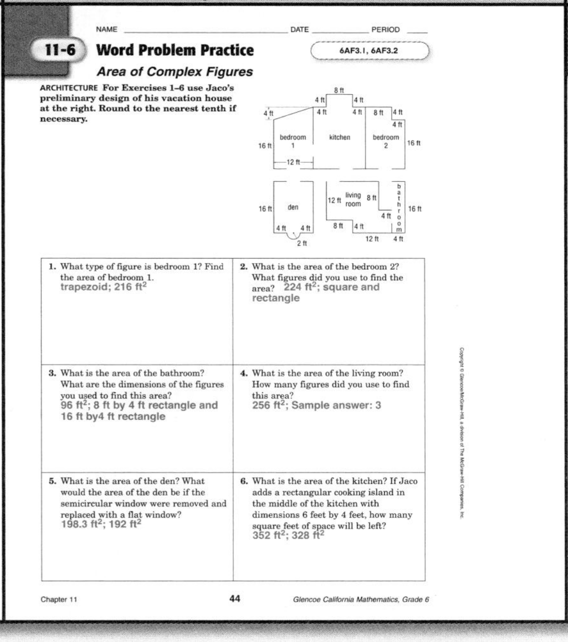

NAME _____ DATE _____ PERIOD _____

11-6 **Word Problem Practice**   6AF3.1, 6AF3.2

Area of Complex Figures

ARCHITECTURE For Exercises 1–6 use Jaco's preliminary design of his vacation house at the right. Round to the nearest tenth if necessary.

1. What type of figure is bedroom 1? Find the area of bedroom 1. trapezoid; 216 ft²

2. What is the area of the bedroom 2? What figures did you use to find the area? 224 ft²; square and rectangle

3. What is the area of the bathroom? What are the dimensions of the figures you used to find this area? 96 ft²; 8 ft by 4 ft rectangle and 16 ft by 4 ft rectangle

4. What is the area of the living room? How many figures did you use to find this area? 256 ft²; Sample answer: 3

5. What is the area of the den? What would the area of the den be if the semicircular window were removed and replaced with a flat window? 198.3 ft²; 192 ft²

6. What is the area of the kitchen? If Jaco adds a rectangular cooking island in the middle of the kitchen with dimensions 6 feet by 4 feet, how many square feet of space will be left? 352 ft²; 328 ft²

Chapter 11   44   Glencoe California Mathematics, Grade 6

Enrichment
p. 45 **OL** **AL**

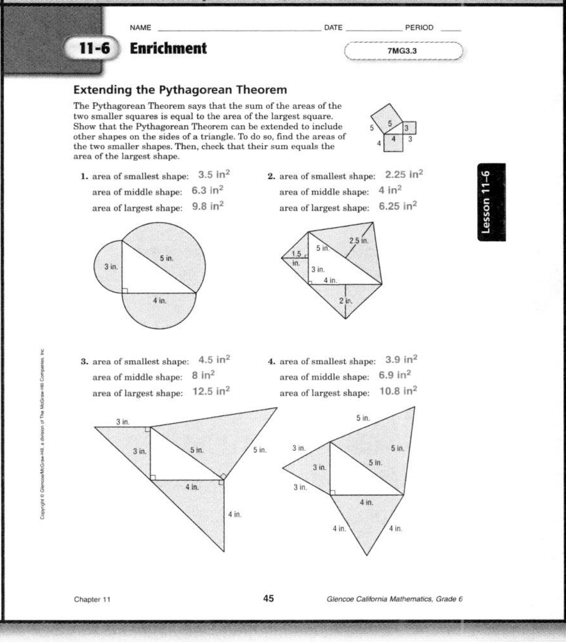

NAME _____ DATE _____ PERIOD _____

11-6 **Enrichment**   7MG3.3

Extending the Pythagorean Theorem

The Pythagorean Theorem says that the sum of the areas of the two smaller squares is equal to the area of the largest square. Show that the Pythagorean Theorem can be extended to include other shapes on the sides of a right triangle. To do so, find the areas of the two smaller shapes. Then, check that their sum equals the area of the largest shape.

1. area of smallest shape: 3.5 in²
   area of middle shape: 6.3 in²
   area of largest shape: 9.8 in²

2. area of smallest shape: 2.25 in²
   area of middle shape: 4 in²
   area of largest shape: 6.25 in²

3. area of smallest shape: 4.5 in²
   area of middle shape: 8 in²
   area of largest shape: 12.5 in²

4. area of smallest shape: 3.9 in²
   area of middle shape: 6.9 in²
   area of largest shape: 10.8 in²

Chapter 11   45   Glencoe California Mathematics, Grade 6

Additional Lesson Resources

Transparencies
- *5-Minute Check Transparency*, Lesson 11-6

Other Print Products
- *Teaching Mathematics with Manipulatives*
- *Noteables™ Interactive Study Notebook with Foldables™*

Teacher Tech Tools
- *Interactive Classroom CD-ROM*, Lesson 11-6
- *AssignmentWorks*, Lesson 11-6

Student Tech Tools
ca.gr6math.com
- Extra Examples, Chapter 11, Lesson 6
- Self-Check Quiz, Chapter 11, Lesson 6

 Area of Complex Figures

1 Focus

Standards Alignment

Before Lesson 11-6
Derive and use the formula for the area of a triangle and of a parallelogram by comparing it with the formula for the area of a rectangle from ◆ Standard 5MG1.1

Lesson 11-6
Use variables in expressions describing geometric quantities (e.g., $A = \frac{1}{2}bh$, $C = \pi d$—the formulas for the area of a triangle and the circumference of a circle, respectively). Express in symbolic form simple relationships arising from geometry from Standards 6AF3.1 and 6AF3.2

After Lesson 11-6
Estimate and compute the area of more complex or irregular two- and three-dimensional figures from Standard 7MG2.2

2 Teach

Scaffolding Questions

Draw the figure shown below on the left (without the dotted segments) on the board. As students name the figures, draw the appropriate dotted lines.

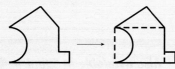

Ask:
- What figures make up this figure?
  triangle, square, rectangle, semicircle

Main IDEA

Find the areas of complex figures.

 Standard 6AF3.1
Use variables in expressions describing geometric quantities (e.g., $P = 2w + 2\ell$, $A = \frac{1}{2}bh$, $C = \pi d$—the formulas for the perimeter of a rectangle, **the area of a triangle, and the circumference of a circle, respectively).**
Standard 6AF3.2 Express in symbolic form simple relationships arising from geometry.

NEW Vocabulary

complex figure
semicircle

🌐 **Vocabulary Link** . . . . .
    Complex
Everyday Use a whole made up of distinct parts
Math Use a figure made of triangles, quadrilaterals, semicircles, and other two-dimensional figures

▶ **GET READY** for the Lesson

ARCHITECTURE Rooms in a house are not always square or rectangular, as shown in the diagram.

1. Describe the shape of the kitchen.

2. How could you determine the area of the kitchen?

3. How could you determine the total square footage of a house with rooms shaped like these?

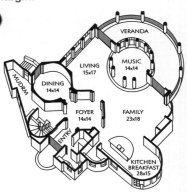

· A **complex figure** is made of triangles, quadrilaterals, semicircles, and other two-dimensional figures. A **semicircle** is half of a circle.

To find the area of a complex figure, separate it into figures with areas you know how to find, and then add those areas.

EXAMPLE   Find the Area of a Complex Figure

① **Find the area of the figure at the right.**

The figure can be separated into a rectangle and a triangle. Find the area of each.

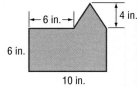

Area of Rectangle	Area of Triangle
$A = \ell w$	$A = \frac{1}{2}bh$
$A = 10 \cdot 6$ or 60	$A = \frac{1}{2}(4)(4)$ or 8

The base of the triangle is $10 - 6$ or 4 inches.

The area is $60 + 8$ or 68 square inches.

✔ **CHECK Your Progress**   Find the area of each figure.

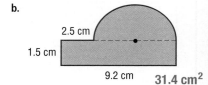

a. 60 ft²   b. 31.4 cm²

596   Chapter 11 Measurement: Two- and Three-Dimensional Figures

✔ Formative Assessment

Use the Check Your Progress exercises after each Example to determine students' understanding of concepts.

Additional Answers

2. Sample answer: Find the areas of the rectangle and the semicircle, then add.

3. Sample answer: Find the area of each room, then add.

2 ARCHITECTURE Refer to the diagram of the house at the beginning of the lesson. The kitchen is 28 feet by 15 feet, as shown at the right. Find the area of the kitchen. Round to the nearest tenth.

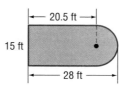

The figure can be separated into a rectangle and a semicircle.

Area of Rectangle

$A = \ell w$

$A = 20.5 \cdot 15$

$A = 307.5$

Area of Semicircle

$A = \frac{1}{2}\pi r^2$

$A = \frac{1}{2}\pi(7.5)^2$ Use 3.14 for π.

$A \approx 88.3$

The area is approximately 307.5 + 88.4 or 395.9 square feet.

CHECK Your Progress

c. **DECKS** Find the area of the deck shown. **672 ft²**

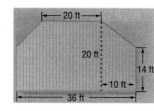

Online Personal Tutor at ca.gr6math.com

★ indicates multi-step problem

CHECK Your Understanding

Example 1
(p. 596)

Find the area of each figure. Round to the nearest tenth if necessary.

1.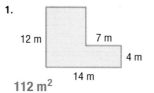

112 m²

2.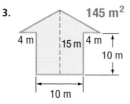

104.1 ft²

3.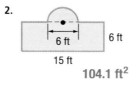

145 m²

Example 2
(p. 597)

4. **APARTMENTS** The manager of an apartment ★ complex will install new carpeting in a studio apartment. The floor plan is shown at the right. What is the total area that needs to be carpeted? **342.5 ft²**

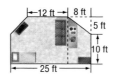

★ 5. **TILING** A kitchen, shown at the right, has a bay window. If the entire kitchen floor is to be tiled, including the section by the bay window, how many square feet of tile are needed? **195 ft²**

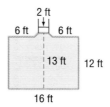

Focus on Mathematical Content

A **complex figure** can be mentally separated into simpler figures. By adding or subtracting the area of each simpler figure, the area of the complex figure can be found.

ADDITIONAL EXAMPLES

1 Find the area of the figure in square centimeters. 160 cm²

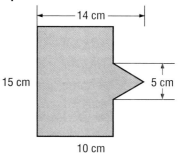

2 **WINDOWS** The diagram below shows the dimensions of a window. Find the area of the window. Round to the nearest tenth. about 23.2 ft²

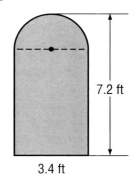

Additional Examples are also in:

- Noteables™ Interactive Study Notebook with Foldables™
- Interactive Classroom PowerPoint® Presentations

Tips for New Teachers

Area of Complex Figures

Make sure students realize that subtraction can also be used to find the area of complex figures. For example, in Exercise 1, the area of the "missing" 8 × 7 rectangle could be subtracted from the area of the 14 × 12 rectangle. Encourage students to analyze each figure and choose the solution method they find easier. Will it be quicker to add or subtract the simpler figures?

Formative Assessment

Use Exercises 1–5 to check for understanding. Then use the chart at the bottom of this page to customize your assignments for students.

Intervention You may wish to use the Study Guide and Intervention Master on page 41 of the *Chapter 11 Resource Masters* for additional reinforcement.

Odd/Even Assignments

Exercises 6–13 are structured so that students practice the same concepts whether they are assigned odd or even problems.

Additional Answer

19. $467.4 \div 350 \approx 1.34$; Since only whole gallons of paint can be purchased, you will need 2 gallons of paint. At $20 each, the cost will be $2 \times \$20$ or $40.

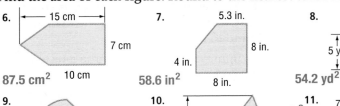

Exercises

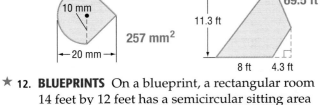

HOMEWORK HELP	
For Exercises	See Examples
6–11	1
12–13	2

Exercise Levels
A: 6–13
B: 14–19
C: 20–22

Find the area of each figure. Round to the nearest tenth if necessary.

6. 15 cm, 7 cm, 10 cm — 87.5 cm^2

7. 5.3 in., 8 in., 4 in., 8 in. — 58.6 in^2

8. 5 yd, 7 yd — 54.2 yd^2

9. 10 mm, 20 mm — 257 mm^2

10. 11.3 ft, 8 ft, 4.3 ft — 69.5 ft^2

11. 7 yd, 4 yd, 5.2 yd, 5.2 yd, 2 yd — 66.2 yd^2

★ **12. BLUEPRINTS** On a blueprint, a rectangular room 14 feet by 12 feet has a semicircular sitting area attached with a diameter of 12 feet. What is the total area of the room and the sitting area? **about 224.5 ft^2**

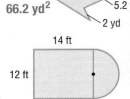
14 ft, 12 ft

★ **13. POOLS** The diagram at the right gives the dimensions of a swimming pool. If a cover is needed for the pool, what will be the approximate area of the cover? **approximately 847.2 ft^2**

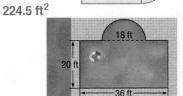
18 ft, 20 ft, 36 ft

Find the area of the shaded region. Round to the nearest tenth if necessary.

14. 33 cm, 34 cm, 46 cm, 18 cm — $1{,}037 \text{ cm}^2$

15. 7 in., 25 in. — 196.1 in^2

For each figure, write an algebraic expression that represents the area in square centimeters of the shaded region.

16. x cm, 8 cm, x cm, 12 cm — $96 - x^2$

17. x cm, 6 cm, x cm — $x^2 + \frac{1}{2}(6x)$ or $x^2 + 3x$

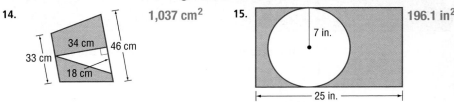

18. 467.4 ft^2
19. See margin.

EXTRA PRACTICE
See pages 710, 725.
Math Online
Self-Check Quiz at
ca.gr6math.com

PAINTING For Exercises 18 and 19, use the diagram that shows one side of a storage barn.

18. This side of the storage barn needs to be painted. Find the total area to be painted.

19. Each gallon of paint costs $20 and covers ★ 350 square feet. Find the total cost to paint this side once. Justify your answer.

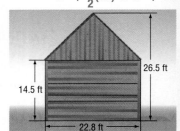
26.5 ft, 14.5 ft, 22.8 ft

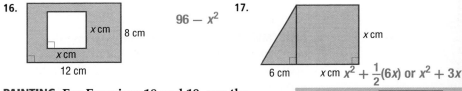

DIFFERENTIATED HOMEWORK OPTIONS

Level	Assignment	Two-Day Option	
BL Basic	6–13, 22–31	7–13 odd, 23, 24	6–12 even, 22, 25–31
OL Core	7–17 odd, 18, 19, 22–31	6–13, 23, 24	14–19, 22, 25–31
AL Advanced/Pre-AP	14–28 (optional: 29–31)		

H.O.T. Problems

20. Sample answer: Add the areas of a trapezoid and a small rectangle. Area of trapezoid: $\left[\frac{1}{2} \times 5 \,(1+2)\right] =$ 7.5; Area of rectangle: $7 \times 2 =$ 14; 7.5 + 14 = 21.5. So, an approximate area is 21.5 × 1,900 or 40,850 mi².

CHALLENGE Describe the figures each state can be separated into. Then use these figures to estimate the area of each state if one square unit equals 1,900 square miles. Justify your answer.

20.

21.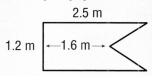

See margin.

22. **WRITING IN MATH** Describe how you would find the area of the figure shown at the right.

Sample answer: Separate it into a rectangle and a triangle, find the area of each, and add.

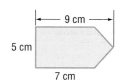

23. Which expression represents the area, in square feet, of the recreation room in terms of x? **B**

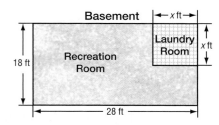

A $504 - 2x$ **C** $504 + x^2$
B $504 - x^2$ **D** $504 + 4x$

24. The shaded part of the grid represents the plans for a fish pond.

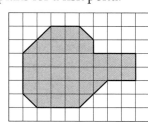

If each square on the grid represents 5 square feet, what is the approximate area of the fish pond? **G**

F 175 ft²   **H** 150 ft²
G 165 ft²   **J** 33 ft²

Spiral Review

25. **MONEY** Over the weekend, Mrs. Lobo spent $534. Of that, about 68% was spent on groceries. About how much money was *not* spent on groceries? Use the *solve a simpler problem* strategy. (Lesson 11-5)
Sample answer: about 30% of $500 or $150

Find the area of each circle. Round to the nearest tenth. (Lesson 11-4)

26. radius = 4.7 cm
69.4 cm²

27. radius = 12 in.
452.2 in²

28. diameter = 15 in.
176.6 in²

GET READY for the Next Lesson

PREREQUISITE SKILL Sketch each object. 29–31. See margin.

29. ice cream cone   **30.** shoe box   **31.** drinking straw

Lesson 11-6 Area of Complex Figures   **599**

Ticket Out the Door Draw the diagram below on the chalkboard. Have students find the area of the figure and write it on a slip of paper.

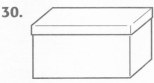

FOLDABLES **Foldables™**
Study Organizer **Follow-Up**

Remind students to take notes about complex figures in their Foldables. Encourage them to draw their own example of a complex figure, marking the simpler figures and showing how to calculate the area of the complex figure.

Additional Answers

21. Sample answer: Add the areas of a trapezoid and a triangle. Area of a trapezoid: $\left(\frac{1}{2} \times 2.5 \,(7+10)\right) =$ 21.25; Area of a triangle: $\frac{1}{2} \times 6 \times 2 = 6$; 21.25 + 6 = 27.25. So, an approximate area is 27.25 × 1,900 or 51,775 mi².

29.

30.

31.

Nets and Surface Area

1 Focus

Materials
- cardboard boxes
- poster paper
- scissors
- rulers

Teaching Tip

Collect several cardboard boxes before the lesson. You may wish to model the Activity on the chalkboard. If you don't have enough boxes for every student in your class (or if the boxes are large), have students work in pairs or groups of three.

2 Teach

Working in Cooperative Groups
You may wish for students to work in pairs. Student 1 can roll the box and hold it still while Student 2 traces the outline of each surface of the box.

Activity

Make sure students realize that it doesn't matter which side of the box they start with as the "bottom." You might want to point out that opposite faces of the box are congruent rectangles. Students can complete the Activity and analysis without cutting out the nets.

Main IDEA

Nets and Surface Area

Preparation for Standard 7MG3.5 Construct two-dimensional patterns for three-dimensional models, such as cylinders, **prisms**, and cones.
Standard 6MR3.3 Develop generalizations of the results obtained and the strategies used and apply them in new problem situations.

Suppose you cut a cardboard box along its edges, open it up, and lay it flat.

The result is a complex figure called a **net**. A net can help you see the regions or faces that make up the surface of a figure.

ACTIVITY

STEP 1 Place the box in the middle of a large sheet of paper as shown. Trace the outline of the bottom of the box.

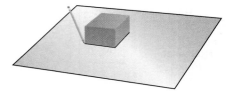

STEP 2 Roll the box onto its right side and label the outline you traced "Bottom". Trace and label each of the sides and top in this same way as shown below.

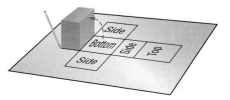

STEP 3 Cut out the resulting complex figure.

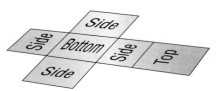

CHECK Your Progress

a–b. Make nets for two other rectangular boxes. **See students' work.**

600 **Chapter 11** Measurement: Two- and Three-Dimensional Figures

3–5. See Ch. 11 Answer Appendix for nets.

ANALYZE THE RESULTS

1. The net shown in the Activity is made of rectangles. How many rectangles are in the net? **6**

2. Explain how you can find the total area of the rectangles.
   Find the sum of the areas of the rectangles.

Draw a net for each figure. Find the area of the net.

3.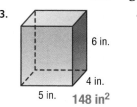
   6 in.
   4 in.
   5 in.   **148 in²**

4.
   8 ft
   92 ft²
   3 ft
   2 ft

5.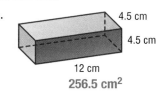
   4.5 cm
   4.5 cm
   12 cm
   256.5 cm²

6. The *surface area* of a prism is the total area of its net. Write an equation that shows how to find the surface area of the prism below using the length ℓ, width w, and height h.
   surface area $= \ell w + \ell w + wh + wh + \ell h + \ell h$

7. Find the surface areas of cubes whose edges are 1 unit, 2 units, and 3 units and graph the ordered pairs (side length, surface area) on a coordinate plane. Describe the graph. **See margin.**

8. **MAKE A CONJECTURE** Describe what happens to the surface area of a cube as its dimensions are doubled? tripled?
   increase by 2^2; increase by 3^2

Draw a net for each figure. 9. See margin. 10. See Ch. 11 Answer Appendix.

9.
   tetrahedron

10.
    square-based pyramid

11. Explain how the net of a tetrahedron differs from the net of a square-based pyramid.

12. Describe how you could find the surface area of a tetrahedron.

13. Describe how you could find the surface area of a square-based pyramid.

14. Find the surface area of a square-based pyramid if the square base has a side length of 8 centimeters and the height of each triangular side of the pyramid has a height of 5 centimeters. **144 cm²**

11. The net for a square-based pyramid is made up of 5 shapes: 4 triangles and a square. The net for a tetrahedron is made of just 4 shapes and all of them are triangles.

12. Find the area of the triangular base and the area of each triangular side. Then find the sum of all these areas.

13. Find the area of one triangular side. Since there are four congruent triangular sides, multiply this area by four. Then find the area of the square base and add this area to the total area of the four triangular sides.

Nets and Surface Area

Make sure students understand that the surface area of a three-dimensional figure is the sum of all the areas of each individual surface. As students draw nets, find the area of each figure in the net, and find the sum of these areas, they are finding the surface area of the figure. While the figure is three-dimensional, its net is two-dimensional and the area of the net will be noted in square units. As an extension, have students draw a net that could be used to find the surface area of a cylinder.

Use Exercises 3–5 to determine whether students understand how to use a net to find the total surface area of a rectangular prism.

From Concrete to Abstract Use Exercise 6 to bridge the gap between using nets to find the surface area of rectangular prisms and writing an equation to find the surface area of rectangular prisms.

Extending the Concept You might want to have students consider the problem of creating a net of a sphere. Have them use the Internet or an encyclopedia to research how mapmakers have tried to show Earth on a flat piece of paper. Encourage volunteers to share their research with the class.

Additional Answers

7.
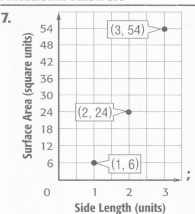

Sample answer: As the side length increases, the surface area increases by a factor equal to the square of the new side length.

9.
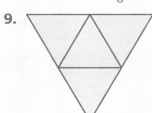

CHAPTER 11 Mid-Chapter Quiz
Lessons 11-1 through 11-6

Find the area of each parallelogram. Round to the nearest tenth if necessary. (Lesson 11-1)

1. base = 7 cm **28 cm²**   height = 4 cm
2. base = 4.3 in. **38.7 in²**   height = 9 in.
3. base = $11\frac{3}{4}$ ft $97\frac{11}{12}$ **ft²**   height = $8\frac{1}{3}$ ft

4. **STANDARDS PRACTICE** A scale drawing of a deck is shown. What is the actual area of the deck if the scale drawing is 10 m = 1 mm? (Lesson 11-1) **A**

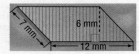

A 7,200 m²

B 720 m²

C 720 mm²

D 24 m²

Find the area of each figure. Round to the nearest tenth if necessary. (Lesson 11-2)

5.
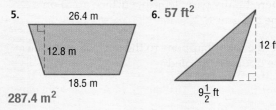
26.4 m
12.8 m
18.5 m
287.4 m²

6. **57 ft²**
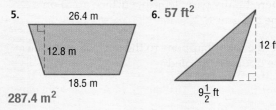
12 ft
$9\frac{1}{2}$ ft

7. **ALGEBRA** Find the area of a triangle with a base of 23 centimeters and a height of 18 centimeters. (Lesson 11-2) **207 cm²**

Find the circumference of each circle. Use 3.14 or $\frac{22}{7}$ for π. Round to the nearest tenth if necessary. (Lesson 11-3)

8. radius = $10\frac{7}{8}$ in.   9. diameter = 21 ft
   $68\frac{5}{14}$ **in.**   **65.9 ft**

10.
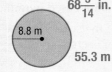
8.8 m
55.3 m

11.
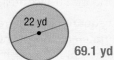
22 yd
69.1 yd

12. **STANDARDS PRACTICE** Which expression could be used to find the circumference of a circular patio table with a diameter of 8.9 feet? (Lesson 11-3) **G**

F $2 \times \pi \times 8.9$

G $\pi \times 8.9$

H $\pi \times 8.9 \times 8.9$

J $\pi \times 4.45 \times 4.45$

Find the area of each circle. Round to the nearest tenth. (Lesson 11-4)

13. radius = $4\frac{1}{4}$ cm   14. diameter = $6\frac{4}{5}$ ft
    56.7 cm²   **36.3 ft²**
15. diameter = 14.6 m   16. radius = $7\frac{3}{4}$ yd
    167.3 m²   **188.6 yd²**

17. **SALES** A manager at the local cell phone store reported to his employees that sales had increased 19.5% over last month's total of $25,688. About how much did the store sell this month? Use the *solve a simpler problem* strategy. (Lesson 11-5) **See margin.**

For Exercises 18 and 19, find the area of the shaded region for each figure. (Lesson 11-6)

18.
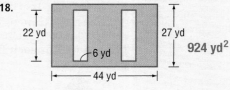
22 yd
6 yd
27 yd
44 yd
924 yd²

19.
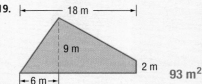
18 m
9 m
2 m
6 m
93 m²

20. **MEASUREMENT** How many square feet of glass is needed to make the window shown? Round to the nearest tenth. (Lesson 11-6) **8.6 ft²**
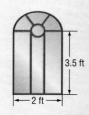
3.5 ft
2 ft

Data-Driven Decision Making	Exercises	Lesson	Standard	Resources for Review
Diagnostic Teaching Based on the results of the Chapter 11 Mid-Chapter Quiz, use the following to review concepts that students continue to find challenging.	1–4	11–1	6AF3.1	CRM Study Guide and Intervention pp. 10, 17, 23, 31, 36, and 41
	5–7	11–2	6AF3.1	Math Online
	8–12	11–3	6MG1.1	• Extra Examples
	13–16	11–4	6MG1.1	• Personal Tutor
	17	11–5	6MR1.3	• Concepts in Motion
	18–20	11–6	6AF3.2	

11-7 Three-Dimensional Figures

Preparation for ➤— Standard 7MG3.6:

Identify elements of three-dimensional geometric objects (e.g., diagonals of rectangular solids) and describe how two or more objects are related in space (e.g., skew lines, the possible ways three planes might intersect).

PACING:

Regular: 1 periods, **Block:** 0.5 period

Options for Differentiated Instruction

ELL = English Language Learner   **AL** = Above Grade Level   **SS** = Struggling Students   **SN** = Special Needs

Using Models SN

Use before presenting Example 1.

Provide several rectangular prisms for students to examine. Have them identify and measure the dimensions of each figure: length, width and height. Then have students orient the prism differently.

Ask:

- If the prism is rotated, do the dimensions of the prism change? no
- If the prism is rotated, do the bases of the prism change? sometimes

Making Real-World Connections ELL SN

Use after presenting the Examples.

Have students define the three-dimensional figures presented in Lesson 11-7 and give real-life examples of each. Also, have them define the parts of a three dimensional figure: face, edge, lateral face, and vertex.

Organizing Student Work and Thinking SS SN

Use before assigning the Exercises.

Provide a copy of the following table for students to use as a resource sheet. Have them classify each three-dimensional figure shown and then complete the rest of the table.

Figure				
	prism	pyramid	cone	cylinder
Number of Faces	5	4	1	2
Number of Edges	9	6	0	0
Number of Vertices	6	4	1	0

BL = Below Grade Level   **OL** = On Grade Level   **AL** = Above Grade Level   **ELL** = English Language Learner

Lesson Reading Guide
p. 46 **BL OL ELL**

NAME _____ DATE _____ PERIOD _____

11-7 Lesson Reading Guide
Three Dimensional Figures   7MG3.6

Get Ready for the Lesson

Complete the Mini Lab at the top of page 603 in your textbook. Write your answers below.

1. Study the shape of each object. Then compare and contrast the properties of each object. Sample answer: cereal box: Each side is a rectangle; soda can: The top and bottom are circles and the side is curved; party hat: The bottom is a circle.

Read the Lesson

Fill in the blanks.

2. The top and bottom faces of a prism are _____ and are _____. bases; parallel

3. The shape of the base tells the name of the _____. pyramid or prism

4. The base of a cone is a _____. circle

5. A _____ has no faces, bases, edges, or vertices. cylinder

6. The bases of a cylinder are _____. circles

7. All of the points on a _____ are the same distance from the _____. cylinder; center or axis

Remember What You Learned

8. Compare and contrast a triangular prism, a triangular pyramid, and a cone.
A triangular prism has 2 triangular bases; it has three lateral faces that are rectangles.
A triangular pyramid has a triangle base; it has one base and three triangle sides.
A cone has a circle base; it has one vertex and no edges.

Chapter 11   46   Glencoe California Mathematics, Grade 6

Study Guide and Intervention*
p. 47 **BL OL ELL**

NAME _____ DATE _____ PERIOD _____

11-7 Study Guide and Intervention
Three Dimensional Figures   7MG3.6

Prisms	At least 3 rectangular lateral faces	Top and bottom bases are parallel	Shape of the base tells the name of the prism
Pyramids	At least three triangular lateral faces	One base shaped like any 3-sided closed figure	Shape of the base tells the name of the pyramid
Cones	Only one base	Base is a circle	One vertex and no edges
Cylinders	Only two bases	Bases are circles	No vertices and no edges
Spheres	All points are the same distance from the center	No faces or bases	No edges or vertices

Example For each figure, name the shape of the base(s). Then classify each figure.

A. parallel triangular bases, three rectangular faces; The figure is a triangular prism.

B. two circular bases, no edges; The figure is a cylinder.

Exercises

For each figure name the shape of the base(s). Then classify each figure.

1. rectangle; rectangular prism
2. triangle, triangular prism
3. circle; cylinder
4. circle; cone
5. triangle; triangular pyramid
6. square; cube or square prism

Chapter 11   47   Glencoe California Mathematics, Grade 6

Skills Practice*
p. 48 **BL OL**

NAME _____ DATE _____ PERIOD _____

11-7 Skills Practice
Three-Dimensional Figures   7MG3.6

For each figure, identify the shape of the base(s). Then classify the figure.

1. circles; cylinder
2. rectangles; rectangular prism
3. squares; cube
4. circle; cone
5. none; sphere
6. triangle; pyramid
7. square; pyramid
8. none; cylinder
9. circle; cone
10. none; sphere
11. triangles; triangular prism
12. rectangles; rectangular prism
13. rectangles; rectangular prism
14. squares; cube
15. circles; cylinder

Chapter 11   48   Glencoe California Mathematics, Grade 6

Practice*
p. 49 **OL AL**

NAME _____ DATE _____ PERIOD _____

11-7 Practice
Three-Dimensional Figures   7MG3.6

For each figure, identify the shape of the base(s), if any. Then classify the figure.

1. pentagons; pentagonal prism
2. circles; cylinder
3. triangles; triangular prism
4. circle; cone
5. hexagon; hexagonal pyramid
6. rectangle; rectangular pyramid
7. none; sphere
8. rectangles; rectangular prism
9. trapezoid; trapezoidal pyramid

10. CANDLES What three-dimensional figure describes the candle shown? cylinder

11. FENCES The basic shape of a fence post is made of two geometric figures. Classify these figures. rectangular prism and rectangular pyramid

Chapter 11   49   Glencoe California Mathematics, Grade 6

Word Problem Practice*
p. 50 **OL AL**

NAME _____ DATE _____ PERIOD _____

11-7 Word Problem Practice
Three-Dimensional Figures   7MG3.6

1. SPORTS A regulation basketball weighs 20-22 ounces. Classify the shape of a regulation basketball as a three-dimensional figure. sphere

2. ICE CREAM The picture shows an ice cream cone with a single scoop on top. What two three-dimensional shapes make up the ice cream and cone? sphere and cone

3. SHIPPING Jessie bought a box to ship her gifts to her grandmother. Classify the shape of a box as a three-dimensional figure. rectangular prism

4. LAUNDRY Classify the shape of the laundry hamper shown as a three-dimensional figure. cylinder

5. SCHOOL PROJECT Jarnel is creating a diorama for his class project. He plans to use a shoebox to build the diorama. Classify the shape of a shoebox as a three-dimensional figure. rectangular prism

6. SOUP Classify the shape of a soup can as a three-dimensional figure. cylinder

7. BABY BLOCKS Classify the shape of the baby block as a three-dimensional figure. cube

8. EARTH Classify the shape of the Earth as a three-dimensional figure. sphere

Chapter 11   50   Glencoe California Mathematics, Grade 6

Enrichment
p. 51 **OL AL**

NAME _____ DATE _____ PERIOD _____

11-7 Enrichment   7MG3.6

Properties of Prisms

Leonard Euler, born in 1707, was one of the world's greatest mathematicians. One of his accomplishments was discovering a formula for calculating the number of faces, edges, and vertices on a three-dimensional figure. He found that $V + F = E + 2$. (Vertices + Faces = Edges + 2)

A triangular prism has 6 vertices, 5 faces, and 9 edges. It has the fewest faces, edges, and vertices of any prism.

1. Complete the table for a hexagonal and an octagonal prism.

Prism	Vertices	Faces	Edges
triangular	6	5	9
rectangular	8	6	12
pentagonal	10	7	15
hexagonal	12	8	18
octagonal	16	10	24

2. If a prism has 14 vertices and 21 edges, how many faces does it have? Use Euler's formula. 9 faces

3. A prism has 20 vertices. How many faces does it have? How many edges? This prism has 12 faces and 30 edges. (It is a "decagonal prism"; the top and base each have 10 sides.)

4. An "n-gonal" prism has two bases, each with n sides. Use the patterns in the table to write expressions to find the number of faces, edges, and vertices an n-gonal prism has. An "n-gonal" prism has n + 2 faces, 3n edges, and 2n vertices.

Chapter 11   51   Glencoe California Mathematics, Grade 6

Additional Lesson Resources

Also available in Spanish **ELL**

Transparencies
- 5-Minute Check Transparency, Lesson 11-7

Other Print Products
- Teaching Mathematics with Manipulatives
- Noteables™ Interactive Study Notebook with Foldables™

Teacher Tech Tools
- Interactive Classroom CD-ROM, Lesson 11-7
- AssignmentWorks, Lesson 11-7

Student Tech Tools
ca.gr6math.com
- Extra Examples, Chapter 11, Lesson 7
- Self-Check Quiz, Chapter 11, Lesson 7

 Main IDEA

Build three-dimensional figures given the top, side, and front views.

Preparation for Standard 7MG3.6 Identify elements of three-dimensional geometric objects (e.g., diagonals of rectangular solids) and describe how two or more objects are related in space (e.g., skew lines, the possible ways three planes might intersect).

NEW Vocabulary

three-dimensional figure
face
edge
lateral face
vertex (vertices)
prism
base
pyramid
cone
cylinder
sphere
center

 **STUDY TIP**

Three-Dimensional Figures In three-dimensional figures, dashed lines are used to indicate edges that are hidden from view.

GET READY for the Lesson

Study the shape of each common object below.
Then compare and contrast the properties of each object.

See Ch. 11 Answer Appendix.
Many common shapes are **three-dimensional figures**. That is, they have length, width, and depth (or height). Some terms associated with three-dimensional figures are shown below.

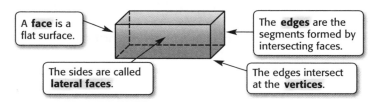

A **face** is a flat surface.

The **edges** are the segments formed by intersecting faces.

The sides are called **lateral faces**.

The edges intersect at the **vertices**.

Two types of three-dimensional figures are prisms and pyramids.

KEY CONCEPT   Prisms and Pyramids

Figure	Properties
Prism	• Has at least three lateral faces that are parallelograms. • The top and bottom faces, called the **bases**, are congruent parallel polygons. • The shape of the base tells the name of the prism. Rectangular prism Triangular prism Square prism or cube
Pyramid	• Has at least three lateral faces that are triangles. • Has only one base, which is a polygon. • The shape of the base tells the name of the pyramid. Triangular pyramid Square pyramid

Lesson 11-7 Three-Dimensional Figures **603**

Differentiated Instruction

Visual/Spatial Learners While presenting the Key Concept box, have students create nets for a rectangular prism, triangular prism, square prism, triangular pyramid, and square pyramid to make visual connections to the properties for each figure. For example, by making a net for a square pyramid, students can visualize the three triangular surfaces and the one square surface of the pyramid.

1 Focus

Standards Alignment

Before Lesson 11-7
Visualize and draw two-dimensional views of three-dimensional objects made from rectangular solids from Standard 5MG2.3

Lesson 11-7
Identify elements of three-dimensional geometric objects from Standard 7MG3.6

After Lesson 11-7
Students compute the volumes and surface areas of prisms, pyramids, cylinders, cones, and spheres from Standard G9.0

2 Teach

Scaffolding Questions

As you ask the following questions, point to a chalkboard eraser, cardboard box, or other rectangular prism.

Ask:
• What shape are the top and the bottom? rectangle

• Are the top and bottom parallel? yes

• How many sides does it have? 4

• Are the sides flat? yes

• How many vertices does it have? 8

 Prisms

Make sure students realize that the bases of a prism can be positioned toward the sides. Also make sure they realize that any pair of opposite faces of a rectangular or square prism can be the bases.

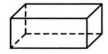

Some three dimensional figures have curved surfaces.

Figure	Properties	
Cone	• Has only one base. • The base is a circle. • Has one vertex.	
Cylinder	• Has only two bases. • The bases are congruent circles. • Has no vertices and no edges.	
Sphere	• All of the points on a sphere are the same distance from the **center**. • No faces, bases, edges, or vertices.	center 

KEY CONCEPT Cones, Cylinders, and Spheres

STUDY TIP

Prisms and Pyramids Prisms and pyramids are examples of *polyhedra*, or solids with flat surfaces that are polygonal regions. Cones, cylinders, and spheres are not examples of polyhedra.

EXAMPLES **Classify Three-Dimensional Figures**

For each figure, identify the shape of the base(s). Then classify the figure.

❶ The figure has one circular base, no edge, and one vertex.

The figure is a cone.

❷ The base and all other faces are squares.

The figure is a square prism or cube.

CHECK Your Progress

a. triangle; pyramid

b.  circle; cylinder

Real-World EXAMPLE

❸ **CAMERAS** Classify the shape of the body of the digital camera, not including the lens, as a three-dimensional figure.

The body of the camera is a rectangular prism.

CHECK Your Progress

c. Classify the shape of the zoom lens as a three-dimensional figure.

cylinder

 Personal Tutor at ca.gr6math.com

3 Practice

Examples 1, 2
(p. 604)

For each figure, identify the shape of the base(s). Then classify the figure.

3. circle; cylinder

1.

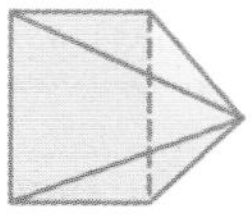

square; square pyramid

2.

triangle; triangular prism

3.

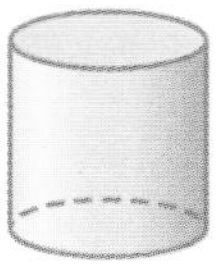

Example 3
(p. 604)

4. SPORTS An official major league baseball has 108 stitches. Classify the shape of a baseball as a three-dimensional figure. **sphere**

Exercises

HOMEWORK HELP

For Exercises	See Examples
5–8	1–2
9–10	3

Exercise Levels
A: 5–10
B: 11–15
C: 16–19

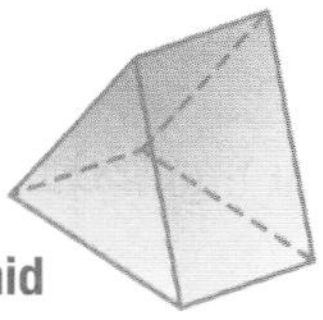

6. triangle; triangular prism

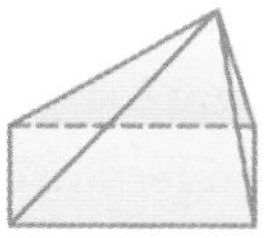

7. rectangle; rectangular pyramid

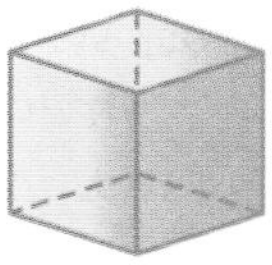

8. square; square prism or cube

For each figure, identify the shape of the base(s). Then classify the figure.

5.

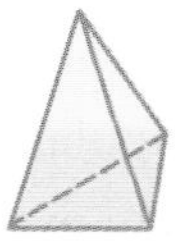

6.

7.

8.

triangle; triangular pyramid

9. FOOD What three-dimensional figure describes the item shown? **cone**

10. SCHOOL SUPPLIES Classify the shape of your math textbook as a three-dimensional figure. **rectangular prism**

11–13. See margin.

For each figure, identify the shape of the base(s). Then classify the figure.

11.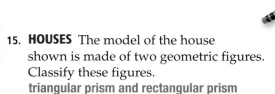

12.

13.

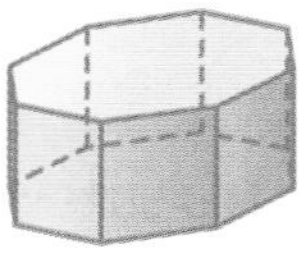

14. SCHOOL SUPPLIES The model of the pencil shown is made of two geometric figures. Classify these figures.
cylinder and cone

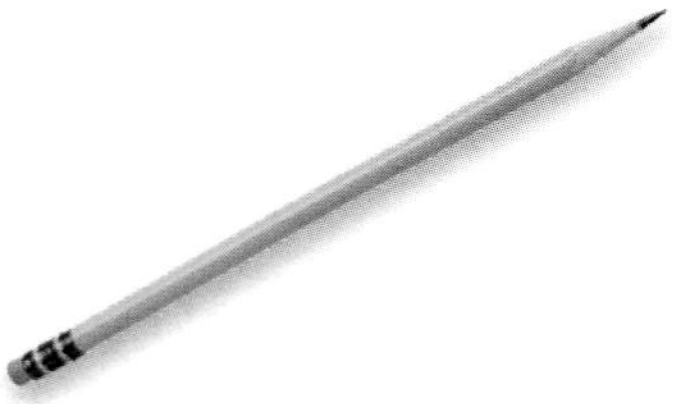

EXTRA PRACTICE
See pages 710, 725.
Math Online
Self-Check Quiz at
ca.gr6math.com

15. HOUSES The model of the house shown is made of two geometric figures. Classify these figures.
triangular prism and rectangular prism

Lesson 11-7 Three-Dimensional Figures **605**

Formative Assessment

Use Exercises 1–4 to check for understanding.

Then use the chart at the bottom of this page to customize your assignments for students.

Intervention You may wish to use the Study Guide and Intervention Master on page 47 of the *Chapter 11 Resource Masters* for additional reinforcement.

Odd/Even Assignments

Exercises 5–10 are structured so that students practice the same concepts whether they are assigned odd or even problems.

Additional Answers

11. trapezoid; trapezoidal prism

12. pentagon; pentagonal pyramid

13. octagon; octagonal prism

DIFFERENTIATED HOMEWORK OPTIONS			
Level	**Assignment**	**Two-Day Option**	
BL Basic	5–10, 16, 18–29	5–9 odd, 20, 21	6–10 even, 16, 18, 19, 22–29
OL Core	5–13 odd, 14–16, 18–29	5–10, 20, 21	11–16, 18, 19, 22–29
AL Advanced/Pre-AP	11–26 (optional: 27–29)		

Ticket Out the Door Have students draw an everyday object that resembles a three-dimensional geometric figure. Have them classify the object according to the figure it resembles, pointing out its properties.

FOLDABLES Study Organizer **Foldables™ Follow-Up**

Remind students to take notes about the classification of three-dimensional figures in their Foldables. Encourage them to give examples of each figure, noting its properties.

Additional Answers

18. Sample answer: rectangular prism; the measures of the areas of the bases of a rectangular prism are equal.

19. Sample answer: A cone has only one base that is a circle. A pyramid also has only one base but its base is a polygon. They both have only one vertex. A cone does not have any lateral faces and a pyramid has at least three lateral faces.

H.O.T. Problems

16. Set A is a list of figures that are made up of flat surfaces only and set B is a list of figures that have curved surfaces.

16. **REASONING** Two sets of figures were sorted according to a certain rule. The figures in Set A follow the rule and the figures in Set B do not follow the rule. Describe the rule.

Set A	Prism	Pyramid	Cube
Set B	Cylinder	Cone	Sphere

17. **CHALLENGE** What figure is formed if only the height of a cube is increased? Draw a figure to justify your answer. **rectangular prism; See students' work for justification.**

18. **OPEN ENDED** Select one three-dimensional figure in which you could use the term *congruent* to describe the bases of the figure. Then write a sentence using *congruent* to describe the figure. **See margin.**

19. **WRITING IN MATH** Apply what you know about the properties of geometric figures to compare and contrast cones and pyramids. **See margin.**

STANDARDS PRACTICE 7MG3.6

20. Which statement is true about all triangular prisms? **C**

   A All of the edges are congruent line segments.

   B There are exactly 6 faces.

   C The bases are congruent triangles.

   D All of the faces are triangles.

21. Which figure is shown? **F**

   F triangular pyramid

   G square pyramid

   H rectangular pyramid

   J triangular prism

Spiral Review

22. **MEASUREMENT** Find the area of the figure shown at the right if each triangle has a height of 3.5 inches and the square has side lengths of 4 inches. (Lesson 11-6) **44 in²**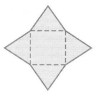

23. **MEASUREMENT** Find the area of a circle with a radius of 5.7 meters. Round to the nearest tenth. (Lesson 11-4) **102.0 m²**

ALGEBRA Find the missing angle measure in each quadrilateral. (Lesson 10-5)

24.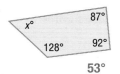
70°
123°
$x°$
77°

25.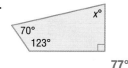
$x°$
87°
128°
92°
53°

26.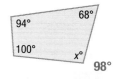
94°
68°
100°
$x°$
98°

GET READY for the Next Lesson

PREREQUISITE SKILL Describe the shape seen when each object is viewed from the top.

27. number cube **square**

28. cereal box **rectangle**

29. soup can **circle**

Pre-AP Activity Use after Exercise 18

Have students write a formula for the total area of the faces of a cube with sides of length x. $A = 6x^2$

Main IDEA

Build three-dimensional figures given the top, side, and front views.

Preparation for Standard 7MG3.6 Identify elements of three-dimensional geometric objects (e.g., diagonals of rectangular solids) and describe how two or more objects are related in space (e.g., skew lines, the possible ways three planes might intersect).
Standard 6MR2.4 Use a variety of methods, such as words, numbers, symbols, charts, graphs, tables, diagrams, and **models, to explain mathematical reasoning.**

Cubes are examples of three-dimensional figures because they have length, width, and depth. In this lab, you will use centimeter cubes to build other three-dimensional figures.

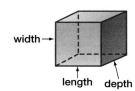

ACTIVITY

The top view, side view, and front view of a three-dimensional figure are shown below. Use centimeter cubes to build the figure. Then make a sketch of the figure.

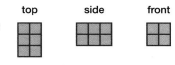

STEP 1 Use the top view to build the figure's base.

STEP 2 Use the side view to complete the figure.

STEP 3 Use the front view to check the figure.

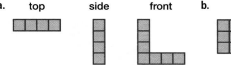

CHECK Your Progress a–b. See margin.

ANALYZE THE RESULTS

1. Explain how you began building the figures in Exercises a and b.

2. Determine whether there is more than one way to build each model. Explain your reasoning. **See students' work.**

3. Build two different models that would look the same from two views, but not the third view. Draw a top view, side view, and front view of each model. **See margin.**

4. Describe a real-world situation where it might be necessary to draw a top, side, and front view of a three-dimensional figure. **See margin.**

Explore 11-8 Geometry Lab: Three-Dimensional Figures **607**

1. Sample answer: start with the base.

1 Focus

Materials
• centimeter cubes

2 Teach

Activity Explain to students that a good strategy for building the three-dimensional figures is first to build the base of the figure by looking at the top view, and then to complete the figure by looking at the side and front views. However, some students may find it easier to visualize the figure by first looking at either the front or side view. Encourage students to use the method that makes most sense to them. Finally, students should check their figures by comparing them with each of the three views.

3 Assess

Formative Assessment

Use Exercises 2 and 3 to determine whether students understand how to build three-dimensional figures when given top, side, and front views.

Moving from Models to Abstract Thought Use Exercise 4 to bridge the gap between building three-dimensional figures with cubes and recognizing that some real-life figures are best described by drawing their top, side, and front views.

Extending the Concept Have students draw the top, side, and front views of a real-life three-dimensional figure (such as a house, tree, book, or egg).

Additional Answers

a.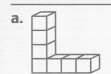

b.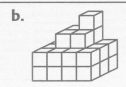

3.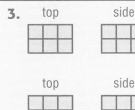

4. Sample answer: building a doghouse

11-8 Drawing Three-Dimensional Figures

Reinforcement of Standard 5MG2.3:	**Visualize and draw two-dimensional views of three-dimensional objects made from rectangular solids.**
Standard 6MR2.4:	**Use a variety of methods, such as** words, numbers, symbols, charts, graphs, tables, **diagrams, and models, to explain mathematical reasoning.**
PACING:	**Regular**: 2 periods, **Block**: 1 period

Options for Differentiated Instruction

ELL = English Language Learner   **AL** = Above Grade Level   **SS** = Struggling Students   **SN** = Special Needs

Kinesthetic Learning **SS**

Use after presenting Example 3.

Have students work in pairs. One partner should build a structure with five centimeter cubes. Both students draw the structure on isometric dot paper, as well as the top, front, and side views. Then have students compare and correct their drawings. The other partner creates a new structure with five cubes, and the students repeat the task.

Spatial Skills **ELL** **SS** **SN**

Use before assigning the Exercises.

Using isometric dot paper is difficult for many students. Model how to use the paper by drawing a single cube first, then two cubes, and so on. It is very helpful for students to shade the top of the cube to help them see the third dimension. Allow students plenty of time to discover how to use this tool.

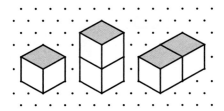

Reinforcement With Models **SS** **SN**

Use with the Exercises.

Have centimeter blocks available for students to build the three dimensional figures and to check their work. This will help students draw the solids on isometric dot paper in Exercises 4 and 12–15.

A model of the solid described in Exercise 4 is shown below.

Exercise 4

Leveled Lesson Resources

Chapter 11 Resource Masters

BL = Below Grade Level   **OL** = On Grade Level   **AL** = Above Grade Level   **ELL** = English Language Learner

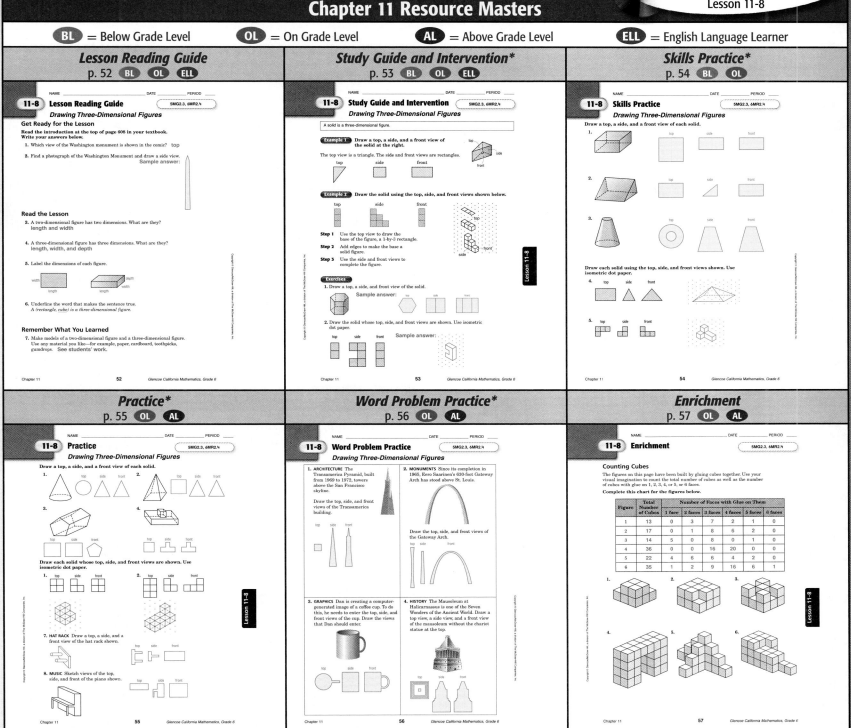

Additional Lesson Resources

* Also available in Spanish **ELL**

Transparencies
- *5-Minute Check Transparency*, Lesson 11-8

Other Print Products
- *Teaching Mathematics with Manipulatives*
- *Noteables*™ *Interactive Study Notebook with Foldables*™

Teacher Tech Tools
- *Interactive Classroom CD-ROM*, Lesson 11-8
- *AssignmentWorks*, Lesson 11-8

Student Tech Tools
ca.gr6math.com
- Extra Examples, Chapter 11, Lesson 8
- Self-Check Quiz, Chapter 11, Lesson 8

1 Focus

Standards Alignment

Before Lesson 11-8
Visualize and draw two-dimensional views of three-dimensional objects made from rectangular solids from Standard 5MG2.3

Lesson 11-8
Use a variety of methods, such as diagrams and models to explain mathematical reasoning from Standard 6MR2.4

After Lesson 11-8
Construct two-dimensional patterns for three-dimensional models from Standard 7MG3.5

2 Teach

Scaffolding Questions

Ask:

• What shape would a water glass look like from above? circle

• What shape would it look like from the side? rectangle, or trapezoid

• What shape would the wheel of a car look like from above? rectangle

• What shape would it look like from the front? rectangle

• What shape would it look like from the side? circle

Formative Assessment

Use the Check Your Progress exercises after each Example to determine students' understanding of concepts.

Additional Answers

2. Sample answer:

11-8 Drawing Three-Dimensional Figures

Main IDEA

Draw a three-dimensional figure given the top, side, and front views.

 Reinforcement of Standard 5MG2.3 Visualize and draw two-dimensional views of three-dimensional objects made from rectangular solids.
Standard 6MR2.4 Use a variety of methods, such as words, numbers, symbols, charts, graphs, tables, **diagrams, and models, to explain mathematical reasoning.**

> **GET READY for the Lesson**

COncepts in MOtion
Interactive Lab ca.gr6math.com

COMICS For Exercises 1 and 2, refer to the comic below.

SHOE

top

1. Which view of the Washington Monument is shown in the comic?

2. Find a photograph of the Washington Monument and draw a side view. **See margin.**

You can draw different views of three-dimensional figures. The most common views drawn are the top, side, and front views.

STUDY TiP

Plane Figures In geometry, three-dimensional figures are *solids* and two-dimensional figures such as triangles, circles, and squares are *plane* figures.

> **EXAMPLE** Draw a Three-Dimensional Figure

1. Draw a top, a side, and a front view of the figure at the right.

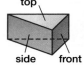

The top view is a triangle.

The side and front view are rectangles.

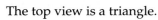

| top | side | front |

 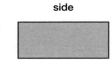

> **CHECK Your Progress**

Draw a top, a side, and a front view of each solid.

a. See margin. b. See margin.

a. top   side   front

b.

top   side   front

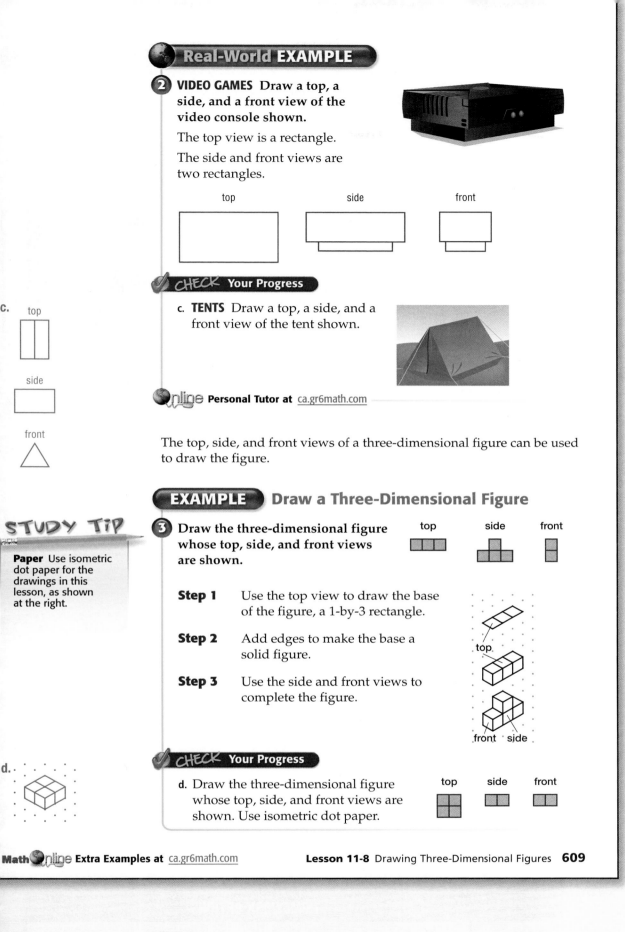

Real-World EXAMPLE

2 VIDEO GAMES Draw a top, a side, and a front view of the video console shown.

The top view is a rectangle.

The side and front views are two rectangles.

top	side	front

CHECK Your Progress

c. TENTS Draw a top, a side, and a front view of the tent shown.

Personal Tutor at ca.gr6math.com

The top, side, and front views of a three-dimensional figure can be used to draw the figure.

EXAMPLE Draw a Three-Dimensional Figure

3 Draw the three-dimensional figure whose top, side, and front views are shown.

top   side   front

Step 1 Use the top view to draw the base of the figure, a 1-by-3 rectangle.

Step 2 Add edges to make the base a solid figure.

Step 3 Use the side and front views to complete the figure.

CHECK Your Progress

d. Draw the three-dimensional figure whose top, side, and front views are shown. Use isometric dot paper.

top   side   front

c.
top

side

front

STUDY TIP

Paper Use isometric dot paper for the drawings in this lesson, as shown at the right.

d.

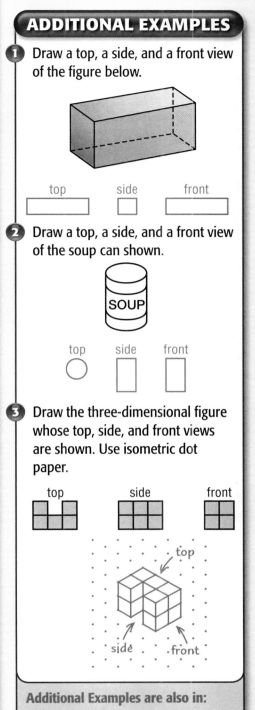

ADDITIONAL EXAMPLES

1 Draw a top, a side, and a front view of the figure below.

top   side   front

2 Draw a top, a side, and a front view of the soup can shown.

SOUP

top   side   front

3 Draw the three-dimensional figure whose top, side, and front views are shown. Use isometric dot paper.

top   side   front

top

side   front

Additional Examples are also in:

• Noteables™ Interactive Study Notebook with Foldables™

• Interactive Classroom PowerPoint® Presentations

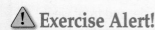

Formative Assessment

Use Exercises 1–4 to check for understanding.

Then use the chart at the bottom of this page to customize your assignments for students.

Intervention You may wish to use the Study Guide and Intervention Master on page 53 of the *Chapter 11 Resource Masters* for additional reinforcement.

Odd/Even Assignments

Exercises 5–16 are structured so that students practice the same concepts whether they are assigned odd or even problems.

⚠️ Exercise Alert!

Use Isometric Dot Paper Exercises 4 and 11–14 require students to draw three-dimensional figures on isometric dot paper.

CHECK Your Understanding

Example 1
(p. 608)

Draw a top, a side, and a front view of each solid. 1–2. See Ch. 11 Answer Appendix.

1.   2.

Example 2
(p. 609)

3. **SCIENCE** A transparent prism can be used to refract or disperse a beam of light. Draw a top, a side, and a front view of the prism shown at the right. See Ch. 11 Answer Appendix.

Example 3
(p. 609)

4. **Draw the solid whose top, side, and front views are shown. Use isometric dot paper.** See Ch. 11 Answer Appendix.

top   side   front

Exercises

HOMEWORK HELP

For Exercises	See Examples
5–10	1
15–16	2
11–14	3

Exercise Levels
A: 5–16
B: 17–24
C: 25–28

Draw a top, a side, and a front view of each solid. 5–10. See Ch. 11 Answer Appendix.

5.   6.   7.

8.   9.   10.

Draw each solid whose top, side, and front views are shown. Use isometric dot paper. 11–14. See Ch. 11 Answer Appendix.

11. top   side   front   12. top   side   front

13. top   side   front   14. top   side   front

DIFFERENTIATED HOMEWORK OPTIONS			
Level	**Assignment**	**Two-Day Option**	
BL Basic	5–16, 26–41	5–15 odd, 29	6–16 even, 26–28, 30–41
OL Core	5–19 odd, 20, 21, 23, 24, 26–41	5–16, 29	17–24, 26–28, 30–41
AL Advanced/Pre-AP	17–37 (optional: 38–41)		

15. SCHOOL Draw a top, a side, and a front view of the eraser shown.

16. TABLES Draw a top, a side, and a front view of a square table.

15–16. See Ch. 11 Answer Appendix.

Draw each solid whose top, side, and front views are shown. Use isometric dot paper.

17. top   side   front   See margin. **18.** top   side   front   See margin.

19. ARCHITECTURE The Quetzalcoatl pyramid in Mexico is the largest pyramid in the world. Use the photo at the left to sketch views from the top, side, and front of the pyramid. **See Ch. 11 Answer Appendix.**

Real-World Link . . . .
The Quetzalcoatl pyramid is about 30 meters tall. It was constructed by the Mayans 1000–1200 A.D.
Source: Guinness World Records

20. RESEARCH Use the Internet or another source to find a photograph of the only Wonder of the Ancient World existing today, the Great Pyramid of Giza. Draw a top view, a side view, and a front view of the pyramid. **See margin.**

Draw a top, a side, and a front view of each solid. 21. See margin.

21.   **22.**   **23.**

22–23. See Ch. 11 Answer Appendix.

EXTRAPRACTICE
See pages 711, 725.
Math online
Self-Check Quiz at
ca.gr6math.com

24. TRANSPORTATION Sketch views of the top, side, and front of the school bus shown at the right. **See Ch. 11 Answer Appendix.**

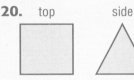

H.O.T. Problems

26. Rectangle, because it is the only two-dimensional figure.

27, 28. See students' work.

25. CHALLENGE Draw a three-dimensional figure in which the front and top views each have a line of symmetry but the side view does not. (*Hint*: Refer to Lesson 10-10 to review line symmetry). **See margin.**

26. Which One Doesn't Belong? Identify the figure that does not have the same characteristic as the other three. Explain your reasoning.

      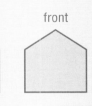

27. OPEN ENDED Choose an object in your classroom or in your home. Sketch any view of the object. Choose among a top, a side, or a front view.

28. WRITING IN MATH Apply what you have learned about views of three-dimensional figures to write a problem about the bridge shown.

Lesson 11-8 Drawing Three-Dimensional Figures **611**

Pre-AP Activity   Use as an Extension

As students complete Exercise 26, have them review the properties of three-dimensional figures including prisms, pyramids, cones, and cylinders. Most students will state that the rectangle is the figure that does not belong since it is a two-dimensional figure while the other figures are three-dimensional. Ask students what properties or characteristics they could use to suggest that the cone does not belong with the other figures. Sample answer: The cone is the only figure that does not contain at least one rectangle surface. The prism is made up of six rectangular surfaces, the two-dimensional figure is a rectangle, and the cylinder contains one rectangular curved surface.

612 **Chapter 11** Measurement: Two- and Three-Dimensional Figures

4 Assess

Crystal Ball Tell students that tomorrow's lesson is about finding the volume of prisms. Have them write how they think what they learned today will connect with tomorrow's material.

 Formative Assessment

Check for student understanding of concepts in Lessons 11-6 through 11-8.

 Quiz 3, p. 74

 Foldables™ Follow-Up

Remind students to take notes about drawing three-dimensional figures in their Foldables. Encourage them to give examples, showing the different views.

Additional Answers

30. rectangular pyramid

31. sphere

32. square prism

 **STANDARDS PRACTICE** 5MG2.3

29. The top, side, and front view of a solid figure made of cubes are shown. **B**

 top   side   front

Which solid figure is best represented by these views?

A   **C**

B   **D**

Spiral Review

Classify each figure. (Lesson 11-7) **30–32. See margin.**

30.   **31.**   **32.**

MEASUREMENT Find the area of each figure. Round to the nearest tenth if necessary. (Lesson 11-6)

33. 10 ft **96 ft²** 8 ft ←14 ft→

34. 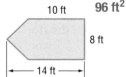 7 m **30.2 m²** 5 m 3 m 3.8 m

35. 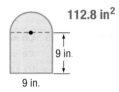 **112.8 in²** 9 in. 9 in.

36. **STATISTICS** Jordan buys a soccer ball for $15, a baseball for $8, a basketball for $18, and a football for $19. Find the mean amount spent. (Lesson 8-2) **$15**

37. **SAVINGS** Ernesto deposited $75 into a savings account earning 4.25% annual interest. What is his balance 9 months later if he makes no withdrawals or no more deposits? Round to the nearest cent. (Lesson 7-8) **$77.39**

GET READY for the Next Lesson

PREREQUISITE SKILL Multiply. (Lesson 5-5)

38. $7\frac{1}{2} \cdot 6$ **45**   **39.** $8 \cdot 2\frac{3}{4}$ **22**   **40.** $\frac{5}{6} \cdot 1\frac{4}{5}$ **$1\frac{1}{2}$**   **41.** $10\frac{1}{5} \cdot 6\frac{2}{3}$ **68**

11-9 Volume of Prisms

Standard 6MG1.3: **Know and use the formulas for the volume of triangular prisms** and cylinders **(area of base × height); compare these formulas and explain the similarity between them and the formulas for the volume of a rectangular solid.**

PACING: **Regular:** 1 periods, **Block:** 0.5 period

Options for Differentiated Instruction

ELL = English Language Learner   **AL** = Above Grade Level   **SS** = Struggling Students   **SN** = Special Needs

Using Manipulatives **ELL** **AL** **SS** **SN**

Use before beginning Lesson 11-9.

Create a rectangular prism with 24 centimeter cubes like the one shown below. Have students determine the three dimensions: length, width and height.

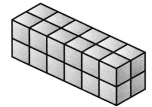

Ask:

- Is there more than one way to use all 24 cubes and make a rectangular prism? Explain.
  Sample answer: Yes; a prism 8 cubes long, 3 cubes wide, and 1 cube high could be made.
- How do the dimensions relate to the total number of cubes, 24?
  The product of the dimensions equals the total number of cubes.
- If you were to use 27 cubes, how many different rectangular prisms could be made that have unique dimensions? Describe the dimensions. three: $1 \times 1 \times 27$; $3 \times 3 \times 3$, $1 \times 3 \times 9$
- How do the dimensions relate to the total number of cubes, 27? The product of the dimensions equals the total number of cubes.

Study Tools **SS** **SN**

Use after presenting Examples.

Have students add the formulas for the volume of rectangular and triangular prisms to their flash card rings. Make sure they include an explanation of what *B* stands for.
- On the top left corner, write the page number where the formula is introduced in the textbook.
- On the top right corner, write the lesson number.
- Write the title of the formula and the formula itself. Also include a drawing if appropriate.
- On the reverse side of the index card, include an example of the formula.

Extensions and Challenges **AL**

Use after presenting Lesson 11-9.

Have students explore what happens to the volume of a rectangular prism when all the dimensions are doubled. Have them discuss how this compares to the area of a rectangle, when its dimensions are doubled. Students should explain their answers by using examples.

Leveled Lesson Resources

Chapter 11 Resource Masters

BL = Below Grade Level   **OL** = On Grade Level   **AL** = Above Grade Level   **ELL** = English Language Learner

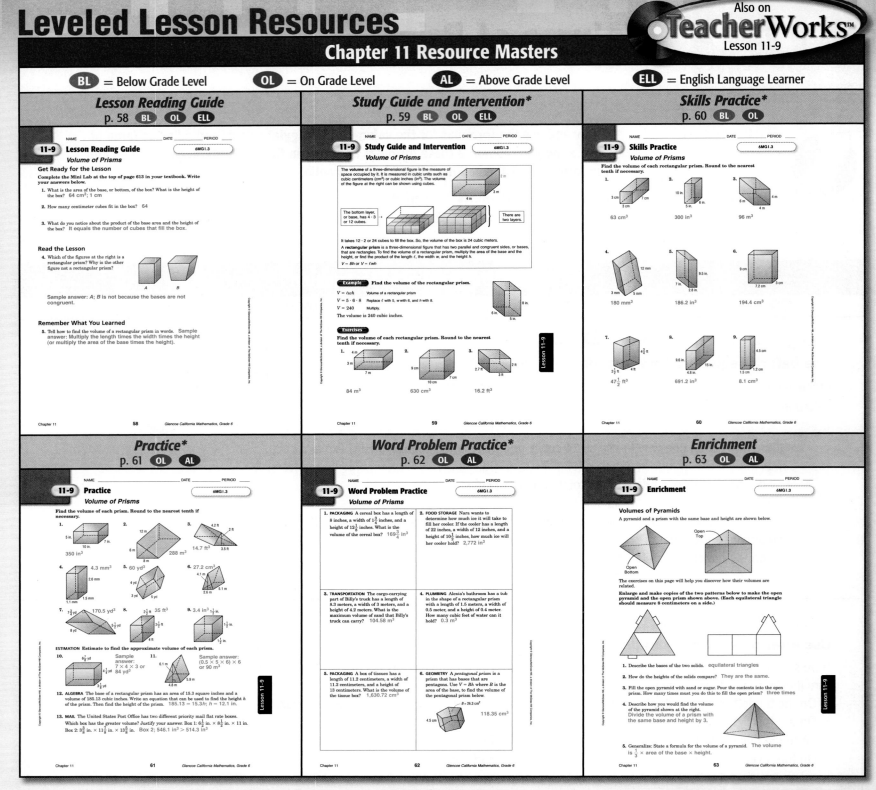

Lesson Reading Guide
p. 58 **BL** **OL** **ELL**

Study Guide and Intervention*
p. 59 **BL** **OL** **ELL**

Skills Practice*
p. 60 **BL** **OL**

Practice*
p. 61 **OL** **AL**

Word Problem Practice*
p. 62 **OL** **AL**

Enrichment
p. 63 **OL** **AL**

* Also available in Spanish **ELL**

Additional Lesson Resources

Transparencies
- 5-Minute Check Transparency, Lesson 11-9

Other Print Products
- Noteables™ Interactive Study Notebook with Foldables™

Teacher Tech Tools
- Interactive Classroom CD-ROM, Lesson 11-9
- AssignmentWorks, Lesson 11-9

Student Tech Tools
ca.gr6math.com
- Extra Examples, Chapter 11, Lesson 9
- Self-Check Quiz, Chapter 11, Lesson 9

Main IDEA

Find the volumes of rectangular and triangular prisms.

Standard 6MG1.3
Know and use the formulas for the volume of triangular prisms and cylinders **(area of base × height); compare these formulas and explain the similarity between them and the formulas for the volume of a rectangular solid.**

NEW Vocabulary

volume
rectangular prism
triangular prism

Vocabulary Link . . . .
Volume
Everyday Use bulk or mass, as in shipping a large volume of merchandise

Math Use measure of space occupied by a three-dimenional figure

▶ MINI Lab

- On a piece of grid paper, cut out a square that is 10 centimeters on each side.
- Cut a 1-centimeter square from each corner. Fold the paper and tape the corners together to make a box. **1. 64 cm²; 1 cm**

1. What is the area of the base, or bottom, of the box? What is the height of the box?
2. How many centimeter cubes fit in the box? **64**
3. What do you notice about the product of the base area and the height of the box?

3. It equals the number of cubes that fill the box.

The **volume** of a three-dimensional figure is the measure of space occupied by it. It is measured in cubic units such as cubic centimeters (cm^3) or cubic inches (in^3). The volume of the figure at the right can be shown using cubes.

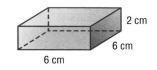

2 cm
6 cm
6 cm

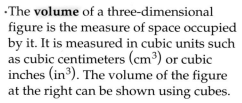

The bottom layer, or base, has 6 · 6 or 36 cubes.

There are two layers.

It takes 36 · 2 or 72 cubes to fill the box. So, the volume of the box is 72 cubic centimeters.

The figure above is a rectangular prism. A **rectangular prism** is a prism that has rectangular bases.

KEY **CONCEPT**   Volume of a Rectangular Prism

Words	The volume V a rectangular prism is the area of the base B times the height h. It is also the product of the length ℓ, the width w, and the height h.	**Model** 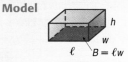 h w ℓ $B = \ell w$
Symbols	$V = Bh$ or $V = \ell wh$	

You can use the formula $V = Bh$ or $V = \ell wh$ to find the volume of a rectangular prism.

1 Focus

Standards Alignment

Before Lesson 11-9
Understand the concept of volume and use the appropriate units in common measuring systems to compute the volume of rectangular solids from Standard 5MG1.3

Lesson 11-9
Know and use the formula for the volume of triangular prisms and cylinders; compare these formulas and explain the similarity between them and the formulas for the volume of a rectangular solid from Standard 6MG1.3

After Lesson 11-9
Use formulas routinely for finding the perimeter and area of basic two-dimensional figures and the surface area and volume of basic three-dimensional figures from Standard 7MG2.1

2 Teach

▶ MINI Lab

Many students will use multiplication to find how many centimeter cubes fit in their boxes. You might want to ask students how many cubes would fit in a box that was 2 centimeters tall. 128

Scaffolding Questions

As students answer the questions, write each formula on the board.

Ask:
- What is the formula for area of a square? $A = s^2$

- What is the formula for area of a rectangle? $A = \ell w$

- How are the formulas for the area of a square and the area of a rectangle the same? Sample answer: The formulas are the same, except the length and the width of a square are equal.

- What is the formula for area of a triangle? $A = \frac{1}{2} bh$

Focus on Mathematical Content

Three-dimensional figures have **volume**, which is measured in cubic units.

To find the volume of a prism, first find the **area of a base**. Then multiply it by the **distance between the two bases**.

Formative Assessment

Use the Check Your Progress exercises after each Example to determine students' understanding of concepts.

ADDITIONAL EXAMPLES

1 Find the volume of the rectangular prism. 24 cm³

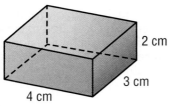

2 cm
3 cm
4 cm

2 GAMES The manufacturer of the game Bugs of Planet Zykon uses the box shown below. If the manufacturer increases the length of the box to 10 inches, how much will the box's volume increase? 36 in.³

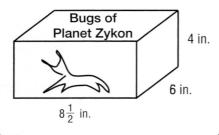

Bugs of Planet Zykon
4 in.
6 in.
$8\frac{1}{2}$ in.

Additional Examples are also in:

- Noteables™ Interactive Study Notebook with Foldables™
- Interactive Classroom PowerPoint® Presentations

EXAMPLE Volume of a Rectangular Prism

1 Find the volume of the rectangular prism.

$V = \ell w h$ Volume of a prism
$V = 5 \cdot 4 \cdot 3$ $\ell = 5, w = 4,$ and $h = 3$
$V = 60$ Multiply.

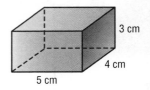

3 cm
4 cm
5 cm

The volume is 60 cubic centimeters or 60 cm³.

CHECK Your Progress

a. Find the volume of the rectangular prism at the right. **142.5 m³**

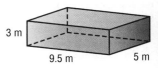

3 m
9.5 m
5 m

Real-World Career . . . .
Market researchers use tools such as statistics, surveys, focus groups, and product tests to determine what drives people to buy a product.

Math **Online**
For more information, go to ca.gr6math.com.

b. Box B; Sample answer: Box A holds 61.25 in³ of popcorn while Box B holds 72 in³ of popcorn.

READING in the Content Area

For strategies in reading this lesson, visit ca.gr6math.com.

Real-World EXAMPLE

2 MARKETING A company needs to decide which size box to use to package its new cereal. Which box shown will hold more cereal?

Box A
2.5 in.
12 in.
7.5 in.

Box B
2.5 in.
11.5 in.
8 in.

Find the volume of each box. Then compare.

Box A
$V = \ell w h$ Volume of a rectangular prism
$V = 7.5 \cdot 2.5 \cdot 12$ $\ell = 7.5, w = 2.5,$ and $h = 12$
$V = 225$ in³   Multiply.

Box B
$V = \ell w h$ Volume of a rectangular prism
$V = 8 \cdot 2.5 \cdot 11.5$ $\ell = 8, w = 2.5,$ and $h = 11.5$
$V = 230$ in³   Multiply.

Since 230 in³ > 225 in³, Box B will hold more cereal.

CHECK Your Progress

b. **PACKAGING** A movie theater serves popcorn in two different container sizes. Which container holds more popcorn? Justify your answer.

Box A
5 in.
3.5 in.
3.5 in.

Box B
4 in.
4.5 in.
4 in.

614 Chapter 11 Measurement: Two- and Three-Dimensional Figures

---

Appropriate Units

Tips for New Teachers

Remind students that when finding the perimeter or circumference of a two-dimensional figure, they should use linear units, such as centimeters (cm) or feet (ft). When finding the area of a two-dimensional figure, they should use square units, such as square centimeters (cm²) or square feet (ft²). This is because area requires the multiplication of one dimension by another, resulting in the multiplication of two uinits (unit × unit = unit²). When finding the volume of a three-dimensional figure, they should use cubic units, such as cubic centimeters (cm³) or cubic feet (ft³). This is because volume requires the multiplication of three dimensions successively (unit × unit × unit = unit³).

A **triangular prism** is a prism that has triangular bases. The diagram below shows that the volume of a triangular prism is also the product of the area of the base B and the height of the prism h.

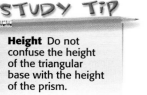
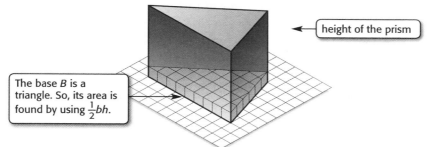

height of the prism

The base B is a triangle. So, its area is found by using $\frac{1}{2}bh$.

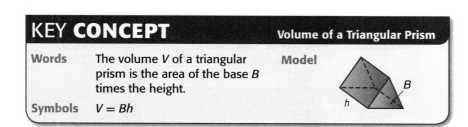
KEY **CONCEPT** — Volume of a Triangular Prism

Words The volume V of a triangular prism is the area of the base B times the height.

Symbols $V = Bh$

Model

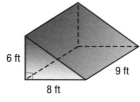

B

h

EXAMPLE Volume of a Triangular Prism

③ Find the volume of the triangular prism shown.

The area of the triangle is $\frac{1}{2} \cdot 6 \cdot 8$ so replace B with $\frac{1}{2} \cdot 6 \cdot 8$.

$V = Bh$ Volume of a prism

$V = \left(\frac{1}{2} \cdot 6 \cdot 8\right)h$ Replace B with $\frac{1}{2} \cdot 6 \cdot 8$.

$V = \left(\frac{1}{2} \cdot 6 \cdot 8\right)9$ The height of the prism is 9.

$V = 216$ Multiply.

6 ft

9 ft

8 ft

The volume is 216 cubic feet or 216 ft³.

CHECK Your Progress

Find the volume of each triangular prism.

c. 7 in.   70 in³   **d.**   46.8 mm³

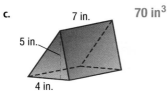

5 in.

4 in.

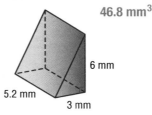

6 mm

5.2 mm

3 mm

Online Personal Tutor at ca.gr6math.com

Differentiated Instruction

Verbal/Linguistic Learners After presenting Examples 1–3, have students create a portfolio that connects the models for the volume of rectangular and triangular prisms to the formulas for the volume of these figures. Their portfolio should include drawings of the three-dimensional figures (at least two rectangular prisms and two triangular prisms of different dimensions), drawings of their nets, and a verbal explanation of how the drawings connect to the formula. Drawings and the verbal explanation should include units. Students should calculate the volume of each of their figures. See students' work.

3 Practice

Formative Assessment

Use Exercises 1–5 to check for understanding.

Then use the chart at the bottom of this page to customize your assignments for students.

Intervention You may wish to use the Study Guide and Intervention Master on page 59 of the *Chapter 11 Resource Masters* for additional reinforcement.

Odd/Even Assignments

Exercises 6–15 are structured so that students practice the same concepts whether they are assigned odd or even problems.

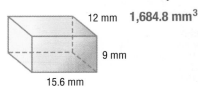

CHECK Your Understanding

Find the volume of each prism. Round to the nearest tenth if necessary.

Example 1 (p. 614)

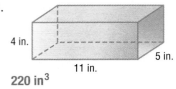 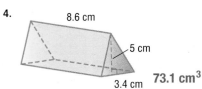

1. **220 in³**

2. **1,684.8 mm³**

Example 3 (p. 615)

3.

5. 37.5 ft³ < 63 ft³; second cabinet

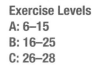

63 yd³

4. **73.1 cm³**

Example 2 (p. 614)

5. **STORAGE** One cabinet measures 3 feet by 2.5 feet by 5 feet. A second ★ measures 4 feet by 3.5 feet by 4.5 feet. Which cabinet has the greater volume?

Exercises

Find the volume of each prism. Round to the nearest tenth if necessary.

HOMEWORK HELP	
For Exercises	**See Examples**
6–9	1
14–15	2
10–13	3

Exercise Levels
A: 6–15
B: 16–25
C: 26–28

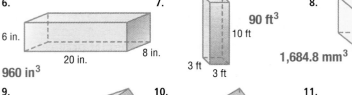

6. **960 in³**

7. **90 ft³**

8. **1,684.8 mm³**

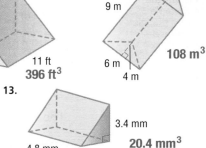

9. **236.3 cm³**

10. **396 ft³**

11. **108 m³**

12. **37.8 yd³**

13. **20.4 mm³**

14. Soapy Suds; 1,248 in³ > 468 in³

★ 14. **PACKAGING** A soap company sells laundry detergent in two different containers. Which container holds more detergent? Justify your answer.

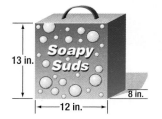

Soapy Suds
13 in.
12 in.
8 in.

CLEAN & BRIGHT
8 in.
9 in.
13 in.

DIFFERENTIATED HOMEWORK OPTIONS

Level	Assignment	Two-Day Option	
BL Basic	6–15, 27–39	7–15 odd, 29, 30	6–14 even, 27–28, 31–39
OL Core	7–19 odd, 20, 21, 23–25, 27–39	6–15, 29, 30	16–25, 27–28, 31–39
AL Advanced/Pre-AP	16–35 (optional: 36–39)		

★ 15. **TOYS** A toy company makes rectangular sandboxes that measure 6 feet by 5 feet by 1.2 feet. A customer buys a sandbox and 40 cubic feet of sand. Did the customer buy too much or too little sand? Justify your answer.

Find the volume of each prism.

16.
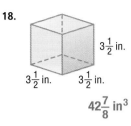

$5\frac{1}{2}$ ft

3 ft $2\frac{1}{4}$ ft

$37\frac{1}{8}$ ft³

17.
$8\frac{3}{4}$ yd

4 yd $9\frac{1}{2}$ yd

$166\frac{1}{4}$ yd³

18.
$3\frac{1}{2}$ in.

$3\frac{1}{2}$ in. $3\frac{1}{2}$ in.

$42\frac{7}{8}$ in³

ARCHITECTURE For Exercises 19 and 20, use the diagram at the right that shows the approximate dimensions of the Flatiron Building in New York City.

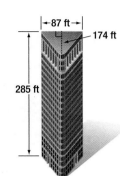

|← 87 ft →|

174 ft

285 ft

Real-World Math....
The Flatiron Building in New York City resembles a triangular prism.

Source:
greatbuildings.com

19. What is the approximate volume of the Flatiron Building? **2,157,165 ft³**

20. The building is a 22-story building. Estimate the volume of each story.
See margin.

15. 40 ft³ > 36 ft³, so too much was bought

★ 21. **ALGEBRA** The base of a rectangular prism has an area of 19.4 square meters and a volume of 306.52 cubic meters. Write an equation that can be used to find the height h of the prism. Then find the height of the prism.
306.52 = 19.4h; 15.8 m

ESTIMATION Estimate to find the approximate volume of each prism.

22. Sample answer:
$\left(\frac{1}{2} \cdot 10 \cdot 6\right) 6$ or
480 cm³

22.
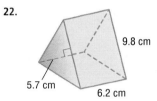

9.8 cm

5.7 cm   6.2 cm

23.
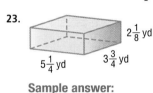

$2\frac{1}{8}$ yd

$5\frac{1}{4}$ yd $3\frac{3}{4}$ yd

Sample answer:
5 • 4 • 2 or 40 ft³

★ 24. **MONEY** The diagram shows the dimensions of an office. It costs about 11¢ per year to air condition one cubic foot of space. On average, how much does it cost to air condition the office for one month? **$88**

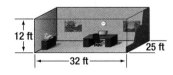

12 ft

25 ft

32 ft

25. **MEASUREMENT** The Garrett family is building a pool in the shape of a rectangular prism in their backyard. The pool will cover an area 18 feet by 25 feet and will hold 2,700 cubic feet of water. If the pool is equal depth throughout, find that depth. **6 ft**

Lesson 11-9 Volume of Prisms **617**

4 Assess

Crystal Ball Tell students that tomorrow's lesson is about finding the volume of cylinders. Have them write how they think what they learned today will connect with tomorrow's material.

FOLDABLES Study Organizer **Foldables™ Follow-Up**

Remind students to take notes about finding the volume of prisms in their Foldables. Encourage them to draw an example of a rectangular prism and a triangular prism, showing the dimensions needed to find the volume.

Additional Answers

28. Sample answer: They are similar in that the volume is the product of the area of the base and the height of the prism. They are different in the formulas used to find the area of the base of the figure.

31.

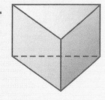

H.O.T. Problems
27. Sample answer: the volumes are the same; the volume of prism B is $8 \times 4 \times 16$ which can be written as $8 \times 4 \times (2 \times 8) = 8 \times (4 \times 2) \times 8 = 8 \times 8 \times 8$.

26. CHALLENGE How many cubic inches are in a cubic foot? **1,728 in³**

27. NUMBER SENSE Without calculating, determine whether the volumes of the two prisms are equal. If so, explain your reasoning. If not, tell which has the greater volume.

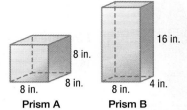

Prism A   Prism B

28. **WRITING IN MATH** Explain the similarities and differences in finding the volume of a rectangular prism and a triangular prism. **See margin.**

 **STANDARDS PRACTICE** 6MG1.3

29. A fish aquarium is shown below.

What is the volume of the aquarium? **D**

A 168 ft³   C 2,016 ft³
B 342 ft³   D 4,032 ft³

30. Use a ruler to measure the dimensions of the paper clip box in centimeters.

Which is closest to the volume of the box? **F**

F 1.5 cm³   H 4.5 cm³
G 2.5 cm³   J 5.5 cm³

Spiral Review

31. GEOMETRY The top, side, and front view of a geometric figure are shown at the right. Make a sketch of the geometric figure. (Lesson 11-8) **See margin.**

top   side   front

For each figure, identify the shape of the base(s). Then classify the figure. (Lesson 11-7)

32. circle; cylinder

33. 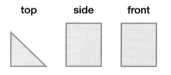 rectangle; rectangular prism

34. triangle; triangular pyramid

35. RATES A car travels 180 miles in 3.6 hours. What is the average rate of speed in miles per hour? (Lesson 6-2) **50 mph**

▶ **GET READY for the Next Lesson**

PREREQUISITE SKILL Estimate. (page 674) 36–39. Sample answers are given.

36. $3.14 \cdot 6$ $3 \cdot 6$ or 18   **37.** $5 \cdot 2.7^2$ $5 \cdot 3^2$ or 45   **38.** $9.1 \cdot 8.3$ $9 \cdot 8$ or 72   **39.** $3.1 \cdot 1.75^2 \cdot 2$ $3 \cdot 2^2 \cdot 2$ or 24

Pre-AP Activity   Use after Exercise 31

Have students use what they know about rectangular and triangular prisms to write a formula for the volume of a trapezoidal prism. Encourage them to draw a diagram illustrating the variables used in the formula.

$V = \frac{1}{2} h(b_1 + b_2) \cdot \ell$, where ℓ is the length of the prism, or distance between bases

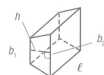

Volume of Cylinders

Standard 6MG1.3: **Know and use the formulas for the volume of** triangular prisms and **cylinders (area of base × height); compare these formulas and explain the similarity between them and the formulas for the volume of a rectangular solid.**

Standard 6AF1.4: Solve problems manually by using the correct order of operations or by using a scientific calculator.

PACING: **Regular:** 1.5 periods, **Block:** 1 period

Options for Differentiated Instruction

ELL = English Language Learner   **AL** = Above Grade Level   **SS** = Struggling Students   **SN** = Special Needs

Study Tools **SS** **SN**

Use after presenting the Examples.

Have students add the formula for the volume of a cylinder to their flash card rings. Have them include an example where the radius of the base is given and an example where the diameter of the base is given.

- On the top left corner, write the page number where the formula is introduced in the textbook.
- On the top right corner, write the lesson number.
- Write the title of the formula and the formula itself. Also include a drawing if appropriate.
- On the reverse side of the index card, include an example of how to use the formula.

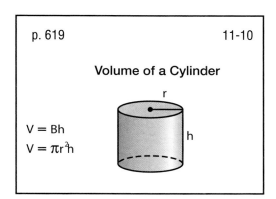

p. 619   11-10

Volume of a Cylinder

$V = Bh$
$V = \pi r^2 h$

Mathematical Displays **AL**

Use after presenting Lesson 11-10.

Have students make posters showing the similarities and differences among the following formulas:
- volume of a rectangular prism,
- volume of a triangular prism, and
- volume of a cylinder.

Have them include examples and diagrams on their posters.

Extensions and Challenges **AL**

Use after students complete Lesson 11-10.

Display the following problem. Have students solve the problem and explain the steps they used.

> A machinist makes a part by drilling a hole through a block of copper. The copper is in the shape of a rectangular prism with a square base that measures 6 centimeters on a side and a height of 11 centimeters. If the hole has a radius of 2 centimeters and a height of 11 centimeters, what is the volume of the resulting solid? about 257.8 cm³

Leveled Lesson Resources

Chapter 11 Resource Masters

BL = Below Grade Level   **OL** = On Grade Level   **AL** = Above Grade Level   **ELL** = English Language Learner

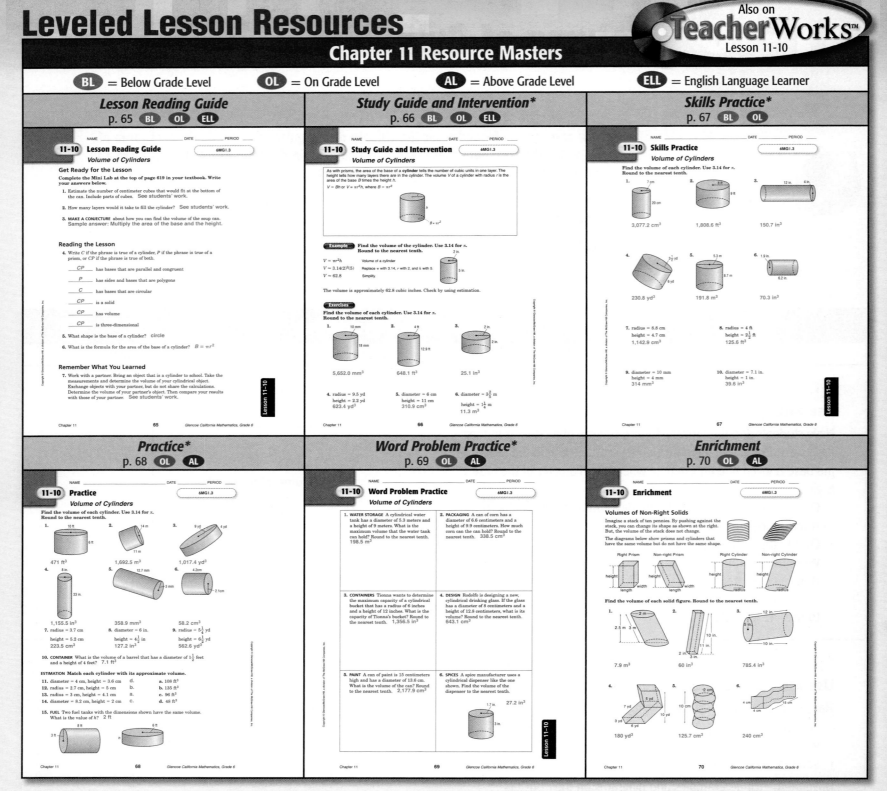

Additional Lesson Resources

* Also available in Spanish **ELL**

Transparencies
- *5-Minute Check Transparency*, Lesson 11-10

Other Print Products
- *Noteables™ Interactive Study Notebook with Foldables™*

Teacher Tech Tools
- *Interactive Classroom CD-ROM*, Lesson 11-10
- *AssignmentWorks*, Lesson 11-10

Student Tech Tools
ca.gr6math.com
- Extra Examples, Chapter 11, Lesson 10
- Self-Check Quiz, Chapter 11, Lesson 10

Main IDEA

Find the volumes of cylinders.

Standard 6MG1.3 Know and use the formulas for the volume of triangular prisms and **cylinders (area of base × height); compare these formulas and explain the similarity between them and the formulas for the volume of a rectangular solid. Standard 6AF1.4** Solve problems manually by using the correct order of operations or by using a scientific calculator.

MINI Lab

Set a soup can on a piece of grid paper and trace around the base, as shown at the right. **1–2. See students' work.**

1. Estimate the number of centimeter cubes that would fit at the bottom of the can. Include parts of cubes.

2. If each layer is 1 centimeter high, how many layers would it take to fill the cylinder.

3. **MAKE A CONJECTURE** How can you find the volume of the soup can?

3. Sample answer: Multiply the area of the base and height.

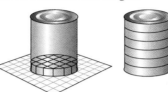

As with prisms, the area of the base of a cylinder tells the number of cubic units in one layer. The height tells how many layers there are in the cylinder.

KEY **CONCEPT**   Volume of a Cylinder

Words The volume V of a cylinder with radius r is the area of the base B times the height h.

Symbols $V = Bh$ where $B = \pi r^2$ or $V = \pi r^2 h$

Model

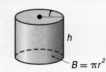

h

$B = \pi r^2$

STUDY TIP

Check for Reasonableness Use estimation to check for reasonableness.

$\pi(5)^2(8.3) \approx 3(5)^2(8)$

≈ 600

Since $600 \approx 651.9$, the answer is reasonable.

EXAMPLE   Find the Volume of a Cylinder

① Find the volume of the cylinder. **Round to the nearest tenth.**

$V = \pi r^2 h$	Volume of a cylinder
$V = \pi(5)^2(8.3)$	Replace r with 5 and h with 8.3.
$V \approx 3.14\,(5^2)(8.3)$	Use 3.14 for π.
$V \approx 651.6$	Multiply.

5 cm

8.3 cm

The volume is about 651.6 cubic centimeters.

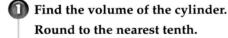 **Extra Examples at** ca.gr6math.com

Lesson 11-10 Volume of Cylinders **619**

 Standards Alignment

Before Lesson 11-10
Understand the concept of volume and use the appropriate units in common measuring systems to compute the volume of rectangular solids from ⬤━ Standard 5MG1.3

Lesson 11-10
Know and use the formulas for the volume of triangular prisms and cylinders; compare these formulas and explain the similarity between them and the formulas for the volume of a rectangular solid from Standard 6MG1.3

After Lesson 11-10
Use formulas routinely for finding the perimeter and area of basic two-dimensional figures and the surface area and volume of basic three-dimensional figures from Standard 7MG2.1

2 Teach

MINI Lab

Many students will use the formula for area of a circle to find how many centimeter cubes would fit in the bottom of their cans. They can also estimate the area of the circle by counting. Students can measure the height of their cans and use pieces of tape to mark where each layer of centimeter cubes would go.

Scaffolding Questions

Ask:

• What are some everyday objects that resemble a cylinder? Sample answers: trash can, water glass, thermos

• How could you find the area of the base of a cylinder? use the formula for the area of a circle, $A = \pi r^2$

• What are the properties of a cylinder? A cylinder has two circular bases and a curved surface.

Find the volume of each cylinder. Round to the nearest tenth.

a.
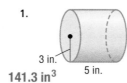
3 in.

1.8 in.

50.9 in³

b. 2.4 m
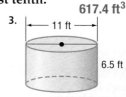

162.8 m³ 9 m

Focus on Mathematical Content

To find the volume of a cylinder, first find the **area of a base**. Then multiply by the **height**, or distance between the two bases.

A good way to check a volume calculation is by **estimating**. Round π to 3, round measurements to the nearest whole number, and then use mental math.

Formative Assessment

Use the Check Your Progress exercises after each Example to determine students' understanding of concepts.

ADDITIONAL EXAMPLES

① Find the volume of the cylinder. Round to the nearest tenth.
854.9 cm³

5.5 cm

9 cm

② **COFFEE** How much coffee can the can hold? 42.4 in³

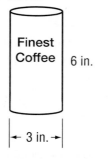
Finest Coffee 6 in.

← 3 in. →

Additional Examples are also in:

• Noteables™ Interactive Study Notebook with Foldables™

• Interactive Classroom PowerPoint® Presentations

STUDY TIP

Circles Recall that the radius is half the diameter.

Real-World EXAMPLE

② **WEATHER** The decorative rain gauge shown has a height of 13 centimeters and a diameter of 3 centimeters. How much water can the rain gauge hold?

$V = \pi r^2 h$ Volume of a cylinder

$V = \pi(1.5)^2 13$ Replace r with 1.5 and h with 13.

$V \approx 91.8$ Simplify.

The rain gauge can hold about 91.8 cubic centimeters.

3 cm

13 cm

CHECK Your Progress

c. **PAINT** Find the volume of a cylinder-shaped paint can that has a diameter of 4 inches and a height of 5 inches. **62.8 in³**

Online Personal Tutor at ca.gr6math.com

★ indicates multi-step problem

CHECK Your Understanding

Find the volume of each cylinder. Round to the nearest tenth.

Example 1 (p. 619)

1.
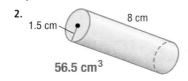
3 in.

5 in.

141.3 in³

2. 1.5 cm
8 cm

56.5 cm³

3. ← 11 ft →
617.4 ft³
6.5 ft

Example 2 (p. 620)

4. **HOCKEY** An official hockey puck has a diameter of 3 inches and a height of 1 inch. What is the volume of the hockey puck? **about 7.1 in³**

5. **CANDLES** A scented candle is in the shape of a cylinder. The radius is 4 centimeters and the height is 12 centimeters. Find the volume of the candle. **about 602.9 cm³**

620 Chapter 11 Measurement: Two- and Three-Dimensional Figures

Differentiated Instruction

Verbal/Linguistic Learners After presenting Examples 1 and 2, have students create a portfolio (or add to their portfolio if they created one in Lesson 11-9 on page 615) that connects the model for the volume of a cylinder to the formula for the volume of a cylinder. Their portfolio should include drawings of at least three cylinders of different dimensions, drawings of their nets, and a verbal explanation of how the drawings connect to the formula. Drawings and the verbal explanation should include units. Students should calculate the volume of each of their figures. See students' work.

Exercises

HOMEWORK HELP

For Exercises	See Examples
6–15	1
16, 17	2

Exercise Levels
A: 6–17
B: 18–29
C: 30–34

Find the volume of each cylinder. Round to the nearest tenth.

6. **401.9 in³**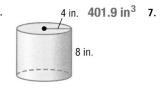
4 in.
8 in.

7. **4,069.4 ft³**
9 ft
16 ft

8. **2,260.8 mm³**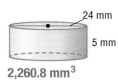
24 mm
5 mm

9. **2,769.5 yd³**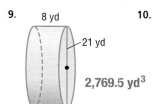
8 yd
21 yd

10. **167.0 cm³**
13.3 cm
2 cm

11. **35.6 m³**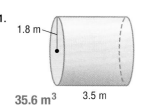
1.8 m
3.5 m

12. diameter = 15 mm **847.8 mm³**
    height = 4.8 mm

13. diameter = 4.5 m **103.3 m³**
    height = 6.5 m

14. radius = 6 ft **602.9 ft³**
    height = $5\frac{1}{3}$ ft

15. radius = $3\frac{1}{2}$ in. **288.5 in³**
    height = $7\frac{1}{2}$ in.

16. **FOOD** What is the volume of a can of potato chips that has a radius of $1\frac{1}{2}$ inches and a height of 8 inches? **about 56.5 in³**

17. **SCIENCE** The Hubble Space Telescope is cylinder-shaped. Use the information at the left to find its volume to the nearest tenth. **163.3 m³**

Find the volume of each cylinder. Round to the nearest tenth.

18.
26 ft
40 ft

19.
75 m
46 m

20.
86 in.
32 in.

18. 84,905.6 ft³
19. 124,579.5 m³
20. 276,521.0 in³

ESTIMATION Match each cylinder with its approximate volume.

21. radius = 4.1 ft, height = 5 ft **d.**   a. 91 ft³

22. diameter = 8 ft; height = 2.2 ft **c.**   b. 48 ft³

23. diameter = 6.2 ft, height = 3 ft **a.**   c. 111 ft³

24. radius = 2 ft, height = 3.8 ft **b.**   d. 264 ft³

25. **PACKAGING** A cylinder-shaped popcorn tin has a height of 1.5 feet and a diameter of 10 inches. Find the volume to the nearest cubic inch. Use 3.14 for π. **1,413 in³**

Lesson 11-10 Volume of Cylinders **621**

③ Practice

Formative Assessment

Use Exercises 1–5 to check for understanding.

Then use the chart at the bottom of this page to customize your assignments for students.

Intervention You may wish to use the Study Guide and Intervention Master on page 66 of the *Chapter 11 Resource Masters* for additional reinforcement.

Odd/Even Assignments

Exercises 6–17 are structured so that students practice the same concepts whether they are assigned odd or even problems.

DIFFERENTIATED HOMEWORK OPTIONS			
Level	**Assignment**	**Two-Day Option**	
BL Basic	6–17, 31–44	7–17 odd, 35, 36	6–16 even, 31–34, 37–44
OL Core	7–25 odd, 26–29, 31–44	6–17, 35, 36	18–29, 31–34, 37–44
AL Advanced/Pre-AP	18–44		

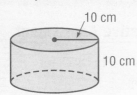
26. Rectangular pan, because its volume is 234 in³; the total volume of the two round pans is approximately 201 in³.

★ **26. BAKING** Which will hold more cake batter, the rectangular pan, or the two round pans? Explain.

2 in.

13 in.

9 in.

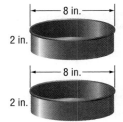

8 in.

2 in.

8 in.

2 in.

★ **27. PACKAGING** The two cans at the right have the same volume. What is the value of *h*? **9 cm**

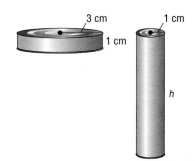

3 cm

1 cm

1 cm

h

MEASUREMENT For Exercises 28 and 29, use the following information.

Firewood is usually sold by a unit of measure called a *cord*. A cord is a stack of wood that is 8 feet long, 4 feet wide, and 4 feet high.

EXTRA PRACTICE

See pages 712, 725.

Math Online

Self-Check Quiz at
ca.gr6math.com

28. What is the volume of a cord of wood? **128 ft³**

29. Suppose a tree has a diameter of 2 feet. Find the height of the tree trunk
★ that would produce about 1 cord of firewood. **about 40.7 ft**

H.O.T. Problems

30. Sample answer: The shorter cylinder, because the radius is larger and that is the squared value in the formula.

30. CHALLENGE Two equal-size sheets of paper are rolled along the length and along the width, as shown. Which cylinder do you think has the greater volume? Explain.

31. OPEN ENDED Draw and label a cylinder that has a larger radius, but less volume than the cylinder shown at the right. **See margin.**

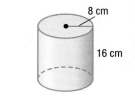

8 cm

16 cm

32. NUMBER SENSE What is the ratio of the volume of a cylinder to the volume of a cylinder having twice the height but the same radius? **1 to 2**

33. NUMBER SENSE Suppose cylinder A has the same height but twice the radius of cylinder B. What is the ratio of the volume of cylinder B to cylinder A? **1 to 4**

34. Sample answer: In both, the volume equals the area of the base times the height.

34. WRITING IN MATH Explain how the formula for the volume of a cylinder is similar to the formula for the volume of a rectangular prism.

Differentiated Instruction

Interpersonal Learners Separate students into pairs. Tell them that a machinist drilled a hole through a block of copper. The block was a rectangular prism measuring 6 cm × 6 cm × 11 cm. The drill bit had a diameter of 4 cm, and the machinist drilled from top to bottom (11 cm). Have students find the volume of the copper solid after the hole was drilled. Encourage them to draw a diagram of the problem.
257.8 cm³

Then have each pair create its own real-life problem involving volume. Finally, have the pairs exchange problems and solve one another's problems.

35. The oatmeal container shown has a diameter of $3\frac{1}{2}$ inches and a height of 9 inches. **D**

Which is closest to the number of cubic inches it will hold when filled?

A 32

B 42.78

C 75.92

D 86.55

36. Which statement is true about the volumes of the cylinders shown? **G**

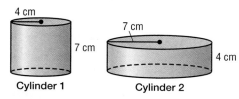

Cylinder 1   Cylinder 2

F The volume of cylinder 1 is greater than the volume of cylinder 2.

G The volume of cylinder 2 is greater than the volume of cylinder 1.

H The volumes are equal.

J The volume of cylinder 1 is twice the volume of cylinder 2.

Spiral Review

37. MEASUREMENT Find the volume of a rectangular prism with a length of 6 meters, a width of 4.9 meters, and a height of 5.2 meters. (Lesson 11-9)

$$152.9 \text{ m}^3$$

Make a sketch of each geometric figure using the top, side, and front views shown. (Lesson 11-8) **38–39. See margin.**

38.

top   side   front

39.

top   side   front

PROBABILITY A coin is tossed and a number cube is rolled. Find the probability of each of the following. (Lesson 9-8)

40. P(heads and 4) $\frac{1}{12}$

41. P(tails and an odd number) $\frac{1}{4}$

42. P(heads and *not* 5) $\frac{5}{12}$

43. P(*not* tails and not 2) $\frac{5}{12}$

44. TEST SCORES The list gives the scores on a recent history test. Find each measure of central tendency and range. Round to the nearest tenth if necessary. Then state which measure best represents the data. Explain your reasoning. (Lesson 8-2)

History Test Scores									
78,	92,	83,	88,	89,	91,	96,	72,	74,	99
81,	88,	86,	95,	73,	97,	78,	78,	60	
84,	85,	90,	92,	98,	74,	76,	80,	83	

mean: 84.3; median: 84.5; mode: 78; range: 39; The mean or median best represents the data. Less than half of the numbers are below the mode and more than half are above the mode.

Lesson 11-10 Volume of Cylinders **623**

---

4 Assess

Ticket Out the Door Tell students that a cylinder has a radius of *x* and height of 3*x*. Have them write an algebraic expression for the cylinder's volume.

Formative Assessment

Check for student understanding of concepts in Lessons 11-9 and 11-10.

CRM Quiz 4, p. 74

FOLDABLES **Foldables™**
Study Organizer **Follow-Up**

Remind students to take notes about finding the volume of cylinders in their Foldables. Encourage them to draw an example of a cylinder, showing the needed dimensions.

Additional Answers

38. Sample answer:

39. Sample answer:

Graphing Calculator Lab
Graphing Geometric Relationships

① Focus

Materials

- TI-83/84 Plus graphing calculators
- centimeter grid paper

Easy-to-Make Manipulatives

Teaching Mathematics with Manipulatives,
Templates for:

- centimeter grid, p. 15

Teaching Tip

If there aren't enough graphing calculators for every student in your class, have students work in pairs or groups of three, sharing the calculators.

② Teach

Working in Cooperative Groups

You may wish for students to work in pairs. The two students can work together to draw the five parallelograms and to complete the chart, and then take turns entering the data into the calculator.

Activity 1 You may need to remind students that the height of a parallelogram is the distance between the base and the opposite side. Encourage students to make the lengths of the bases of their parallelograms whole numbers.

Additional Answer

2.

The graph of the data forms a straight line that increases from left to right.

Main IDEA

Use technology to graph data in order to demonstrate geometric relationships.

 Standard 6AF3.2 Express in symbolic form simple relationships arising from geometry. **Standard 6MR1.2** Formulate and justify **mathematical conjectures based on a general description of the mathematical question or problem posed.**

In this lab, you will use a TI-83/84 Plus graphing calculator to analyze geometric relationships among the base, height, and area of several parallelograms.

ACTIVITY

① **STEP 1** Draw five parallelograms that each have a height of 4 centimeters on centimeter grid paper.

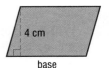

STEP 2 Copy and complete the table shown for each parallelogram.

Base (cm)	Height (cm)	Area (cm²)
	4	
	4	
	4	
	4	
	4	

STEP 3 Next enter the data into your graphing calculator. Press [STAT] 1 and enter the length of each base in L1. Then enter the area of each parallelogram in L2.

STEP 4 Turn on the statistical plot by pressing [2nd] [STAT PLOT] [ENTER] [ENTER]. Select the scatter plot and enter or confirm L1 as the Xlist and L2 as the Ylist.

STEP 5 Graph the data by pressing [ZOOM] 9. Use the Trace feature and the left and right arrow keys to move from one point to another.

1. For each ordered pair, *x* represents the length of the parallelogram's base and *y* represents the area of the parallelogram.

3. $y = 4x$; The area of each parallelogram is 4 times the length of its base.

4. As the length of the base of the parallelogram increases, the area increases at a constant rate. In the table, for every 1 cm increase in the length of the base, the area increases by 4 cm². The graph of the relationship forms a straight line.

ANALYZE THE RESULTS

1. What does an ordered pair on your graph represent?

2. Sketch and describe the shape of the graph. **See margin.**

3. **MAKE A CONJECTURE** Write an equation for your graph. Check your equation by pressing [Y=], entering your equation into Y1, and then pressing [GRAPH]. What does this equation mean?

4. As the length of the base of the parallelogram increases, what happens to its area? Does this happen at a constant rate? How can you tell this from the table? from the graph?

Math **Online** Other Calculator Keystrokes at ca.gr6math.com

5. For each ordered pair, *x* represents the length of the rectangle and *y* represents the width of each rectangle.

6.

The graph of the data forms a curve that decreases from left to right.

7. $y = \frac{36}{x}$; The width of each rectangle is the quotient of the area, 36 square centimeters, and its length.

8. As the length of the rectangle increases, the width decreases. In the table, for every 1 cm increase in the length of the base, the width does not decrease at a constant rate. The graph of the relationship forms a curve.

11. $y = x^3$; The volume of the cube is the cube of the edge length.

12. As the length of the cube's edge increases, the volume of the cube increases.

ACTIVITY

2 **STEP 1** Draw five rectangles that each have an area of 36 square centimeters on centimeter grid paper. The length should be greater than or equal to its width.

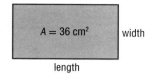

$A = 36 \text{ cm}^2$ width

length

STEP 2 Copy and complete the table shown for each rectangle.

Length (cm)	Width (cm)	Area (cm²)
		36
		36
		36
		36
		36

STEP 3 Clear list L1 and L2 by pressing [STAT] 4 [2nd] [L1] , [2nd] [L2] [ENTER]. Then press [STAT] 1 and enter the length of each rectangle in L1 and the width of each rectangle in L2.

STEP 4 Follow Steps 4 and 5 of Activity 1 to graph the data.

ANALYZE THE RESULTS

5. What does an ordered pair on your graph represent?

6. Sketch and describe the shape of the graph.

7. **MAKE A CONJECTURE** Write an equation for your graph. Use the calculator to graph and check your equation. What does this equation mean?

8. As the length of the rectangle increases, what happens to its width? Does this happen at a constant rate? How can you tell this from the table? from the graph?

9. **MAKE A PREDICTION** Draw five cubes with different edge lengths. Predict the shape of the graph of the relationship between the edge length and volume of the cube. **See students' work.**

10. Create a table to record the edge length and volume of each cube. Then graph the data to show the relationship between the edge length and volume of the cube. Sketch and describe the shape of the graph. **See margin.**

11. **MAKE A CONJECTURE** Write an equation for your graph. Use the calculator to graph and check your equation. What does this equation mean?

12. As the length of the cube's edge increases, what happens to the volume?

Extend 11-10 Graphing Calculator Lab: Graphing Geometric Relationships **625**

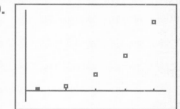

Download Vocabulary
Review from ca.gr6math.com

FOLDABLES™
Study Organizer

Dinah Zike's Foldables

Have students look through the chapter to make sure they have included notes and examples about the key concepts of each lesson in their Foldables.

Encourage students to refer to their Foldables while completing the Study Guide and Review and while preparing for the Chapter Test.

 Formative Assessment

Key Vocabulary The page references after each word denote where that term was first introduced. If students have difficulty answering Exercises 1–7, remind them that they can use these page references to refresh their memories about the vocabulary terms.

Math Online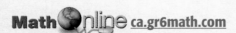

Vocabulary PuzzleMaker improves students' mathematics vocabulary using four puzzle formats—crossword, scramble, word search using a word list, and word search using clues. Students can work online or from a printed worksheet.

FOLDABLES™
Study Organizer   **GET READY to Study**

Be sure the following Key Concepts are noted in your Foldable.

Key Concepts

Area (Lessons 11-1, 11-2, and 11-6)

parallelogram   triangle   trapezoid

$A = bh$ $A = \frac{1}{2}bh$ $A = \frac{1}{2}h(b_1 + b_2)$

Circles (Lessons 11-3 and 11-4)
- circumference
  $C = \pi d$ or $C = 2\pi r$
- area
  $A = \pi r^2$

Volume (Lessons 11-9 and 11-10)

rectangular   triangular   cylinder
prism   prism

$V = Bh$ $V = Bh$ or $\pi r^2 h$

---

626 Chapter 11 Two- and Three-Dimensional Figures

Math Online Vocabulary Review at ca.gr6math.com

Key Vocabulary

base (p. 572)	π (pi) (p. 584)
center (p. 584)	prism (p. 603)
circle (p. 584)	pyramid (p. 603)
circumference (p. 584)	radius (p. 584)
complex figure (p. 596)	rectangular prism (p. 613)
cone (p. 604)	semicircle (p. 596)
cylinder (p. 604)	sphere (p. 604)
diameter (p. 584)	three-dimensional figure (p. 603)
edge (p. 603)	
face (p. 603)	triangular prism (p. 615)
height (p. 572)	vertex (p. 603)
lateral face (p. 603)	volume (p. 613)

Vocabulary Check

Choose the correct term or number to complete each sentence.

1. A (rectangular prism, rectangle) is a three-dimensional figure that has three sets of parallel congruent sides. **rectangular prism**

2. The (volume, surface area) of a three-dimensional figure is the measure of the space occupied by it. **volume**

3. $A = \frac{1}{2}h(b_1 + b_2)$ is the formula for the area of a (triangle, trapezoid). **trapezoid**

4. Volume is measured in (square, cubic) units. **cubic**

5. A (cylinder, prism) is a three-dimensional figure that has two congruent, parallel circles as its bases. **cylinder**

6. The volume of a rectangular prism is found by (adding, multiplying) the length, the width, and the height. **multiplying**

7. The formula for the area of a (square, circle) is $A = \pi r^2$. **circle**

 Summative Assessment

 Vocabulary Test, p. 76

Lesson-by-Lesson Review

11-1 Area of Parallelograms (pp. 572–576)

Find the area of each parallelogram.
Round to the nearest tenth if necessary.

8.
10 cm
9.9 cm
99 cm²

9.
60 in.
42 in.
2,520 in²

10. ALGEBRA A parallelogram has an area of 57 square inches. Find the base of the parallelogram if the height is 6 inches. $9\frac{1}{2}$ in.

Example 1 Find the area of a parallelogram if the base is 15 inches and the height is 8 inches.

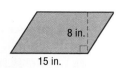
8 in.
15 in.

$A = bh$ Area of a parallelogram
$A = 15 \cdot 8$ Replace b with 15 and h with 8.
$A = 120\ \text{in}^2$.   Multiply.

Lesson-by-Lesson Review

Intervention If the given examples are not sufficient to review the topics covered by the questions, remind students that the page references tell them where to review that topic in their textbooks.

Two-Day Option Have students complete the Lesson-by-Lesson Review on pages 627–630. Then you can use ExamView® Assessment Suite to customize another review worksheet that practices all the objectives of this chapter or only the objectives on which your students need more help.

For more information on ExamView® Assessment Suite, see page 570C.

Differentiated Instruction

Super DVD: MindJogger Plus
Use this DVD as an alternative format of review for the test. For more information on this game show format, see page 570D.

11-2 Area of Triangles and Trapezoids (pp. 578–582)

Find the area of each figure. Round to the nearest tenth if necessary.

11.
12 ft
6 ft
36 ft²

12.
5 in.
5 in.
10 in.
37.5 in²

13. trapezoid: bases 22 yd and 35 yd height 18.5 yd **527.3 yd²**

14. ALGEBRA The area of a triangle is 26.9 square inches. If the base is 9.6 inches, what is the height of the triangle? **about 5.6 in.**

Example 2 Find the area of a triangle with a base of 8 meters and a height of 11.2 meters.

$A = \frac{1}{2}bh$ Area of a triangle
$A = \frac{1}{2}(8)(11.2)$ or $44.8\ \text{m}^2$ $b = 8, h = 11.2$

Example 3 Find the area of the trapezoid.

10 in.
3 in.
2 in.

$A = \frac{1}{2}h(b_1 + b_2)$
$A = \frac{1}{2}(3)(2 + 10)$ $h = 3, b_1 = 2, b_2 = 10$
$A = \frac{1}{2}(3)(12)$ or $18\ \text{in}^2$ Simplify.

11-3 Circles and Circumference (pp. 584–588)

Find the circumference of each circle. Use 3.14 or $\frac{22}{7}$ for π. Round to the nearest tenth if necessary.   **15. 75.4 in.**
    87.9 m
15. radius = 12 in.   **16.** diameter = 28 m

17. diameter = $8\frac{2}{5}$ ft   **18.** radius = 4.4 cm
    27.6 cm

19. LIFE SCIENCE A circular nest built by bald eagles has a diameter of $9\frac{1}{2}$ feet. Find the nest's circumference. $29\frac{6}{7}$ ft

17. $26\frac{2}{5}$ ft

Example 4 Find the circumference of a circle with a diameter of 12.2 meters.

12.2 m

$C = \pi d$ Circumference of a circle
$C \approx 3.14(12.2)$ $\pi \approx 3.14$ and $d = 12.2$
$C \approx 38.3$ Multiply.
The circumference is about 38.3 meters.

11-4 Area of Circles (pp. 589–593)

Find the area of each circle. Round to the nearest tenth.

20. radius = 11.4 in. **408.1 in²**

21. diameter = 44 cm **1,519.8 cm²**

22. **GARDENING** A lawn sprinkler can water a circular area with a radius of 20 feet. Find the area that can be watered. Round to the nearest tenth.

22. **1,256 ft²**

Example 5 Find the area of a circle with a radius of 5 inches.

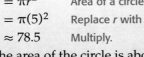

$A = \pi r^2$ Area of a circle

$A = \pi(5)^2$ Replace r with 5.

$A \approx 78.5$ Multiply.

The area of the circle is about 78.5 square inches.

11-5 PSI: Solve a Simpler Problem (pp. 594–595)

23. **BAKING** The local baker can make 10 cakes in 2 days. How many cakes can 8 bakers make working at the same rate in 20 days? **800 cakes**

24. **TRAVEL** Mrs. Whitmore left Chicago at 6:45 A.M. and arrived in St. Louis at 11:15 A.M., driving a distance of approximately 292 miles. Find her approximate average speed. **65 mph**

25. **$105**
25. **SHOPPING** Mercedes spent $175.89 over the weekend. Of the money she spent, 40% was spent on shoes. About how much money was *not* spent on shoes?

Example 6 A total of 950 residents voted on whether to build a neighborhood playground. Of those that voted, 70% voted for the playground. How many residents voted for the playground?

Find 10% of 950 and then use the result to find 70% of 950.

10% of 950 = 95

Since there are seven 10%s in 70%, multiply 95 by 7.

So, 95 × 7 or 665 residents voted for the playground.

11-6 Area of Complex Figures (pp. 596–599)

Find the area of each figure. Round to the nearest tenth if necessary.

26.

15 ft ← 11 ft → **341.6 ft²**

27. **67.8 yd²**

9 yd

4 yd

28. **PATIOS** The McAllister family is installing a brick patio like the one shown. What is the total area of the patio? **about 182.7 in²**

8 in.

8 in.

Example 7 Find the area of the figure. Round to the nearest tenth.

10 cm

7 cm

10 cm

5 cm

16 cm

The figure can be separated into a parallelogram and a trapezoid.

parallelogram: $A = 10 \cdot 7$ or 70

trapezoid: $A = \frac{1}{2}(10)(16 + 5)$ or 105

The area is 70 + 105 or 175 cm².

Mixed Problem Solving
For mixed problem-solving practice,
see page 725.

CHAPTER
11
Study Guide
and Review

29. triangle; triangular prism
30. hexagon; hexagonal pyramid

11-7 **Three-Dimensional Figures** (pp. 603–606)

For each figure, identify the shape of the base(s). Then classify the figure.

29.   30.

31. **VEGETABLES** Classify the shape of a can of green beans. **cylinder**

DOGHOUSES For Exercises 32 and 33, use the figure of the doghouse shown.

32. What geometric figure is represented by the main part of the doghouse?

33. Identify the top figure of the doghouse.

32. rectangular prism   33. rectangular pyramid

Example 8 For the figure, identify the shape of the base(s). Then classify the figure.

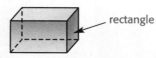 rectangle

Since the figure has 6 rectangular faces, parallel bases, and a rectangular base, the figure is a rectangular prism.

Example 9 Classify the shape of a basketball.

The figure has no faces, bases, edges, or vertices. The figure is a sphere.

11-8 **Drawing Three-Dimensional Figures** (pp. 608–612)

Draw a top, a side, and a front view of each solid. 34–37. See margin.

34.   35.

36. Draw a solid using the top, side, and front views shown. Use isometric dot paper.

        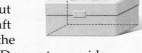

top   side   front

37. **CRAFTS** Alejandra put all of her craft supplies in the box shown. Draw a top, a side, and a front view of the box.

Example 10 Draw the solid by using the top, side, and front views shown.

top   side   front

The side view is a square. The top and front views are rectangles.

The figure drawn is a rectangular prism.

Tips for New Teachers

Properties of Figures

As students complete Exercises 34–35, have them also identify the shape of the base and classify the figures using their properties. Ask the students to compare the solids in Exercises 34–35 based on the similarities and differences of their properties. Sample answer: The figure in Exercise 34 is a pyramid since there are at least three lateral faces that are triangles and it has only one base. The figure in Exercise 35 is a cone since it has only one base, the base is a circle, and has one vertex.

Additional Answers

34. top   side   front

35. top   side   front

36.

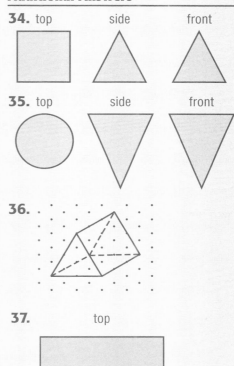

37.   top

side   front

CHAPTER 11 Study Guide and Review

Problem Solving Review

For additional practice in problem solving for Chapter 11, see the Mixed Problem Solving Appendix, page 725 in the Student Handbook section.

Anticipation Guide

Have students complete the Chapter 11 Anticipation Guide and discuss how their responses have changed now that they have completed Chapter 11.

CRM Anticipation Guide, p. 7

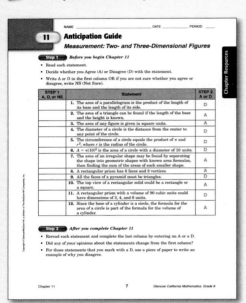

11-9 **Volume of Prisms** (pp. 613–618)

Find the volume of each prism. Round to the nearest tenth if necessary.

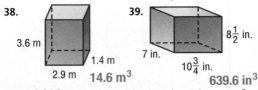

38. 3.6 m, 1.4 m, 2.9 m **14.6 m³**

39. $8\frac{1}{2}$ in., 7 in., $10\frac{3}{4}$ in. **639.6 in³**

40. **POOLS** A competition swimming pool is 25 yards long and has 8 lanes that are each 3 yards wide. The pool is filled to a depth of 6 feet. Find the number of cubic feet of water in the pool. **32,400 ft³**

41. **TRUCKS** The dimensions of the bed of a dump truck are length 20 feet, width 7 feet, and height $9\frac{1}{2}$ feet. What is the volume of the bed of the dump truck? **1,330 ft³**

Example 11 A local city provides residents with a rectangular container for recycling products. Find the volume of the rectangular container.

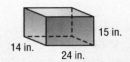
15 in., 14 in., 24 in.

$V = \ell wh$ Volume of a rectangular prism

$V = (24)(14)(15)$ Replace ℓ with 24, w with 14 and h with 15.

$V = 5,040$ Multiply.

The volume of the rectangular container is 5,040 cubic inches.

11-10 **Volume of Cylinders** (pp. 619–623)

Find the volume of each cylinder. Round to the nearest tenth.

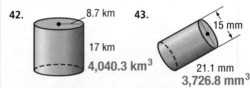

42. 8.7 km, 17 km **4,040.3 km³**

43. 15 mm, 21.1 mm **3,726.8 mm³**

44. **POTTERY** In his art class, Benjamin made a vase in the shape of a cylinder. The diameter is 5 inches, and the height is 10 inches. Find the maximum volume of water the vase can hold. **about 196.3 in³**

45. **COOKIES** Mrs. Delagado stores cookies in a cylinder-shaped jar that has a height of 12 inches and a diameter of 10 inches. Find the volume to the nearest cubic inch. Use 3.14 for π. **942 in³**

Example 12 Marquez stores his toys in a cylinder-shaped can like the one shown below. Find the volume of the cylinder-shaped can. Round to the nearest tenth.

3 ft, 7 ft

$V = \pi r^2 h$ Volume of a cylinder

$= \pi 3^2(7)$ Replace r with 3 and h with 7.

≈ 197.8 Multiply.

The volume of the cylinder-shaped can is 197.8 cubic feet.

630 **Chapter 11** Measurement: Two- and Three-Dimensional Figures

---

Additional Answers (p. 631)

14.
top   side   front

15. top   side   front

10. rectangle; rectangular prism
11. triangle; triangular prism

Find the area of each figure. Round to the nearest tenth if necessary.

1.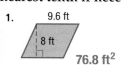
9.6 ft
8 ft
76.8 ft²

2.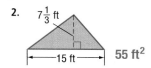
$7\frac{1}{3}$ ft
15 ft
55 ft²

3.
8 yd
6 yd
5 yd
39 yd²

4.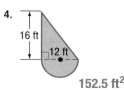
16 ft
12 ft
152.5 ft²

5. **MEASUREMENT** Mrs. Torres has a circular rug underneath her dining room table. What is the approximate circumference of the rug if it has a radius of $3\frac{1}{2}$ yards? **22.0 yd**

Find the area of each circle. Round to the nearest tenth.

6. radius = 9 ft
254.3 ft²

7. diameter = 5.2 m
21.2 m²

8. **STANDARDS PRACTICE** A fountain is in the shape of a circle. If the fountain has a diameter of 8.8 meters, which equation could be used to find the area of the base of the fountain? **B**

A $A = \pi \times 8.8^2$ C $A = 2 \times \pi \times 4.4$
B $A = \pi \times 4.4^2$ D $A = \pi \times 8.8$

9. no; see margin for justification.

9. **MEASUREMENT** The Gruseser family wants to build a swimming pool like the one shown below. If they have 85 square feet of land available for the pool, do they have enough space for the swimming pool? Justify your response.

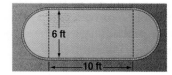
6 ft
10 ft

For each figure, identify the shape of the base(s). Then classify the figure.

10.

11.

12. **GEOMETRY** Classify the shape of a roll of paper towels. **cylinder**

13. **GEOMETRY** Which geometric shape has at least three lateral faces that are triangles and only one base? **pyramid**

Draw a top, a side, and a front view of each solid. 14–15. See margin.

14.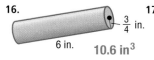

15.

Find the volume of each prism and cylinder. Round to the nearest tenth.

16.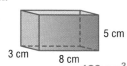
$\frac{3}{4}$ in.
6 in.
10.6 in³

17.
5 cm
3 cm
8 cm
120 cm³

18.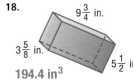
$9\frac{3}{4}$ in.
$3\frac{5}{8}$ in.
$5\frac{1}{2}$ in.
194.4 in³

19.
6 ft
12 ft
1,356.5 ft³

20. **STANDARDS PRACTICE** The standard-size drinking straw has a radius of $\frac{1}{8}$ inch and a height of $7\frac{3}{4}$ inches. How much liquid is contained in the straw if it is only half full? **F**

F 0.2 in³   H 3.4 in³
G 1.5 in³   J 3.8 in³

Summative Assessment

CRM **Chapter 11 Resource Masters**

Leveled Chapter 11 Tests			
Form	**Type**	**Level**	**Pages**
1	MC	BL	77–78
2A	MC	OL	79–80
2B	MC	OL	81–82
2C	FR	OL	83–84
2D	FR	OL	85–86
3	FR	AL	87–88

MC = multiple-choice questions
FR = free-response questions
BL = below grade level
OL = on grade level
AL = above grade level

- Vocabulary Test, p. 76
- Extended-Response Test, p. 89

ExamView Assessment Suite
Customize and create multiple versions of your chapter test and their answer keys. All of the questions from the leveled chapter tests in the *Chapter 11 Resource Masters* are also available on ExamView Assessment Suite with the California Standard that each item assesses.

Additional Answers

9. Sample answer: The area of the pool shown is about 88.3 ft² and 88.3 > 85.

Data-Driven Decision Making	Exercises	Lesson	Standard	Resources for Review
Diagnostic Teaching Based on the results of the Chapter 11 Practice Test, use the following to review concepts that students continue to find challenging.	10–13	11–7	Preparation for 7MG3.6	CRM Study Guide and Intervention pp. 47, 53, 59, and 66 Math Online
	14, 15	11–8	Reinforcement of 5MG2.3	• Extra Examples
	17, 18	11–9	6MG1.3	• Personal Tutor
	16, 19, 20	11–10	6MG1.3	• Concepts in Motion

CHAPTER
11 California Standards Practice
Cumulative, Chapters 1–11

 Read each question. Then fill in the correct answer on the answer document provided by your teacher or on a sheet of paper.

1 Stephanie shaded part of a circle like the one shown below. What is the approximate area of the shaded region? **A**

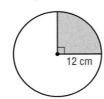

12 cm

A 113 cm²

B 364 cm²

C 452 cm²

D 728 cm²

TEST-TAKING TIP

Question 1 Many tests include a Mathematics Chart in the test booklet. Refer to the chart for area and volume formulas.

2 The circular floor rug shown has a diameter of 6 feet. Which expression can be used to find its circumference, C, in feet? **H**

6 ft

F $C = 3 \times \pi$

G $C = 3^2 \times \pi$

H $C = 6 \times \pi$

J $C = 2 \times 6 \times \pi$

3 Angle D and angle E are complementary angles. If $\angle D$ is 35°, what is the measure of $\angle E$? **B**

A 35°   **C** 90°

B 55°   **D** 145°

4 If the corresponding angles of 2 trapezoids are congruent and the lengths of the corresponding sides of the trapezoids are proportional, the trapezoids are — **J**

F regular   **H** symmetric

G congruent   **J** similar

5 Which description shows the relationship between a term and n, its position in the sequence? **C**

Position	1	2	3	4	5	n
Value of Term	2	5	8	11	14	

A Add 1 to n

B Multiply n by 2 and add 3

C Multiply n by 3 and subtract 1

D Add 9 to n

6 A metal toolbox has a length of 11 inches, a width of 5 inches, and a height of 6 inches. What is the volume of the toolbox? **J**

F 22 in³   **H** 210 in³

G 121 in³   **J** 330 in³

7 A bag contains 5 red, 2 yellow, and 8 blue marbles. Xavier removed one blue marble from the bag and did not put it back. He then randomly removed another marble. What is the probability that the second marble removed was blue? **C**

A $\frac{8}{14}$ **C** $\frac{1}{2}$

B $\frac{8}{15}$ **D** $\frac{7}{15}$

632 **Chapter 11** Measurement: Two- and Three-Dimensional Figures

More California
Standards Practice
For practice by standard,
see pages CA1–CA39.

CHAPTER
11
California
Standards Practice

8 In the figure shown, all the corners form right angles. What is the area of the figure in square feet? **G**

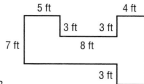

F 91 ft²

G 107 ft²

H 115 ft²

J 122 ft²

9 Ms. Williams recorded the time it took six of her top students to complete a math quiz. The results are shown in the table below. What is the median time for these six students? **C**

Math Quiz Times	
Student	**Time (minutes)**
1	12.8
2	23.1
3	19.6
4	15.7
5	27.3
6	20.5

A 12.8 minutes   **C** 20.05 minutes

B 16 minutes   **D** 27.3 minutes

10 Katie has 3 apples to serve to her friends. If Katie serves each friend $\frac{1}{3}$ of a whole apple, how many friends can she serve? **H**

F 1   **H** 9

G 3   **J** 12

11 The circles shown have radii of 4 feet and 8 feet.

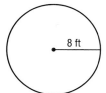

What is $\dfrac{\text{circumference of Circle } x}{\text{circumference of Circle } y}$? **D**

A $\dfrac{\pi}{4}$

B $\dfrac{\pi}{2}$

C $\dfrac{1}{4}$

D $\dfrac{1}{2}$

Pre-AP

Record your answers on a sheet of paper. Show your work.

12 Suppose you bought a new tent with the dimensions shown below.

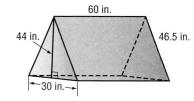

a. Is the area of the parallelogram-shaped side of the tent greater than or less than the area of the floor? Explain. **See margin.**

b. The front and back triangular regions are covered with screens. What is the total area of the screens? **1,320 in²**

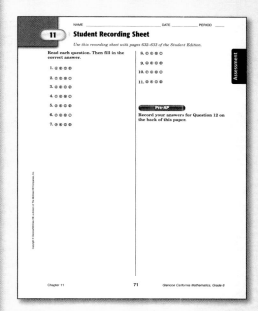
NEED EXTRA HELP?

If You Missed Question...	1	2	3	4	5	6	7	8	9	10	11	12
Go to Lesson...	11-4	11-6	10-1	10-6	1-9	11-9	9-1	11-6	8-2	5-7	11-3	11-2
For Help with Standard...	MG1.2	AF3.1	MG2.2	NS1.3	AF1.2	MG1.3	SDAP3.3	AF3.1	SDAP1.1	NS2.2	MG1.2	AF3.1

Homework Option

Get Ready for Chapter 12 Assign students the exercises on page 635 as homework to assess whether they possess the prerequisite skills needed for the next chapter.

Page 576, Lesson 11-1

32.

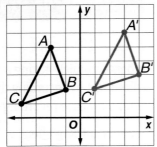

33. Sample answer: The sum of the measures of an octagon is 1,080°. Each angle measure is 1,080° ÷ 8 or 135°. Since 135 does not go into 360 evenly, an octagon does not tessellate the plane.

Pages 594–595, Lesson 11-5

1. Sample answer: Finding the areas of the separate geometric figures and then adding is easier than trying to find the area of the irregular figure as a whole.

2. Sample answer: Find the area of each smaller rectangle and the area of each semicircle and then add.

3. Sample answer: Find the area of the wall below to determine how much paint to buy. To solve, find the area of the triangle and the area of the rectangle, then add. The answer is 77 ft².

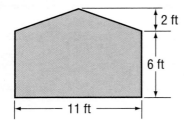

2 ft

6 ft

11 ft

10. division followed by multiplication followed by division; $\frac{60 \text{ in.}}{36 \text{ in.}} = 1\frac{1}{3}$ yd; $1\frac{1}{3}$ yd × 20 yd = $33\frac{1}{3}$ yd², $15\frac{1}{2}$ yd × $5\frac{3}{4}$ yd = $89\frac{1}{8}$ yd²; $89\frac{1}{8}$ yd² ÷ $33\frac{1}{3}$ yd² = $2\frac{539}{800}$; 3 bolts

11. multiplication followed by division; 150 × 108 = 16,200; 16,200 ÷ 10 = 1,620; 1,620 h

Page 601, Extend 11-6

3.

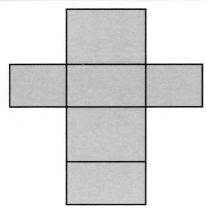

4.

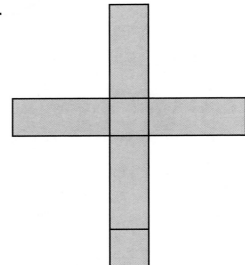

5.

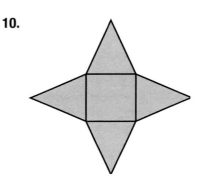

10.

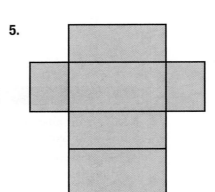

Page 603, Lesson 11-7 (Get Ready for the Lesson)

Sample answer: The cereal box has six rectangular faces. The soda can has only two faces, both of which are circular. The cylinder has no vertices and no edges. The birthday hat has one circular base and one vertex.

Pages 610–611, Lesson 11-8

1.   top   side   front

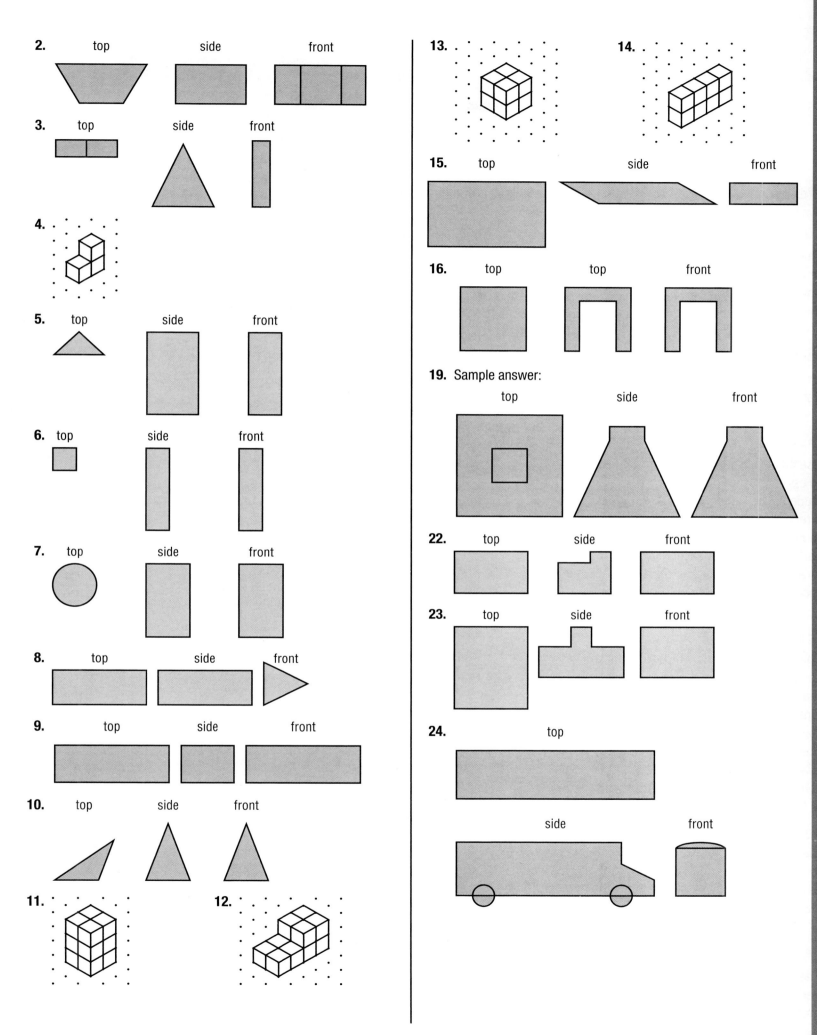

2. top   side   front

3. top   side   front

4.

5. top   side   front

6. top   side   front

7. top   side   front

8. top   side   front

9. top   side   front

10. top   side   front

11.   **12.**

13.   **14.**

15. top   side   front

16. top   top   front

19. Sample answer:

top   side   front

22. top   side   front

23. top   side   front

24. top

side   front

Standards Review

Standards Review

Mastering the California Mathematics Standards

This consumable workbook includes multiple assessment tools to determine how well your students have mastered the Grade 6 Standards.

Diagnose

Use the Diagnostic Test to pinpoint which California Standards need reinforcement.

Prescribe

Use the results from the Diagnostic Test to assign practice pages for each student. The student workbook includes a recording chart so that students monitor their own progress in mastering each Standard. The Teacher Edition also includes a class recording chart to monitor all of your students' progress.

Practice

There are two ways in which students can practice multiple-choice questions that relate to the Grade 6 Standards. One practice set is organized by standard and has at least one page of questions per standard. The other practice set is organized by the sequence in which the topics are taught in this textbook.

A *Standard Assessment* is modeled after the CST blueprint for Grade 6 and includes multiple-choice questions to assess student progress in mastering the standards.

Periodic Assessment

The workbook also includes four Periodic Assessment tests that help you monitor your students progress in

Throughout the school year, you may be required to take several tests, and you may have many questions about them. Here are some answers to help you get ready.

How Should I Study?

The good news is that you've been studying all along—a little bit every day. Here are some of the ways your textbook has been preparing you.

- **Every Day** Each lesson had practice questions that cover the California Standards.

- **Every Week** The Mid-Chapter Quiz and Practice Test had several practice questions.

- **Every Month** The California Standards Practice pages at the end of each chapter had even more questions similar to those on tests.

Are there Other Ways to Review?

Absolutely! The following pages contain even more practice for each California Standard.

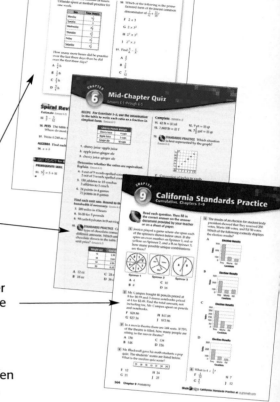

Math Online Additional California Standards at ca.gr6math.com

mastering the California Standards through the year. These tests can be used to pinpoint those Standards that need more instruction. The Teacher Edition includes answers for ease in grading as well as additional diagnostic tools.

Tips for SUCCESS

Prepare

- Go to bed early the night before the test. You will think more clearly after a good night's rest.
- Become familiar with common formulas and when they should be used.
- Think positively.

During the Test

- Read each problem carefully. Underline key words and think about different ways to solve the problem.
- Watch for key words like *not*. Also look for order words like *least, greatest, first,* and *last.*
- Answer questions you are sure about first. If you do not know the answer to a question, skip it and go back to that question later.
- Check your answer to make sure it is reasonable.
- Make sure that the number of the question on the answer sheet matches the number of the question on which you are working in your test booklet.

Whatever you do...

- Don't try to do it all in your head. If no figure is provided, draw one.
- Don't rush. Try to work at a steady pace.
- Don't give up. Some problems may seem hard to you, but you may be able to figure out what to do if you read each question carefully or try another strategy.

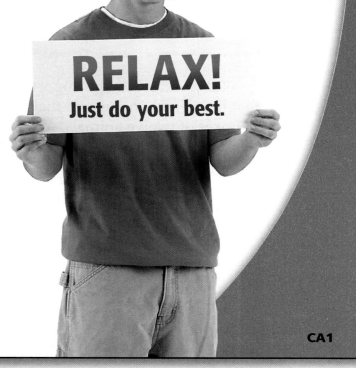

RELAX! Just do your best.

CA1

 The questions from the *Mastering the California Standards* workbook are also available in an electronic format on the ExamView Assessment Suite. These standard-based questions can easily be incorporated into your tests or used separately for California Standards practice.

The Teacher Management System allows you to automatically grade tests and track students' progress using multiple reporting features.

Multiple-Choice Questions

In multiple-choice questions, you are asked to choose the best answer from four possible answers. To record a multiple-choice answer, you will be asked to shade in a bubble that is a circle. Always make sure that your shading is dark enough and completely covers the bubble.

Incomplete shading

Too light shading

Correct shading
(A) (B) (●C) (D)

STANDARDS EXAMPLE

1 **Mrs. Hon's sixth grade students are purchasing stuffed animals to donate to a charity. They bought 3 boxes containing eight animals each and 5 boxes containing twelve animals each. Which expression *cannot* be used to find the total number of animals they bought to give to the charity?**

A $8 + 8 + 8 + 12 + 12 + 12 + 12 + 12$

B $3 \times 8 + 5 \times 12$

C $3(8) + 5(12)$

D $8 \times 8 \times 8 + 5(12)$

> Notice that the problem asks for the expression that *cannot* represent the situation.

Read the problem carefully and locate the important information. There are 3 boxes that have eight animals, so that is 3×8, or 24 animals. There are 5 boxes of twelve animals, so that is 5×12, or 60 animals. The total number of animals is $24 + 60$, or 84.

You know from reading the problem that you are looking for the expression that *does not* simplify to 84. Simplify each expression to find the answer.

A $8 + 8 + 8 + 12 + 12 + 12 + 12 + 12$
$= (8 + 8 + 8) + (12 + 12 + 12 + 12 + 12)$
$= 24 + 60$
$= 84$

B $3 \times 8 + 5 \times 12 = 24 + 60$
$= 84$

C $3(8) + 5(12) = 24 + 60$
$= 84$

D $8 \times 8 \times 8 + 5(12) = 512 + 60$
$= 572$

The only expression that *does not* simplify to 84 is D.
The correct choice is D.

STANDARDS EXAMPLE

2 On a hiking trip, Grace and Alicia traveled 10 miles south and 4 miles west as part of a rectangular hiking path. If they complete the path back to their starting point, how far will they have hiked?

F 14 mi   **G** 20 mi   **H** 28 mi   **J** 32 mi

STRATEGY

Diagrams Draw a diagram for the situation. If you cannot write in the test booklet, draw a diagram on scratch paper.

To solve this problem, you need to draw a diagram of the situation. Label the directions and the important information from the problem.

To find the total distance hiked, find the perimeter of the rectangle.

$$P = 2\ell + 2w \qquad \text{Perimeter of a rectangle}$$
$$P = 2(10) + 2(4) \qquad \text{Replace } \ell \text{ with 10 and } w \text{ with 4.}$$
$$P = 20 + 8 \qquad \text{Multiply.}$$
$$P = 28 \qquad \text{Add.}$$

The total distance hiked will be 28 miles. The correct choice is H.

Some problems give more information than needed to solve the problem. Read the question carefully to determine the information you need.

STANDARDS EXAMPLE

3 One of the biggest pieces of cheese ever produced was made in 1866 in Ingersoll, Canada. It weighed 7,300 pounds. It was shaped as a cylinder with a diameter of 7 feet and a height of 3 feet. To the nearest cubic foot, what was the volume of the cheese? Use 3.14 for π.

A 462 ft^3 **B** 143 ft^3 **C** 115 ft^3 **D** 63 ft^3

You need to use the formula for the volume of a cylinder. The diameter is 7 feet, so the radius is $\frac{7}{2}$ or 3.5 feet. The height is 3 feet.

$$V = \pi r^2 h \qquad \text{Volume of a cylinder}$$
$$V \approx (3.14)(3.5)^2(3) \qquad \text{Replace } \pi \text{ with 3.14, } r \text{ with 3.5, and } h \text{ with 3.}$$
$$V \approx 115.395 \qquad \text{Simplify.}$$

STRATEGY

Formulas Use the Mathematics Chart to find the correct formula.

The volume of the cheese is about 115 cubic feet. The correct choice is C.

Practice by Standard: Number Sense

Standard Set 1.0: Students compare and order positive and negative fractions, decimals, and mixed numbers. Students solve problems involving fractions, ratios, proportions and percentages.

DIRECTIONS
Choose the best answer.

QUICK Practice

1 Which list of numbers is ordered from *least* to *greatest*? (6NS1.1) **B**

A $0.8, \frac{1}{8}, 1.8, 1\frac{1}{8}$

B $\frac{1}{8}, 0.8, 1\frac{1}{8}, 1.8$

C $0.8, \frac{1}{8}, 1\frac{1}{8}, 1.8$

D $\frac{1}{8}, 1.8, 1\frac{1}{8}, 0.8$

QUICK Review

STRATEGY **Think:** Which answers can you eliminate because they are not reasonable?

Graph the numbers on a number line and compare.

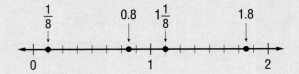

For more help with ordering rational numbers, see page 215.

---

2 Korin and her family took a vacation over her summer break. The first day they drove 180 miles in 3 hours. What ratio represents their rate in miles per hour? (6NS1.2) **F**

F 60:1

H 1:6

G 180:1

J 1:180

READING HINT A ratio is a comparison of two numbers by division.

You can answer this by first writing the ratio as a fraction. Then write the fraction in simplest form.

For more help with ratios, see page 282.

---

3 In 6 hours, Mr. Williams drove a total of 330 miles. If Mr. Williams drives at the same rate, which proportion could be solved to find x, the number of miles he could drive in 9 hours? (6NS1.3) **D**

A $\frac{9}{330} = \frac{6}{x}$

C $\frac{6}{330} = \frac{x}{9}$

B $\frac{6}{9} = \frac{x}{330}$

D $\frac{6}{330} = \frac{9}{x}$

STRATEGY Solve the proportion to see whether the answer makes sense.

First, write a ratio comparing the number of hours to miles when Mr. Williams drove 6 hours. Then write an equivalent ratio that compares the number of hours to miles for 9 hours.

For more help with proportions, see page 306.

4 The rectangles below are similar. What is the value of x in the diagram below? (6NS1.3) **G**

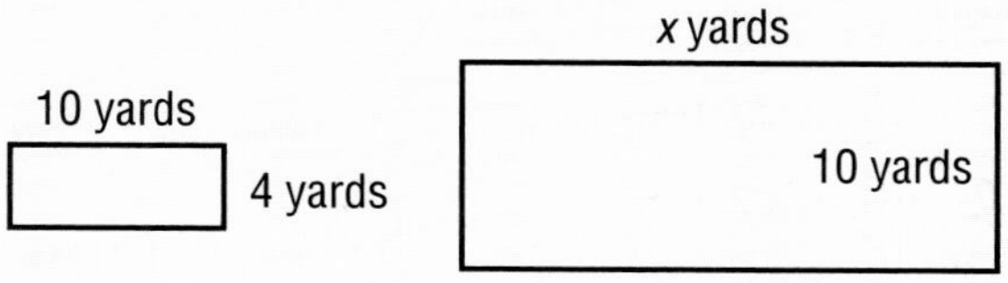

x yards

10 yards

4 yards

10 yards

 F 4 yards

 G 25 yards

 H 30 yards

 J 40 yards

> **READING HINT** Remember that similar figures have corresponding sides that are proportional.

Since the two rectangles are similar, the ratios of their corresponding sides are equivalent. Write and solve a proportion to find x.

$$\frac{10 \text{ yards}}{4 \text{ yards}} = \frac{x \text{ yards}}{10 \text{ yards}}$$

For more help with similar figures, see page 540.

---

5 Miguel bought a guitar for $159.99. If the original price was $229.99, what is the approximate percent of the discount? (6NS1.4) **A**

 A 30%

 B 40%

 C 70%

 D 144%

> **STRATEGY** Solve a simpler problem.

To find the percent of the discount, first find the amount of the discount. Then determine what percent of the original price the discount represents.

For more help with percent of change, see page 369.

---

6 The principal of Harvey Middle School has determined that for every 15 students on a field trip, there should be 2 chaperones. How many chaperones should attend a field trip with 90 students? (6NS1.3) **J**

 F 6

 G 8

 H 10

 J 12

> **STRATEGY** **Think:** Which answers can you eliminate because they are not reasonable?

This problem can be answered using a proportion.

$$\frac{2 \text{ chaperones}}{15 \text{ students}} = \frac{x \text{ chaperones}}{90 \text{ students}}$$

For more help with proportions, see page 306.

7 During softball practice on Tuesday, Maya had 9 hits out of 24 at-bats. Which of the following ratios represents Maya's batting average? (6NS1.2) **A**

A $\frac{3}{8}$

B $\frac{1}{4}$

C $\frac{1}{2}$

D $\frac{2}{3}$

8 When gear B turns 3 revolutions, gear A turns 8 revolutions. When gear A turns 104 revolutions, how many revolutions does gear B turn? (6NS1.3) **J**

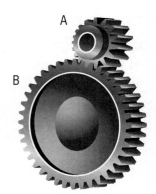

F 99

G 62

H 48

J 39

9 Elyse and her grandmother went to a restaurant for dinner. Their bill came to $48. They added a 20% tip. How much total did they spend on dinner? (6NS1.4) **C**

A $9.60

B $38.40

C $57.60

D $68

10 Noah typed a 1,500 word essay in 24 minutes. At this rate, how long would it take him to type a 2,500 word essay? (6NS1.3) **G**

F 35 minutes

G 40 minutes

H 48 minutes

J 56 minutes

11 Which point shows the location of $-2\frac{3}{4}$ on the number line? (6NS1.1) **A**

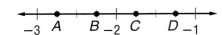

A point A

B point B

C point C

D point D

12 Selia wants to buy a sweater that costs $58. The sales tax is 7.5%. About how much will she pay in sales tax? (6NS1.4) **H**

F $62.35

G $43.50

H $4.35

J $6.35

13 Leticia ran 3 miles in 25 minutes. At this rate, which of the following proportions can be used to find x, the number of minutes it would take her to run 5 miles? (6NS1.3) **B**

A $\frac{3}{25} = \frac{x}{5}$

B $\frac{3}{25} = \frac{5}{x}$

C $\frac{5}{25} = \frac{3}{x}$

D $\frac{25}{5} = \frac{3}{x}$

Practice by Standard: Number Sense

Standard Set 2.0: Students calculate and solve problems involving addition, subtraction, multiplication, and division.

DIRECTIONS
Choose the best answer.

QUICK*Practice*

1 What is the least common multiple of 3, 5, and 6? (6NS2.4) **C**

  A 15

  B 18

  C 30

  D 35

2 The Student Council is wrapping gifts for a fund-raiser. Each gift uses $1\frac{1}{4}$ feet of ribbon. How many gifts can be wrapped using the spool of ribbon below? (6NS2.1) **G**

Total Length = 10 ft

  F 2   **G** 8

  H 6   **J** 12

3 What is $-13 + (-27)$? (6NS2.3) **D**

  A 14

  B 40

  C −14

  D −40

QUICK*Review*

> **READING HINT** Recall that the least common multiple is the least of their common multiples, excluding zero.

Make a list of the common multiples of 3, 5, and 6. Then choose the least multiple, excluding zero.

For more help with the least common multiple, see page 211.

> **STRATEGY** **Think:** Which operation can be used to solve the problem?

If each gift uses $1\frac{1}{4}$ feet of ribbon, then the number of gifts that can be wrapped using a 10 foot length of ribbon can be found by dividing 10 by $1\frac{1}{4}$.

For more help with division of fractions, see page 265.

> **STRATEGY** Use a number line to visualize the situation.

To add integers with the same sign, add their absolute values. The sum is negative if both integers are negative.

For more help with adding integers, see page 95.

QUICKPractice

4 At 7 A.M., the temperature was −5°F. By noon, the temperature had risen 18°F. What was the temperature at noon? (6NS2.3) **H**

   F −23°F

   G −13°F

   H 13°F

   J 23°F

5 What is $\frac{15}{16} \times \frac{16}{27}$? (6NS2.1) **B**

   A $\frac{1}{11}$

   B $\frac{5}{9}$

   C $\frac{2}{3}$

   D $\frac{31}{43}$

6 The table shows Laura's golf scores, in number of strokes above or below par, for the first five holes of a game. What was her total golf score for the first five holes? (6NS2.3) **H**

Holes	Score
1	0
2	1
3	−1
4	−2
5	3

   F −1   **H** 1

   G 0   **J** 2

QUICKReview

STRATEGY Use the information presented in the problem to write an addition expression.

To find the temperature at noon, add 18°F and −5°F. To add two integers with different signs, subtract their absolute values. The sum has the same sign as the integer with the larger absolute value.

For more help with adding integers, see page 95.

STRATEGY First, estimate. Then, eliminate unreasonable answers.

To multiply fractions, multiply the numerators and multiply the denominators. Be sure to simplify your answer. It is best to simplify before multiplying, if possible.

For more help with multiplying fractions, see page 252.

STRATEGY Use properties of addition to check your answer.

To find her total score for the first five holes, you need to find $0 + 1 + (−1) + (−2) + 3$, or 1.

For more help with adding integers, see page 95.

Practice on Your Own

7 Which answer choice best describes the meaning of $4 \div \frac{1}{2}$? (6NS2.2) **B**

A The number of fourths that are in 2 wholes.

B The number of halves that are in 4 wholes.

C The number of times 4 divides into 2.

D The number of times 4 divides into $\frac{1}{2}$.

8 What is $-4 - (-18)$? (6NS2.3) **G**

F −14

G 14

H 22

J −22

9 What length of tablecloth will be needed to cover the two tables pictured below if they are put together as shown? (6NS2.4) **D**

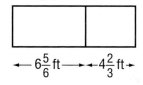

$\leftarrow 6\frac{5}{6}$ ft $\longrightarrow$ $\leftarrow 4\frac{2}{3}$ ft $\rightarrow$

A $2\frac{7}{9}$ feet

B $10\frac{1}{2}$ feet

C $10\frac{7}{9}$ feet

D $11\frac{1}{2}$ feet

10 The elevation of Hikers Peak is 708 feet and the elevation of Greene Lake is −22 feet. What is the difference between these elevations? (6NS2.3) **F**

F 730 feet

G 686 feet

H −686 feet

J −730 feet

11 What is the greatest common divisor of 18, 45, and 54? (6NS2.4) **C**

A 3

B 6

C 9

D 18

12 The table shows the average daily temperatures in degrees Fahrenheit for the past five days for Snow Valley.

Day	Temperature (°F)
1	−7
2	4
3	10
4	−13
5	−9

What was the average temperature of Snow Valley for the past five days? (6NS2.3) **G**

F −15°F   H 3°F

G −3°F   J 5°F

13 What is $\frac{1}{15} + \frac{4}{9}$? (6NS2.4) **C**

A $\frac{1}{9}$ C $\frac{23}{45}$

B $\frac{5}{24}$ D $\frac{2}{3}$

14 The Traverse Valley Junior High football team lost 18 yards on the first play, gained 6 yards on the second play, and lost 9 yards on the third play. If they gained 14 yards on the fourth play, which of the following expressions can be used to represent the total amount of yards gained? (6NS2.3) **F**

F $(-18) + 6 + (-9) + 14$

G $18 + 6 + 9 + 14$

H $(-18) - 6 + (-9) - 14$

J $(-18) + 6 + 9 + (-14)$

Practice by Standard: Algebra and Functions

Standard Set 1.0: Students write verbal expressions and sentences as algebraic expressions and equations; they evaluate algebraic expressions, solve simple linear equations, and graph and interpret their results.

DIRECTIONS
Choose the best answer.

QUICKPractice

1 The total cost of a movie ticket t, soda s, and popcorn f is $12.50. If the soda and popcorn together cost $4.50, which algebraic equation can be used to find t, the cost of the movie ticket? (6AF1.1) **A**

A $12.50 - t = $4.50

B $2t + $4.50 = $12.50

C $t + $12.50 = $4.50

D $t - $4.50 = $12.50

2 The area of a triangle can be found using the equation $A = \frac{1}{2}bh$. What is the height h of the triangle pictured below if the area is 36 square inches? (6AF1.1) **H**

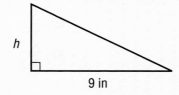

9 in

F 31.5 inches   **H** 8 inches

G 9 inches   **J** 2 inches

3 Which value of n makes the following equation true? (6AF1.1) **C**

$$n + 5.4 = 18.7$$

A 24.1   **C** 13.3

B −13.3   **D** 6.6

QUICKReview

> **READING HINT** An equation is a sentence in mathematics that contains an equals sign.

The cost of the movie ticket plus the cost of the soda plus the cost of the popcorn is $12.50. Thus, $t + s + p = 12.50$. The soda and the popcorn together cost $4.50. Substitute this amount for $s + p$ in the equation.

For more help with writing equations, see page 128.

> **READING HINT** In the formula $A = \frac{1}{2}bh$, A is the area of the triangle, b is the base of the triangle, and h is the height of the triangle.

Replace A with 36 and b with 9 in the equation $A = \frac{1}{2}bh$. Then solve the equation for h.

For more help with solving multiplication equations, see page 142.

> **STRATEGY** Think: Which answers can you eliminate because they are not reasonable?

To solve this addition equation, subtract 5.4 from each side of the equation.

For more help with solving addition equations, see page 136.

4 Which expression can be used to find the cost of buying s sweaters at \$35 each, j pairs of jeans at \$30 each, and h hats at \$12 each? (6AF1.2) **J**

  F $35 + 30 + 12 + s + j + h$

  G $35j + 30s + 12h$

  H $77(j + s + h)$

  J $35s + 30j + 12h$

> **READING HINT**   An expression contains variables, numbers, and at least one operation.
>
> To find the total cost of s sweaters, multiply s by the cost of each sweater, \$35. To find the total cost of j pairs of jeans, multiply j by the cost of each pair of jeans, \$30. To find the total cost of h hats, multiply h by the cost of each hat, \$12. Add these quantities.
>
> For more help with writing expressions, see page 128.

5 The steps Gina took to evaluate the expression $5y + 5 \cdot 5$ when $y = 2$ are shown below.

$$5y + 5 \cdot 5 \text{ when } y = 2$$
$$5 \cdot 2 = 10$$
$$10 + 5 = 15$$
$$15 \cdot 5 = 75$$

What should Gina have done differently in order to evaluate the expression? (6AF1.3) **C**

  A   multiplied $(10 + 5)$ by $(10 \cdot 5)$

  B   multiplied $(10 + 5)$ by 2

  C   added $(5 \cdot 5)$ to 10

  D   added $(5 \cdot 5)$ to 15

> **READING HINT**   To evaluate expressions, use the correct order of operations.
>
> Recall that multiplication comes before addition in the order of operations. Gina should evaluate $5y$ when $y = 2$, which is 10, and multiply $5 \cdot 5$, which is 25. She then should find the sum of 10 and 25.
>
> For more help with evaluating expressions, see page 38.

6 Evaluate the expression below. (6AF1.4) **J**

$$9 + 9 \div 3 + 3$$

  F   3   **H**   12

  G   9   **J**   15

> **READING HINT**   To evaluate expressions, use the correct order of operations.
>
> Recall that division comes before addition. Find $9 \div 3$ before adding in order from left to right.
>
> For more help with evaluating expressions, see page 38.

Practice on Your Own

7 Félix has a cell phone plan that allows him to talk for 500 minutes each month. If he uses 75 minutes of his monthly minutes each day, which expression represents how many minutes he has left after x days? (6AF1.2) **B**

A $500x - 75$

B $500 - 75x$

C $500x$

D $500 + 75x$

8 Which of the following algebraic equations best describes the total distance D traveled by a commercial jet airliner after h hours if the airliner travels 480 miles per hour? (6AF1.1) **F**

F $D = 480h$

G $D = 480 + h$

H $D = \dfrac{480}{h}$

J $D = 480 - h$

9 The table shows the price per pound of several kinds of produce.

Produce	Price ($ per lb)
Peaches	2.79
Apples	1.89
Bananas	1.19
Apricots	3.19

Which of the following equations can Miranda use to find the number of pounds of bananas b she can buy with $10 if she also buys 2 pounds of peaches? (6AF1.1) **D**

A $\$10 - \$1.19(2) = b$

B $\$10 + b = \$2.79(2)$

C $\$10 + 2b = \$2.79$

D $\dfrac{\$10 - \$2.79(2)}{\$1.19} = b$

10 Lauren earns $8 per hour selling jewelry. How many hours does she need to work to earn $68? (6AF1.1) **G**

F 8 hours

G 8.5 hours

H 60 hours

J 544 hours

11 What value of g makes the following equation true? (6AF1.1) **A**

$$g \div 6 = -2$$

A -12

B -3

C 4

D 12

12 A movie ticket at Maximum Cinemas costs $9 and a small drink costs $1.50. Kayla reasoned that the cost of 4 movie tickets and four small drinks can be found using the expression 4($9 + $1.50). Which property shows that this cost is also equivalent to $4 \times \$9 + 4 \times \$1.50$? (6AF1.3) **J**

F Commutative Property of Addition

G Commutative Property of Multiplication

H Associative Property of Addition

J Distributive Property

13 What is the value of the expression $\dfrac{mn}{p}$ if $m = 6, n = -7$, and $p = 2$? (6AF1.2) **A**

A -21

B $-\dfrac{1}{2}$

C 21

D 43

Practice by Standard: Algebra and Functions

Standard Set 2.0: Students analyze and use tables, graphs, and rules to solve problems involving rates and proportions.

DIRECTIONS
Choose the best answer.

QUICKPractice | QUICKReview

1 A piece of string is 125 inches long. About how long is the string in centimeters? (6AF2.1) **C**

  A 3 centimeters

  B 49 centimeters

  C 321 centimeters

  D 4,875 centimeters

> **STRATEGY** **Think:** Which answers can you eliminate because they are not reasonable?

Use 1 inch ≈ 2.54 centimeters. Multiply the unit ratio $\frac{2.54 \text{ centimeters}}{1 \text{ inch}}$ by 125 inches to find about how many centimeters are in 125 inches.

For more help with converting measurements, see page 300.

---

2 The cost of oranges at several grocery stores is listed in the table below. Which store has the least unit cost for oranges? (6AF2.2) **G**

Store	Cost
Casey's Corner	5 oranges for $3
Mark's Market	4 oranges for $2
Geraldine's Grocery	8 oranges for $5

  F Casey's Corner

  G Mark's Market

  H Geraldine's Grocery

  J All three stores have the same unit cost for oranges.

> **STRATEGY** Recall that unit cost is the cost of one unit, or in this case, the cost of one orange.

First, find each unit cost for each grocery store. To do this, simplify each ratio of number of oranges to dollar amount of cost. Then compare the unit costs to determine which grocery store has the least unit cost.

For more help with unit rates, see page 287.

---

3 Jordan drives at a rate of 70 miles per hour on the interstate. At this speed, how long will it take him to drive 280 miles? (6AF2.3) **B**

  A 3 hours   **C** 4.5 hours

  B 4 hours   **D** 5 hours

> **STRATEGY** Use the equation $d = rt$, where d represents the distance, r represents the rate of travel, and t represents the time.

Solve the equation $280 = 70t$ to find the time t it will take Jordan to drive 280 miles.

For more help with problems involving average speed, distance, and time, see page 287.

QUICKPractice

QUICKReview

4 The table below shows the average resting heart rate, in beats per minute, of selected mammals.

Mammal	Average Resting Heart Rate (beats per minute)
Gray Whale	9
Cow	50
Mouse	376

At this rate, how many times would the average cow's heart beat in the course of 12 minutes? (6AF2.2) **H**

F 42 times   **H** 600 times

G 450 times   **J** 800 times

> **STRATEGY** **Think:** Which answers can you eliminate because they are not reasonable?

You can multiply the unit rate $\frac{50 \text{ beats}}{1 \text{ minute}}$ by 12 minutes to find the number of times the average cow's heart will beat in the course of 12 minutes.

For more help with unit rates, see page 287.

---

5 Which ratio below shows a unit rate? (6AF2.2) **A**

A $\frac{65 \text{ words}}{1 \text{ minute}}$

B $\frac{40 \text{ hours}}{\$450}$

C $\frac{900 \text{ miles}}{2 \text{ days}}$

D $\frac{9 \text{ songs}}{47 \text{ minutes}}$

> **READING HINT** Recall that a unit rate is a measure of one quantity per unit value of another quantity.

The only ratio that compares a measure of one quantity per unit value of another quantity is the ratio in answer choice A.

For more help with unit rates, see page 287.

---

6 Yolanda drove 310 miles in 5 hours. At this rate, how many miles could she drive in 9 hours? (6AF2.2) **J**

F 62 miles

G 172 miles

H 525 miles

J 558 miles

> **STRATEGY** You can use unit rates, proportions, or equations to solve this problem.

You can simplify the ratio $\frac{310 \text{ miles}}{5 \text{ hours}}$ to find the number of miles Yolanda drove, on average, per hour. Then multiply this unit rate by 9 hours to find the number of miles she could drive in 9 hours.

For more help with unit rates, see page 287.

Practice on Your Own

7 Seki, Odell, and Brady took their bicycles on a week-long vacation. The table shows the total distances and length of time each person biked during the week.

Person	Distance	Time
Seki	100 miles	5 hours
Odell	143 miles	6.5 hours
Brady	133 miles	7 hours

Which person had the fastest average unit rate of travel? (6AF2.2) **B**

A Seki

B Odell

C Brady

D Each biker had the same unit rate of travel.

8 In training for a half-marathon, Isabel ran 5.5 miles on Friday. About how many kilometers did she run on Friday? (1 mile ≈ 1.61 kilometers) (6AF2.1) **J**

F 3.4 kilometers

G 3.9 kilometers

H 7.1 kilometers

J 8.9 kilometers

9 A certain river flows at a rate of 10,000 gallons of water every 20 minutes. Which of the following is true concerning the unit rate of flow of the river (in gallons per minute)? (6AF2.2) **A**

A The unit rate of flow of the river is 500 gallons per minute.

B The unit rate of flow of the river is 500 minutes per gallon.

C The unit rate of flow of the river is 50 gallons per minute.

D The unit rate of flow of the river is 200,000 gallons per minute.

10 The table shows the prices of several beverages. Which beverage has the lowest unit price? (6AF2.2) **H**

Beverage	Amount	Price
Soda	12 oz.	$1.20
Juice	16 oz.	$2.40
Bottled Water	20 oz.	$1.60
Iced Tea	8 oz.	$1.20

F Soda

G Juice

H Bottled Water

J Iced Tea

11 Nick's Laundromat charges $1.75 to wash and dry one load of laundry. If a customer spent $7.00 doing laundry at Nick's Laundromat, how many loads of laundry did the customer wash and dry? (6AF2.2) **B**

A 3   C 5

B 4   D 6

12 Which rate listed below is the slowest? (6AF2.2) **J**

F 132 miles in 2 hours

G 28 miles in 5 hours

H 180 miles in 10 hours

J 30 miles in 15 hours

13 Marla's car averages 22 miles per gallon of gasoline. At this rate, how many gallons of gasoline are needed for a 330 mile trip? (6AF2.3) **C**

A 11 gallons

B 12 gallons

C 15 gallons

D 18 gallons

Practice by Standard: Algebra and Functions

Standard Set 3.0: Students investigate geometric patterns and describe them algebraically.

DIRECTIONS
Choose the best answer.

QUICKPractice	QUICKReview
1 The rectangle shown below has length 27 centimeters and perimeter P centimeters.	**READING HINT** The perimeter of a rectangle is found by using the formula $P = 2\ell + 2w$.

27 centimeters

Which equation could be used to find the width of the rectangle?
(6AF3.1) **C**

A $P = 27 + \dfrac{w}{2}$ **C** $P = 54 + 2w$

B $P = 27 - w$ **D** $P = 54 + w$

Replace ℓ with 27 in the equation $P = 2\ell + 2w$, since the length of the rectangle is 27 centimeters.

For more help with the perimeter of a rectangle, see page 156.

---

2 Which equation could be used to find the area in square yards of a circle with a diameter of 14 yards?
(6AF3.2) **J**

F $A = 14 \times \pi$ **H** $A = \pi \times 11^2$

G $A = 28 \times \pi$ **J** $A = \pi \times 7^2$

READING HINT Use the correct value for the radius. The area of a circle is found by using the formula $A = \pi r^2$, but the problem gives you the diameter.

Recall that the radius is half of the diameter.

---

3 Which expression is equivalent to the area, in square units, of the triangle below? (6AF3.1) **B**

y

18

A $18y$ **C** $18 + y$

B $9y$ **D** $\dfrac{18}{y}$

STRATEGY The area of a triangle is found by using the formula $A = \frac{1}{2}bh$.

Replace b with 18 in the expression $\frac{1}{2}bh$. Remember to simplify the expression.

For more help with the area of a triangle, see page 578.

QUICK Practice | QUICK Review

4 A square with side length x is inside a rectangle that measures 8 by 5, as pictured below. Which expression represents the area of the shaded region in terms of x? (6AF3.2) **H**

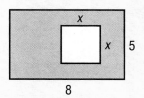

F $13 - x$ **H** $40 - x^2$

G $26 + x$ **J** $40 - 2x$

> **READING HINT** Recall that the area of the rectangle is found by multiplying the length by the width.

Find the area of the rectangle. Write an expression for the area of the square. Then, write an expression that represents the area of the square subtracted from the area of the rectangle.

For more help with the area of a rectangle, see page 156.

---

5 A circle has a circumference of 20 inches and a diameter of d inches. Which equation below could be used to find the diameter, in inches, of the circle? (6AF3.1) **B**

A $d = 20 - \pi$ **C** $d = 20 \times \pi$

B $d = \frac{20}{\pi}$ **D** $d = \frac{\pi}{20}$

> **READING HINT** The circumference of a circle is found by using the formula $C = \pi d$.

In the equation $C = \pi d$, replace C with 20. Then solve the equation for d.

For more help with the circumference of a circle, see page 584.

---

6 The triangle below has a height of 15 meters and an area of 45 square meters. Which equation below could be used to find the length of the base b of the triangle? (6AF3.2) **F**

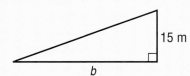

F $45 = \frac{15b}{2}$ **H** $45 = 15b$

G $15 = \frac{45b}{2}$ **J** $15 = 45b$

> **STRATEGY** Notice that you do not need to solve the equation for b.

Replace A with 45 and h with 15 in the equation, $A = \frac{1}{2}bh$.

For more help with the area of a triangle, see page 578.

Practice on Your Own

7 A clock has a radius of 5 inches. Which expression could be used to find the circumference of the clock? (6AF3.1) **B**

A 5π

B 10π

C 25π

D $\dfrac{5}{\pi}$

8 Which equation could be used to find the area of a circle with a diameter of 6 centimeters? (6AF3.1) **H**

F $A = 6^2 \times \pi$

G $A = 6 \times \pi$

H $A = 3^2 \times \pi$

J $A = 12 \times \pi$

9 The rectangle below has a length of 7 inches and a width of x inches. The square has side lengths of 3 inches. Which is an expression for the area of shaded region? (6AF3.2) **C**

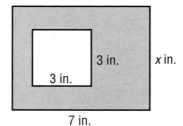

3 in.

3 in.

x in.

7 in.

A $7 + x + 9$

B $23 + 2x$

C $7x - 9$

D $7x + 9$

10 Bryn has a water wheel in her backyard. It has a diameter of d feet. Which expression can be used to find its circumference, C, in feet? (6AF3.1) **F**

F πd

G $\dfrac{\pi d}{2}$

H $2\pi d$

J πd^2

11 Which of the following expressions represents the area in square yards of the triangle shown below? (6AF3.2) **C**

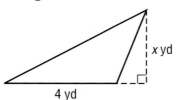

x yd

4 yd

A $8x$

B $4x$

C $2x$

D $4x^2$

12 Which of the following expressions gives the perimeter of a rectangle whose length is three times its width, w? (6AF3.2) **G**

F $5w$

G $8w$

H $3 + w$

J $3w^2$

Practice by Standard: Measurement and Geometry

Standard Set 1.0: Students deepen their understanding of measurement of plane and solid shapes and use this understanding to solve problems.

DIRECTIONS
Choose the best answer.

QUICK**Practice**	QUICK**Review**
1 Marcy has a circular swimming pool in her backyard with a diameter of 15 feet. Which measure is the *closest* to the length of the circumference of the pool? (6MG1.1) **D**	**STRATEGY** The circumference of a circle is found by using the formula $C = \pi \times d$. Replace d with 15 and multiply by π. For more help with the circumference of a circle, see page 584.
A 24 feet **C** 45 feet **B** 40 feet **D** 47 feet	
2 Mavis is filling the cylinder shown below with water. What is the closest estimate to the volume of the cylinder? (6MG1.2) **H** 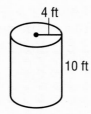 4 ft 10 ft	**STRATEGY** The volume of a cylinder is found by multiplying the area of the base by the height. Since the base is a circle, the area of the base is found by using the formula $A = \pi r^2$. Replace r with 4 and multiply by π. Then multiply the area of the base by the height. For more help with the volume of a cylinder, see page 619.

F 46 cubic feet
   G 80 cubic feet
   H 480 cubic feet
   J 2,010 cubic feet	

3 Which fraction is closest to the value of π? (6MG1.2) **B**	**READING HINT** The decimal approximation for π is 3.14. Which fraction is closest to 3.14? For more help with common estimates of π, see page 584.
A $\frac{21}{7}$ **C** $\frac{7}{21}$ **B** $\frac{22}{7}$ **D** $\frac{7}{22}$	

QUICKPractice

QUICKReview

4 Which of the following formulas would give the area of the circular tabletop shown? (6MG1.1) **G**

F $A = \pi \times d$

G $A = \pi \times r^2$

H $A = \pi \times d^2$

J $A = 2 \times \pi \times r$

▶**STRATEGY** It is helpful to memorize common formulas.

The area of a circle is found by using the formula $A = \pi r^2$.

For more help with the area of a circle, see page 589.

5 Ariel is filling the sand box shown below with sand. What is the volume of the sand box? (6MG1.3) **B**

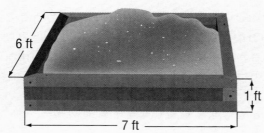

6 ft

1 ft

7 ft

A 21 cubic feet

C 84 cubic feet

B 42 cubic feet

D 168 cubic feet

▶**STRATEGY** The sandbox is in the shape of a rectangular prism.

The volume of a rectangular prism is found by multiplying the area of the base by the height of the prism. Since the base is a rectangle, this is the same as multiplying the length by the width of the prism and then multiplying this product by the height of the prism.

For more help with finding the volume of a rectangular prism, see page 613.

6 In the formula for the circumference of a circle, $C = \pi \times d$, which of the following represents a constant? (6MG1.1) **G**

F C only

G π

H d only

J Both C and d are constants.

▶**READING HINT** A constant is a value that remains unchanged.

Both C and d are variables; they can represent the values for circumference and diameter, respectively. These values can change depending on the dimensions of the circle. The only value that remains unchanged is π.

For more help with the circumference of a circle, see page 584.

Practice on Your Own

7 Which value below is the best estimate for the area of the circle shown below? (6MG1.2)

C

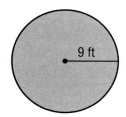

9 ft

A 28 square feet

B 57 square feet

C 254 square feet

D 486 square feet

8 Which of the following statements is true concerning the formulas for the area and circumference of a circle? (6MG1.1) **G**

F The area of a circle is found by multiplying the radius by π.

G In both formulas, π is a constant.

H The circumference of a circle is found by multiplying the diameter by its radius.

J The circumference of a circle is found by multiplying the radius by π.

9 Which of the following formulas would give the area in square centimeters of the circle shown below? (6MG1.1) **C**

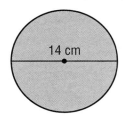

14 cm

A $A = \pi \times 7$

B $A = \pi \times 14$

C $A = \pi \times 7^2$

D $A = \pi \times 14^2$

10 Which of the following equations gives the circumference in meters of a circle with a diameter of 10 meters? (6MG1.1) **G**

F $C = \pi \times 5$

G $C = \pi \times 10$

H $C = \pi \times 5^2$

J $C = \pi \times 10^2$

11 Which of the following expressions gives the area in square centimeters of a circle with a radius of 2 centimeters? (6MG1.2) **A**

A 4π

B 2π

C 8π

D 12π

12 How do the volumes of the two prisms below compare? (6MG1.3) **G**

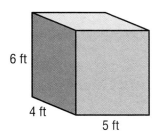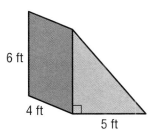

6 ft   6 ft

4 ft   4 ft

5 ft   5 ft

F The rectangular prism has a volume that is 4 times the volume of the triangular prism.

G The rectangular prism has a volume that is 2 times the volume of the triangular prism.

H The rectangular prism has a volume that is $\frac{1}{2}$ times the volume of the triangular prism.

J The rectangular prism has a volume that is $\frac{1}{4}$ times the volume of the triangular prism.

Practice by Standard: Measurement and Geometry

Standard Set 2.0: Students identify and describe the properties of two-dimensional figures.

DIRECTIONS

Choose the best answer.

QUICK Practice

1 Which is a true statement about angles 1 and 2 shown below? (6MG2.1) **A**

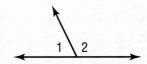

- **A** ∠1 is adjacent to ∠2.
- **B** ∠1 is complementary to ∠2.
- **C** Both angles are obtuse.
- **D** Both angles are acute.

2 What is the value of x in the triangle below? (6MG2.2) **G**

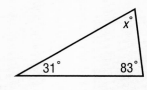

- **F** 60
- **G** 66
- **H** 86
- **J** 246

3 A walkway is built from one corner of a garden to the opposite corner as shown. What is the value of m? (6MG2.2) **A**

- **A** 36°
- **B** 45°
- **C** 54°
- **D** 126°

QUICK Review

> **STRATEGY** Look at the terms listed. Define the ones that you know and eliminate any choices that are unreasonable.

When two angles share a common vertex, a common side, and do not overlap, they are adjacent angles.

For more help with identifying angles, see pages 510 and 514.

> **READING HINT** The sum of the measures of the angles of a triangle is equal to 180 degrees.

Solve the equation $83° + 31° + x° = 180°$ for x.

For more help with the sum of the measures of the angles of a triangle, see page 524.

> **STRATEGY** Think: Which answers can you eliminate because they are not reasonable?

Solve the equation $54° + m° = 90°$, to find the value of m.

For more help with complementary angles, see page 514.

QUICK Practice

4 Which drawing below is a right isosceles triangle? (6MG2.3) **G**

F

G

H

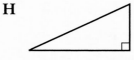

J

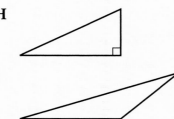

QUICK Review

▶ **READING HINT** An isosceles triangle has at least two congruent sides, and a right triangle has one right angle.

The only triangle shown that has at least two congruent sides and one right angle is the triangle shown in answer choice G.

For more help with classifying triangles, see page 524.

---

5 Angles R and S are supplementary. If $m\angle R = 68°$, what is $m\angle S$? (6MG2.2) **C**

A 22°   C 112°

B 32°   D 292°

▶ **READING HINT** Two angles are supplementary if the sum of their measures is equal to 180 degrees.

Solve the equation $68° + m\angle S = 180°$ for $m\angle S$.

For more help with the supplementary angles, see page 514.

---

6 In the figure below $\overleftrightarrow{AD}$ intersects $\overleftrightarrow{BE}$ at F, $m\angle AFB = 70°$, and $\angle CFD \cong \angle EFD$. What is $m\angle BFC$? (6MG2.2) **J**

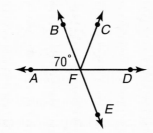

F 170°   H 110°

G 140°   J 40°

▶ **READING HINT** The symbol $\cong$ means *is congruent to.*

You know $m\angle AFB = 70°$. Use the fact that vertical angles are congruent to find $m\angle EFD$. Since $\angle CFD \cong \angle EFD$, they have the same measure, 70°. Use the fact that $m\angle AFB + m\angle BFC + m\angle CFD = 180°$ to find $m\angle BFC$ given that you know $m\angle AFB = m\angle CFD = 70°$.

For more help with finding an unknown angle, see page 514.

Practice by Standard: Measurement and Geometry **CA23**

Practice on Your Own

7 Which pair of angles below are supplementary? (6MG2.1) **A**

A

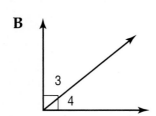

B

C

D

8 In the figure below $\overleftrightarrow{MN}$ intersects $\overleftrightarrow{XY}$ at W, $m\angle YWN = 40°$, and $\angle ZWY \cong \angle MWZ$. What is $m\angle ZWY$? (6MG2.2) **G**

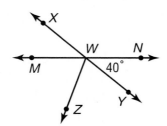

F 40°

G 70°

H 140°

J 180°

9 Which drawing below is a parallelogram with 4 congruent sides and no right angles? (6MG2.3) **C**

A

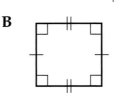

B

C

D

10 Angles XYZ and RST are complementary. If $m\angle XYZ = 34°$, what is the measure of angle RST? (6MG2.2) **G**

F 146°   **H** 32°

G 56°   **J** 23°

11 Corey drew two angles, x and y, as shown below. What must be the relationship between these two angles? (6MG2.1) **C**

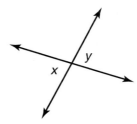

A $\angle x$ and $\angle y$ are complementary.

B $\angle x$ and $\angle y$ are supplementary.

C $\angle x$ and $\angle y$ are are vertical angles.

D $\angle x$ and $\angle y$ are are adjacent angles.

Practice by Standard: Statistics, Data Analysis, and Probability

Standard Set 1.0: Students compute and analyze statistical measurements for data sets.

DIRECTIONS
Choose the best answer.

QUICKPractice

1 The table shows the number of pages that Theo read each day for a week. What is the mean number of pages that he read? (6SDAP1.1) **C**

Day	Pages Read
Monday	7
Tuesday	12
Wednesday	12
Thursday	6
Friday	5
Saturday	10
Sunday	4

A 6   **C** 8

B 7   **D** 12

2 The line plot shows the number of gold medals won by each country participating in the 2006 Winter Olympic games. What is the mode of this data? (6SDAP1.1) **F**

2006 Winter Olympics Gold Medals Won

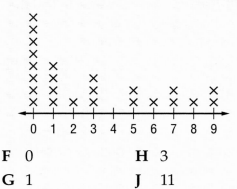

F 0   **H** 3

G 1   **J** 11

QUICKReview

> **READING HINT** The mean of a set of data is the sum of the data divided by the number of items in the data set.

To find the mean, first find the sum of the data. Then divide the sum by 7, the number of items in the data set.

For more help with finding the mean, see page 402.

> **READING HINT** The mode of a set of data is the number or numbers that occur most often.

Look for the number that occurs most often. On the line plot, the value 0 occurs most often.

For more help with finding the mode, see page 402.

QUICKPractice

QUICKReview

3 The following table shows the scores that students received on Mr. Hill's science quiz.

Quiz Scores									
10	6	9	5	10	9	7	8	3	8

How would the range of the above data set change if a score of 2 was added? (6SDAP1.2) **A**

A The range would increase.

B The range would decrease.

C The range would stay the same.

D There is not enough information.

> **READING HINT** The range of a data set is the difference between the greatest and least values in the data set.

Since 2 is lower than the lowest value of the original data set, the range would increase.

range of original data set : $10 - 3$, or 7

range when a score of 2 is added: $10 - 2$, or 8

Since $8 > 7$, the range would increase.

For more help with understanding how additional data values affect the range, see page 396.

---

4 In the data set below, how would the median be affected if the outlier was excluded? (6SDAP1.3) **F**

$$1, 14, 16, 18, 13, 11, 15, 16$$

F The median would increase.

G The median would decrease.

H The median would stay the same.

J There is not enough information.

> **READING HINT** Outliers are data points that are quite separated from the rest of the data points.

First, find the median of the original data set by writing the numbers in order from least to greatest and finding the middle number. Then repeat this process with the outlier, 1, excluded from the data set. Compare the two medians.

For more help with understanding how the exclusion of outliers affect the median, see page 410.

---

5 Luisa has scores of 85, 78, 95, and 100 on four of her math tests. How would a score of 65 on her fifth test affect the mean of her previous test scores? (6SDAP1.2) **B**

A The mean would increase.

B The mean would decrease.

C The mean would stay the same.

D There is not enough information.

> **READING HINT** You are not asked to find the mean. It is not necessary to perform any calculations to solve this problem.

Since a score of 65 is lower than any of her first four test scores, the mean would decrease.

For more help with understanding how additional data values affect the mean, see page 402.

Practice on Your Own

6 Lizzie recorded the number of T-shirts that her boutique sold each day for 10 days. What is the median of the data set? (6SDAP1.1) **G**

6, 7, 20, 16, 10, 25, 14, 18, 2, 24

F 14.2 **H** 16

G 15 **J** There is no median.

7 What is the mode of the data set below? (6SDAP1.1) **B**

Number Of TVs per Household

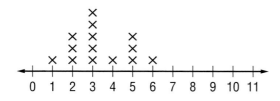

A 1 **C** 5

B 3 **D** 6

8 Chet's batting averages are 0.287, 0.216, 0.167, 0.287, and 0.325.

If an average of 0.344 is added to this list, then which of the following is true? (6SDAP1.2)

F The mean would increase. **F**

G The mean would decrease.

H The median would decrease.

J The mode would increase.

9 How would the mode of the data set below be affected if the outlier was removed? (6SDAP1.3) **C**

High Temperatures (°F)					
85	84	85	78	74	85
74	82	84	85	101	80

A The mode would increase.

B The mode would decrease.

C The mode would remain unchanged.

D There is not enough information.

10 Hector priced the cost of a movie ticket at five theaters in his hometown. How does the outlier affect the mean of the data set? (6SDAP1.3) **G**

Movie Ticket Prices				
$8.50	$7.50	$1.00	$8.25	$8.00

F The mean would be less if the outlier was excluded.

G The mean would be greater if the outlier was excluded.

H The mean would remain unchanged if the outlier was excluded.

J There is not enough information.

11 The hourly wages of several employees at a department store are listed below. Suppose the wages $7.50, $8.75, and $12.00 are added to this set. How does the additional data affect the median of the new data set? (6SDAP1.2) **B**

Department Store Wages				
$8.25	$10.00	$15.25	$18.75	$9.25
$9.00	$9.50	$9.50	$10.25	$11.25

A The median would increase.

B The median would decrease.

C The median would stay the same.

D There is not enough information.

12 Julian priced eight DVDs. The prices are shown below.

DVD Prices							
$20	$20	$23	$24	$21	$26	$22	$23

What is the range of these prices? (6SDAP1.1)

F 26 **H**

G 20

H 6

J 4

Practice by Standard: Statistics, Data Analysis, and Probability

Standard Set 2.0: Students use data samples of a population and describe the characteristics and limitations of samples.

DIRECTIONS
Choose the best answer.

QUICKPractice

1 The student council wants to determine the student body's favorite sport. They decide to survey the basketball team. What type of sampling is this? (6SDAP2.2) **B**

  A random sampling

  B convenience sampling

  C voluntary response sampling

  D none of the above

2 The table shows the income made by Rollie's Music in one week.

Day of The Week	Income
Monday	$525
Tuesday	$850
Wednesday	$325
Thursday	$380
Friday	$975

Which statement is valid about the income of the store? (6SDAP2.5) **H**

  F There were no days with an income less than $400.

  G Friday's income was more than $600 greater than Thursday's.

  H There was no day that had over $1,000 in income.

  J The combined income of Wednesday and Thursday was greater than $900.

QUICKReview

READING HINT Convenience sampling can occur when sampling is not taken randomly.

The survey is a convenience sample since it includes members of a population that are easily accessed; i.e., the members of the basketball team.

For more help with types of sampling, see page 438.

READING HINT You are looking for only one valid conclusion.

Check each answer choice to see if it is valid.

For more help with identifying valid claims, see page 438.

QUICKPractice

QUICKReview

3 Which sample below is *not* random? (6SDAP2.2) **A**

A To determine the favorite dessert of a community, 250 people at the local ice cream parlor are surveyed.

B To determine the favorite sport of the sixth grade class, every 10th student in an alphabetical list is surveyed.

C To determine whether the community should build a swimming pool, every 25th person in the phone book is surveyed.

D To determine whether the high school should get a water polo team, two students from every homeroom are surveyed.

READING HINT You are looking for a sample that is *not* random. Recall that in a random sample, each member of the population has an equal chance of being selected.

Check each answer choice to determine if it is a random sample. Select the answer choice that is *not* random.

For more help with random sampling, see page 438.

4 Carlos is trying to decide which sandwich to add to his sandwich shop menu. Which of the following methods is the *best* way for him to choose a random sample of his customers to survey? (6SDAP2.2) **G**

F Survey every customer who orders a combo meal at lunch time.

G Survey every 10th customer who enters the sandwich shop for one week.

H Survey every customer who orders a turkey sandwich.

J Give his customers a telephone survey response card.

STRATEGY You are looking for the *best* way to choose a random sample.

Eliminate answer choice F because people's preferences at lunch time may be different than at other times of the day.

Eliminate answer choice H because people that order turkey sandwiches probably already prefer turkey.

Eliminate answer choice J because everyone may not respond to a phone survey.

For more help with random sampling, see page 438.

Practice on Your Own

5 Marcus wants to find what type of pizza is preferred by most students at his school. Which of the following is the best method of choosing a random sample of the students in his school? (6SDAP2.2) **C**

A selecting all the students on his bus

B selecting all the students in his math class

C selecting 8 students from each third period class

D selecting students that like the same kind of pizza as Marcus

6 Lily wants to predict who will win the local Mayoral election. Which of the following is the best method of choosing a random sample that could predict which candidate might be elected? (6SDAP2.2) **F**

F selecting every 20th person in the phone book

G selecting the first 50 customers at Lily's favorite restaurant

H selecting the teachers at her school

J selecting her parents' friends

7 Eliot surveyed his sixth grade class to determine their favorite subject.

Subject	Percent of Sixth Grade Students
Math	35%
English	25%
Science	20%
Spanish	20%

Which statement is a valid conclusion based on the survey results? (6SDAP2.5) **C**

A English is the favorite subject.

B Math is the least favorite subject.

C Math is the favorite subject.

D Science is the least favorite subject.

8 Mr. Carter surveyed the students in his third period science class to determine their favorite food. The following table shows the results of the survey.

Favorite Food	Number of Students
Pizza	12
Hamburgers	6
Tacos	8
Spaghetti	5
Chinese	2

Which of the following claims is valid based upon this survey? (6SDAP2.5) **J**

F More students chose pizza as their favorite food than tacos and spaghetti combined.

G The number of students that chose spaghetti was the same as the number of students that chose tacos.

H Ten times as many students chose pizza as their favorite food as Chinese.

J Twice as many students selected pizza as their favorite food as hamburgers.

9 Carson wants to survey the students at his middle school to determine how many hours they spend on homework each weeknight. Which of the following methods would be the best way to generate a random sample? (6SDAP2.2) **C**

A Every student is asked to visit a website to complete a survey.

B A questionnaire is handed out to all students taking Spanish.

C Two people from each homeroom are surveyed.

D Randomly selected parents at a parent meeting are surveyed.

Practice by Standard: Statistics, Data Analysis, and Probability

Standard Set 3.0: Students determine theoretical and experimental probabilities and use these to make predictions about events.

DIRECTIONS
Choose the best answer.

*QUICK*Practice

1 What is the probability that a number cube will turn up a 5 or a 6 when it is rolled? (6SDAP3.3) **D**

   A $\frac{5}{6}$ **C** $\frac{1}{2}$

   B $\frac{2}{3}$ **D** $\frac{1}{3}$

*QUICK*Review

> **READING HINT** A number cube has 6 faces. The probability that any one face will turn up is $\frac{1}{6}$.

The probability that either a 5 or a 6 will turn up is $\frac{2}{6}$, or $\frac{1}{3}$.

For more help with theoretical probability, see page 486.

---

2 Claudio has 2 different shirts, green and yellow, and 2 different pairs of pants, blue and black, to wear to work. What is the probability that he will wear the green shirt and the black pants if he is equally likely to select any shirt-pants combination? (6SDAP3.1) **G**

   F 15%   **H** 50%

   G 25%   **J** 75%

> **STRATEGY** Make an organized list of all possible outcomes.

You can draw a tree diagram or make a table to find the probability. There are 2 choices for the shirt and 2 choices for the pair of pants for a total of 2 × 2, or 4 combinations. One outcome is favorable, so the probability is $\frac{1}{4}$, or 25%.

For more help with finding probabilities, see page 471.

---

3 To win at a carnival booth, the spinner below is spun. What is the probability that the spinner does *not* land on red? (6SDAP3.3) **C**

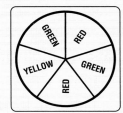

   A 20%   **C** 60%

   B 40%   **D** 80%

> **STRATEGY** **Think:** Which answers can you eliminate because they are not reasonable?

The question asks for the probability that the spinner does *not* land on red. The probability that the spinner lands on green or yellow is $\frac{3}{5}$.

For more help with finding the probability of an event *not* occurring, see page 460.

QUICKPractice

4 Xavier will choose one item from each of the following lists. (6SDAP3.1) **J**

Frozen Yogurt
chocolate
strawberry
vanilla

Cone
sugar
waffle

Which set shows *all* the possible choices of frozen yogurt and cone?

F {(chocolate, strawberry, vanilla)}

G {(chocolate, sugar), (chocolate, waffle)}

H {(chocolate, sugar), (strawberry, waffle), (vanilla, sugar)}

J {(chocolate, sugar), (chocolate, waffle), (strawberry, sugar), (strawberry, waffle), (vanilla, sugar), (vanilla, waffle)}

5 Which of the following are two dependent events? (6SDAP3.5) **A**

A choosing a book from a bookshelf, not replacing it, and then choosing a second book from the same shelf

B rolling 2 number cubes

C spinning a spinner twice

D tossing a coin three times

6 A number cube is rolled and a coin is tossed. What is the probability that a multiple of 3 will be rolled and tails will be tossed? (6SDAP3.4) **J**

F $\frac{3}{8}$ **H** $\frac{1}{5}$

G $\frac{2}{5}$ **J** $\frac{1}{6}$

QUICKReview

READING HINT The items in this set are listed as ordered pairs inside braces { }.

Read through the answer choices. You are looking for an answer choice where each element in the frozen yogurt list is paired with each element in the cone list.

For more help with listing the sample space, see page 465.

READING HINT Dependent events are events in which the outcome of one affects the outcome of the other.

Read through the answer choices. You are looking for an answer choice where the first event affects the second event.

For more help with dependent events, see page 492.

READING HINT The probability of one event following another, in independent trials, is the product of the two individual probabilities.

The probability that a multiple of 3 will turn up is $\frac{2}{6}$, or $\frac{1}{3}$. Multiply this by $\frac{1}{2}$, the probability that tails will turn up on the coin.

For more help with disjoint events, see page 492.

Practice on Your Own

7 Andrés is choosing colors for his new car. He has three choices for the exterior, red, blue, or white and two choices for the interior, black or brown. Which tree diagram represents all of his choices? (6SDAP3.1) **B**

A
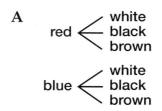

B
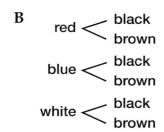

C
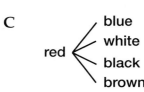

D   red — brown
    blue — brown
  white — brown
  black — brown

8 Sam's Sandwich Shop offers a variety of sandwiches. You can choose one type of meat from turkey, ham, or roast beef, one kind of cheese from American or Provolone, and then either sourdough or wheat bread. How many choices does each customer have if they must select a meat, a cheese, and a type of bread? (6SDAP3.1) **H**

  F 6
  G 7
  H 12
  J 24

9 Which of the following are independent events? (6SDAP3.5) **D**

  A choosing two coins from a purse without replacing the first coin

  B choosing a pizza topping and then choosing a second pizza topping that is different from the first topping

  C choosing a shirt to wear on Sunday and then choosing a different shirt to wear on Monday

  D choosing a CD from a collection of 5 CDs and then choosing a DVD from a collection of 15 DVDs

10 What is the approximate probability of the spinner below landing on either red or blue? (6SDAP3.3) **H**

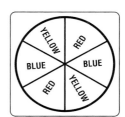

  F 25%
  G 40%
  H 67%
  J 75%

12 There are 125 sixth grade students at Belgrade Intermediate School. 62 of these are girls. If a student is chosen at random, what is the probability that the student is *not* a girl? (6SDAP3.3) **B**

  A $\frac{62}{125}$

  B $\frac{63}{125}$

  C $\frac{62}{63}$

  D $\frac{63}{62}$

Practice by Standard: Mathematical Reasoning

Standard Set 1.0: Students make decisions about how to approach problems.

DIRECTIONS
Choose the best answer.

QUICK Practice | QUICK Review

1 Which is a correct first step to solve the equation $-4 + 9x = -49$ for x? (6MR1.3, 6AF1.1) **C**

  A Divide each side by 9.

  B Add -4 to each side.

  C Add 4 to each side.

  D Multiply each side by 9.

> **STRATEGY** Recall that to solve a two-step equation, you must undo the operations in reverse order of the order of operations.
>
> To work backward, first subtract -4 from each side of the equation. To subtract -4, add positive 4.
>
> For more help with solving two-step equations, see page 151.

---

2 On Tuesday, a gas station charged $24.56 for 8 gallons of gasoline. At this rate, which conjecture below is valid concerning the cost of g gallons of gasoline? (6MR1.2, 6AF2.3) **J**

  F The cost of g gallons is $24.56g$.

  G The cost of g gallons is $8.00g$.

  H The cost of g gallons is $3.70g$.

  J The cost of g gallons is $3.07g$.

> **STRATEGY** **Think:** Which answers can you eliminate because they are not reasonable?
>
> You can find the cost per gallon by dividing the cost of 8 gallons, $24.56, by the number of gallons, 8.
>
> For more help with unit rates, see page 287.

---

3 Two quantities x and y are related in the following way.

x	y
4	12
7	21
11	33
14	42

Identify the relationship between x and y. (6MR1.1, 6AF1.2) **A**

  A $y = 3x$ **C** $x = 3y$

  B $y = x + 8$ **D** $y = 3 + x$

> **STRATEGY** Check each row in the table to make sure that the pattern continues. By considering only the first row, either answer choice A or B would be appropriate.
>
> Observe the pattern in the table. Notice that each y-coordinate is found by multiplying its corresponding x-coordinate by 3. This relationship can be represented by the equation $y = 3x$.
>
> For more help with identifying relationships from a table, see page 63.

Practice on Your Own

4 If the pattern below continues, what will be the next number? (6MR1.1, 6NS2.0) **H**

5, 10, 15, ?

F 10   **H** 20

G 15   **J** 30

5 Consider the following problem.

> A plane flew from New York to Los Angeles at 450 miles per hour. On the return flight, it flew at 410 miles per hour. If the return trip took 5 hours and 58 minutes, what was the distance traveled?

Identify the irrelevant information in the problem. (6MR1.1, 6AF2.3) **A**

A the rate at which the plane flew from New York to Los Angeles

B the rate at which the plane flew from Los Angeles to New York

C the length of time of the return flight

D the distance between New York and Los Angeles

6 Which expression can be used to find the area in square yards of the complex figure below? (6MR1.3, 6AF1.4) **F**

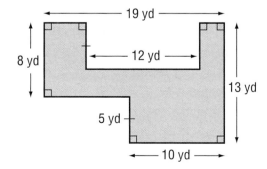

F $(19 \times 13) - (9 \times 5) - (12 \times 5)$

G $(10 \times 5) + (8 \times 5) + (12 \times 13)$

H $(13 \times 10) + (19 \times 8) - (12 \times 5)$

J $(19 \times 13) - (8 \times 5) - (12 \times 8)$

7 Carla is twice as old as her younger sister, Emilia. Emilia's age is $\frac{1}{3}$ that of her older brother, Lucas. Lucas is half the age of their father, Pedro. To find all of their ages, which of the following could you find first, given that you know Pedro's age? (6MR1.3, 6NS2.0) **B**

A Emilia's age

B Lucas' age

C Carla's age

D the sum of Carla's and Emilia's ages

8 A coin was tossed 6 times and each time, it turned up heads. Which of the following statements below is valid concerning the probability that the coin will turn up heads on the 7th time it is tossed? (6MR1.2, 6SDAP3.3) **G**

F The probability is 0.

G The probability is $\frac{1}{2}$.

H The probability is $\frac{20}{21}$.

J The probability is 1.

9 A light bulb manufacturer determines that 0.025 of the bulbs produced are defective. Which conjecture below is valid concerning the number of defective light bulbs in a batch of 280 light bulbs produced? (6MR1.2, 6SDAP3.2) **A**

A About 7 light bulbs are expected to be defective.

B About 5 light bulbs are expected to be defective.

C About 3 light bulbs are expected to be defective.

D About 2 light bulbs are expected to be defective.

Practice by Standard: Mathematical Reasoning

Standard Set 2.0: Students use strategies, skills, and concepts in finding solutions.

DIRECTIONS
Choose the best answer.

QUICKPractice

1 The table below shows the scores of the students in Mrs. Meyer's Spanish class on their final exam.

95	88	72	91	80	65	85	77	66	96	90
74	86	72	81	92	93	70	80	68	72	84

Mrs. Meyer calculated that the mean of the scores was 70. Which of the following shows that her calculation is invalid? (6MR2.7, 6SDAP1.1) **C**

A No one scored below 70.

B The mode is 72, not 70.

C Most of the students have scores higher than the mean.

D Most of the students have scores lower than the mean.

QUICKReview

STRATEGY You do not have to calculate the mean in order to answer this problem.

You are looking for a true statement that shows that 70 cannot be the mean. Read through each answer choice, checking for its validity and how it shows that the Mrs. Meyer's calculation of the mean cannot be true.

For more help with calculating the mean of a data set, see page 402.

---

2 Which expression represents the perimeter in centimeters of the rectangle below? (6MR2.4, 6AF3.2) **F**

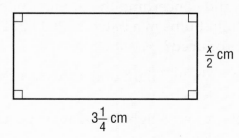

$\frac{x}{2}$ cm

$3\frac{1}{4}$ cm

F $6\frac{1}{2} + x$

G $6\frac{1}{2} + \frac{x}{2}$

H $3\frac{1}{4} + \frac{x}{2}$

J $6\frac{1}{2} + 2x$

READING HINT The perimeter of a rectangle is found by using the formula $P = 2\ell + 2w$.

Replace ℓ with $3\frac{1}{4}$ and w with $\frac{x}{2}$ in the formula for the perimeter of a rectangle. Then simplify the expression.

For more help with the perimeter of a rectangle, see page 156.

Practice on Your Own

3 Which of the following is true concerning the circumference in feet of the circle shown? (6MR2.6, 6AF3.1) **B**

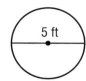
5 ft

A The exact circumference can be found by multiplying 3.14 by 5.

B The approximate circumference can be found by multiplying 3.14 by 5.

C The exact circumference can be found by multiplying $\frac{22}{7}$ by 5.

D The approximate circumference can be found by multiplying 3.14 by 10.

4 A caterer made 12 batches of muffins with 21 cups of flour. Which of the following proportions can be used to find x, the number of cups of flour needed to make 28 batches of muffins? (6MR2.5, 6NS1.3) **G**

F $\frac{12}{21} = \frac{x}{28}$

H $\frac{12}{28} = \frac{x}{21}$

G $\frac{12}{21} = \frac{28}{x}$

J $\frac{12}{x} = \frac{28}{21}$

5 Describe the relationship between x and y on the graph below. (6MR2.4, 6AF1.1) **A**

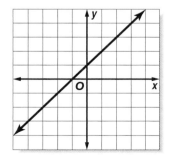

A Each y-coordinate is one unit greater than each x-coordinate.

B $y = x - 1$

C $y = x$

D $y = -x$

6 Parker can mow one lawn in 3.9 hours. He determined that it would take him 15.6 hours to mow 4 lawns. Which of the following verifies that his solution is reasonable? (6MR2.1, 6NS1.3) **F**

F $3.9 \times 4 \approx 4 \times 4$, or 16, and $15.6 \approx 16$

G $3.9 \times 4 \approx 3 \times 4$, or 12, and $12 \div 4 = 3$

H $15.6 - 3.9 \approx 16 - 4$, or 12, and $12 + 4 = 16$

J $3.9 + 4 \approx 4 + 4$, or 8, and $8 + 4 = 12$

7 Myra determines that there are 16 possible outcomes when a coin is tossed four times. Which of the following shows that her calculation is valid? (6MR2.7, 6SDAP3.1) **D**

A There are two possible outcomes for each toss and $2 \times 4 = 8$.

B There are two possible outcomes for each toss and $2 + 14 = 16$.

C There are two possible outcomes for each toss and $2 \times 16 = 32$.

D There are two possible outcomes for each toss and $2 \times 2 \times 2 \times 2 = 16$.

8 Which of the following equations can be used to find the area A in square inches of the regular octagon below? (6MR2.2, 6AF3.2) **G**

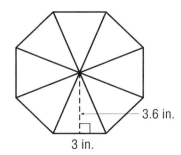
3.6 in.
3 in.

F $A = 3 \times 3.6 \times 8$

G $A = \frac{1}{2} \times 3 \times 3.6 \times 8$

H $A = \frac{1}{2} \times 3 \times 3.6$

J $A = \frac{1}{2} \times (3 + 3.6) \times 8$

Practice by Standard: Mathematical Reasoning

Standard Set 3.0: Students move beyond a particular problem by generalizing to other situations.

DIRECTIONS
Choose the best answer.

QUICKPractice

1 A diagonal drawn on a rectangle splits a rectangle into two congruent triangles. Using the formula for the area of a rectangle, which of the following would give the area of each triangle? (6MR3.2, 6AF3.2) **D**

A $A = \ell w + 2\ell w$

B $A = \ell w^2$

C $A = 2\ell w$

D $A = \frac{1}{2}\ell w$

2 The measures of several pairs of complementary angles are shown in the table.

m∠x	m∠y
31°	59°
72°	18°
47°	43°

Use the table to make a generalization about the measures of any two complementary angles x and y. (6MR3.3, 6MG2.1) **H**

F $m\angle x + m\angle y = 180°$

G $m\angle x - m\angle y = 90°$

H $m\angle x + m\angle y = 90°$

J $m\angle x + 90° = m\angle y$

QUICKReview

READING HINT Recall that the area of a rectangle can be found by using the formula $A = \ell w$.

Since the rectangle is split into two congruent triangles, the area of each triangle can be found by halving the area of the rectangle.

For more help with the area of a triangle, see page 578

STRATEGY Recall that the sum of the measures of complementary angles is 90°.

Use the definition of complementary angles to verify that the sum of each angle pair in the table is 90°. Then write an equation representing the sum of any two complementary angles x and y.

For more help with complementary angles, see page 514.

Practice on Your Own

3 Liseli read a 250-page book in 10 hours. Which of the following is a reasonable calculation for the number of hours it would take her to read a 325-page book at this rate? (6MR3.1, 6NS1.3) **C**

A 25

B 15

C 13

D 8

4 A circle with diameter *d* is inside a square with side length *d*, as shown. Which expression represents the area of the shaded region in terms of *d*? (6MR3.2, 6AF3.1) **H**

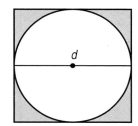

F $d^2 - (\pi \times d^2)$

G $d^2 - (\pi \times 2d^2)$

H $d^2 - [\pi \times (\frac{d}{2})^2]$

J $d^2 + (\pi \times \frac{1}{2}d^2)$

5 The parallelogram below is split into two congruent trapezoids.

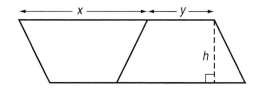

Which of the following represents the area of each trapezoid? (6MR3.2, 6AF3.2) **B**

A $A = \frac{1}{2}xyh$

B $A = \frac{1}{2}(x + y)h$

C $A = \frac{1}{2}(x + y + h)$

D $A = (x + y)h$

6 Alfonso decides to leave a 20% tip on a restaurant bill of $14.75. He determines that the tip should be about $5.00. Which of the following shows that his solution is *not* reasonable? (6MR3.1, 6NS1.4) **G**

F 20% of $14.75 ≈ $\frac{1}{3}$ of $15.00, or $5.00

G 20% of $14.75 ≈ $\frac{1}{5}$ of $15.00, or $3.00

H 20% of $14.75 ≈ $\frac{1}{2}$ of $15.00, or $7.50

J 20% of $14.75 ≈ $\frac{1}{4}$ of $15.00, or $3.75

7 The table shows the number of possible outcomes when a coin is tossed a certain number of times.

Number of Tosses	Number of Outcomes
1	2
2	4
3	8

Use the table to make a generalization about the number of possible outcomes *p* when a coin is tossed *m* times. (6MR3.3, 6SDAP3.1) **C**

A $p = m \times 2$

B $p = m^2$

C $p = 2^m$

D $p = m + m$

8 The sum of $\frac{3}{5}$ and $\frac{1}{5}$ is $\frac{4}{5}$, the sum of $\frac{2}{7}$ and $\frac{4}{7}$ is $\frac{6}{7}$, and the sum of $\frac{1}{11}$ and $\frac{5}{11}$ is $\frac{6}{11}$. Use this pattern to make a generalization about the sum of the fractions $\frac{a}{b}$ and $\frac{c}{b}$. (6MR3.2, 6NS2.1) **F**

F $\frac{a}{b} + \frac{c}{b} = \frac{a + c}{b}$

G $\frac{a}{b} + \frac{c}{b} = \frac{ac}{b}$

H $\frac{a}{b} + \frac{c}{b} = \frac{a + c}{b + b}$

J $\frac{a}{b} \times \frac{c}{d} = \frac{ac}{bd}$

Chapter Overview

Looking Ahead to Grade 7: Geometry and Measurement

Standards-Based Lesson Plan		Pacing Your Lessons	
LESSONS AND OBJECTIVES	California Standards	40–50 Minute Periods	90-Minute Periods
12-1 Estimating Square Roots (pp. 636–639) • Estimate square roots.	7NS2.4	2	1
12-2 The Pythagorean Theorem (pp. 640–645) • Find length using the Pythagorean Theorem.	7MG3.3	2	1
12-3 Problem–Solving Investigation: Make a Model (pp. 646–647) • Solve problems by making a model.	6MR2.4 6NS2.1	2	1
12-4 Surface Area of Rectangular Prisms (pp. 649–653) • Find the surface areas of rectangular prisms. **Extend 12-4 Measurement Lab: Changes in Volume and Surface Area** (pp. 654–655) • Investigate changes in volume and surface area.	7MG2.1 7MG2.4 6MR2.4 6AF3.2	2	1
12-5 Surface Area of Cylinders (pp. 656–659) • Find the surface areas of a cylinder.	7MG2.1	2	1
REVIEW		2	1
ASSESSMENT		1	1
TOTAL		13	7

*The complete **Assessment Planner** for Chapter 12 is provided on page 635.*

Professional Development

California Standards Vertical Alignment

Before Chapter 12

Related Topics from Grade 6

- Know and use the formulas of triangular prisms and cylinders from Standard 6MG1.3

Chapter 12

Topics from Grade 7

- For an integer that is not square, determine without a calculator the two integers between which its square root lies and explain why

- Know and understand the Pythagorean theorem and its converse and use it to find the length of the missing side of a right triangle and the lengths of other line segments and, in some situations, empirically verify the Pythagorean theorem by direct measurement ◄—

- Use formulas routinely for finding the surface area of basic three-dimensional figures, including prisms

See individual lessons for specific Standards covered.

After Chapter 12

Preparation for Grade 7

- Know and understand the Pythagorean theorem and its converse and use it to find the length of the missing side of a right triangle and the lengths of other line segments and, in some situations, empirically verify the Pythagorean theorem by direct measurement
  ◄— Standard 7MG3.3

- Students prove the Pythagorean Theorem ◄— StandardG14.0

- Compute the length of the perimeter, the surface area of the faces, and the volume of a three-dimensional object built from rectangular solids. Understand that when the lengths of all dimensions are multiplied by a scale factor, the surface area is multiplied by the square of the scale factor and the volume is multiplied by the cube of the scale factor Standard 7MG2.3

Preparation for Geometry

- Students prove the Pythagorean Theorem Standard G14.0

Back-Mapping

California Mathematics: *Concepts, Skills, Problem Solving* was conceived and developed with the final result in mind, student success in Algebra I and beyond. The authors, using the California Mathematics Standards as their guide, developed this brand-new series by "back-mapping" from the desired result of student success in Algebra I and beyond. McGraw-Hill's K-7 intervention program, *California Math Triumphs: Intensive Intervention* as well as *California Algebra 1, California Geometry, California Algebra 2,* and *California Algebra Readiness* were developed utilizing the same philosophy.

What the Research Says . . .

According to Lampert and Cobb in "Communication and Language," talking helps students move from concrete objects to related mathematics concepts. The process of coming to see concrete situations in mathematical terms is called *mathematizing*.

- In Lesson 12-3, a student is shown communicating her strategy of using a model to solve a problem. This is to encourage students to also discuss how to proceed from visual representations to mathematical solutions.

Mc Graw Hill Professional Development

Targeted professional development has been articulated throughout the *California Mathematics: Concepts, Skills, and Problem Solving* series. The **McGraw-Hill Professional Development Video Library** provides short videos that support the ◄— Key Standards. For more information, visit ca.gr6math.com.

| Model Lessons | Instructional Strategies |

Technology Solutions

Teacher Resources

TeacherWorks™ All-in-One Planner and Resource Center

All of the print materials from the Classroom Resource Masters are available on your TeacherWorks™ CD-ROM.

BL = Below Grade Level **OL** = On Grade Level **AL** = Above Grade Level **ELL** = English Language Learner

			Chapter Resource Masters	12-1	12-2	12-3	12-4	12-5
BL	**OL**	**ELL**	Lesson Reading Guide	9	16		26	32
BL	**OL**	**ELL**	Study Guide and Intervention*	10	17	22	27	33
BL	**OL**		Skills Practice*	11	18	23	28	34
	OL	**AL**	Practice*	12	19	24	29	35
	OL	**AL**	Word Problem Practice*	13	20	25	30	36
	OL	**AL**	Enrichment	14	21		31	37
	OL	**AL**	Calculator and Spreadsheet Activities	15				38
	OL	**AL**	Chapter Assessments*	39–60				
BL	**OL**	**AL**	5-Minute Check Transparencies	✓	✓	✓	✓	✓
BL	**OL**		Teaching Mathematics with Manipulatives				✓	

Also available in Spanish.

AssignmentWorks

Differentiated Assignments, Answers, and Solutions

- Print a customized assignment worksheet using the Student Edition exercises along with an answer key or worked-out solutions.
- Use default lesson assignments as outlined in the Differentiated Homework Options in the Teacher Wraparound Edition.
- Includes modified questions from the Student Edition for students with special needs.

Interactive Classroom

This CD-ROM is a customizable Microsoft® PowerPoint® presentation that includes:

- In-Class Examples
- Your Turn Exercises*
- 5-Minute Check Transparencies*
- Links to Online Study Tools
- Concepts in Motion

compatible with response pad technology

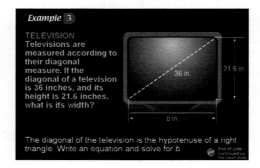

ExamView® Assessment Suite

- Create, edit, and customize tests and worksheets using QuickTest Wizard
- Create multiple versions of tests and modify them for a desired level of difficulty
- Translate from English to Spanish and vice versa
- Build tests aligned with your state standards
- Track students' progress using the Teacher Management System

Student Tools

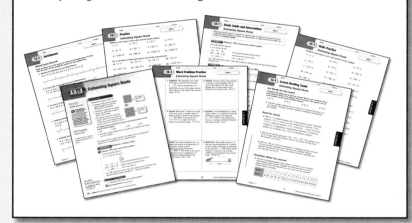
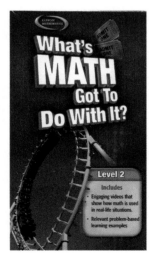
Internet Resources

Math Online ca.gr6math.com

TEACHER	STUDENT	PARENT	
			Online Study Tools
	●	●	Online Student Edition
●	●	●	Multilingual Glossary
			Lesson Resources
	●	●	BrainPOP®
●	●	●	Concepts in Motion
●	●	●	Extra Examples
●			Group Activity Cards
●			Problem of the Week Cards
	●	●	Other Calculator Keystrokes
	●	●	Reading in the Content Area
	●	●	Real-World Careers
	●	●	Self-Check Quizzes
			Chapter Resources
	●	●	Chapter Readiness
	●	●	Chapter Test
	●	●	Family Letters and Activities
	●	●	Standardized Test Practice
	●	●	Vocabulary Review/Chapter Review Activities
			Unit Resources
●	●		Cross-Curricular Internet Project
			Other Resources
●			Dinah Zike's Foldables
●	●		Game Zone Games and Recording Sheets
	●	●	Hotmath Homework Help
●			Key Concepts
●	●	●	Math Skills Maintenance
●	●	●	Meet the Authors
●			NAEP Correlations
	●	●	Personal Tutor
●			Project CRISS℠
	●	●	Scavenger Hunts and Answer Sheets
●			Vocabulary PuzzleMakers

Noteables™ Interactive Study Notebook with Foldables™

This workbook is a study organizer that provides helpful steps for students to follow to organize their notes for Chapter 12.

- Students use Noteables to record notes and to complete their Foldables as you present the material for each lesson.
- Noteables correspond to the Examples in the *Teacher Wraparound Edition* and *Interactive Classroom CD-ROM*.

READING in the Content Area

This online worksheet provides strategies for reading and analyzing Lesson 12-1, Estimating Square Roots. Students are guided through questions about the main idea, subject matter, supporting details, conclusion, clarifying details, and vocabulary of the lesson.

ca.gr6math.com

Recommended Outside Reading for Students

Mathematics and Activities

- *From Crystals to Kites: Exploring Three Dimensions* by Ron Kremer ©1997 [nonfiction]

In this activity book, students explore the properties of three-dimensional figures by building straw models, making kites with tetrahedrons, and finding the volume of prisms and pyramids.

Mathematics and Fantasy

- *Flatland A Romance of Many Dimensions* by Edwin Abbot ©2002 [fiction]

This short, classic fantasy novel takes the reader to a two-dimensional world occupied by geometric figures. When one such shape discovers the existence of a third dimension, the reader begins to understand how a fourth dimension, or beyond, might relate to our three-dimensional existence.

Project CRISS℠ STUDY SKILL

A comparison chart can help students understand mathematical relationships, especially when new formulas are being learned. The chart at the right shows a comparison of the formulas for the surface area of rectangular prisms and the surface area of cylinders. Students should note that the surface area of any three-dimensional figure is the sum of the areas of all of its surfaces. Have students draw a comparison chart or charts for other material as they read through Chapter 12. Then, allow time for a class discussion so students can compare charts and formulas.

Figure	Sketch	Surface Area Formula
rectangular prism		$S = 2\ell w + 2\ell h + 2wh$
cylinder		$S = 2\pi r^2 + 2\pi rh$

CReating **I**ndependence through **S**tudent-owned **S**trategies

Differentiated Instruction

Quick Review Math Handbook*

is Glencoe's mathematical handbook for students and parents.

Hot Words includes a glossary of terms.

Hot Topics consists of two parts:

- explanations of key mathematical concepts
- exercises to check students' understanding.

Lesson	Hot Topics Section	Lesson	Hot Topics Section
12-1	3•2	12-4	7•6, 7•7, 9•3
12-2	3•2, 7•9	12-5	7•6

Also available in Spanish

Teacher To Teacher

Sandy Gavin
Tieton Middle School
Tieton, WA

USE WITH LESSON 12-5

"I use empty toilet paper rolls to model the surface area of a cylinder. By cutting down the tube, I can open the tube to show that the surface area can be found by multiplying the circumference of the base by the height of the cylinder."

Intervention Options

Intensive Intervention

Math Triumphs can provide intensive intervention for students who are at risk of not meeting the California standards addressed in Chapter 12.

Diagnose student readiness with the Quick Check and Quick Review on page 635. Then use *Math Triumphs* to accelerate their achievement.

Algebra: Integers

Prerequisite Skill	*Math Triumphs*
Evaluate exponents 4NS4.1	Volume 1, Chapter 4
Evaluate algebraic expressions 6AF1.2	Volume 4, Chapter 3

See chart on page T24 for other *Math Triumphs* lessons that will support the prerequisite skills needed for success in *Glencoe California Mathematics, Grade 6*.

Strategic Intervention

For strategic intervention options, refer to the Diagnostic Assessment table on page 635.

FOLDABLES™ Study Organizer Dinah Zike's Foldables

Focus This Foldable is designed to help students organize their notes about surface area of three-dimensional figures.

Teach Have students make their Foldables and label the rows and columns. Explain to students that they should draw examples and record definitions, equations, and procedures in the cells of the table.

When to Use It

Column	Use with Lesson(s)
Rectangular Prisms	12-3, 12-4, Extend 12-4
Cylinders	12-5

A version of a completed Foldable is shown on p. 660.

Differentiated Instruction

CRM Student-Built Glossary, p. 1

Students complete the chart by providing the definition of each term and an example as they progress through Chapter 12.

This study tool can be used to review for the chapter test.

Materials Needed for Chapter 12
- algebra tiles (Lesson 12-1)
- grid paper (Lessons 12-2 and 12-5)
- scissors (Lessons 12-2, 12-3, and 12-5)
- cardboard (Lesson 12-3)
- masking tape (Lesson 12-3)
- centimeter cubes (Lesson 12-4)
- isometric dot paper (Extend 12-4)
- cans (Lesson 12-5)

CHAPTER 12 Looking Ahead to Grade 7: Geometry and Measurement

BIG Idea

- **Preparation for Standard 7MG3.3**
  Know the Pythagorean Theorem and deepen the understanding of plane and solid geometric shapes by constructing figures that meet given conditions and by identifying attributes of figures.

Key Vocabulary

hypotenuse (p. 640)

irrational number (p. 637)

Pythagorean Theorem (p. 640)

surface area (p. 650)

Real-World Link

SPAGHETTI The shape of many spaghetti boxes is a rectangular prism, and the shape of many cans is a cylinder. You can use the formula $S = 2lw + 2lh + 2wh$ to find the surface area of a box of spaghetti given the length *l*, the width *w*, and the height *h* of the box.

FOLDABLES™ Study Organizer

Geometry and Measurement Make this Foldable to help you organize your notes. Begin with a piece of 11" by 17" paper.

❶ **Fold** the paper in fourths lengthwise.

❷ **Open** and fold a 2" tab along the short side. Then fold the rest in half.

❸ **Draw** lines along the folds and label as shown.

GET READY for Chapter 12

Diagnose Readiness You have two options for checking Prerequisite Skills.

Option 1

Take the Quick Check below. Refer to the Quick Review for help.

Option 2

Math Online Take the Online Readiness Quiz at ca.gr6math.com.

QUICKCheck

(Used in Lessons 12-1 and 12-2)
Evaluate each expression. (Lesson 1-2)

1. 4^2 **16**
2. 7^2 **49**
3. 13^2 **169**
4. 24^2 **576**
5. $5^2 + 8^2$ **89**
6. $10^2 + 6^2$ **136**
7. $9^2 + 12^2$ **225**
8. $15^2 + 17^2$ **514**

9. **AGES** Samuel's mother is 7^2 years old, and his grandmother is 9^2 years old. Find the sum of their ages. (Lesson 1-2) **130 yr**

(Used in Lesson 12-4)
Evaluate the expression
$2ab + 2bc + 2ac$ **for each value of the variables indicated.** (Lesson 1-4)

10. $a = 4, b = 5, c = 8$ **184**
11. $a = 2, b = 7, c = 11$ **226**
12. $a = 3.1, b = 2.4, c = 9.9$ **123.78**
13. $a = 2.1, b = 1.7, c = 4.6$ **42.1**

(Used in Lesson 12-5)
Evaluate each expression below. Round to the nearest tenth. Use 3.14 for π. (Lesson 11-3)

14. $(2)(\pi)(3^2) + (2)(\pi)(3)(8)$ **207.2**
15. $(2)(\pi)(7^2) + (2)(\pi)(7)(5)$ **527.5**

QUICKReview

Example 1
Evaluate $3^2 + 5^2$.

$3^2 + 5^2 = 9 + 25$ Evaluate 3^2 and 5^2.
$ = 34$ Add 9 and 25.

Example 2
Evaluate the expression
$2ab + 2bc + 2ac$ for $a = 3, b = 5$, and $c = 6$.

$2ab + 2bc + 2ac$
$= 2(3)(5) + 2(5)(6) + 2(3)(6)$ Replace a with 3, b with 5, and c with 6.
$= 30 + 60 + 36$ Multiply.
$= 126$ Add.

Example 3
Evaluate $(2)(\pi)(4^2) + (2)(\pi)(4)(6)$. Round to the nearest tenth. Use 3.14 for π.

$(2)(\pi)(4^2) + (2)(\pi)(4)(6)$
$= (2)(\pi)(16) + (2)(\pi)(4)(6)$ Evaluate 4^2.
$= (32)(3.14) + (48)(3.14)$ Multiply.
≈ 251.2 Multiply and add.

Diagnostic Assessment

Exercises	California Standards	Strategic Intervention
1–9	6AF1.3; 6AF1.4	SE Review Lesson 1-4, pp. 38–41
10–13	6AF1.2; 6AF1.4	SE Review Lesson 1-6, pp. 44–47
14–15	6MG1.1; 6MG1.2	SE Review Lessons 11-3 and 11–4, pp. 584–593

✓ Formative Assessment

CRM Anticipation Guide, pp. 7–8
Spotting Preconceived Ideas
Students compete this survey to determine prior knowledge about ideas from Chapter 12. Revisit this worksheet after completing the chapter. Also see page 662.

TWE Lesson Activities

- Ticket Out the Door, pp. 639, 659
- Crystal Ball, p. 647
- Name the Math, p. 653
- Yesterday's News, p. 645

Chapter Checkpoints

SE Mid-Chapter Quiz, p. 648
SE Study Guide and Review, pp. 660–662
SE California Standards Practice, pp. 664–665
CRM Quizzes, pp. 41 and 42
CRM Standardized Test Practice, pp. 58–60

Math Online ca.gr6math.com

- Self-Check Quizzes
- Practice Test
- Standardized Test Practice

✓ Summative Assessment

SE Chapter Practice Test, p. 663
CRM Mid-Chapter Test, p. 43
CRM Vocabulary Test, p. 44
CRM Extended-Response Test, p. 57
CRM Leveled Chapter Tests, pp. 45–56
⊙ ExamView Pro® Assessment Suite

KEY

CRM *Chapter 12 Resource Masters*
SE Student Edition
TWE Teacher Wraparound Edition
⊙ CD-ROM

Estimating Square Roots

Preparation for Standard 7NS2.4

Use the inverse relationship between raising to a power and extracting the root of a perfect square; **for an integer that is not square, determine without a calculator the two integers between which its square root lies and explain why.**

PACING: **Regular:** 2 periods, **Block:** 1 period

Options for Differentiated Instruction

ELL = English Language Learner   **AL** = Above Grade Level   **SS** = Struggling Students   **SN** = Special Needs

Verbal Explanations **SN**

Use after presenting Example 1.

Write the following numbers on the board.

30   96

Have students explain in their own words how to estimate the square root of each number to the nearest whole number. Sample answer: 30 is between the perfect squares 25 and 36. Since 30 is closer to 25, $\sqrt{25} \approx 5$. 96 is between the perfect squares 81 and 100. Since 96 is closer to 100, $\sqrt{100} \approx 10$.

You may wish to write some numbers on small cards, place the cards in a bag, and have each student draw out a number. Have students explain how to estimate the square root of the number that they drew.

Verbal Representations **ELL** **AL** **SS** **SN**

Use after presenting Example 1.

Have each student make a number line with the numbers 1 through 10 evenly spaced above the line and the squares of 1 through 10 evenly spaced below the line, as shown below.

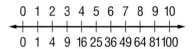

```
   0 1 2 3 4 5 6 7 8 9 10
  <+-+-+-+-+-+-+-+-+-+-+->
   0 1 4 9 16 25 36 49 64 81 100
```

Write a number between 1 and 100 on the board. Ask students to place the number in its approximate location below the number line and circle the closest square root to it. Repeat this using several different numbers.

Communication Understanding **ELL** **SS**

Use before assigning the Exercises.

Have students write in their own words the difference between rational and irrational numbers. Ask, "How can you look at a number and know what type of number it is?"

Have them give some examples of each type of number. Then have them exchange papers with a classmate to make sure that their explanations are clear and concise.

Chapter 12 Resource Masters

BL = Below Grade Level   **OL** = On Grade Level   **AL** = Above Grade Level   **ELL** = English Language Learner

---

Lesson Reading Guide
p. 9 **BL OL ELL**

NAME _____ DATE _____ PERIOD _____

12-1 Lesson Reading Guide   7NS2.4
Estimating Square Roots

Get Ready for the Lesson

Complete the Mini Lab at the top of page 636 in your textbook. Write your answers below. Use algebra tiles to estimate the square root of each number to the nearest whole number.

1. 40 6   2. 28 5   3. 85 9   4. 62 8

5. Describe another method that you could use to estimate the square root of a number. **Sample answer: square numbers using guess and check**

Read the Lesson

6. Why is $\sqrt{4}$ a rational number and $\sqrt{2}$ an irrational number? **Sample answer: $\sqrt{4} = 2$, and 2 can be written as a fraction: $\frac{2}{1}$. So, $\sqrt{4}$ is a rational number. $\sqrt{2} = 1.4142135...$, which is not an integer or a repeating or terminating decimal. It cannot be written as a fraction. So, $\sqrt{2}$ is an irrational number.**

7. How do you read the statement $\sqrt{64} < \sqrt{75} < \sqrt{81}$? **The square root of 64 is less than the square root of 75, which is less than the square root of 81.**

8. Why are $\sqrt{64}$ and $\sqrt{81}$ used in Example 1? **Sample answer: 64 and 81 are perfect squares, and they are the closest integer perfect squares to 75. They are used to find an estimate for the square root of 75.**

Remember What You Learned

9. The key to estimating square roots without a calculator is to be familiar with common perfect squares. Complete the following table of common perfect squares then test yourself to see how many you can remember without using a calculator.

Number	5	6	7	8	9	10	11	12	13	14	15	16	20	25
Square	25	36	49	64	81	100	121	144	169	196	225	256	400	625

Chapter 12   9   Glencoe California Mathematics, Grade 6

Study Guide and Intervention*
p. 10 **BL OL ELL**

NAME _____ DATE _____ PERIOD _____

12-1 Study Guide and Intervention   7NS2.4
Estimating Square Roots

Recall that a perfect square is a square of a rational number. In esson 5-8, you learned that any number that can be written as a fraction is a rational number. A number that cannot be written as a fraction is an irrational number.

Example 1 Estimate $\sqrt{40}$ to the nearest whole number.

List some perfect squares.
1, 4, 9, 16, 25, 36, 49, ...
$36 < 40 < 49$ 40 is between the perfect squares 36 and 49.
$\sqrt{36} < \sqrt{40} < \sqrt{49}$ Find the square root of each number.
$6 < \sqrt{40} < 7$ $\sqrt{36} = 6$ and $\sqrt{49} = 7$

So, $\sqrt{40}$ is between 6 and 7. Since 40 is closer to 36 than to 49, the best whole number estimate is 6.

Example 2 Use a calculator to find the value of $\sqrt{28}$ to the nearest tenth.

2nd √ 28 ENTER 5.291502622

$\sqrt{28} = 5.3$

Check Since $5^2 = 25$ and 25 is close to 28, the answer is reasonable.

Exercises

Estimate each square root to the nearest whole number.

1. $\sqrt{3}$ 2   2. $\sqrt{8}$ 3
3. $\sqrt{26}$ 5   4. $\sqrt{41}$ 6
5. $\sqrt{61}$ 8   6. $\sqrt{94}$ 10
7. $\sqrt{152}$ 12   8. $\sqrt{850}$ 29

Use a calculator to find each square root to the nearest tenth.

9. $\sqrt{2}$ 1.4   10. $\sqrt{27}$ 5.2
11. $\sqrt{73}$ 8.5   12. $\sqrt{82}$ 9.1
13. $\sqrt{105}$ 10.2   14. $\sqrt{395}$ 19.9
15. $\sqrt{846}$ 29.1   16. $\sqrt{2,298}$ 47.9

Chapter 12   10   Glencoe California Mathematics, Grade 6

Skills Practice*
p. 11 **BL OL**

NAME _____ DATE _____ PERIOD _____

12-1 Skills Practice   7NS2.4
Estimating Square Roots

Estimate each square root to the nearest whole number.

1. $\sqrt{5}$ 2   2. $\sqrt{10}$ 3   3. $\sqrt{21}$ 5
4. $\sqrt{28}$ 5   5. $\sqrt{78}$ 9   6. $\sqrt{102}$ 10
7. $\sqrt{179}$ 13   8. $\sqrt{274}$ 17   9. $\sqrt{303}$ 17
10. $\sqrt{563}$ 24   11. $\sqrt{592}$ 24   12. $\sqrt{755}$ 27
13. $\sqrt{981}$ 31   14. $\sqrt{1,356}$ 37   15. $\sqrt{1,688}$ 41
16. $\sqrt{3,287}$ 57   17. $\sqrt{3,985}$ 63   18. $\sqrt{4,125}$ 64

Use a calculator to find each square root to the nearest tenth.

19. $\sqrt{6}$ 2.4   20. $\sqrt{19}$ 4.4   21. $\sqrt{30}$ 5.5
22. $\sqrt{77}$ 8.8   23. $\sqrt{114}$ 10.7   24. $\sqrt{125}$ 11.2
25. $\sqrt{149}$ 12.2   26. $\sqrt{182}$ 13.5   27. $\sqrt{212}$ 14.6
28. $\sqrt{436}$ 20.9   29. $\sqrt{621}$ 24.9   30. $\sqrt{853}$ 29.2
31. $\sqrt{918}$ 30.3   32. $\sqrt{1,004}$ 31.7   33. $\sqrt{1,270}$ 35.6
34. $\sqrt{5,438}$ 73.7   35. $\sqrt{4,215}$ 64.9   36. $\sqrt{5,786}$ 76.1

37. Order $\frac{25}{7}$, 4.91, and $\sqrt{23}$ from least to greatest. $\frac{25}{7}$, $\sqrt{23}$, 4.91

38. Graph $\sqrt{42}$ and $\sqrt{62}$ on the same number line.

$\sqrt{42}$ $\sqrt{62}$
0 1 2 3 4 5 6 7 8

Chapter 12   11   Glencoe California Mathematics, Grade 6

Practice*
p. 12 **OL AL**

NAME _____ DATE _____ PERIOD _____

12-1 Practice   7NS2.4
Estimating Square Roots

Estimate each square root to the nearest whole number.

1. $\sqrt{8}$ 3   2. $\sqrt{19}$ 4   3. $\sqrt{47}$ 7   4. $\sqrt{70}$ 8
5. $\sqrt{91}$ 10   6. $\sqrt{125}$ 11   7. $\sqrt{150}$ 12   8. $\sqrt{389}$ 20
9. $\sqrt{2,468}$ 50   10. $\sqrt{899}$ 30   11. $\sqrt{4,840}$ 70   12. $\sqrt{8,080}$ 90

Use a calculator to find each square root to the nearest tenth.

13. $\sqrt{6}$ 2.4   14. $\sqrt{21}$ 4.6   15. $\sqrt{53}$ 7.3   16. $\sqrt{79}$ 8.9
17. $\sqrt{190}$ 13.8   18. $\sqrt{624}$ 25.0   19. $\sqrt{427}$ 20.7   20. $\sqrt{3,178}$ 56.4
21. $\sqrt{0.36}$ 0.6   22. $\sqrt{0.81}$ 0.9   23. $\sqrt{1.44}$ 1.2   24. $\sqrt{2.25}$ 1.5

25. **ALGEBRA** What whole number is closest to $\sqrt{a + b}$ if $a = 24$ and $b = 38$? 8

26. **ALGEBRA** Evaluate $\sqrt{x - y}$ to the nearest tenth if $x = 10$ and $y = 4.5$. 2.3

27. **QUILTING** A queen-size quilt in the shape of a square has an area of 51 square feet. What is the approximate length of one side of the quilt to the nearest tenth? 7.1 ft

28. **PENDULUM** The formula below can be used to estimate the time it takes for a pendulum to swing back and forth once. Use the formula to find the time it takes for a pendulum with a length of 0.8 meter to swing back and forth once. Round to the nearest tenth. 1.8 seconds

$$T = 2 \times \sqrt{L}$$
- T = time (seconds)
- L = length (meters)

Chapter 12   12   Glencoe California Mathematics, Grade 6

Word Problem Practice*
p. 13 **OL AL**

NAME _____ DATE _____ PERIOD _____

12-1 Word Problem Practice   7NS2.4
Estimating Square Roots

1. **GEOMETRY** The diameter d of a circle with area A is given by the formula $d = \sqrt{\frac{4A}{\pi}}$. What is the diameter of a circle with an area of 56 square inches? Use 3.14 for π and round to the nearest tenth. 8.4 in.

2. **FENCING** Carmen wants to buy fencing to enclose a square garden with an area of 500 square feet. How much fencing does Carmen need to buy? Round to the nearest tenth. 89.4 ft

3. **OCEANS** The speed v in feet per second of an ocean wave in shallow water of depth d in feet is given by the formula $v = \sqrt{32d}$. What is the speed of an ocean wave at a depth of 10 feet? 17.9 ft/s

4. **LIGHTING** A new flashlight has a beam whose width w at a distance d from the flashlight is given by the formula $w = 1.2\sqrt{d}$. What is the width of the beam at a distance of 30 feet? Round to the nearest tenth. 6.6 ft

5. **SOUND** The speed of sound in air c in meters per second at a temperature T in degrees Celsius is given approximately by the formula $c = \sqrt{402(T + 273)}$. What is the speed of sound in air at a temperature of 25 degrees Celsius? Round to the nearest tenth. 346.1 m/s

6. **PROJECTILES** The muzzle velocity v in feet per second necessary for a cannon to hit a target x feet away is estimated by the formula $v = \sqrt{32x}$. What muzzle velocity is required to hit a target 3,000 feet away? Round to the nearest tenth. 309.8 ft/s

3,000 ft

Chapter 12   13   Glencoe California Mathematics, Grade 6

Enrichment
p. 14 **OL AL**

NAME _____ DATE _____ PERIOD _____

12-1 Enrichment   7NS2.4

World Series Records

Each problem gives the name of a famous baseball player. To find who set each record, graph the points on the number line.

1. pitched 23 strikeouts in one World Series
U at $\sqrt{3}$, X at 3.3, K at 0.75, O at $\frac{9}{4}$, F at $\sqrt{6}$, A at $2\frac{7}{8}$

K   O   U   F   A   X
0   1   2   3   4

2. 71 base hits in his appearances in World Series
B at $\sqrt{5}$, R at $\sqrt{12}$, A at 3.75, G at $\frac{16}{13}$, E at $\frac{3}{2}$, Y at 0.375, R at $\frac{13}{4}$, I at 1.6, and O at 0.7

Y   O   G   I   B   E   R   R   A
0   1   2   3   4

3. 10 runs in a single World Series
N at $\sqrt{60}$, K at $\sqrt{30}$, A at 4.3, S at 6.2, C at $\frac{46}{9}$, O at $\sqrt{45}$, and J at $\sqrt{17}$

J   A   C   K   S   O   N
4   5   6   7   8

4. batting average of 0.625 in a single World Series
E at $\sqrt{32}$, U at $6\frac{5}{9}$, A at $\frac{14}{3}$, T at $\sqrt{55}$, B at 5.3, R at $\sqrt{40}$, H at 7.75, B at $\frac{21}{5}$

B   A   B   E   R   U   T   H
4   5   6   7   8

5. 42 World Series runs in his career
E at $\sqrt{140}$, Y at 9.6, L at 8.6, E at $\sqrt{90}$, A at $\frac{21}{2}$, M at $\sqrt{70}$, C at $8\frac{7}{8}$, M at $\sqrt{100}$, N at 10.7, K at $9\frac{1}{11}$, T at $\sqrt{120}$, L at 11.4

M   I   C   K   E   Y   M   A   N   T   L   E
8   9   10   11   12

Chapter 12   14   Glencoe California Mathematics, Grade 6

Additional Lesson Resources

*** Also available in Spanish ELL**

Transparencies
- *5-Minute Check Transparency*, Lesson 12-1

Other Print Products
- *Noteables™ Interactive Study Notebook with Foldables™*

Teacher Tech Tools
- *Interactive Classroom CD-ROM*, Lesson 12-1
- *AssignmentWorks CD-ROM*, Lesson 12-1

Student Tech Tools
ca.gr6math.com
- Extra Examples, Chapter 12, Lesson 1
- Self-Check Quiz, Chapter 12, Lesson 1

 Estimating Square Roots

1 Focus

Standards Alignment

Before Lesson 12-1
Understand and compute positive integer powers of nonnegative integers; compute examples as repeated multiplication from Standard 5NS1.3

Lesson 12-1
For an integer that is not square, determine without a calculator the two integers between which its square root lies and explain why from Standard 7NS2.4

After Lesson 12-1
Know and understand the Pythagorean theorem and its converse and use it to find the length of the missing side of a right triangle and the lengths of other line segments and, in some situations, empirically verify the Pythagorean theorem by direct measurement from Standard 7MG3.3

2 Teach

▶ MINI Lab

Make sure students realize that the square roots of the large tile squares are represented by the number of tiles in a square's side. Many students will be able to estimate the square roots by using the guess and check strategy.

Scaffolding Questions

Draw a number line from 15 to 25 on the chalkboard. As students answer the following questions, mark each square and approximate square on the number line.

Main IDEA

Estimate square roots.

Preparation for Standard 7NS2.4 Use the inverse relationship between raising to a power and extracting the root of a perfect square; for an integer that is not square, determine without a calculator the two integers between which its square root lies and explain why.

NEW Vocabulary

irrational number

5. Sample answer: Square numbers using guess and check.

READING
in the Content Area

For strategies in reading this lesson, visit ca.gr6math.com.

▶ MINI Lab

Estimate the square root of 27.

- Arrange 27 tiles into the largest square possible. You will use 25 tiles and 2 will remain.

- Add tiles to make the next larger square. So, add 9 tiles to make a square with 36 tiles.

- The square root of 27 is between 5 and 6. Since 27 is much closer to 25 than 36, we can expect that the square root of 27 is closer to 5 than 6.

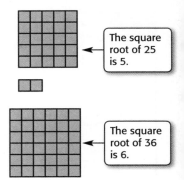
The square root of 25 is 5.
The square root of 36 is 6.

Use algebra tiles to estimate the square root of each number to the nearest whole number.

1. 40 **6**   2. 28 **5**   3. 85 **9**   4. 62 **8**

5. Describe another method that you could use to estimate the square root of a number.

The square root of a perfect square is an integer. You can estimate the square root of a number that is *not* a perfect square.

EXAMPLE   Estimate a Square Root

1 Estimate $\sqrt{78}$ to the nearest whole number.

List some perfect squares.

1, 4, 9, 16, 25, 36, 49, 64, 81, ...

78

$64 < 78 < 81$ 78 is between the perfect squares 64 and 81.

$\sqrt{64} < \sqrt{78} < \sqrt{81}$ Find the square root of each number.

$8 < \sqrt{78} < 9$ $\sqrt{64} = 8$ and $\sqrt{81} = 9$

So, $\sqrt{78}$ is between 8 and 9. Since 78 is much closer to 81 than to 64, the best whole number estimate is 9.   Verify with a calculator.

CHECK Your Progress

a. Estimate $\sqrt{50}$ to the nearest whole number. **7**

 Personal Tutor at ca.gr6math.com

636   Chapter 12 Looking Ahead to Grade 7: Geometry and Measurement

---

Ask:

- What is the square of 4? 16

- What is the square of 5? 25

- What is the approximate square of 4.5?
  about 20

- What is the approximate square of 4.9?
  about 24

✓ Formative Assessment

Use the Check Your Progress exercises after each Example to determine students' understanding of concepts.

A number that cannot be expressed as the quotient of two integers is an **irrational number**.

Irrational Numbers $\sqrt{2}$, π, 0.636336333...

The square root of any number that is not a perfect square is an irrational number. You can use a calculator to estimate square roots that are irrational numbers.

Vocabulary Link . . . .
Irrational
Everyday Use lacking usual or normal clarity, as in irrational thinking

Math Use a number that cannot be expressed as the quotient of two integers

b. $\sqrt{6}$
┼─┼─┼─┼─┼
0 1 2 3 4

c. $\sqrt{23}$
┼─┼─┼─┼─┼─┼
1 2 3 4 5 6

d. $\sqrt{309}$
┼─┼─┼─┼─┼
14 15 16 17 18

EXAMPLE   **Graph Square Roots on a Number Line**

2 Graph $\sqrt{42}$ on a number line.

[2nd] [√] 42 [ENTER]   6.480740698

$\sqrt{42} \approx 6.5$

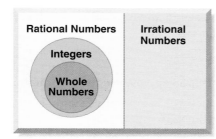

$\sqrt{42}$
┼─┼─┼─┼─┼─┼─┼─┼
1 2 3 4 5 6 7 8

Check for Reasonableness
$6^2 = 36$ and $7^2 = 49$. Since 42 is between 36 and 49, the answer, 6.5, is reasonable.

CHECK Your Progress

Graph each square root on a number line.

b. $\sqrt{6}$ c. $\sqrt{23}$ d. $\sqrt{309}$

The Venn diagram shows the relationship among sets of numbers.

```
┌─────────────────────┬──────────────┐
│ Rational Numbers    │ Irrational   │
│                     │ Numbers      │
│    Integers         │              │
│   ┌─────────┐       │              │
│   │ Whole   │       │              │
│   │ Numbers │       │              │
│   └─────────┘       │              │
└─────────────────────┴──────────────┘
```

Whole Numbers: 0, 1, 2, 3, ...
Integers: ..., −2, −1, 0, 1, 2, ...
Rational Numbers: $\frac{1}{2}$, 0.25, −0.2, 0.333...
Irrational Numbers: π, $\sqrt{2}$, 0.124543...

★ indicates multi-step problem

CHECK Your Understanding

Example 1   Estimate each square root on a number line.
(p. 636)

1. $\sqrt{39}$ 6   2. $\sqrt{106}$ 10   3. $\sqrt{90}$ 9   4. $\sqrt{140}$ 12

Example 2   Graph each square root on a number line. 5–8. See margin.
(p. 637)

5. $\sqrt{7}$ 6. $\sqrt{51}$ 7. $\sqrt{135}$ 8. $\sqrt{462}$

9. **MEASUREMENT** The diagram at the right shows the floor plan of a square kitchen. What is the approximate length of one side of the kitchen floor to the nearest tenth? **9.7 cm**

Area = 95 cm²   x

x

Additional Answers

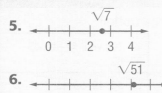

5. $\sqrt{7}$
┼─┼─┼─┼─┼
0 1 2 3 4

6. $\sqrt{51}$
┼─┼─┼─┼─┼─┼
3 4 5 6 7 8

7. $\sqrt{135}$
┼─┼─┼─┼─┼
9 10 11 12 13

8. $\sqrt{462}$
┼─┼─┼─┼─┼
18 19 20 21 22

Focus on Mathematical Content

The **square root of a number can be estimated** by comparing the number to the perfect square less than it and to the perfect square greater than it.

A calculator can be used to find the **decimal approximation** of a square root of a nonperfect square.

ADDITIONAL EXAMPLES

1 Estimate $\sqrt{96}$ to the nearest whole number. 10

2 Use a calculator to find the value of $\sqrt{37}$ to the nearest tenth. 6.1

Additional Examples are also in:

• Noteables™ Interactive Study Notebook with Foldables™

• Interactive Classroom PowerPoint® Presentations

3 Practice

Formative Assessment

Use Exercises 1–9 to check for understanding.

Then use the chart at the bottom of the next page to customize your assignments for students.

Intervention You may wish to use the Study Guide and Intervention Master on page 10 of the *Chapter 12 Resource Masters* for additional reinforcement.

638 **Chapter 12** Looking Ahead to Grade 7: Geometry and Measurement

Odd/Even Assignments

Exercises 10–27 are structured so that students practice the same concepts whether they are assigned odd or even problems.

Additional Answers

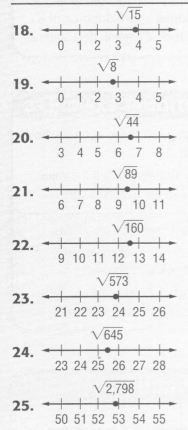

$\sqrt{15}$

18. ├──┼──┼──┼──●┼──┤
       0 1 2 3 4 5

$\sqrt{8}$

19. ├──┼──┼──●┼──┼──┤
       0 1 2 3 4 5

$\sqrt{44}$

20. ├──┼──┼──●┼──┼──┤
       3 4 5 6 7 8

$\sqrt{89}$

21. ├──┼──┼──●┼──┼──┤
       6 7 8 9 10 11

$\sqrt{160}$

22. ├──┼──┼──●┼──┼──┤
       9 10 11 12 13 14

$\sqrt{573}$

23. ├──┼──●┼──┼──┼──┤
       21 22 23 24 25 26

$\sqrt{645}$

24. ├──┼──●┼──┼──┼──┤
       23 24 25 26 27 28

$\sqrt{2,798}$

25. ├──┼──●┼──┼──┼──┤
       50 51 52 53 54 55

Exercises

HOMEWORK HELP

For Exercises	See Examples
10–17, 26, 27	1
18–25	2

Exercise Levels
A: 10–27
B: 28–41
C: 42–49

Estimate each square root to the nearest whole number.

10. $\sqrt{11}$ 3   **11.** $\sqrt{20}$ 4   **12.** $\sqrt{35}$ 6   **13.** $\sqrt{65}$ 8

14. $\sqrt{89}$ 9   **15.** $\sqrt{116}$ 11   **16.** $\sqrt{137}$ 12   **17.** $\sqrt{409}$ 20

Graph each square root on a number line. 18–25. See margin.

18. $\sqrt{15}$ **19.** $\sqrt{8}$ **20.** $\sqrt{44}$ **21.** $\sqrt{89}$

22. $\sqrt{160}$ **23.** $\sqrt{573}$ **24.** $\sqrt{645}$ **25.** $\sqrt{2,798}$

26. MEASUREMENT The bottom of the square baking pan has an area of 67 square inches. What is the approximate length of one side of the pan? **8.2 in.**

27. ALGEBRA What whole number is closest to $\sqrt{m-n}$ if $m = 45$ and $n = 8$? **6**

Estimate each square root to the nearest whole number.

28. $\sqrt{925}$ 30   **29.** $\sqrt{2,480}$ 50   **30.** $\sqrt{1,610}$ 40   **31.** $\sqrt{6,500}$ 81

Estimate each square root to the nearest tenth.

32. $\sqrt{0.25}$ 0.5   **33.** $\sqrt{0.49}$ 0.7   **34.** $\sqrt{1.96}$ 1.4   **35.** $\sqrt{2.89}$ 1.7

ALGEBRA For Exercises 36 and 37, evaluate each expression to the nearest tenth if $a = 8$ and $b = 3.7$.

36. $\sqrt{a+b}$ 3.4   **37.** $\sqrt{6b-a}$ 3.8

STAMPS For Exercises 38 and 39, use the information below.

The Special Olympics' commemorative stamp is square in shape with an area of 1,008 square millimeters.

38. Find the length of one side of the postage stamp to the nearest tenth. **31.7 mm**

39. What is the length of one side in centimeters? **3.17 cm**

★ **40. ALGEBRA** The formula $D = 1.22 \times \sqrt{h}$ can be used to estimate the distance D in miles you can see from a point h feet above Earth's surface. Use the formula to find the distance D in miles you can see from the top of a 120-foot hill. Round to the nearest tenth. **13.4 mi**

EXTRA PRACTICE

See pages 712, 726.

Math Online
Self-Check Quiz at ca.gr6math.com

41.  **FIND THE DATA** Refer to the California Data File on pages 16–19. Choose some data and write a real-world problem in which you would estimate a square root. **See students' work.**

H.O.T. Problems

42. $\sqrt{81}$; It is not irrational.

42. Which One Doesn't Belong? Identify the number that does not have the same characteristic as the other three. Explain your reasoning.

$\sqrt{5}$	π	$\sqrt{81}$	0.535335333...

DIFFERENTIATED HOMEWORK OPTIONS

Level	Assignment	Two-Day Option	
BL Basic	10–27, 42–44, 49–62	11–27 odd, 50–52	10–26 even, 42–44, 49, 52–62
OL Core	11–25 odd, 26, 27, 29–37 odd, 38–44, 49–62	10–27, 50–52	28–44, 49, 53–62
AL Advanced/Pre-AP	28–58, (optional: 59–62)		

44. 51 is between
the perfect
squares 49 and 64.
Since 51 is closer
to 49 than 64, $\sqrt{51}$
s closer to $\sqrt{49}$,
or 7.

43. **OPEN ENDED** Select three numbers with square roots between 4 and 5.
Sample answer: 17, 18, 19

44. **NUMBER SENSE** Explain why 7 is the best whole number estimate for $\sqrt{51}$.

CHALLENGE A cube root of a number is a number whose cube is that number.
Estimate the cube root of each of the following to the nearest whole number.

45. $\sqrt[3]{9}$ 2 46. $\sqrt[3]{26}$ 3 47. $\sqrt[3]{120}$ 5 48. $\sqrt[3]{500}$ 8

49. **WRITING IN MATH** Apply what you know about numbers to explain
why $\sqrt{30}$ is an irrational number. **It cannot be written as a fraction.**

4 Assess

Ticket Out the Door Tell students
that a square has an area of 912 square
feet. Have them estimate the length of
a side and write it on a slip of paper.
a little more than 30 feet

STANDARDS PRACTICE 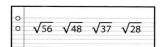 7NS2.4

50. Reina wrote four numbers on a piece
of paper. She then asked her friend
Tyron to select the number closest to 5.
Which number should he select? **D**

$\sqrt{56}$ $\sqrt{48}$ $\sqrt{37}$ $\sqrt{28}$

A $\sqrt{56}$
B $\sqrt{48}$
C $\sqrt{37}$
D $\sqrt{28}$

51. Which of the following is an irrational
number? **G**

F $\sqrt{25}$ H -13
G $\sqrt{7}$ J $\frac{4}{5}$

52. Find $\sqrt{169}$. **B**
A 15
B 13
C 12
D 11

Spiral Review

53. **MEASUREMENT** Find the volume of a can of vegetables with a diameter of 3 inches
and a height of 4 inches. (Lesson 11-10) **28.3 in³**

54. **MEASUREMENT** A rectangular prism is 14 inches long, 4.5 inches wide, and
1 inch high. What is the volume of the prism? (Lesson 11-9) **63 in³**

GEOMETRY For Exercises 55–58, use the graph
at the right. Classify the angle that represents
each category as *acute*, *obtuse*, *right*, or
straight. (Lesson 10-1)

55. 30–39 hours **acute**   56. 1–29 hours **acute**
57. 40 hours **obtuse**   58. 41–50 hours **obtuse**

Hours Worked in a Typical Week

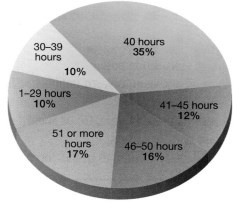

30–39 hours 10%
40 hours 35%
1–29 hours 10%
41–45 hours 12%
51 or more hours 17%
46–50 hours 16%

Source: Heldrich Work Trends Survey

▶ **GET READY for the Next Lesson**

PREREQUISITE SKILL Solve each equation.
(Lesson 1-7)

59. $7^2 + 5^2 = c$ **74**   60. $4^2 + b = 36$ **20**
61. $3^2 + a = 25$ **16**   62. $9^2 + 2^2 = c$ **85**

Differentiated Instruction

Bodily/Kinesthetic Learners Before class, write a number between 10 and 150 on each of
approximately 100 index cards. Do not write any perfect squares. Separate students into groups of
three. Distribute 10 index cards to each group. Have each group shuffle its cards and turn them face
down in the middle of the group. One student turns a card over, and all three students estimate the
square root (without using calculators). The person with the closest estimate gets a point. The first
person with 5 points wins.

The Pythagorean Theorem

12-2

Preparation for
⚬— **Standard 7MG3.3**

Know and understand the Pythagorean theorem and its converse and use it to find the length of the missing side of a right triangle and the lengths of other line segments and, in some situations, empirically verify the Pythagorean theorem by direct measurement.

PACING: **Regular:** 2 periods, **Block:** 1 period

Options for Differentiated Instruction

ELL = English Language Learner   **AL** = Above Grade Level   **SS** = Struggling Students   **SN** = Special Needs

Drawing and Measuring **SS** **SN**

Use after presenting the Examples.

Have students use centimeter grid paper to draw and label one of the triangles described in the lesson. Tell them to let 1 centimeter represent 1 unit. A drawing of the triangle in Exercise 4 is shown at right.

Have them work through the Pythagorean Theorem equation step by step with a partner, and then check their results by actually measuring with a centimeter ruler. For students with fine motor skills difficulties, provide a figure already drawn on grid paper.

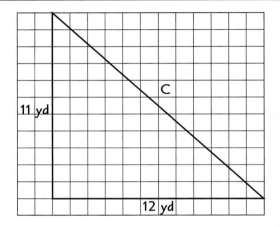

Kinesthetic Learning **ELL** **SS** **SN**

Use before assigning the Exercises.

Have students work in pairs to calculate the length of a "human hypotenuse."
• Have one student stand an arm's length from a wall and lean forward until his or her arms reach as high on the wall as possible.
• The other student should mark the spot using a small piece of tape. He or she then measures the distance from the floor to the tape and the distance from the wall to their partner's heels.
• Students then use the Pythagorean Theorem to calculate the length of the "human hypotenuse."

Researching **AL**

Use after students complete Lesson 12-2.

The Pythagorean Theorem was named after a Greek mathematician named *Pythagoras*.
Have students research to find out about the life of Pythagoras:
• when and where he lived,
• the branches of mathematics in which he was interested, and
• any other interesting facts about Pythagoras.

Tell students to be prepared to share their research with the class.

Leveled Lesson Resources

Chapter 12 Resource Masters

BL = Below Grade Level   **OL** = On Grade Level   **AL** = Above Grade Level   **ELL** = English Language Learner

Lesson Reading Guide
p. 16 **BL** **OL** **ELL**

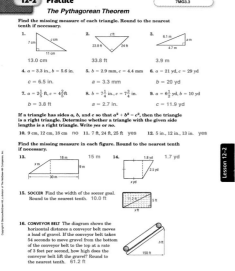

Study Guide and Intervention*
p. 17 **BL** **OL** **ELL**

Skills Practice*
p. 18 **BL** **OL**

Practice*
p. 19 **OL** **AL**

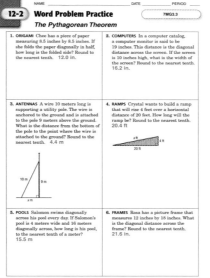

Word Problem Practice*
p. 20 **OL** **AL**

Enrichment
p. 21 **OL** **AL**

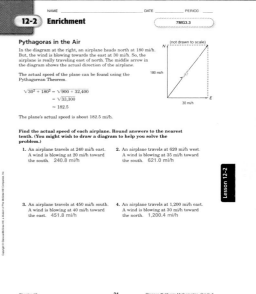

Additional Lesson Resources

*** Also available in Spanish ELL**

Transparencies
• *5-Minute Check Transparency*, Lesson 12-2

Other Print Products
• *Noteables™ Interactive Study Notebook with Foldables™*

Teacher Tech Tools
• *Interactive Classroom CD-ROM*, Lesson 12-2
• *AssignmentWorks CD-ROM*, Lesson 12-2

Student Tech Tools
ca.gr6math.com
• Extra Examples, Chapter 12, Lesson 2
• Self-Check Quiz, Chapter 12, Lesson 2

12-2 The Pythagorean Theorem

640 Chapter 12 Looking Ahead to Grade 7: Geometry and Measurement

1 Focus

Standards Alignment

Before Lesson 12-2
Use variables in expressions describing geometric quantities. Express in symbolic form simple relationships arising from geometry from Standards 6AF3.1 and 6AF3.2

Lesson 12-2
Know and understand the Pythagorean theorem and its converse and use it to find the length of the missing side of a right triangle and the lengths of other line segments and, in some situations, empirically verify the Pythagorean theorem by direct measurement from 🔑 Standard 7MG3.3

After Lesson 12-2
Students prove the Pythagorean Theorem from 🔑 Standard G14.0

2 Teach

▶ MINI Lab

You might wish to have students write an addition sentence for the areas of the squares in both triangle models. $9 + 16 = 25$, $25 + 144 = 169$

Then have them rewrite the sentences using square notation for each term. $3^2 + 4^2 = 5^2$, $5^2 + 12^2 = 13^2$

Make sure they see that the base of each term in the square notation is the length of one side of the triangle.

Main IDEA
Find length using the Pythagorean Theorem.

🔑 **Preparation for ● Standard 7MG3.3** Know and understand the Pythagorean theorem and its converse and use it to find the length of the missing side of a right triangle and the lengths of other line segments and, in some situations, empirically verify the Pythagorean theorem by direct measurement.

NEW Vocabulary

leg
hypotenuse
Pythagorean Theorem

1. 9 units², 16 units², 25 units²
2. They are the same.
3. 25 units²; They are equal.
4. They are the same.

READING Math

Square Roots Read $\pm\sqrt{5}$ as *plus or minus the square root of* 5.

▶ MINI Lab

COncepts in MOtion
BrainPOP® ca.gr6math.com

Three squares with sides 3, 4, and 5 units are used to form the right triangle shown.

1. Find the area of each square.
2. How are the squares of the sides related to the areas of the squares?
3. Find the sum of the areas of the two smaller squares. How does the sum compare to the area of the larger square?
4. Use grid paper to cut out three squares with sides 5, 12, and 13 units. Form a right triangle with these squares. Compare the sum of the areas of the two smaller squares with the area of the larger square.

In a right triangle, the sides have special names.

The two sides adjacent to the right angle are the **legs**.

The side opposite the right angle is the **hypotenuse**.

The **Pythagorean Theorem** describes the relationship between the length of the hypotenuse and the lengths of the legs.

KEY CONCEPT — Pythagorean Theorem

Words	In a right triangle, the square of the length of the hypotenuse equals the sum of the squares of the lengths of the legs.	Model
Symbols	$c^2 = a^2 + b^2$	

When using the Pythagorean Theorem, you will encounter equations that involve square roots. Every positive number has both a positive and a negative square root. By the definition of square roots, if $n^2 = a$, then $n = \pm\sqrt{a}$. The notation $\pm\sqrt{\ }$ indicates both the positive and negative square root of a number. You can use this relationship to solve equations that involve squares.

Scaffolding Questions
Ask:
• What is the square of 7? 49
• What is the square of −7? 49
• What is 7 times −7? −49
• Can a negative number have a square root? no

EXAMPLE   Find the Length of the Hypotenuse

1 Find the length of the hypotenuse of the triangle.

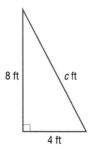
8 ft   c ft
4 ft

$$c^2 = a^2 + b^2$$ Pythagorean Theorem
$$c^2 = 8^2 + 4^2$$ Replace a with 8 and b with 4.
$$c^2 = 64 + 16$$ Evaluate 8^2 and 4^2.
$$c^2 = 80$$ Add.
$$c = \pm\sqrt{80}$$ Definition of square root
$$c \approx \pm 8.9$$ Simplify.

The length of the hypotenuse is about 8.9 feet.

CHECK Your Progress

a. Find the length of the hypotenuse of a right triangle with legs 5 yards and 7 yards. Round to the nearest tenth. **8.6 yd**

Real-World Career . . . .

How Does an Archeologist Use Math? Before digging, archaeologists use the Pythagorean Theorem to calculate the diagonal of an excavation site to be sure that the area is a rectangle.

Math Online
For more information, go to ca.gr6math.com.

Real-World EXAMPLE

2 **ARCHAEOLOGY** Archaeologists placed corner stakes to mark a rectangular excavation site as shown at the right. If their stakes are placed correctly, what is the measure of the diagonal of the excavation site?

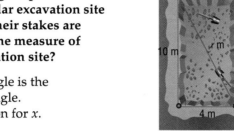
10 m   x m
4 m

The diagonal of the rectangle is the hypotenuse of a right triangle. Write and solve an equation for x.

$$c^2 = a^2 + b^2$$ Pythagorean Theorem
$$x^2 = 4^2 + 10^2$$ Replace c with x, a with 4, and b with 10.
$$x^2 = 16 + 100$$ Evaluate 4^2 and 10^2.
$$x^2 = 116$$ Add.
$$x = \pm\sqrt{116}$$ Definition of square root
$$x \approx \pm 10.8$$ Simplify.

The length of the diagonal of the excavation site is about 10.8 meters.

CHECK Your Progress

b. **SOFTBALL** A softball diamond is a square measuring 60 feet on each side. How far does a player on second base throw when she throws from second base to home? Round to the nearest tenth. **84.9 ft**

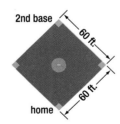
2nd base   60 ft.
60 ft.
home

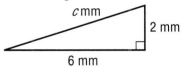
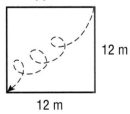

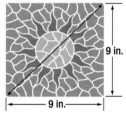
You can also use the Pythagorean Theorem to find the measure of a leg if the measure of the other leg and the hypotenuse are known.

EXAMPLE Find the Length of a Leg

3 Find the missing measure of the triangle. Round to the nearest tenth if necessary.

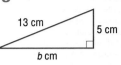

13 cm

5 cm

b cm

The missing measure is the length of a leg.

$c^2 =$	$a^2 + b^2$	Pythagorean Theorem
$13^2 =$	$5^2 + b^2$	Replace a with 5 and c with 13.
$169 =$	$25 + b^2$	Evaluate 13^2 and 5^2.
$-25 = -25$		Subtract 25 from each side.
$144 =$	b^2	Simplify.
$\pm\sqrt{144} =$	b	Definition of square root
$12 =$	b	Simplify.

The length of the leg is 12 centimeters.

CHECK Your Progress

c.

a ft

17 ft

15 ft

d.

4 cm

9.2 cm

b cm

e. $b = 7$ in., $c = 25$ in.

STANDARDS EXAMPLE   7MG3.3

4 Mr. Thomson created a mosaic tile in the shape of a square to place in his kitchen.

9 in.

9 in.

Which is closest to the length of the diagonal of the tile?

A 10 in.   **C** 15 in.

B 13 in.   **D** 17 in.

Read the Item

You need to use the Pythagorean Theorem to find the length of the diagonal.

Solve the Item

$$c^2 = a^2 + b^2 \qquad \text{Pythagorean Theorem}$$
$$c^2 = 9^2 + 9^2 \qquad \text{Replace } a \text{ with 9 and } b \text{ with 9.}$$
$$c^2 = 81 + 81 \qquad \text{Evaluate } 9^2 \text{ and } 9^2.$$
$$c^2 = 162 \qquad \text{Add.}$$
$$c = \pm\sqrt{162} \qquad \text{Definition of square root}$$
$$c \approx \pm 12.7 \qquad \text{Simplify.}$$

The length is about 12.7 inches.
The answer choice closest to 12.7
inches is 13 inches. So, the answer is B.

 CHECK **Your Progress**

f. A painter leans a ladder against the side
   of a building. How far from the bottom
   of the building is the top of the ladder? **F**

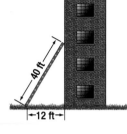

   F 38.2 ft   **H** 21.8 ft
   G 28.0 ft   **J** 20.0 ft

 Personal Tutor at ca.gr6math.com

★ indicates multi-step problem

CHECK Your Understanding

Examples 1, 3
(pp. 641–642)

Find the missing measure of each triangle. Round to the nearest tenth if necessary.

1. 26 mm
2. 24.5 in.
3. 18.5 cm
4. 16.3 yd

1.
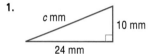

2.
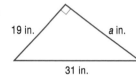

3. $b = 21$ cm, $c = 28$
4. $a = 11$ yd, $b = 12$ yd

Example 2
(p. 641)

5. **ARCHITECTURE** What is the width of the
   the fence gate shown at the right? Round
   to the nearest tenth. **4.0 ft**

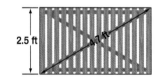

Example 4
(pp. 642–643)
7MG3.3

6. **STANDARDS PRACTICE** A company
   designed a public play area in the
   shape of a square. The play area will
   include a pathway, as shown. Which is
   closest to the length of the pathway? **C**

   A 100 ft   **C** 140 ft
   B 125 ft   **D** 175 ft

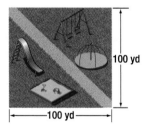

Lesson 12-2 The Pythagorean Theorem **643**

ADDITIONAL EXAMPLE

④ **STANDARDS EXAMPLE**
Televisions are measured
according to their diagonal
measure. If the diagonal of a
television is 36 inches, and its
height is 21.6 inches, what is
its width? B

A 42.0 in.
B 28.8 in.
C 14.4 in.
D 57.6 in

3 **Practice**

✓ **Formative Assessment**

Use Exercises 1–6 to check for
understanding.

Then use the chart at the bottom of
the next page to customize your
assignments for students.

Intervention You may wish to use the
Study Guide and Intervention Master
on page 17 of the *Chapter 12 Resource
Masters* for additional reinforcement.

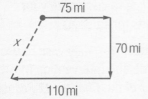
Exercises

Find the missing measure of each triangle. Round to the nearest tenth if necessary.

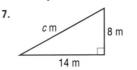

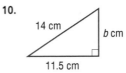

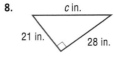

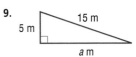

7.

8.

9.

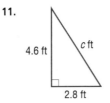

10.

11.

12.

13. $a = 2.4$ yd, $c = 3.7$ yd **2.8 yd**

14. $b = 8.5$ m, $c = 10.4$ m **6.0 m**

15. $a = 7$ in., $b = 24$ in. **25 in.**

16. $a = 13.5$ mm, $b = 18$ mm **22.5 mm**

MEASUREMENT For Exercises 17 and 18, find each distance to the nearest tenth.

17.

18.

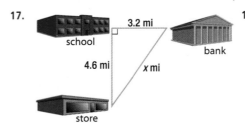

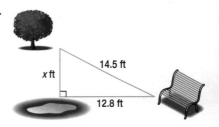

SPORTS For Exercises 19 and 20, find the length or width of each piece of sports equipment. Round to the nearest tenth.

19.

20.

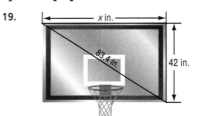

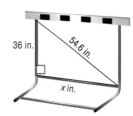

21. **MEASUREMENT** The doorway of a house is 3 feet wide and 6.5 feet tall. A square mirror 7 feet on each side must be delivered through the doorway. Can the mirror fit through the doorway? Justify your answer. **See margin.**

22. **MEASUREMENT** On a weekend trip around California, Sydney left her home in Modesto and drove 75 miles east to Yosemite National Park, then 70 miles south to Fresno, and finally 110 miles west to Monterey Bay. About how far is she from her starting point? Justify your answer with a drawing. **See margin.**

644 Chapter 12 Looking Ahead to Grade 7: Geometry and Measurement

DIFFERENTIATED HOMEWORK OPTIONS

Level	Assignment	Two-Day Option	
BL Basic	7–20, 24–34	7–19 odd, 26, 27	8–20 even, 24, 25, 28–34
OL Core	7–19 odd, 21, 22, 24–34	7–20, 26, 27	21, 22, 24, 25, 28–34
AL Advanced/Pre-AP	21–33, (optional: 34)		

23. **CHALLENGE** What is the length of the diagonal shown in the cube at the right? **about 10.4 in.**

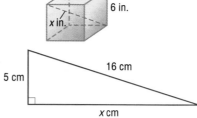
6 in.
x in.

24. **FIND THE ERROR** Devin and Jamie are writing an equation to find the missing measure of the triangle at the right. Who is correct? Explain.

5 cm
16 cm
x cm

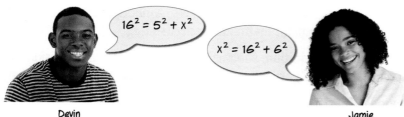

$16^2 = 5^2 + x^2$

$x^2 = 16^2 + 6^2$

Devin   Jamie

25. **WRITING IN MATH** Write a problem about a real-world situation in which you would use the Pythagorean Theorem. **See students' work.**

STANDARDS PRACTICE 7MG3.3

26. Which triangle has sides a, b, and c so that the relationship $a^2 + b^2 = c^2$ is true? **B**

A
a c b

B a c b

C a b c

D b c a

27. An isosceles right triangle has legs that are each 8 inches long. About how long is the hypotenuse? **G**

F 12.8 inches
G 11.3 inches
H 8 inches
J 4 inches

Spiral Review

28. **ESTIMATION** Which is closer to $\sqrt{55}$: 7 or 8? (Lesson 12-1) **7**

29. **MEASUREMENT** A cylinder-shaped popcorn tin has a height of 1.5 feet and a diameter of 10 inches. Find the volume to the nearest cubic inch. Use 3.14 for π. (Lesson 11-10) **1,413 in³**

Write each percent as a decimal. (Lesson 4-7)

30. 45% **0.45**   31. 8% **0.08**   32. 124% **1.24**   33. 265% **2.65**

GET READY for the Next Lesson

34. **PREREQUISITE SKILL** The average person takes about 15 breaths per minute. At this rate, how many breaths does the average person take in one week? Use the *solve a simpler problem* strategy. (Lesson 11-5) **151,200 breaths**

12-3 Problem-Solving Investigation
MAKE A MODEL

Standard 6MR2.4 **Use a variety of methods, such as** words, numbers, symbols, charts, graphs, tables, diagrams, and **models, to explain mathematical reasoning.**

Standard 6NS2.1 **Solve problems involving addition,** subtraction, **multiplication,** and division **of positive fractions and explain why a particular operation was used for a given situation.**

PACING: **Regular:** 2 periods, **Block:** 1 period

Options for Differentiated Instruction

ELL = English Language Learner   **AL** = Above Grade Level   **SS** = Struggling Students   **SN** = Special Needs

Organizing Student Work and Thinking   **ELL** **SS** **SN**

Use before assigning the Exercises.

Have students add the strategy of making a model to their problem-solving booklets. They should include the following about the strategy:
- a description of the strategy
- an explanation of the best time to use the strategy
- examples of problems that are solved using the strategy
- advantages and disadvantages of using the strategy

Cooperative Groups   **ELL** **AL** **SS** **SN**

Use after students complete Exercises 1 and 2.

Display the following figures on the board or overhead. Have students describe a real-world object that each figure could be used to model. Sample answers are given.

a stadium   an office building   a house roof

Research   **AL**

Use after students complete Lesson 12-3.

Have students work in small groups to research different occupations in which people make models to solve work-related problems. If possible, have students interview people in their community who use models in their professions. Have students report their findings to the class, including pictures of the models, if possible.

Chapter 12 Resource Masters

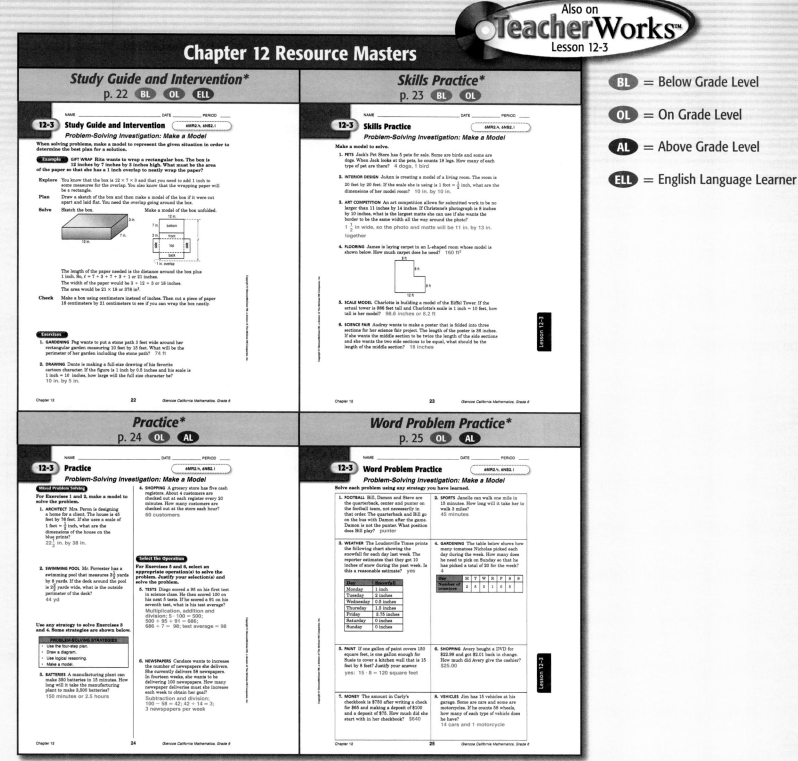

Study Guide and Intervention*
p. 22 **BL** **OL** **ELL**

Skills Practice*
p. 23 **BL** **OL**

Practice*
p. 24 **OL** **AL**

Word Problem Practice*
p. 25 **OL** **AL**

BL = Below Grade Level

OL = On Grade Level

AL = Above Grade Level

ELL = English Language Learner

* *Also available in Spanish* **ELL**

Additional Lesson Resources

Transparencies
- *5-Minute Check Transparency*, Lesson 12-3

Other Print Products
- *Noteables™ Interactive Study Notebook with Foldables™*

Teacher Tech Tools
- *Interactive Classroom CD-ROM*, Lesson 12-3
- *AssignmentWorks CD-ROM*, Lesson 12-3

Student Tech Tools
ca.gr6math.com
- Extra Examples, Chapter 12, Lesson 3
- Self-Check Quiz, Chapter 12, Lesson 3

1 Focus

Make a Model Real-world mathematical problems can often be solved by making a model or drawing a diagram. Models and diagrams make clear what information needs to be found and how best to find it. This problem-solving strategy could be applied to many real-world problems involving the Pythagorean Theorem (Lesson 13-2) and will be useful in Lesson 13-4, in which students will find the surface area of rectangular prisms.

2 Teach

Scaffolding Questions

Ask:

- If I am trying to visualize a problem about a sphere, what could I use as a model? Sample answers: globe, ball

- If I am trying to visualize a problem about a rectangular prism, what could I use as a model? Sample answers: shoe box, chalkboard eraser

- How could I model the shapes needed to make a cylinder? Sample answers: create a paper cylinder and then cut it apart; cut apart a tin can

---

ADDITIONAL EXAMPLE

1 **Solve. Use the make a model strategy.**

STORAGE A daycare center plans to make simple wooden storage bins for the 3-inch square alphabet blocks. If each bin will hold 30 blocks, give two possible dimensions for the inside of the bin. Sample answers: 15 in. by 9 in. by 6 in., or 18 in. by 15 in. by 3 in.

12-3 **Problem-Solving Investigation**

MAIN IDEA: Solve problems by making a model.

Standard 6MR2.4 Use a variety of methods, such as words, numbers, symbols, charts, graphs, tables, diagrams, and **models, to explain mathematical reasoning. Standard 6NS2.1 Solve problems involving addition,** subtraction, **multiplication,** and division **of positive fractions and explain why a particular operation was used for a given situation.**

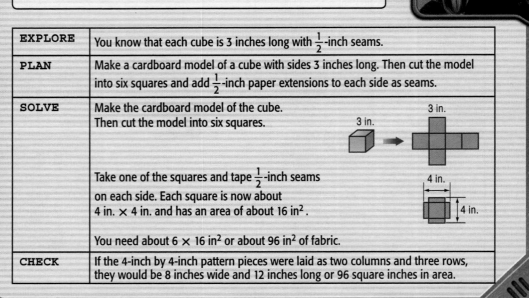

P.S.I. TEAM +

e-Mail: MAKE A MODEL

YOUR MISSION: Make a model to solve the problem.

THE PROBLEM: How much fabric is needed to make one cube if there is a $\frac{1}{2}$-inch seam on each side?

> **Libby:** I'm going to help my mom make 3-inch soft alphabet blocks for the children at her daycare center. A model can be used to find out how much fabric is needed.

EXPLORE	You know that each cube is 3 inches long with $\frac{1}{2}$-inch seams.
PLAN	Make a cardboard model of a cube with sides 3 inches long. Then cut the model into six squares and add $\frac{1}{2}$-inch paper extensions to each side as seams.
SOLVE	Make the cardboard model of the cube. Then cut the model into six squares. Take one of the squares and tape $\frac{1}{2}$-inch seams on each side. Each square is now about 4 in. × 4 in. and has an area of about 16 in². You need about 6 × 16 in² or about 96 in² of fabric.
CHECK	If the 4-inch by 4-inch pattern pieces were laid as two columns and three rows, they would be 8 inches wide and 12 inches long or 96 square inches in area.

Analyze The Strategy

1. Explain why you think Libby started with the three-dimensional model to make her pattern. **See margin.**

2. **WRITING IN MATH** Write a problem that can be solved by making a model. Then solve the problem. **See Ch. 12 Answer Appendix.**

646 **Chapter 12** Looking Ahead to Grade 7: Geometry and Measurement

---

Additional Answer

1. Sample answer: A three-dimensional object allows you to physically change the object. This makes it easier to make the pattern and then solve the problem.

Additional Examples are also in:

- Noteables™ Interactive Study Notebook with Foldables™

- Interactive Classroom PowerPoint® Presentations

Mixed Problem Solving

★ indicates multi-step problem

For Exercises 3–5, make a model to solve the problem.

3. **ART** Rodrigo is creating a layout of his bedroom for art class. The room measures 15 feet by 12 feet. If he uses a scale of $1 \text{ ft} = \frac{3}{4}$ inch, what are the dimensions of his bedroom on the model? **11.25 in. by 9 in.**

4. **BICYCLES** Eight customers stood outside The Bike Shop with either a bicycle or a tricycle that needed repaired. If there was a total of 21 wheels, how many tricycles and bicycles were there? **5 tricycles, 3 bicycles**

5. **MEASUREMENT** Francis has a photo that measures 10 inches by $8\frac{1}{2}$ inches. If the frame he uses is $1\frac{1}{4}$ inches wide, what is the perimeter of the framed picture? **47 in.**

Use any strategy to solve Exercises 6–9. Some strategies are shown below.

> **PROBLEM-SOLVING STRATEGIES**
> • Use the four-step plan.
> • Draw a diagram.
> • Use logical reasoning.
> • Make a model.

6. **COMMUNITY SERVICE** There are four drop-off centers for the community food drive. The table shows the total collections for each center. Suppose a newsletter reports that over 13,000 cans of food were collected. Is this estimate reasonable? Explain.

Center	Number of Cans
A	3,298
B	2,629
C	4,429
D	2,892

yes; 3,300 + 2,600 + 4,400 + 2,900 > 13,000

7. **SPORTS** Len can swim one 20-meter lap in $1\frac{1}{4}$ minutes. How long will it take her to swim 100 meters at the same rate? $6\frac{1}{4}$ min

★ 8. **TRAFFIC** At the four-way intersection shown below, the traffic lights change every 90 seconds. About 8 cars in one lane travel through each light change. Determine the approximate number of cars in all lanes that travel through the intersection in 3 minutes. **about 64 cars**

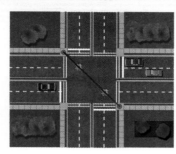

9. **MEASUREMENT** How many square feet of wallpaper are needed to cover a wall that measures $9\frac{3}{4}$ feet by $16\frac{1}{2}$ feet? $160\frac{7}{8}$ ft²

Select the Operation

For Exercises 10–12, select the appropriate operation(s) to solve the problem. Justify your selection(s) and solve the problem.

10. **MONEY** Duante deposited $450 in a new savings account in January, withdrew $175 in February, and then began monthly deposits of $75 from March through December. How much money does he have in his savings account? **Subtraction followed by multiplication and addition; $1,025**
★

11. **BASEBALL** A regulation baseball diamond is a square with an area of 8,100 square feet. If it is laid out on a field that is 172 feet wide and 301 feet long, how much greater is the distance around the whole field than the distance around the diamond? **Take the square root followed by addition followed by subtraction; 586 ft**
★

12. **DVDS** Marc currently has 68 DVDs in his collection. By the end of the next four months, he wants to have 92 DVDs in his collection. How many DVDs must he buy each month to obtain his goal? **Subtraction followed by division; 6 DVDs**
★

---

3 Practice

Using the Exercises

Exercises 1 and 2 can be used to check students' understanding of the make a model strategy.

Exercises 3–5 give students an opportunity to practice the make a model strategy.

Exercises 6–9 are structured so that students have the opportunity to practice many different problem-solving strategies. You may wish to review some of the strategies they have studied.

• use the four-step plan (p. 25)
• draw a diagram (p. 314)
• use logical reasoning (p. 530)
• make a model (p. 646)

Exercises 10–12 require students to select the appropriate operation(s) to solve a problem. Have students analyze each problem and its wording, asking themselves what kind of information is needed. Which operation(s) must be performed to get the information?

4 Assess

Crystal Ball Tell students that tomorrow's lesson is about finding the surface area of rectangular prisms. Have them write how they think what they learned today will connect with tomorrow's material.

 Formative Assessment

Check for student understanding of concepts in Lesson 12-3.

📀 Quiz 2, p. 41

Differentiated Instruction

Visual/Spatial Learners Have students draw a three-dimensional figure such as a prism, pyramid, cone, or cylinder. Then have them make a model of the figure, using paper (or cardboard), scissors, and tape. What shapes are needed to make the model?

CHAPTER 12 **Mid-Chapter Quiz**
Lessons 12-1 through 12-3

Formative Assessment

Use the Mid-Chapter Quiz to assess students' progress in the first half of the chapter.

Have students review the lesson indicated for the problems they answered incorrectly.

Summative Assessment

 Mid-Chapter Test, p. 43

ExamView Customize and
Assessment Suite create multiple versions of your Mid-Chapter Test and their answer keys.

 **Dinah Zike's Foldables**

Before students complete the Mid-Chapter Quiz, encourage them to review the notes in their Foldables tables.

Estimate each square root to the nearest whole number. (Lesson 12-1)

1. $\sqrt{32}$ 6
2. $\sqrt{80}$ 9
3. $\sqrt{105}$ 10
4. $\sqrt{230}$ 15

MEASUREMENT Estimate the side length of each square to the nearest whole number. (Lesson 12-1)

5.
Area = 14 m²

4 m

6.
Area = 110 ft²

10 ft

ALGEBRA Evaluate each expression to the nearest tenth if $a = 20$ and $b = 7$. (Lesson 12-1)

7. $\sqrt{a + b}$ 5.2
8. $\sqrt{a - b}$ 3.6

9. **STANDARDS PRACTICE** Imani is playing a review game in math class. She needs to pick the card that is labeled with a number closest to 8. Which should she pick? (Lesson 12-1) **C**

| $\sqrt{37}$ | $\sqrt{52}$ | $\sqrt{70}$ | $\sqrt{83}$ |

A $\sqrt{37}$

B $\sqrt{52}$

C $\sqrt{70}$

D $\sqrt{83}$

Find the length of the hypotenuse of each triangle. Round to the nearest tenth if necessary. (Lesson 12-2)

10.
6.7 ft

6 ft c ft

3 ft

11.
18.0 cm
7 cm
16.6 cm
c cm

Find the missing measure of each triangle. Round to the nearest tenth if necessary. (Lesson 12-2)

12.
10 in.   22.9 in.
25 in.
a in.

13. 4.9 cm
5.4 cm b cm
2.2 cm

14. **MEASUREMENT** On a computer monitor, the diagonal measure of the screen is 17 inches.

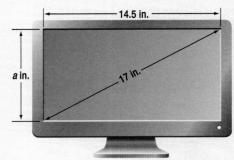
14.5 in.
a in.   17 in.

If the screen length is 14.5 inches, what is the height of the screen to the nearest tenth? (Lesson 12-2) **8.9 in.**

15. 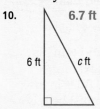 **STANDARDS PRACTICE** Eduardo jogs 5 kilometers north and 5 kilometers west. To the nearest kilometer, how far is he from his starting point? (Lesson 12-2) **H**

F 25 km   H 7 km

G 10 km   J 5 km

16. **SCIENCE** A certain type of bacteria doubles every hour. If there are two bacteria initially in a sample, how many will be present after five hours? Use the *make a model* strategy. (Lesson 12-3) **64 bacteria**
17. 8 in. by 5 in. by 3 in.
17. **SCALE MODELS** A scale model is made of a building measuring 120 feet long, 75 feet wide, and 45 feet high. If the scale is 1 inch = 15 feet, what are the dimensions of the model? Use the *make a model* strategy. (Lesson 12-3)

648   **Chapter 12** Looking Ahead to Grade 7: Geometry and Measurement

---

Data-Driven Decision Making	**Exercises**	**Lesson**	**Standard**	**Resources for Review**
Diagnostic Teaching Based on the results of the Chapter 12 Mid-Chapter Quiz, use the following to review concepts that students continue to find challenging.	1–9	12–1	**Preparation for 7NS2.4**	**CRM** Study Guide and Intervention pp. 10, 17, and 22
	10–15	12–2	**Preparation for ➤ 7MG3.3**	**Math** Online • Extra Examples • Personal Tutor
	16, 17	12–3	**6MR2.4**	• Concepts in Motion

12-4 Surface Area of Rectangular Prisms

Standard 6AF3.2 **Express in symbolic form simple relationships arising from geometry.**

Preparation for Standard 7MG2.1 **Use formulas routinely for finding** the perimeter and area of basic two-dimensional figures and **the surface area** and volume **of basic three-dimensional figures, including** rectangles, parallelograms, trapezoids, squares, triangles, circles, **prisms,** and cylinders.

PACING: **Regular:** 2 periods, **Block:** 1 period

Options for Differentiated Instruction

ELL = English Language Learner   **AL** = Above Grade Level   **SS** = Struggling Students   **SN** = Special Needs

Using Measurement   ELL SS SN

Use before presenting Example 1.

Have students work in pairs. Give each pair an empty box to open up and cut as necessary to create a net. Have them follow these steps:

1. Measure the length and width of each rectangular face.
2. Find the area of each face.
3. Add the areas to find the surface area.

Then have pairs trade boxes, measure the sides, and find the surface area. Have them compare answers with their classmates. Have students explain how their calculations are related to the formula $S = 2\ell w + 2\ell h + 2wh$.
Sample answer: If ℓ = length, w = width, and h = height, then the area of the faces are ℓw, ℓh, and wh.

Cooperative Groups   ELL SS SN

Use after presenting Examples 1 and 2.

Arrange students in small groups, placing students who prefer using nets or visual models with those who prefer to calculate surface area using the formula $S = 2\ell w + 2\ell h + 2wh$. Give each group the dimensions for several rectangular prisms and ask them to use two different methods to calculate the surface area of each prism.

Creating Models   AL SS

Use after presenting Lesson 12-4.

Give each student a piece of masking tape and six congruent squares cut out of cardstock. Have them tape together the squares to test if a net will form a cube when it is folded. Have them sketch the nets on grid paper. Tell students to find as many different nets as possible for a cube. (*Hint:* There are 11 different nets.)

Make sure that students understand that rotations or reflections of a net only count as one solution.

Lesson 12-4 Surface Area of Rectangular Prisms   **649a**

Leveled Lesson Resources

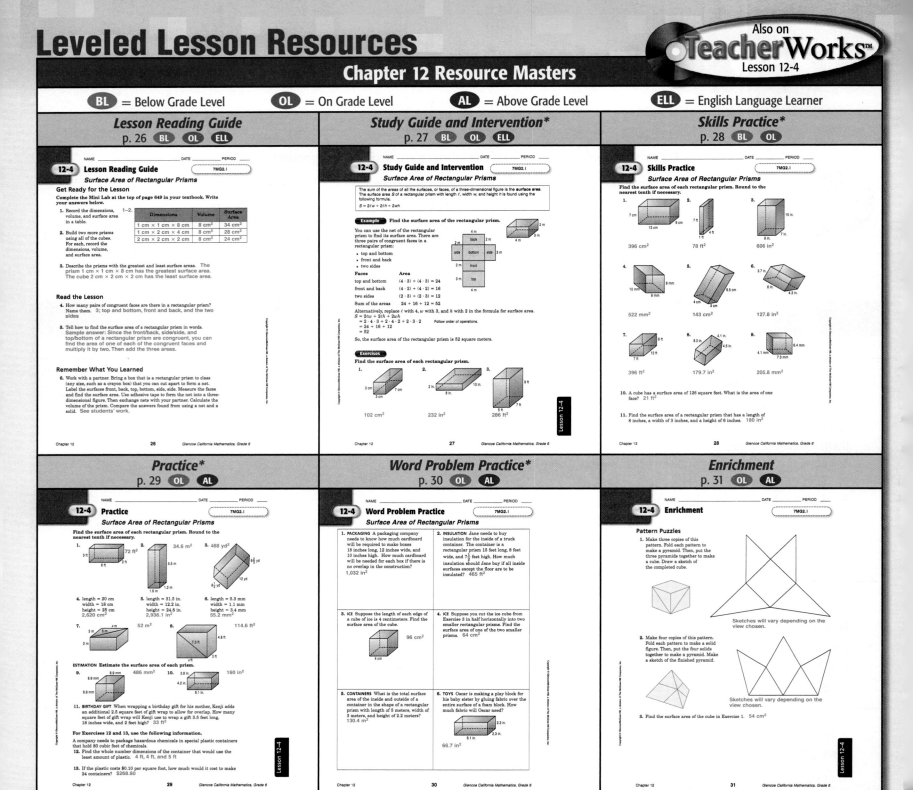

Chapter 12 Resource Masters

BL = Below Grade Level **OL** = On Grade Level **AL** = Above Grade Level **ELL** = English Language Learner

Lesson Reading Guide
p. 26 **BL** **OL** **ELL**

Study Guide and Intervention*
p. 27 **BL** **OL** **ELL**

Skills Practice*
p. 28 **BL** **OL**

Practice*
p. 29 **OL** **AL**

Word Problem Practice*
p. 30 **OL** **AL**

Enrichment
p. 31 **OL** **AL**

Additional Lesson Resources

Transparencies
- *5-Minute Check Transparency*, Lesson 12-4

Other Print Products
- *Teaching Mathematics with Manipulatives*
- *Noteables™ Interactive Study Notebook with Foldables™*

Teacher Tech Tools
- *Interactive Classroom CD-ROM*, Lesson 12-4
- *AssignmentWorks CD-ROM*, Lesson 12-4

Student Tech Tools
ca.gr6math.com
- Extra Examples, Chapter 12, Lesson 4
- Self-Check Quiz, Chapter 12, Lesson 4

* Also available in Spanish **ELL**

649b **Chapter 12** Looking Ahead to Grade 7: Geometry and Measurement

Main IDEA

Find the surface areas of rectangular prisms.

 Preparation for Standard 7MG2.1 Use formulas routinely for finding the perimeter and area of basic two-dimensional figures and **the surface area** and volume **of basic three-dimensional figures, including** rectangles, parallelograms, trapezoids, squares, triangles, circles, **prisms,** and cylinders. **Standard 6AF3.2 Express in symbolic form simple relationships arising from geometry.**

NEW Vocabulary

surface area

. The prism 1 cm × cm × 8 cm has the greatest suface area. The ube 2 cm × 2 cm × 2 cm as the least surface area.

▶ MINI Lab

- Use the cubes to build a rectangular prism with a length of 8 centimeters.

- Count the number of squares on the outside of the prism. The sum is the *surface area*.

1–2. See margin.

1. Record the dimensions, volume, and surface area in a table.

2. Build two more prisms using all of the cubes. For each, record the dimensions, volume, and surface area.

3. Describe the prisms with the greatest and least surface areas.

The sum of the areas of all of the surfaces, or faces, of a three-dimensional figure is the **surface area**.

KEY CONCEPT — Surface Area of a Rectangular Prism

Words	The surface area S of a rectangular prism with length ℓ, width w, and height h is the sum of the areas of its faces.
Symbols	$S = 2\ell w + 2\ell h + 2wh$

Model

EXAMPLES — Find Surface Area

1 Find the surface area of the rectangular prism.

There are three pairs of congruent faces.

- top and bottom
- front and back
- two sides

Faces	Area
top and bottom	$2(5 \cdot 4) = 40$
front and back	$2(5 \cdot 3) = 30$
two sides	$2(3 \cdot 4) = 24$
sum of the areas	$40 + 30 + 24 = 94$

The surface area is 94 square centimeters.

Additional Answers

1–2.

Dimension	Volume	Surface Area
1 cm × 1 cm × 8 cm	8 cm³	34 cm²
1 cm × 2 cm × 4 cm	8 cm³	28 cm²
2 cm × 2 cm × 2 cm	8 cm³	24 cm²

- **What is the formula for the area of a rectangle?** area = length × width

- **How could I find the area of all the faces of a rectangular prism?** Sample answer: Use the area formula for each face and find the sum of the six areas.

1 Focus

 Standards Alignment

Before Lesson 12-4
Visualize and draw two-dimensional views of three-dimensional objects made from rectangular solids from Standard 5MG2.3

Lesson 12-4
Use formulas routinely for finding the surface area of basic three-dimensional figures including prisms from Standard 7MG2.1

After Lesson 12-4
Compute the length of the perimeter, the surface area of the faces, and the volume of a three-dimensional object built from rectangular solids. Understand that when the lengths of all dimensions are multiplied by a scale factor, the surface area is multiplied by the square of the scale factor and the volume is multiplied by the cube of the scale factor from Standard 7MG2.3

2 Teach

▶ MINI Lab

After the second step, you might wish to ask students how many different prisms can be made with the 8 cubes. 3 Make sure they realize that reordering the dimensions of a prism doesn't make it a different prism. Thus, a 1 × 2 × 4 prism is the same as a 2 × 1 × 4 prism.

Scaffolding Questions

Ask:
- **What are the properties of a rectangular prism?** It has 2 parallel, congruent, rectangular bases and 4 lateral faces.

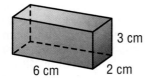
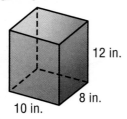
STUDY TIP

Surface Area
When you find the surface area of a three-dimensional figure, the units are square units, not cubic units.

2 **Find the surface area of the rectangular prism.**

Replace ℓ, with 9, w with 7, and h with 13.

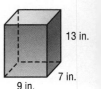
13 in.
9 in.   7 in.

surface area $= 2\ell w + 2\ell h + 2wh$

$= 2 \cdot 9 \cdot 7 + 2 \cdot 9 \cdot 13 + 2 \cdot 7 \cdot 13$

$= 126 + 234 + 182$ Multiply first. Then add.

$= 542$

The surface area of the prism is 542 square inches.

CHECK Your Progress

Find the surface area of each rectangular prism.

a.

6 m
10 m   3 m   216 m²

b.
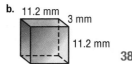
11.2 mm   3 mm
11.2 mm
385.28 mm²

Real-World EXAMPLE

3 **GIFTS** Rafael is wrapping a gift. He places it in a box 8 inches long, 2 inches wide, and 11 inches high. If Rafael bought a roll of wrapping paper that is 1 foot wide and 2 feet long, did he buy enough paper to wrap the gift? Justify your answer.

STEP 1   Find the surface area of the package.
Replace ℓ with 8, w with 2, and h with 11.

surface area $= 2\ell w + 2\ell h + 2wh$
$= 2 \cdot 8 \cdot 2 + 2 \cdot 8 \cdot 11 + 2 \cdot 2 \cdot 11$
$= 252$ in²

STEP 2   Find the area of the wrapping paper.

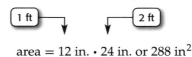
1 ft   2 ft

area $= 12$ in. $\cdot$ 24 in. or 288 in²

Since 288 > 252, Rafael bought enough wrapping paper.

STUDY TIP

Consistent Units
Since the surface area of the package is expressed in inches, convert the dimensions of the wrapping paper to inches so that all measurements are expressed using the same units.

c. Yes; the surface area of the box is 926 ft² and 950 ft² > 926 ft².

d. No; the surface area of the new box would be 1,092 ft² and 950 ft² < 1,092 ft².

CHECK Your Progress

c. **BOXES** The largest corrugated cardboard box ever constructed measured about 23 feet long, 9 feet high, and 8 feet wide. Would 950 square feet of paper be enough to cover the box? Justify your answer.

d. **BOXES** If 1 foot was added to each dimension of the largest corrugated cardboard box, ever constructed, would 950 square feet of paper still be enough to cover the box? Justify your answer.

nline **Personal Tutor at** ca.gr6math.com

Formative Assessment

Use the Check Your Progress exercises after each Example to determine students' understanding of concepts.

EXAMPLE   Use the Pythagorean Theorem

4 **Find the surface area of the rectangular prism.**

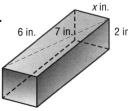
x in.

6 in. 7 in. 2 in.

The width and height of the prism are given. To find the surface area, you need to find the length of the prism. Notice that the diagonal, length, and width of the top face of the prism form a right triangle.

$c^2 = a^2 + b^2$	Pythagorean Theorem
$7^2 = 6^2 + x^2$	Replace c with 7, a with 6, and b with x.
$49 = 36 + x^2$	Evaluate 7^2 and 6^2.
$49 - 36 = 36 + x^2 - 36$	Subtract 36 from each side.
$13 = x^2$	Simplify.
$\pm\sqrt{13} = x$	Definition of square root
$\pm 3.6 \approx x$	Simplify.

STUDY TIP

Square Roots
The equation $13 = x^2$ has two solutions, 3.6 and −3.6. However, the length of the prism must be positive, so choose the positive solution.

The length of the prism is about 3.6 inches. Find the surface area.

$$\text{surface area} = 2\ell w + 2\ell h + 2wh$$
$$= 2(3.6)(6) + 2(3.6)(2) + 2(6)(2) \text{ or } 81.6$$

The surface area of the prism is about 81.6 square inches.

CHECK Your Progress

e. Find the surface area of the rectangular prism to the nearest tenth. **95.6 cm²**

5 cm
1.5 cm
x cm
8 cm

★ indicates multi-step problem

CHECK Your Understanding

Examples 1, 2 (pp. 649–650)   **Find the surface area of each rectangular prism. Round to the nearest tenth if necessary.**

1.
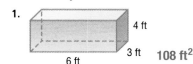
4 ft
3 ft **108 ft²**
6 ft

2.

8.2 cm
5.5 cm
3.4 cm **183.4 cm²**

Example 3 (p. 650)   **3. PAINTING** Lars built a toy box 5 feet long, 2 feet wide, and 2 feet high. If he has 1 quart of paint that covers about 87 square feet, does he have enough to paint the toy box twice? Justify your answer. **See margin.**

Example 4 (p. 651)   **4. MEASUREMENT** Find the surface area of the rectangular prism at the right. Round to the nearest tenth if necessary. **152.8 m²**

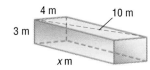
4 m 10 m
3 m
x m

ADDITIONAL EXAMPLE

4 Find the surface area of the rectangular prism. about 130.8 m²

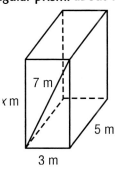
7 m
x m
5 m
3 m

3 Practice

Formative Assessment

Use Exercises 1–4 to check for understanding.

Then use the chart at the bottom of the next page to customize your assignments for students.

Intervention You may wish to use the Study Guide and Intervention Master on page 27 of the *Chapter 12 Resource Masters* for additional reinforcement.

Additional Answer

3. No; The surface area of the toy box is 48 ft². To paint it twice would require enough paint for 48 × 2 or 96 ft². Since 87 ft² < 96 ft², he does not have enough paint.

Odd/Even Assignments

Exercises 5–14 are structured so that students practice the same concepts whether they are assigned odd or even problems.

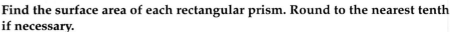

HOMEWORK HELP

For Exercises	See Examples
5–10	1, 2
11–12	3
13–14	4

Exercise Levels
A: 5–14
B: 15–18
C: 19–21

9. 125.4 in^2 or 124$\frac{3}{8}$ in^2
10. 659.7 yd^2 or 6591318 yd^2
12. Yes; there are 2,520 ft^2 of fencing. Since 8 gallons of paint will cover 350 • 8 or 2,800 ft^2 and 2,800 ft^2 > 2,520 ft^2, 8 gallons is enough paint.

13. 243.8 ft^2
14. 303.7 m^2

Find the surface area of each rectangular prism. Round to the nearest tenth if necessary.

5.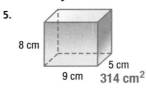
8 cm, 9 cm, 5 cm **314 cm^2**

6.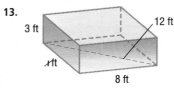
13 m, 4 m, 5 m **274 m^2**

7.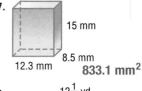
15 mm, 8.5 mm, 12.3 mm **833.1 mm^2**

8.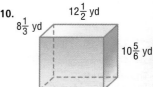
12 ft, 1.7 ft, 6.4 ft **216.2 ft^2**

9.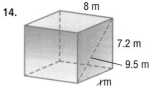
3 in., 4$\frac{3}{4}$ in., 6$\frac{1}{4}$ in.

10.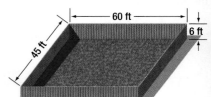
12$\frac{1}{2}$ yd, 8$\frac{1}{3}$ yd, 10$\frac{5}{6}$ yd

★ **11. BOOKS** When making a book cover, Anwar adds an additional 20 square inches to the surface area to allow for overlap. How many square inches of paper will Anwar use to make a book cover for a book 11 inches long, 8 inches wide, and 1 inch high? **234 in^2**

12. FENCES If one gallon of paint covers 350 square feet, will 8 gallons of paint be enough to paint the inside and outside of the fence shown once? Explain.

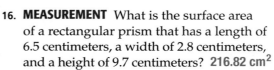
60 ft, 45 ft, 6 ft

Find the surface area of each rectangular prism. Round to the nearest tenth if necessary.

13.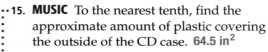
3 ft, 12 ft, x ft, 8 ft

14.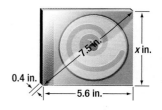
8 m, 7.2 m, 9.5 m, x m

Real-World Link . . . .
The recording industry in California employs over 27,000 people and adds billions of dollars annually to the California economy.
Source: California Music Coalition

15. MUSIC To the nearest tenth, find the approximate amount of plastic covering the outside of the CD case. **64.5 in^2**

16. MEASUREMENT What is the surface area of a rectangular prism that has a length of 6.5 centimeters, a width of 2.8 centimeters, and a height of 9.7 centimeters? **216.82 cm^2**

7.5 in., 0.4 in., 5.6 in., x in.

17. ALGEBRA Write a formula for the surface area s of a cube in which each side measures x units. $s = 6x^2$

★ **18. PACKAGING** A company needs to make a trial size cereal box that holds 100 cubic centimeters of cereal. If cardboard costs $0.05 per 100 square centimeters, how much would it cost to make 100 boxes? **$6.50**

652 Chapter 12 Looking Ahead to Grade 7: Geometry and Measurement

DIFFERENTIATED HOMEWORK OPTIONS

Level	Assignment	Two-Day Option	
BL Basic	5–14, 19, 21–26	5–13 odd, 22, 23	6–14 even, 19, 21, 24–26
OL Core	5–13 odd, 15, 16, 17–19, 21–26	5–14, 22, 23	15–19, 21, 24–26
AL Advanced/Pre-AP	15–26, (optional: 27–30)		

19. REASONING The bottom and sides of a pool in the shape of a rectangular prism will be painted blue. The length, width, and height of the pool are 18 feet, 12 feet, and 6 feet, respectively. Explain why the number of square feet to be painted is *not* equivalent to the expression $2(18)(12) + 2(18)(6) + 2(12)(6)$. **See margin.**

EXTRA PRACTICE

See pages 714, 726.

Math Online

Self-Check Quiz at
ca.gr6math.com

20. CHALLENGE The figure at the right is made by placing a cube with 12-centimeter sides on top of another cube with 15-centimeter sides. Find the surface area.
1,926 cm²

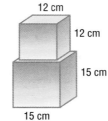

12 cm

12 cm

15 cm

15 cm

21. WRITING IN MATH Explain why surface area of a three-dimensional figure is measured in square units rather than in cubic units.
Surface area measures the area of the faces, and area is measured in square units.

STANDARDS PRACTICE 7MG2.1

22. Which of the following expressions represents the surface area of a cube with side length w? **B**

  A w^3

  B $6w^2$

  C $6w^3$

  D $2w + 4w^2$

23. How much cardboard is needed to make a box with a length of 2.5 feet, a width of 1.6 feet, and a height of 2 feet? **G**

  F 37.5 square feet

  G 24.4 square feet

  H 8 square feet

  J 6.1 square feet

Spiral Review

24. MEASUREMENT A rectangular-shaped yard that measures 50 feet by 70 feet is bordered by a flowerbed that is 2 feet wide. What is the perimeter of the entire yard? Use the *make a model* strategy. (Lesson 12-3) **256 ft**

25. MEASUREMENT What is the missing measure of a right triangle in which $a = 13$ feet and $c = 18$ feet? Round to the nearest tenth. (Lesson 12-2) **12.4 ft**

26. MEASUREMENT What is the volume of the cylinder shown at the right? Round to the nearest tenth. (Lesson 11-10) **351.7 in³**

4 in.

7 in.

GET READY for the Next Lesson

PREREQUISITE SKILL Find the area of each circle. Round to the nearest tenth. (Lesson 11-4)

27.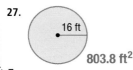
16 ft
803.8 ft²

28.
21 m
346.2 m²

29. diameter = 13.6 yd
145.2 yd²

30. radius = 23 km
1,661.1 km²

Name the Math Tell students that an architect is trying to find the surface area of a skyscraper shaped like a rectangular prism. Have them write what mathematical procedures they would suggest to the architect. You may want to remind students that their answers should not include the bottom of the building.

Formative Assessment

Check for student understanding of concepts in Lesson 12-4.

Quiz 3, p. 42

FOLDABLES Study Organizer **Foldables™ Follow-Up**

Remind students to take notes about finding the surface area of rectangular prisms in their Foldables tables. Encourage them to draw an example of a prism, labeling its dimensions and showing how they relate to the formula.

Additional Answer

19. Sample answer: Not all sides of the rectangular prism will be painted. The top will not be painted. The number of square feet to be painted is $(18)(12) + 2(18)(6) + 2(12)(6)$ or 576.

Pre-AP Activity Use after Exercise 22

Have students find the dimensions of two rectangular prisms with a volume of 64 cm³—the prism with the least possible surface area, and the prism with the greatest possible surface area. Make sure they explain their steps and reasoning. Did they draw diagrams? Did they use prime factorization? Did they look for a pattern? The prism with the least surface area has the following dimensions: 4 cm × 4 cm × 4 cm. The prism with the greatest surface area has the following dimensions: 64 cm × 1 cm × 1 cm.

1 Focus

Materials

- isometric dot paper

Easy-to-Make Manipulatives

Templates for:
- isometric dot paper, p. 17

Teaching Tip

You might want to have students predict by how much the surface area (and the volume) of a cube will increase when the cube's dimensions are doubled and tripled. Record their predictions on the chalkboard. When students finish the Activity, have them discuss their results and compare them with their predictions.

2 Teach

Activity 1 Have students make their tables before they begin drawing the cubes. Make sure students remember that each side of a cube is congruent. Encourage students to write the ratios in simplest form (for example, 2:8 can be written as 1:4, 2:24 can be written as 1:12).

Extend
12-4

Measurement Lab
Changes in Volume and Surface Area

Main IDEA

Investigate changes in volume and surface area.

 Preparation for Standard 7MG2.4 **Relate the changes in measurement with a change of scale to the units used** (e.g., square inches, cubic feet) and to conversions between units (1 square foot = 144 square inches or [1 ft²] = [144 in²], 1 cubic inch is approximately 16.38 cubic centimeters or [1 in³] = [16.38 cm³]). **Standard 6MR2.4 Use a variety of methods, such as words, numbers, symbols, charts, graphs, tables, diagrams, and models, to explain mathematical reasoning.**

Suppose you have a model of a rectangular prism and you are asked to create a similar model whose dimensions are twice as large. In this lab, you will investigate how changing the dimensions of a three-dimensional figure affects the surface area and volume.

ACTIVITY

1 **STEP 1** Draw a cube on dot paper that measures 1 unit on each side. Calculate the volume and the surface area of the cube. Then record the data in a table like the one shown below.

 1 unit

STEP 2 Double the side lengths of the cube. Calculate the volume and the surface area of this cube. Record the data in your table.

 2 units

STEP 3 Triple the side lengths of the original cube. Now each side measures 3 units long. Calculate the volume and the surface area of the cube and record the data.

 3 units

STEP 4 For each cube, write a ratio comparing the side length and the volume. Then write a ratio comparing the side length and the surface area. The first one is done for you.

Side Length (units)	Volume (units³)	Surface Area (units²)	Ratio of Side Length to Volume	Ratio of Side Length to Surface Area
1	$1^3 = 1$	$6(1^2) = 6$	1:1	1:6
2	$2^3 = 8$	$6(2^2) = 24$	1:4	1:12
3	$3^3 = 27$	$6(3^2) = 54$	1:9	1:18
4	$4^3 = 64$	$6(4^2) = 96$	1:16	1:24
5	$5^3 = 125$	$6(5^2) = 150$	1:25	1:30
s	s^3	$6s^2$	$s:s^3$	$s:6s^2$

 **CHECK Your Progress**

a. Complete the table above. **See table.**

ACTIVITY

2 **STEP 1** Draw a cube on dot paper that measures 8 units on each side. Calculate the volume and the surface area of the cube. Record the data in a table like the one shown below.

STEP 2 Halve the side lengths of the cube in Step 1. Calculate the volume and the surface area of this cube and record the data.

STEP 3 Halve the side lengths of the cube in Step 2. Calculate the volume and the surface area of the cube and record the data.

STEP 4 For each cube, write a ratio comparing the side length and the volume and a ratio comparing the side length and the surface area. The first one is done for you.

Side Length (units)	Volume (units³)	Surface Area (units²)	Ratio of Side Length to Volume	Ratio of Side Length to Surface Area
8	$8^3 = 512$	$6(8^2) = 384$	8:512 or 1:64	8:384 or 1:48
4	$4^3 = 64$	$6(4^2) = 96$	1:16	1:24
2	$2^3 = 8$	$6(2^2) = 24$	1:4	1:12
s	s^3	$6s^2$	$s:s^3$	$s:6s^2$

CHECK Your Progress

b. Complete the table above. **See table.**

ANALYZE THE RESULTS

1. Write a formula for the volume V of a cube with side length s. **$V = s^3$**

2. Write a formula for the surface area A of a cube with side length s.
 $A = 6s^2$

MAKE A CONJECTURE Complete each sentence.

3. 2^3 or 8

3. If the side length of a cube is doubled, the volume is times greater.

4. If the side length of a cube is doubled, the surface area is ■ times greater. **2^2 or 4**

5. If the side length of a cube is tripled, the volume increases by ■ times and the surface area increases by ■ times. **3^3 or 27; 3^2 or 9**

6. If the side length of a cube decreases by $\frac{1}{2}$, the surface area decreases by ■. **$\frac{1}{4}$**

Extend 12-4 Measurement Lab: Changes in Volume and Surface Area **655**

Teaching Tip

You might want to have students predict by how much the surface area (and the volume) of a cube will decrease when the cube's dimensions are halved. Record their predictions on the chalkboard. When students finish the Activity, have them discuss their results and compare them with their predictions.

Activity 2 Have students make their tables before they begin drawing the cubes. Encourage students to write the ratios in simplest form (for example, 8:512 can be written as 1:64, 4:64 can be written as 1:16).

3 Assess

Formative Assessment

Use Exercises 3–6 to determine whether students understand how changing the dimensions of a cube affects its surface area and volume.

From Concrete to Abstract Use Exercise 1 and 2 to bridge the gap between using models of three-dimensional figures to find surface area and volume and using formulas to find surface area and volume.

Extending the Concept Ask students to predict by how much the surface area of a cylinder will increase when its dimensions are doubled.

Surface Area of Cylinders

Preparation for Standard 7MG2.1

Use formulas routinely for finding the perimeter and area of basic two-dimensional figures and **the surface area** and volume **of basic three-dimensional figures, including** rectangles, parallelograms, trapezoids, squares, triangles, circles, prisms, and **cylinders.**

PACING: **Regular:** 2 periods, **Block:** 1 period

Options for Differentiated Instruction

 = English Language Learner   = Above Grade Level   = Struggling Students   = Special Needs

Reviewing Concepts

Use before beginning Lesson 12-5.

Prior to starting the lesson, have students prepare a card that lists all the formulas and vocabulary terms they know involving circles. This card should include the following:
- formula for area of a circle
- formula for circumference of a circle
- definition of diameter
- definition of radius
- definition of pi

Have students include any diagrams or examples that will help them review concepts involving circles.

Explaining the Steps

Use after presenting the Examples.

Students will have a better understanding of surface areas of cylinders if they use their own words to describe the formula. Have students explain verbally or write a detailed description of the procedure for finding the surface area of a cylinder.

Their descriptions should include the following:
- an explanation of the different parts of the formula, and
- the reason there are two parts to this formula.

Challenge Beyond the Lesson Content

Use after students complete Lesson 12-5.

Have students find the dimensions of a cylinder and a rectangular prism that fit the following criteria:
- Both figures have a surface area between 250 and 300 square centimeters.
- The height of the cylinder is twice the height of the prism.

Have them explain how they determined their solution. Sample answer: prism: 5 cm long, 6 cm wide, 10 cm high (280 cm^2); cylinder: 2 cm radius, 20 cm high (276.5 cm^2); use the guess and check strategy.

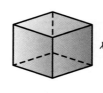
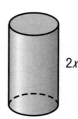

BL = Below Grade Level   **OL** = On Grade Level   **AL** = Above Grade Level   **ELL** = English Language Learner

---

Lesson Reading Guide
p. 32 **BL OL ELL**

NAME _____ DATE _____ PERIOD _____

12-5 Lesson Reading Guide   7MG2.1
Surface Area of Cylinders

Get Ready for the Lesson
Complete the Mini Lab at the top of page 656 in your textbook. Write your answers below.

1. Make a net of the cylinder. Sample answer:

2. Name the shapes in the net. circle, rectangle

3. How is the length of the rectangle related to the circles? The length of the rectangle is the circumference of the circle. So, the length is $2\pi r$.

4. Explain how to find the surface area of the cylinder. Add the areas of both circles and the area of the rectangle.

Read the Lesson
Write the formula to use to find each of the following.

5. the area of a circle _____ $A = \pi r^2$

6. the circumference of a circle _____ $C = 2\pi r$

7. the area of a rectangle _____ $A = bh$

8. How would you find the surface area of a cylinder with no top? Give your answer in words and symbols. Sample answer: Find the area of the base and add it to the area of the curved surface; $S = \pi r^2 + 2\pi rh$.

Remember What You Learned
9. Complete the table.

Words	The surface area of a cylinder	equals	the area of two bases	plus	the area of the curved surface.
Symbols	S	=	$2(\pi r^2)$	+	$(2\pi r)h$

Chapter 12   32   Glencoe California Mathematics, Grade 6

Study Guide and Intervention*
p. 33 **BL OL ELL**

NAME _____ DATE _____ PERIOD _____

12-5 Study Guide and Intervention   7MG2.1
Surface Area of Cylinders

The diagram below shows how you can put two circles and a rectangle together to make a cylinder.

the surface area of a cylinder	equals	the area of two bases	plus	the area of the curved surface.
S	=	$2(\pi r^2)$	+	$(2\pi r)h$

In the diagram above, the length of the rectangle is the same as the circumference of the circle. Also, the width of the rectangle is the same as the height of the cylinder.

Example Find the surface area of the cylinder. Use 3.14 for π. Round to the nearest tenth.

$S = 2\pi r^2 + 2\pi rh$ Surface area of a cylinder.
$S = 2\pi(6)^2 + 2\pi(6)(20)$ Replace π with 3.14, r with 6, and h with 20.
≈ 979.7 Simplify.

The surface area is about 979.7 square meters.

Exercises
Find the surface area of each cylinder. Use 3.14 for π. Round to the nearest tenth.

1. 408.2 in^2
2. 508.7 ft^2
3. 440.2 cm^2

Chapter 12   33   Glencoe California Mathematics, Grade 6

Skills Practice*
p. 34 **BL OL**

NAME _____ DATE _____ PERIOD _____

12-5 Skills Practice   7MG2.1
Surface Area of Cylinders

Find the surface area of each cylinder. Use 3.14 for π. Round to the nearest tenth.

1. 1,607.7 in^2
2. 602.9 mm^2
3. 276.3 m^2

4. 355.7 yd^2
5. 107.3 ft^2
6. 506.4 cm^2

7. Find the surface area of a can with a radius of 4 centimeters and a height of 11 centimeters. 376.8 cm^2

8. Find the surface area of the outside of a cylindrical barrel with a diameter of 10 inches and a height of 12 inches. 533.8 in^2

9. Find the area of the curved surface of a D battery with a diameter of 3.2 centimeters and a height of 5.8 centimeters. 56.3 cm^2

Chapter 12   34   Glencoe California Mathematics, Grade 6

Practice*
p. 35 **OL AL**

NAME _____ DATE _____ PERIOD _____

12-5 Practice   7MG2.1
Surface Area of Cylinders

Find the surface area of each cylinder. Use 3.14 for π. Round to the nearest tenth.

1. 50.2 ft^2
2. 331.6 m^2
3. 90.3 in^2

4. 227.1 m^2
5. 332.1 cm^2
6. 395.6 ft^2

7. diameter = 15.2 mm, height = 9.4 mm 811.4 mm^2
8. diameter = 28.4 yd, height = 15.1 yd 2,612.9 yd^2
9. radius = 50 cm, height = 70 cm 37,680 cm^2

ESTIMATION Estimate the area of each cylinder.

10. Sample answer: $2 \cdot 3 \cdot 2^2 + 2 \cdot 3 \cdot 2 \cdot 7$ or 108 ft^2
11. Sample answer: $2 \cdot 3 \cdot 10^2 + 2 \cdot 3 \cdot 10 \cdot 7$ or 1,020 mm^2
12. Sample answer: $2 \cdot 3 \cdot 3^2 + 2 \cdot 3 \cdot 3 \cdot 4$ or 126 yd^2

13. **FUEL STORAGE** A fuel storage tank needs to be painted on the inside. If the height of the tank is 40 feet and the diameter is 120 feet, what is the surface that needs to be painted? Round to the nearest hundred square feet. 37,680 ft^2

14. **PAPER TOWELS** Each of the three rolls of paper towels in a package are individually wrapped in plastic. The radius of each roll is 5.6 centimeters and the height is 27.9 centimeters. How much plastic is used to individually wrap the three rolls? Round to the nearest tenth. 3,534.4 cm^2

Chapter 12   35   Glencoe California Mathematics, Grade 6

Word Problem Practice*
p. 36 **OL AL**

NAME _____ DATE _____ PERIOD _____

12-5 Word Problem Practice   7MG2.1
Surface Area of Cylinders

1. **PACKAGING** What is the area of the label on a box of oatmeal with a radius of 9.3 centimeters and a height of 16.5 centimeters? Round to the nearest tenth. 963.7 cm^2

2. **TIRES** Betty wants to know the total surface area of the tread on one of her tires. If the diameter of the tire is 18 inches and the width of the tire is 5 inches, what is the total surface area of the tire's tread? Round to the nearest tenth. 282.6 in^2

3. **CANS** A cylindrical can has a diameter of 6 inches and a height of 7.3 inches. What is the surface area of the can? Round to the nearest tenth. 194.1 in^2

4. **CANS** A cylindrical can has a height of 14 centimeters and a radius of 4.2 centimeters. Find the surface area of the can. Round to the nearest tenth. 480.0 cm^2

5. **MANUFACTURING** How much sheet metal is required to make a cylindrical trash can with a diameter of 2 feet and height of $4\frac{1}{2}$ feet? Round to the nearest tenth. (*Hint*: Do not include the top.) 29.8 ft^2

6. **PLUMBING** How much steel is needed to make a hollow pipe with a radius of 3 inches and a height of 15 inches? Round to the nearest tenth. 282.6 in^2

Chapter 12   36   Glencoe California Mathematics, Grade 6

Enrichment
p. 37 **OL AL**

NAME _____ DATE _____ PERIOD _____

12-5 Enrichment   7MG2.1

Cross Sections
In each diagram on this page, a plane cuts through a solid figure. The intersection of the plane with the solid figure is called a *cross section*.
Sketch the cross section formed in each diagram.

1.
2. (pyramid with a square base)
3.
4.
5. (pyramid with a triangular base)
6.
7.
8. (pyramid with a triangular base)

Chapter 12   37   Glencoe California Mathematics, Grade 6

*** Also available in Spanish ELL**

Additional Lesson Resources

Transparencies
- *5-Minute Check Transparency*, Lesson 12-5

Other Print Products
- *Noteables™ Interactive Study Notebook with Foldables™*

Teacher Tech Tools
- *Interactive Classroom CD-ROM*, Lesson 12-5
- *AssignmentWorks CD-ROM*, Lesson 12-5

Student Tech Tools
ca.gr6math.com
- Extra Examples, Chapter 12, Lesson 5
- Self-Check Quiz, Chapter 12, Lesson 5

12-5 Surface Area of Cylinders

1 Focus

1 Focus

Standards Alignment

Before Lesson 12-5
Know and use the formulas for the volume of triangular prisms and cylinders from Standard 6MG1.3

Lesson 12-5
Use formulas routinely for finding the surface area of basic three-dimensional figures, including cylinders from Standard 7MG2.1

After Lesson 12-5
Compute the length of the perimeter, the surface area of the faces, and the volume of a three-dimensional object built from rectangular solids. Understand that when the lengths of all dimensions are multiplied by a scale factor, the surface area is multiplied by the square of the scale factor and the volume is multiplied by the cube of the scale factor from Standard 7MG2.3

Main IDEA

Find the surface area of a cylinder.

 Preparation for Standard 7MG2.1 Use formulas **routinely for finding** the perimeter and area of basic two-dimensional figures and **the surface area** and volume **of basic three-dimensional figures, including** rectangles, parallelograms, trapezoids, squares, triangles, circles, prisms, and **cylinders.**

3. Sample answer:
The length of the rectangle is the circumference of the circle. So, the length is $2\pi r$.
4. Add the areas of both circles and the area of the rectangle.

REVIEW Vocabulary

circumference the distance around a circle (Lesson 11-3)

▶ MINI Lab

STEP 1 Trace the top and bottom of the can on grid paper. Then cut out the shapes.

STEP 2 Cut a long rectangle from the grid paper. The width of the rectangle should be the same as the height of the can. Wrap the rectangle around the side of the can. Cut off the excess paper so that the edges just meet.

1. Make a net of the cylinder. **See margin.**
2. Name the shapes in the net. **circle, rectangle**
3. How is the length of the rectangle related to the circles?
4. Explain how to find the surface area of the cylinder.

You can put two circles and a rectangle together to make a cylinder.

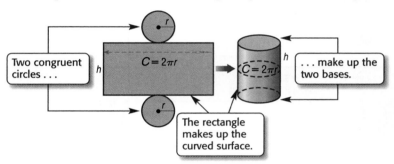

In the diagram above, the length of the rectangle is the same as the circumference of the circle. Also, the width of the rectangle is the same as the height of the cylinder.

The surface area of a cylinder	equals	the area of two bases	plus	the area of the curved surface.
S	$=$	$2(\pi r^2)$	$+$	$(2\pi r)h$

KEY CONCEPT
Surface Area of a Cylinder

Words The surface area S of a cylinder with height h and radius r is the sum of the areas of the circular bases and the area of the curved surface.

Model

Symbols $S = 2\pi r^2 + 2\pi rh$

2 Teach

▶ MINI Lab

Some students may suggest using a ruler to measure the length of the rectangle and, thus, to find its area. Make sure everyone realizes that the rectangle's length is the same as the circumference of the circle. If students don't remember the formula for the circumference of a circle, have them review their Foldables for Chapter 11.

Scaffolding Questions

Ask:
• What is the radius of a circle?
distance from its center to any point on the circle

• What is the diameter of a circle? distance across the circle through its center

• What is the circumference of a circle? distance around the circle

• What is π? ratio of any circle's circumference to its diameter, approximated by 3.14 or $\frac{22}{7}$

Additional Answer

1. Sample answer:

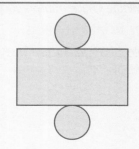

Value of π
Use 3.14 as the approximate value of π.

EXAMPLE Find the Surface Area of a Cylinder

1 Find the surface area of the cylinder. Round to the nearest tenth.

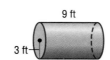
2 m
7 m

$S = 2\pi r^2 + 2\pi rh$ Surface area of a cylinder

    $= 2\pi(2)^2 + 2\pi(2)(7)$ Replace *r* with 2 and *h* with 7.

    ≈ 113.0 Simplify.

The surface area is about 113.0 square meters.

CHECK Your Progress

a. Find the surface area of the cylinder. Round to the nearest tenth. **226.1 ft²**

9 ft
3 ft

Real-World EXAMPLE

2 **DESIGN** A can of soup is 5 inches high, and its base has a diameter of 4 inches. How much paper is needed to make the label on the can?

Chicken Noodle Soup

Since the diameter is 4 inches, the radius is 2 inches. Only the curved side of the can has a label.

$S = 2\pi rh$ Curved surface of a cylinder

    $= 2\pi(2)(5)$ Replace *r* with 2 and *h* with 5.

    ≈ 62.8 Simplify.

So, about 62.8 square inches of paper is needed to make the label.

CHECK Your Progress

b. **DESIGN** Find the area of the label of a can of tuna with a radius of 5.1 centimeters and a height of 2.9 centimeters. **about 92.9 cm²**

Online Personal Tutor at ca.gr6math.com

★ indicates multi-step problem

CHECK Your Understanding

Example 1
(p. 657)

Find the surface area of each cylinder. Round to the nearest tenth.

1. 5 mm
2 mm
87.9 mm²

2. ←11 in.→
8 in.
466.3 in²

Example 2
(p. 657)

3. **STORAGE** The height of a water tank is 10 meters, and it has a diameter of 10 meters. What is the surface area of the tank? **about 471 m²**

Math Online Extra Examples at ca.gr6math.com

Focus on Mathematical Content

The **curved surface of a cylinder** can be mentally "unrolled" into a rectangle. The bases of a cylinder are circles. So, students can use what they know about the area of rectangles and the area of circles to find the surface area of a cylinder.

Formative Assessment

Use the Check Your Progress exercises after each Example to determine students' understanding of concepts.

ADDITIONAL EXAMPLES

1 Find the surface area of the cylinder. Round to the nearest tenth. 169.6 cm²

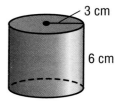
3 cm
6 cm

2 **GIFT WRAP** A poster is contained in a cardboard cylinder that is 10 inches high. The cylinder's base has a diameter of 8 inches. How much paper is needed to wrap the cardboard cylinder if the ends are to be left uncovered? about 251.2 in²

Additional Examples are also in:
- Noteables™ Interactive Study Notebook with Foldables™
- Interactive Classroom PowerPoint® Presentations

Formative Assessment

Use Exercises 1–3 to check for understanding.

Then use the chart at the bottom of this page to customize your assignments for students.

Intervention You may wish to use the Study Guide and Intervention Master on page 33 of the *Chapter 12 Resource Masters* for additional reinforcement.

Odd/Even Assignments

Exercises 4–11 are structured so that students practice the same concepts whether they are assigned odd or even problems.

Additional Answers

12. Sample answer: $2 \cdot 3 \cdot 5^2 + 2 \cdot 3 \cdot 5 \cdot 2$ or 210 cm^2

13. Sample answer: $2 \cdot 3 \cdot 4^2 + 2 \cdot 3 \cdot 4 \cdot 4$ or 192 m^2

14. Sample answer: $2 \cdot 3 \cdot 7^2 + 2 \cdot 3 \cdot 7 \cdot 13$ or 840 ft^2

17. No; the surface area of the side of the cylinder will double, but the area of the bases will not.

19. A cylinder with radius 6 cm and height 3 cm has a greater surface area than a cylinder with height 6 cm and radius 3 cm; Sample answer: The first cylinder has a surface area of 339.3 cm^2 while the second cylinder has a surface area of 169.6 cm^2.

Exercises

HOMEWORK HELP

For Exercises	See Examples
4–9	1
10–11	2

Exercise Levels
A: 4–11
B: 12–16
C: 17–19

Find the surface area of each cylinder. Round to the nearest tenth.

4. 6 yd, 10 yd — **602.9 yd^2**

5. 12.5 m, 9 m — **1,215.2 m^2**

6. 3 ft, 18 ft — **183.7 ft^2**

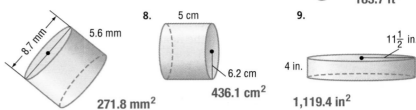

7. 8.7 mm, 5.6 mm — **271.8 mm^2**

8. 5 cm, 6.2 cm — **436.1 cm^2**

9. $11\frac{1}{2}$ in., 4 in. — **1,119.4 in^2**

10. CANDLES A cylindrical candle has a diameter of 4 inches and a height of 7 inches. What is the surface area of the candle? **113 in^2**

11. PENCILS Find the surface area of an unsharpened cylindrical pencil that has a radius of 0.5 centimeter and a height of 19 centimeters. **61.2 cm^2**

ESTIMATION Estimate the surface area of each cylinder

12–14. See margin.

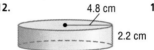

12. 4.8 cm, 2.2 cm

13. 8.2 m, 3.7 m

14. 12.8 ft, 6.5 ft

★ **15. BAKING** Mrs. Jones baked a cake 5 inches high and 9 inches in diameter. If Mrs. Jones covers the top and sides of the cake with frosting, find the area that the frosting covers to the nearest tenth. **204.9 in^2**

EXTRA PRACTICE
See pages 714, 726.
Math Online
Self-Check Quiz at ca.gr6math.com

16. PACKAGING The mail tube shown is made of cardboard and has plastic end caps. ★ Approximately what percent of the surface area of the mail tube is cardboard? **about 85.7%**

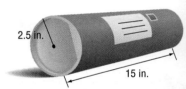

2.5 in., 15 in.

H.O.T. Problems

17. CHALLENGE If the height of a cylinder is doubled, will its surface area also double? Explain your reasoning. **See margin.**

18. WRITING IN MATH Write a problem about a real-world situation in which you would find the surface area of a cylinder. Be sure to include the answer to your problem. **See students' work.**

19. See margin.

19. REASONING Which has more surface area, a cylinder with radius 6 centimeters and height 3 centimeters or a cylinder with radius 3 centimeters and height 6 centimeters? Explain your reasoning.

DIFFERENTIATED HOMEWORK OPTIONS

Level	Assignment	Two-Day Option	
BL Basic	4–11, 18–27	5–11 odd, 20, 21	4–10 even, 18, 19, 22–27
OL Core	5–15 odd, 16, 18–27	4–11, 20–21	12–16, 18, 19, 22–27
AL Advanced/Pre-AP	12–27		

20. Stacey has a cylindrical paper clip holder with the net shown. Use a centimeter ruler to measure the dimensions of the net in centimeters. **C**

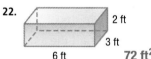
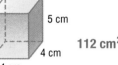

Which is closest to the surface area of the cylindrical paper clip holder?

A 6.0 cm^2

B 6.5 cm^2

C 7.5 cm^2

D 15.5 cm^2

21. The three containers below each hold about 1 liter of liquid. Which container has the greatest surface area? **G**

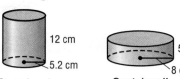

12 cm
5.2 cm
Container I

5 cm
8 cm
Container II

10 cm
5.7 cm
Container III

11 cm
5.4 cm
Container IV

F Container I

G Container II

H Container III

J Container IV

Spiral Review

MEASUREMENT Find the surface area of each rectangular prism. (Lesson 12-4)

22.

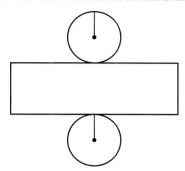

2 ft
3 ft
6 ft
72 ft^2

23.

5 cm
4 cm
4 cm
112 cm^2

24.

15 m
7 m
11.2 m
702.8 m^2

MEASUREMENT Find the missing measure of each right triangle. Round to the nearest tenth if necessary. (Lesson 12-2)

25. $a = 8$ in., $b = 10$ in. **12.8 in. 26.** $a = 12$ ft, $c = 20$ ft **16 ft** **27.** $b = 12$ cm, $c = 14$ cm **7.2 cm**

Cross-Curricular Project

Math and History

It's All Greek to Me It's time to complete your project. Use the information and data you have gathered about Pythagoras to prepare a Web page or poster. Be sure to include the three-dimensional solid you created with your project.

Math Online **Cross-Curricular Project at** ca.gr6math.com

Ticket Out the Door Tell students that a cylinder has a diameter of 2 feet and a height of 1 foot. Have students find the cylinder's surface area and write it on a slip of paper. 12.6 ft^2

Formative Assessment

Check for student understanding of concepts in Lesson 12-5.

CRM Quiz 4, p. 42

FOLDABLES **Foldables™**
Study Organizer **Follow-Up**

Remind students to take notes about finding the surface area of cylinders in their Foldables tables. Encourage them to draw an example of a cylinder, labeling its dimensions and showing how they relate to the formula.

Differentiated Instruction

Interpersonal Learners Have students write step-by-step instructions for finding the surface area of a real-world cylinder, such as a soup can. You might wish to have students direct their instructions to a friend or family member. Encourage them to exchange instructions with a partner and test them. Is enough information included? too much? Could a friend or family member use the instructions to find the cylinder's surface area without any help from the student?

Dinah Zike's Foldables

Have students look through the chapter to make sure they have included notes and examples about the key concepts of each lesson in their Foldables.

Encourage students to refer to their Foldables while completing the Study Guide and Review and while preparing for the Chapter Test.

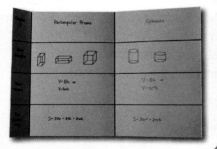

Formative Assessment

Key Vocabulary The page references after each word denote where that term was first introduced. If students have difficulty answering Exercises 1–10, remind them that they can use these page references to refresh their memories about the vocabulary terms.

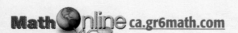 ca.gr6math.com

Vocabulary PuzzleMaker improves students' mathematics vocabulary using four puzzle formats—crossword, scramble, word search using a word list, and word search using clues. Students can work online or from a printed worksheet.

 Download Vocabulary Review from ca.gr6math.com

FOLDABLES Study Organizer — GET READY to Study

Be sure the following Key Concepts are noted in your Foldable.

Key Concepts

Irrational Numbers (Lesson 12-1)
• An irrational number is a number that *cannot* be written as a fraction.

Pythagorean Theorem (Lesson 12-2)
• In a right triangle, the square of the length of the hypotenuse equals the sum of the squares of the lengths of the legs.

Surface Area (Lessons 12-4, 12-5)
• The surface area S of a rectangular prism with length ℓ, width w, and height h is the sum of the areas of the faces. $S = 2\ell w + 2\ell h + 2wh$

• The surface area of S of a cylinder with height h and a radius r is the sum of the area of the circular bases and the area of the curved surface. $S = 2\pi r^2 + 2\pi rh$

1. false; right triangle
4. false; sum
6. false; rectangular prism

Summative Assessment

 Vocabulary Test, p. 44

Key Vocabulary

hypotenuse (p. 640)   Pythagorean Theorem
irrational number (p. 637)   (p. 640)
leg (p. 640)   surface area (p. 648)

Vocabulary Check

State whether each sentence is *true* or *false*. If *false*, replace the underlined word or number to make a true sentence.

1. The side opposite the right angle in a <u>scalene triangle</u> is called a hypotenuse.

2. Either of the two sides that form the right angle of a right triangle is called a <u>hypotenuse</u>. **false; leg**

3. An <u>irrational number</u> is a number that cannot be expressed as the quotient of two integers. **true**

4. In a right triangle, the square of the length of the hypotenuse equals the <u>difference</u> of the squares of the lengths of the legs.

5. The sum of the areas of all the surfaces of a three-dimensional figure is called the <u>surface area</u>. **true**

6. The formula for finding the surface area of a <u>cylinder</u> is $S = 2\ell w + 2\ell h + 2wh$.

7. Rational numbers include <u>only positive</u> numbers. **false; positive and negative**

8. The <u>Pythagorean Theorem</u> can be used to find the length of the hypotenuse of a right triangle if the measures of both legs are known. **true**

9. To find the surface area of a <u>rectangular prism</u>, you must know the measurements of the height and the radius. **false; cylinder**

10. The square root of a perfect square is a <u>rational number</u>. **true**

Mixed Problem Solving
For mixed problem-solving practice,
see page 726.

CHAPTER 12 **Study Guide and Review**

Lesson-by-Lesson Review

12-1 **Estimating Square Roots** (pp. 636–639)

Estimate each square root to the nearest whole number.

11. $\sqrt{6}$ **2**   12. $\sqrt{99}$ **10**   13. $\sqrt{48}$ **7**

14. $\sqrt{76}$ **9**   15. $\sqrt{19}$ **4**   16. $\sqrt{52}$ **7**

Estimate each square root to the nearest tenth.

17. $\sqrt{61}$ **7.8**   18. $\sqrt{132}$ **11.5**

19. $\sqrt{444}$ **21.1**   20. $\sqrt{12}$ **3.5**

21. **SWIMMING POOL** The bottom of Marcia's square swimming pool has an area of 118 square feet. What is the approximate length of one of the sides?

   21. 11 ft

Example 1 Estimate $\sqrt{29}$ to the nearest whole number.

$25 < 29 < 36$ 29 is between the perfect squares 25 and 36.

$\sqrt{25} < \sqrt{29} < \sqrt{36}$ Find the square root of each number.

$5 < \sqrt{29} < 6$ $\sqrt{25} = 5$ and $\sqrt{36} = 6$

So, $\sqrt{29}$ is between 5 and 6. Since 29 is closer to 25 than to 36, the best whole number estimate is 5.

12-2 **The Pythagorean Theorem** (pp. 640–645)

Find the missing measure of each triangle. Round to the nearest tenth if necessary.

22.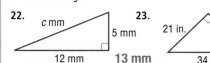

23.
   26.7 in.

24. $a = 5$ ft, $b = 6$ ft **7.8 ft**

25. $b = 10$ yd, $c = 12$ yd **6.6 yd**

26. $a = 7$ m, $c = 15$ m **13.3 m**

27. **COMMUNICATION** Find the length of the wire x that is attached to the telephone pole. Round to the nearest tenth. **29.8 ft**

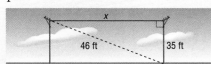

28. **LADDERS** Bartolo has a 26-foot ladder.
24 ft He places it 10-feet away from the base of a building. What is the height of the building where the top of ladder rests?

Example 2 Find the missing measure of the triangle shown at the right. Round to the nearest tenth if necessary.

Use the Pythagorean Theorem to solve for c.

$c^2 = a^2 + b^2$ Pythagorean Theorem

$c^2 = 4^2 + 12^2$ $a = 4$ and $b = 12$

$c^2 = 16 + 144$ Evaluate.

$c^2 = 160$ Add.

$c = \pm\sqrt{160}$ Definition of square root

$c \approx \pm 12.6$ Simplify.

Since length cannot be negative, the length of the hypotenuse is about 12.6 centimeters.

Lesson-by-Lesson Review

Intervention If the given examples are not sufficient to review the topics covered by the questions, remind students that the page references tell them where to review that topic in their textbooks.

Two-Day Option Have students complete the Lesson-by-Lesson Review on pages 661–662. Then you can use ExamView® Assessment Suite to customize another review worksheet that practices all the objectives of this chapter or only the objectives on which your students need more help.

For more information on ExamView® Assessment Suite, see page 634C.

Differentiated Instruction

Super DVD: MindJogger Plus
Use this DVD as an alternative format of review for the test. For more information on this game show format, see page 634D.

Problem Solving Review

For additional practice in problem solving for Chapter 12, see the Mixed Problem Solving Appendix, page 726 in the Student Handbook section.

Anticipation Guide

Have students complete the Chapter 12 Anticipation Guide and discuss how their responses have changed now that they have completed Chapter 12.

CRM Anticipation Guide, p. 7

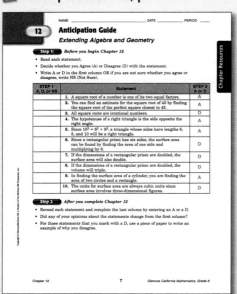

12-3 PSI: Make a Model (pp. 646–647)

Solve the problem by using the *make a model* strategy.

29. FRAMING A painting 15 inches by 25 inches is bordered by a mat that is 3 inches wide. The frame around the mat is 2 inches wide. Find the area of the picture with the frame and mat. **875 in²**

30. DVDS A video store arranges its best-selling DVDs in their front window. In how many different ways can five best-seller DVDs be arranged in a row? **120**

Example 3 The bottom layer of a display of soup cans has 6 cans in it. If there is one less can in each layer above it and there are 4 layers in the display, how many cans are there in the display?

So, based on the model there are 18 cans.

12-4 Surface Area of Rectangular Prisms (pp. 649–653)

Find the surface area of each rectangular prism. Round to the nearest tenth if necessary. **202 yd²**   **531.3 m²**

31.   **32.**

33. MOVING A large wardrobe box is 2.25 feet long, 2 feet wide, and 4 feet tall. How much cardboard is needed to make the box? **43 ft²**

Example 4 Find the surface area of a rectangular prism.

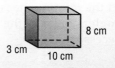

$$\text{surface area} = 2\ell w + 2\ell h + 2wh$$
$$= 2(10)(3) + 2(10)(8) + 2(3)(8)$$
$$= 268$$

The surface area is 268 square centimeters.

12-5 Surface Area of Cylinders (pp. 656–659)

Find the surface area of each cylinder. Round to the nearest tenth.

34.   **35.**

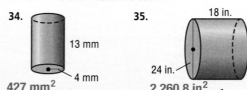

427 mm²   **2,260.8 in²**

36. DESIGN A can of black beans is $5\frac{1}{2}$ inches high, and its base has a radius of 2 inches. How much paper is needed to make the label on the can?

about 69.1 in²

Example 5 Find the surface area of the cylinder. Round to the nearest tenth.

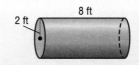

$$\text{surface area} = 2\pi r^2 + 2\pi rh$$
$$= 2(3.14)(2^2) + 2(3.14)(2)8$$
$$\approx 125.6 \text{ ft}^2$$

The surface area is about 125.6 square feet.

CHAPTER 12 Practice Test

Estimate each square root to the nearest whole number.

1. $\sqrt{500}$ **22**   2. $\sqrt{95}$ **10**   3. $\sqrt{265}$ **16**

Estimate each square root to the nearest tenth.

4. $\sqrt{570}$ **23.9**   5. $\sqrt{7}$ **2.6**   6. $\sqrt{84}$ **9.2**

7. **STANDARDS PRACTICE** The length of one side of a square sandbox is 7 feet. Which number is closest to the length of the diagonal of the sandbox? **A**

A $\sqrt{100}$
B $\sqrt{50}$
C $\sqrt{14}$
D $\sqrt{7}$

Find the missing measure of each right triangle. Round to the nearest tenth if necessary.

8. $a = 5$ m, $b = 4$ m **6.4 m**
9. $b = 12$ in., $c = 14$ in. **7.2 in.**
10. $a = 7$ in., $c = 13$ in. **11.0 in.**

11. **MEASUREMENT** Use the diagram below to find the distance from the library to the post office. Round to the nearest tenth. **22.2 ft**

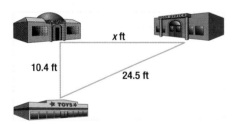

12. **CHAIRS** Chris is responsible for arranging the chairs at the meeting. There are 72 chairs, and he wants to have twice as many chairs in each row as he has in each column. How many chairs should he put in each row? How many rows does he need?
6 rows of 12 chairs each

Find the surface area of each rectangular prism and cylinder. Round to the nearest tenth if necessary.

13.

5 cm, 3 cm, 8 cm
158 cm²

14.

26.1 m, 14 m, 19.6 m
2,302.7 m²

15.

$9\frac{3}{4}$ in., $3\frac{5}{8}$ in., $5\frac{1}{2}$ in.
$217\frac{13}{16}$ in²

16.

6 ft, 12 ft
678.2 ft²

17.

11.5 mm, 20.7 mm
955.1 mm²

18.

$\frac{1}{4}$ in., 6 in.
9.8 in²

19. **PACKAGING** Mrs. Rodriguez is wrapping a gift. What is the least amount of wrapping paper she will need to wrap the box below?
540 in²

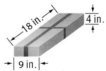
18 in., 4 in., 9 in.

20. **STANDARDS PRACTICE** The dimensions of four containers are given below. Which container has the greatest surface area? **J**

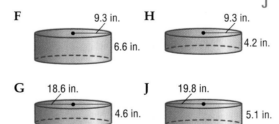

F 9.3 in., 6.6 in.
H 9.3 in., 4.2 in.
G 18.6 in., 4.6 in.
J 19.8 in., 5.1 in.

Math Online **Chapter Test at** ca.gr6math.com

Summative Assessment

Chapter 12 Resource Masters

Leveled Chapter 12 Tests

Form	Type	Level	Pages
1	MC	BL	45–46
2A	MC	OL	47–48
2B	MC	OL	49–50
2C	FR	OL	51–52
2D	FR	OL	53–54
3	FR	AL	55–56

MC = multiple-choice questions
FR = free-response questions
BL = below grade level
OL = on grade level
AL = above grade level

• Vocabulary Test, p. 44
• Extended-Response Test, p. 57
• Unit 5 Test, pp. 61–62

ExamView Assessment Suite Customize and create multiple versions of your chapter test and their answer keys.

All of the questions from the leveled *Chapter 12 Resources Masters* are also available on Exam View Assessment Suite® with the California Standard that each item assesses.

Data-Driven Decision Making	Exercises	Lesson	Standard	Resources for Review
Diagnostic Teaching Based on the results of the Chapter 12 Practice Test, use the following to review concepts that students continue to find challenging.	13–15, 19	12-4	**Preparation for 7MG2.1**	**CRM** Study Guide and Intervention pp. 27 and 33 **Math Online** • Extra Examples • Personal Tutor • Concepts in Motion
	16–18, 20	12-5	**Preparation for 7MG2.1**	

California Standards Practice
Cumulative, Chapters 1–12

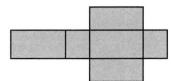

Read each question. Then fill in the correct answer on the answer document provided by your teacher or on a sheet of paper.

1 Which of the following three-dimensional figures could be formed from this net? **D**

A Cube

B Rectangular pyramid

C Triangular prism

D Rectangular prism

2 Which of the following nets could be used to make a cylinder? **J**

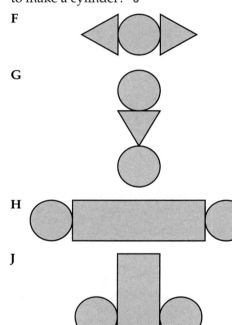

F

G

H

J

3 Carla has an above-ground swimming pool with a circumference of 20 feet. Which of the following equations could be used to find r, the radius of the pool? **A**

A $r = \frac{10}{\pi}$ C $r = \frac{10}{2\pi}$

B $r = \frac{40}{\pi}$ D $r = \frac{\pi}{20}$

4 Of the following figures that Ryan drew, which 2 figures have the same area? **J**

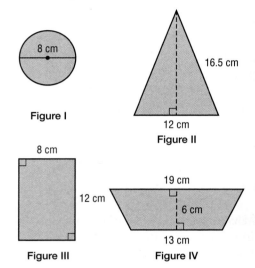

Figure I

Figure II

Figure III

Figure IV

F Figure I and II

G Figure II and III

H Figure II and IV

J Figure III and IV

5 Cassandra drew a circle with a radius of 12 inches and another circle with a radius of 8 inches. What is the approximate difference between the areas of the 2 circles? Use $\pi = 3.14$. **B**

A 452.16 in^2 C 50.24 in^2

B 251.2 in^2 D 25.12 in^2

664 Chapter 12 Looking Ahead to Grade 7: Geometry and Measurement

More California
Standards Practice
For practice by standard,
see pages CA1–CA39.

CHAPTER
12 California
Standards Practice

6 Which equation could be used to find the area of a circle with a radius of 10 centimeters? **J**

F $A = 5 \times \pi$

G $A = \pi \times 5^2$

H $A = 10 \times \pi$

J $A = \pi \times 10^2$

7 Dave can run 30 yards in 8.2 seconds. During a race, he ran 120 yards. If Dave's rate of speed remained the same, how long did it take him to run the race? **B**

A 43 seconds   **C** 24.6 seconds

B 32.8 seconds   **D** 18.4 seconds

8 Which of the following equations gives the surface area S of a cube with side length m? **G**

F $S = m^3$

G $S = 6m^2$

H $S = 6m$

J $S = 2m + 4m^2$

TEST-TAKING TIP

Question 9 Be sure to read each question carefully. In question 9, you are asked to find which statement is *not* true.

---

9 Which statement is *not* true about an equilateral triangle? **C**

A The sum of the angles is 180°.

B It has three congruent angles.

C It has one right angle.

D It has exactly three congruent sides.

---

10 Bill's Electronics bought 5 computers for a total of $3,000. The business later bought another computer for $600. What was the mean price of all the computers? **F**

F $600.00   **H** $3,600.00

G $3,200.00   **J** $6,100.00

11 A jar contains 9 yellow marbles and 1 red marble. Ten students will each randomly select one marble to determine who goes first in a game. Whoever picks the red marble goes first. Lily will pick first and keep the marble that she picks. Heath will pick second. What is the probability that Lily will pick a yellow marble and Heath will pick the red marble? **D**

A $\frac{9}{10}$ **C** $\frac{1}{9}$

B $\frac{4}{5}$ **D** $\frac{1}{10}$

Pre-AP

Record your answers on a sheet of paper. Show your work.

12 A square with a side of y inches is inside a square with a side of 6 inches, as shown below.

a. Write an expression that can be used to find the area of the shaded region in terms of y. **$36 - y^2$**

b. If the dimensions of both squares are doubled, write an expression that could be used to find the area of the new shaded region. **$144 - (2y)^2$ or $144 - 4y^2$**

Answer Sheet Practice

Have students simulate taking a standardized test by recording their answers on a practice recording sheet.

[CRM] Student Recording Sheet, p. 39

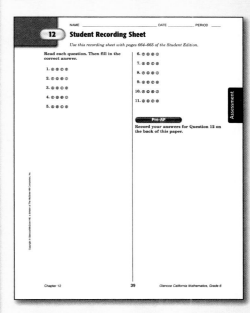

NEED EXTRA HELP?

If You Missed Question...	1	2	3	4	5	6	7	8	9	10	11	12
Go to Lesson...	11-8	11-8	11-3	11-2	11-4	11-4	6-5	12-4	10-3	8-2	9-8	11-1
For Help with Standard ...	MR2.4	MR2.4	AF3.1	AF3.1	MR1.2	MG1.2	NS1.3	AF3.2	SDAP3.1	SDAP1.1	SDAP3.5	AF3.1

2. Sample answer: How many feet of chrome edging do you need to finish a table-top 54 inches long and 30 inches wide? 14 ft

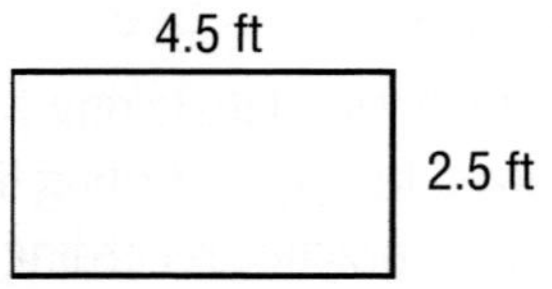

4.5 ft

2.5 ft

NOTES